JAGUAR

SPORTS RACING & WORKS COMPETITION CARS FROM 1954

JAGUAR

SPORTS RACING & WORKS COMPETITION CARS FROM 1954

Andrew Whyte

This book is the second in a two-volume set, the first of which was entitled,

Jaguar Sports Racing & Works Competition Cars to 1953 (F277)

Together with the following Foulis titles, they form a comprehensive history of Jaguar:

Jaguar Saloon Cars by Paul Skilleter with Andrew Whyte (F263)
Jaguar Sports Cars 2nd Edition by Paul Skilleter (F453)

ISBN 0 85429 319 1

A Foulis Motoring Book

First published 1987
Revised edition published 1988
© Andrew J. A. Whyte 1987

Published by:
Haynes Publishing Group
Sparkford, Near Yeovil, Somerset BA22 7JJ

Haynes Publications Inc.
861 Lawrence Drive, Newbury Park, California 91320, USA

Library of Congress catalog card number 86–83364

British Library Cataloguing in Publication Data
Whyte, Andrew
    Jaguar sports, racing & works competition cars from 1954 on.
    1. Automobile racing——History 2. Jaguar automobile——History
    I. Title
    796.7′2   GV1029.15
    ISBN 0-85429-319-1
Page Design: Mike King and Tim Rose
Editor: Mansur Darlington
Printed in England by: J. H. Haynes & Co. Ltd

Author's notes
The title of this book and, indeed, that of the first volume are notably unwieldy. Thus, throughout they will be referred to simply as Vol. 1 and Vol. 2.

*   *   *   *

I have always preferred to use the form: C-type, D-type, E-type. It is difficult, however, to claim a definitive form, inverted commas often being seen.

*   *   *   *

This revised edition has been updated to record the completion of the 1987 racing season and Jaguar's historic attainment of the World Sportscar Championship.

Front endpaper shows Tony Rolt springing from his D-type for the last change-over with Duncan Hamilton in the 1954 Le Mans.

Contents

1987 XJR-8: Brilliant 6.9-litre sports-racing car that brought Jaguar the World titles for teams *and* drivers (see p. 427).

Introduction

Five years have passed since I wrote the preface to *Jaguar Sports Racing & Works Competition Cars, to 1953*, the first book in this two-volume work. I did not mean the second volume to be so delayed: but, as it was being planned, the news was already out .... Jaguar was to return to racing! Although never intended to grow so big, this book might well have ended on a low note if Jaguar had not made its pronouncement. It could, even, be argued that a third volume should have been added to cover the new era of Jaguar, since (Sir) John Egan took the marque in hand – but that era is not yet over. Who knows what Jaguar's racing involvement may be in five, ten, or twenty years ... let alone another thirty-three?

I think it is right to embrace the period from one 'high' – the D-type's début – to another: the re-establishment of the name of Jaguar in competitions.

Since the motor industry was born, there has not been a manufacturer who did not look at competitions as a means of promoting, if not improving, the product. It is true that some of them became twice shy, once bitten. Rolls-Royce has stayed aloof since early in the century (though it has been interesting to note the new look being given to Bentley in the 1980s, implying a sporting past); General Motors has tended to stay at the fringes of the sporting side of the business, though individual marques (e.g., Chevrolet, Holden, Opel) have established pedigrees of their own. Look at most of the famous names, and there is a competitive element somewhere in their past, if not their present. Indeed, many a company would have survived if it had not become obsessed by this element, at the expense of its business development. Only a few companies – BMW, Ferrari, and Porsche spring to mind – have a competitive thread that passes through their complete histories, unbroken.

Jaguar's competition history has passed in spasms. Volume 1 tells of the days before Jaguar, when two motor-cycling enthusiasts – William Walmsley and William Lyons – got together to make Swallow sidecars in Blackpool. It tells of successes in the Sidecar TT races and other events, and of how the partners went on to make special Swallow bodywork for cars. These were award winners, but only at *Concours d'Elegance*, for they were built on mundane chassis.

Volume 1 goes on to describe how the company moved from Blackpool to Coventry and, in 1931, created the flamboyant SS marque. They were beautiful to look at, comfortable, and competitively-priced; but, though they performed adequately on the road, their uncompetitive performances in the tough Alpine Trials of 1933 and 1934 made William Lyons very wary of risking the reputation of his products in events other than static ones.

By the end of 1934, when SS Cars Ltd was expanding quickly, Walmsley lost interest and retired. Shortly after Walmsley's departure, Lyons – now sole proprietor of the car business and the sidecar business – brought in a Humber-trainee engineer, William Heynes.

That was in April 1935. Within six months a new range of SS cars was announced, featuring a Harry Weslake overhead valve conversion for the Standard six-cylinder engine. Introduced to the World in September 1935, these

D-type under wraps, 1956.

first ohv SS motor cars were given the suffix which was to mean so much for so long afterwards – they were called SS *Jaguars*.

There were saloons and open models, the most famous (though hardly numerous) being the SS Jaguar 100. It made best performance in the 1936 Alpine Trial proving that Lyons' creations were not *just* pretty faces. From 1938 it had a $3\frac{1}{2}$-litre engine which propelled it to a genuine 100 mph. A successful production year in 1938/39 ensured that there was sufficient confidence for SS Cars Ltd to obtain sufficient military contracts to stay in business throughout the 1939/45 period, after which the original product – the Swallow sidecar – was sold-off. In 1945, Jaguar Cars Ltd was formed (thus discarding the SS

name), and a new range was developed.

The combined talents of William Heynes (chief engineer), Harry Weslake (consultant), Walter Hassan (development engineer) and Claude Baily (designer) gave the early post-war Jaguars a robust heart in the form of their dohc six-cylinder XK engine. Its days may be numbered now but, after close on forty years of production, this power unit remains (and will go down in history as) one of the finest series-production engines the world has ever seen. It is at the heart of both of these volumes.

For racing, the Jaguar XK engine proved ideal. Even in the 1980s it was still earning its laurels – particularly in USA national sports car championships and in various

8

Above:
Before Jaguar there was Swallow. Williams Lyons and his fiancée, Greta Brown, toured Scotland with this outfit in 1923. (*Courtesy: Lady Lyons*)

Above right:
The Swallow competition model as raced in the late 1920s by Lyons's first overseas agent, Emil Frey of Zürich. The size of the letters indicates that racing was a business from the start. (*Courtesy: Emil Frey*)

European historic events.

Back in 1950, privately-entered Jaguar XK 120 sports cars showed their potential in the French 24-hour race at Le Mans, observed by Bill Heynes and Jaguar's service manager Raymond ('Lofty') England. They reported back to William Lyons who authorised the manufacture of three special versions for the next year.

The XK 120C – 'C' stood for competition – scored a fairytale victory in that 1951 Le Mans race. It was, in fact, quite a lucky win. Two of the Jaguars retired before half-time when an internal oil pick-up pipe fractured; the pipe had had to be rerouted and, with insufficient support, it failed due to the constant vibration at racing speeds. Fortunately, the third Jaguar had pulled out such a lead that it could be driven with care for the rest of the race, which it won easily. Jaguar's Le Mans era had begun – with justifiable pride tempered by sighs of relief.

The year of 1952 was one of new developments (like the disc brake) and lessons learned (like Le Mans). This was the year in which Mercedes-Benz returned to racing with a flourish, their new 300 SLs finishing second and fourth in the Mille Miglia in May – barely six weeks prior to Le Mans. Stirling Moss drove a lone works Jaguar in the Italian road race, but went off-course and damaged the steering at a late stage when well placed to beat all but one of the Mercedes. Moss's subsequent pressure on Coventry resulted in William Lyons giving the go-ahead to some

last-minute modifications to the proved C-type shape. A lowered bonnet meant redesigning the cooling system. Restricted water circulation led to overheating and no Jaguar finished at Le Mans. It was all such a pity for Jaguar; that the mistakes should happen at the very race where superiority over Mercedes-Benz *could* have been demonstrated. Even the French Gordini and Talbot outstripped the silver coupés initially. In the end, Mercedes gamesmanship reaped its reward with a lucky but nonetheless deserved 1–2 result in the French classic. The

The SSs of the early 1930s looked more sporting than they were. Their only regular competition successes were in *concours d'elegance*, which emphasised their superb value. This November 1934 advertisement shows the embellished SS1 saloon, *Aether VI*, owned by commercial radio pioneer Leonard Plugge.

What is a Sports Car?

The Autocar

FOUNDED 1895

LARGEST CIRCULATION 4D

6 14 46 21 25

...e of the many 1934 *Concours* successes

William Lyons in his first SS two-seater, the 1935 SS90, which inspired the more successful SS Jaguar 100.

Germans went on to win the Mexican road race, before disappearing from the sports car racing scene for two more seasons.

Photographs of a prototype sports-racing Jaguar had been issued to *The Autocar, Autosport,* and *The Motor* on 29 May 1953. A fortnight later, the works Jaguar C-types – looking very much like the 1951 cars but, beneath the surface, extensively modified mechanically (see Appendix 4) had swept to a 1-2-4 walkover in the 24-hour *Grand Prix d'Endurance* of Le Mans. This time, Jaguar had done everything right, and victory was sweet – for the opposition was stronger than ever, despite Mercedes' absence.

The year 1953 was Jaguar's year of maturity in more ways than one – above all, in the company's single-minded approach to the matter of winning on the Sarthe circuit. Even the closeness of the World Sports Car Championship had been considered of little consequence by comparison with mastery of Le Mans.

Having won so decisively, Jaguar's next priority was simply to win Le Mans again in 1954.

So impressive had the old C-type been that it might have seemed almost unnecessary to alter the car for 1954.

The Jaguar XK120, starting point for Jaguar's serious post-war competition activity. This one is being driven by the brilliantly successful partnership of Ian and Pat Appleyard, whose achievements in the Alpine Rally in particular are covered in detail in Volume 1. (*Courtesy: Bernard Viart*)

Jaguar's first win (of five) in 1950s Le Mans 24-hour races. Peter Whitehead takes the chequered flag at 1951's magic moment. It had been the very first race for the C-type Jaguar.

Jaguar did learn some lessons the hard way, as at Le Mans in 1952 with their modified but untested C-types, all of which retired when the race was theirs for the taking. Here Ian Stewart leads Zora Duntov (Allard) and P.-L. Dreyfus (Ferrari), better known as 'Heldé', in the early stages. The C-type story is told in full in Volume 1, which covers Jaguar's competition activities up to and including the marvellous 1953 season in which the C-type totally dominated Le Mans once again. (*Courtesy: Robert Blake*)

So it was that the new prototype went almost unremarked even when it was photographed for a second time, in October 1953, after Norman Dewis had driven it at nearly 180 mph on the Jabbeke highway. Very few people can have realised the extent of Jaguar's engineering commitment to a new competition car in that winter of 1953/1954 – yet the resulting car would become one of *the* ultimate sports-racing machines.

In his Foreword to Volume 1, Lofty England pointed out that the competition work was additional to the normal duties of the management and staff concerned, adding that besides the C-type and the D-type Bill Heynes and his handful of engineers got into production four completely new roadgoing Jaguars – the Marks V and VII, the XK120, and the 2·4 – *and* many variations of them in the first post-war decade. England added:

'Racing and rally successes played a big part in the expansion of export markets, and in promoting enthusiasm throughout the workforce and the companies supplying Jaguar with vital components or services. I also believe that, apart from the benefit to Jaguar itself, the worldwide publicity given to major successes did much to promote Britain and British trade *generally* abroad.

Those words seem remarkably apt today, as Jaguar rebuilds the reputation that was lost *generally* by the British motor industry particularly in the period immediately after British Leyland was nationalised in 1975.

It is with the birth of the D-type that this book, takes up the Jaguar competition story, at the start of 1954. (Certainly, there are rally elements to consider, but in this volume they are, mainly, interspersed chronologically with the main text.)

The Jaguar D-type – three times a Le Mans winner – is admired, prized, and copied wherever great cars are appreciated. There were eighty-seven of them, and each is listed in a special appendix (Appendix 5). The C-type was treated similarly in Volume 1.

Although the works team, as such, was disbanded for 1957, many of its members – engineers, mechanics, and drivers – continued to use their knowledge, to assist private teams and individuals. The service department also continued to play a major part.

The late 1950s and early 1960s saw the 3·4, and then the 3·8-litre Mark 2 saloons come into their own, culminating in victory in the first-ever European Touring Car Drivers' Championship. There was an abortive and, truth be told, halfhearted attempt to combat Ferrari's GTO in GT racing with the so-called 'lightweight' E-type. Even in the mid-1960s there was a clear desire to keep Jaguar's name in the headlines as a race-winner; but the XJ13 Le Mans project never made it to the start line. There was a disastrous attempt by British Leyland (in conjunction with the infectiously enthusiastic Ralph Broad) to race the two-door version of the stylish XJ12; it was ill-judged. No races were won, and the programme was scrapped on the eve of Michael Edwardes's arrival at BL in autumn 1977.

By contrast, Robert Tullius of the USA had been campaigning V12-powered Jaguars successfully at home since 1974. This activity had kept the flag flying in the most important export market of all, and would continue to do

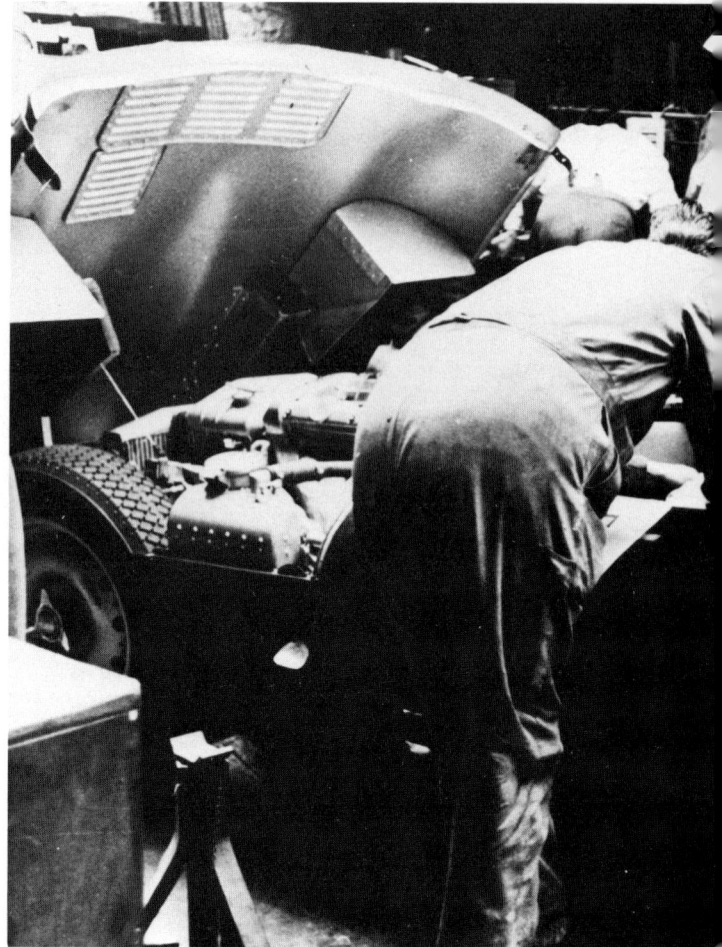

Above:

William Lyons at the wheel of XKC 402 in the Jaguar team garage just before the D-type made its début – Le Mans 1954. Beyond can be seen Mary Lyons, Gérard Levecque, Lofty England, and Frank Rainbow. The car would come a close second in the race, which is described in this book. (*Courtesy: Les Hughes*)

Top right:

The men who created and raced the D-type Jaguar: Technical Director Bill Heynes (*left*), Service (and Racing) Manager Lofty England in consultation with William Lyons behind the pits at Reims, scene of so many Jaguar victories including the D-type's first one.

Middle right:

Newly-knighted Sir William Lyons in New York in 1956, with Johannes Eerdmans (President of Jaguar's North American subsidiary) and (*right*) Briggs Cunningham who ran a US-based team of works-owned long-nose D-types with success from 1955 – the year in which he gave up making his own brand of sports-racing car.

Right:

First public demonstration of the previously-secret XJ13 was made at Silverstone in 1973 by Lofty England, shortly to retire as Jaguar's Chairman.

so in the troubled times that still lay ahead.

Since 1980, Jaguar has begun to look healthy again. Its

Duel of the 1980s – 1: Jaguar v. BMW. The winning TWR Jaguar XJ-S and its chief rival, the works-backed Schnitzer BMW 635CSi, in the 1984 Spa-Francorchamps 24-hour race.

Duel of the 1980s – 2: Jaguar v. Porsche. In sports-prototype racing on both sides of the Atlantic, Jaguar provided the first consistently successful challenge to the might of Porsche. Seen here at Sebring in 1986 are the Porsche 962 of A1 Holbert and the American-built Jaguar XJR-7s numbered 04 and 44. (*Courtesy: Karen Miller*)

own engineers have been busy putting the road cars back firmly on the pedestal from which they had been threatening to fall, due to lack of incentive in the BL days. So there has been no attempt to form an in-house racing team. However, Tullius's Group 44 team in Virginia and Tom Walkinshaw's Oxford-based race engineering business have come up with positive results on Jaguar's behalf.

Tullius's XJR-5 and XJR-7 mid-engined prototypes had scored seven outright victories by the end of 1986, and had paved the way for a new assault on Le Mans with official two-car entries at the Sarthe in 1984 and 1985.

Walkinshaw spent three seasons running XJ-Ss in the new Group A Touring Car Championship before winning it in 1984: after which he turned his attention to Group C sports-prototype racing with the XJR-6 which won the 1986 Silverstone 1000 km race before making its presence felt at Le Mans. It ran strongly, as the 'American' Jaguars had done, none of the three cars finished – the last of them retiring from a potential second place early on the second day, due to damage caused by tyre failure. The years 1987 and 1988 promised to see this team – the Silk Cut Jaguar Team – renew its effort to win the French marathon.

Bob Tullius and John Egan are advised of the XJR-5's Le Mans potential by Derek Bell (*right*), Silverstone 1983. (*Courtesy: Maurice Rowe, Motor*)

Jaguar's Director of Vehicle Engineering, James Randle, with Tom Walkinshaw – the man who put Jaguar back on the racing map in Europe – Monza, 1983.

Perhaps a future edition of this book may record that the mission was accomplished?

Jaguar plc now runs its own affairs. It was officially 'privatised' in 1984, has been breaking all previous production and profit records, and launched its XJ40 road car – the new XJ6. John Egan received his knighthood in 1986. To win Le Mans again, which he was determined his company *would* do, meant the same as a knighthood for everyone who had played a part in Jaguar's latterday success. If that determination was anything to go by, it was only a matter of time ...

Note to the revised edition
The foregoing introduction was written last year. Since then, the determination of Jaguar to score that elusive sixth Le Mans win has become stronger than ever – and, in the meantime, victory in the 1987 World Sports-Prototype Championship has been achieved. Details of the success are included on Page 427 and in the endpapers of this revised edition.

Andrew Whyte, February 1988.

Acknowledgements

It goes without saying that all the people and organisations whose help I acknowledged in Volume 1 are doubly thanked including Jaguar people past and present, and the magazine editors who allowed me to reproduce photographs and/or extracts from their pages, to add to the period atmosphere I've tried to put over. Besides renewing my appreciation of the opportunity provided by *Autocar*, *Motor*, and by Jaguar itself, I am most grateful to Hazleton Publishing for permission to reprint the D-type feature from *Autocourse*.

Many people have helped by supplying photographs, and I have tried to acknowledge them individually. Where an illustration is not acknowledged, it is almost certainly from my own library or from Jaguar's. In the case of the latter, I owe particular thanks to Roger Clinkscales, Jim Callaghan and Mike Cann of the works photographic unit; also to Malcolm Bryan and Hal Crocker, suppliers of race pictures to Jaguar Cars Ltd and Jaguar Cars Inc. respectively.

For the co-operation they have given me during my work with Group 44 and TWR – Jaguar's contracted race teams of the 1980s – I am especially grateful to Pamela Compton, Michael Cook, Michael Dale, John Dugdale, Lee Dykstra, Lawton ('Lanky') Foushee, Karen Miller, Brian Redman, Bob Tullius, and Graham Whitehead in the USA; Arnold Bolton, David Boole, Martin Brundle, Colin Cook, Paul Davis, Pierre Dieudonné, Peter Dodd, Sir John Egan, Ron Elkins, Alan Hodge, Ian Luckett, George Mason, Charles Nickerson, Ian Norris, Malcolm Oliver, Win Percy, Roger Putnam, Jim Randle, Allan Scott, Roger Silman, Tony Southgate, and Tom Walkinshaw in Europe; Peter Bedwell, John Crawford, Ian Cummins, John Goss, Les Hughes, and Terry McGrath in Australia. For their help with earlier periods (not covered by Volume 1) my thanks are due to many more people including 'John' Gordon Benett, Briggs Cunningham, Lou Fidanza, Walter Hill, Graham Gauld, John Pearson, and Paul Skilleter (who has, as usual, come to my rescue by filling numerous photographic gaps).

Michael MacDowel wrote his recollections specially for Chapter 11, and Roger Woodley (one of his successors) read the main body of text and commented on it. They did these major time-consuming tasks with their usual good humour; I cannot thank them enough. I am grateful to Walter Hassan, from whose published views on the 5-litre V12 I have taken an extract.

I am sorry I haven't named absolutely everyone, but the list of people who have encouraged or advised, or in some other way helped the project is endless when I take into account the amount of material (pictures *and* information) which I have had to omit – though only with great reluctance. Here I must add that I owe a particular debt of gratitude where the patience of my publishers is concerned; they have done their best to include everything I asked them to include – but here and there they had to draw the line; and who can blame them? The forbearance shown by my wife, Wendy, while I disappeared further and further into this sea of paperwork, calls for something extra-special. She says that a bonfire would do very nicely, thank you.

Andrew Whyte,
Ettington, 1987

Chapter One

From C-type to D-type

The new Jaguar sports-racing car for 1954, the D-type, would remain on the secret list until shortly before the Le Mans race – virtually in the middle of the season. Meanwhile, the Company did show some support for the more enthusiastic users of its products.

All three 1953 works C-types had been sold to *Ecurie Ecosse*, and one of these came fourth in the first round of the 1954 World Sports Car Championship – the Argentine 1000 km in January. Another entrant was America's most successful 1953 Jaguar driver, Masten Gregory. He was but one of many independent drivers who would have liked a disc-braked 'works-spec' C-type to race in 1954. William Lyons wrote to him making it clear that no discs would be available in time, so Gregory ran his own C-type Jaguar on drums at Buenos Aires; then he abandoned the marque to find fame with Ferrari.

For Jaguar's Competition Manager, Mortimer Morris-Goodall, January 1954 was devoted almost entirely to providing works support for Monte Carlo rally entrants.

Ian Appleyard, Britain's most successful rallyist of the early fifties, had announced his retirement from serious rallying – although he would compete irregularly over the next few years – and did not take part in the 'Monte'. Along with Appleyard, however, two rally drivers stood out from the rest; both came from Ireland and both had proved their ability to make the big Jaguar saloons competitive. Ulsterman Ronald Adams had been quite well-placed in 1953, and Goodall arranged (through the Belfast distributor, Victor Ltd) for Adams's MkVII to come to Coventry for thorough preparation. Cecil Vard had done

even greater things; moreover, he had done them with the obsolete MkV saloon, taking third place in 1951 and fifth in 1953. Gentle, diplomatic pressure from this quiet Dubliner led to a good rapport with Coventry and, in 1954, the loan of a works MkVII.

Announced in late 1950, this elegant XK-engined saloon had already proved agile enough to do well in competitions, and the car borrowed by Vard was the already well-known grey war-horse, LWK 343, with which Stirling Moss had won the 1952 and 1953 touring car races at Silverstone.

For 1954, there were more MkVII entrants in the 'Monte' than ever, most of whom made contact with Goodall and obtained varying degrees of works advice or service preparation. It was decided that the Adams and Vard cars should form an official Jaguar team, to be completed by the MkVII of Midland motor-trade men Frank Grounds and Ken Rawlings.

The aid of Jaguar distributors and importers along the 'Monte' route was enlisted for Jaguar competitors and Dick Jeffrey of Dunlop lent Goodall some $7 \cdot 00 \times 16$ snow tyres on $5\frac{1}{2}$ inch rims for those who wanted them.

Philip Weaver of the works competition shop was sent to Llandrindod Wells to see the Glasgow starters safely through Wales. 'Mort' Goodall had, meantime, taken a hack MkVII (KRW 621) to the south of France for reconnaissance of the regularity test on the common route from Gap to Monaco, the highlight of which was the icy Col des Lècques. The Adams and Vard Jaguars started from Monte Carlo to take advantage of the recce-ing

The 1952 Alfa Romeo *Disco Volante*'s Superleggera Touring bodywork (*above*): influenced Malcolm Sayer when he shaped the 'XK 120C Mk II', seen (*below*): at Jabbeke in 1953 with Norman Dewis driving. From it emerged the 'XK 120C Mk IV', or D-type.

possibilities. This contributed to their arrival back in the principality in first and fifth places respectively at the end of the rally-proper; but a final dash round the houses, on the tight Grand prix circuit, took them down a few places in the final reckoning. Louis Chiron won in a Lancia GT, although this was not confirmed until several weeks later when Alfa driver Georges Houel withdrew a protest relating to the Lancia's eligibility.

Still, easily best of the British cars were the two 'Irish' Jaguars. Ronald Adams, Leslie Rawlinson, and Desmond Titterington were given sixth position; Cecil Vard and Arthur Jolley came eighth in the works car. They should have been well-placed for the team award but the Grounds/Rawlings MkVII was a long way down the results table and the Jaguars were pipped by Rootes for that prize.

In the five-lap race at Monaco, the Jaguars had performed with great credit, however. Adams's best lap time was 2 min. 24·6 sec. compared with Chiron (Lancia) 2 min. 20·9 sec., and Houel (Alfa Romeo) 2 min. 22·7 sec.

In the post-rally hill-climb at Mont Agel, the winner was again Chiron followed by Houel and Vard. Adams was fifth here, behind Arnaud's Lancia.

No official photographer went to the first 1954 test session at Silverstone, and it is thanks to the specialist restorer John Pearson of Whittlebury that a record exists at all. As a boy he would skip school in Towcester when he knew the Jaguar team was coming. Norman Dewis would pick him up at the corner and take him to the circuit.

Young John took these pictures of the XK120C and the 'XK120C MkII' at Silverstone. Norman Dewis appears in three pictures – one with Pete Blackmore from Jaguar Experimental, one with Stirling Moss and Bob Knight, and another with Moss's fancy Standard 8. Moss was on hand to test the Francis Beart Cooper 500, and happened upon the Jaguar group; it seems he did not drive the new Jaguar that day. (John Pearson always dreamed of having a D-type of his own; in 1987 it looked as if he had re-created one, using many authentic parts in a long-nose structure made for him by Lynx Engineering.)

Cecil Vard's eighth position in the rally was the highest yet achieved by a works Jaguar in the Monte Carlo Rally. Vard reported back to Jaguar afterwards:

REPORT ON MARK VII (LWK 343) MONTE CARLO RALLY 1954

ENGINE   No comment. Excellent.

STEERING   Apart from the note under the heading of 'Brakes', the
& GENERAL   steering and handling of the car were excellent. The
HANDLING   high ratio greatly improved the control of the car.
               Before reporting this item I will mention that the car
               was officially weighed at 38 cwt. With crew of three and
               full petrol tanks the rally weight would be 43/44 cwt.
               When taking the car from the factory, the brakes were
               perfectly smooth. When returning the car they were very
               rough slowing down from high speeds. There was also
               a lot of pedal reaction, as if there was ovality in the
               drums. On LWK 343 I felt an increased proportion of
               rear braking would be desirable. On extreme braking
               the front wheels would lock solid even on dry tarmac,
               while the rear wheels were still rotating. When the
               brakes had to be used cornering on ice, no matter how
               gently they were applied, the front end was away. This
               also applied (but not to the same extent) under racing
               conditions, on hairpin turns especially downhill.

TYRES   The Dunlop snow tyres also are well worthy of comment.
               The treads have a good balance for snow and ice. Under
               fast cornering, the soft studs allow the car to act and

feel as if the tyres were very soft, but if this was eliminated they probably would not serve their original purpose. We found that, after driving a lot on dry roads, it was a great benefit to change over the front wheels, thus reversing their rotation, as the wear from braking had worn the studs on an angle. The increased adhesion braking on ice, after this change, was astonishing.

TYRE PRESSURE. 24 lb front – 26 lb rear would seem about right for give and take rally conditions.
    18 lb front – 20 lb rear would be better for continuous icy conditions.
    30 lb front – 32 lb rear was used in all the speed events.

ELECTRICAL   Trouble free. Would suggest cover plate for master
EQUIPMENT   switch. The passenger is inclined to switch it accidentally with his feet. This happened twice during the Rally.
               HEADLIGHTS. Le Mans type, as fitted, are the best I have ever driven behind. Despite the yellow bulbs, the car could be driven as fast as possible, road conditions being the only limiting factor. They illuminated an exceptional distance, combined with a very good spread of light. The dipping arrangement was adequate and never questioned by oncoming traffic.
               HEATER. Good under normal conditions; when the outside temperature was near freezing, the engine (even with the radiator blind fully up) was not hot enough to feed the heater properly. It was only reasonably warm in the front of the car, but very cold in the back.

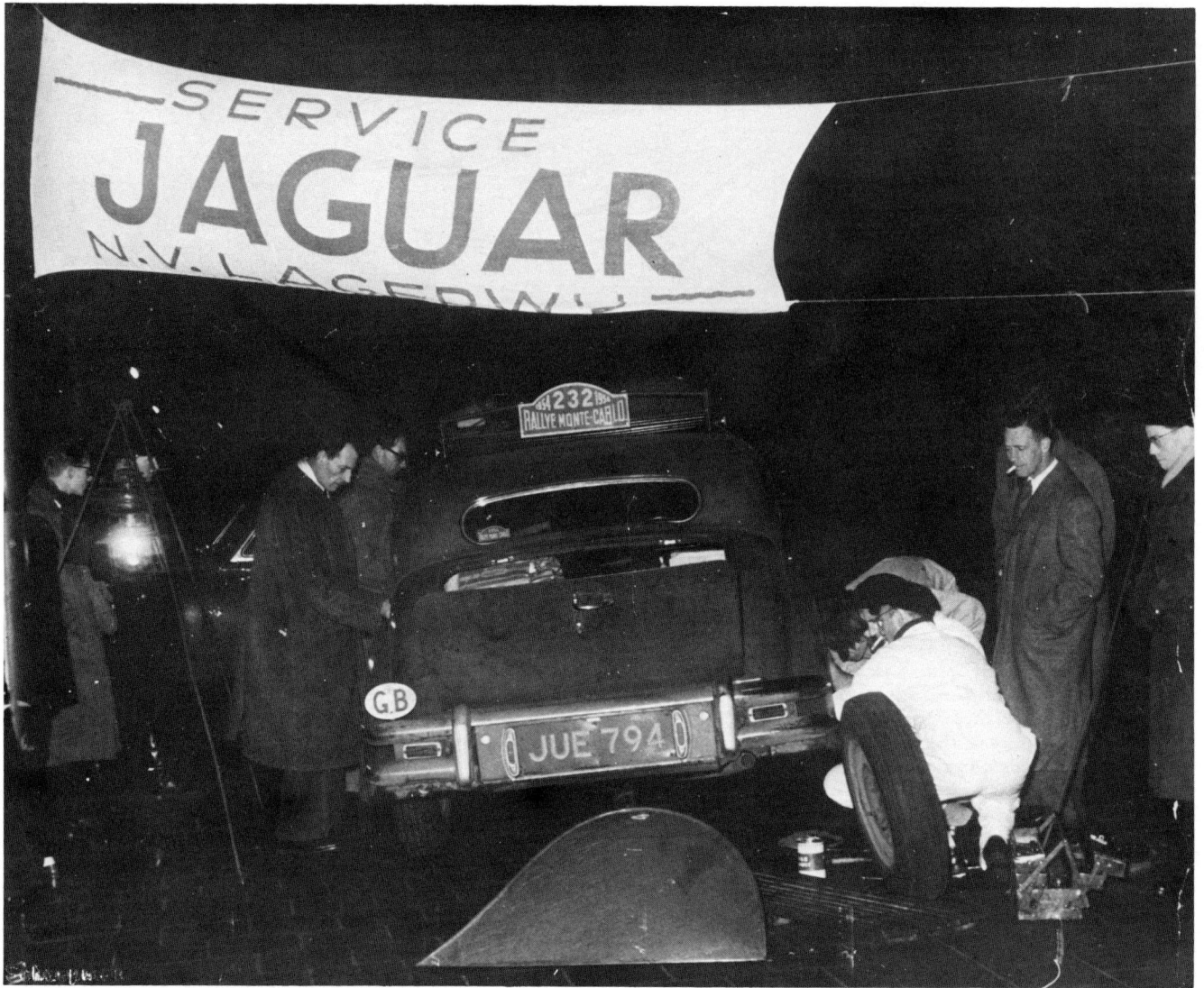

N. V. Lagerwij of The Hague was typical of Jaguar's enthusiastic Continental representatives in providing service for rally competitors – in this case John Lucas and Lawrence Handley with their MkV saloon on the 1954 'Monte'.

DRIVING POSITION   *(This is my own preference and probably would not apply to others.) To sit a comfortable distance from the steering wheel, I find I am not near enough to the pedals for maximum control. Also from this position I have to stretch forward to make all the gear changes.*

Cecil Vard   5 February 1954

1954 was not destined to be a great year for Jaguar in rallies. With no works car on offer from Browns Lane for the RAC Rally in March, Ronnie Adams borrowed one from Alvis just down the road to win the over-2·6-litre saloon car class. Tenth overall and second in class to Adams was Ashworth in a Jaguar MkVII.

While Jaguar saloons remained competitive in certain events, the XK120's days as a rally car were numbered. Henri Peignaux (see vol. 1), winner of the 1953 Lyon–Charbonnières, was not so lucky this time – nor were his customers, some of whom had had their cars rebodied.

French organisers, in particular, were seeking ways of being fair to all contestants, often at the expense of bigger cars. Peignaux found Coventry sympathetic rather than helpful as he tried to get round his local rally regulations.

Morris-Goodall moves on

Not long after returning from Monte-Carlo, 'Mort' Morris-Goodall left the Company. Clearly, Morris-Goodall was not happy at Jaguar. He had been brought in little more than a year before, to reduce the work-load on Lofty England's department, the main function of which was, after all, the servicing of customers' cars. Morris-Goodall's job had, however, turned out to be administrative and largely clerical. The policy-making remained firmly in the hands of Bill Heynes on engineering matters and Lofty England on team organisation – with William Lyons, naturally, taking the major decisions based on his wishes and their advice. A close-knit team.

'Mort' Morris-Goodall was at least able to share in the pleasure of that winter's accolades, so many of which reflected Jaguar's brilliant 1953 season. The Malcolm Campbell Memorial Trophy and the ERA Club Trophy

The Mk VII was a favourite Monte Carlo rally car. The entrant of this one was Ken Rawlings who worked for P. J. Evans, Jaguar Midland distributor. (*Courtesy: K. Rawlings*)

A privately-owned Mk VII spins on the Col des Lecques during the 1954 Monte Carlo Rally. Manchester butcher Charles Merrill and his chums were typical of the once-a-year-adventure enthusiasts for whom there is less opportunity nowadays. Jaguar helped and encouraged such entries as best it could. (*Courtesy: Frederick Merrill*)

LWK 343 was the most used, most developed works-owned Jaguar saloon. It was a regular winner at Silverstone, and in 1954 Cecil Vard took it to eighth place on the 'Monte'. This nice action picture was taken on the Motor Industry Research Association (MIRA) test track at Lindley near Nuneaton. (*Courtesy: N. Dewis*)

went jointly to Duncan Hamilton and Tony Rolt for their great Le Mans victory; the John Cobb Memorial Trophy was won by the Appleyards for their superb season in which only a quirky scoring system had prevented them from being the European Rally Champions; and the Ferodo Trophy was presented to Jaguar Cars Ltd, for its 'outstanding British contribution to the sport of motor-racing'.

Winter revelries over, Mort Morris-Goodall moved office from Coventry to Warwick to join the Donald Healey Company, while Lofty England – who, in reality, had never relinquished any of the competition responsibilities – got down to securing the Jaguar racing team members for 1954.

It had been a good team in 1953 and no changes to the three existing pairings were planned. Stirling Moss and Peter Walker were two of Britain's fastest drivers. Walker was past his prime. Moss, on the other hand, was just

approaching his, and was now commanding a retainer of £2,000 from Jaguar for a racing programme much thinner than he would have liked. His personal manager, Ken Gregory, wrote to Coventry from time to time to say that Moss would like a Jaguar for this or that race, only to be reminded by England that Jaguar's racing activities were strictly limited.

Duncan Hamilton and Tony Rolt were naturals, with a proved Le Mans record: fourth in 1950 and sixth in 1951 for Donald Healey, then victors for Jaguar in 1953. These two extrovert ex-servicemen understood one another well and, through racing, their families had become close

friends, too.

One member of the third Jaguar pair was to be the quiet and steady Peter Whitehead, who drove well to team orders. With his good friend Peter Walker he had given Jaguar their first Le Mans victory back in 1951. Now his regular co-driver was the brilliant young Scot, Ian Stewart, one of *Ecurie Ecosse*'s originators.

Lofty England prepared the 1954 contracts for signing. Jaguar's programme alone could not possibly provide 'full employment', so the wording made it quite feasible for team members to drive other makes – except that potentially competitive sports car events could not be entered without the Company's prior permission. This is how the contract read:

AGREEMENT
1954 MOTOR RACING SEASON

An Agreement between Mr (so-and-so), hereafter called the Driver, and Jaguar Cars Ltd, Coventry hereafter called The Company.

I hereby agree to drive a Jaguar car in races during the 1954 Motor Racing Season on the following conditions:—

1. *That the cars will be entered by and will be the property of The Company.*
2. *That The Company will draw up a programme and advise the Driver of the races in which they desire him to drive The Company's cars during the 1954 Season.*
3. *That The Company will pay to the Driver a retaining fee in the sum of (such-and-such).*
4. *That The Company will pay all entrance fees and all charges connected with the running of the car in the race.*
5. *That The Company will be responsible for the preparation of the cars and the transport of the cars to and from races and for the servicing and control of the cars in all races in which they compete.*
6. *That The Company will hand over to the Driver all prize and/or bonus money which may be paid to The Company for successes gained in The Company's cars with the following exceptions:—*
   (a) That where two drivers compete in one car the percentage of prize and bonus money to be allocated to each Driver will be 50% of the amount won.
   (b) That where during the course of the race the Drivers of two or more cars running in consecutive positions receive orders from the Team Manager to maintain those positions any prize or bonus money which may be won will be pooled and divided equally among the drivers concerned and in this matter the ruling of The Company will be final.
7. *That in the event of a driver disobeying pit signals The Company reserve the right to withhold payment of any prize or bonus money which may be due to the Driver concerned.*
8. *That The Company retain any trophies which may be awarded for successes won in The Company's cars.*
9. *That the Driver agrees to absolve The Company from all liability from injury, loss of life or any contingent liability caused by or arising from an accident while driving The Company's cars.*
10. *That the Driver will provide himself with a personal accident insurance policy if required so to do by race regulations.*
11. *That the Driver agrees to make no private contract with fuel oil or tyre companies that will prevent him competing with The Company's cars using fuel oil, tyres or accessories selected by The Company.*
12. *That the Driver agrees not to drive cars of another make in sports car events without first obtaining The Company's approval.*
13. *That The Company agrees to pay all travelling expenses to and from races in which the Driver is driving a Company car and to pay all reasonable hotel expenses involved in such races.*
14. *That the Driver agrees to act in accordance with any instruction he may receive from The Company's Team Manager and to obey all pit*

Jaguar's Lyon distributor, Henri Peignaux, enlisted Lofty England's aid in obtaining approval for a special-bodied lightweight XK 120 to take part in the 1954 Lyon-Charbonnière Rally, which he had won the previous year. Apparently, the plan did not go ahead, although it is on record that Peignaux did compete and retire. This picture shows the bodywork Peignaux envisaged – one of three XK 120s built upon previously by the *carossier* Jean Barou of Tournon. (One of them had finished second in the 1952 Liège-Rome-Liège Rally.)

signals during races in which he drives a Company car.

15. That in the event of the Driver persistently disobeying pit signals or acting in a manner considered prejudicial to the proper running of The Company's cars The Company reserve the right to terminate this Agreement.

(Followed by two witnesses' signatures and the Driver's signature.)

Above right:
'XK 120C Mk II' at Reims in the spring of 1954. Lofty England is behind the bonnet and M. Lallement of Dunlop France faces the camera. (*Reims pits photos by courtesy of F. R. W. England*)

Importeuse Joska Bourgeois and export sales chief Ben Mason (*in profile, centre*) **with Belgian team C-type on the Jaguar stand, Brussels Show, 1954.**

Peter Whitehead and his C-type in Australia shortly before his return to Europe and tests of the 1954 racing Jaguars.

The one man who proved difficult to locate immediately was Ian Stewart. He had been driving one of the ex-works C-type Jaguars for *Ecurie Ecosse* in the Argentine in January when, according to Scottish team boss David Murray, he had been forced off the road by a couple of Porsche drivers having their own private scrap. Although much less-badly damaged than the car, Stewart was taken to hospital for a check-up and treatment for 'a few scratches'. Then he set off for North America where, eventually, the Jaguar works contract found him.

Ian Stewart returned the contract to Lofty England from Manhasset, Long Island, confirming a rumour that he was giving up racing: 'Unfortunately the accident in Buenos Aires makes it all look rather bad,' confessed Stewart. 'During the past two years my father has been moaning quite a lot about my absence from the family business, and in November last year I received, by letter, his final ultimatum. I had hoped to talk him out of it while in BA (he was there on holiday just before the race) but all to no avail. He gave me the choice of racing or pursuing my normal course at home. Quite frankly, apart from the fact that I don't want to disappoint my father who has been very good to me, I am loth to give up the wonderful chances which are open to me at home and so, to my very great regret, I must give up racing. I have thoroughly enjoyed all the racing I have done and cannot thank you enough ...'

By the time England read this news, he had also heard from *Autosport* editor Gregor Grant that Stewart was to be married in New York shortly. Thus, what no-one would ever know was whether Ian Stewart really *was* the world-class driver his short racing career had suggested. 'I suppose you will have some team troubles,' ventured Grant in his note to England, suggesting the 'experienced' Philip Fortheringham-Parker and young Ian Burgess as possible replacements. England thanked Grant, saying he thought Stewart's decision wise in the circumstances and that he felt there would be no difficulty in replacing the Scot.

Paul Frère was due to drive for Mercedes-Benz at Le Mans, and heard of the German team's withdrawal just at the time the news of Ian Stewart's retirement filtered out. The Belgian engineer and writer was always something of a Jaguar enthusiast. He had worked for the Belgian Jaguar importeuse, Joska Bourgeois, for a while and knew England well enough to sound him out. England congratulated him on being requested to drive for Mercedes. 'You are I think the first Belgian to receive such an offer,' England told Frère (referring to living memory only) adding, significantly, his own regret that Mercedes had cancelled their Le Mans entries, 'which does you out of a drive and us out of opposition'.

England went on: 'I have just completed arrangements with a front rank British driver. If there should be any opportunity of giving you a drive I will certainly bear you in mind. In the meantime, is there not any possibility of you driving with Laurent whose car should be quite good since we will be bringing it up to 1953 Le Mans standard.' In fact Frère knew this wouldn't work, because there were two cars in the *Ecurie Francorchamps* team – Roger Laurent's C-type Jaguar and Jacques Swaters's GP Ferrari – and,

since Laurent sometimes drove the Ferrari it was natural for him to share his Le Mans entry with Swaters. Paul Frère moved quickly, however, and got a drive with Carroll Shelby in a DB3S Aston Martin.

The driver chosen by Jaguar to replace Ian Stewart was in fact West Midlander Ken Wharton.

Early events of 1954

By the end of March, therefore, Jaguar once again had a complete team of six drivers. What it did not have was a competitive sports car for them to try. The three 1953 Le Mans cars were sold and the only other really up-to-date C-type (XKC038) had just been purchased by Duncan Hamilton to race privately.

Actually, private owners all over the world were giving Jaguar a good start to the 1954 racing season. It began in Australia on the first day of February, when Mrs 'Geordie' Anderson shared the driving of her XK120 coupé with

Right:
Peter Whitehead at Thillois in the 'XK 120C Mk II', Spring 1954.

Bill Pitt and Charles Swinburn to win the 24-hour race on the rough Mount Druitt circuit, where the early leader had been works driver Peter Whitehead in his own C-type; but the bumps had wrecked the rear axle location, and the car (XKC039) had to be withdrawn.

Another previously unpublished shot of the 1954 Reims tests. Pete Blackmore and Len Hayden are at left. Dunlop men include George Brookes (at cockpit) and Vic Barlow, in blazer, attending to latest wheel and tyre.

New Dunlop wheels on C-type for Reims test session. Norman Dewis and Lofty England are on the left. Frank Lees is on the extreme right (next to Dunlop disc brake man Harold Hodkinson in flat hat).

With the works Aston Martins, the private Ferraris and the lone C4R Cunningham all disappearing from the lap charts, suddenly it was Osca's finest hour – four of the diminutive Italian cars finishing in the top eight! Assisted by the American Bill Lloyd, Stirling Moss – released by Jaguar to drive the $1\frac{1}{2}$-litre Osca of Briggs Cunningham – scored an amazing victory.

In the production car classes of SCCA (Sports Car Club of America) events, the Jaguar XK120 was still a regular

C-type Jaguars did not figure at Sebring either. Florida's 12-hour round in the world championship for sports cars, on the first weekend of March, should have been a walkover for the works Lancias; but genuine bad luck prevented this.

Peter Whitehead, Norman Dewis (*nearest to camera*) and Lofty England are entertained by Raymond Roche (*left*) and his colleagues of the *AC de Champagne*, April 1954. (*Courtesy: F. R. W. England*)

winner but, by the spring of 1954, even the better-driven C-types were finishing runners-up in the 'modified' category more often than they were winning – their owners frustrated at not being able to bring them up to 1953 works specification.

In Europe, things looked better for Jaguar's obsolescent competition model. Michael Head did well in Scandinavia with XKC 005, as recorded on Pages 323–327 of Volume

Shell-Mex and BP Chairman C. M. Vignoles presents a Roy Nockolds painting to Ian Appleyard and his wife, formerly Patricia Lyons, in the spring of 1954 – by which time their most famous rally car (NUB 120, as illustrated) had been put out to pasture. The Appleyards – Britain's best rally partnership of the early 1950s – did relatively little competitive motoring after this.

Bill Heynes chats to Norman Dewis. Behind the new (as yet un-named) Jaguar are (*Left to right*) Malcolm Sayer, Bob Knight, Joe Sutton, Arthur Ramsay, Keith Cambage, Philip Weaver, Gordon Gardner, Bob Penney and Len Hayden.

The spring session at Le Mans, 1954. Weaver is in the car; England and Dewis confer with him. No-one had yet noticed the wrong registration number ('OKV' instead of 'OVC').

Lyons (Heynes beside him) talks to Lallement, as Rolt tries the cockpit of XKC 401.

One. Hans Davids (XKC006, ex-Ian Stewart) was winning races in Belgium and Holland. In France, Jacques Jonneret won the Nîmes sports car race in pouring rain, driving XKC027 which he had just bought from John Simone who had moved into the Maserati camp for his motor-racing – thus sowing the seeds of Maserati-France. Jonneret's car also appeared in a spectacular new feature film, *The Racers* (see next Chapter).

After their costly visit to the Argentine, *Ecurie Ecosse* wisely concentrated on the British scene, with Jimmy Stewart emerging as the team's leading light.

It was, however, Duncan Hamilton in his own ex-works C-type (XKC038) who enjoyed more success than any other Jaguar driver in the early part of 1954. In a brilliant drive at Oulton Park he was the fastest finisher of the British Empire Trophy race, though the handicap system placed him fourth in the official classification. His victories included the Paris Cup at Linas-Montlhéry in April and, in May, the first-ever Aintree *car* race which was run anti-clockwise for this one meeting. Hamilton was in terrific form and, in constant rain, pulled ahead of a fierce battle he had been having with Carroll Shelby (Aston Martin DB3S) at the rate of two seconds a lap to win easily – but only after Jimmy Stewart's dominant *Ecosse* C-type developed a misfire and dropped from first to third.

Naturally, the other Jaguar works drivers were keeping their hand in at the racing game. Peter Whitehead, for example, having sold his C-type in New Zealand, returned to European sports car racing with his weird new Cooper-Jaguar which had a works-prepared XK engine. Tony Rolt and Peter Walker were given occasional drives in *Ecurie Ecosse* C-types. Stirling Moss and Ken Wharton could and did drive brilliantly in anything, so it didn't matter (from the training point of view) that most of their early-season driving was in single-seaters.

Like the motor-racing public, Jaguar's six team drivers spent the first part of 1954 longing for 'their' new Jaguars.

The *Mille Miglia* came and went, and still there was no new Jaguar – although HWM did receive a new Jaguar engine from Coventry in time for George Abecassis to take part. The dangerous, exciting Italian classic always took its toll, and this time the HWM-Jaguar of Abecassis and Denis Jenkinson was posted among the non-finishers, due basically, to the failure of a rear shock absorber, the work of which had not been taken up by the bump stops. The car was quite driveable at reduced speed but, as the last one to start, it had to cope with the ever-increasing problem of home-going crowds, as time slipped away. Abecassis and Jenks called it a day at Ravenna and headed west for Bologna where they met Frank Kennington who was using John Heath's Citroën Big Six as service car. After a good lunch and an improvement in the weather, they had an enjoyable run back to Brescia with the early numbers, causing great alarm for their well-wishers by turning off-course shortly before the finish, and returning quietly to Count Maggi's castle.

It was left to a young Belgian, who had arrived hot-foot from Holland (where he had just won the Tulip Rally with Pierre Stasse in an Alfa Romeo) to give Jaguar the best British-car placing of the 1954 *Mille Miglia*. His name was Olivier Gendebien, and he was a friend of Jacques Swaters of the *Ecurie Francorchamps*. With the car's owner, Charles Fraikin, he finished twenty-first in the XK120 coupé. Gendebien and Fraikin had been runners-up in the previous year's Liège–Rome–Liège and won a *Coupe des Alpes* in the same car, so their achievement was based on experience of marathons.

Ascari's *Mille Miglia* victory brought Lancia up level with Ferrari at the top of the world sports car table after three rounds, with Jaguar down in seventh place thanks to the few points earned by Ninian Sanderson and Sir James Scott Douglas for the Scottish team's fourth place in Argentina.

The fourth round, however, was Jaguar's own special event – the 24-hours of Le Mans, to be held on 12 and 13 June 1954.

Tyre tests at Reims

In the Snippets column of *Autosport* it was stated, on 2 April 1954, that 'Jaguars will probably go to Monza to test their Le Mans cars, the circuit being considered the best closed venue to simulate Sarthe conditions'. A week later the same column corrected the location to Reims – but by then those particular tests had taken place, though *not* with the cars destined for Le Mans.

In fact, the plan to hold tests of the latest racing tyres had been laid during the winter and, on 10 March, the three objects of the test were set out by D. W. Badger of the Fort Dunlop research division in a letter to Jaguar Technical Director Bill Heynes:

1) To establish satisfactory high speed performance and fatigue resistance of the new Stabilia racing tyres.
2) To evaluate road-holding at Le Mans pressures (probably 45 to 50 lb per square inch), and
3) To compare the tread wear resistance of the 1954 Stabilia race covers with the 6·50-16 RI covers as used at Le Mans 1953.

The letter also set out a list of tyre equipment on slightly differing wheel and rim sizes. Heynes circulated it to Messrs England (services and competitions) and Knight (chassis engineer) on 16 March, stressing confidentiality amongst themselves and Dewis (test engineer).

It was much easier to maintain secrecy in those days. Inter-industry 'pressure' was there, all right; but it was gentlemanly. Nor was there today's press requirement for 'scoop' material. The other point of view, always worthy of consideration, is whether or not it is better to be totally open about one's plans (within reason) if one believes – as Jaguar had a right to believe – that one is 'top dog' anyway? Nowadays, not one track test session can pass without an immediate conjectural follow-up in the press – for the press must be competitive, too, if a publication is to survive: maybe at the expense of another. (The appearance of an XJR-5 in TWR colours, in the early part of 1985, was a good example of how modern racing politics hid the more obvious clues as to Jaguar's intentions for that season.)

Back in 1954, the atmosphere was different. Except over road tests, *Autocar* and *Motor* were not scoop-minded; they were the 'fair-thinking establishment'. *Autosport* was new,

**Walker in 'XKC 054' ('XK 120C Mk II') and Rolt in
XKC 401 ('XKC 120C Mk IV', or D-type); Norman Dewis
in overalls; Bob Knight bending over from pit counter.**

growing, still one on its own. Secrecy, if required, was
assured.

So it was that when Henri Lallement of Dunlop France
set the ball rolling for his parent company and for Jaguar
he was able, through Raymond Roche, to secure the Reims
circuit for several days without (as far as I can tell) any
press pictures appearing: well, certainly not in the UK.

The high-speed Reims circuit was more-or-less a
triangle, all of it on public roads, one section being part
of RN31, the main road between Soissons and Reims.

Lofty England recalls what was achieved: 'We had the
circuit for a week. The police diverted the traffic throughout *and* we had third party insurance – all for something
like £40 – to the accompaniment of French diplomacy,
certain quantities of champagne, a special lunch, and a
signing of the 12-hour race entry forms for three Jaguar
motor cars. These forms were slid across the table at
the appropriate moment.' In fact, with two consecutive
successes at Reims, Jaguar had already decided to attend.
It was known that the new Mercedes-Benz grand prix car

could be expected to make its début there on the first
weekend of July. If Germany was about to make a spectacular comeback in Grand Prix racing, then at least
Jaguar must ensure success for Britain in the accompanying sports car race.

Two cars were taken to Reims for the private tests
between 5 and 11 April. Jaguar staff were Lofty England,
Norman Dewis and Bob Knight plus fitters Len Hayden,
Peter Blackmore, and Frank Lees.

The cars were a C-type (XKC 011) and the nameless
one-off prototype, existence of which had been made
public knowledge nearly a year earlier. I tend to refer to
the latter car as 'XKC 054', since there is a pencilled note
of this number in Jaguar's sales records. At the time of its
high-speed runs in Belgium in October 1953, airflow
expert Malcolm Sayer described it as the 'XKC 120C
MkII'. In his Reims engine preparation report, Jack
Emerson noted: 'Engine No. E1054-9, wet sump lubrication, Weber DCO3 carburetters, 246 bhp at 6000 rpm,
installed light alloy chassis XP11, preparations completed
in chassis 3-4-54.' Later memos described the car as
'XKC 201'.

XKC 011 was a two-year-old C-type. For the 1954 tyre
tests its engine, E1005-8, was developing 214·5 bhp at

29

5750 rpm with Weslake-flowed head and twin SU H8 carburetters.

The prototype, with its Sayer-designed body, was fitted with wire spoke wheels, as before. The C-type, now allocated to Dunlop for development purposes, had a set of smart new Dunlop perforated light alloy disc wheels, the outcome of the experience of spoke-breakages – and in expectation of greater forces expected to be generated by the latest tyres.

With Peter Whitehead and Norman Dewis doing the driving, these tests enabled Jaguar to decide to go ahead with the new tyres and wheels.

A (fairly) private view at Le Mans

It was not until Saturday 8 May that the definitive new Jaguar made its public début – and in fact it had quite a large audience.

Right inset:
(**left to right**) **Joe Wright and Harold Hodkinson of Dunlop; Bill Heynes and William Lyons of Jaguar. (Gérard Levecque is standing.)**

Thanks to the enthusiasm of XK racer Elmer Richard Protheroe and the co-operation of his commanding officer, RAF Gaydon – notable for its long runway – had been made available for the first tentative tests of the D-type by Norman Dewis, Duncan Hamilton, and Tony Rolt. (Hamilton claims to be the first to spin the car!) MIRA (the Motor Industry Research Association's track), near Nuneaton was used, too, but it was no substitute for Le Mans itself. It so happened that 8/9 May 1954 was the weekend of France's international *Rallye de Sablé Solesmes*, during which one of the tests included five laps of the Sarthe circuit, especially closed for the occasion. (Perhaps it was not surprising that the OSCA of a racing driver, Jacques Péron, should be the rally winner.) With the co-operation of the *Automobile Club de l'Ouest* – in the persons of the President, Jean-Marie Lelièvre, and the Secretary of the *Commission Sportive*, Raymond Acat – Jaguar obtained permission to fit in a brief test session during that road closure.

It was an opportunity not to be missed. Two cars were identified by Lofty England to Peter Brotchie of J. H. Minet Ltd, London, Jaguar's insurers for racing purposes, as follows:

Type	Ch. No.	Eng. no.	Reg. No.
XK120C Series 4	XKC 401	E2001-9	0VC 501
XK120C Series 2	XKC 201	E1054-9	—

The latter was, of course, the car I call XKC 054. Its engine, incidentally, was the one used originally in the C-type which had come fourth at Le Mans in 1953, and was now fitted experimentally with SU fuel injection. What is interesting too, is the temporary designation 'XK120C Series 4' for the newest prototype, which was in fact the first true D-type (though that name was yet to be coined).

Unfortunately Peter Walker was delayed because of a forgotten passport; he was brought to the circuit late by Eric Adlington of Temple Press. The other hold-up was caused when XKC 401's clutch slave cylinder needed

Rolt accelerates away in XKC 401. The spectators were there to watch a rally speed-test. The Jaguars were a bonus for them.

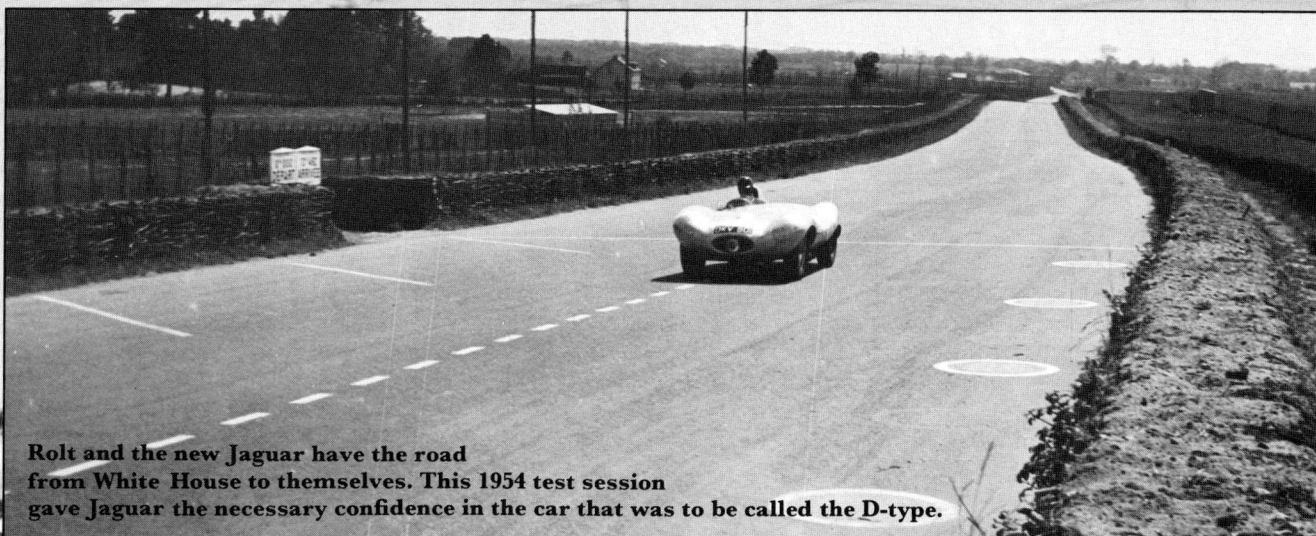

Rolt and the new Jaguar have the road
from White House to themselves. This 1954 test session
gave Jaguar the necessary confidence in the car that was to be called the D-type.

Joe Wright (father of the disc brake)
with Stirling Moss.

Clandestine 1955 snapshot by Australian Ron Gaudion of his pal (later best man) Roy Cole in the racing shop at Browns Lane one lunch hour. New car in foreground; 1954 works car, centre; Belgian 'production' car beyond. The high partition on the left kept this small shop well hidden, even from the main experimental department next door. Gaudion joined *Ecurie Ecosse* shortly afterwards.

changing; that item was very inaccessible, but Phil Weaver worked out a way of doing it. All the same, there was much less time for testing than had been allotted. It was

Tony Rolt who 'delivered the goods', by taking XKC401 round the circuit fully five seconds below Ascari's official 1953 lap record (4 min. 27·4 sec. with the 4½-litre works Ferrari). It caused a few problems when Rolt conveniently failed to note that the officials wanted to open the roads again, but it was his time for that extra lap that was to show the opposition Jaguar truly meant business. Research engineer Bob Knight had been so confident beforehand that he had bet Lyons a packet of Players that Rolt would lap in 4 min. 22 sec. Rolt did 4 min. 22·2 sec. 'I never got the Players,' twinkled Knight, years later. As a chain-smoker he *would* remember.

Before a race, the main Experimental Department workshop tended to be over-run with racers. XKC 401 is in the foreground with Tom Jones's brother Bill holding the bonnet. Next to it, is a C-type with disc brakes (XKC 011 or 012), while a D-type takes shape in the background. The 'C/D' car is just visible, far left. Beyond the far wall in this 1954 (pre-Le Mans) shot is the small competition section.

Only when the cars were being checked back through Customs at Eastleigh airport was it noticed that the papers did not tally. Harry Andrews of the service department paint shop in Coventry had been told to paint OKV 501 on the otherwise unpainted body – which accounts for the erroneous number plate seen in photographs of that Le Mans session. Fortunately, the officials let the Jaguar party go home to Coventry where the registration number was quickly corrected to OVC 501.

Silverstone diplomacy

On the following Wednesday, 12 May, readers of *The Motor* saw the first one-page description of the 1954 Le Mans Jaguar. (It is reproduced elsewhere in this book.) That Saturday, 15 May, was to be the date of Britain's first major international race-meeting of the year – the BRDC *Daily Express* International Trophy – and the pro-

gramme was already printed. There, listed among the sports car race entries were two Jaguars: 'ENTRANT – W. Lyons'. Back in March, it *had* been thought that the British public might be treated to the sight of the new Jaguars in action. After all, six cars were scheduled – three for Le Mans, one 'spare' prototype, and (therefore) two that might be earmarked for Silverstone. In fact, it would be a panic to get any of the cars to Le Mans.

On 12 May, Lyons wrote to Desmond Scannell, the BRDC secretary:

Dear Mr Scannell,

I am very sorry indeed that the two Le Mans cars which we entered for the Sports Car Race on Saturday will not be competing, and I would like you to know that the decision for them not to do so in no way indicates that we underestimate the value of this event, nor that we do not understand that it may cause some disappointment.

The reason for our decision is that we do not wish to interfere with the final preparation of the cars for the event for which they were primarily produced. We wish to take full advantage of the 18 days which remain between now and the date on which the cars leave for Le Mans.

I do hope you will agree that our decision is the right one. I think you will be pleased to know that the cars are progressing very satisfactorily, and all the tests are quite up to expectations.

Wishing you a successful event on Saturday.

Kindest regards,

Yours sincerely   (W. Lyons)

Norman Dewis demonstrating XKC 401 (properly registered by now) at a special MIRA event. (Courtesy: The Motor)

Next day he wrote to Basil Cardew, Motoring Correspondent of the *Daily Express* – the newspaper which, five years earlier, had precipitated Jaguar's entry into motor racing by its sponsorship of the very first Silverstone production-car race:

Dear Basil,

I tried several times yesterday to speak to you on the telephone, but unfortunately without success.

I promised to give consideration to your request that we should enter at least one of the Le Mans cars in the Sports Car Race on Saturday, but I was ringing you to tell you that I am sorry that I have not been able to do other than come to the conclusion again that it would be most unwise to interrupt the preparation of the cars for the main objective.

This, I know, does mean that we are opening ourselves to some criticism, but then I think, to be thorough, which we are trying very hard to be, one has to put up with these things, so I hope you will not judge us too harshly.

One thing I do wish to assure you, and that is that I much appreciate your helpfulness at all times, and you may be certain that we shall always, when it is practicable for us to do so, give our whole-hearted support to the Daily Express events.

Kind regards,
Yours sincerely, (W. Lyons)

It is interesting to note that Lyons never, ever, forgot the free publicity the *Daily Express* had given him, when he announced the SS1 in 1931.

With the works Jaguars non-starting, and Paolo Marzotto's works 4·9 Ferrari being taken over by Froilan Gonzalez, the result of the sports car race at Silverstone became a foregone conclusion – or did it? *Ecurie Ecosse* had entered the three 1953 ex-works C-type Jaguars, and Pete Walker was driving one of them. Indeed it was fortunate that the itchy-footed works-contracted Jaguar drivers – all six of them – had something to race. Three drove in the sports car race: Walker in an *Ecurie Ecosse* C-type (XKC 051, the 1953 Le Mans winner), Duncan Hamilton in his own very successful C-type and Peter Whitehead in his brand new Type 33 Cooper with works-tested 240 bhp wet-sump Jaguar engine. This was a most impressive looking machine with very compact, curving lines and a driving position so far offset that the driver looked as if he was falling out of the cockpit.

Walker made a superb start on the soaking track and led the race on Lap 1; but the great Gonzalez was on top form and soon sailed away in the big Ferrari. The other star of the race was George Abecassis, who climbed from fifth to second place with the Jaguar-powered HWM. Walker was a busy third, closely followed by Jimmy

33

Jimmy Stewart en route to fourth place at Silverstone, May 1954, in the *Ecurie Ecosse* ex-works C-type, XKC 052. The promoters (the *Daily Express*) had asked Lyons for the new car but he wouldn't budge; but the Scottish team – as it did so often – served the marque well. (*Courtesy: J. R. Stewart*)

Inset:
Froilan Gonzalez in the winning 4.9 Ferrari – Silverstone, May 1954.

Ian Appleyard scores a surprise victory in the *Daily Express* touring car race, 1954, in his own Mk VII.

Stewart (*Ecurie Ecosse* C-type XKC 052). Next came plucky old Reg Parnell in the very latest, but poor-handling, V12 Lagonda with Hamilton (XKC 038) right behind him. Peter Whitehead and the new Cooper-Jaguar tiptoed neatly to ninth behind Roy Salvadori and Peter Collins in factory Aston Martins.

Jaguar fulfilled their obligations after the lunch break by bringing two MkVIIs for the touring car race as listed, one for Stirling Moss and one for Tony Rolt.

The regulations were fairly liberal, and the power units were well up to C-type specification. Moss had LWK 343, with which he had won this race in 1952 and 1953; its engine, A4212–9, was developing 202 bhp at 5750 rpm.

Rolt's sister car (LHP 5 – an even older vehicle) had engine A1315-9 giving out exactly 200 bhp at 5500 rpm. Ronald Adams and Ian Appleyard had their own MkVIIs. Appleyard's was a rare appearance in a pure race; but, after the scuttle across the track and the failure of Moss's car to fire-up at once because the starter had jammed (plus an initial spurt into the lead, followed on lap 2 by a lurid spin at Stowe Corner for Lyndon Sims's Riley $2\frac{1}{2}$-litre) it was Appleyard who stayed in front until the finish. Rolt and Moss – seventh and twelfth at the end of the first lap – moved up quickly to hold station behind

the Yorkshireman rather than battle with him. Some way behind at the finish was Reg Parnell, fourth in one of Daimler's Conquest Century saloons, managing to hold off the Adams Jaguar. Another Daimler dicer that day was Ken Wharton – until he rammed a spinning Tony Crook (Lancia).

The only non-starter, significantly, was the Armstrong-Siddeley Sapphire entered by Charles Goodacre. Ian Appleyard had corresponded with Lofty England about this possible menace, which he had examined with his usual thoroughness; but on the day the threat did not materialise and, for the third year running, the MkVIIs dominated the proceedings with their 1-2-3 finish and the team prize.

It was Gonzalez's day though, for not only did he win the sports car race: he was just as clearly superior in the Formula One International Trophy race too, winning his heat *and* the final for Ferrari.

By now Le Mans loomed only four weeks away.

The 1954 Le Mans car, with two of its most important associates: Malcolm Sayer (the tall one) and Norman Dewis. The picture was taken at MIRA, primarily to provide a 'catalogue' picture.

Chapter Two

D-type Racing, 1954

On 27 April 1954, Lofty England sent this note to Jaguar's technical overlord, Bill Heynes.

The following is a list of items which, in my view, need attention or consideration on the new type Le Mans car. It is, of course, understood that some of these items have been or are being, dealt with already.

1. Provisions of bonnet straps and wire prop to hold bonnet when open.

2. Type of mounting to be used for headlamps and foglamps.

3. Provisions of sealing tags for water, oil and petrol caps.

4. Provision of self-aligning bushes on throttle control rod.

5. Leather cover for accelerator pedal slot to prevent fumes, oil etc. getting in the cockpit.

6. Driving mirror.

7. Illumination for rear racing number.

8. Provision for visibly observing oil tank level, I would suggest tube in baffle.

9. Improved leak-proof breather pipe for engine to oil tank.

10. Filters for engine breather pipes.

11. Type of tail light fitted appears easily damaged.

12. Provision of adjustable seat for driver or cushions and squabs to suit various drivers.

13. Foot rest for driver.

14. Clutch pedal set more to left.

15. Pad for driver's left knee at left-hand corner of dash.

16. Set gear lever forward and to right.

17. Rev. counter and oil and water gauges poorly positioned. Difficult to observe when driving. Note: Existing rev. counter is sluggish and should be changed before further tests are made.

18. Fitment of lighting switches agreed with Lucas.

19. Provision of instrument lighting.

20. Cockpit ventilation.

21. Amend brake ratio to give more rear braking.

22. Provision of two stoplamp switches (one to be coupled up in case of failure).

23. Insufficient clutch clearance when car last tested.

24. Suspension bump through at rear on damper buffers.

25. Positioning of coil and spare coil in accessible position.

26. Fitment of large headed crown-wheel fixing bolts in rear axle.

27. Construction of passenger seat to meet regulations and to contain tools and spares, preferably in two compartments.

28. Provision of suitable jack to be carried in car.

29. Fitment of baffle in petrol filler neck. At present loss of fuel from cap.

30. Fuel tank capacity not really adequate to meet race requirements.

31. Provision of handbrake.

32. Fitment of dummy silencers and tail pipes extended to exhaust outside tyre wall.

33. Provision of fire extinguisher.

The countdown to Le Mans was well under way. Before that, the month of May 1954 saw private owners performing well in a tougher-than-usual Tulip Rally, Boardman and Duckworth (Mk VII) winning their class and being placed fourth overall. ('The car ran magnificently and maintained its tune perfectly; the brakes were completely troublefree.' So wrote John Boardman to William Lyons afterwards, in response to the latter's congratulatory telegram.) Eric Haddon and Charles Vivian (XK 120) dropped from first to second in their class because of throttle linkage failure in the final test at Zandvoort.

In the USA, the Sports Car Club of America was developing better and better race meetings across the land, still taking full advantage of military airbases and the enthusiasm of forces personnel. For example, the official programme for the Nation's Capital Sports Car Races at Andrews Air Force Base, held near Washington DC in May 1954, contained no fewer than twelve pages of Jaguar

LES 24 HEURES DU MANS 1954
PROGRAMME OFFICIEL

Prix : **200** francs

Le Mans programme cover artist Georges Hamel evidently thought the works would run the 'XK 120C Mk II' in 1954.

Gordon Gardner and the Bedford spares truck snapped in France by the late Bob Penney. (Jaguar never had a race-car transporter but the loss of a car en route to Le Mans in 1954 would lead to air transport charter for 1955.)

ar/Porsche event. In the 200-mile President's Trophy race, C. ('John') Gordon Benett retired from third place when his Frank Miller-owned C-type began making 'expensive noises'. Best Jaguar result was fourth by Doc Wyllie (C-type), the winner being Bill Spear (4·5 Ferrari). At West-hampton in Suffolk County, a week later, Russell Boss

advertising, instigated by the energetic east-coast importer, Max Hoffman – although the Jaguar Cars North American Corporation (JCNA) had been formed several weeks earlier to give Jaguar greater control over its transatlantic operations. Hoffman also took eight pages in the following weekend's Suffolk County AFB, NY, race programme. Hoffman had both publications sent to William Lyons as part of an unsuccessful last-ditch campaign to retain his Jaguar connections. Jaguars did well at both meetings, despite their obsolescence. At Washington, Ernie Erickson (C-type) and Charles Schott (fuel-injected XK special: *see picture in Vol. 1, page 293*) came second and third behind Jim Kimberly (4·5 Ferrari) in 'Class C Modified'. The XK 120s of Charles Wallace, Jack Crusoe and John Bird took the top places in the production Jagu-

Alfred Moss talks to Peter Whitehead in the scrutineering queue, Le Mans 1954. (*Courtesy: Paul Skilleter*)

beat Walter Hansgen and Jack Crusoe (soon to be injured at Mount Equinox) in the production sports car race, all in XKs; but again Jaguar were outclassed by the Italian jobs for overall victory in the main 150-mile 'modified' event. (UK racing at this period is covered in Appendix 2.)

On the continent of Europe, the C-type was still a winner: probably most significant were the victories by Michael Head in Scandinavia (*fully described in Volume One*) and by Hans Davids at Spa-Francorchamps after a tussle with Benoit Musy (Maserati).

Although there was still no Monaco Grand Prix – the last one had been for sports cars two years earlier (*see vol 1, pages 167–169*) Monte Carlo's harbour did *look* all set for a race in 1954; and among the participants was the C-type of Jacques Jonneret, fresh from his victory over Auguste Veuillet (Porsche) in the Nîmes GP. It was all a sham, though, for the 'props' were artificial; Monaco was being used for the making of *The Racers* by 20th Century Fox. Translated for Britain as *Such Men are Dangerous*, this film should have benefited from the advice and driving techniques of John Fitch, Emanuel de Graffenried, Louis Chiron, Paul Frère, Harry Schell and other great drivers; but, despite all attempts to create realism, the combination of Kirk Douglas (cast as an Italian) and dreadful continuity ensured that it would not be memorable. Even so, it would be worth trying to see again, if only for the few well-located shots that weren't speeded-up far beyond realism.

May 1954 was, above all, the month of the new sports-racer. This is what Ernest William Rankin (Jaguar's head of public relations from 1934) told the press on 5 May.

NEW JAGUARS FOR LE MANS

Interest in Le Mans this year will be heightened by the news that JAGUAR, twice winners in the past three years, will enter three cars embodying many new features, some of which will remain secret until the day of the race.

For the past eighteen months an entirely new outline shape has been under development, and wind tunnel and secret road tests have revealed that greatly lessened wind resistance has been obtained. The prototype car, which achieved the speed of 178 m.p.h. at Jabbeke last year, showed an increase in maximum speed over the existing XK120 'C' type having the same engine power. Since then, further important development work has been carried out, both in streamlining and in power output. The engine is again the 3½ litre twin overhead camshaft engine which is, in basic principle, identical with all XK engines fitted to XK120 and Mark VII production cars, all major units such as cylinder block, cylinder head and crankshafts being actually taken from the production line. Dunlop disc brakes will again be used.

With their reduced frontal area, overall improved aerodynamic shape, reduced weight, higher power output and superior handling characteristics, the new Jaguars must be accounted formidable opponents to all who seek to wrest the title of Le Mans Record Holders from them.

The six drivers will, except for one change, be the same as in previous years and are paired as follows:
Stirling Moss with Peter Walker
Tony Rolt with Duncan Hamilton
Peter Whitehead with Ken Wharton.

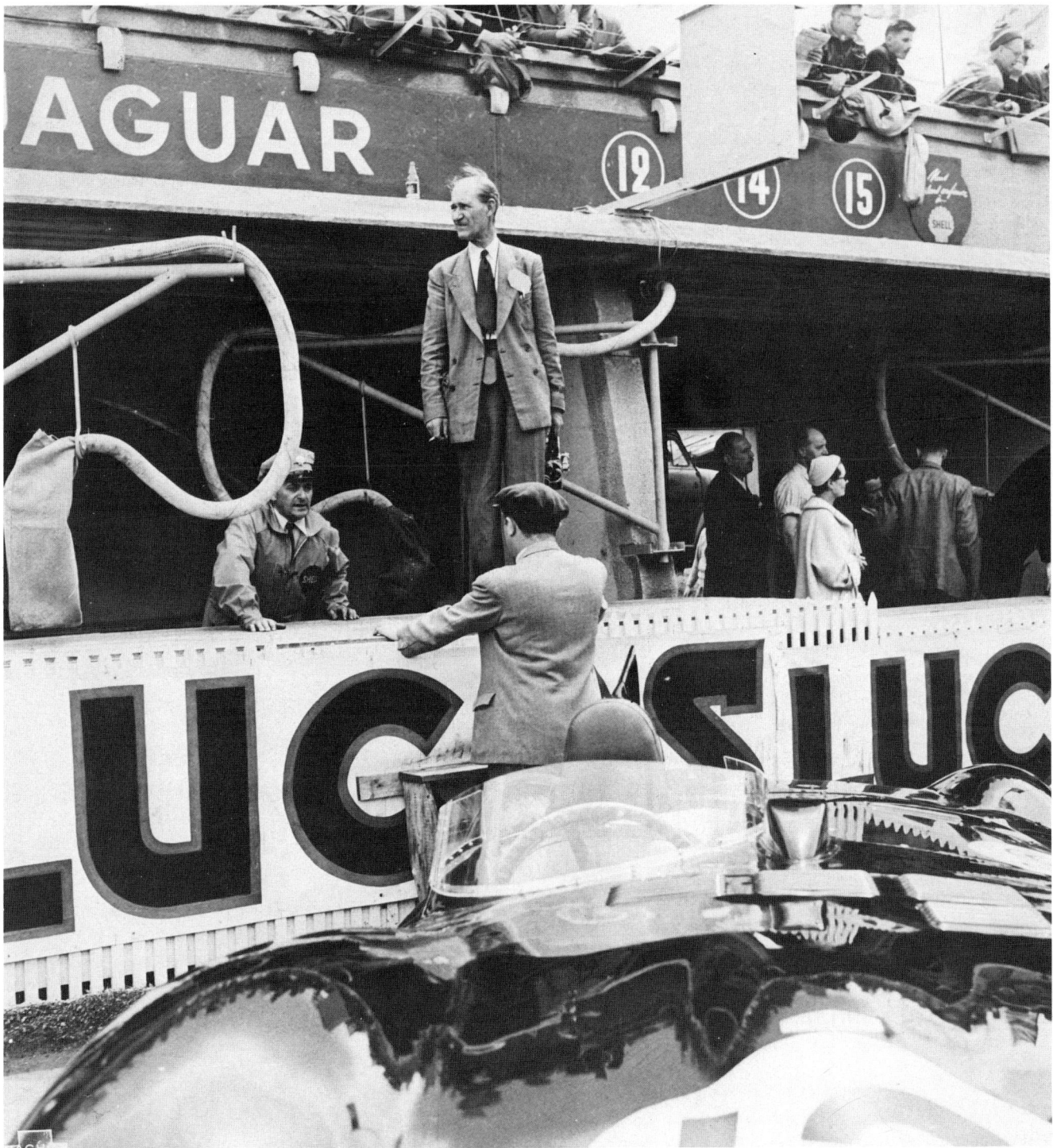

Ernest William Rankin, Jaguar's publicity chief at Le Mans for the D-type's début.

The press release was accompanied by a 'features' item on similar *Jaguar News Bulletin* yellow-headed foolscap sheet:

FEATURES OF THE NEW LE MANS JAGUAR
1. *Body and chassis built as one unit.*
2. *Special magnesium alloy used in body-chassis.*
3. *Super streamlining derived from wind tunnel tests gives lessened drag and increased speed.*
4. *Extremely low build, car is only 32 inches high – 6 inches lower than 1953 car.*
5. *Engine is inclined at an angle of 8 degrees from the vertical to gain lower frontal area.*
6. *Dry sump lubrication with oil cooler.*
7. *Larger carburettors and other secret developments have increased the horse-power to over 250 bhp but no official figure can be released.*
8. *Disc brakes as last year, but further developed and with improved efficiency.*
9. *Light alloy ventilated disc wheels replace the wire-spoke wheels of the 1953 car.*

DIMENSIONS:–
Wheelbase 7′ 6″   (1953 8′ 0″)
Front Track 4′ 2″   (1953 4′ 3″)
Rear Track 4′ 0″   (1953 4′ 3″)
Overall length 12′ 10″   (1953 13′ 1″)
Overall width 5′ 5½″   (1953 5′ 4½″)
Overall height 2′ 8″   (1953 3′ 2½″)

WEIGHT is secret.   MAXIMUM SPEED is secret.

Several pictures of the new un-named car were published just before the International Trophy meeting so, at least, visitors to Silverstone were not completely in the dark.

Inside the official Le Mans programme was a photograph of Bill Heynes at the wheel of his new 'baby' still captioned as an 'XK120C'. The colour cover of the programme must have had to go to press before artist Georges Hamel knew about it, however, for his painting was, clearly, based on the experimental Jabbeke/Reims car, the shape of which had been known publicly for over a year.

Running second to the Jaguar in Hamel's speculative scene was a Lancia – an even less accurate prediction!

On 17 May 1954 the French sporting newspaper *L'Équipe* published a story which could be translated like this:

Jaguar and Ferrari men meet; (*left to right*) William Lyons, race-winner Froilan Gonzalez, Ken Wharton, Ferrari driver Umberto Maglioli, Stirling Moss and, barely visible, Bob Berry.

Works team practice line-up, Le Mans 1954.

WITHDRAWAL OF LANCIA FROM THE LE MANS 24 HR RACE

Following the withdrawal of Mercedes from the Le Mans 24-hr Race announced some weeks ago, the Italian firm of Lancia has just made it known (as stated in Équipe last Saturday) that due to unforeseen delays they will not be able to compete in this famous race. This statement does not refer to nine Lancia cars, as a cabling error made us state, but to three cars.

Nevertheless Lancia has said that at best one car might participate in the 24 Hour Race, but in a purely experimental form – a cautious move to safeguard the future!

Far be it for us to question the reason given by LANCIA any more than

that given by MERCEDES, except that in the case of the German firm, its directors made known their decision before they even knew the results of the first trials carried out by their rivals. It is equally curious to note that, in these days, one does not enter a competition unless it is virtually won beforehand – or nearly so. At least this is the impression (perhaps incorrect) that emerges; and it is the impression in the motoring circles in which we have been moving since Saturday.

In general, it is said that Jaguar has had the effect of a scarecrow. After the first very satisfactory tests carried out by the English concern on the Reims circuit, and the no-less convincing tests on the Le Mans circuit eight days ago, during which a lap was completed at an average speed of 185·174 km/hr, beating the record by nearly 4 km/hr, Jaguar has shown its hand and its opponents now prefer to withdraw.

We repeat that this is only an opinion based on impressions received and cannot in consequence have the force of a judgement, but one's awareness of the situation is disturbing enough.

41

It is only fair to remind the reader that Lancia, like Mercedes-Benz was about to embark on a programme for the new Grand Prix formula.

In any case, the opposition at Le Mans *did* still look strong. Italy's entries were led by Ferrari, of course; their new 375 Plus was the biggest they had fielded – nearly 5-litres – and the driver line-up was equally impressive. Maserati and OSCA did not constitute such a threat. France's Gordini was fast – but would it last? – and no amount of modern clothing could now update the old Talbot sufficiently to give it more than an outside chance. Germany's Porsches could be expected to do well in their class, but the only real opposition to the Ferraris and Jaguars for overall honours came from Briggs Cunningham's and David Brown's teams – the latter including the new V12 Lagonda.

Donald Healey felt that his new 100S model, which had run well at Sebring, was at an unfair disadvantage compared with most of the entries – so he withdrew in a fit of uncharacteristic picque. ('B. Bira' and Lance Macklin were given places by Aston Martin and Osca respectively but Louis Chiron, Ron Flockhart and George Huntoon were all left without a drive.)

Besides the three new works cars, a fourth Jaguar was entered. In 1953, Roger Laurent's *Ecurie Francorchamps* C-type (XKC 047) had finished a steady ninth at Le Mans. Laurent's young co-driver Charles de Tornaco had been killed later that year – while practising in a Ferrari at Modena – and for 1954 their mutual friend Jacques Swaters was to assist Laurent with the driving.

Through the liaison work of Joska Bourgeois, Jaguar's Belgian importeuse, and her service manager Arthur Martin, the C-type had gone back to Coventry to be brought up to a specification approximating to that of the 1953 factory cars – including the fitting of disc brakes and triple Weber carburetters.

Preparing for Le Mans
XKC 401, the definitive D-type prototype, was not used for racing at any time. The three works cars for the 1954 Le Mans 24-hour race were XKC 402, 403 and 404, registered OKV 1, 2 and 3 respectively. The only major problem in the regulations concerned the use of lamps and bulbs approved by the French *Service des Mines*. Lofty England had written to Raymond Acat about this in early April, tipping off John Wyer of Aston Martin and Nello Ugolini of Ferrari that he had done so. A prompt reply from Acat had stated that his committee would rule that foreign competitors could use lighting equipment of their choice, provided that it shed a yellow light. This overcame a potentially difficult situation for, as England had written to Acat:

I think you will agree that this year the fastest cars will be achieving 165 mph, or over, on the Mulsanne Straight. While this in itself presents no great danger it is, in my view, a great hazard for drivers to pick out the small cars running at a speed not much in excess of half that of our cars, with the length of headlamp beam permitted.

At 3 pm on Friday 28 May 1954, Jaguar's technical over-

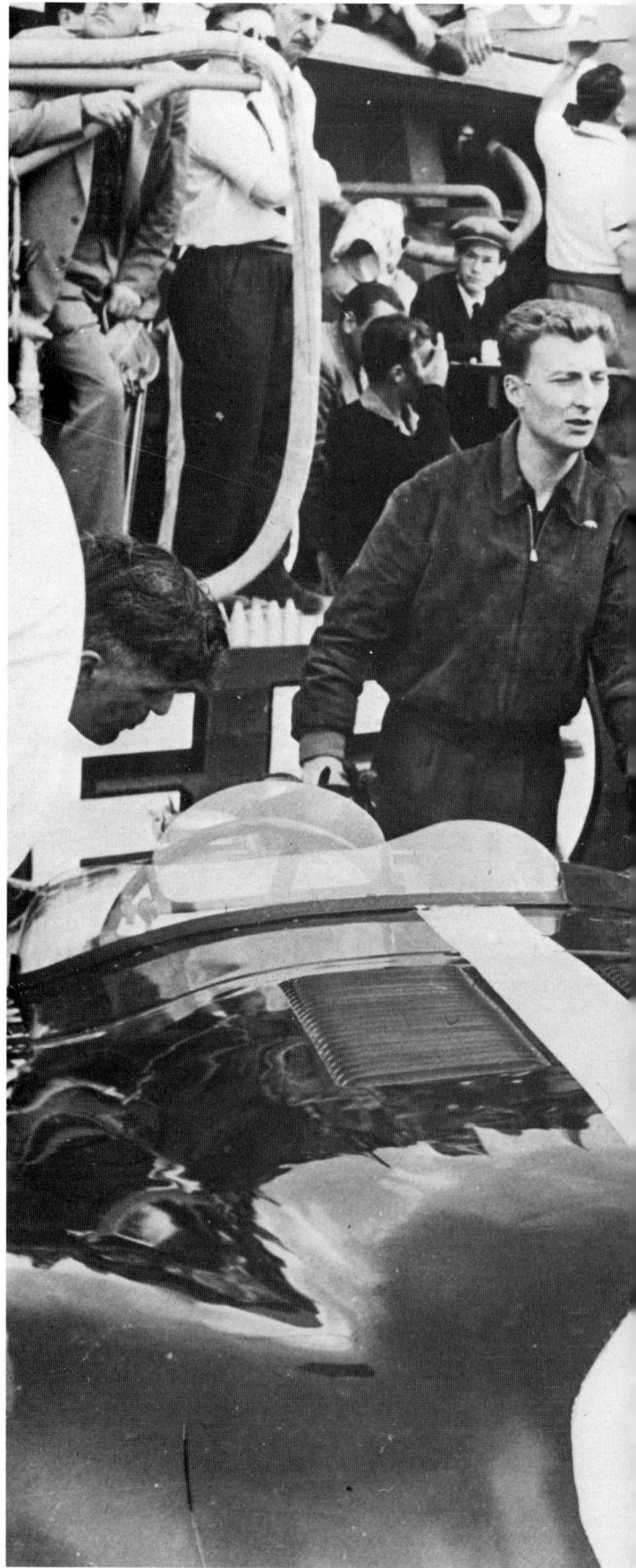

Swaters looks worried as Laurent does up his helmet; they would finish a resounding fourth with their quickly-assembled C-type.

lord Bill Heynes issued the following note to Messrs Weaver, Knight, Robinson, England, Harris, Jones and Sayer:

GENERAL POINTS STILL TO BE ATTENDED ON LE MANS CARS

1. *Instrument Panel.*
2. *Inconel exhaust manifolds and pipes.*
3. *Mechanical jack. Re-check Lake & Elliott jacks for lift.*
4. *Pit Jacks. Design quick-lift jack for pit cars.*
5. *Gearbox Locking device.*
6. *Headlamps – method of mounting and covers.*
7. *Additional lamp and cover.*
8. *Conical windscreen.*
9. *Sharp corners on door shut pillar.*
10. *Coupe top bonnet handles.*
11. *Centre bonnet fixing.*
12. *Additional bonnet louvres.*
13. *Bonnet louvre over oil tank.*
14. *Improved oil dipstick.*
15. *General insulation of bulkhead.*
16. *Sticking wheels.*
17. *Sliding panel to windscreen as requested by Stirling Moss.*
18. *Petrol resisting rubber for air box.*
19. *Foot rest for driver to be checked at Gaydon on Sunday.*
20. *Tyre fouling on full lock.*

Attached were three further sheets. The references to No 3, No 4, and No 5 cars may give a clue as to the existence of an 'XKC 405' at some stage; but I am still unable to

Crowds gather for the start as Moss talks to Rolt, watched by Gardner and Sutton.

account for that car's history, although recently retired chassis engineer Tom Jones reckons that the car was kept in reserve, never being assembled fully.

WORK OUTSTANDING ON LE MANS CARS. No. 3 car

Mr Weaver	1)	Brakes – calipers and discs. O.K. to run.
Dunlop	2)	Fit handbrake assembly.
Mr Robinson	3)	Fit latest conical windscreen.
Mr Robinson	4)	Fit stabilizing fin.
Mr Robinson	5)	Modify bonnet and fit extra lamps.
Mrs Robinson	6)	Remove fine gauze from air intake duct.
Mr Weaver	7)	Modify steering Wheel rivets (3 off).
Mr Weaver	8)	Fit latest short oil pipe (pump to cooler) with single union. (Material ? T.J.)
Mr Robinson	9)	Modify main air intake duct as found necessary by development.
Mr Weaver	10)	Fit safety clips between exhaust down pipes.
Mr England	11)	Paint car (service dept)
Mr Weaver	12)	Fit revised exhaust system if this is found necessary.

NO. 4 CAR

Mr Robinson	1)	Modify bonnet for extra lamps.
Mr Harris	2)	Modify headlamp wiring and reposition junction box.
Mr Robinson	3)	Remove fine gauze from air duct in bonnet.
Mr Robinson	4)	Modification to main air entry of bonnet as found necessary by development.
Mr Weaver	5)	Fit front side shields and wire up junction boxes.
Mr Weaver	6)	Fit correct calipers and discs and bleed system.
Mr Robinson	7)	Fit correct windscreen.
Mr Robinson	8)	Fit lock to petrol filler cover in head fairing. (? Design).
Mr Weaver	9)	Fit correct petrol balance pipe between tanks and provide clips. (Material 1–30 F).
Mr Jones	10)	Provide proper rivetting for steering wheel. (Design).
Mr James	11)	Modify gearbox lid as found necessary to restrain 1st and 2nd gears. (Design).
Mr Weaver	12)	Provide duplicated systems for stop lights – switches, springs, wiring and lamps.
Mr Robinson	13)	Fit regulation mirror and cowl.
Mr Weaver	14)	Fit handbrake assembly and brackets to axle to torque member.
Mr England	15)	Paint car.
Mr Weaver	16)	Fit revised exhaust system if this is found necessary.

NO. 5 CAR

Mr Robinson	1)	Modify bonnet for extra lamps and air duct as found necessary by development.
Mr Robinson	2)	Remove fine gauze from air duct.
Mr Weaver	3)	Fit side plates and junction box. ? production box mounting.
Mr Weaver	4)	Fit correct oil pipes, cooler to pump and engine. Monday.

Right:
Tony Rolt streaks up the outside after a hesitant start in Jaguar No. 14, passing the Cunningham of Spear/Johnston and the Cunningham-modified Ferrari of Fitch/Walters. (*Courtesy: Robert Blake*)

Inset:
Hamilton at Mulsanne. He did not cause the scar, though.

Mr Weaver	5)	Fit undershield to front.
Mr Weaver	6)	Caster, camber, track and torsion bar setting.
Mr Weaver	7)	Fit latest brake set-up and discs, etc. (Dunlop).
Mr Weaver	8)	Bleed brakes.
Mr Robinson	9)	Fit battery and proper clips.
Mr Weaver	10)	Grease chassis.
Mr Robinson	11)	Fit seats. Driver's OK. passenger seat in hand.
Mr Robinson	12)	Fit windscreen.
Mr Weaver	13)	Calibrate fuel tanks.
Mr Weaver	14)	Fit handbrake assembly. Awaiting caliper and cable.
Mr Weaver	15)	Fit modified rear dampers and identify. Friday.
Mr England	16)	Paint car.
Mr Weaver	17)	Fit revised exhaust system.

On 10 June former racing motor-cyclist Jack Emerson, Jaguar's experimental engine tuning wizard, amended his 'Le Mans Salient Engine Features' reports (issued 25 May) to provide this interesting information:

Engine No: E2001–9, previously installed in 'Series IV Car No. XKC 401' was now fitted to XKC 405.
Engine No: E2004–9, previously installed in XKC 405 was now fitted into XKC 402.
Engine No: E2002–9, previously installed in XKC 402, was now fitted into XKC 401.

E2003–9 and E2005–9 appear to have remained in

Ken Wharton (seen here) and Peter Whitehead would take their crinkled D-type up to second place by midnight, only to retire in the early hours of Sunday morning.

A photograph from Sir William Lyons's personal files. He and Bill Heynes are centre stage. His own caption reads: 'Examining dirt from petrol which stopped our cars at Le Mans'.

XKC 403 and XKC 404 respectively for the race. Most engines had Weslake-flowed cylinder heads, and developed between 246 and 247 bhp at 6000 rpm, except E2004–9, which gave 255·5 bhp on test.

At Le Mans most of the management – including the Lyonses and the Whittakers from Jaguar, plus Joe Wright and Harold Hodkinson, the men responsible for the Dunlop disc brake – stayed at the Hotel de Paris in the Avenue General Leclerc. The Hamiltons, Rolts and Walkers were among those who returned to Mme Lamo-

the's hospitable and thoroughly pro-Coventry accommodation in the Rue Premartine. 'If you haven't bedrooms enough for Les 24 Haures,' she told Lofty England (who was doing the spadework again, now that Goodall was gone), 'say it me simply and I shall find some ones for you with comfort if I know quickly. Now . . . defeat for Mercedes! and victory for Jaguar!!' That was before it became clear that Daimler–Benz and Lancia would not be taking part in the French classic which – despite strong-looking opposition from Aston Martin, Cunningham, Gordini, Maserati and Talbot–Lago – was to turn into a simple and enthralling duel between the 4·9-litre Ferraris and the 3·4-litre Jaguars.

An accident en route

Things started badly when the 'Belgian' C-type was virtually written-off against a concrete pylon. 'We were bringing up the rear of the Jaguar convoy,' Frank Rainbow told me, long afterwards. 'Near Montebourg, as we pulled out to overtake a small Renault at a regular speed – about 60 – I managed to get into a spin. It all seemed to be in slow motion. I even had time to look over my shoulder. When I picked myself up off the road as a wheel bounced off into the distance I had only one shoe. The other one turned up under the clutch pedal. Then I saw Les, and I thought he'd had it.' Les Bottrill (who would be the tester of production D-types) had flown out of the passenger's seat and landed on his elbow. Remarkably neither man was badly hurt and the rest of the team rallied round.

The Bedford lorry and van had gone by the shorter Channel crossing. Gordon Gardner and Bob Penney had the job of going back to Montebourg and getting the C-type – which had lost its complete nearside front suspension and was very bent – transported to Le Mans. Meanwhile, XKC 012, the 1953 works C-type Le Mans practice car, was rushed from Coventry. It was fitted with the more important removable mechanical components from XKC 047, including the works-prepared engine, and assumed the identity of the wrecked yellow car. There was no time for a repaint but the dark green car was given a yellow stripe as a gesture to the patient if somewhat bemused Belgians, while the scrutineers showed benevolence.

Jaguar v Ferrari

The new Jaguars looked superbly modern and sleek, lined up in echelon. From near the head of the fifty-seven car queue, the three red 4·9-litre Ferraris emerged at the end of the first lap leading three works 3·4-litre Jaguars in the order Gonzalez, P. Marzotto, Manzon, Moss, Rolt and Wharton – the latter's car already the worse for wear, following the inevitable barging match of the Le Mans-type start.

It was to be a bad-weather race and, as the first rain began to fall, the Jaguars closed in.

The story of this dramatic race has been told many times. The Jaguar race log tells the story. All the works cars suffered from misfiring, eventually traced to blocked fuel filters, quite unsuitable for the task: *their* removal removed the problem, but only at the expense of stops which were to cost Rolt and Hamilton the race. Later, Moss had a fright when he 'lost' the brake pedal at the end of the Mulsanne Straight, though he managed not to hit anything. (He put it down to pad 'knock back' in retrospect, although the servo was blamed at the time). Moss's and Walker's race was run. Gearbox trouble meant slogging in top, eventually affecting the engine and leading to the retirement of the Whitehead/Wharton car shortly before 'half-time'; this car had been as high as second during the night.

Malcolm Sayer's subsequent notes for Lofty England tell the story of each of the four Jaguars.

RECORD OF RUNNING AT LE MANS, 1954
CAR NO. 12 (OKV 2)

A. *32 laps at 4 min. 28 sec. average. Moss. In at 6.23pm for fuel stop of 1 min. 29 sec. No oil added, no water.*

B. *6 laps at 4 min. 51 sec. average. Walker. In at 6.53pm for removal of fuel filter in 2 min. 58 sec.*

C. *1 lap at 7 min. 5 sec. by Walker. In at 7.05pm for plug checking etc. in 14 min. 22 sec.*

D. *1 lap at 33 min. 9 sec. by Walker. Did not stop at pits.*

E. *23 laps at 4 min. 40 sec. average by Walker. In at 9.41pm for fuel stop of 2 min. 4 sec. 7 pints of oil added, no water.*

F. *28 laps at 4 min. 42 sec. average by Moss. In at 11.54pm reporting brake failure.*

G. *1 lap into dead car park by Walker at 0hr 28 min. am. 7 pints of oil added in garage.*

TOTALS:

Total running time:	7 hr. 21 min.	
	(excluding last lap).	
Total time in pits:	57 min	
	Total: 8 hr. 18 min.	

14 pints of oil, no water.

CAR NO. 14 (OKV 1)

A. *31 laps at 4 min. 31 sec. average Rolt. In at 6.20pm for fuel stop of 1 min. 13 sec. 4 pints of oil added, no water.*

B. *2 laps at 5 min. 7 sec. average by Hamilton. In at 6.32pm for change of plugs, 3 min. 18 sec.*

C. *11 laps at 4 min. 53 sec. average by Hamilton. In at 7.29pm for removal of filter, 8 min. 47 sec.*

D. *20 laps at 4min. 16 sec. average by Hamilton. In at 9.14pm for fuel stop of 1 min. 50 sec. 1 pint of oil added, no water.*

E. *35 laps of 4min. 38 sec. average by Rolt. In at 11.58pm for fuel stop of 1 min. 58 sec. 8 pints of oil added, 1 gallon water.*

F. *35 laps at 4 min. 34 sec. average by Hamilton. In at 2.40am for fuel stop of 4 min. 54 sec. Oil not recorded, 1 gallon water.*

G. *35 laps at 4 min. 48 sec. average by Rolt. In at 5.28pm for fuel stop of 1 min. 52 sec. Oil not recorded, 1 gallon water, OSR tyre change.*

H. *34 laps at 4 min. 36 sec. average by Hamilton. In at 8.14am for fuel stop of 1 min. 25 sec. 8 pints oil, 1 gallon water.*

I. *35 laps at 4 min. 47 sec. average by Rolt, (including approx. 2½ min. lost in hitting sandbank and knocking out damage at pit on 27th at these laps).*
  In at 10.52am for fuel stop of 2 min. 5 sec. 4 pints oil added, 1 gallon water, NSR tyre changed.

J. *35 laps at 4 min. 39 sec. average by Hamilton. In at 1.37pm for fuel stop of 1 min. 41 sec. 10 pints oil added, 1 gallon water.*

K. *15 laps, average 5 min. 6 sec. by Rolt. In at 2.55pm for goggle trouble, change of drivers 35 sec.*

L. *12 laps, average 5 min. 2 sec. by Hamilton. End of race 4.00pm.*

TOTALS:
Total running time	23 hr. 33 min.
Total time in pits	27 min.
	24 hr. 0 min.

Oil, at least 35 pt. Water, 6 gallons.

CAR NO. 15 (OKV 3)

A. 36 laps at 4 min. 36 sec. by Wharton. In at 6.45pm for fuel stop of 6 min. 29 sec. Fuel filter removed. 2 pints of oil, no water.

B. 35 laps at 4 min. 43 sec. by Whitehead. In at 9.37pm for fuel stop of 1 min. 35 sec. 1 pint of oil added, no water.

C. 34 laps at 4 min. 47 sec. by Wharton. In at 12.20 midnight for fuel stop of 1 min. 35 sec. 1 pint of oil added, no water.

D. 18 laps at 4 min. 45 sec. by Whitehead. In at 1.45am for stop of 7 min. 41 sec.

E. 1 lap in 5 min. 39 sec. by Whitehead. In at 1.59am for stop of 22 min. 18 sec.

F. 1 lap in 5 min. 37 sec. by Whitehead. In at 2.18am for stop of 9 min. 53 sec.

G. 1 lap in 6 min. 2 sec. by Whitehead. In at 2.33am for stop of 18 min.

H. 5 laps at 6 min. 20 sec. by Whitehead. In finally at 3.25am.

TOTALS:
Total running time	10 hr. 17 min.
Total time in pits	1 hr. 8 min.
	11 hr. 25 min.

Oil, 4 pints. Water, none.

CAR NO. 16 (C-TYPE)

A. 38 laps at 4 min. 58 sec. average by Laurent. In at 7.9pm for fuel stop of 1 min. 22 sec.

B. 37 laps at 5 min. 12 sec. average by Swaters. In at 10.22pm for fuel stop at 2 min. 30 sec. 3 pints oil.

C. 12 laps at 5 min. 11 sec. average by Laurent. In at 11.27pm for removal of fuel filter 3 min. 57 sec. 3 pints oil.

D. 27 laps at 4 min. 56 sec. average by Laurent. In at 1.44am for fuel stop of 2 min. 7 sec. 3 pints oil.

E. 37 laps at 5 min. 3 sec. average by Swaters. In at 4.56am for fuel stop of 1 min. 25 sec. 3 pints oil.

F. 39 laps at 5 min. 3 sec. average by Laurent. In at 8.18am for fuel stop of 2 min. 2 sec. 3 pints oil, near side rear tyre changed.

G. 38 laps at 5 min. 14 sec. average by Swaters. In at 11.36am for fuel stop of 1 min. 24 sec. 3 pints oil. 2 pints water.

H. 27 laps at 5 min. 14 sec. average by Laurent. In at 1.59pm to change drivers – approx 5 sec (?).

I. 10 laps at 5 min. 40 sec. average by Swaters. In at 2.55pm for fuel stop of 1 min. 3 sec. 3 pints of oil.

J. 10 laps at 5 min. 43 sec. average by Swaters. End of race 4.00pm.

TOTALS:–
Total running time	23 hr. 44 min.
Total time in pits	16 min.
	24 hr. 0 min.

Oil, 21 pints. Water, 2 pints.

The C-type was, of course, the hastily-prepared Belgian entry, assisted in the pits by the works team. Its steady run to fourth place was a fine reward for the Belgians, who would gain outstandingly high positions at Le Mans in subsequent years.

It was Car No. 14 which provided the drama, however.

Top: **The final drama: Rolt, goggles in hand, calls for a visor.**

Above right:
Rolt leaves the car and heads for shelter. England tells Hamilton (visor on already) to take over for a final assault on the Ferrari. (Frank Rainbow is at the car door, as a Bristol splashes by.)

For over twelve hours Duncan Hamilton and Tony Rolt held second place, always looking capable of repeating their 1953 victory – and thus of giving Jaguar's D-type a début win (as Walker and Whitehead had done for the C-type three years earlier).

The weather got worse rather than better, and No.14 was consuming considerable quantities of oil and water although this characteristic was at least fairly consistent. The D-type was on the same lap as the leading Ferrari of Gonzalez/Trintignant when, as the race entered its final six-hour phase, Rolt was carved up by a Talbot driver. He got through the only gap but arrived too fast to get through Arnage without locking up. His trip into the sandbank led to the unscheduled stop noted by Sayer. This misfortune put the Jaguar just over a lap down on the Ferrari which came in for its final pit stop just after 2.20pm. In the teeming rain, drama struck the Ferrari pit as Gonzalez could not get the engine to restart; so he had

Wharton passes Eric Thompson who, hammer in hand, is trying to clear the bodywork from the wheels of his stricken Lagonda.

Hamilton charges under the Dunlop Bridge in the pouring rain.

to clamber out while mechanics worked frantically. At last, with an hour and a half of racing left, the big V12 spluttered into life. It was at this stage that Rolt, blinded by the rain, paused to ask for a visor instead of goggles but was shooed away without ceremony. When he saw the dead-looking Ferrari he realised why, of course! Nevertheless, Rolt *had* to come in for a second time, unable to drive effectively with goggles during this particularly treacherous session. Instead of letting Rolt finish his stint,

Desperate work on the leading Ferrari (which was refusing to fire) would result in an exciting final hour and one of the closest finishes ever: Le Mans 1954.

Hamilton (already kitted-up) was told to get in and finish the race. This incident rankled afterwards, despite a diplomatic letter from Rankin to *The Autocar* and other publications, explaining the background to the decision.

Le Mans '54: a close-run thing

Everyone realised later that, with a pitstop less, Jaguar No. 14 could have won. The surviving Ferrari and Jaguar, which had provided race-goers with one of the most exciting battles they had ever witnessed, lost a lot of time in the pits, dealing with their niggling troubles. Indeed the British car had spent considerably longer at a halt. Yet they ended the 24-hour marathon an estimated 2·5 miles apart – less than the length of the Mulsanne Straight! – in the closest finish yet, between rival marques at Le Mans. (An even closer finish would, however, take place fifteen years later, with the winning Ford and the runner-up Porsche crossing the line in sight of each other.) By all calculations, the difference between the Jaguar's and the colours flying, and the intensity and excitement added a new lustre to the reputation of the event itself. That said, no amount of post-race analysis could take away from the brilliance of Gonzalez's wet-weather driving. The Argentinian heavyweight was credited with a record lap, although the race average itself (at 105 mph) was down on that of 1953 due to the conditions; his brilliant handling of the monster for ever laid to rest his early reputation as the charging *II Cabezon* or pampas bull. Sadly José Froilan Gonzalez would never regain his true form after the death of his compatriot Onofre Marimon at Nürburgring and a crash of his own in practice for the Tourist Trophy race later in the season.

Lofty England made it clear afterwards that no-one would protest about the rulebook infringements during the Ferrari's last frantic pit-stop. Certainly, that would have taken the edge off a great motor race, captured so excitingly by Random Films in the first of five annual contracts to make 16 mm colour films for Jaguar at Le Mans.

Hamilton takes the chequered flag, officially 4 km behind the winner, Gonzalez, after 24 hours.

Ferrari's total pit-stop times was measurably greater than the 87 seconds which separated the two cars at the end of their titanic struggle.

Both Ferrari and Jaguar came out of the arena with

The Aston Martin, Lagonda and Talbot challengers faded to nil but Cunningham and Gordini showed well, to equal their best-ever performances. As usual it had been a race of attrition, but the 2-litre Bristol 450 coupés completely dominated their class, running steadily to 7th, 8th and 9th places overall. There had been 57 starters and 18 finishers, these being the leaders:

General Classification	Total Distance Covered	Best Speed over 1km on Mulsanne Straight
1st: José Froilan Gonzalez/Maurice Trintigant (4954 Ferrari 375 Plus)	2523½ miles	160·1 mph
2nd: Duncan Hamilton/Tony Rolt (3441 Jaguar D-type)	2521 miles	172·8 mph
3rd: Sherwood Johnston/Bill Spear (5482 Cunningham C-4R)	2368 miles	148·1 mph
4th: Roger Laurent/Jacques Swaters (3441 Jaguar C-type)	2315 miles	147·0 mph
5th: John Gordon Benett/Briggs Cunningham (5482 Cunningham C-4R)	2289 miles	(?)
6th: André Guelfi/Jacques Pollet (2473 Gordini)	2202 miles	147·3 mph

In a nutshell, Jaguar's Le Mans performance came from outstanding speed and braking; Ferrari's came from acceleration.

Peter Walker wrote to Lofty England on 17 June:

We were being left behind in the wet, out of slow corners.... These were literally the only places where we could not hold the Ferraris, and on the fast corners we could gain on them. ... the Jaguars are extremely good to handle, compared to the Ferraris.

Walker's only really adverse criticism of the D-type was the pedal layout and movement. 'We will have our revenge on July 3rd!' he concluded – and he was right.

On 20 June, one week after Le Mans, Jacques Pollet – the young man who had helped provide France its only high placing – gave Gordini a win over Jaguar (the C-type of Dutchman Hans Davids) in the Picardy Grand Prix near Amiens. Jean Estager, later a noted Jaguar touring car driver, came third in a Maserati.

On 27 June Peter Whitehead – whose Cooper–Jaguar had suffered an engine failure at Hyères earlier in the month with Duncan Hamilton was at the wheel – came third to Villoresi and Castellotti in Lancias, and ahead of the local Ferrari brigade in the Grand Prix of Oporto, the first in-the-money result for this new Surbiton car. There was no Jaguar representation at the same day's Supercorte-maggiore GP, which was limited to 3-litre cars. This Ferrari benefit was led by Hawthorn and Maglioli, with Peter Whitehead's half-brother Graham and Carroll Shelby taking 5th for Aston Martin. All the Jaguar-retained drivers had to keep in practice somehow and, although William Lyons was careful to guard Jaguar interests, he could not be adamant about releasing them within reason. Stirling Moss, in particular, continued to 'hustle' Coventry for cars to drive: but the pattern emerging clearly was that, despite its 'near-miss' in 1953 (see vol. 1), Jaguar was not interested in the new World Sports Car Championship series. The D-type had been built to win Le Mans, and would be raced only as often as the Coventry management – essentially Lyons and Heynes, as advised by England – saw fit. No D-types would be sold until the next season, so private race entries still consisted of XKs, C-types and a few hybrids of which Cooper and HWM were the most significant. Frank Le Gallais was still recording fine hill-climb times in his LGS Jaguar-powered rear-engined special; but in this branch of the sport it was Ken Wharton who remained the undisputed British champion in ERA and Cooper.

A worthwhile journey to Reims

While much of Lofty England's correspondence was to turn down invitations, one event tailor-made for acceptance was the 12-hour race at Reims, run by the helpful Raymond Acat for the *AC de Champagne* on 3/4 July as a prelude to the Grand Prix for which Daimler–Benz had promised to make its comeback. Jaguar were well set, as Walker had suggested, for revenge. Jaguars had won at Reims in 1952 and 1953 and the three Le Mans D-types plus the Belgian C-type were prepared in Coventry with a view to ensuring victory. *Ecurie Ecosse* were, reportedly,

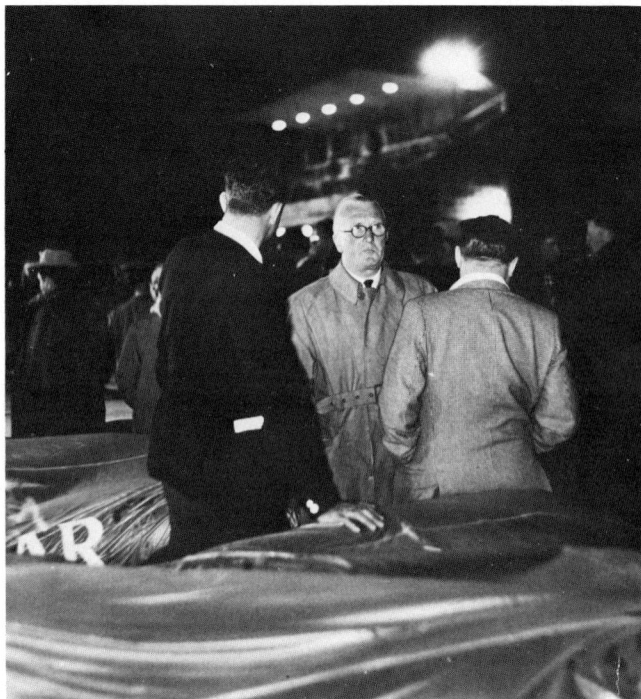

Heynes and England (backs to camera) with Lyons and sheeted cars awaiting the night start of the Reims 12-hour race.

Dewis and Hayden at work during a night stop at Reims. Whitehead settles into the cockpit. England is on the left.

turned down; but another C-type did appear in the form of XKC 037, an ex-works car owned by John Manussis from Nairobi. His co-driver would be Gerry Dunham – Luton Jaguar dealer, and son of Lofty England's former Alvis racing colleague (*see vol. 1*) – who had raced before, and was looking after the car in Britain. As he always did at Le Mans, England once again 'borrowed' Gérard Levecque from French importer Charley Delecroix, to be Jaguar's general factotum on the spot.

The opposition, though not as strong as at Le Mans, was not insignificant: several Ferraris of up to 4·5 litres; sundry Maseratis; and the two Cunninghams which had done so well three weeks earlier. Levegh was there with

Swaters in the C-type ploughs through the murk at Reims.

his Talbot, and four Gordinis were listed to swell the French effort. Aston Martin steered clear, but there *was* British back-up in the form of two Jaguar-powered HWMs and the three weird Bristol 450s. For Germany there was a strong Porsche presence.

This was Malcolm Sayer's practice report to his boss Bill Heynes, with copies to Messrs England, Knight, Weaver and Dewis:

SUMMARY OF PRACTICE FOR REIMS 1954

CAR NO 1. MOSS–WALKER
a. 48 laps av. 2.m. 48.s. = 347 ml. at 110¼ m.p.h.
b. Consumption: – Fuel, 8·6 m.p.g. Oil 308 m.p.g.
c. Fastest laps, Moss 2.m. 40.s. = 116 m.p.h.
   Walker 2.m. 42.s. = 114½ m.p.h.

CAR NO 2. ROLT–HAMILTON
a. 63 laps av. 2.m. 47.s. = 325 ml. at 111 m.p.h.
b. Consumption: – Fuel, 10·0. m.p.g. Oil 640 m.p.g.
c. Fastest laps, Rolt 2.m. 38.s. = 117 m.p.h.
   Hamilton 2.m. 41.s. = 115 m.p.h.

CAR NO 3. WHITEHEAD–WHARTON
a. 46 laps av. 2.m. 47.s. = 237 ml, at 111 m.p.h.
b. Consumption: – Fuel 9·65 m.p.g. Oil 1320 m.p.g.
c. Fastest laps, Whitehead 2.m. 41.s. = 115 m.p.h.
   (2.m. 42.s. = 114 m.p.h. in dark)
   Wharton 2.m. 38.s. = 117 m.p.h.

CAR NO 4. MANUSSIS–DUNHAM
a. 70 laps av. 3.m. 5.s. = 360 ml. at 100 m.p.h.
b. Fastest laps, Manussis 2.m. 57.s. = 105 m.p.h.
   Dunham 2.m. 51.s. = 108½ m.p.h.

CAR NO 9. LAURENT–SWATERS
a. 58 laps av. 3.m. 9.s. = 196 ml. at 98 m.p.h.
b. Fastest laps, Laurent 2.m. 55.s. = 106 m.p.h.
   Swaters 2.m. 54.s. = 106½ m.p.h.

The D-types were driven by the same crews as at Le Mans and the chief opposition would, clearly, come from the Cunninghams and from the 4·5 Ferrari of two former C-type Jaguar drivers – the youthful Masten Gregory (22) of Kansas City and Clemente Biondetti from

Florence, 55 years old and soon to die of cancer: a generation apart but each a driver of unquenchable spirit.

The race started in thin rain at midnight. Moss forged into an immediate lead and was soon lapping the tiddlers, always considered such a danger, especially at night. Umberto Maglioli in a works 3-litre Ferrari made a particularly daring job of picking off the little Panhards. This 4-cylinder Ferrari could not get quite close enough to challenge the Jaguar – especially after Moss put in some daunting sub-2 min. 50sec. laps to draw clear – and Maglioli retired after 25 laps, the gearbox useless.

At 21 laps Tony Rolt, running third in OKV 1, was shunted from behind by Jean Behra whose Gordini appeared to need the Jaguar's assistance to slow for Thillois. The D-type went down the escape road, then made a pit-stop to tidy the rear end and to top up with fuel.

Rolt didn't notice the latter operation, however, and so became worried.

Moss and Wharton began to look secure in first and second places but then Moss came in for an unscheduled plug change (one plug had lost an electrode). He stayed at the wheel for another stint, then handed over to Walker; eight laps later, the propellor shaft failed and Walker had no choice but to leave OKV 2 out on the circuit.

As dawn approached, John Fitch (Cunningham) was running second to Peter Whitehead and when it began to rain again, and the latter came in for a visor, the American took the lead; but the Jaguars had a pit-stop in hand and soon it was Jaguar first and second again; and as Gordinis and Maseratis succumbed one by one, the Belgian C-type moved up the field to challenge the Cunninghams. The second C-type spun off into retirement, however, Dunham doing the deed. After nine hours the D-types were running close together at the head of the field, with Rolt just ahead of Wharton. Then, after what should have been the final pit-stops (during which the leading car took on less fuel, and got away quicker), Hamilton led Whitehead by nearly a lap.

Although well behind the leaders, Laurent and Swaters had shaken off all the other opposition by the eleventh hour. Jaguars were 1st, 2nd and 3rd! Then Gregory began

England shows Hamilton where to stop ...

... examining the damage ...

to fly in the big Ferrari, Malcolm Sayer giving him a best lap of 2min. 42sec. compared to Wharton's 2min. 43sec. – although official timing recorded a 2min. 43·8sec. lap record for Wharton. (Both lap times, recorded late in a 12-hour event, were of the order of ten seconds longer than the best to be achieved by the Mercedes-Benz 'silver arrows' in the afternoon's Grand Prix event.)

The race was well into its last hour when OKV 1 shunted in the tail for the second time in a month – came into the pits with a noisy rear axle and, as Peter Whitehead took OKV 3 into a confident lead once again, the Hamilton car was examined closely. Now it was apparent that the differential casing had been punctured by a bent subframe member – a legacy of the Behra incident – and the teeth were running in the dry. (Could Dunham have spun on the lost oil, one wonders?) So near was midday that second place seemed certain; a temporary seal was made and Hamilton crawled round for a lap and a bit until the flag came out for his team-mate.

Meantime, Gregory's late charge was reaching its dramatic conclusion and Laurent was very nearly caught at the finishing line; the young American's Ferrari slammed into the tail of Briggs Cunningham's car which had been

... Bob Penney fills the syringe (held by Frank Rainbow) with axle oil while Weaver (behind pit counter), England, Rolt, Heynes and Lyons show varying degrees of worry. Vic Barlow of Dunlop looks over England's shoulder.

minding its own business in fifth place. Fortunately Cunningham managed to avoid the barrier in front of the grandstand and all was well. The other Cunningham had dropped back already, with overheating. This is Malcolm Sayer's post-race record of the three D-types and the fourth-placed Ferrari:

CAR NO 1: MOSS/WALKER

1. 39 laps by Moss, av. 2m. 56s. = 201 miles at 105 m.p.h.
2. 4m. 38s. in pit. Fuel 20 gal. Oil none. Water none. All plugs changed. Electrode missing from No. 3 plug.
3. 42 laps by Moss, av. 2m. 55s. = 216m. at 106 m.p.h.
4. 46s. in pit. Fuel 22 gal. Oil $\frac{1}{2}$ gal. Water none.
5. 8 laps by Walker, av. 2m. 59s. = 41m. at $103\frac{1}{2}$ m.p.h.
6. Propshaft failed, Walker walked in.
   Running time 4 hr. 21m. 46s. at 105 m.p.h. av.
   Pit stops 5m. 24s.

   Total _____ 4hr. 27m. 10s.

Consumption: 9·9 mpg. fuel, 834 mpg. oil. Water none.
Fastest laps, Moss 2m. 49s. = 109·8 m.p.h. in dark.
Walker 2m. 56s. = 105·2 m.p.h.

Lofty England keeps the leading driver informed.

CAR NO 2: ROLT/HAMILTON

1. 21 laps by Rolt, av. 2m. 57s. = 108 m. at $104\frac{1}{2}$ m.p.h.
2. 2m. 15s. in pit. Fuel 8·8 gal. oil none. Water none. Damaged spare wheel lid wired on, rear lamp repaired.
3. 60 laps by Rolt, av. 3m. 0s. = 309 m. at 105 m.p.h.
4. 1m. 4s. in pit. Fuel 27 gal. Oil 1 gall. Water $\frac{1}{2}$ gal.
5. 61 laps by Hamilton av. 2m. 54s. = 314m. at $106\frac{1}{2}$ m.p.h.
6. 1m. 2s. in pit. Fuel 32 gal. Oil 1 gal. Water $\frac{3}{4}$ gal.
7. 51 laps by Rolt av. 2m. 51s. = 263 m. at $108\frac{1}{2}$ m.p.h.
8. 56s. in pit. Fuel 23 gal. Oil $\frac{3}{4}$ gal. Water $\frac{3}{4}$ gal.
9. 40 laps by Hamilton av. 2m. 50s. = 206 m. at 109 m.p.h.
10. 12m. 10s. in pit. Axle cover patched with masking tape, refilled with oil.
11. 1 lap by Hamilton in 14m. 9s. then partial lap to end race.
    Running time 11 hr. 42m. 33s. at 103 m.p.h. (before axle trouble)
    Pit stops _____ 17m. 27s.

    Total _____ 12 hr. 0m. 0s.

Consumptions: 10·95 mpg fuel; 361 mpg oil; 497 mpg water.
Fastest laps: Rolt 2m. 51s. = 108·5 in dark.
2m. 45s. = 112·5 in light
Hamilton 2m. 44s. = 112·9 in light.

First win for a D-type! The chequered flag comes down for OKV 3 at Reims 1954.

CAR NO 3: WHITEHEAD/WHARTON

1. *61 laps by Wharton av. 3m. 2s. = 314 m. at 102 m.p.h.*
2. *1m. 0s. in pit. Fuel 27 gals. Oil 1 pint. Water 1 pint.*
3. *48 laps by Whitehead av. 2m. 58s. = 247 m. at 104 m.p.h.*
4. *48s. in pit adjusting visor.*
5. *16 laps by Whitehead av. 2m. 56s. = 82m. at 105 m.p.h.*
6. *1m. 3s. in pit. Fuel 33 gal. Oil ½ gal. Water none.*
7. *62 laps by Wharton av. 2m. 51s. = 319 m. at 108½ m.p.h.*
8. *1m. 3s. in pit. Fuel 33 gal. Oil ½ gal. Water none.*
9. *56 laps by Whitehead av. 2m. 53s. = 289 m. at 107 m.p.h.*

Running time	*11 hr. 56s. 6s. at 105 m.p.h.*
Pit stops	*3m. 54s.*
Total	*12 hr. 0m 0s.*

*Consumptions: 10·35 m.p.g. fuel 453 m.p.g. Oil
Water none.*
*Fastest laps, Whitehead 2m. 56s. = 105·2 in dark.
2m. 47s. = 111 in light.
Wharton 2m. 51s. = 108·5 in dark.
2m. 43s. = 113·8 in light.*

4·5 FERRARI. GREGORY–BIONDETTI

1. *43 laps by Gregory av. 3m. 3s. = 222 m. at 101 m.p.h.*
2. *2m. 53s. in pit.*
3. *13 laps by Gregory av. 3m. 16s. = 67 m. at 94½ m.p.h.*
4. *1m. 3s. in pit.*
5. *25 laps by Biondetti av. 3m. 12s. = 129m. at 96½ m.p.h.*
6. *2m. 15s. in pit.*
7. *5 laps by Biondetti av. 3m. 0s. = 26m. at 103 m.p.h.*
8. *5m. 25s. in pit.*
9. *33 laps by Biondetti av. 3m. 2s. = 170 m. at 102 m.p.h.*
10. *2m. 1s. in pit.*
11. *46 laps by Gregory av. 2m. 55s. = 237 m. at 106 m.p.h.*
12. *2m. 51s. in pit*
13. *42 laps by Biondetti av. 2m. 52s. = 216 min. at 108 m.p.h.*
14. *1m. 51s. in pit.*
15. *26 laps by Gregory av. 2m. 51s. = 134 at 108½ m.p.h.*
16. *Final partial lap.*

Running time	*11h. 41m. 41s. at 103 m.p.h.*
Pit stops	*18m. 19s.*
Total	*12h. 0m. 0s.*

*Fastest laps—Gregory 2m. 57s. = 104·7 in dark.
2m. 42s. = 114·5 in light.
Biondetti 2m. 45s. = 112·5 in light.*

As at Le Mans, OKV 1 showed by far the greatest thirst for oil and water. The top six positions at the finish were:

1st Ken Wharton/Peter Whitehead (3441 Jaguar D-type) 1254 miles.

2nd Duncan Hamilton/Tony Rolt (3441 Jaguar D-type) 1210 miles.

3rd Roger Laurent/Jacques Swaters (3441 Jaguar C-type) 1204½ miles.

4th Clemonte Biondetti/Masten Gregory (4523 Ferrari) 1204½ miles.

5th Briggs Cunningham/Sherwood Johnston (5482 Cunningham) 1194 miles.

6th John Fitch/Phil Walters (5482 Cunningham) 1171 miles.

Tony Gaze and Graham Whitehead brought the surviving HWM-Jaguar home seventh ahead of a Porsche, a Ferrari and the three Bristols.

It is interesting to note that the fuel consumed by the works and Belgian Jaguars cost just over 200,000 francs (or

around £200), which Shell paid, together with bonuses. Dunlop also paid some bonus money and this, with prize money, produced the following rewards for Jaguar works-contracted drivers, representing Le Mans and Reims combined. It was not done on an equal-share basis, except that the first and second place money for Reims was divided equally between the four drivers, because the cars had been running to strict orders at the time of Hamilton's emergency stop (as itemised earlier in the 1954 contract):

	Le Mans 24-hr	Reims 12-hr	Total
J. D. Hamilton A. P. R. Rolt	£983 10s. 0d. each	£603 15s. 0d. each	£1587 5s. 0d. each
S. C. Moss P. D. C. Walker	£15 0s. 0d. each	£30 11s. 3d. each	£35 11s. 3d. each
F. C. K. Wharton P. N. Whitehead	£15 0s. 0d. each	£603 15s. 0d. each	£618 15s. 0d. each

As Moss's manager, Ken Gregory sent Lofty England an almost-too-polite 'thank you' letter for the cheque. In addition to these sums, the drivers received £75 in starting money for each of the two races. On the whole, expenses were covered without formal commitment. Retainers were nominal, although Stirling Moss received special treatment as a full-time professional race driver of world class.

An Alpine without Appleyard

There was not the same direct interest in rallying now that Ian Appleyard had sold RUB 120, his XK 120 Roadster, which (*as described in vol. 1*) had been rebodied as a drop-head coupé in the autumn of 1953. This car had made its début in the 1953 Alpine Trial and Appleyard had been quickest in four of the six special tests (*see vol. 1, page 253*). More important, he had gained his fifth *Coupe des Alpes* an unparalleled individual performance.

Now business was limiting his competitive motoring to the occasional appearance in Jaguar saloons or MG sports cars: but Appleyard did find time to write to Lofty England in the spring of 1954, commenting on the latest Alpine regulations and the implications of revised handicapping.

Success in the Alpine had become something of a speciality for Jaguar and, with three promising private entries, Dunlop proved particularly co-operative in the supply of specially constructed 6·00 × 16 Fort Racing covers and tubes, which Appleyard had found very effective in 1953. Help for the entries in question was co-ordinated by Lofty England. The three cars were XK 120s, namely:

Roadster *661165* (RJH 400); owner Eric Haddon of Wealdstone; co-driver Charles Vivian.

Fixed-head coupé *669024* (GFE 111); owners Reg and Joan Mansbridge, Jaguar dealers of Lincoln and winners of a *Coupe des Alpes* in 1953.

Drophead coupé *661071* (RUB 120); ex-Appleyard, owned by Denis Scott of Prestbury, Cheshire: co-driver John Cunningham.

The Mansbridges retired at St-Moritz, the end of the first stage, with loss of power at high altitude. Haddon and

Eric Haddon, class-winner with his XK 120 in the 1954 Alpine Trial.

Vivian drove prudently, sacrificing many road marks; but they were rewarded with a win in the over 2·6-litre class. It was Denis Scott, however, usually a Ford man, whose driving made the greatest impression. He made best performance in the *autobahn* speed test. In the second test, the Circuit of the Dolomites, he was again fastest, taking 43 min. 9·8 sec. compared with the rally-winning Denzel's 43 min. 35 sec. In test three, he beat everyone in the 14 km race up the Stelvio Pass. It was during the fourth timed test, towards the end of the rally, on the Col de la Cayolle, that a rear spring broke. Scott and Cunningham did struggle on, to finish second in the class – but, for the first time in many years there would be no *Coupes des Alpes* for Jaguar drivers. (The *Coupe des Alpes* was awarded to all competitors who lost no road marks on the Alpine Trial, and was among the most coveted awards in rallying. In 1952 Appleyard had become the first recipient of the supreme accolade – The Alpine Gold Cup, or 'third Alpine Cup in a row'. This time, in 1954, Stirling Moss became the second winner of a 'Gold' driving a Sunbeam for the Rootes team.) Later in the month (July), Denis Scott wrote to Lofty England, telling him that 'no-one could have wished for better performance' from the car, and continued:

There was no sign of any lack of power at high altitudes, and the rear axle ratio of 3·77 to me seemed quite suitable, although it would have been interesting to compare our times for the hills with those of Mansbridge if he had carried on, but as I have said before with the use of 1st and 2nd gears for the hairpins the car never gave any impression of being too highly geared.

Conditions were so foul for the flying 1½ kms that water drag

Norman Dewis (XKC 404) and Bob Berry (XK 120 lightweight) at Brighton. The D-type's best time for the standing start Kilometre that day was 26.14 seconds. (*Courtesy: Bob Berry*)

and wind must have reduced the car's maximum by a good 10 m.p.h.

Now for the 'bitter bit': just after the start of the timed climb of the Col de la Cayolle, owing to a moment's relaxation of concentration I had to brake heavily for a corner. This, three hours from the finish, caused the off-side rear spring to snap off at the forward mounting; this was discovered at the top of the timed climb, as at the time of breaking we did not stop, thinking that it was probably the shock absorber that had gone.

On reaching the top and seeing what the trouble was the only thing we could do was to lash the end of the spring to the chassis and press on as fast as possible, hoping the crownwheel & pinion would stand up to it and that the front brakes would give us a little stopping, the rear brake pipe being cut when the spring broke.

Talking about brakes, we never had any trouble with these at all, the rear ones were taken up twice, a total of 6 or 7 clicks.

Scott also enclosed a copy of his letter to Dunlop, commenting favourably on the even and gradual wear of the tyres: the rear ones had been changed once, the fronts not at all. Rainy conditions for much of the event had played a part here.

This was to be one of the last competitive international rally performances for a Jaguar XK120, which was to be succeeded by the XK140 range at the London show in October. From now on, most rally success for Jaguar would be gained by the saloon models. Rallying, in general, was entering a long period of great change. Time will tell whether or not 1986's highly specialised rally cars were the ultimate machines for this sport, which finally got out of hand, and had to be curbed. On the other hand it *has* become a spectator sport which, thirty years ago, it was not.

The 1954 Alpine Trial gave Jaguar the chance to advertise in the British Grand Prix Report issue of *Autosport*, for the marque had a quiet day at Silverstone. There were no works cars in the sports car race there, and *Ecurie Ecosse* had a bad day with their ex-works C-types against a strong Aston Martin–Lagonda entry. Tony Rolt made best practice laps for the Scottish team but dropped back when the car went off-colour. Desmond Titterington from Belfast managed a commendable sixth place in a strong field; Sanderson was eighth, Rolt tenth. With none of the latest cars yet available to private owners, there was frustration for those who preferred Jaguar to any other power source.

In August 1954, Peter Whitehead made the Jaguar-powered Cooper look really promising, however, with wins at Snetterton and The Curragh. The latter was the Wakefield Trophy race, in which Duncan Hamilton and Joe Kelly shared second place in their C-types. In fifth position, behind Anthony Powys-Lybbe's glorious monoposto Alfa Romeo came Bob Berry in the very fast lightweight XK120 prepared by former Jaguar racing mechanic John Lea. So unexpectedly fast was this car that Berry – who, on weekdays, was Rankin's publicity assistant at the Jaguar works – came within 3 seconds of wresting the O'Boyle Handicap Trophy from Redmond Gallagher (Gordini) despite having given away nearly a lap to the Irishman's nimble little French car.

Autumn Cancellation

For international sports car racing, the autumn of 1954 proved a somewhat uncertain period. The Goodwood 9-hour race was missing from the calendar, and for a while it looked as if the Jaguar works team's next race would be the Nürburgring 1000 Km event in which an *Ecurie Ecosse* C-type had been the 1953 runner-up. Jaguar was about to place an entry when word came through that the race, due for 29 August, would be cancelled – largely because its public appeal might be lost when it was revealed that the new Mercedes-Benz 300SLR sports-racers would not make their début in this WSCC event. The Lancia team was already working hard at the 'Ring when the announcement was made, and joined Jaguar in rebuking the ADAC for its late decision.

The Reims-winning car (OKV 3, chassis XKC 404) was rebuilt but not raced again in 1954. It took part in several demonstrations at traditional British meetings, as something of a PR exercise, since no-one had seen the new Jaguars in action on mainland Britain. Ken Wharton, star of the late-August Shelsley Walsh meeting anyway, took the car up the famous hill in an impressive 40·70 seconds – but only unofficially, for Leslie Wilson the Midland AC would not accept late entries. It was at this meeting that serious sports-car competitors began breaking the 40-second barrier.

On 4 September, Jaguar's chief experimental test engineer/driver, Norman Dewis, took part in the Brighton Speed Trials – a standing start 1 Km Sprint along the Madeira Drive – running the car with a 3·54 to 1 axle ratio and 17-inch wheels. The engine number at this point – and for the next year – was E2006–9. In the competition proper, Dewis (29·14 sec.) had to give best to Maurice Wick (Allard–Cadillac: 28·36 sec.), the surface being damp. During his 'demonstration', however, the Coventry driver was able to get more grip and, with slick gear-changes at just the right moments, he set a new sports car standard of 26·14 sec. which compared favourably with the BTD of 23·57 sec. achieved by a 998 cc Vincent motor cycle.

Unhappy handicap

Under threat all year, through lack of finance, the Tourist Trophy – run at Dundrod by the Ulster Automobile Club for the RAC – was by now a racing certainty, the confirmation of entries from Ferrari, Lancia and Maserati settling the matter.

Animated correspondence had been passing between Lofty England and Ulster AC secretary Gordon Neill since the regulations had been issued, mainly on the handicap system of credit laps against engine capacity, which (for the bigger cars) was broken down like this:

Engine Capacity	Credit Laps	Estimated Average mph
Over 6283 cc	0	90·47
5220–6283 cc	1	89·51
4448–5220 cc	2	88·55
3862–4448 cc	3	87·59
3403–3862 cc	4	86·62
3036–3403 cc	5	85·66
2734–3036 cc	6	84·70
2483–2734 cc	7	83·74
2266–2483 cc	8	82·77

2082–2266 cc	9	81·81
1922–2082 cc	10	80·85
and so on down to:		
757–794 cc	26	65·45
Under 757 cc	27	64·49

An estimated race time of 7 hr. 42 min. 42 sec. had been calculated for the theoretical 'scratch' distance of 94 laps, and the system had been chosen so that the whole field would start together with a view to pleasing the crowds who had bought grandstand seats. England had expressed Jaguar's dissatisfaction with the system but, despite saying that the decision to race or not rested with Mr Lyons, he got nowhere.

On 10 August, Heynes told Messrs Lyons, England, Knight and Baily in a memo:

Reference the letter received from the T.T. Authorities regarding the handicap, this position looks unsatisfactory and I am going ahead with the preparation of one 2½ litre car for use in this race, which will be 2483 c.cs., to take full advantage of the handicap.

Providing pistons are available in time it would be possible for us to enter a team of three 2½ litre cars instead of the three 3½ litre and one 2½ litre, and I am endeavouring to make arrangements so that this can be done if tests prove outstandingly satisfactory. I would, however, recommend that one 3½ litre car at least is entered with a view to obtaining the greatest distance. Although there does not appear to be any award for this it is always a creditable achievement.

On 20 August, Lofty England formally advised the regular team drivers that they would be required in Belfast in time to race on 11 September. As had happened before, David Yorke and Arthur Birks of the Whitehead personal *équipe* were drafted in to assist, Yorke to be in charge of sorting out the complex timing information system which would be necessary. Local competition driver Chris Lindsay also joined the Jaguar pit team for the occasion.

In 1953, the surface had been particularly abrasive but this problem was now said to be less acute, yet the circuit itself seemed no faster: slower if anything, or was it the Jaguar cars? (John Bolster would speculate afterwards, 'One cannot help wondering for how much longer this make is to be handicapped by having a conventional rear axle.')

In the end it was decided to enter two of the new cars with a reduced engine capacity, and one with the regular long stroke dimension. This was the works line-up:

XKC 402 with its usual 3441 cc power unit (E2004–9), a 3:54 to 1 axle ratio, and 17-inch wheels. Drivers: Rolt and Hamilton; race number 5.

XKC 403 with converted engine (basically E2005–9); 9·05 to 1 compression ratio; 76·5 mm stroke crankshaft in 3·4 block giving 2482 cc; tested (on 9 September) by Jack Emerson to give 190 bhp at 6000 rpm; 4·09 to 1 axle ratio and 17-inch wheels. Drivers: Whitehead and Wharton; race number 6. (This number reflected the original entry as a '3½'.)

XKD 406, a new car (misleadingly registered OKV 3) with made-up 2482 cc (76·5 mm stroke in 3·4 block) engine, probably numbered 'DB 1000' or E2003–9 converted, 9·66 to 1 compression ratio; tested (9 Sept) to give 193 bhp at 6000 rpm; 3·92 to 1 axle ratio and 16-inch wheels with Dunlop 'Stabilia' tyres. Drivers: Moss and Walker; race number 20.

The 1954 TT did not go well for Jaguar. Here Moss takes the Dundrod hairpin in XKD 406 – a brand new D-type fitted with a 2½-litre engine which was chosen in an attempt to beat the handicappers.

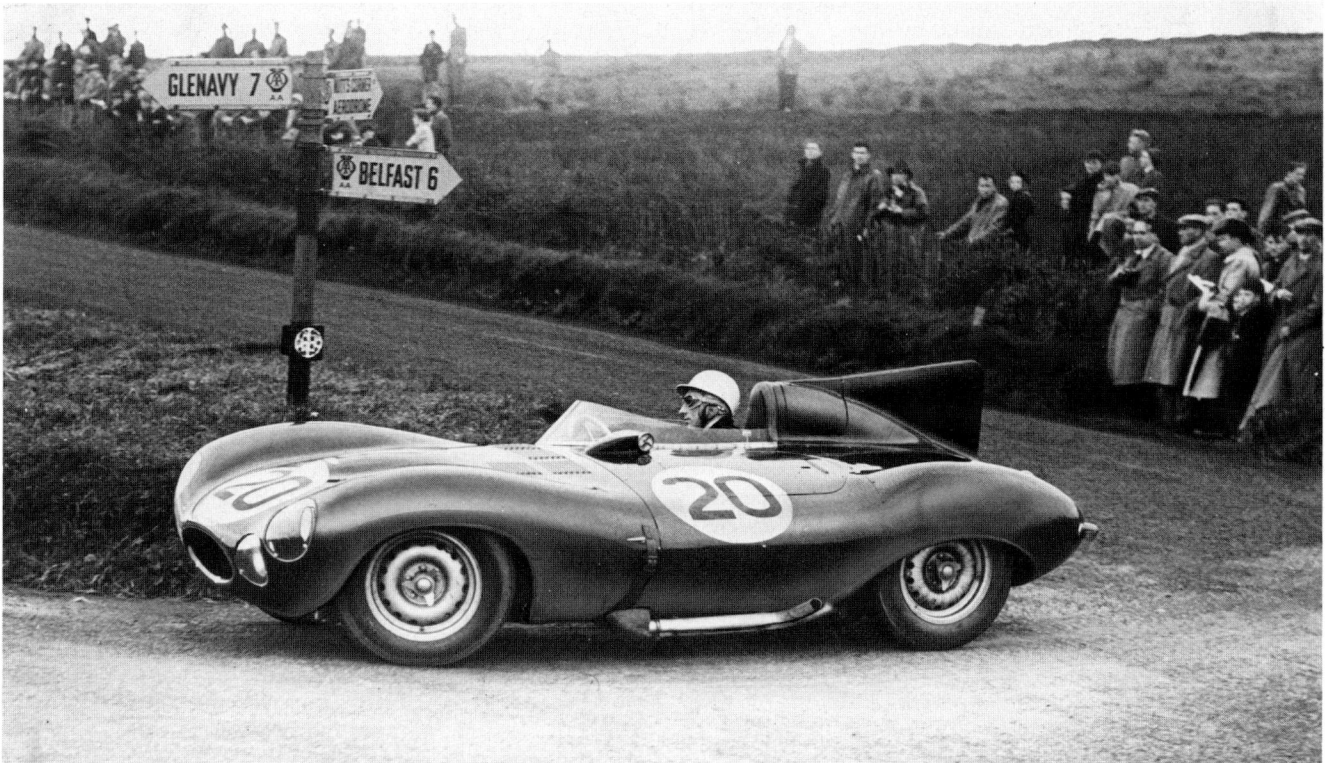

It was not a successful outing, for Jaguar was already looking towards the 1955 season. Several important developments were being considered, and experimental work for the TT formula was an intrusion. Jaguar had never been over-staffed and motor-racing was something that had to be fitted in with the everyday business of car-making.

Practice on the difficult and narrow Dundrod road circuit on the high ground between Belfast and Lough Neagh began spectacularly enough. It was dull, damp and windy as Jaguar No. 5 became the first car to complete a lap.

Shortly afterwards Le Mans winner Froilan Gonzalez got into trouble at Tornagrough, the highest point on the course. He lost his Ferrari under braking. The car hit a bank tail-first; then it rebounded and struck it again with the nose. The burly Gonzalez was thrown out into the road and it took him some time to regain his senses. Eventually he sat up, and even managed to take off his helmet before the ambulancemen arrived. He was taken to hospital, accompanied by a concerned Mike Hawthorn who had been one of the first on the scene. Gonzalez recovered well, but did not return to a serious big-time racing career, and competed only occasionally afterwards. He was a great driver, however, and is underrated by history. His compatriot, Fangio (3·8 Lancia), had an altercation with a bank at Quarry Corner soon afterwards but was unhurt.

Star of this (drying) practice session was reigning World Grand Prix Champion Alberto Ascari, whose 3·8 Lancia was the first machine to beat the official sports car lap record of 5 m. in 01 sec. (88·70 mph) set in 1953 by Peter Walker in a works C-type Jaguar. Ascari finally got down to 4 mm. 54 sec., only three seconds short of the outright motor-cycle record, then held by Geoff Duke and Ken Kavanagh. Only a second slower over the 7 mile 732 yard course was Ulsterman Desmond Titterington in Joe Kelly's 3-litre Ferrari which would retire with a broken gearbox. No-one else broke the old record. Piero Taruffi (3·3 Lancia) did 5 min. 03 sec. followed by Poore/G White-head (Aston Martin DB3S) in 5 min. 08 sec. The Jaguars came next with Moss (2·5) on 5 min. 09 sec. and his team-mates on 5 min. 10 sec.

Those treating this session as a preliminary canter were to be disappointed next day, when the heavens opened. Even so, Mike Hawthorn (3-litre, four-cylinder Ferrari) managed 4 min. 58 sec. as conditions eased.

Race day was largely dry and the first lap was completed in the order: Ascari, Hawthorn, Rolt, Fangio. This soon changed to Hawthorn, Ascari, Fangio, Rolt. When Lancia's 3·8 engine gave trouble Fangio became Taruffi's co-driver in the 3·3. Ascari later retired when the prop-shaft came through the floor after his 3·8 Lancia had covered the 1 km straight at a record 144·6 mph. Despite doing 'only' 132 mph here, however, Hawthorn set the best race lap time of 4 min. 49 sec. (92·38 mph). After 33 laps in a car that was well down on its known performance, Rolt came in with the oil pressure gone. One slow lap by Hamilton confirmed serious engine trouble, incurable that day.

Moss had been making good progress in relation to the handicap, however, getting to within a second of Walker's old record before handing over to the man himself; but Walker was not able to get near his old C-type pace. At Moss's speed, third place on handicap was a distinct possibility – until a piston failed with an hour to go and Moss, who had had to do the same thing in 1953, waited to chug across the finishing line in a lowly eighteenth place. This was a poor reward, if a not surprising one, for the efforts of the previous night when the engine had had to be rebuilt – after the holing of a piston!

By contrast, the Wharton/Whitehead '2½' had a steady race with only a plug change. Its main time-loss was due to a puncture when Wharton was on the far side of the circuit. This car was the sixth fastest finisher and fifth on handicap, fractionally slower than George Abecassis and Jim Mayers in one of two HWM-Jaguars.

It *should* have been Hawthorn's day, he and Trintignant being fastest finishers; but the Frenchmen Paul Armagnac and Gérard Laureau had the last laugh. Their nimble little 750 cc DB-Panhard buzzed round at an average of 68·75 mph to beat their target by over 4 mph. The final handicap order was: 1st, Laureau/Armagnac (745 DB-Panhard); 2nd Hawthorn/Trintignant (3-litre Ferrari); 3rd, Musso/Mantovani (2-litre Maserati); 4th, Taruffi/Fangio (3·3 Lancia); 5th, Whitehead/Wharton (2·5 Jaguar); 6th Manzon/Valenzano (3·3 Lancia). Only the first three achieved their set targets.

On race speed alone, the top ten would have been:

3·0 Ferrari	Hawthorn/Trintignant	86·08 mph
3·3 Lancia	Taruffi/Fangio	85·64 mph
3·3 Lancia	Manzon/Valenzano	83·60 mph
3·4 HWM-Jaguar	Abecassis/Mayers	80·91 mph
2·0 Maserati	Musso/Mantovani	80·88 mph
2·5 Jaguar (D-type)	P. Whitehead/Wharton	80·85 mph
3·4 Jaguar (C-type)	Laurent/Swaters	79·92 mph
3·0 Aston Martin	G. Whitehead/Poore	79·00 mph
2·0 Ferrari	Gregory/Said	76·67 mph
2/0 Cooper–Bristol	Brown/Keen	75·87 mph

It is noteworthy that the Belgians, their rebuilt C-type Jaguar now resplendent in bright yellow livery, had driven another fast and steady race, though handicapped down from seventh to sixteenth in the results. Even further down the field came Joe Kelly's C-type, on loan to Joe Flynn and Torrie Large.

John Bolster's TT remarks about the Jaguar's non-independent rear end appeared to be borne out a week later at Prescott Hill, where Peter Walker was nominated to demonstrate the Reims-winning car (the genuine OKV 3). It poured with rain, and the lack of traction was embarrassing, even for an *ascension d'honneur*.

The car ran with a works-built 4·27 to 1 final drive and 16-inch wheels, with cut Dunlop R1 tyres – 6·00 front and 6·50 rear.

On 20 September, OKV 3 (XKC 404) was fitted with a 3·54 to 1 axle and tested. On 18 October the gearbox was replaced by a three-synchro C-type unit for use at Goodwood six days later. This was to be the Guild of Motoring Writers' annual motor show test day, which it got through unscathed.

Showtime drama

The three works TT cars were shipped home for long work lists to be issued on 20 September. XKC 402's engine had broken its crankshaft and E2004–9 was replaced by E2005–9 in 3·5-litre form. Such was the internal chaos that the oil radiator and other components were discarded to guard against contamination or obstruction. The gearbox needed a rebuild with many new components. Gearbox and water and oil radiators were transferred from OKV 2 (XKC 403) as no new spares were available and (as the most successful Le Mans car) OKV 1 had to be mobile in order to get to Paris for the motor show. On test the car had proved 'virtually undrivable' due to long clutch pedal travel, so modifications were incorporated in the rebuild on 27 September, to include a different master cylinder and an altered pedal fulcrum giving 45 lb sq in load and 6 inches travel. The bulkhead was modified to suit. After much cosmetic surgery the car was driven on Saturday 2 October from Coventry to Folkestone by Gordon Gardner. He was met at Calais by Charles Delecroix's man-of-all-work, Gérard Levecque, and they continued towards Paris in convoy. Almost at once Gardner was in trouble with the clutch withdrawal mechanism, and bent the 1–2 selector fork badly; so he drove in third

Poul Petersen (service manager of Jaguar Denmark importer) contemplates the battered nose and tail of XKD 402 in France, October 1954. (*Courtesy: Ole Sommer*)

Erik Nørregard (winner of a trip to Coventry) watches Joe Sutton fill up XKD 402 after its road accident on the way back from Paris, 1954. (*Courtesy: Ole Sommer*)

and top and, wisely, took a tow through the streets of Paris to the Delecroix garage. Tidied up, and given its old Le Mans race number, the car made a fine exhibit at the Paris Salon where the XK 120 model was displayed for the last time – albeit on the stand of the coachbuilder, Ghia, in the typical coupé style which would become more familiar when Volvo announced the P1800 five years later.

On 19 October, Joe Sutton set off for Paris with gearbox number 403 and a standard clutch cylinder. His instructions were to bring OKV 1 'back to standard in every respect ... car being sold to Duncan Hamilton on return from France' (according to the competition department's handwritten notes for the car).

OKV 1 received its new gearbox, its *Salon* appearance over, and Joe Sutton headed north. All went well until, approaching the coast near Abbeville, he swerved to avoid a cow – or was it a bull? Joe thought so. XKD 402's front end was damaged in a ditch, almost exactly as it had been at Le Mans. This time it also hit a tree backwards, being damaged even more than at Reims!

Poul Petersen (service manager for Sommer, Jaguar's Danish importer) and Erik Nørregard – a fitter who had won a trip to Coventry and the motor show as an incentive prize – happened upon the embarrassing scene to record it for posterity. The rubber fuel tank was damaged, but there was no apparent hurt in the main frame or suspension, and Sutton got the car to the ferry and back to Coventry without further incident. At Browns Lane a new rear axle cover plate was fitted to replace the dented one. The rear sub-frame skin was removed and replaced while

two cross-members were straightened. A new head fairing, fin, and bootlid were also fabricated. The Marston company repaired and tested the tanks, and new pipework was fitted. In its final specification for sale to Hamilton, the car had engine E2005-9, gearbox 403, a 3·54 to 1 axle and a new set of 6·00 × 16 front and 6·50 × 16 rear Dunlop R1 tyres. Lucky man. The first private owner of a D-type, Hamilton drove it home in the snow later that winter. 'If a so-called sports-racing car cannot be driven on the road,' he would say, 'it is not what it purports to be.'

There was less hurry to rebuild OKV 2 (XKC 403), for it had no immediate commitments. It was given the rebuilt engine (E2004-9) and other checked or rebuilt components including the OKV 1's pre-Paris gearbox (No. 401) and its oil and water radiators. In November, the wide calipers and the old discs were removed so that standard-width calipers could be fitted, thus enabling 16-inch wheels to be used. Bob Penney did most of the work on this car which went out on road test on 30 November and had to be towed in from Princethorpe after gearbox failure. Various work was carried out in December including the removal of a 3-inch blanking strip from the upper radiator in favour of a controllable blind, and the fitting of 16-inch wheels instead of the 17-inch ones. Third gear failed during driver tests at Silverstone on 31 December.

XKD 406 had also needed considerable mechanical rebuilding after Dundrod. These 2·5-litre engines would never be raced again and E2003-9 became a 3·4 unit once more. This car was bulled-up for Earls Court where it was shown alongside the recently-introduced Mark VII 'M' and the debutante XK 140 range. It was run at Silverstone soon afterwards, developing a serious oil leak. At Lindley (The Motor Industry Research Association's test establishment near Nuneaton) on 20 November, pre-Sebring tests revealed third and top gear selection problems. Final preparations, including the fitting of an adjustable radiator blind and tonneau cover stiffener brackets were completed by 21 December when the car was considered ready for shipment to America.

In Britain the year ended, as usual, with 'Boxing Day Brands'. Stirling Moss played Santa Claus, leaving the driving to others. Among the winners that day were Syd Creamer (Creamer 500) and John Coombs (Lotus–Connaught) both of whom would become leading Jaguar dealers as the Coventry firm built up its home market which had to be sacrificed in favour of exports so far.

Third place in the unlimited sports car race was gained by Dan Margulies in XKC 038 which he had just bought from Duncan Hamilton. During 1955, with help from Graham Hill, Margulies would prove that there was plenty of life in the old C-type yet.

More important, the D-type for 1955 was beginning to look a much more practical proposition – for the customer, and for the works team, too.

Chapter Three

A New-look Team for 1955

If there had been any serious dissent about Jaguar works drivers up to this stage, it had been kept well below the surface. From the drivers' point of view, however, 1954 had been an even less satisfactory year than usual. The 1953 C-types had been sold to *Ecurie Ecosse* long before the new cars were ready – so there had not been any old cars to race prior to Le Mans.

The new cars had been raced as a team only three times – at Le Mans, Reims and Dundrod – by the end of a season in which Jaguar's understandably obsessive concentration upon Le Mans had become more obvious than ever.

In each of its six 'full' seasons of racing as a factory-based team, from 1951 to 1956, Jaguar never allowed its new Le Mans cars to take part in a race beforehand (except in 1956 when the 24–hour event would be postponed until late July). Once that event was over, Jaguar thoughts usually turned to the immediate business in Coventry, the next year's Le Mans and the rest of the racing season – in that order. Le Mans was always the focal point of the year.

The person most affected by the Jaguar policy was, of course, Stirling Moss, whose father mentioned on the telephone to Bill Heynes that, 'the drivers were disappointed that the full share-out of prize money for the team did not occur, although as far as Stirling was concerned he was not prepared to raise this matter as he was completely satisfied with his own overall treatment'. (Moss, as recorded earlier, received a £2,000 retainer for 1954). Heynes next spoke to Moss's manager Ken Gregory, who assured him that 'Stirling would be only

too pleased' to demonstrate a car at Sebring (a race in which the Jaguar works team had not yet participated). On the same day, 17 November 1954, Heynes – writing to Lyons with a copy to England – reported his conversations:

I spoke to Mr Moss this morning and asked the question as to whether we could take it as certain that Stirling would be driving for us again on the same terms as before. He told me that Stirling had already been to Italy and tried out the Ferrari, and had definitely turned down the proposals they had put to him.

He had had conversations with Mercedes and put it to them that as he was signed with Shell he could not undertake a contract with Mercedes, who were running on Esso/Castrol, and the matter had reached that stage when he left for America. Since he has left for America, Mercedes have wired that they have made arrangements that if Stirling signs up to drive with them his car can run on Shell fuel and lubricants. They wish him to go to Germany and try out the cars, which they state have been redesigned since last season in respect of the steering, and wish to make him a proposal, and as I see it the matter rests there until Stirling's return and he has had an opportunity to go over and discuss this matter with Mercedes.

Mr Moss assures me that even if Stirling finds the offer so attractive that he feels compelled to accept it, he would still endeavour to make the contract for Grand Prix racing only so that he can remain with the Jaguar on sports cars, but personally, I feel that if he signs with Mercedes they will be likely to enforce a sports car clause as well.

He added some general remarks about Ken Gregory's advice on Transatlantic logistics. 'I feel the whole matter calls for a further conference at the earliest possible moment,' Heynes concluded; but it was too late.

Moss's Formula 1 career had been a disaster so far, due in part to his attempts to stay with British constructors. He had driven a new 250F Maserati for most of 1954, often looking a winner (even against Fangio's Mercedes-Benz) but usually failing to finish. Three late-season non-championship victories were small consolation, and in his three Jaguar sports car drives he had done a fine pacemaking job; but the D-type was not giving *him* the results he needed so badly at this crucial stage of his career. Suggestions to Jaguar, on the matter of a car for this or that race, brought little positive response and much frustration. For example, on the subject of the *Carrera Panamericana*, which Moss had reconnoitred with England in 1953, Lyons wrote to him about his idea of a vehicle for the touring section:

I have no doubt that we can prepare a MkVII with a performance capable of winning the race, and I agree with you that success in this event is of greater value in America than the Le Mans Race. The chief obstacle, I think, from our point of view, apart from the cost which we may be able to raise in some way (although we most certainly do not want our cars to race blazoned with the name of someone's beer or similar product), is the organisation which it is necessary to provide; likewise the personnel, which would have to be very considerable – as much, in fact, for one car as for three. However, now that you have raised this, we will have a think round it.

That was as far as it ever got.

Moss leaves, Mike arrives

Eventually Stirling Moss decided not to sign-up with Maserati for 1955. It was all very well being honoured at home by awards, and by selection for Madame Tussaud's; but becoming a Grand Prix *winner* was now a matter of urgency. In the first week of December Daimler-Benz (as Heynes had predicted) announced the retention of Moss not only for Grands Prix but also for their new World Sports Car Championships contender, the Mercedes-Benz 300SLR. It was an unparalleled offer for the British driver for whom 1955 would prove an outstanding season.

Britain's other star driver Mike Hawthorn, who had missed a Jaguar works drive due to injury in 1952 (*See Vol. 1*) was already a fully-fledged Grand Prix *and* sports car driver for Enzo Ferrari – a taskmaster for whom Moss was never prepared to work. 1954 had not been a bed of roses, though. Hawthorn had been burned severely at Syracuse, and his father had been killed in a road accident. Late in the season he had scored his second championship Grand Prix win – a superb performance with the 'Squalo' Ferrari – but had to follow that with a visit to Guy's Hospital, London, for a kidney operation. (This got a merciless press off his back when the authorities, at last, indicated openly that he was quite unfit for National Service.)

Since he wanted to spend more time at the family garage in Farnham, and less of it commuting to Italy, Hawthorn accepted Tony Vandervell's invitation to drive the F1 Vanwall. When this was announced, England wrote to Hawthorn, still in Guy's, asking him to join Jaguar for 1955.

Lofty England had prepared his first tentative short-list of 1955 drivers just after the TT back in September. Beside each name he put in the driver's age where known, suffixed by a simple '1' or '2' classification. This was not an official memo – just an *aide memoire*:

500cc Types	Age	Classification
J Russell	34	1
I Bueb	–	2
S Lewis-Evans	24	1
R Bicknell	–	2
Sports		
P Gammon	30	1
J R Stewart	23	1
D Beauman	–	2
J Riseley-Pritchard	–	2
D Titterington	26	2
N Sanderson	29	1/2
P Collins	23	1
R Parnell	44	1
A Crook	34	2
R Salvadori	31	1/2
R Nuckey	25	2
A Brown	35	2
C A S Brooks	–	2
L Macklin	35	2
M Keen	35	1
T Line	30	2
G Dunham	34	–
R Jacobs	38	–

There was no written indication as to which drivers might be approached. By the end of September, Desmond Titterington had tested a car at Silverstone and been accepted.

For the next Silverstone session, Jimmy Stewart (his arm, injured at Le Mans, improving well) and Ninian Sanderson were invited down from Scotland. Peter Walker and Jaguar's own Bob Berry were the other two to drive D-types on that wet and murky November day. Both Stewart (XKD 406) and Sanderson (XKC 404) did 2min. 11sec. in the wet. As the surface dried, their times came down to 2min. 5sec. and 2min. 9sec. respectively. Best times for each driver by the end of the day were: Berry (XKC 404) 1min. 54.5sec.; Walker (XKD 406) 1min. 57sec.; Stewart (XKC 404) 1min. 58sec.; and Sanderson (XKC 404) 2min. 01sec. Although there is no record of exact changes in weather, it is known that the cars, with their 16-inch wheels and 3.54 to 1 axle ratios, were to similar specifications. (XKC 404 would be tidied up afterwards for January's Brussels show.)

Although, as a Jaguar employee, Berry was probably not in the running for a works drive as such, there is no doubt that it was this performance which earned him his seat (at Heynes' recommendation) when XKC 403 was sold to Jack Broadhead. Afterwards, Ninian Sanderson received a polite letter from England telling him that he would not be required for 1955 but: 'I trust you will be seen at the wheel of a Jaguar car again next year.' Jimmy Stewart was asked to wait in hope. Roy Salvadori had been invited along, but declined when John Wyer took exception to his plan to buy a D-type for his own use (when not racing for Aston Martin).

In December, Lofty England stayed with the Titteringtons (who were flax and yarn merchants in Belfast) when fulfilling a speaking engagement with the Ulster Automobile Club. He also showed the dramatic Random Films production *Le Mans, 1954*, and answered questions. *Belfast Newsletter* columnist Billy McMaster reported some of his comments, though not those relating to the TT handicapping arrangements. England acknowledged that Jaguar had been experimenting with fuel injection for 'the past two years', and forecast an international sports car racing top-limit of 3 or $3\frac{1}{2}$ litres – probably for 1956. (These figures were being discussed by the International Sporting Commission.) England obtained Titterington's signature before returning to Coventry to finalise the 1955 team. This was done at another Silverstone test session on 31 December, when Donald Beauman made a very good impression. ('I must say you did not do too badly,' wrote England a few days later, confirming that Beauman would be invited to a final selection day.)

The main hold-up in announcing the 1955 team was the settling of Hawthorn's contract, announcement of his signing for Jaguar being made on 31 January. By then, there was just one place to fill, for Hamilton and Rolt were virtually automatic reselections due to their excellence as a partnership; and Hawthorn, Stewart, and Titterington were using the final session with XKC 401 and 403 as a familiarisation one, for they had already passed muster. Times were somewhat irrelevant again due to mixed weather.

On 10 February, England wrote to Ivor Bueb explaining that Don Beauman would be the sixth man because of his sports car experience: 'There was practically nothing between the times put up by you, Beauman and Berry, your performance at Silverstone being equal to theirs.... I feel you have a very good attitude to motor racing.... I do hope that should, for some reason, one of our drivers not be able to drive in some event in which we are running, we may be able to obtain your services.' Those services would, indeed, come into their own sooner rather than later.

The following Jaguar press release was issued on 14 February:

JAGUAR RACING TEAM FOR 1955
The following drivers will form the official Jaguar team in all those sports car races in which Jaguar cars will compete during the 1955 season:
  J M Hawthorn
  A P R Rolt
  J D Hamilton
  J R Stewart
  J D Titterington
  D B Beauman

A tentative programme of events has been arranged covering the following events; Le Mans entries have already been made.
  Silverstone – Sports and Touring Car Races
  Le Mans
  Rheims
  Aintree – Sports Car Race
  1,000 Km. Race – Nürburgring
  Tourist Trophy Race

The backlash came the next day, and Lyons immediately issued the following statement:

I was surprised to read in this morning's press that statements have been made by two of the drivers who have driven our cars in past competitions, regarding the fact that they will not be driving in our JAGUAR Team this year, and I should be glad if you would be good enough to give equal publicity to our point of view in this matter. A spokesman of the Company has already stated that contracts are arranged annually only, and that we have made changes in our team in order to bring along some younger drivers we have discovered.

As far as I am concerned, in the case of Mr Wharton he has never been considered as a driver in our 1955 team. Since he drove for us last year he has taken up an appointment as Competition Manager of another manufacturer. He did this without consulting us, and I assumed he would realise that in view of this appointment, he would not be nominated as a driver for us in this year's racing.

In the case of Mr Walker, I have the greatest admiration for him, both as a driver of great ability, and as a man, and I am sure he knows it, but as racing is a very serious matter for my Company, he was asked by us to take part in private speed trials in company with other drivers under consideration for team places, but he declined and subsequently signed up for another Company. With regard to Mr Whitehead who has left this country for a visit to Australia, he was informed before he went that it was unlikely that we would ask him to sign for us for 1955.

In the foregoing circumstances we have done no more than to build up an already depleted team from the best available sources and the question of 'dropping' drivers for reasons of age does not arise.

The sourness did not last long, however. Peter Whitehead (like Duncan Hamilton) had his own Jaguar-powered cars to race; and Peter Walker had already written to Lofty England: 'I do feel you should know my driving by now without recourse to further testing at Silverstone.... I have with great regret decided to drive for another firm this year.' Thanking Jaguar for 'a great deal of fun in the past,' Walker moved to Aston Martin. Ken Wharton had received an unusually diplomatic letter from England (following a telephone conversation) explaining the selection of 'new blood' and congratulating him on winning the Malcolm Campbell Trophy, with Whitehead, for their Reims drive – but not mentioning Wharton's 'freelance' appointment as Daimler competition manager. Lyons, who had been on a tour of the United States (including opening his new Park Avenue showrooms in New York) when the trouble was brewing, took the trouble to send the three sacked drivers a suitable letter – quite courteous yet utterly direct. This was the telling comment Lyons addressed to Walker at his Herefordshire farm: '... as racing costs us several hundred thousand pounds a year, we cannot afford to be sentimental about it. It is your hobby, but it is a very serious business matter for us.'

In six seasons of Jaguar works racing activity, that shake-up of the winter of 1954–55 was the only one of its kind.

Of the other possibilities at that stage, it is interesting to note that England made informal approaches to Alberto Ascari and Luigi Villoresi; also that, without his boss's knowledge, Tom Lush of the Allard company asked England if Sydney Allard might be considered as a member of the Le Mans Jaguar as 'he likes this event more than any other'. England would have liked to help the enthusiastic Clapham car maker, but had to point out that the team was complete.

Team prize on the 'Monte'

Racing contracts were quite unrelated to rallying, in which Jaguar took a more-than-passing interest – naturally being keen to win the Monte Carlo Rally for the prestige attached, rather than for any technical lessons that might be learned from this event which was unpredictable in terms of weather and in quality of organisation. In January 1955, Lofty England was in Monaco to see the MkVII saloons carry off the Charles Faroux Trophy for the best performance by a nominated team of three cars. Ronald Adams and Ernest McMillen came eighth overall in the works car, PWK 700; Cecil Vard and Arther Jolley were twenty-seventh in another – PWK 701 – having been caught out at a secret check; Ian and Pat Appleyard nearly didn't make it at all, after blowing a core plug in their own car, SUM 7 – but despite relegation from a leading position to eighty-third in the final placings, they helped make sure of a major award for Jaguar even though that outright win remained elusive. Private Jaguars were still

the RAC. Jaguars were often successful in French rallies, and began this season well with the Parsy brothers' victory in a very wintry *Rallye des Routes du Nord*. In March's tough Lyon-Charbonnières Rally, however, the modified XK120 of 1953 winner Henri Peignaux (proprietor of Jaguar's Lyon dealership) would run out of tyres and time – leaving the Babolat brothers' XK140 to finish second in class, but well down the general classification. In April, M. & Mme Monjo won the *Tour d'Algerie* in an XK120; only four crews were unpenalised in this tough one. So the XK was not yet outclassed altogether.

Hamilton: the first 'D' privateer

Back on the racing scene, Duncan Hamilton was now the first private owner of a D-type (XKC 402, the original OKV 1) having driven it home from Coventry in the snow. In the 11 February edition of *Autosport*, John Bolster reported on his brief drive in this car from Hamilton's Byfleet premises. He commented favourably on its engine

The Appleyards flanked by Adams, Vard, and their team-prize winning crews, Monte Carlo 1955.

forming a good proportion of the entry of many of the major rallies, although the early part of 1955 would produce no further significant results for the marque, other than a repeat class-win (and eighth overall) for John Boardman in the Tulip Rally.

For the RAC Rally, Adams would once again switch to an Alvis and Appleyard to an MG, taking first and third places in their respective classes. At Easter, in the Circuit of Ireland, the Triumphs of Adams, Titterington and McKinney would take a team prize while the Appleyards' MG TF was to finish an excellent fourth overall. In neither event did Jaguars shine in 1955, although the Stross/Pointing car would score a heavily-penalised class win on

performance, its braking, its ease of handling (by comparison with the C-type), and its tautness, which added up to a car of 'breeding':

'It is, indeed, a new conception in sports-racing cars,' – but, Bolster also warned:

I do not approve of the possession of very fast cars by inexperienced drivers, but I feel that this is one of the easiest of the real flyers to handle. Unlike some of the latest speed models it does allow some margin for error, and there is nothing tricky about it. Obviously its full potentialities on a road circuit can be extracted only by the higher echelon of racing drivers, but one's nearest and dearest could drive it through the West End without demur ... There remains the usual Jaguar miracle, which is the price. [This was quoted as a basic £1895, although production preparations were still at an early stage in the Browns Lane works.]

Prepared by Robin Freeman, the D-type was shipped via Antwerp to Casablanca. The first race was to be at Agadir, whence Hamilton sent Lofty England a postcard of *une jeune femme Marocaine dans une jardin exotique* on 24 February: 'Just the place for a motor race,' he wrote, 'also to get into training! Had to remove the engine in Casablanca and change the clutch. Old one all rust and worn out. There are six 3-litre Ferraris and three 3-litre Gordinis here, all the Italian outfit are present, even Enzo. Very twisty and hilly course. Regards, Duncan.' The garage services of former Jaguar racer Guy Berthomier (*See Vol. 1*) had proved a boon for this work, which was done in Casablanca prior to the 300-mile drive to earthquake-torn Agadir. The journey was undertaken in convoy with the Aston Martin of Graham Whitehead (Peter's half-brother) and the former Hamilton C-type Jaguar now being campaigned by Dan Margulies with Graham Hill assisting. This trip was described graphically by Hamilton in his enjoyable and informative yarn, published as *Touch Wood*. The Circuit of Agadir on 27 February was won by Mike Sparken of the Paris-based *Los Amigos* racing team, in a new Ferrari 750, with Margulies seventh in the C-type.

A week later, Hamilton wrote to England from the Vichy hotel in Dakar, Senegal, a thousand miles further south:

Arrived last night after a very hectic journey by air. Very nearly finished up in the desert. What with being shot at in Casa, bombed etc., you can take it from me this is some trip.

Well the news on the car is not good. First of all in Casablanca ... we had to change the clutch. The one that came out was finished up to 2500 rpm when it would take up. It was not adjustment or free movement as all this was in perfect order. Just wear and what would appear to be rust on the splines, from standing.

Hamilton went on to talk about Agadir, where the Ferrari entourage turned out to be 'Ugolini and 18 mechanics' rather than 'Enzo'. Here Hamilton reported using a 4.09 to 1 axle ratio:

It was about right as it gave me 5850 rpm down the straight. The course is very twisty and hilly, like Prescott and Shelsley in reverse. I did exactly six laps and, as I came over the brow of a left-hand downhill corner at about 5000 in 2nd gear on the overrun, the flaming back wheels locked up solid. I got the clutch out but to no effect – also too late, as I spun right round and hit the wall a glancing blow and went backwards into the straw-bales. They stopped me from going over a 250 ft. cliff, and there I was stuck. No flag marshals, so I hopped out pretty quickly. The car was stuck in gear and after about 20 minutes we managed to get it free, and I let it coast down the hill. After about 150 yards it seized up again, but eventually we reached the garage. The only thing to do was to take the engine out for the second time and dismantle the gearbox. This meant I would not be able to practise on the second day, and therefore I had no practice times as only the 2nd day counted for position on the grid. I took the whole gearbox to pieces and I think the following happened: The layshaft 1st motion gear, which is located by a circlip on the layshaft, moved backwards as the circlip was broken and had obviously been taking up the load – presumably by the high torque reversal due to the low axle ratio. As this gear moved backwards it dragged off the 4th gear

syncromesh cone and dogs which are a press fit on the first motion shaft, thus reducing the clearance between 3rd and 4th gears to zero. This resulted in the top gear seizing up when I was in 2nd gear, which gave the effect of engaging two gears at once. Well I rushed around the town at 2 in the B. morning and found a lathe and electric welding gear turned up a sleeve, split it and fitted it over the shaft in place of the circlips. Then Hamilton did a wonderful piece of electric welding and it now is on there permanently. The cones on third and top are not in a very good state but run well enough and in fact show no difference at all. During my hectic four laps, I found the car quite unsuitable for the circuit and it just stood still out of corners. All the Ferraris were fitted with ZF diffs and it was worth 8 to 10 sec. a lap. On the straight we were about the same, but around the corners on the back leg it was hopeless. The Aston Martin DB3S and also my old C with discs were all in the same trouble. I also had trouble with the offside rear back brake locking on. That is also the wheel that spins on the straight and I am wondering if the body and chassis was not twisted a little more than one thought after its (road) accident in France. The front suspension is not set right as one side has degrees down on the wishbone and the other up. I am hoping to be able to weigh each wheel with a Citroën scale in the morning to check the torsion bars etc. Life is hell as I have a roaring cold and seem to spend my life in changing from one hotel to another. In the race at Agadir I retired after 12 laps as the locking back brake was far too dangerous on that circuit and also I would have been well beaten up. Working on the car now and hope it goes better here. Please excuse spelling etc but I have such a B. head I can hardly write at all. Regards all and give Angela a ring for me. Regards. Duncan X.

The Dakar circuit proved a complete contrast to Agadir and, here, the D-type proved thoroughly competitive, its disc brakes compensating for the sluggish getaway resulting from 17-inch wheels and a 'high' axle ratio. The Grand Prix of Dakar was run in intense heat on 13 March. The Ferraris of Piero Carini and Louis Rosier were first and second in the 230-mile race, followed by the Jaguar. Hamilton and Rosier slipstreamed each other until the Jaguar came in for a tyre check. The Frenchman recorded fastest lap of the event at over 122 mph, the straight being long enough for sustained maximum speed. The subsequent report from Dunlop's tyre design division to Jaguar engineering read as follows:

6.5–17 R.1. Stabilia Race Tyres
D Type Jaguar – Duncan Hamilton – Agadir and Dakar

The two tyres which Duncan Hamilton returned under complaint after these races have been examined and we give below our assessment.

(1) AGADIR – *Tyre No. 20A-543*

The tread bias joint has opened on this tyre and a piece of the tread has subsequently torn out.

There is no question of normal tread stripping, the tread-to-case bond is perfect.

Very special care is taken with the tread joints of Stabilia tyres.

As an added precaution there is a directional arrow on Stabilia tyres, so that the joint is laid down during running on the road. The Agadir tyre had been run in the wrong direction, which would aggravate the joint opening.

Of the 200 Stabilia tyres made and used last year this is the only instance of an open tread joint.

Action:

This tread joint will be carefully examined by microscope to check the cause of opening. The Factory will, we are sure, co-operate with us to make quite sure a very high standard is maintained in making the race tyre tread joints.

(2) DAKAR – Race speed 119 mph. Maximum speed on straight 183 mph. Tyre No 3HA 040.

The only damage on this tyre is a series of hair line folds in the rubber surface, occurring in the shoulder pattern channels. These are only in the surface of the rubber and would not have developed to cause any damage.

It is understandable that in view of the tread stripping of Englebert tyres, all drivers would be super critical of their tyres, but in the case of the Stabilia tyre, there was no reason for concern, and certainly no cause to make a special stop to examine the tyres during the race. Mr Lallement expressed this view to Duncan Hamilton at Dakar. The rear tyres sent for the Dakar race are severely scarred, showing evidence of very hard acceleration as we expect from Duncan Hamilton, who is a hard driver. In view of the hard driving, high speeds and high air temperature, the Stabilia tyres stood up very well in this race.

(Signed) D. W. Badger

So the D-type Jaguar returned from its first trip in private hands with at least one reasonable result to its credit.

The D-type reaches America

On the same day as Dakar, another D-type was making its Transatlantic race début – at Sebring – and a most successful début, too.

Long-awaited by North American sports car drivers, the D-type would not be readily available to them for many months yet. The first sign of positive activity had come with two Rankin press releases from Coventry in February:

JAGUAR NEWS BULLETIN, 1ST FEBRUARY 1955

AMERICAN COMPANY TO RACE JAGUARS
BRIGGS CUNNINGHAM SURPRISE

Briggs Cunningham, millionaire American sportsman and head of the Briggs Cunningham Company, will race with 'D' type Jaguars this year. For the past three years, Cunningham cars have been America's challenge in the 24-hours Le Mans Race in which they finished third last year.

The decision to race Jaguars was made last week following secret trials in America at the Sebring Circuit when Briggs Cunningham himself and top ranking American drivers, Phil Walters, Bill Spear and Bill Lloyd, all drove a 'D' type Jaguar for several laps and expressed themselves amazed and delighted at its performance. The trials were carried out against Cunningham's Ferrari with which Spear achieved so much success last year and with which he won the President Eisenhower Trophy. Despite the fact that Spear was in great form, Walters, driving the Jaguar for the first time, consistently returned several laps two or three seconds faster than the Ferrari.

Cunningham has entered a Jaguar for this year's Le Mans and will also enter another Jaguar for the big Sebring Race. Thus, British cars, wearing the American racing colours of blue and white, will be seen in two, and probably more, big international events this year.

JAGUAR NEWS BULLETIN, 22ND FEBRUARY 1955

NEW SPEED RECORD FOR JAGUAR

At the two-day Daytona Beach Speed Trials held on Saturday and Sunday last, which attracted a strong international entry, a production Jaguar 'D' type, driven by Phil Walters, demonstrated its complete superiority by returning a record average speed for the meeting of 164·138 m.p.h. over a measured mile. The former record for this meeting, one of the most important on the American Sporting Calendar, was 136 m.p.h. set up by an Italian Ferrari last year.

This year, the Jaguar proved to be a clear 12 mph faster than the Le Mans winning Ferrari which also gained the President Eisenhower Trophy as the championship car of America last year, and no less than 31 mph faster than the much vaunted German Mercedes Type 300 SL.

The NASCAR News Bulletin recorded the following as the top six sports cars over the smooth sands of Daytona (scene of several British world speed records in earlier days):

3·4 Jaguar (Phil Walters)	164·136 mph
4·5 Ferrari (Jack Rutherford)	152·275 mph
4·9 Ferrari (Jim Kimberly)	151·700 mph
4·5 Ferrari (John Shakespeare)	148·755 mph
4·9 Ferrari (Bill Frick)	145·115 mph
5·5 Cunningham (Briggs Cunningham)	144·405 mph

Phil Walters ('Ted Tappett') in XKD 406 at Daytona.

XKD 406 in action on Daytona Beach, early 1955.

Jack Rutherford, the former record-holder, had also run Jaguars (*see Vol. 1*). Phil Walters (who raced in his younger days as 'Ted Tappett') and Bill Frick had been partners in Frick-Tappett Motors of Long Island, the firm which had co-operated in the preparation of Briggs Cunningham's 1950 Le Mans Cadillacs, forerunners of the Cunningham sports-racing cars. Those Cunningham cars were now on their way out.

The Daytona D-type, although entered in Cunningham's name, was in fact XKD 406, and it was attended chiefly by Len Hayden of the Jaguar competition shop. There were several good reasons for making this a Cunningham entry, including the use of Firestone tyres as opposed to Dunlops. Jim Sterland (then representing Jaguar Service in the USA) recalled that this car had been shipped originally for display purposes. The result was a testimony to Len Hayden's skills.

Victory at Sebring

Ultimate victory in the 1955 Sebring was preceded by a chapter of adventure for the D-type, which Mike Hawthorn and Phil Walters shared for twelve wearisome hours over the rough Florida concrete that characterised America's premier sports car event. It was not so much a case of which cars were in good condition at the finish as: which cars had deteriorated the least. The details are in the American chapter. Suffice it to say here, the lone D-type led virtually from the start (when Hawthorn drove) to the finish, apart from a brief challenge from the Taruffi/Schell Ferrari. Walters kept up the furious pace, before settling down to team orders as the attrition began. Frequent pit stops towards the end of the race made for a dramatic final phase – but the Jaguar was nursed to the chequered flag in one of the marque's most significant wins of all time. Moreover, this victory for Hawthorn in his first race for Coventry, ably backed by Walters, had been achieved in one of last year's models. Many improvements were now in hand for 1955 production and works team cars.

The only sour note was caused by a post-race protest

from oil baron Allen Guiberson, entrant of the Phil Hill/Carroll Shelby Ferrari which had eroded the Jaguar's two-lap lead to 25·4 seconds when the twelve hours were up. His protest – based on an erroneous public-address announcement (late in the race) that his car was in the lead, *and* a scoring error in his team's pit – was thrown out, but not soon enough to permit Jaguar to get maximum publicity from its biggest US race win to date.

In England no new D-types were emerging. Hamilton's car got back from Dakar only just in time for the Empire Trophy race at Oulton Park on 2 April. The car was not in very raceworthy condition, and the track was greasy and very slippery. In those conditions, Hamilton did well to pass Peter Collins (Aston Martin) and finish second in the over 2·7-litre heat to Mike Sparken's Ferrari, while others slowed or had accidents. The final became a benefit for the smaller cars whose handicap advantage was further improved by what had become a downpour. The D-type showed up badly, being the second 'big' car behind Dick Shattock's Jaguar XK-engined glass-fibre bodied RGS-Atalanta which had independent suspension all round. The easy winner was Archie Scott-Brown in the nimble Lister-Bristol, Shattock and Hamilton being fifth and seventh.

Mike Hawthorn in XKD 406 at Sebring.

Phil Walters, Hawthorn's co-driver in the winning D-type, Sebring 1955.

Nine days later, at Goodwood on Easter Monday, Sparken and Hamilton continued their sparring, finishing the over 2-litre sports car race four seconds apart – but Roy Salvadori (Aston Martin) had the last laugh being presented with the race on a plate, the leaders losing 15 seconds apiece for jumping the start.

Next race for OKV 1 was the *Coupe de Paris* at Montlhéry, where Hamilton (with shock absorbers which did little to help him keep control on the braking) did well to keep André Pilette's Grand Prix Gordini in sight. (The latter had not even practised, yet was a front-row starter.) Behind the Jaguar came Ferraris driven by Picard, de Portago and Piotti followed by Levegh's streamlined Talbot-Lago of Le Mans fame.

Silverstone 1955

The *Daily Express* International Trophy meeting at Silverstone in early May was always a major event and on this occasion Lofty England was able to confirm to BRDC secretary Desmond Scannell that Hawthorn, Rolt and Hamilton would drive works D-types in the sports car race; Hawthorn, Stewart, and Titterington would drive Mark Sevens in the saloon car event. Stewart and Titterington had been nominated by David Murray to drive

Although doubt is expressed in the Wide World Photos picture caption, Hawthorn, Walters and Cunningham *know* they have won; but it took several days for the Sebring organisers to confirm it.

(SEB5) SEBRING, Fla., Mar. 13—THE WINNERS?—Mike Hawthorne (left) of England, wears the floral wreath of victory after driving a D-Jaguar through the 12 hours of the Grand Prix of endurance here today. Center is his co-driver, Phil Walters, while at right is Briggs Cunningham of West Palm Beach, Fla., American sports-man who imported the new type sports car. A protest was entered against the Jag's victory. (See wire story) (APWirephoto) (jm1231sjpk-stf)1955

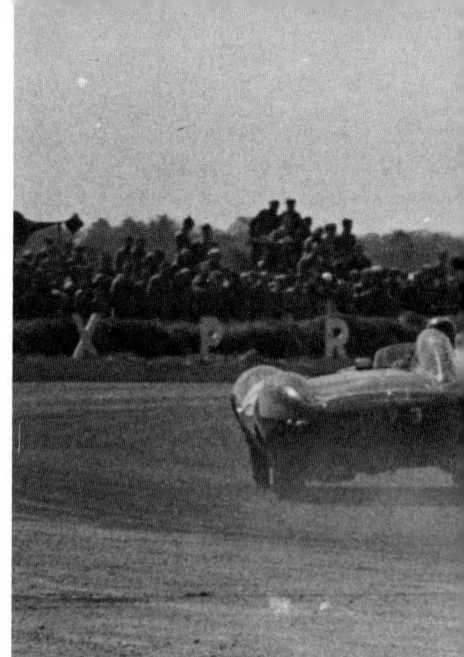

All Above: **Mike Hawthorn in action at Silverstone, May 1955.**

the new *Ecurie Ecosse* D-types which were prepared just in time. This arrangement suited England very well, as he knew he could not keep all his drivers happy all of the time. Don Beauman had to put up with being reserve driver.

First item on the programme was the sports car race – a Jaguar v. Aston Martin battle in the making, with Sparken's Ferrari looking on. Jimmy Stewart had been quick in practice but aquaplaned off course in the wet second session, damaging the brand new metallic blue *Ecurie Ecosse* car XKD 501 ('Don't worry . . . in those conditions anyone could have done it,' England wrote afterwards. 'Repair has not proved as much of a problem as I anticipated.')

Hawthorn (XKC 404) dominated practice and most of the 40-lap race, breaking the sports car record in 1 min. 49 sec. on the thirty-second lap. Five laps later, to quote from Hawthorn's book *Challenge Me The Race*:

The D-type was leading fairly comfortably, about 10 seconds ahead of Parnell's Aston Martin, when there was a loud plopping noise from the engine and a lot of water came back into the cockpit. I stopped, found that a top water hose had burst, tried the engine and found it ran reasonably well, so carried on gingerly and finished fourth.

The records show that the lap in which Hawthorn stopped took him 2 min. 31 sec. and that for the remaining three he was able to circulate within 10 seconds of normal. The engine (E2006-9) was running with a compression ratio of 9·4 to 1 and 35/40 cylinder head, and had shown 272·5 bhp at 5500 rpm on Jack Emerson's test bed beforehand. Afterwards, however, it was removed for loss of oil pressure and rebuilt with new bearings.

Tony Rolt (XKC 403) held second place initially, but slipped back to third behind Parnell and Salvadori in works Aston Martins at the finish. Duncan Hamilton (XKD 406) was fifth behind Hawthorn, followed by Desmond Titterington in the second new 'Scottish' D-type (XKD 502) ahead of Collins and Walker (Astons) and Sparken (Ferrari).

Below: **Rolt in XKC 403 at Silverstone in May 1955, after which the car was transferred to Jack Broadhead's stable.**

Hawthorn's mount for the touring car event was the old MkVII, LWK 343 (Chassis 711195), its engine having been run up to 6000 rpm and shown 218·8 bhp. As with the other two cars – PWK 700 for Stewart and PWK 701 for Titterington – England had confirmed beforehand that it was to catalogue specification and FIA recognition form, and included the following modifications:

9 to 1 CR pistons
Special vibration damper
Lightened flywheel
2-inch SU carburetters
D-type cylinder head

Competition-type clutch
Close-ratio gearbox
High-geared steering
Twin exhaust pipes
and bucket type front seats

Hawthorn went ahead of Stewart and they finished the 25 laps an orderly 2 seconds apart, Hawthorn creating another lap record of 2 min. 10 sec: Ian Appleyard ran third in his own car, until as in the 'Monte', it expired in a cloud of steam, leaving Titterington to complete a

Heynes, Weaver, Dewis and (almost certainly) Harry Rogers in the Experimental workshops with three 1955 long-nose cars. (*Courtesy: William Heynes*)

comfortable 1-2-3 for the works team. Fourth overall came the ever-popular Ken Wharton in a very fast Ford Zephyr, as if to show that the whole Daimler episode had been misrepresented at the Jaguar end.

The record of prize money makes interesting reading. It consists of BRDC awards, plus bonuses from Shell, Champion, Dunlop, Mintex, Girling and Lucas. Hawthorn earned £702. 15s. 4d. for his two wins. Rolt's fee came to £228. 10s., Stewart's £373. 15s., Titterington's £250. 7s. 4d., Hamilton's £79. 14s. and Beauman got £25 for playing gooseberry.

On the day after Silverstone, at Djurgard Park, Helsinki, Michael Head was driving the Hamilton D-type (XKC 402) to victory in the main race from the fast Finn, Curt Lincoln, in XKC 044.

Adventures for Ecurie Ecosse

Six days later, on 14 May, Desmond Titterington won the Ulster Trophy at his home circuit, Dundrod, averaging 89.86 mph for over two hours in the *Ecurie Ecosse* D-type, XKD 502. Hero of the day, though, was a young RAF National Serviceman – Bill Smith from Lincoln. His average speed of 86.79 mph in XKC 051, (the ex-*Ecurie Ecosse*, ex-works 1953 Le Mans-winning C-type, now

painted bright red), was second quickest of all, and made him an easy winner from Titterington on handicap. Lofty England would have his eye on Smith throughout that summer.

With customer D-types still in short supply, earlier models were continuing to represent the Jaguar marque. Dan Margulies, for example, was beginning a season-long trek around Europe, taking part in some of the most unlikely road races. In May (following a fine Easter victory at Castle Combe) Margulies and XKC 038 came eighth in the Bari night event, third in the Cagliari-Sassari-Cagliari road race with his mechanic Graham Hill alongside, and seventh in the over-1500cc Eifelrennen.

The latter took place at the Nürburgring, with Fangio winning in a Mercedes-Benz 300SLR. Dutifully in second place was Stirling Moss, still fresh from an historic victory in the Mille Miglia. No D-types had been to the Nürburgring before, and it was *Ecurie Ecosse* which had to learn its lessons the hard way: Jimmy Stewart (XKD 501) and Desmond Titterington (XKD 502) both 'lost' their brakes in practice and went off the road and into the undergrowth. Stewart was pinned beneath his upturned car with fuel dripping on him, but managed to switch off the ignition with his foot. Stirling Moss, circulating in a 300SL (rather than his race car) was first on the scene and helped get Stewart out of his predicament; he then drove him back to the pits, *en route* becoming the first person to know that the young Scot had just decided to give up

76

racing – despite being due to drive for the Jaguar works team at Le Mans only a few days later. It was not that Stewart had frightened himself more than usual (he knew the crash hadn't been his fault) nor that his arm was damaged too badly – although this was a reason he gave. The real reason was that he knew the anguish his mother suffered at home every time he went racing, especially since his 1954 Le Mans accident. In order to get David Murray his starting money, he did agree to do one lap of the Eifelrennen in the cobbled-up Titterington car – but that was the end of Jimmy Stewart's career as a potentially-brilliant racing driver. A decade later his kid brother Jackie would take up where he had left off – but no-one knew *that* at the time.

Desmond Titterington wrote to Lofty England on Monday, 30 May:

First reserve: Ivor Bueb (seen 'debriefing' with Lofty England at the White Horse, Silverstone) was to join the Jaguar team after Jimmy Stewart hung up his gloves.(*Courtesy: John Pearson*)

I am writing to you from my bed in Adenau Hospital, following a 90 mph crash on the Nürburgring on Friday afternoon. I am far from satisfied that there has been an improvement in the Dunlop Disc Brakes since my last two events (Silverstone and Dundrod). The brakes are totally unreliable: whereas at Dundrod the pedal needed pumping on every braking occasion, on Friday it only began to be apparent after the first two laps (28 miles) and then only on occasion did I need to pump. This was even worse, for I didn't know beforehand if a few pumps were necessary or not. Unfortunately I must have forgotten to pump on that occasion, for there was no time for the car to slow after it came to ground following a hump on the road before the bend.

The car also showed very peculiar handling properties. We had about 25 gallons on board but the tail seemed very light, bouncing about like my Allard, and taking a long time to come down after bumps – altogether an unpleasant experience. David and Wilkie seem very worried about these things, while Jimmy and I are most disappointed with our cars.

I hope to be absolutely fit by next week but bring a reserve for me just in case . . .

On the Wednesday, however, the Ulsterman wrote again:

The doctor advises that I stay here at least a week more. The results of the X-ray are satisfactory but there has been considerable damage to the back and shoulder muscles and it will all take time to mend. More important is that I should not risk driving for at least three weeks due to a certain commotion in the old head! This news was most distressing to me, and I'm sorry I won't be in the team on this occasion. I hope it will give Bob a chance but tell him to take it easy! [*It was to be Norman Dewis, and not Bob Berry, who would take Titterington's place at Le Mans.*]

Good Luck and Good Hunting – I hope I can be fit enough to clear myself by the end of next week.

Sure enough he got to Le Mans to cheer on the team.

1955 long-nose D-type. (*Courtesy: William Heynes*)

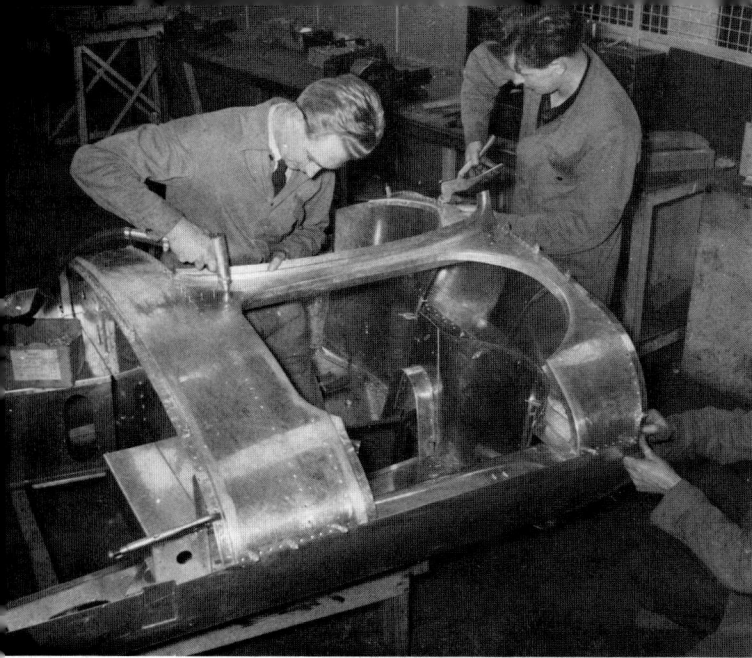

Three views showing 1955 D-type body construction, using Avdel rivets. Note new-style tail-fin.

Below:
Norman Dewis testing in the wet at MIRA.

Jack Emerson and a competition engine on the bench.

Below:
1955 long-nose D-type.

79

The Nürburgring problem was in fact brake pad 'knock-off'.

May 29 witnessed an excellent result in Belgium, where Meunier (driving the old but highly-tuned XK 120 of Jaguar dealer De Ridder – *see Vol. 1*) came second to Musy (Maserati) in the *Grand Prix des Frontières* at Chimay. At home on the Whit-Monday, 30 May, Duncan Hamilton won two races from Bob Berry at Goodwood. Hamilton had been under the weather with delayed concussion since crashing a Gordini at the Silverstone meeting but it didn't show as he went on his spectacular way with XKC 402, newly prepared after its Finnish trip. (Hamilton was also in the process of buying his Silverstone works car, XKC 406, newly registered RRW 21, on behalf of Michael Head, although the latter was still using his own C-type XKC 005, on this occasion.) At Goodwood Berry was having his first drive in XKC 403, which had come into Jack Broadland's possession after Silverstone.

Suddenly, with Le Mans in the offing, the world racing picture became clouded. First in a sequence of accidents came the death of the personable former world champion, Alberto Ascari, while practising for the Monza 1000 Km sports car race. (This being limited to 3-litre cars, England let Hawthorn drive for Ferrari here. He came second.) Then Bill Vukovich – winner in 1953 and 1954 – died when his Meyer-Drake-engined 'roadster' piled into someone else's accident while he was leading the Indianapolis 500.

However, few – least of all the Aston Martin, Ferrari, Jaguar and Mercedes-Benz team members preparing for their great confrontation – could have anticipated that the 1955 Le Mans 24-hour race would cast a shadow over the whole sporting world.

Close-up of 1955 car.

Chapter Four

Le Mans 1955

In addition to its clever adaption of the D-type for limited production programme (dealt with in Chapter 7), Jaguar used the experience of the D-type to develop an improved version for the 1955 Le Mans 24-hour race, which had all the makings of a mighty battle between the finest machines of Germany, Italy and the United Kingdom, if not France itself.

In that this was to be a confrontation with Mercedes-Benz, following an outstanding Mille Miglia result for the Stuttgart firm, there was a certain similarity to the 1952 situation, when Jaguar had introduced a late modification to the C-type's coolant system without checking if it would work.

The improvements to the D-type for the 1955 race were, as before, based upon the need for higher performance and more speed on the straight. As early as 16 December 1954, Claude Baily had issued Project Specification ZX.501/50, itemised as: 'Preparation of 8 engines for Le Mans 1955 – $3\frac{1}{2}$ L.' Baily's comments included:

Cylinder Block: as D-type with modified rear bearing.
Bearing Cap – Rear: To suit cylinder block.
Main Bearing – Rear: Reduced by $\frac{1}{8}''$ in width.
Crankshaft: E.N.40.3/4 Forgings, stiffened front end, stiffened rear web. Polish all over and crack detect.

There were numerous parts modifications, due to increased crankshaft diameter at the front end. The project specification included fittings to suit fuel injection, twin-plug combustion chambers and 35/40 degree angled

cylinder head – but of those three features, only the last-named would be used in the race, in conjunction with 15/32 inch lift cams and larger-diameter valves (preventing overlap).

For 1955, 'D-type' was accepted terminology and the new chassis number series began at XKD 501. XKD 501 and 502 were for *Ecurie Ecosse*, whose 1955 programme did not include Le Mans which was just as well, in view of the state both cars were in after their visit to the Nürburgring in May.

The various slight shunts, which caused structural kinks in the 1954 cars, had led to the substitution of a steel frame for the original magnesium alloy type, which had been integral with the unique cockpit or tub. The new frame was bolted at the front and rear bulkheads and for convenience of repair along the floor of the tub. Interchangeability was a boon although, historically, it has become the basis for many an identity crisis. (This problem would increase throughout the 1970s and 1980s as 'classic' cars moved into the Great Masters price category, and 'new' cars began to emerge.) This form of structure would be taken a stage further when the E-type came along, and is described in full elsewhere.

The 1955 D-types had a further demountable front sub-frame for the water and oil radiators – again with a view to ease of repair after minor front end damage.

The third 'production' D-type (XKD 503) was sent direct to the Browns Lane competition shop, for preparation on behalf of Roger Laurent's *Ecurie Francorchamps* whose C-type had done so well at Le Mans in 1953 and

Don Beauman at Le Mans scrutineering, 1955. Bob Penney and Frank Wright are on the left, Lofty England and Frank Rainbow on the right. (*Courtesy: Frank Rainbow*)

Works long-nose car for Cunningham team drivers Spear and Johnston, Le Mans 1955. This car, considerably modified, would remain in the Cunningham collection once it became obsolete. Art Mayhew holds the door. (*Courtesy: Bob Blake*)

1954. Because of the works involvement, Phil Weaver gave it a reference notebook of its own. (All the works D-types had individual notebooks which have helped greatly in piecing together their early history.)

The following additions were made to XKD 503's specification for Le Mans 1955: a cylinder head of 'known characteristics' (but not the new 35/40 type); standard exhaust system (no explanation given); 'wide' brake calipers; 17 inch wheels and tyres; mirror-operating rod; stabilising fin; new type radiator (details not given); spares box and rubber straps; front and rear air-scoops.

In May, Laurent was injured while practising (in a Ferrari) for the Bari Grand prix, and so his regular colleague Jacques Swaters was partnered by Johnny Claes for the race at Le Mans, where the 'Belgian' D-type scored a resounding third place, as detailed later in this chapter. After Le Mans, the car was brought back to Browns Lane where the 'works' cylinder head was replaced by a standard one. (The engine, E2011-9, was not otherwise stripped, and stayed with the car.) The gearbox was stripped, as was the rear axle (ratio changed from 2·79:1 to 3·54:1). Standard calipers and 16-inch wheels were fitted, as was a new air box – the old one having 'numerous' fractures. The prototype light alloy master cylinder was

82

John Cooper and Malcolm Sayer co-cogitate over the new six-cylinder 4·4-litre Ferrari 121 LM with which Castellotti would soon be setting the initial pace at Le Mans. (*Courtesy: Bob Blake*)

removed and replaced by the cast-iron production type. The other post-Le Mans work was to remove the tail fin, weld the fractures at its base and refit it. On final test it was noted that the exhaust downpipes were loose in the silencer and that there was a slight oil leak from the gearbox end cover (the drawing office was notified of the latter). The final entry in the Competition Shop notebook on XKD 503 was: 'Delivered to London Docks for shipping to Brussels 8-7-55, by L. Bottrill.' Les Bottrill was the

The 1955 Le Mans winner at pre-race scrutineering, as yet without its identifying nose band. (*Courtesy: Walter Hassan*)

man who would spend much of that year testing and reporting on the new production D-Types.

XKD 504 was a works long-nose car – the 'spare' one for Le Mans, then retained for experimental work on Lucas fuel-injection equipment.

XKD 505, XKD 506 and XKD 508 were fitted (as were all D-types which raced in 1955) with the regular triple DC03 Weber carburetter set-up. The bigger valves and detail modifications gave an increase of some 20 bhp, typical output being 270 bhp. An interesting remark about the cylinder head was included in a typed engine report: '35/40 Twin sparking plug position'. This had been altered in ink by Jack Emerson to read: '35/40 Twin sparking plug pattern, plugs fitted in new position only.' Here is Emerson's full June 1955 Experimental Report on the build specifications of 'XK 120 D' engines E3002-9, E3003-9 and E3005-9 (used in cars XKD 505, 506 and 508 respectively), issued to Bill Heynes under the heading:

LE MANS 1955, SALIENT FEATURES
A 91 Specification

COMPONENT	DRG. NO.	DESCRIPTION
Cylinder Head	XK 1987	35/40 Twin sparking plug pattern, plugs fitted in new position only.
Compression Ratio		9:1
Camshaft	XK 1825/6	7/16 in lift, Steel
Valve Springs	XK 2070/1	'Terry' 15/32 in Lift. Green identifications.
Tappets	XK 1403	Brice Parker luberised X Ray Supply.
Inlet Valve	XK 1980	Farnboro' Eng. KE 965 2 in Dia.
Exhaust Valve	XK 1981	Farnboro' Eng. Nimonic 80 111/16 in Dia.
Valve Timing		Inlet open 30° B.T.D.C. Exhaust Close 35° A.T.D.C.
Tappet Clearance		Inlet ·006/7 in Exhaust ·010/11 in
Cyl. Head Joint	67861	Steel ·015 in Transverse Corrigation.
Pistons	XK 2026	Brice issue 2 Slipper Type.
Crankshaft	XK 1958	Stiffened Rear Web Nitrided.
Crankshaft Bolt	XK 2019	with integral washer.
Main Bearings	G 5891/2	Vandervell Lead Indium.
" " Rear	XK 1979A/B	" " " (narrow type)
Connecting Rod Bearings	C 5893	Vandervell Lead Indium.
Chain Tensioner	C 10332	Renold Hydraulic, selected supply.
Oil Pump	C 9809	Pressure Alum. Body.
" " Gear	C 9234	Driving length 1¼ in steel.
" " "	C 6546	Driven, cast iron, length 1¼ in.
" " Spring	XK 2078	Relief Valve. Inbuilt discharge.
Oil Pump	C 9805	Scavenge, alum body.
" " Gear	C 9242	Driving, steel, length 1 in.
" " "	C 9281	Driven, Cast Iron, length 1 in 2 off.
Oil Sump	XK 1764	Bottom half. 1954 pattern.
Oil Seal	XK 1974	Front, Super Oil Seals Ltd.
Water Pump	XK 1551	Light Alloy body, 2 in Dia. Intake. Split Pulley.
Induction Pipe	XK 1834	Boris steel sleeved.
Carburetters	45 m/m	Weber dual DC03 Horizontal.
Setting	Choke 40 m/m	Main Jet 1·85 m/m Air Jet 1·95 m/m Pump ·75 m/m S.R. 70 m/m 2·50 m/m Needle Valve. Petrol level 1 in Less Primary venturi.
Air Trumpet	XK 2079	Cornercroft supply.
Distributer	Lucas	L.T. series 15790/1/4/5/6/779 EN 16 Driving dog, Taper pinned. X Ray, Rotor Arms. Timed 14° B.T.D.C. Crankshaft.
Coil	Lucas	H.V. 12 Rig tested.
Sparking Plug	Champion	NA 10 Gap. ·018/20 in Solid Copper Washer.
Dynamo	Lucas	4·5 in Dia. Rig tested. End 2408.
Starter Motor	Lucas	M4189/GC 25549A
Fuel Filter	CAV	Cylinderical Paper Carton Type F2/9
Flywheel	C 9192	8 in Diameter.
Starter Ring	C 9193	Clutch mounted.
Clutch	C 9194	Triple Plate (Red Springs Pressure).

Further 'salient features' lists were made for E3004-9, the engine for XKD 507, the car prepared for Briggs Cunningham to run at Le Mans. Like the Belgian car, it was given the regular configuration cylinder head, with valve angle and sizes, and 3/8 in lift cams. Likewise its triple Weber carburetters had 33 mm choke, 1·75 mm main jet, and 1·85 mm air jet.

The main technical worries of the spring of 1955 were the braking system (not the brakes themselves) as described earlier, and the tendency for D-type gearboxes to seize in third gear. These were the points noted by Bill Heynes on 29 April:

1) The direct cause of the trouble was the 3rd gear moving off its housing due to the interference fit being insufficient.
2) Seizure had taken place on the mainshaft 3rd speed. This may have been a subsidiary to the movement of the 3rd speed gear; on the other hand, it is possible that the sharp corner which was left on the inside of the gear may have started a pick-up on the thrust face and have been partially responsible for the gear moving.
3) It was noticed that 1st speed and 2nd speed gears have had no chamfer in the internal bore. Mr Jones is arranging for this to be added to the drawing, but in the meantime Mr Thomson will arrange for these chamfers to be introduced on all boxes.
4) Ball Races. On this first box Italian races, which appeared to be well below the standard quality used in production, had been used and showed considerable roughness and float. These must all be replaced by either Hoffman or Skefco races as used in production.
5) End float on mainshaft had permitted the reverse gear hub to touch the rear roller bearing sleeve, and although no serious damage had resulted it is possible that trouble might be caused at this point. It is desirable, therefore, that ·010″ to ·015″ clearance should be allowed either side of this rear roller bearing sleeve.
6) Layshaft. The constant, 3rd and 2nd speed gears are all loose on the splines, despite the fact that these have been coppered, with the result that the split rings had been rotating and worn badly, and Mr Thomson stated that he was aware that this first box was a poor fit but it was the only layshaft available at the time of assembly. Care is being taken that when the boxes are re-built they are made a close fit at this point.
7) Layshaft Split Ring. Despite the fitting of the screw sleeve on the layshaft instead of the circlips, the split rings still rotate in the groove. Mr Jones is arranging to have some new split rings designed which have a step on the side to fit into the spline, which should effectively overcome this trouble.

(The names are those of Jock Thomson, builder of racing gearboxes, and Tom Jones who had joined SS Cars Ltd as a trainee draughtsman and would progress to Jaguar Group Chief Vehicle Engineer in the 1980s, retiring in 1985.)

Mercedes-Benz's fascinating high-speed transporter carries a preserved 300SLR, demonstrating 'air-brake'. (*Courtesy: Daimler-Benz*)

PERSONNEL AND DUTIES

Pit Manager :
F. R. W. ENGLAND

Chief Mechanic :
P. WEAVER

●

JAGUAR FACTORY ENTRIES

CAR No. 6

DRIVER I	... ...	J. M. HAWTHORN
DRIVER 2	... ...	I. BUEB
MECHANIC I	... ...	J. SUTTON
MECHANIC 2	... ...	R. GAUDION

CAR No. 7

DRIVER I	... ...	A. P. R. ROLT
DRIVER 2	... ...	J. D. HAMILTON
MECHANIC I	... ...	L. HAYDEN
MECHANIC 2	... ...	R. PENNEY

CAR No. 8

DRIVER I	... ...	J. D. TITTERINGTON
DRIVER 2	... ...	D. B. BEAUMAN
MECHANIC I	... ...	F. RAINBOW
MECHANIC 2	... ...	R. WRIGHT

INDEPENDANT ENTRIES

Ecurie Francorchamps :

Car No. 10

DRIVER I	... ...	J. CLAES
DRIVER 2	... ...	J. SWATERS
MECHANIC I	... ...	L. BOTTRILL
MECHANIC 2	... ...	E. BROOKES

Briggs Cunningham Entry :

Car No. 9

DRIVER I	... ...	W. SPEAR
DRIVER 2	... ...	P. WALTERS

●

Jaguar Technicians ::
J. EMERSON, R. KNIGHT, M. SAYER, W. WILKINSON
Timekeepers ::
T. JONES, I. APPLEYARD, R. BERRY
Fueling ::
G. LEVECQUE

JAGUAR HEADQUARTERS : HOTEL DE PARIS.   Phone 35.28
GARAGE AND WORKSHOP : 12, RUE DE SARTHE.

The 1955 Le Mans Jaguar personnel directory.

DIRECTORY

Name	Firm	Address	Telephone
Mr. Appleyard	—	Hotel de Paris	35.28
Mr. Allerton	Lucas	Hotel de Paris	35.28
Mr. Baily	Jaguar	Hotel de Paris	35.28
Mr. Beauman	Driver	Hotel de Paris	35.28
Mr. Bedinham	Dunlop	Hotel des Ifs	8.87
Mr. Berry	Jaguar	Hotel de Paris	35.28
Mr. Bottrill	Jaguar	Hotel des Ifs	8.87
Mr. Brookes	Jaguar	Hotel des Ifs	8.87
Mr. Brooks	Dunlop	Hotel des Ifs	8.87
Mr. Bueb	Driver	Hotel de Paris	35.28
Mr. Chadwick	Cov'try Teleg'h	Hotel Moderne	0.05
Mr. Cole	Lucas	Hotel de Paris	35.28
Mr. Claes	Driver	Hotel de Paris	35.28
Mr. Delecroix	Delecroix	80, Rue de Longchamp, Paris XVI	Passy 16
Mr. Dewis	Jaguar	Hotel de Paris	35.28
Mr. Emerson	Jaguar	Hotel de Paris	35.28
Mr. England	Jaguar	Hotel de Paris	35.28
Mr. Freeman	Dunlop	Hotel de Paris	35.28
Mr. Gardner	Jaguar	Hotel des Ifs	8.87
Mr. Gaudion	Jaguar	Hotel des Ifs	8.87
Mr. Hamilton	Jaguar	Hotel de Paris	35.28
Mr. Hands	Champion	Hotel Moderne	0.50
Mr. Hawthorn	Driver	Hotel de Paris	35.28
Mr. Hayden	Jaguar	Hotel des Ifs	8.87
Mr. Heynes	Jaguar	Hotel Central	8.93
Mr. Hodkinson	Dunlop Brakes	Hotel de Paris	35.28
Mr. Huckvale	Jaguar	Hotel de Paris	35.28
Mr. Jones	Jaguar	Hotel de Paris	35.28
Mr. Knight	Jaguar	Hotel de Paris	35.28
Mr. Laurent	Driver	Hotel de Paris	35.28
Mr. Levecque	Delecroix	Hotel de Paris	35.28
Mr. Lyons (J)	Jaguar	Hotel de Paris	35.28
Mr. Lyons (W)	Jaguar	Hotel de Paris	35.28
Mintex	Mintex	Hotel de Paris	35.28
Mr. Penney	Jaguar	Hotel des Ifs	8.87
Mr. Rainbow	Jaguar	Hotel des Ifs	8.87
Mr. Rankin	Jaguar	Hotel Lion d'Or Sable sur Sarthe	0.34
Mr. Rolt	Driver	Hotel de Paris	35.28
Mr. Rowe	Dunlop	Hotel des Ifs	8.87
Mr. Sayer	Jaguar	38, Rue Premartine	—
Mr. Sutton	Jaguar	Hotel des Ifs	8.87
Mr. Swaters	Driver	Hotel de Paris	35.28
Mr. Thomson	Jaguar	Hotel des Ifs	8.87
Mr. Titterington	Driver	Hotel de Paris	35.28
Mr. Turle	Shell	Hotel de Paris	35.28
Mr. Turner	A & A	Hotel Central	8.93
Mr. Whittaker	Jaguar	Hotel de Paris	35.28
Mr. Weaver	Jaguar	Hotel des Ifs	8.87
Mr. Wilkinson	Jaguar	Hotel de Paris	35.28
Mr. Wright	Dunlop	Hotel de Paris	35.28
Mr. Wright	Jaguar	Hotel des Ifs	8.87

As early as March it was decided by Heynes that 6·50 × 16 in Dunlop Stabilia tyres would be used on 'Lightweight' 16-inch wheels all round at Le Mans, although he was anticipating specifying normal R1 tyres at Reims, subject to tests there beforehand.

The determination to achieve speed *with reliability* before Le Mans was paramount at every stage. A repeat of 1952 was not to be risked under any circumstances. Everything would be fully tested.

Improving D-type airflow

Of the six cars (including spare) prepared for the 1955 race, all but XKD 503 were given the improved 'long-nose' bodywork – 7·5 inches longer in the bonnet – with brake-cooling ducts on each side and rear exhausts. The cockpit had a higher windscreen which wrapped around the driver more snugly to reduce tiresome buffeting and improve airflow over the new and more streamlined one-piece headrest and tail fin. Although the airflow performance might not look so good against modern aerodynamics, the 1955 D-type was a technical work of art in its day. Chiefly responsible for its shape was the now-legendary, self-effacing Malcolm Sayer, who had had at his disposal the facilities of the Royal Aircraft Establishment at Farnborough from the outset. Apart from the foregoing changes, there seemed little else to do to improve the shape except (the RAE staff suggested) to ensure airtight riveting and to wax-fill the body joints before a race. It was calculated that a white circle on the bonnet could cost up to 4 mph at 160 mph; but I have found no evidence that the idea of using the RAF's special low-drag paint finish was ever adopted. With a bigger dynamo and battery, and 100-watt lighting, the need to build-in an extra spot lamp (as 1954) was eliminated.

Work still to be carried out by 10 May (Heynes noted to Weaver) included:

REAR AXLE
ZF Diff. These have been received from Germany, but unfortunately they have been broached with the wrong spline, and in order to use these it is necessary for new axle shafts to be obtained from Salisbury. We have already been in touch with Salisbury and are expecting a call back on the position of these shafts.

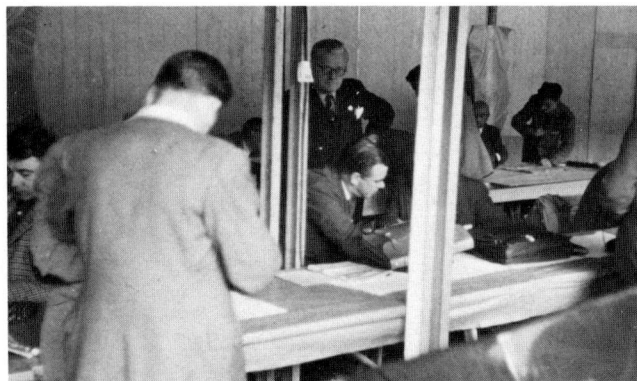

Lofty England talks to the scrutineer – maybe about the lack of a nearside door? – at Le Mans in 1955. (*Courtesy: Walter Hassan*)

ZF Diff. (English Manufacture). One of these diffs. we used at Silverstone in Mr Hawthorn's car. At the earliest opportunity this must be removed and inspected to see what wear has taken place. Cooling tests will, however, have to take priority on this car.

2·53 Gear Ratios. These are now promised from Salisbury on Friday next. As soon as one of these axles is received it must be fitted to a car and tested round the high-speed track by Mr Dewis after a period of running-in.

Cunningham Axle. A decision has to be obtained as early as possible from Cunningham on the make of tyre he is proposing to employ. If Firestone tyres are used 2·79 axle ratio will be required, whereas if the Stabilia tyres are used, as on our own Le Mans cars, either 2·53 or 2·67 will be required.

COOLING SYSTEM
The cooling trouble which was experienced at Silverstone by Hawthorn is the subject of a most serious investigation, as at the moment the cause of the trouble is not definitely clear. Tests are being carried out on the radiator matrix, the cylinder block and the cylinder head. The cylinder head is being pressure tested. The relief valve has already been checked and is found to blow off at 4 lbs/p.s.i. The water pump has been examined and is apparently in perfect condition. It has been pointed out that this particular car has a finer mesh gauze than we used last year, which might contribute something to overheating, and tests will be made with the Le Mans type gauze, which gives approximately 10% improvement in the amount of air passed. The whole system on this particular car must be regarded with the gravest suspicion until the cause of the trouble is located.

GEARBOXES
From reports received all five gearboxes of the new type which were running at Silverstone behaved faultlessly. At a convenient time one of the gearboxes, preferably from Mr Hawthorn's car, will be stripped and examined to see whether any wear has taken place.

The same note mentioned progress on dynamos, brake and tyre developments. On the latter subject, Heynes stated:

TYRES
As yet we have received no samples of the Le Mans type tyres for test purposes. It is felt that it is desirable to obtain one or two sets of these tyres to test for handling under really high-speed conditions. If possible, Gaydon would be the most suitable venue.

Although not affecting the Le Mans issue, it is desirable for further comparative tests to be carried out between the new Dunlop, the Pirelli, the Firestone (when they arrive) and, additionally, the Avon Rubber Company are interested in submitting a set of tyres for test.

On the administration side, Duncan Hamilton's contribution of a caravan for off-duty drivers and staff was accepted ironically but gratefully by Lofty England.

Once again, garage premises owned by Monsieur A Carré (a Parisian XK120 owner) were to be made available, these being situated in the Rue de Sarthe, Le Mans. With M. Carré's ready agreement, Gérard Levecque – general factotum for Charley Delecroix, Jaguar's French importer – arranged for a four-poster car lift and a suitable engine hoist to be installed. Earlier Le Mans missions had suffered somewhat through lack of these facilities. For the first time – to reduce the risk of transit damage, rather than because they might not be suitable to drive on the road – the works cars were to be flown from Elmdon Airport, Birmingham, to Le Mans direct by Silver City charter aircraft on 7 June. They would return by the usual Cherbourg-Southampton route – much used.

Accompanying personnel listed on the original April bookings to travel with them were: F. R. W. England, J. Emerson, E. W. Rankin, C. P. Weaver, L. Weaver, L. Sullivan, D. B. Beauman, W. Wilkinson (the works man, not *Ecurie Ecosse*'s 'head lad'), L. W. Hayden, J. Sutton, R. J. Penney, E. Brookes, R. Gaudion (later of *Ecurie Ecosse*), S. F. Rainbow, G. H. ('Jock') Thomson, L. T. Bottrill and an 'ABC Television Unit Representative'. Scheduled to fly by the normal Silver City service from Southampton to Cherbourg were: M. Sayer, N. Dewis, R. E. Berry, J. Lyons, W. Lyons and W. M. Heynes. (Dewis and Berry were to be reserve drivers, as well as deliverers of the 'American' and 'Belgian' D-types.) Spares and tools would travel via Dunkerque on two works Bedfords – a 3-ton van (OWK 380) and a 5-ton wagon (OWK 86) – which were due to stay on after Le Mans for the Reims 12-hour.

Death of John Lyons

The first tragedy occurred on the Monday before the race, soon after 25-year-old John Michael Lyons – the only son of William and Greta Lyons – set out from Cherbourg for Le Mans. Driving alone in one of the works MkVIIs (PWK 701), he was returning *The Motor* Trophy to the race organisers when the car collided with a US military bus on the straight but heavily cambered N13, at the village of St Joseph near Valognes. John Lyons, who died instantly, was quiet, and popular with everyone he met. He was an experienced and skilful driver, too.

The movement of Jaguar equipment and personnel took place in an atmosphere of gloom, but certainly not of foreboding.

Identification of the six Jaguars was as follows:

Race No.	Ch. No.	Eng. No.	Drivers	Reg. No.
10	XKD 503	E2011-9	Claes/Swaters	070 DU (red on white)
(N/A)	XKD 504	E3001-9	(spare car)	164 WK (white on red)
6	XKD 505	E3002-9	Hawthorn/Bueb	774 RW (red on white)
7	XKD 506	E3003-9	Hamilton/Rolt	032 RW (red on white)
9	XKD 507	E3004-9	Spear/Walters	210 RW (red on white)
8	XKD 508	E3005-9	Beauman/Dewis	194 WK (white on red)

The spare engines were E2012-9 and E3006-9. A further engine (E2013-9) had been verified by the RAC and supplied to Cooper's of Surbiton for Peter Whitehead's new 'Mark II' Cooper-Jaguar. This car was scheduled to be co-driven by Graham Whitehead, but would retire early in the race with loss of oil pressure.

Tommy Wisdom – who had masterminded Stirling Moss's first great TT drive for Jaguar back in 1950 – was taking part in the event for the seventh year in a row. (This year he would come ninth, assisted by Jack Fairman, in a Bristol 450.) As always, Wisdom filed stories, too – and there would be plenty after *this* race. Before it, he wrote a nice piece for the Friday 10 June edition of *Sporting Life*: TEST DRIVER GETS HIS BIG CHANCE. This

referred to the selection of Norman Dewis to replace a Desmond Titterington still under doctor's orders. 'At long last a British motor racing team has given a chance to a man from the bench. Three years ago I chose Norman Dewis, Chief test driver of Jaguar firm, for a place in the racing team.' Having watched him in practice, Wisdom went on to say: 'Dewis seems to me to be in the same class as Moss and Hawthorn but (*he digressed*) their story after yesterday morning's practice is a sorry one – Hawthorn blew up the engine of a new Jaguar [XKD 504] – and then Moss's Mercedes collided opposite the pits with two other cars.' In fact, Moss had been signalled by Alfred Neubauer to leave the pits as a little DB was coming in. It was dusk and drizzly. Moss nearly 'escaped', as he accelerated away, but the French car hit the Mercedes in the rear and bounced into the pit wall, hitting several people including Jean Behra whose injuries were sufficient for him to have to forego his works Maserati drive.

The new long-nose D-types looked absolutely beautiful, despite the necessity to cut out a small panel in the nearside, only to screw it back on again – thus overcoming a scrutineering argument about access to the passenger's seat. (*See next chapter.*) Fastest in that final practice session with a time of 4 min. 14·1 sec. was Eugenio Castellotti in the new 4·4-litre six-cylinder Ferrari 121LM: not quite as heavy or bulky as the V12 4·9 with which Gonzalez had broken the race lap record in 4 min. 16·8 sec. the previous year. All eyes were on Moss and Hawthorn, and their expected duel took up many of the pre-race headlines.

Bob Berry did some practice laps as second works reserve; but it was Ivor Bueb – the man so nearly selected for the works team at the start of the season – who was now the last-minute substitute (for the retired Jimmy Stewart) as Mike Hawthorn's co-driver. He would prove a tower of strength.

Hawthorn v Fangio

Race-day dawned dry, and the early laps were run in sunshine. Castellotti took an immediate, sprinting lead which was whittled down by Hawthorn and by Fangio (Moss's co-driver – what a combination, potentially!). On Lap 16, about seventy minutes into the race, the Jaguar swept past the Ferrari when it spun at Mulsanne Corner.

Fangio had made a poor start but was now engaging Hawthorn in an enthralling duel. The cars seemed evenly matched. The Jaguar had the slippery shape and the disc brakes; The Mercedes-Benz 300SLR had all-independent suspension to assist traction and cornering at lower speeds, but it had the disadvantage of drum brakes. Daimler-Benz had compensated for this by fitting a controversial driver-controlled air brake and dashboard mounted plungers which *could* be used to lubricate each lining individually.

Practice times rarely meant much at Le Mans and Fangio and Hawthorn pulverised the lap record between them, the Jaguar driver leaving it at 4 min. 06·6 sec. – over 122 mph – towards the end of the second hour.

Speeds on the Mulsanne Straight were recorded officially (but not very convincingly) over a kilometre in which many cars were still accelerating. The 1955 information suggests that the best Ferrari and Jaguar averages over the kilometre were about 176 mph to the

The Hawthorn/Bueb Jaguar (XKD 505) and the
Whitehead/Whitehead Cooper-Jaguar are pushed to
their starting positions.

Left:
Hawthorn's D-type
wings its way under the Dunlop
Bridge with half an hour gone.

Hawthorn momentarily ahead
of Castellotti and Fangio at Mulsanne.
(*Courtesy: William Heynes*)

Hawthorn and Fangio leaving the Esses.

Right:
**Hawthorn and Fangio neck and neck as they accelerate
from White Horse corner, as Castellotti (Ferrari)
begins to lose ground.** (*Courtesy: Paul Skilleter*)

Mercedes's 169 mph, but such figures are academic at Le Mans, except in the context of *completing* 24 hours of racing.

At two hours there was still nothing between Hawthorn and Fangio, neither giving anything away – two of the world's very finest drivers duelling brilliantly and with mutual respect. They had pulled out one minute on the Castellotti Ferrari. One lap back came Maglioli (Ferrari), Kling (Mercedes-Benz), 'Levegh' (Mercedes-Benz), Walters (Jaguar), Rolt (Jaguar) who had made a bad start, and Beauman (Jaguar). Another lap down, in tenth place, lay the leading Maserati followed by the 'Belgian' Jaguar. Then came the David Brown team V12 Lagonda and the first of his works Aston Martins. So, all five Jaguars were in the top twelve and looking confident, as were the three Mercedes.

Left:

Hawthorn's 3·4-litre disc-braked D-type and Fangio's 3-litre (fuel-injection, desmodromic-valve) 300 SLR lean on a back-marker at Arnage. (*Courtesy: Daimler-Benz*)

The Tragedy

Hawthorn was in the lead by six to seven seconds just before the 2½-hour mark when he was due to make his first pit-stop. Before doing so, he overtook Lance Macklin in the works disc-braked Austin-Healey 100S. Macklin's car was struck shortly afterwards by the Mercedes-Benz of Pierre 'Levegh', which was launched into the air. 'Levegh' died as his car crashed down, abruptly, against the parapet of a tunnel passing beneath the circuit. Almost anywhere else, the energy could have been dissipated less cruelly. As it was, the instantaneous deceleration had the effect of an explosion as parts from the 300SLR scythed through the densely-packed spectator enclosure. The appalling devastation was greeted with stunned incredulity – just as at Bradford City FC in 1985, when another freak tragedy would rock the world of sport.

Among those deeply affected was Mike Hawthorn, who, like most people – drivers included – just wanted Le Mans 1955 to end there and then. While there was still a race, however, team managers stuck to the rules. Hawthorn was

told by England to get back into his car and complete another lap, before handing over to Bueb.

The race organisers kept the race going. Basically, the argument was to prevent further panic and massive crowd movements while the injured were being rushed to hospital. At some point, presumably after the emergency work had been completed, another decision must have been taken: To see the race through to its so-bitter ending.

Malcolm Sayer's post-race summary (see Appendix 6) was based on the Jaguar team's timesheets (to the nearest second). Average speeds for individual drivers did not include stopping or starting laps. Average running speeds for the cars *did* include those laps, but not the time spent at rest.

'Unfortunately,' wrote Sayer, 'a complete record of oil and water replenishments was not kept; what is known is included. The Mercedes accident appears to have occurred at approximately 18 hrs. 27 min. 40 sec. by our timing, on No. 6's 35th lap, No. 7's 34th, No. 8's 34th, and No. 10's 33rd.' As can be seen by its inclusion in the summary clearly, Malcolm Sayer's brief had been to include the 'Belgian' car, which was also serviced throughout the race by works mechanics Les Bottrill and Ted Brookes. XKD 507 was controlled by the self-contained Cunningham team which had been coming to Le Mans with its own cars for the past five years. Indeed on this occasion Briggs Cunningham was once again driving one of his own cars – a somewhat Jaguar-looking machine with a 3-litre Meyer-Drake engine – which expired in the nineteenth hour after a slow run. The team's brand new Jaguar was well-placed initially, driven by Phil Walters. He and Bill Spear retired the car in the sixth hour. After-

Sequence from pits shows how Fangio escaped involvement in the accident, as Macklin's Healey spun beside him while Levegh's 300SLR disintegrated and burned, and Hawthorn's D-type continued to slow. In particular, these pictures show that few people in the pit area could have seen how the accident was caused.

wards it was noted at the works that this car's engine failure was 'presumed to be due to a piece of air box (which broke up) getting under a valve.'

Below:
Rolt at the Esses.

Dewis at Indianapolis. (*Courtesy: Norman Dewis*)

Below:
Bueb passes the pits. Note cut-out panel to satisfy scrutineers' 'passenger access' requirements. (Maybe someone had leaned on it.)

Following a fine drive by Norman Dewis – who (like Bueb) began his first-*ever* start at Le Mans only a few minutes after the accident – Don Beauman lost fourth place by going into the sand. He might have got going again if Colin Chapman's Lotus had not hit the stationary D-type. Soon afterwards, in the early hours of Sunday, Alfred Neubauer called in his two remaining 300SLRs on orders from the Daimler-Benz works; the team then packed up and returned to Stuttgart. Fangio/Moss had been leading, with Kling/Simon third, sandwiching the Bueb/Hawthorn Jaguar.

Sunday, 12 June, was bleak and wet and in the morning the Rolt Hamilton car, at one time secure in second place, was withdrawn. Its first and second gears had seized due

Spear passes the pits in XKD 507. (*Courtesy: Bob Blake*)

Bueb leaves the pits at night, passing the stricken Rolt/Hamilton car. (Dunlop's Harold Hodkinson is on extreme right.)

Below Right:
Len Hayden does up the bonnet strap as Hawthorn jumps in for a Sunday morning spell. Missing advertising banners show where the Levegh Mercedes-Benz had landed. Far left can be seen the distinct kink in the barrier line which made it impossible for anyone to use the extreme left-hand side of the road at that point. (See picture sequence at end of chapter.)

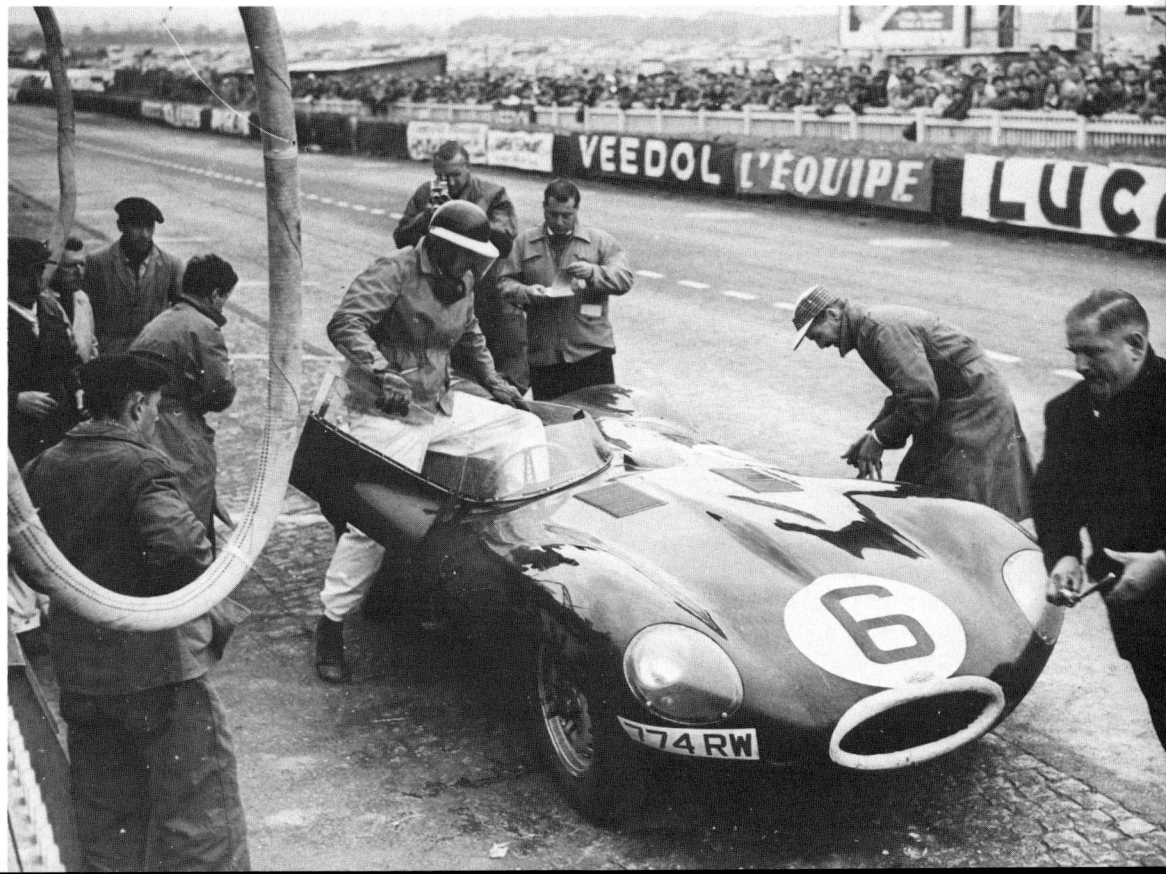

Johnny Claes en route for third place in XKD 503, shortly before the finish.

Right:
England helps Hawthorn on with his waterproofs; he was soaked already.

to an oil-seal failure and, though it was driveable, the car would certainly suffer if allowed to continue. (XKD 505, 506 and 508 were fitted with very 'high' 2·67 to 1 ZF final drive units and non-standard half-shafts. XKD 503 and 507 ran 2·79 to 1 ratios.)

With all five Ferraris long gone, it was a lonely day for Jaguar No. 6, droning on to an unchallenged victory in the lashing rain. The last of the Maseratis ground to a halt in the twentieth hour, leaving British cars in the first three places, followed by three Porsches – their days of outright victory yet to come – and the three-car Bristol team. The winning Jaguar averaged over 107 mph to cover a record distance, despite the miserable weather and some very slow laps as the end came in sight.

There were 21 classified finishers, the top six in the General Classification being:

1st	Hawthorn/Bueb	(3·4 Jaguar)	4135 km
2nd	Collins/Frère	(2·9 Aston Martin)	4073 km
3rd	Claes/Swaters	(3·4 Jaguar)	3987 km
4th	Polensky/v. Frankenberg	(1·5 Porsche)	3830 km
5th	Gendebien/Seidel	(1·5 Porsche)	3716 km
6th	Glöckler/Juhan	(1·5 Porsche)	3680 km

The Polensky Porsche won the Index of Performance prize with the works Jaguar second and the Aston Martin third. William, Greta and Mary Lyons and Ian and Pat Appleyard, mourning the loss of John, sent a joint telegram of congratulation.

Hawthorn first, Claes third, at the chequered flag.

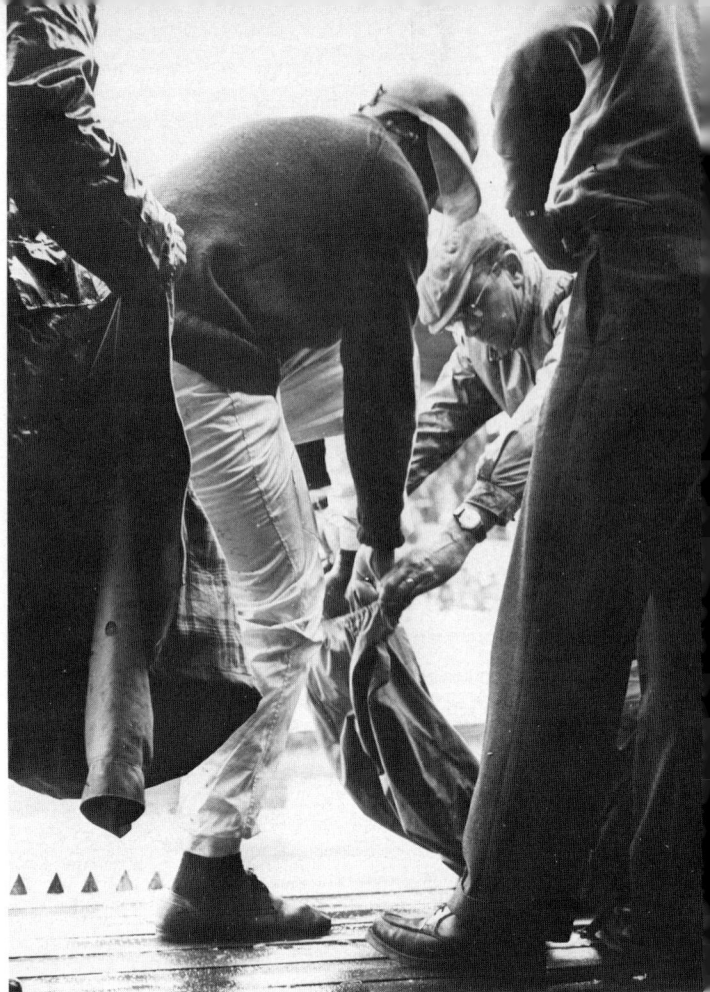

Above:
Lofty England's weariness finally shows as he takes a post-race lift from Mike Hawthorn and Ivor Bueb.

Len Hayden, Bill Heynes, Mike Hawthorn and Ivor Bueb – soaked to the skin and thoroughly thankful it's all over.

Johnny Claes, Jacques Swaters, Ted Brookes and Les Bottrill at the finish.

Instead of being driven, the works cars were flown to Le Mans by Silver City Airways in 1955. Len Hayden sits in the winning car on return to Elmdon, Birmingham airport. Apart from the one gentleman on the extreme left, the group reads (*left to right*) Les Bottrill, Ted Brookes, Bob Penney, Joe Sutton, Ron Gaudion, Jock Thomson, Frank Rainbow, Phil Weaver, Jack Emerson and Bill Wilkinson. (*Courtesy: Ron Gaudion*)

Jaguar had no intention of making any comment at all. There were, however, unfortunate inferences in a speech by Daimler-Benz chief engineer Fritz Nallinger; and on the same day, Wednesday 15 June, the Associated Press agency reported on the judicial enquiry which had followed the race. Lance Macklin had had to abandon the damaged Austin-Healey in front of the pits where it had skated to a halt after hitting the pit-wall and ricocheting across the track. He had been shaken but uninjured; now he was back at Le Mans where he gave evidence for 'more than an hour'. The AP report quoted Macklin as saying that Hawthorn had passed him about 200 yards from the supply pits: 'After passing me, Hawthorn turned too sharply towards the right and braked. In turn I braked my car as hard as I could to avoid him, my wheels locked

and I was carried towards the left. Levegh's car hit the back of my car. I was spun around. I saw the Mercedes knocked aside – and you know the rest.'

After saying that in his view Hawthorn committed an error (the AP story went on) Macklin was asked directly if he thought Hawthorn responsible for the accident. He replied:

In an affair of this kind it is difficult to speak of responsibility. Hawthorn no doubt committed an error, but the real responsibility was the speed of our cars. Going at a speed of 220 to 240 km/hr Hawthorn could not halt within a distance of 200 metres, and he had made a mistake in passing me. . . . In the excitement of this struggle, Hawthorn executed a manoeuvre which astonished me, and he left me no other alternative than to either run into him or turn to the left.

This appeared nationally on 17 June – the date upon which Jaguar's public relations officer E. W. Rankin issued the following Jaguar statement as a press release:

In view of the fact that all the circumstances surrounding the Le Mans disaster are in the course of official investigation by the French authorities, we would not have thought it incumbent upon any firm or individual to make any comments which seek to fix responsibility or apportion blame for the tragic occurrence. Nevertheless, certain statements have been quoted in the press implicating one of our drivers and, in fairness to him, we have no option but to make it known that, as a result of close questioning of the Jaguar pit personnel and others who witnessed the occurrence, there is no evidence to establish that Hawthorn acted in any way contrary to accepted racing practice.

In the course of our own enquiry, Hawthorn made the following statement:

'After passing Levegh's Mercedes at Arnage, I passed the Austin-Healey between White House Corner and the Pits and, having given the necessary hand signal, I braked and pulled into my pit in accordance with pit instructions given during the course of the preceding lap. In my judgement I allowed sufficient time for the driver of any following car to be aware of my intentions and for him to take such action as might be required without danger to others.'

In view of the foregoing statement and the evidence of the Jaguar pit personnel who witnessed the occurrence, The Company is of the opinion that any adverse criticism of Hawthorn's driving is without justification.

Many years have passed since the tragedy of Le Mans 1955, and many words have been written based upon eye-witness accounts.

No individual sees any high-speed sequence from all angles; so, no individual can tell the whole story. (An horrific parallel – the Bradford FC grandstand fire – took place at the time this chapter was being written.) I have decided, however, to include what I believe to be far-and-away the most complete, single, account of the sequence of events which led to the deaths of over eighty people. The events are described dispassionately by the multilingual Belgian engineer/writer/driver Paul Frère who wrote the original in German, for the June 1975 edition of *Autorevue* of Austria, just twenty years after the event. His reason for writing the feature is obvious from the first paragraph.

The pictures (from a film) were given to me by Lofty England, who had obtained them on Jaguar's behalf. In 1976, some of them appeared without the all-important Frère commentary, in a book entitled *Death Race, Le Mans 1955* – written by *Sunday Mirror* journalist Mark Kahn as the result of a telephone call from Lance Macklin. Except in these two publications, I am not aware of this sequence of pictures having appeared in print before. The reader who studies the words and the pictures closely may form an opinion and, maybe, reach a personal conclusion. I am particularly grateful to Paul Frère, who has given me his permission to print the full English translation; it was done by Lofty England's Austrian wife, Doris, and approved by Frère. This relieves me of the responsibility of tackling this matter myself.

THE 1955 LE MANS ACCIDENT

A clarification of the greatest tragedy in Motor-Racing history

In his book *Die Schnellsten* (The Fast Ones) published in 1974 by Ueberreuter, Helmut Zwickl devotes one chapter to Mike Hawthorn. That Hawthorn (and not Hawthorne as spelt by the author) actually gets a mention could be taken as a worthy posthumous acclamation of a first-class driver, especially since other great post war drivers like Stirling Moss and Jim Clark have not even been given a separate chapter. The title of the Hawthorn chapter 'Mike Hawthorn's Guilt and Retribution' raises the question: Should the most horrible accident in motor racing history be resurrected only for sensation-hungry readers, and the blame for the accident put at Hawthorn's door?

Although the protracted official investigation of the accident found that no individual driver was to blame for the accident which caused the death of approximately 90 people, the public will always find a scapegoat and who could better fill this requirement than one who can no longer defend himself? Since he is no longer here to do so, I would like to do so on his behalf since Mike was one of my racing contemporaries with whom I had extremely friendly relations. In the tragic Le Mans race, as the driver of an Aston Martin, I was one of his competitors and the next year we both drove for the Jaguar team, in fact we even shared the same car in the Reims 12-Hour Race in which we finished second behind another Jaguar. Helmut Zwickl bases his accusations against Hawthorn on an excerpt from Fangio's memoirs which, anyway, were not written by Fangio himself but by his Manager Marcello Giambertone and, furthermore, then translated into German; so it could hardly be called a first-hand account.

As the first point in leading up to my verdict of 'not guilty' for Mike Hawthorn, I would like to restate the quotation made by Zwickl from Fangio's memoirs. 'It was the 36th lap. This number will always remain in my memory. Hawthorn's Jaguar was approximately 90 metres in front of me. Behind him and a little to his right and already lapped was the Austin-Healey of Lance Macklin. To the left behind him was my team-mate Levegh. We were driving on full throttle. Suddenly Hawthorn pulled sharply to the right to go to the pits. His unexpected braking surprised the two drivers behind him. Macklin braked hard and steered his car to the left. However, Levegh was there. For my being alive to-day, I thank Levegh. He threw his right hand up to warn me that he was pulling out to the left. At that moment I slammed my brakes on'. Then Zwickl goes on: 'Levegh's Mercedes touched the Austin-Healey and went like a torpedo to the left into the protective bank, behind which tens of thousands of spectators stood shoulder to shoulder watching the race. Cars ran at a speed of 200 kph on the start/finishing straight, which at that time was only wide enough for two cars. For a third car to overtake there was no more room'.

And further: 'Mike Hawthorn, under the stress of his duel with the Mercedes, had already twice missed seeing his pit signals. In the 36th lap he outbraked Macklin before turning in to refuel. With this violent manoeuvre he started the events leading to the catastrophe.' I would straight away make a correction as it is important in the turn of events. Zwickl writes of Hawthorn's duel with the Mercedes cars and in another paragraph of the battle between three cars – Fangio and Levegh in Mercedes 300SLR and Hawthorn on the Jaguar. In reality there was not a battle between three cars and only a duel between Hawthorn and Fangio. On the lap before the accident the Jaguar had an 8-second lead over Fangio's Mercedes and, on the lap on which the accident occurred, Hawthorn had lapped the two Mercedes of Kling and Levegh. On the same lap, Fangio had also lapped Karl Kling, but not Pierre Levegh who, after White House Corner, was slightly in front of him. Here I would like to point out that in those days one drove through White House Corner at approximately 185 kph and that the speed before the pit-area was considerably higher than 200 kph – for a Jaguar or Mercedes probably 230 kph. Further, the accompanying photographs show that, while at that time the track was relatively narrow, it was wide enough for three cars to be alongside each other without problems.

Undoubtedly it is wrong to suggest that Hawthorn had twice missed seeing his pit signals. It is highly unlikely that a driver of Hawthorn's calibre would miss pit signals in broad day-light, but to avoid just such a possibility, Jaguar showed their Fuel Stop pit signal three times: 'FUEL 3 LAPS', three laps before the Fuel stop and in the two following laps 'FUEL 2 LAPS' and 'FUEL IN'. Perhaps others did not understand these signals, but to suggest that Hawthorn did not know exactly when he had to stop is utter nonsense.

That the accident was set in motion by Hawthorn's Jaguar going into the pits and that the accident would not have occurred had he not been making that pit stop, cannot be disputed. However, I would like to reject, emphatically, the suggestion that his pulling into the pits was a violent manoeuvre based not only on what I myself saw from the pits (where, at that time, I was ready and waiting to take over the car driven by Peter Collins: and I am no better an eye-witness than others) but also from a film on which the whole sequence of the accident is seen clearly.

This film was taken by a spectator who was badly injured by flying vehicle debris and was in hospital for three months. In taking this film, he substantially helped in Mike Hawthorn being cleared of all responsibility for the accident. From this film I have selected a number of photographs which clearly show the sequence of events of the accident.

Picture 1. A group of cars is coming out of a slight bend on the right that follows the left hand corner of White House on to the 'finishing straight'. According to the precise circuit plan, this bend is situated approximately 700 metres before the first of the pits. The group of cars is led by Hawthorn's Jaguar which has just overtaken Macklin's Austin-Healey, which can be seen in the photo on the extreme left (in the direction the cars were being driven: on the far right of the road). One can also identify two Mercedes of which Levegh's car is in front and on the outside (that is on the extreme right of the photo). The leading Jaguar is estimated to be approximately 550 metres from the pit area in this photograph, that is a good 600 metres away from the Jaguar pits. It is also already well to the right of the centre of the road.

Picture 2. The Jaguar gradually moves further to the right and the Austin-Healey still remains on the right of the road behind Hawthorn. The two Mercedes of Levegh and Fangio are on the left side of the road and behind them one can recognise the third Mercedes driven by Karl Kling which is just coming out of the bend.

Picture 3. The Jaguar is now fully to the right hand side of the road and on the correct line for the approach to the pits. The Austin-Healey is now directly behind the Jaguar and cannot be seen in this photo. Hawthorn has evidently been braking for some time, since the Mercedes are quickly catching up.

Picture 4. Hawthorn is on the extreme right and Macklin from close behind him starts to pull out. The whole of the left side of the track (right side on photo) and half of the right side of the track are completely clear for overtaking by the Mercedes.

Picture 5. Macklin pulls out abruptly after he has probably been braking behind the Jaguar, but there is no reaction from Levegh.

Picture 6. Macklin goes slightly over the centre line to the left side but there is still no visible reaction from Levegh.

Picture 7. Macklin has his car straightened up with the two left side wheels just over the centre line, but Levegh has still not reacted. With the substantial speed difference a collision now seems unavoidable although, apart from a few centimetres, the left hand side of the track was completely clear. Hawthorn continues correctly on the right side of the road to his pit.

Picture 8. The sloping tail of the Austin-Healey forms a springboard for the Mercedes.

Picture 9 (*the last on the film*). Due to the change of attitude and the speed of the Mercedes still being around 200 kph, the car becomes airborne and goes on to crash into a concrete section of the protective bank and disintegrates. Levegh was thrown out

2

3

5

6

8

9

and killed instantly and flying parts of the car which included the complete engine killed nearly another 90 people. The Austin-Healey, from the impact, went across the road into the pit wall and then back across to the middle of the track. Macklin was not injured. From the statement in the Fangio book referring to Levegh's arm being raised in warning, nothing can be seen in the film. What seems much more likely is that Fangio, driving behind Levegh, appreciated that a collision would occur and reacted accordingly.

It is completely clear from the photographs that Hawthorn did not make a sudden-brake-and-pull-sharp-right manoeuvre only a short distance from the pits, thereby endangering the cars near him. At least 500 metres before the pit area, he was already well to the right side of the road even though at that time there was no pit lane forcing him to do so. How then, since all the drivers concerned were experienced people, did this dreadful accident come about? My explanation is as follows: Hawthorn was involved in a dogfight with Fangio and was leading the race. It would have been unthinkable for him to stay behind the much slower Austin-Healey of Macklin, after the White House corner which is approximately 1 km before the pits, since his car was much quicker out of the corner and could rapidly overtake Macklin. Having done so, he had ample time to get over to the right hand side of the road and then, at approx. 400 metres before the pits, to brake.

That the Jaguar was braking, *Macklin did not immediately see,* since once the much quicker Jaguar had overtaken him, he was much more concerned with the two Mercedes coming up behind him. Had he, Macklin, enough time to get on the left side of the road in order to take the Dunlop Bridge corner after the pits at full speed? Or must he stay on the right side of the road and allow the two Mercedes to pass before the Dunlop curve? The answer to this question could only be found from watching the rear view mirror and understandably Macklin concentrated more on that, than on what was happening ahead of his car.

Normally, the Jaguar would, long since, have disappeared into the distance. So Macklin (who, considering the following Mercedes, remained well to the right) did not notice that Hawthorn had started to brake in the meantime. Had he looked in front, it would have been no problem for him to pull to the left and pass the Jaguar again. He could even have done it without crossing the centre line to the left and obstructing the Mercedes. Hawthorn must have had the same thoughts. But Macklin's attention was concentrated on the situation behind him and when he looked to the front again, he found himself so close to the Jaguar, that only by a sudden avoiding action (probably with simultaneous braking) could he avert a collision. However, the entire left side of the track remained free and nothing obstructed the passing of the two Mercedes. The photographs show further more that Macklin was in complete control of his vehicle.

Why, therefore, did Levegh not take advantage of the left side of the track in order to pass Macklin without problem? Undoubtedly, because he also paid far more attention to the events behind him than those in front of him. He surely did not fail to observe that Fangio, his team-mate, had caught him up and was about to lap him. In the role of a guest-driver with the Mercedes stable, he was anxious not to obstruct him in the overtaking manoeuvre and his sight was on the mirror. Otherwise he must have seen what was happening in front of him and anticipated that Macklin would pull out to the left. But he saw nothing. The photo shows, that he showed no reaction whatsoever to the events going on in front of him and made no effort to evade to the left, thereby ramming the Austin-Healey in full force from behind.

Undoubtedly the accident would not have happened if Hawthorn had not made for the pits; but nor would it have happened if Macklin had reacted in time to the Jaguar's slowing down; and the fatally-crashing Levegh could be accused of hitting the Austin-Healey despite having the complete left track at his disposal for passing.

No. One cannot burden any of the involved drivers with the responsibility. Hawthorn's manoeuvre was correct and he could have no idea of the fact that Macklin was not becoming aware of his braking for the pits and acting accordingly.

One cannot accuse Macklin of not anticipating that the normally much quicker Jaguar would suddenly go slower. That he was paying more attention to events behind him than those in front could be taken as a positive point on his part.

And the case of Levegh has great similarity with Macklin's. At most, one could accuse the Frenchman of paying too much attention to his rear; since Fangio's Mercedes was not faster than his, it would not be substantially obstructed by his on the straight. He (Levegh), on the other hand, had the much slower Austin-Healey in front of him, which he must overtake within the next 200 to 300 metres. However, if Levegh was concentrating too much on the approaching Fangio, it was undoubtedly with the best intention.

In any case, it is wrong to burden the guilt for this catastrophe on Mike Hawthorn and one has, after unemotional investigation of the facts, also appreciation of the decision of the racing manager of Jaguar at that time, 'Lofty' England, to let his cars remain in the race after the withdrawal of Mercedes.

Paul Frère

An indication of how little could be seen by most people in the pits may be obtained by studying 'stills' from Jaguar's ciné film made by Random Films, reproduced on pages 92 and 93.

Chapter Five

An Unfulfilled Season (June~Dec ´55)

Among the immediate post-Le Mans cancellations were those of the Alpine Trial and the Reims 12-hour race – two of Jaguar's happiest hunting grounds. Jaguar had been all set to participate in both.

Back in the Spring Ian Appleyard, in reply to a letter from Lofty England, had said that he believed the XK 140 to be 'a greatly improved motor car', finding its handling 'certainly quite exceptional'. Appleyard went on: 'I agree with you that we can put up a much better show in the Alpine now, even with the same amount of power available. Mr Lyons seemed quite interested in the idea of the same three drivers [as in Monte Carlo Rally] forming an Alpine team and ... it would be a good idea to get Vard and Adams definitely organised ....' which England did. In May, Jaguar's home sales distribution manager Alec Blythe noted the allocation of two dark green XK 140s – RHP 474 (S800033DN) and RHP 575 (S800034DN) for Adams/McMillen and Vard/Jones respectively – and a cream one, RRW 460 (S800035DN); but in June, William Lyons's son-in-law, Appleyard, changed his mind about making an Alpine 'comeback'. This was for the sake of the Lyons family. In his place was nominated the 1954 over-2·6-litre class winner, Eric Haddon of Haddon Transformers Ltd, Harrow, who signed a one-off works contract for this event, only to hear of its cancellation on 25 June, barely a fortnight before it was due to start. Peter Brotchie of J. H. Minet & Co., the London insurers, was a happy man when he acknowledged Lofty England's cancellation advice: 'Although sorry for the three gents concerned, frankly I couldn't be more

delighted,' he said.

In the Portuguese sports car GP at Oporto on 26 June, XK engines came 3rd, 4th and 5th – Hamilton (XKC 402), P. Whitehead (Cooper-Jaguar), and Berry (XKC 403) respectively. Bob Berry's personal account of this event is included in the appendices. The Hamilton and Whitehead cars stayed on in Portugal for the Lisbon GP four weeks later, but both were destined to retire. There had been an intention to send XKD 506 to Lisbon for Mike Hawthorn, until it was declared that the organisers had run out of starting money.

There was more agony to come before the season was out. Poor Don Beauman was killed on 9 July, driving Sir Jeremy Boles's GP Connaught. Having just made fastest lap of the Leinster Trophy Race at Wicklow, he lost control and was thrown out as the car crashed. His was by no means the only accident in this heat-wave event – but it was the only fatal one. Desmond Titterington was having his first race since his *Eifelrennen* crash and won the over 2-litre scratch race in the *Ecurie Ecosse* D-type XKD 501 from Mike Heather (whose XK 120 would go on to win the Munster 100-mile race at Carrigohane a week later) but the Jaguar men were out-handicapped at Wicklow where a young man named David Piper won the main prize in his supercharged 750cc MG-powered Lotus 6.

Stirling Moss scored his first-ever Championship Grand Prix victory on 16 July at the Aintree circuit, now in its second season and being used clockwise. It was a long-awaited Formula One win for him, and a walkover for the

Mercedes-Benz W196 cars which took the first four places. Hawthorn, back with Ferrari's Grand Prix team, was suffering from the heat and Castellotti took over from him to take sixth place. Macklin spun off into the strawbales in Moss's 250F Maserati but was allowed to re-start and finished eighth.

Earlier in the day, four DB3S Aston Martins had taken the top places in the sports car race, their slow-corner behaviour proving ideal for the Aintree circuit.

A single works D-type was entered for Hawthorn, and two cars were brought for test. XKD 505, the winner at Le Mans, had had its engine and gearbox removed, stripped and reassembled with no recorded problems. New inner and outer members had been fitted to the ZF differential, enabling standard 19-spline halfshafts to be used: The ratio was changed to 3·31 to 1. The oil system had been flushed out and examined carefully. A few days before the Aintree date both fuel pumps were found to be inoperative after standing in the workshop. SU diagnosed corrosion due to water evaporation in the armature housing. The pumps were replaced and the car taken to Aintree, but it did not seem to go well. The list of work afterwards included complete steering and throttle linkage checks, and an instruction to fit copper washers to the bottom studs and set-bolt of the gearbox rear cover.

The four-spoke steering wheel, which Hawthorn always specified, was transferred to XKD 506 which had had similar post-Le Mans checks. The gearbox (which had seized at Le Mans due to failure of an oil seal) was replaced and a complaint of steering stiffness had led to the discovery of a slight 'pick-up' condition between the rack and the support tube outer bush. When the Lisbon plans were scrubbed, just as the car was due to leave for the docks, XKD 506 was diverted to Aintree where it performed better than 505 – perhaps partly because of a change from 3·31 to 3·54 axle with German 12-spline axle shafts.

Attended by Phil Weaver and Bob Penney, this car was chosen for race day, running on Dunlop R4s and Champion NA8 plugs (as opposed to NA10s). The engine for this race was E3007-9.

Outpaced at Aintree

The Aintree corners were no help to the Jaguar with its non-independent rear end, and Hawthorn's best practice lap of 2 min. 10·2 sec. was 1·4 seconds off the top Aston Martin pace. Nevertheless the Jaguar charged through from the second row to lead gloriously for one race lap. Then the Aston Martins went through one by one. So Hawthorn was fifth, having discovered only one corner, Melling Crossing, which the D-type could really take in its stride. The D-types of Bob Berry and Ninian Sanderson battled for sixth and seventh; Berry settled for the lower place after flying off course at Melling, still keeping ahead of Mike Keen (HWM-Jaguar). (Keen would die in a crash at Goodwood a few weeks later. 1955 was proving a costly year in terms of human life.)

While D-types were not yet a familiar sight in national and club racing, privately-owned C-types continued to put up impressive performances. Curt Lincoln of Finland brought XKC 044 to Britain; and Archie Scott-Brown was

spectacular in XKC 049 at Snetterton and Brands Hatch.

Bill Smith (XKC 051) continued to impress, and was catching the eye of many a team manager. Poor Dan Margulies and Graham Hill came a cropper with XKC 038 after running as high as fifth in the Messina 10-hour race.

The *Ecurie Ecosse* D-types, usually driven by Titterington and Sanderson, became increasingly successful in UK events as 'Wilkie' Wilkinson and his team from Edinburgh's Merchiston Mews got to know the cars better.

The private Hamilton *équipe* (XKC 402 and XKC 406) would soon expand with the acquisition of XKD 510, and cars would be lent to friendlier rivals such as Michael Head (who never received the new car he'd wanted), George Abecassis, and Graham Whitehead. As a dealer

Unmistakably Aintree atmosphere in this July 1955 paddock shot taken by Bob Penney, showing XKD 506 which he and Phil Weaver looked after, on that weekend.

in specialist cars, Hamilton would buy and sell a number of D-types over the years.

After Lisbon (where XKC 402 ran out of brakes) and Kristianstad (where Head brought XKC 406 home sixth in the Swedish Grand Prix), the Hamilton cars spent the latter part of 1955 in England, where racing was affected less than most countries by the aftermath of Le Mans – probably because of the high standards of circuit management, marshalling, and safety. Duncan Hamilton himself scored worthily at Goodwood, Silverstone and Snetterton, which helped to make up for the lack of works drives.

Hamilton and Rolt, the longest-serving members of the works team, did manage to obtain the loan of a works car for the revived Goodwood 9-hour race in mid-August. Jaguar had had this event 'in the bag' in 1952 and 1953, only to lose out to Aston Martin due to late-race drama. After missing 1954, the fixture had now returned to the calendar for a third (and final) time.

The loan car was OKV 3 (XKC 404), the Silverstone

lap record holder – but it had been standing around since May. On 3 and 4 August however, the engine was removed (for loss of oil pressure) and rebuilt with new bearings and 1955-type relief-valve spring. Before the race a 3·54 to 1 axle was fitted and several other updating modifications carried out, including borrowing the full power brake master cylinder and reservoir from XKD 505. Three extra number-illuminating lamps were fitted to comply with the regulations for this race, which ran from 3 pm until

midnight. Tony Rolt took the first stint in the race, making a fine start to run fourth initially – then the distributor drive gear sheared. Len Hayden would return to Coventry in the car next day – at the end of a towrope. Rolt was on the point of giving up racing but this was a particularly depressing way to finish. One of Hamilton's own cars was driven by Michael Head and former works team-member Peter Whitehead who went off backwards at Woodcote Corner with an engine seizure at about half-time.

Three other Jaguar-powered machines performed extremely well, however. The Titterington/Sanderson *Ecosse* D-type was always in the hunt and sometimes in the lead in this battle of tyre-wear and pitstops. In the end it was running strongly in second place and catching the leaders – Dennis Poore and erstwhile Jaguar driver Peter

Dunlop's tireless tyre men, Vic Barlow and Dick Jeffrey at Aintree.

The Hamilton-entered D-type of Peter Whitehead and Michael Head tops up at the Shell tanker ahead of the Moss/von Hanstein Porsche, Goodwood 9-hr race 1955.

Walker in a works Aston Martin DB3S. In fourth and fifth places, behind the Brooks/Collins DB3S, came Bill Smith and Lance Macklin (HWM-Jaguar) and Jaguar's 'reserves' Bob Berry and Norman Dewis (XKC 403), the latter pair wishing they'd set the Broadhead D-type a less conservative race schedule (see Appendix 3).

Berry and Dewis with the Broadhead D-type. (*Courtesy: Bob Berry*)

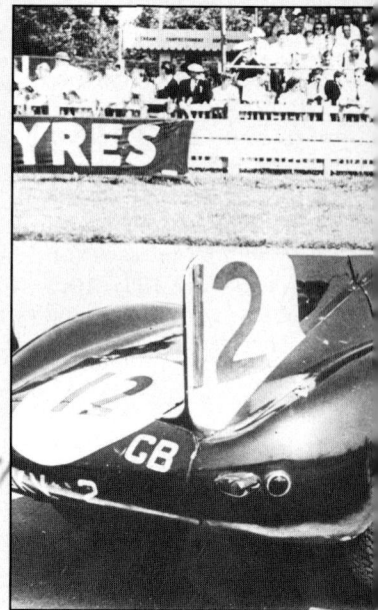

Dewis with D-type lined u
(*Courtesy: Tom Rowe*)

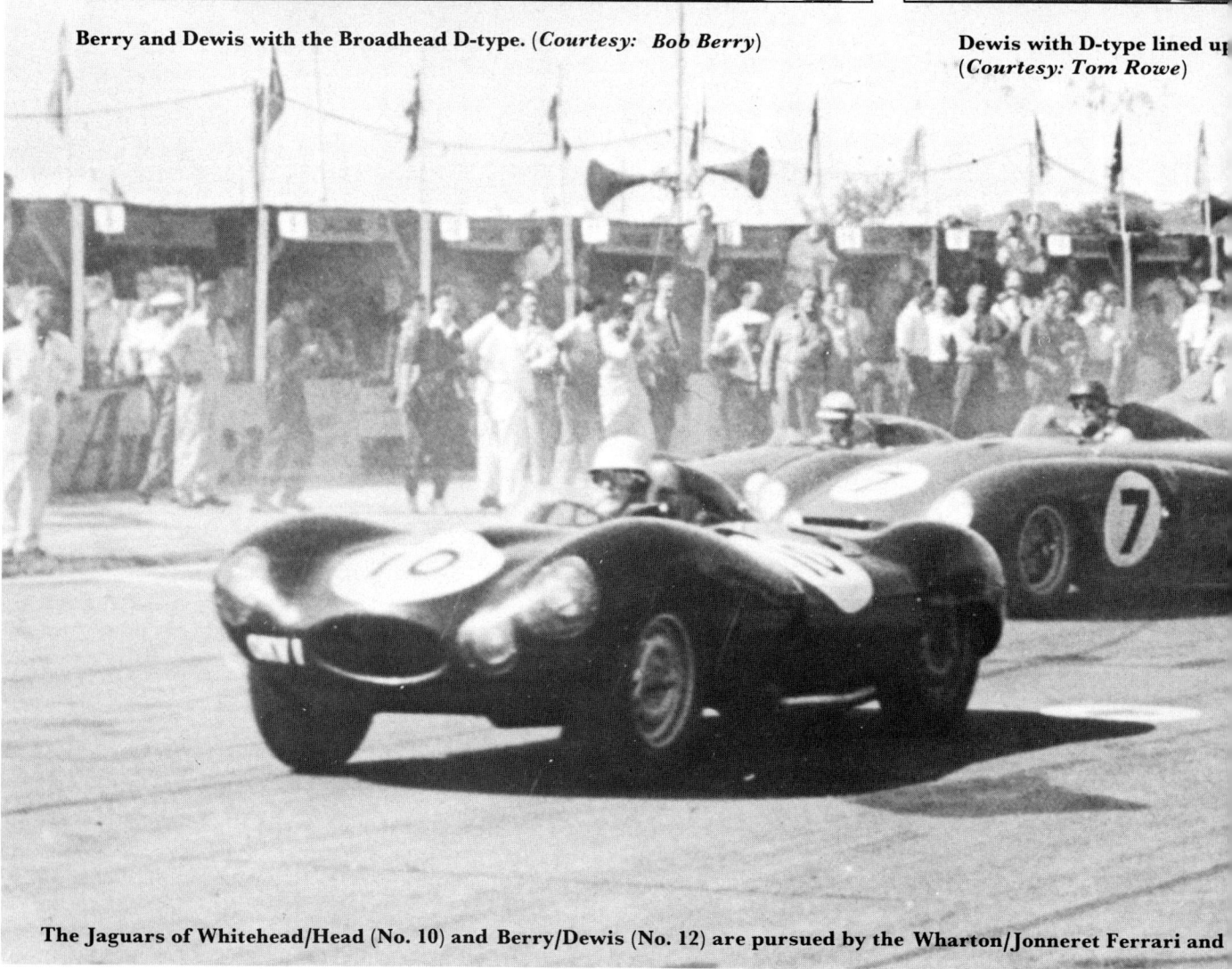

The Jaguars of Whitehead/Head (No. 10) and Berry/Dewis (No. 12) are pursued by the Wharton/Jonneret Ferrari and

wood 9-hour race.

Night stop for XKC 403 at Goodwood. (*Courtesy: John Lea*)

t of the field: Goodwood 9-hrs 1955. (*Courtesy: Bob Berry*)

Mike Hawthorn, whose 3-litre 'Monza' led in the early stages, had now been released to Ferrari for sports car as well as Grand Prix racing. This was only reasonable, as it was now clearer than ever that Jaguar would never field a *full* Browns Lane team for a *full* season's racing. There was an occasion at about this time that Jaguar had to deny rumours that it was giving up racing altogether.

Looking for improvement

Jaguar was in fact working on its problem areas, with regular test sessions by Norman Dewis. Here is an example of a report from Lofty England to Bill Heynes and Bob Knight after a Silverstone test by Mike Hawthorn on 29 July 1955, with XKC 401. (There was a Ferrari on hand too):

ROLL BAR AND TYRE TESTS – SILVERSTONE 28th JULY, 1955

> Car: OVC.501
> Driver: J. M. Hawthorn.
> Wheel Camber: 2°.

Tests with Roll Bar fitted.

(1) 650 x 16 R.1. Dunlop front and rear. Tyre pressures 30 front 35 rear. Best lap time 1–54. Excess over-steer reported.

(2) 6·0 x 17 Dunlop Stabilia front 6·5 x 17 1954 type Stabilia rear. Tyre pressures 35 front and rear. Reported lack of control, variation of over-steer and under-steer and wheel jumping. Generally unsatisfactory.

(3) 600 x 16 R.1. Dunlop front 6·5 x 17 1955 type Stabilia rear. Tyre pressures 35 front and rear. Best lap time 1–52·4. Reported less under-steer than test (2) and best handling condition of tests (1), (2) and (3).

(4) Tyres as test (3) but front tyre pressures reduced to 30. Best lap time 1–51·8. Reported best handling conditions of tests (1) to (4) with slight under-steer.

Tests with Rear Roll Bar removed.

(5) Tyres as test (4). Tyre pressures 35 front and rear. Best lap time 1–51·8. Handling satisfactory but more under-steer than in test (4).

(6) Firestone 170 tyres 600 x 16 front 650 x 16 rear. Tyre pressures 35 front and rear. Best lap time 1–52·4. Reported less under-steer than test (5) but unable to obtain same R.P.M. on given point on acceleration from corner. Tyre temperature 11°C higher than Dunlop (86°C).

(7) Pirelli 600 x 16 Stelvio front 650 x 16 Corsa rear. 35 front and rear tyre pressures. Best lap time 1–50·7. Handling satisfactory with a little under-steer. No holding back on R.P.M.

(8) Dunlop R.4. 550 x 16 front 650 x 16 rear. Tyre pressures 35 front and rear. Best lap time 1–53·5. Handling satisfactory but slight over-steer due to rear slipping out.

(9) Tyres as test (8) but front tyre pressures reduced to 30. Best lap time 1–51. Reported better handling than test (8).

(10) Ferrari 750.S. Tyres Dunlop R.1. 525 x 16 front 650 x 16 rear. Tyre pressures 34 front and 38 rear. Best lap time 1–53·5.

Conclusions.

(A) Rear roll bar produces definite over-steer characteristics; would be more advantageous if softened. Does not appear to have great effect on lap time but could prove advantageous under racing conditions when full width of corner not available.

(B) Reduction of wheel camber might produce better results than roll bar or a combination of reduced wheel camber and a soft rear roll bar might work.

(C) I think cornering speeds are still limited by the inside wheel lifting, which cannot be overcome with solid rear axle.

(D) The Pirelli tyres undoubtedly give the best handling characteristics.

(E) The Dunlop R.4. tyre does not appear to give the best results until partially worn.

(F) For the Dundrod Circuit, the 1955 6·5 x 17 Stabilia would seem to give the best results consistent with long life on the rear wheels but the 6·0 x 17 Stabilia is definitely not satisfactory on the front wheels. In my opinion the 600 x 16 R.1. tyre used on the front wheels would give satisfactory handling and a tread life comparable to the 6·5 x 17 Stabilia rear tyre. As an alternative Mr Badger says he can produce an R.1. tyre in the 6·0 x 17 Stabilia size but tests of this tyre would have to be made to decide whether it would be satisfactory.

It should be noted that for these tests the car was fitted with a set of standard production brakes and that early on in the tests it was necessary to pump the pedal, which trouble became more pronounced as the tests continued during the latter part of the tests three or four pumps of the pedal prior to each corner being necessary.

This may have had some bearing on the lap times with the latter tests carried out and would also point to the fact that the production 'D' type brake set-up cannot be considered satisfactory in its present condition.

Soon afterwards, XKC 401 was being fitted with a de Dion rear end – something completely new at Jaguar – for it was difficult to ignore the great UK success of the Aston Martin which came up trumps again in the 220-mile Oulton Park International Trophy in late August, when veteran Reg Parnell kept his DB3S ahead of Hawthorn's Ferrari. Here Collins (Aston Martin) was third from Gregory (Ferrari). Jack Broadhead had let Stirling Moss have a go in XKC 403 on Friday's practice (Bob Berry was finding it increasingly difficult to take weekdays off and pursue his career ambitions with Jaguar at the same time); but Berry did race and came in fifth, well ahead of Harry Schell who drove the works HWM-Jaguar which had beaten the Berry car at Goodwood. Stirling Moss zoomed through from the rear of the grid to take seventh place in Peter Bell's Connaught ALSR, which Les Leston had been due to drive.

A week later, at Aintree on 3 September, *Ecurie Ecosse* D-types driven by Sanderson and Titterington took a convincing 1–2 in the last British mainland international sports car race of the season. Salvadori (Aston Martin DB3S) was third, Harry Schell (Ferrari) fourth, and Peter Whitehead (Cooper-Jaguar) fifth.

TT rules revised

There remained one special home event: the RAC International Tourist Trophy race, by now celebrating its 50th anniversary as well as its fifth running on the daunting Dundrod road course officially measuring 7 miles 732 yards per lap, and varying in altitude by some 500 ft. This time there would be a race length of 84 laps – 1000 km – and the main awards would be allocated on a 'scratch' basis. (There *would* still be good prizes on handicap, the top one once again going to Armagnac and Laureau; their DB-Panhard would cover 70 laps.)

When he saw the regulations Lofty England was delighted. That he considered this TT an important race for Jaguar was shown by his expressed intention to enter three cars. At Le Mans he had had a chat to that effect with Charles Gordon Neill, Hon. Sec. of the Ulster Automobile Club.

There had followed a period of silence until 25 August when they spoke on the telephone. England wrote immediately, apologising for not being able to present a full team because, 'we have so much on our hands other than competition work that we just cannot spare the labour force'. (There was little more than a month to go before the announcement of the new, compact, 2·4 saloon – a completely new departure for Jaguar.)

On the same day, Neill also sent a letter to England:

I am writing to you in connection with the Tourist Trophy Race with particular regard to the scrutiny of cars for compliance with the Regulations. This matter has been discussed between myself and the scrutineers who will be doing the job and it has been realised that due to the very keen competition this year and to the very great degree of support which has been given to us by the manufacturers both British and Continental, that the scrutineering will have to be carried out on a fairly strict basis possibly more so than has been the case in previous years.

I understand that you had a little bit of difficulty at Le Mans over the question of an extra door due to the fact that access to the passenger seat could not be directly attained from the drivers seat. I know that an extra door was cut and I presume that it was made to the correct size and that hinges were fitted but I would like to take this opportunity of advising you that our scrutineers over here have come to the conclusion that if you are running the same cars as at Le Mans this door would have to be in place if the car is to comply with the Regulations. Please do not think that I am trying to tell you your business but I am most anxious to avoid any difficulties arising at the last moment which are so much more difficult to settle in the tense atmosphere then prevailing.

This was England's reply, dated 31 August, explaining the scrutineering incident at Le Mans, mentioned in the previous chapter:

Thank you for your letter of the 25 August and for writing to me regarding scrutineering of cars for this year's Tourist Trophy Race.

With regard to the question which arose at Le Mans, I think perhaps you do not know the whole story. This year's Le Mans regulations did not in any way vary from those which applied in the past and which are similar to those contained in Appendix C of the International Sporting Code as applicable to sports cars. No query had ever been raised in the past on the question of access to the passenger's side.

What happened is that when the Nardi car was being scrutineered, this car being a twin boom job, the scrutineers insisted that there should be some direct access to the passenger's side seat which was, of course, completely apart from the Driver's side. The entrant of that car then suggested that if this was to be done to his car it should be done on all other cars where there was no form of division of the body between the driver's and passenger's seat and, unfortunately for us, at the time his car was being scrutineered the Belgian 'D' type was adjacent to it.

Although other 'D' types had been scrutineered prior to this time, we were told that all our cars would have to have some form of access door put in and a letter was, in fact, put out to all entrants, drawing their attention to this particular requirement.

Since there had been no change in that regulation, nobody did anything about it except us, as we were the only people with whom it had been taken up directly. The Organisers in actual fact appreciated that they had not handled the matter too well and asked us to co-operate more or less to save their face on the job, but it is interesting to note that a similar condition applied to something like 40% of the cars in the Race and that no-one, other than us, did anything about it.

For the T.T., therefore, although the car we have entered will still have the door on the passenger's side, swiftly detachable by undoing only four bolts, if you are going to insist on this condition for all cars you scrutineer, I am afraid that you are going to cause a lot of trouble, since there are bound to be a number of cars which will not comply with this requirement

and, since I cannot see that there is anything in the International Regulations which justifies such a requirement, I honestly think that it would be best for your scrutineers to accept the fact that only one door is called for by the International Regulations and that bodies should be accepted on the basis on which they have always been accepted in every race in which we have competed, with the exception of this year's Le Mans Race, where the little drama mentioned above occurred.

No doubt you will let me have some definite news on this subject.

Neill wrote back to the Jaguar Competitions Manager on 4 September:

I have your letter of the 31 August on the subject of the scrutineering of cars in the Tourist Trophy Race together with a full account of what transpired at Le Mans. Unfortunately our Chief Scrutineer Mr C A Stuart is on leave at the moment and will not be back until Thursday so I cannot advise him of the contents of your letter until then.

For your information may I quote the Article in the international Sporting Code relevant to the matter:-

(b) All cars must have at least one rigid door with proper fastenings and hinges. At its upper part, each door shall have a width of at least 40 cms measured horizontally. Furthermore, minimum dimensions over the floor board shall be such as to be sufficient to enclose a rectangle having 40 cms measured horizontally, and 20 cms measured vertically. These doors must be such that real and direct access is given to the front seats.

Mr C A Stuart's contention is that due to the construction of the Jaguar it is not possible to move from the driver's seat to the passenger's seat and therefore real direct access cannot be gained to the passenger's seat. This obviously applied in the case of the Nardi about which the original trouble arose and must have been the reason why you were made to put an extra door in the Jaguar at Le Mans.

I did have a look at most of the cars running in France when I heard of this trouble and while I was not aware at that time of the full facts it did appear to me that in most other cars where there was only one door it was possible to slide from the driver's seat to the passenger's seat without difficulty if the metal cover over the passenger's seat was removed.

This is probably the reason why our scrutineer feels that the Jaguars should have a proper door and I should be glad to have your views on this matter so that I can hand them to him when he returns on Thursday morning.

Here the correspondence ended and, on Thursday 15 September, the scrutineering at Harry Ferguson's premises at Alfred Street, Belfast, went without a hitch. The courtesies would be renewed, however, in some lengthy post-race correspondence.

XKD 505, the nominated entry had been overhauled completely for the TT. A decision to fit an experimental De Dion rear suspension (previously tried on XKC 401) was taken shortly before shipment. The car (according to the Competition Department notebook for it) was withdrawn before the race because 'practice results were unfavourable in that outer Metalastik drive shaft couplings were not reliable'.

The race number (and the front calipers) were switched to XKD 506, which had been intended as a spare car and Hawthorn and Titterington raced it, with its 'Aintree' engine, E3007-9. The only other D-type was the hard-worked Broadhead D-type XKC 403 prepared, as usual, by John Lea with works co-operation. On this occasion Berry was due to share the driving with Sanderson (since *Ecurie Ecosse* were not taking part). Except in practice the Scot was to be out of luck, however.

Berry shot away from the Le Mans type start ahead of

Hawthorn, both Jaguars wagging their tails eagerly, and led the pack into the fast downhill section towards the Lethemstown crossroads. Half way around the first lap, however, Moss (Mercedes-Benz 300SLR) moved ahead, with Hawthorn chasing. Towards the end of Lap 2 Berry, going strongly in third position, went off-course irretrievably after feeling a tyre go soft (*see appendix*) and the order was Moss, Hawthorn, von Trips – Mercedes, Jaguar, Mercedes – with Fangio moving up quickly in the third 300SLR to leave the Aston Martins, Ferraris and Maseratis fighting a separate battle.

TT jeopardizes road-racing

On the third lap, a bad accident claimed the life of Jim Mayers whose Cooper-Coventry Climax broke-up when it hit an enclosing bank and then a gatepost, before coming to rest in the middle of the road. Several cars had no chance of avoiding the burning wreck and injuring their drivers – among them the Connaught of Bill Smith, who had just raced an *Ecurie Ecosse* D-type in Scotland for the first time and had been promised a works drive in the 'fairly near future' by Lofty England. The unfortunate Lincoln lad did not live through this multiple accident and it is ironic to think that if he had been Bob Berry's TT partner (as England had hoped) he would have been waiting in the pits or ahead of the conflagration. This was one of the unhappiest twists of fate in a year of disastrous events. (Richard Wainwaring would crash his Elva later, making it three fatalities in the one day.)

The masters were, meanwhile, showing their prowess to an appreciative audience as yet unaware of the extent of the tragedy on the far side of the course. While Moss established a lead, despite hitting a bank, Hawthorn and Fangio renewed their Le Mans duel and brought the grandstand crowd to its feet. Hawthorn held second place until Lap 14 when Fangio dived past; but the Jaguar driver fought back, swapping places with the World Champion several times before drawing clear again on Lap 17. Two laps later Hawthorn set what was to be an all-time lap record for cars at Dundrod, in 4 min. 42 sec (94·67 mph). Both Moss and Fangio did 4 min. 44 sec. on the same lap, just over $1\frac{1}{2}$ hours into the race. Fangio could not better this; but Moss got down to his personal best time of 4 min. 43 sec. on Lap 25 – only to lose a full ten seconds somewhere on the next one. It was at the end of Lap 25 that Hawthorn came in for his first scheduled pit-stop which took only 48 seconds. Fangio completed 29 laps before handing over to Kling; Moss came in after 30 laps (nearly $2\frac{1}{2}$ hours) with a ruined rear tyre, the tread of which had ripped the body open like a tin can. A large area of offside bodywork above and around the wheel was cut away completely and John Fitch took over. The German team was, apparently, not fully aware of the notorious abrasiveness of the road surface.

Now being handled on home ground by Desmond Titterington, the D-type increased its lead as rain began to become a hazard. Here was a works Jaguar being driven at its reasonable limit by two top-flight drivers, whereas all three Mercedes team cars had 'Number Two' drivers who (though very experienced) were well past their

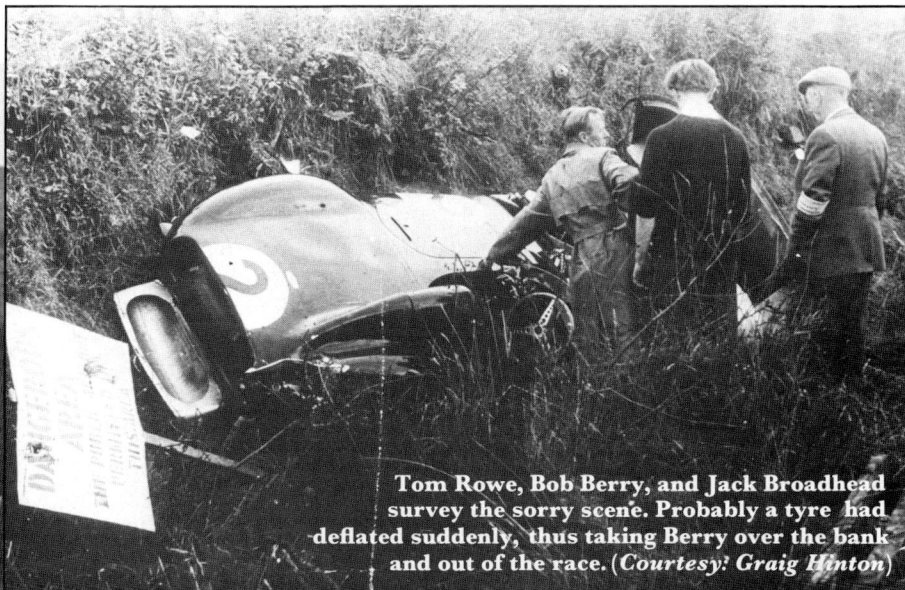

Tom Rowe, Bob Berry, and Jack Broadhead survey the sorry scene. Probably a tyre had deflated suddenly, thus taking Berry over the bank and out of the race. (*Courtesy: Graig Hinton*)

Berry (No. 2) leads Hawthorn (No. 1) at the start of the 1955 Dundrod TT – but Moss is charging forward to catch them in the Mercedes-Benz. Amongst the other cars clearly seen are Peter Whitehead's Cooper-Jaguar 'Mark 2' (No. 3), and the Ferraris (Nos. 4 and 5) of Castellotti and Maglioli. (*Courtesy: Paul Skilleter*)

respective peaks – and while they were at the wheel, the lone car from Coventry was in command.

John Fitch was brought in after only seven laps, Kling after sixteen. In the rain, Moss and Fangio began to make up the deficit; but Titterington was still more than two minutes clear of Moss and over a lap up on Fangio when he came into the pits at the end of Lap 51. In the wet the Jaguar, even with Hawthorn driving, could not hold off the Mercedes which came past on Lap 56 – only to make an emergency stop for new rear tyres and more fuel after 62 laps, when Hawthorn swept ahead again! Moss was off like a rocket, however, and outfumbled Hawthorn when he caught him up a lap later at the hair-pin, Hawthorn dropping a good half-minute regaining the course. Weather conditions were improving – but not enough to

missing). Then, on Lap 82, Hawthorn (as he wrote later) 'felt something go in the engine'. He declutched and would have coasted in to take third place quite easily, had the car not spun on (Hawthorn believed) its own oil.

In today's racing, the car might have been classified fourth (as in the case of Andy Rouse in the TT 22 years later) but, as it was, the Jaguar did not finish at the Finishing Line and was therefore unplaced.

If Mercedes-Benz carried the day, taking the top three places with the 300SLR – which, despite the nomenclature, was based on their W196 Grand Prix car – Desmond Titterington created a local legend for himself, having led the Golden Jubilee TT for twenty glorious laps or more . . .

XKD 506 had broken its crankshaft. Afterwards the

This picture at Leathemstown doesn't include a Jaguar but it does show the country-lane nature of the Dundrod circuit. The 1955 pile-up took place half a mile or so beyond this point; there was no room for the victims to take evasive action. The cars in this picture are the Baxter/Trimble Kieft, the Poore/Walker Aston Martin, and the Behra/Musso/Bordoni Maserati. (*Courtesy: Max Trimble*)

give Jaguar the chance of more than an honourable second place (although an unavailing protest had been put in by England, relating to the continued eligibility of the Moss/Fitch car, now that so much of its bodywork was

engine (E3007-9) was changed for E3005-9, and the brakes completely overhauled, with new discs, calipers and pump. (The Plessey pump drive spindle seal had failed.) Among many other jobs was the replacement of the rear hubs, both of which had suffered damage.

William Lyons wrote to the two drivers, thanking them warmly for upholding British and Jaguar prestige, and sending each a personal bonus cheque.

There followed an unusually protracted correspondence between Lofty England and Gordon Neill of the Ulster Automobile Club.

'As far as the protest is concerned,' wrote England. 'I

QUARTERLAND BUDORE

IRELAND'S CORNER

COCHRANSTOWN

JORDAN'S CROSS

M ANTRIM

N

WHEELER'S CORNER

TO BELFAST

HAIRPIN

LEATHEMSTOWN BRIDGE

LEATHEMSTOWN CORNER

RUSHYHILL

START & FINISH

PITS

THE QUARRY

ARMAGH START, FINISH & PITS ENCLOSURE

SPECTATOR ENCLOSURES

CAR PARKS

COVERED GRAND STANDS

LONDONDERRY STAND

BELFAST STAND

Plan of the 7-mile 732-yard Dundrod circuit in the hills outside Belfast. The year 1955 was its last as a car racing venue, though motorcycle racing continued

Length of Course 7 miles 732 yards

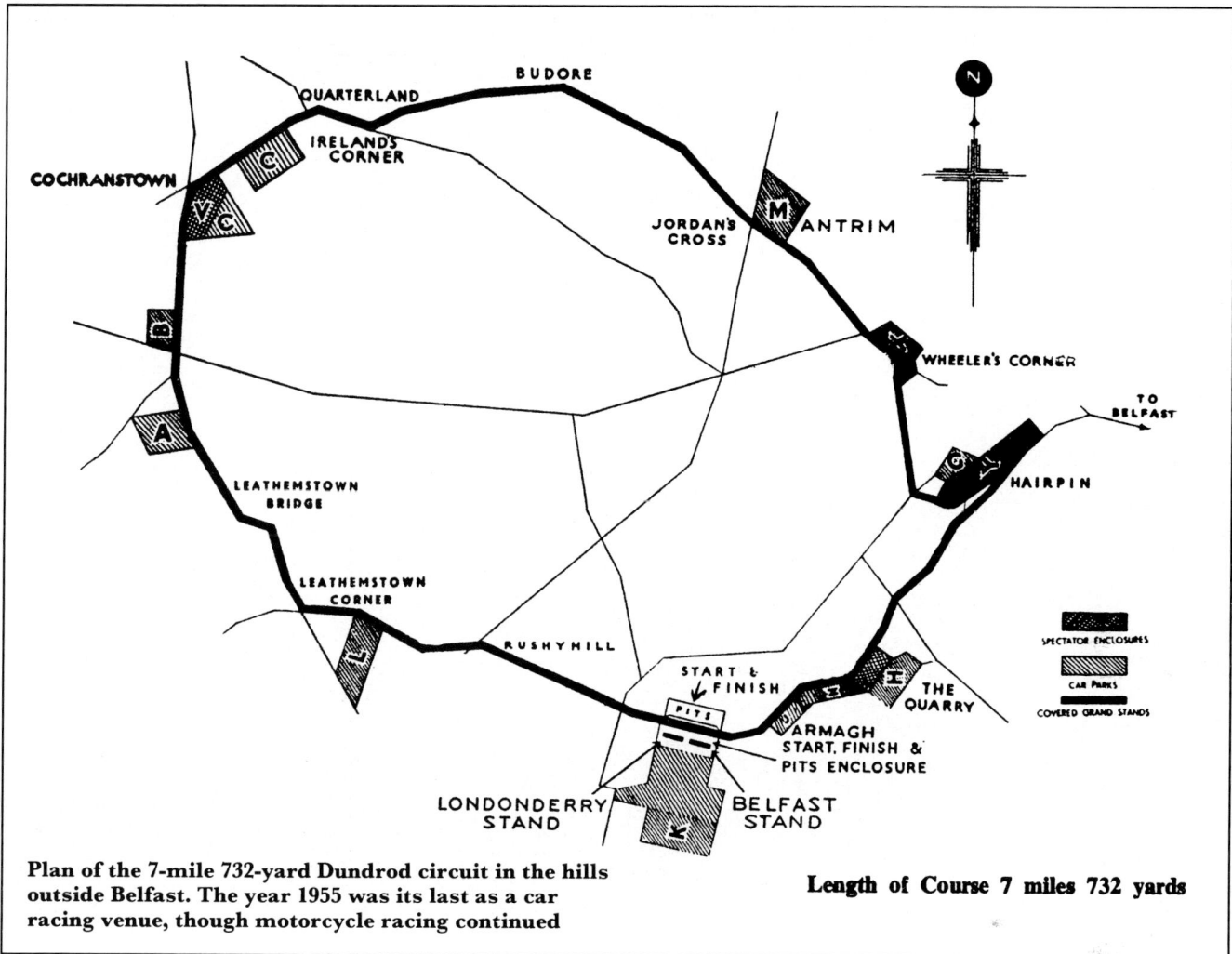

am sorry it was necessary ... but I feel we were quite justified, since the Mercedes did not comply with the regulations. Had the boot been on the other foot I feel sure that they would have taken similar action.' [This was incidental to expressions of thanks, and commiseration about the accident.]

'With regard to the protest,' replied Neill, after complimenting Jaguar on a magnificent run, 'the official reason for it being turned down was that it [the body damage] conferred no advantage on the Mercedes, secondly that it was not dangerous to the car, and thirdly that its absence was not causing difficulties for other competitors.'

England responded at length, saying that the damage to the Mercedes 'was caused by a misjudgement of tyre wear'. He suggested that Mercedes had been 'allowed to ignore regulations', but that Jaguar proposed to take the matter no further.

'For a car to lose a race on a technicality I believe is very bad for the sport ... It is certainly not my intention to allow any person, no matter how important they are, to ride roughshod over Regulations,' responded Neill.

England wrote again comparing Dundrod with Le Mans: If the same thing had happened to Mercedes there, he ventured, the organisers 'certainly would not have allowed them to continue until some repair had been carried out.' His most telling comment in this letter: 'None of the major companies who compete in sports car racing do so through sporting instincts but purely as a serious commercial function to obtain publicity.'

'Basically I must agree with your comments,' England added, in that final letter of the 'series', on 18 October. Each man had made his respective point while maintaining courtesy. Each now looked forward to a 1956 Ulster Tourist Trophy – but there would not be a TT at all until 1958. Then it would be on a disused Sussex airfield, far from the fast, narrow, unforgiving hill roads of County Antrim. By then, the Jaguar works team would be disbanded.

Though the Ulster GP for motorcycles would continue, no car would ever race again at Dundrod.

The England approach

So much had Alfred Neubauer admired Desmond Titterington's TT performance that the Ulsterman was invited to join the 300SLR team for the sixth and final round of the World Sports Car Championship – the Targa Florio in October. How could Lofty England refuse permission? If Jaguar did not attend, Mercedes-Benz or Ferrari must take the title anyway.

XKD 506 in which Desmond Titterington proved an excellent co-driver for Mike Hawthorn. The car's crankshaft broke (a truly rare occurrence) during Hawthorn's final spell when second place, if not victory, seemed certain. Dundrod TT, 1955.

Titterington, who had sidestepped David Murray's quizzings about the TT practice car, was less tactful when he wrote to Lofty England from Palermo during the Targa Florio practice: 'The organisation is awe-inspiring. We have six trucks and around twenty mechanics so far. The rest of the entourage arrives this afternoon. Of the car itself – a wonderful experience with such good roadholding and such usable power. It feels like a big car and has to be driven with care ... the brakes are surprisingly good. Very positive and no locking at all (I suppose because of the low unsprung weight); altogether a wonderful experience.'

Certainly not a Jaguar circuit – that was Titterington's conclusion, especially after a first trip around the circuit with Fangio. England waited until after the race before replying.

So far in 1955 Stirling Moss had won two races for Mercedes-Benz – the Mille Miglia and the TT; Mike Hawthorn had won two for Jaguar – the Sebring 12-hour and Le Mans; but the two marques shared second place behind Ferrari – winner of the poorly-supported opening round in Buenos Aires, and a steady picker-up of points subsequently.

Even if Jaguar were just not interested in Championships for their own sake, the rough and mountainous Madonie circuit of central Sicily was hardly D-type territory.

On the other hand, Mercedes-Benz – having nearly done so after Le Mans – had decided to withdraw from motor racing altogether in 1956. The SLR had proved itself capable of taking hard knocks, and so the Targa Florio just might produce a Grand Finale. A victory would clinch the title for Stuttgart; and indeed, despite the frenzied efforts of Eugenio Castellotti, Ferrari had to give in. The order was Mercedes 1, 2, and 4 (Moss/Collins, Fangio/King, Titterington/Fitch) with the Ferrari of Castellotti and Manzon third.

'Mein lieber Desmond ... I eagerly read the paper on Monday morning, quite expecting to see that you had won the Targa Florio but found to my amazement that two relatively inexperienced characters called Moss and Fangio had finished first and second ... Heil Neubauer, mein lieber Freund.' (More often than not, the heavy sarcasm was Lofty England's way of saying: 'Well done!')

In the meantime, the long-nose 'Cunningham' D-type had started winning in the USA, and 'production' D-types were beginning to make more frequent appearances, too. (These aspects of the D-type's development have chapters of their own, further on in this book.)

As in the past, England received regular approaches from aspiring drivers, each case being dealt with according to its merits or the time available. Jack Fairman was one driver who always liked to keep in touch. One of his letters of 1955 read as follows:

Dear Lofty,

1. *My apologies for disturbing your peace at home last night.*
2. *I have nothing to drive in the T T. (Bristols being non-runners)*
3. *I know the circuit intimately: 2nd in Class 1953 (Jaguar) and 1955 (Connaught).*
4. *Despite your aversion to 40-year-old drivers (according to the popular Press) I have never been fitter.*
5. *I would very much like to drive a potential winner before I am too old.*
6. *As I was a pioneer member of the Jaguar team (1951) I earnestly hope you will give this some serious thought.*
7. *I can present myself at Silverstone or Lindley at short notice for any tests you may consider necessary.*
8. *I propose to take you out to lunch in the near future to chat about all this.*
9. *My regards to Mrs. F. R. W. E. and particular apologies to her for phoning your residence.*

Yours sincerely
(Signed) Jack Fairman

Back came the reply:

1. *It was a pleasure.*
2. *I am surprised that Mercedes have not approached you.*
3. *You omit the intimate knowledge of the circuit gained in 1951 [See Vol. 1 – A. W.]*
4. *Your statement does not really give any clue as to how fit you may be.*
5. *Your ever-increasing family proves you have not yet reached senility.*
6. *I am always serious.*
7. *Excellent.*
8. *I am amazed.*
9. *My wife thinks you are wonderful.*

England also told Fairman that 'I cannot but admire your press-on attitude in trying to get another drive with us.' The fact remained that a few more letters *would* do the trick!

The FIA meeting in Paris in mid-October was to help Jaguar make its decision not to pull out of racing right away. Even in November, however, the 1956 Le Mans regulations were not absolutely clear.

By 12 December, though, there was enough information to hand for Rankin to issue this press release:

JAGUAR NEWS BULLETIN

SENT TO YOU WITH THE COMPLIMENTS OF JAGUAR CARS LTD., TO BRING YOU NEWS OF THE COMPANY'S ACTIVITIES AND ITEMS OF INTEREST IN THE MOTOR INDUSTRY AND IN THE WORLD OF MOTORING.

ISSUED BY JAGUAR CARS LTD., COVENTRY, ENG.   TELEGRAMS: "JAGUAR" COVENTRY   PHONE: 62677

PRESS ONLY

12th December, 1955.

JAGUARS TO RACE NEXT SEASON.

The decision has now been made that Jaguar will enter an official team in selected sports car races in 1956.

For some time it appeared likely that heavy pressure of work in the Design and Development Department would prevent the continuance of competition work next year. Furthermore, the uncertainty which prevailed concerning the regulations for Le Mans has delayed a decision. However, the introduction of the new 2.4-litre has gone through smoothly, and the new Le Mans regulations now encourage the use of standard production sports cars thus eliminating the need for building special prototypes which were becoming a necessity in order to compete with the highly specialised Continental machines of semi-racing types bearing no relation to production cars.

As is well known, the Jaguar "D" type which won Le Mans this year came into series production at the beginning of the year and is eligible to compete at Le Mans, thus relieving the Engineering Department of the work of constructing a new prototype sports car which would have been necessary had specialised semi-racing cars from the Continent still been permitted to compete on equal terms.

An early announcement will be made regarding the drivers, but it can be stated that Mike Hawthorn has already signed up for Jaguar.

Issued by E. W. Rankin, Public Relations Officer, Jaguar Cars Ltd., Coventry, England

---

Chapter Six

The Works
Team's Final Fling, 1956

The Mercedes-Benz withdrawal and the merging of Ferrari and Lancia racing interests under FIAT's 'umbrella' – plus a strengthening of resolve at both Aston Martin and Maserati to achieve better results – made for many top-level team switchings among the world's great drivers at the end of 1955.

In December 1955, Mike Hawthorn was authorised to say that:

In view of the speculation that has been voiced in the press concerning the relative positions which Stirling Moss and myself might occupy in the Jaguar team next year, I would like to make my own feelings in the matter clear should Stirling sign up for Jaguar. For me, any question of 'rivalry' with a team-mate does not exist, and I shall be quite content to do my best for the team as joint No. 1 driver with Stirling, and to act as directed by the team manager who, I know from past experience, is concerned less with personalities than with a smooth working and successful team.

That speculation had resulted from Stirling Moss's announcement early in the month that he had chosen to drive for Maserati in GP racing. According to a letter to the press from Alfred Moss, however, his son 'should be free to drive British cars in six of the major sports car events, and the Maserati company have agreed to release him for this purpose.'

Lofty England had cabled Moss in Nassau on 6 December 1955: 'Following announcement re-Maserati etc, can we rely on you driving for us long distance races next season subject satisfactory agreement with you on

return.' Back came the reply: 'Ken [Gregory] will contact you immediately on return, approx 19th Dec.' but there was no further comment. In the end, an appointment was made for 30 December between Lofty England and the Mosses, father and son, at their home, White Cloud Farm, Tring.

Moss wanted to be 'No. 1' and, knowing that Hawthorn had already signed a 1956 contract, realised that he could not be the sole team leader at Jaguar. It was on 4 January 1956, after much press speculation, that Rankin issued this communique:

MOSS NOT TO DRIVE FOR JAGUAR
In view of the various statements which have appeared in the Press concerning the probability of Stirling Moss driving for JAGUAR in 1956, the Company wish to state that it is true that negotiations with Moss have taken place and that there was a mutual desire that he should drive Jaguars. The Company would have welcomed him to the team, but it was not possible to engage him as Number 1 driver as, of course, the team will be led, as last year, by Mike Hawthorn whose outstanding performance for Jaguar included winning Le Mans, the Sebring 12-Hours Race and the establishment of a new lap record in the T.T. For these achievements Hawthorn was awarded the John Cobb Memorial Trophy for the most meritorious performance by a British driver driving a British car.

Moss would sign for Aston Martin, Britain's other great sports car team, which was still campaigning its well-tried DB3S – a fine-handling car, down on power in its fourth season of racing; but before trying the car he would score two excellent victories for Maserati. On 30 January 1956, William Lyons – knighted in the New Year honours list –

wrote to thank Stirling Moss for his congratulatory telegram:

May I reciprocate by congratulating you on your great success in New Zealand, and on your magnificent win in the Argentine 1000 km Sports Car Race.

I would also like to say how very sorry I am that it has not been possible for you to return to the JAGUAR team. I had thought that the suggestion that you should not join the team officially, but participate as a guest driver in the three principal races, would have been attractive to you. Quite a few members of the Press to whom I mentioned this, thought it provided the complete solution for you. However, apparently your father thought otherwise.

Whilst I must, of course, express the hope that you are not too successful in the sports car field, I sincerely trust that you will achieve your ambition and become World Champion Driver.

By then the 1956 team was as good as settled, the first scheduled race being the Florida 12-hour in which Hawthorn and Walters had been the 1955 winners.

A 'Monte' win, at last

The 1956 season started with a real flourish for Jaguar.

Despite the constant element of luck, which still besets many rallies, it seemed unfortunate that a Jaguar car had not yet won the Monte Carlo Rally outright. The team

prize had been won in 1955, and on previous occasions Jaguars had been 6th, 5th, 4th, 3rd and even 2nd – but never 1st.

All that changed for 1956 when, as had become the custom, Jaguar provided notes on the 'operation of MkVII cars after preparation for the Monte Carlo Rally'. Customer cars, of course, could also be prepared in the Browns Lane service department.

The official factory team consisted of these works MkVIIs:

Ch. No.	Reg. No.	Crew
711195	LWK 343	Cecil Vard, Arthur Jolley, Jimmy Millard
723510	PWK 700	Ronald Adams, Frank Bigger, Derek Johnston
733507	OVC 69	Reg Mansbridge, Joan Mansbridge, P. Strawson

All three cars were tested at MIRA and had their instruments checked there.

The Mansbridges were not without mechanical trouble but finished the rally a respectable forty-fifth. Faithful

1956 saw (*left to right*) Frank Bigger, Ronald Adams and Derek Johnston give Jaguar its finest hour in the Monte Carlo Rally. Here the works Mk VII comes off the specially chartered plane.

LWK 343, which had been rallied and raced for close on five years, suffered (according to the driver's report) 'a fair amount' of body damage in a contretemps which helped keep Vard out of the top 90 places, i.e. those qualifying for the final mountain circuit.

It *had* looked as though the main road section would penalise all competitors, but that was not to be. The weather was too kind, and nineteen crews were 'clean', so the tie-decider took on more importance than it should have done. This was an 1100-metre timed downhill section of the Mont des Mules, with precise braking to a standstill required at the finish. The six fastest drivers were: Vileron (Porsche) 41·0 sec., Adams (Jaguar MkVII) 42·4 sec., Dobler (Porsche) 42·8 sec., Nuthall (Jaguar XK140) and Leston (Aston Martin) 43·4 sec., and Schock (Mercedes-Benz) 43·8 sec.

In the end, the Jaguars were beaten to the team award by the Sunbeam and Citroën teams; but such was the superb teamwork of Derek Johnston and Frank Bigger for their driver, Ronnie Adams, that PWK 700 completed the final mountain run unscathed – giving Jaguar its first outright victory in the 'Monte', edging out the Mercedes-Benz 220 of Walter Schock and Rolf Moll. Later in the season the German pair would use a 300SL to score two wins and become European Champions. Meantime, however, Jaguar had stolen the early-season limelight – and beaten Mercedes!

Ernest ('Bill') Rankin was galvanised into action by the glad news, and PWK 700 was flown back from Nice to Blackbushe in one of Silver City Airways' Bristol freighters. There followed considerable media coverage including some wintry 'road impressions' by John Bolster who drove the big car through several snowdrifts in a blizzard. 'The eventual completion of this foolhardy journey gave me an extremely high regard for the Jaguar,' admitted the honest *Autosport* reporter.

Early March saw Ian and Pat Appleyard, in a new XK140 coupé, come second to Lyndon Sims and Tony

Ambrose (Aston Martin DB2) in the RAC Rally. This was an impressive one-off drive for the couple who had retired from serious rallying in Jaguars.

Equally noteworthy was the performance of Bill Bleakley and Ian Hall whose 2·4 saloon won its class and came fourth overall behind Dr Spare's Morgan Plus Four. This was the first of many international successes for Jaguar's new range of compact saloons.

The official works team was led by the Appleyards (XK140, S804340DN), Ian Appleyard as usual acting as Jaguar's unofficial rally adviser. Vard in his 'Monte' MkVII was ill on the first night, and Adams's XK140 roadster (SHP 575, one of the cars built for 1955's aborted 'Alpine') – despite winning its class in several tests – lost many road marks, probably due to misinterpretation of a new timing rule.

Race testing, 1956

With the decision to race a team of works D-types for a third season, the winter was a busy one in Jaguar's competition shop. More testing than usual was carried out, too – using Lindley (better known as MIRA), Goodwood and Silverstone. Most of these tests were carried out with XKC 404, XKD 504 and XKD 505.

XKD 504, the spare 1955 Le Mans car, was the fuel injection prototype (see chassis appendix). Hawthorn and Bueb had run it at Silverstone in late 1955. In mid-January, Bueb, Fairman, Hamilton and Titterington all tried the car, over 500 miles of tyre and PI testing being achieved before Bueb spun and damaged a fuel tank and

Ian Appleyard (XK 140) pictured at Prescott on his way to second place in the 1956 RAC Rally. This was the Yorkshireman's last major rally achievement.

Snowy arrival at New York (*en route* to Sebring) for Messrs England, Hawthorn (fraternising already), Bueb and Hamilton. (*Courtesy: F. R. W. England*)

Snowbound diners in New York, pre-Sebring 1956: (*left to right*) Colin Chapman of Lotus, Lofty England, Jo Eerdmans (President, Jaguar Cars of North America), Duncan Hamilton, Jock Reid) Jaguar service chief in US), 'John' Gordon Benett (V-p, Jaguar Cars of North America), Ivor Bueb, Bryan Turle (Shell Mex-BP), and Mike Hawthorn. (*Courtesy: R. Graham Reid*)

rear wing, which were repaired at Browns Lane by Bob Blake, an American and a brilliant body man who had been responsible for all the Cunningham panel work. Married to an English girl, it was logical (when Cunningham car manufacture ceased in 1955) for Blake to settle in Britain and join the British company whose cars Briggs Cunningham was now racing. In late March XKD 504 and 505 swapped engines: i.e. XKD 504 acquired E3002-9 fitted with Webers and was used for brake pad development; XKD 505 was given E3003-9, with fuel injection equipment, and prepared for the Goodwood Easter meeting. Hawthorn was entered to race XKD 505, the 'De Dion' car, but (as its notebook records) it was 'subsequently withdrawn owing to poor handling characteristics.' An interesting modification to XKD 505 at this stage was the fitting of a rear axle oil sump of 6 pints capacity.

XKD 506, the hero of Dundrod, was prepared for Sebring and would stay on in the USA afterwards, with XKD 507, for the Cunningham team's use. XKD 508, with engine E3006-9, was also prepared for Sebring.

Drivers to try – but not race – the works D-types at this time included motor-cyclists Geoff Duke and John Surtees. (Johnnie Lockett sought a drive, but it didn't materialise.)

'Sammy' Davis's son Colin, Gerry Dunham Jr, Les Leston, and Ernest McMillen were amongst the other lucky ones to have a go.

While three of the 1955 long-nose D-types were either in America or about to go there, a final batch of six 1956 cars was being laid down. Visually similar to the 1955 series, these were again powered by the 3·4-litre XK engine, featuring the '35/40' cylinder head, and developing some 275 bhp gross at 5750 rpm. Modifications included extra breathing space in the oil return tank and a felt-element filter in the lubrication system. Transmission was not altered significantly, but detail improvements were made to the suspension. The front anti-roll bar diameter was increased by $\frac{1}{8}$ inch, while at the rear, a $\frac{3}{4}$-inch anti-roll bar was added between the two upper trailing arms; these modifications to improve roll-stiffness had been tried out successfully on XKD 506 in the 1955 Ulster TT. The body retained its super-smooth 1955 'works' shape, but a reduction in the gauge of some of the unstressed panelling and bracketry resulted in a weight loss of 50 to 60 lb per car. For this small advantage innumerable body and chassis parts were redesigned. At this time, too, there was some experimental work to see if glass-fibre might provide a key to lighter weight.

The first of the new cars, XKD 601, with fuel injection, went as 'team leader' to Sebring when the Works/Cunningham entries ran into serious brake trouble. XKD 601 was completed (with engine no. E3005-9) on 22 February and tested at Goodwood three days later. Owing to porosity in the aluminium casing, a cast iron gearbox was fitted afterwards. The car was painted in American racing colours using Cellon High Speed Coating. The fuel injection system was inhibited by the Lucas representative on 27 February, the day before the car's shipment via Liverpool to New York.

Meanwhile, tended by Robin Freeman and Arthur Birks, two of Duncan Hamilton's private D-types were in tropical Senegal for the Dakar Grand Prix. This turned out to be the fastest-ever sports car race to date. After nearly two hours of racing, Maurice Trintignant beat Harry Schell by less than one second; their Ferrari shared fastest lap at over 125 mph, Trintignant averaging nearly 124 mph for the whole distance – emphasising the exciting nature of the event. Eight seconds ultimately covered a third place battle, won by Jean Behra (Maserati) from Jean Lucas (Ferrari) and Graham Whitehead in Duncan Hamilton's latest D-type (XKD 510). One of Hamilton's older cars, registered OKV 1, was part of this joust for most of the race but, despite having the highest available gearing *and* 17-inch wheels, it blew up (to use his words), 'when I was going full bore down the straight. Suddenly I was covered in oil . . . My surprise was exceeded only by that of Graham who was close behind.'

Effective fuel-injection

XKD 601's race appearance at Sebring on 24 March was the first in public anywhere for a fuel-injected Jaguar.

Stirling Moss (Aston Martin DB3S) made the best start but he was well down the line in the 'Le Mans' start, and at the end of the first lap Mike Hawthorn (XKD 601) led from 1955 Indianapolis winner Bob Sweikert in Jack Ensley's private D-type (XKD 538) with Hamilton (XKD 508) sixth. Fangio (Ferrari) led briefly from Lap 40 when Titterington took over from Hawthorn, but the PI Jaguar was still leading strongly at the four-hour mark. At this stage XKD 506 (Johnston/Spear) and 508 (Bueb/Hamilton) were fourth and seventh with several private D-types providing good back-up.

Despite a long pit-stop, Hawthorn and Titterington still led at half-time; but brake pad wear and temperature were proving excessive and the car fell back (the brakes finally seized after ten hours). A similar fate befell the Hamilton/Bueb car earlier; while Johnston and Spear, who had driven for some 7½ hours without second gear, retired with valve failure in the No. 1 cylinder and an rpm telltale reading of 6200.

'John' Gordon Benett and Briggs Cunningham shared XKD 507, and lost a lot of time early in the race because of a broken steering wheel boss and other undefined problems; later they got cracking and came twelfth.

It was, however, left to private owners to salvage a reasonable result for Jaguar. The 3·5-litre Ferraris of Fangio/Castellotti and Musso/Schell came first and second. Jack Ensley and Bob Sweikert (XKD 538) came

third, Alfonso Gomez Mena and Santiago Gonzales (XKD 521) eighth. Afterwards, Fangio expressed his admiration for Sweikert's abilities, and it looked as if the former 'Indy' winner might join the international circus. Sadly, he would lose his life at Salem, Indiana, a few weeks later.

Back in Europe, the racing season featured privately-owned D-types from the start – most competitive being

Right Inset:
Jaguar works/Cunningham team cars, Sebring 1956.
No. 10, XKD 504 (Johnston/Spear)
No. 8, XKD 601 (Hawthorn/Titterington)
No. 9, XKD 508 (Bueb/Hamilton)
No. 11, XKD 507 (Benett/Cunningham).
(Courtesy: James Sitz)

the familiar Broadhead, Hamilton and Murray team cars which continued to excel.

At the traditional Easter Monday Goodwood meeting came the first-ever of only a very few D-type fatalities. Duncan Hamilton lent XKD 510 to an inexperienced friend, Tony Dennis, who selected first gear in error at high-speed, and died in the ensuing crash.

Another sad death in April 1956 was that of HWM

Sebring's Le Mans-type start, 1956, with Lou Brero's D-type in centre of picture.

Sebring was a troubled race for the 'official' D-types, but Jack Ensley's car (co-driven by Bob Sweikert), seen here, saved the day for Jaguar with a good run to third place. (*Courtesy: James Sitz*)

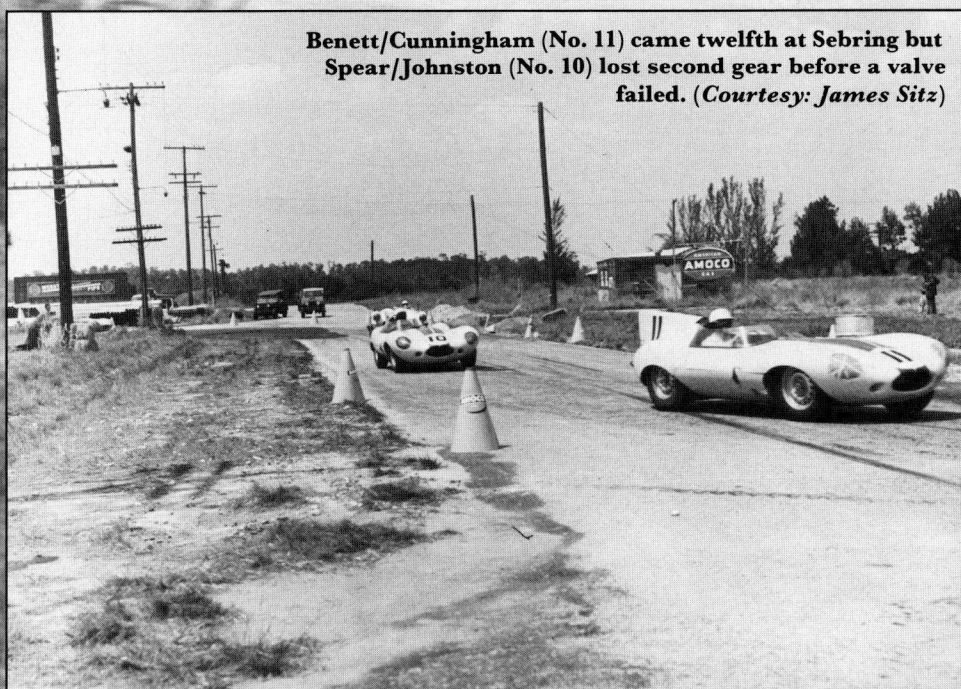
Benett/Cunningham (No. 11) came twelfth at Sebring but Spear/Johnston (No. 10) lost second gear before a valve failed. (*Courtesy: James Sitz*)

Lucas sliding-throttle fuel injection as raced by Jaguar (XKD 601) for the first time at Sebring in 1956.

Labels in diagram:
VACUUM TAPPING TO MIXTURE CONTROL
AIR INTAKE HOLES IN SLIDE
INDUCTION TRACT
INJECTOR NOZZLE
VACUUM TAPPING
RACK-AND-PINION
TO ACCELERATOR
THROTTLE SLIDE (SHOWN IN FULLY CLOSED POSITION)

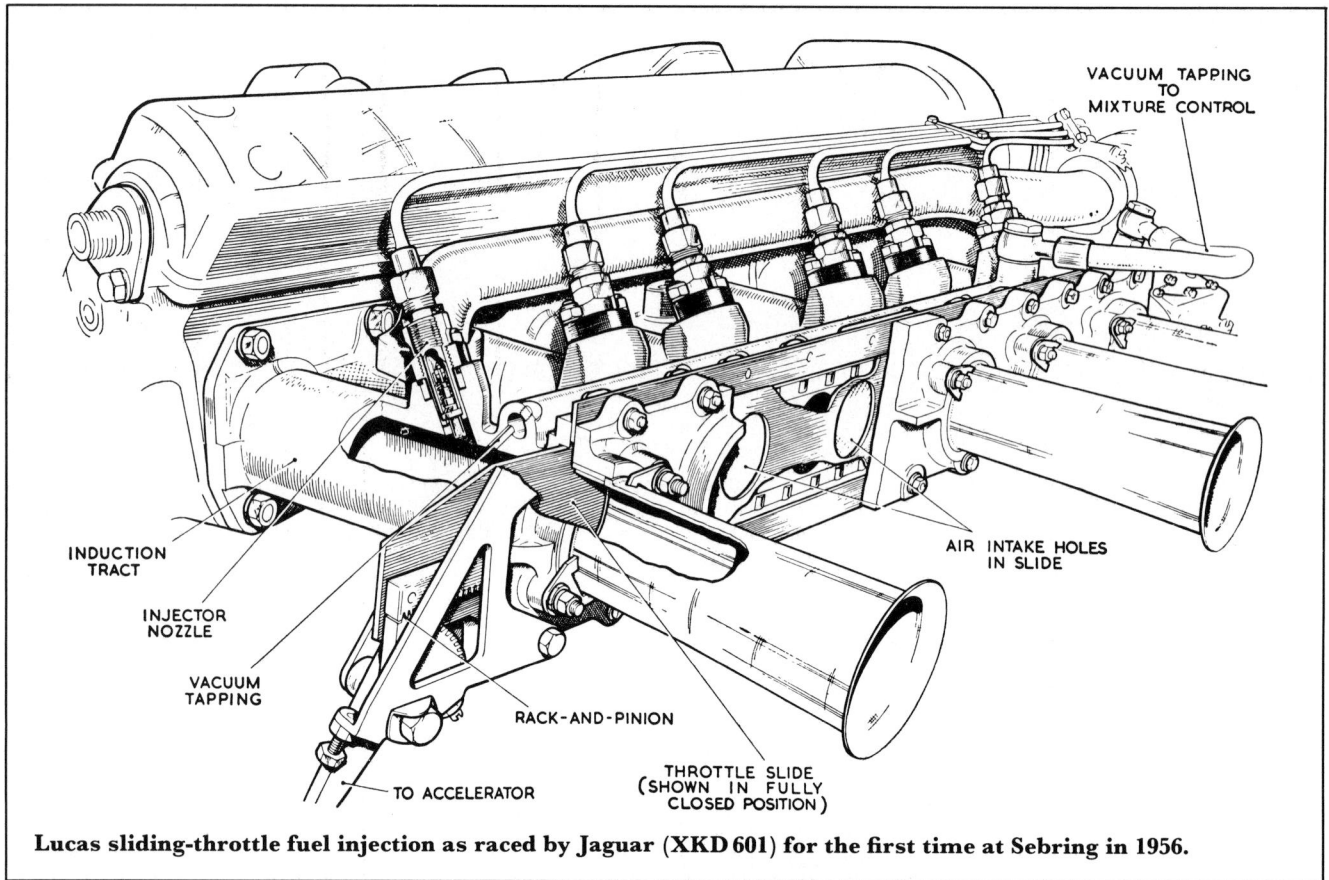

The standard triple-Weber installation compared with the new fuel injection one. (*Courtesy: Paul Skilleter*)

co-proprietor John Heath (HWM-Jaguar) in the Mille Miglia – always a controversial and doomed event, because of the impossibility of proper safety precautions, whether for competitors, or spectators. While this classic provided yet another Ferrari walkover, it is noteworthy that Guyot's Jaguar XK140 (fifth in the over 3-litre sports car class) won the price-related category – a category dear to Sir William's heart, in the market-place.

April was an important month for testing, and Hawthorn and Fairman (rewarded for his persistence) covered a considerable mileage with XKD 505 until a contretemps brought proceedings to an end. According to the car's personal notebook report: 'Fairman crashed at Becketts; damage to N/S/F suspension assembly and also to bonnet. New bonnet assembly ordered from Abbey Panels 18/4/56. Heavy wear taken place at drive-shaft spigot bearings. Drive-shaft assemblies dismantled 20/4/56. Spigots shimmed up & new bushes made, incorporating oil groove and greasing facilities. Engine (E3003-9 fuel injection) removed for power check on test bench 23/4/56.'

It was also noted that on 17 April (the day of the Silverstone tests), the maximum oil temperature in the 3·77 to 1 De Dion rear-end sump reached 120°C.

XKD 505, the 1955 Le Mans winner, did not race again as a works car; but it would cover many miles on experimental work.

Mark VII saves Silverstone

On the 19, 24 and 26 April the compact 2·4-litre saloon – forerunner of the 3·4 and 3·8 – was given its first circuit tests. Norman Dewis did eight laps with Bob Knight as observer. Dewis reported sudden loss of oil pressure

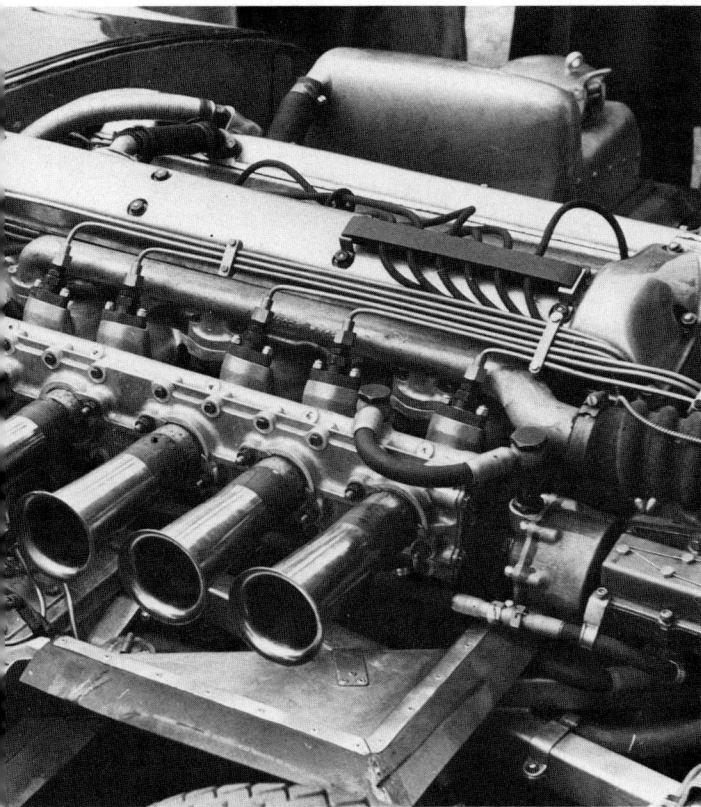

between Copse and Becketts but, 'the handling and cornering qualities were very good and docile and at no time showed any vices'. Hawthorn took over and did a best lap of 2 min. 10·5 sec.

The second test was undertaken with a specially-prepared engine and a 4·88 to 1 (instead of 4·55 to 1) final drive ratio. Bill Nicholson (better known for his motorcycle and MGB prowess, perhaps, than for his Jaguar period in between) drove this time, with the brave Bob Knight as passenger. I say 'brave' advisedly. I had joined Jaguar by this time, and was getting to know some of the Browns Lane legends. One of these concerned the observer who was so keen to bale out of the car, which Bill Nicholson was driving, that he did so while it was still on the move, somewhere near the London Road roundabout at Ryton. No lap time is recorded for Nicholson in the report now in question, however; but he did experience serious axle tramp under braking from the higher speeds of which the car was now capable. The third test was, unfortunately, held in wet weather, and so neither Ivor Bueb nor Mike Hawthorn could reproduce the tramping effect.

This was all done in preparation for the annual touring car race at the BRDC Daily Express meeting on 5 May. Fastest in practice, Hawthorn led the race for two laps before retiring with engine failure.

Ivor Bueb in a MkVII (OVC 69) took over the lead and just managed to hold off Ken Wharton whose Austin A90 Westminster – even more modified than the Jaguars – threatened throughout. Duncan Hamilton – fresh from a fine 'D' victory in the *Coupe de Paris* at Montlhéry – came third in a 2·4 with the MkVII of Paul Frère, the new boy of the Jaguar team, taking fourth place.

At the same meeting, the sports car race went to pieces on Lap 1, when Roy Salvadori (Aston Martin) crowded Desmond Titterington (Jaguar) in the braking area for Club Corner, mistaking him for Hawthorn. Titterington spun out of this melée and was avoided by Hawthorn, Moss and Sanderson, although the latter's *Ecurie Ecosse* D-type went up the bank backwards. The Aston Martins of Collins and Parnell hit the Titterington car (XKD 604) hard and all three retired on the spot. Hawthorn (XKD 603) chased after Salvadori and broke the sports car lap record in doing so, with a time of 1 min. 47 sec.; but the steering began to seize as a ball-joint began to pick up on its seating and, after one pit-stop, Hawthorn came in for good – the car virtually undrivable. So, for the second year running, Hawthorn's luck was out. Jack Fairman (XKD 504 with E3003-9 carburetter engine) was well placed initially, but dropped back and retired with a broken N/S drive shaft.

Not for the first time – nor the last – it was left to privateers to uphold Jaguar honour. Fastest of these was Bob Berry (XKC 403) who came third to the Aston Martins of Salvadori and Moss. Afterwards Moss blamed Salvadori – a fearless and stylish driver – but Moss had been treated in roughly the same way by Salvadori at the previous corner, Stowe, and may have been biased. While tenseness prevailed in the Aston Martin camp, Jaguar could only shovel up the bits and go home. It had been XKD 604's first race, *and* the only one in which a works 'De Dion D' ever participated. The last entry in XKD 604's

Bob Berry steps in at Silverstone, 1956, when the works cars hit trouble. OKV 2 came third.

Inset:
This picture shows how rear end control was achieved by using the differential casing as a mounting point. (*Courtesy: Autocar*)

notebook says: 'Driver, Titterington. Result, crashed – complete write-off. Towed home on trailer and stripped down 7 and 8 May 1956.' For the record, its engine for two-thirds of a lap of the one-and-only race had been E4003-9, on Weber carburetters.

The meeting was notable in providing the Vanwall GP car with its first big win, Moss up. Salvadori crashed his Maserati in the same race and was taken to hospital – but it was not long before the tough independent was back in action, this time in the Nürburgring 1000 km race on 27 May. Before then, another driver – Bob Berry – would find himself in hospital after winning one race at the Goodwood Whitsun meeting, only to fly off-course with XKC 403 in another (see his own story, in Appendix 3). Happier D-type news in May 1956 were a second at Chimay for Hamilton and a first at Spa-Francorchamps for Sanderson. Paul Frère did a good job at the same meeting winning the touring car race in a works 2·4 but not before Norman Dewis had stayed up all night to rebuild the gearbox.

Two works D-types were taken to Nürburgring for the 1000 km race on 27 May. Hawthorn and Titterington shared the ex-Sebring PI car (601). Hawthorn led away from the start, to be passed first by Fangio (3·5 Ferrari) and then Moss (3·0 Maserati); after a lap, however, it was Moss leading from Hawthorn, Fangio and Collins (Aston

Martin). When Titterington took over from Hawthorn he retained the Jaguar's stabilised third position; however, during his second spell Hawthorn, in fourth place, had a problem passing a Porsche and had to stop to unbend bodywork and plug fuel leaks – particularly annoying for him, since he had previously been called in and given a lecture about passing slower cars on the 'wrong' side, whether they were in the way or not. Shortly before the finish, a half-shaft failed while the Ulsterman was driving, and the Jaguar's race was run. Only two works cars had been sent to Nürburgring and Paul Frère had crashed the other one (XKD 603) in practice. A replacement – XKD 504 – had been driven out from Coventry by Dewis, arriving too late for practice; so Frère had started from the back of the grid – only to retire with a broken gearbox after six laps (having worked up to sixth place) depriving Hamilton of his turn at the wheel.

Stirling Moss and Jean Behra gave Maserati a rare and fine win here.

Works car 1, 2 & 3 at Reims
Before going to Nürburgring, the Jaguar team had spent two days at Reims, with XKD 504 (E3002-9) and XKD 605 (E4001-9), a new PI car which had been tried

XKD 601 was brought back to Europe and repainted green after Sebring. This underbonnet shot was taken in the Nürburgring paddock. (*Courtesy: Henry Elwes*)

the general buffeting effect of the Nürburgring. New items fitted for Reims included: front sub-frame, N/S/F suspension unit; front suspension rubbers; oil tank; dampers; axle gears, bearings, and half-shafts; discs, fuel tank, engine mountings, and water hoses.

An equally comprehensive rebuild – including new frame and bonnet – was carried out on XKD 603 following Frère's practice roll in Germany, with odd bits from XKD 604 coming in very handy.

XKD 605 had been the subject of much testing, being the definitive new 'fuel injection car'. Reims was its first race – and a most satisfactory one, too, for it led home a 1, 2, 3, 4 Jaguar procession.

The entry could have been more impressive. Of four Ferraris, only one was really competitive – the 3-litre

at Silverstone but rejected for the race there, having been reported 'unstable at rear'. Much of the driving was done by Paul Frère and Ivor Bueb. Frère reported the same experience as the Sebring drivers – the attempted welding of brake-pad to disc. Selection of new pad material was just one valuable result of this test session.

At the end of June came the Reims 12-hour race proper – revived after a year's absence from the racing calendar.

Jaguar needed a boost before Le Mans (which had been postponed by six weeks for road-widening operations) and Reims provided the perfect tonic.

The Reims line-up was:

XKD 601	E4002-9	(Webers)	Hawthorn/Frère
XKD 603	E4003-9	(Webers)	Titterington/Fairman
XKD 605	E4001-9	(PI)	Hamilton/Bueb

Besides its Porsche encounter XKD 601 had suffered from

The team at Reims, with the Ecurie Ecosse entry (No. 23) just visible. (*Courtesy: Paul Skilleter*)

Ivor Bueb and Duncan Hamilton, the Reims winners, fool about beforehand.

'Monza' of Harry Schell and Jean Lucas – and, on form alone, the two Maseratis could be counted upon *not* to go the full distance. The only serious French opposition was a lone Gordini, and so the Jaguar team was all set for a Le Mans dress-rehearsal.

In the early laps, the Leston/Cunningham-Reid HWM-Jaguar was competitive with the faster Ferrari and Maserati, but it was destined to retire. There were no Aston Martins. The works Jaguars ran well, and there was little to report – the most famous incident being the sacking of Duncan Hamilton who took the lap record in the closing stages when team discipline dictated: 'Maintain Position'. He might have got away with it if he had not also passed the leading car which Frère had taken over for a long stint while Hawthorn took some rest (he was due to race in the afternoon's Formula One Grand Prix). Until Hamilton was brought 'to heel', he was able to show Frère that the new fuel injection engine – even if it was a little less

125

1955-type windscreens were admitted at Reims in 1956.   In this picture is Paul Frère.

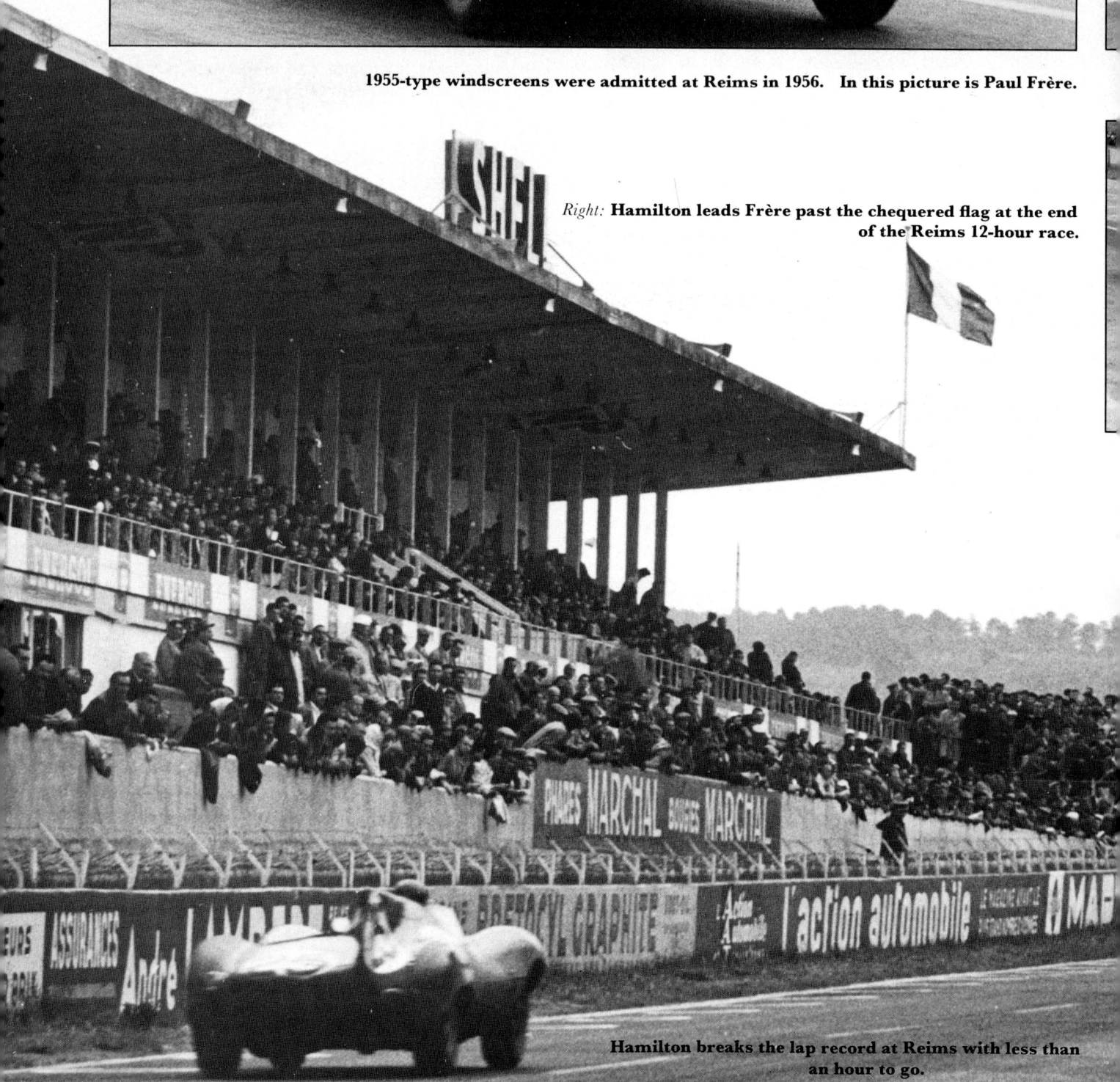

Right: **Hamilton leads Frère past the chequered flag at the end of the Reims 12-hour race.**

Hamilton breaks the lap record at Reims with less than an hour to go.

Jaguar and Ferrari attitudes at Reims.

Right: **Lofty England is less than happy with Hamilton's disobedience.**

powerful so far – did have the edge, to the extent that the Belgian driver could not hang on to XKD 605's slipstream. In his book *Touch Wood* Hamilton tried to explain that in attempting to go slower he found himself going faster – adding: 'I had tried to put much back into the game,' (but, he also admitted, 'on this occasion I took something out'). His lap record was 2 min. 37·2 sec. (118·14 mph), compared with Titterington's 2 min. 35·3 sec. in practice and a new F1 race lap record the same weekend by Fangio (Lancia-Ferrari) in 2 min. 25·8 sec. (127·29 mph). Lofty England, who dismissed Hamilton on the spot, later received a mortar board and cane addressed: 'To teacher with love.' The prize money was shared equally between the works drivers – Hamilton included.

The winners averaged 111·01 mph, and the top six placings after the twelve hours were:

1st	Bueb/Hamilton	Jaguar	1332 miles
2nd	Frère/Hawthorn	Jaguar	1327 miles
3rd	Fairman/Titterington	Jaguar	1322 miles
4th	Flockhart/Sanderson	Jaguar	1303 miles
5th	Manzon/Picard	Ferrari	1225 miles
6th	Bayol/da Silva Ramos	Gordini	1218 miles

The fourth-placed car was entered by *Ecurie Ecosse*, and finished 'on the diff' after a halfshaft failure. (The Scottish team would also take part at Rouen the following weekend. The sports car race there was for cars of 1·5 to 3 litres, and 'Wilkie' Wilkinson had adapted an XKD engine to comply with the regulations. Titterington took a creditable seventh in this event.)

Hamilton continued to race Jaguars privately, but took pleasure in being offered a place in the Ferrari team for Le Mans, rescheduled for 28/29 July.

Just before Le Mans, England replied to a letter from Frère: 'Regarding Reims I do realise that you found it difficult to understand what was going on with Duncan. I am afraid that once again he decided to run things his own way and completely disobeyed my instructions, and for that reason, he will not be driving for us again. I have put you as first driver of the second car at Le Mans with Titterington as your co-driver. Fairman will be first driver of the third car, with Ken Wharton driving with him.' So after nearly two years' absence, the Smethwick all-rounder was back in the team, too!

Regulations for the twenty-fourth 24-hour Le Mans race – subtitled 'Reliability Grand Prix' on the cover of the English edition – began with a MOST IMPORTANT ANNOUNCEMENT, explaining the many changes for 1956.

Only 52 cars (instead of 60) would be allowed to start, even though the pits and main grandstands had been rebuilt further back, enabling the course itself to be widened and realigned. A system of warning lights had been installed around the circuit, and signals were to be given at the exit from Mulsanne, the slow corner at the end of the longest straight.

'You must be kidding. I just won a race for you.' 'Sorry Duncan, you're fired'.

Right:
1956 D-type with the regular gang (*left to right*) Len Hayden, Bob Penney, Peter Jones, Phil Weaver, Bob Blake, Frank Rainbow, Joe Sutton, and Ted Brookes.

Left:
**Body modifications for
Le Mans 1956 meant a big
increase in frontal area.
Bob Blake squats
thoughtfully while Phil
Weaver confers with
Joe Sutton.**

As regards the cars themselves, the rules were new and stringent, to the extent that (for 1956 only) Le Mans would not count towards the World Sports Car Championship: not that Jaguar was any more interested in that than it had ever been.

Prototypes of up to 2·5 litres were permitted, and this category brought entries from Aston Martin (their new

Right:
**1956 long-nose
wide-screen D-type.**

Norman Dewis, Ted Brookes and Gordon Gardner at the MIRA control tower with a 1956 D-type.

Hawthorn, Bueb, and the law: Le Mans practice 1956.

DBR1/250), Ferrari (three 625 LMs), Talbots (two cars powered by Maserati) and Gordini (two cars). The key to Jaguar's wholehearted entry was the acceptance of series production cars with their regular engine size. 'Series production' meant '50 models sold, built, or provided for' – and the D-type could be shown to qualify. There was no argument about long-nose bodywork but, after lengthy correspondence between Raymond Acat and Lofty England, it was established by Malcolm Sayer that the effect the new regulations on the existing Jaguars would be as follows (the dimensions in his note to England are minima):

1. *Driver's door aperture, increase to 18·7″ long at top, 15·7″ at bottom.*
2. *New door on passenger's side to above dimensions, with body fore & aft of door built up to give 7·85″ height above sill.*
3. *Windscreen 7·85″ high for a width of 39·4″.*
4. *Spare windscreen.*
5. *Automatic windscreen wiper.*
6. *New fuel tank, 130 litres.*
7. *Separate stop & tail lights.*
8. *Passenger's lid replaced by flexible tonneau cover.*
9. *Increase seat cushions to 19·7″ wide.*
10. *Width across cockpit level with steering wheel needs checking – some are under 47·2″. (This can be adjusted when doing item 2.)*

Up to and including the 1956 Reims race, the D-type Jaguar had been shaped to meet a simple set of regulations. Now it took on a somewhat odd appearance to meet the needs of Le Mans. Most ingenious was Sayer's smoothly-

contoured flexible 'Vybak' covering for the passenger's seat, which did its best to maintain the original car's beautiful flowing lines.

Item 6 (the new, small fuel tank) was the most significant single requirement. A new rule stated that no car could refuel after a stint of less than 34 consecutive laps (just under 300 miles), and then it could take on a maximum of 120 litres. Thus fuel consumption had to be kept to 11 mpg at worst, throughout the event – the first serious attempt to link speed with economy on the race track.

The 1956 team at Le Mans, 1956. Under wraps is the *Ecurie Ecosse* entry, and beyond it the impressive XK 140.

Below:
Bob Blake works on Fairman's ill-fated car.

On the mechanical side, the main D-type modifications were to the combustion chambers (in search of fuel efficiency) and in the provision of quick-change disc-brake pads. As far back as November 1955, Acat had confirmed to England that fuel injection would be acceptable in the prototype *and* series production categories, both of which permitted 'the type and number of carburetters to be changed'.

Ecurie Ecosse took up the opportunity to take part at Le Mans. As with the works cars and the Belgian entry (a new car, XKD 573), the 'Scottish' machine (XKD 501) was modified at Browns Lane. Whereas the other D-types' engines were also factory prepared and tested, *Ecurie Ecosse* did their own.

A sixth Jaguar was entered by Robert Walshaw, with Peter Bolton (original nomination, Ronnie Adams) co-driving. This XK140 was the only car of its type ever to compete at Le Mans. (It was en route for eighth or ninth place when, after more than twenty hours' running, it was disqualified for refuelling a lap too soon: sad then, that a lack of pit management should spoil this outstanding performance from a relatively unmodified road car.)

The works cars were as follows:

Right:
The works cars, including the spare; Le Mans 1956.
(*Courtesy: Bob Blake*)

Rainbow *en route* for scrutineering in the Fairman/Wharton D-type. (*Courtesy: Frank Rainbow*)

Car	Trade plate	Race No.	Drivers
XKD 602	351 RW	3	Fairman/Wharton
XKD 603	774 RW	2	Frère/Titterington
XKD 605	393 RW	1	Hawthorn/Bueb
XKD 606	032 RW	(2)	

* N.B. Power-tested before conversion to PI

Engine no. (type)	Performance on test
E4004-9 (PI)	272·5 bhp at 5750 rpm*
E4005-9 (carb)	272·2 bhp at 6000 rpm
E4007-9 (PI)	263·5 bhp at 6000 rpm
E4006-9 (carb)	277·5 bhp at 6000 rpm

Blake and Sayer. (*Courtesy: Bob Blake*)

Fairman/Wharton car in practice. (*Courtesy: Frank Rainbow*)

Practice began quite eventfully with Titterington causing superficial damage to XKD 606 during his first lap. Consequently, the spare car (XKD 603) became race car No. 2.

XKD 605 suffered a burnt piston (a result of experimenting with weak mixtures) and its engine was changed (to E4003-9) for the race – a crucial factor, as things would turn out.

There had been five-speed gearbox experiments, but these were not followed up. These cars did, however, have an extra-high axle ratio (2·54 to 1), and the rear ends were modified for easy jacking.

Because this was to be the final event for a fully-fledged factory-run Jaguar race team, it is worth identifying the salient features of a typical works D-type 3·4-litre XK engine: E4007-9. This memo from Bill Wilkinson to Lofty England was dated 16 July 1956:

Engine No. (3·4)	E4007-9
Car No.	XKD 605
Assembly specification	A 97
Compression ratio	9.09 : 1
Cylinder head XK 1987/B	A 52
Inlet valve XK 2133	2″ Nimonic 80. Farnborough Eng.
Exhaust Valve XK 1981	1 11/16″ Nimonic 80. Farnborough Eng.
Valve springs XK 2097/8	Terry 7/16″ lift chrome vanadium, red stripe.
Tappets XK 1403	Brico drilled on skirts.

Above right:
Frère (XKD 603) and Fairman (XKD 602) begin their crawl to retirement at Le Mans. De Portago (Ferrari) is about to do likewise.

Right:
Peter Walker's Aston Martin slides as it passes the accident scene, followed by Ron Flockhart's *Ecurie Ecosse* Jaguar.

Hawthorn, Frère, Fairman and Flockhart run for their Jaguars.

Hawthorn in action.

Camshafts XK 2134/5	Cast iron 7/16″ lift 35°–35° timing.
Tappet clearances	Inlet ·010″ Exhaust ·015″
Cylinder head gasket XK 2131	Nimonic transverse corrugations.
Cylinder block XK 1977	3½ Litre 83 m/m bore.
Crankshaft XK 1958	E.N. 40 Nitrided 5/32″ rad. bow ·060″
Conn-rods C 7917	Polished crack tested.
Crankshaft damper C 8129	Metalastik specially tested.
Triple Plate Clutch	C 9194 Red spring.
Triple Plate flywheel	C 9192
Triple Plate Starter ring	C 9193 Drilled
Timing Gear	To suit Lucas P.I. or carburettors.
Main bearing XK 2161/2 XK 1979A/B	Vandervell lead indium, narrow type.
Conn-rod bearings XK 2163	Vandervell lead indium, narrow type.
Pistons XK 2129	Brico, slipper skirt, dome crown.
Oil pump pressure C 9808	Steel driving gear, cast iron driven gear
Oil relief valve C 6283	Pressure pump. Inbuilt.
Oil relief valve spring XK 2078	Pressure pump. Rate 10·8 lb.in. 75 lb.sq.in
Oil pump scavenge C 9240	Steel driving gear, cast iron driven gear.
Oil sump top half XK 1976	Aluminium dry.
Oil sump bottom half XK 2138	Electron dry.
Oil intake XK 1831	Modified thermo and P.I. tapping.
Water pump XK 1551	Aluminium, 2″ intake Hoffman bearing.
Water pump belt C 9197	Goodyear narrow wedge.
Dynamo belt C 9263	Goodyear narrow wedge.
Distributor	Lucas ENM 3488 J 10. certified by Lucas.
Static setting	12° B.T.D.C. on crankshaft.
Dynamo	Lucas 4·5″
Coil	Lucas HV 12
Sparking plugs	Champion N A 10 Gap ·017″
Inlet manifold XK 2150	Lucas Petrol injection 40 m/m upstream.
Injection timing	17° B.T.D.C. No.4. Cyl. Inlet opening.
Maximum B.H.P.	263·5 at 6000 R.P.M.
Maximum B.M.E.P.	191· at 4500 R.P.M.
Maximum torque	266·0 at 4500 R.P.M.
Oil pressure	65 lbs. at 6000 R.P.M. 100°C oil temp.
Engine Oil	Shell X 100 SAE 30.
Fuel	Le Mans.
Despatch	12-7-56 Comp. Dept.

Fuel feed details for the triple-Weber works engines were as follows:

Inlet manifold XK1834	45 mm integral water pipe
Carburetters	Weber 45 DCO3
Revised spray stem	Choke 42 mm
	Main petrol 185 mm
Discharge tube	Main air 195 mm
	Slow running 70 mm
	Pump jet 50 mm
	Needle valve 25 mm

In addition to one for each factory unit, a list of features was issued for the Belgian car's engine (E2079-9). Again, the memo was dated 16 July 1956:

The XK 140 went extremely well.

Left:
A frustrated Hawthorn explains the symptoms of the infuriating misfire to England. (*Courtesy: F. R. W. England*)

Engine No. (3·4)	*E2079-9*
Car No.	*XKD 573*
Assembly specification	*A 79 Dry sump.*
Compression Ratio	*9 : 1*
Cylinder Head C 7896	*AY610 Jaguar Flowed.*
Inlet Valve C 4708	*$1\frac{7}{8}''$ Dia. KE 965*
Exhaust Valve XK 2202	*$1\frac{5}{8}''$ Dia. Nimonic 90*
Valve springs XK 1238/9	*Terry Chrome Vanadium Black stripe.*
Tappets C 7213	*Brico Rockwell Tested.*
Camshafts C 8512/3	*3/8'' lift 30°–30° Cast iron.*
Tappet clearance	*Inlet .006'' Exhaust .012''*
Pistons C 7710	*Brico, Dykes Comp. Rings.*
Cyl. Head Joint XK 2131	*Nimonic Transverse Corrugation.*
Main Bearings C 5891/2	*Vandervell lead indium.*
Conn. Rod Bearings C 5893	*Vandervell Lead Indium.*
Oil Pressure Pump C 9808	*Driving Gear steel. Driven Gear Cast Iron.*
Oil Scavenge Pump C 9240	*Driving Gear steel. Driven Gear Cast Iron.*
Oil Sump	*Steel suction channel.*
Oil relief Valve spring XK 2078	*Rate 10·8 lb. in 75 lb. sq. in.*
Oil relief Valve C 6283	*Inbuilt Pressure Pump.*
Water Pump XK 1550	*Aluminium screwed adjustable pulley.*
Water Pump Belt XK 1902	*Goodyear narrow wedge*
Dynamo Belt XK 1845	*Goodyear narrow wedge.*
Oil Intake housing XK 1831	*With Thermo connection.*
Clutch C 9194	*Triple Plate Red springs.*
Flywheel C 9192	*For Triple plate clutch.*
Engine Damper C 8129	*Metalastik Comp. Type.*
Distributor	*Lucas LT 40473 A static setting 6° B.T.D.C.*
Sparking Plugs	*Champion NA 8 General Road work*
Sparking Plugs	*Champion NA 10 Race purposes.*
Induction Pipe C 9284	*With adaptor plate.*
Carburetters	*Weber Dual 45 DCO 3*
Setting	*Choke 38 m.m. Main 1.75 m.m. Main Air 170 m.m. Acc. Pump. .35 m.m. SR .70 m.m. modified Diffusers. Less Primary venturi.*
Air Entry	*Collected box. Frontal aperture.*
Maximum BHP	*255·5 at 6000 R.P.M.*
Maximum BMEP	*179·5 lb, sq.in. at 4500 R.P.M.*
Maximum Torque	*250·0 lb. ft. at 4500 R.P.M.*
Oil pressure	*70 P.S.I. at 6000 R.P.M. Oil Temp 85°C*
Oil Pressure Idle	*71.0 P.S.I. 580 R.P.M. Oil Temp 100°C*
Engine Oil	*Shell X 100 SAE 30.*
Fuel	*Le Mans Sample.*
Despatch	*Comp. Dept. 7-7-56.*

A week earlier, this car (XKD 573), which had been assembled on the production line, was taken over by the competition department for preparation to the latest 'production D' thinking. Bill Heynes issued the instruction on 29 June, and the following work was (according to the car's works notebook) put in hand:

1. *Engine and gearbox removed. Engine passed over to Jack Emerson for strip, inspection, fitting of known cylinder head and test.*
2. *Gearbox passed over to service dept for strip, inspection and rebuild to full racing standard.*

3. *Rear axle passed over to service dept for fitting special axle shafts, keys, ZF unit and 2·69 to 1 gears. New races, oil seals, and wirelocking.*
4. *Oil filter and pipes fitted.*
5. *Full power m/c, reservoir, and pipes to suit.*
6. *Armoured rear brake hoses.*
7. *Shortened front brake hoses.*
8. *Standard wide calipers at rear; new single-pad at front.*
9. *Front and rear brake scoops.*
10. *1¼″ & 5/16″ stops on rack.*
11. *⅛″ split pins for sway-bar pins.*
12. *Large dynamo and N/S mounting bracket to suit.*
13. *Complete electrical wire changeover to 1956 standards.*
14. *Twin stop-lamp switches & bracket. Wire to suit.*
15. *Tail and wire altered to suit separation of tail and stop lamps.*
16. *Fit modified upper wishbone ball seats.*
17. *Air duct discarded; tray fitted.*
18. *Steering wheel with steel hub.*
19. *Modified throttle lever.*
20. *Stiffened throttle pedal and shaft to suit.*
21. *'Red' cap fuel pumps.*
22. *11/16″ front sway bar.*
23. *¾″ old-type rear sway bar.*
24. *Discard alum. distance pieces and rubber 'O' rings from rear suspension.*
25. *Latest 'red' A-link.*
26. *Latest header tank with separate relief valve.*
27. *Fuel filter.*
28. *Modified windscreen.*
29. *Passenger's door.*
30. *Tail-fin.*
31. *Wide seats.*
32. *Modified gearbox cowlings.*
33. *Windscreen wiper.*
34. *Tonneau cover.*
35. *Large mirror.*
36. *130-litre fuel-tank & mods. to tank bay.*
37. *Fire extinguisher.*

Perhaps the most noteworthy modification was that to the steering wheel hub, the alloy units used at Sebring having cracked.

Ecurie Ecosse saves the day

It was drizzling as the flag fell at four o'clock on race day and as Paul Frère (XKD 603, Webers) and Jack Fairman (XKD 602, Lucas PI) approached *Les Esses* for the second time in fifth and sixth positions, they both lost control. Frère smote the wall hard with the tail of his car, but Fairman managed to stop without hitting him. Nevertheless, de Portago (Ferrari) arrived on the scene equally out-of-control and collected the front of the Fairman car before it could move-off – the result, three retirements in quick succession! So neither Titterington nor Wharton got a drive. Subsequently, the two wrecked cars – although basically drivable – were cannibalised to make a 'new' XKD 603. Meanwhile, Hawthorn had shot off into an unassailable lead, only to come into the pits after several laps for the first of numerous visits. After seven hours of racing the infuriating misfire was traced to a tiny crack in a fuel line, causing the pressure in the fuel injection system to drop. (Could this have been a result of the engine change?)

When the trouble was found, it was quickly remedied and the car went perfectly for the rest of the race, picking up from twentieth place (22 laps down) at midnight to sixth (20 laps behind the winner – another Jaguar, happily!) at the finish. Hawthorn put in the fastest lap but the 1956 D-type's increased frontal area reduced his lap speed by some 6½ mph to 115·8 mph and his speed on the straight by about 20 mph compared with 1955. An *Ecurie Ecosse* victory, by Flockhart and Sanderson, saved the day for Jaguar. XKD 573 kept up the Belgian tradition, of performance and reliability, by finishing fourth. (Although Roger Laurent had nominated himself and André Pilette originally, the drivers selected for the race were Jacques Swaters and 'Freddy' Rousselle – the latter making an impressive Le Mans début.)

Although the little Porsches were getting quicker every year – one of them finished ahead of the flying Hawthorn/Bueb D-type – the main opposition had come from

the 2·5 Ferraris (one came third) and the 2·9 Aston Martins. The DB3S had managed to get in as a 'series production' car on the basis that Aston Martin had 'made provision' for fifty to be built, although the final total production was in fact thirty-one. At the end of the race, just one Aston Martin was still running – the DB3S of Stirling Moss and Peter Collins. It had given the winning Jaguar a hard time throughout and was little more than a lap behind at the end. Other former Jaguar works drivers were less lucky, Peter Walker (Aston Martin DB3S) being injured in a crash, and Duncan Hamilton failing to get a drive – as a result of his co-driver, 'Fon' de Portago, crashing the Ferrari into Fairman's virtually stationary Jaguar on Lap 2.

Mike Hawthorn's new race lap record did not compare with his previous one of 4 min. 06·6 sec. in the 1955 D-type – but it did count as a record because of all the detail changes to the circuit. The new figure in the wide-screened 1956 car was 4 min. 20·0 sec.; Malcolm Sayer's records show that, during practice, the works drivers had lapped as follows: Hawthorn 4 min. 16 sec.; Titterington 4 min. 19 sec.; Fairman 4 min. 21 sec.; Frère 4 min. 22 sec.; Bueb 4 min. 23 sec.; and Wharton 4 min. 25 sec. Practice calculations had also shown that, if the cars came in after *exactly* the permitted 34 laps, the 120-litre refuelling rule could be met by the D-types without too much anxiety.

The works contingent for this last 'official' visit by Jaguar to Le Mans included Bob Blake, Les Bottrill, Ted Brookes, Norman Dewis, Jack Emerson, Gordon Gardner,

Ron Flockhart forges ahead in the car which he and Ninian Sanderson drove to victory at Le Mans in 1956 – a very important success for the Scottish team, *Ecurie Ecosse*.

Ron Gaudion, Len Hayden, Tom Jones, Bob Knight, Bob Penney, Frank Rainbow, Malcolm Sayer, Joe Sutton, Jock Thomson, Phil Weaver and Bill Wilkinson. All, from Lofty England down, were profoundly grateful to the Scottish team (for whom Ron Gaudion was working by now).

Although Jaguar was not interested in the World Sports Car Championship, the marque found itself placed third in the table by the end of the season – for the third year in succession, thanks to the Whitehead brothers' steady run to fourth place in the Swedish GP at Kristianstad behind three Ferraris. They drove one of the old Hamilton D-types. (Hamilton himself had a drive in the third-placed Ferrari.) Even if Le Mans *had* counted towards the Championship – which it had not – the Jaguar position would not have improved.

The saddest item of Jaguar news for September was that reporting the death of Jack Emerson at the age of 65.

In pre-war days he had been renowned for the tuning and racing of motorcycles. Afterwards he became the XK engine development wizard, and his contribution to Jaguar's Le Mans and other successes was immeasurable. Bill Wilkinson was his successor.

On 13 October 1956, this press release was issued:

JAGUAR TO SUSPEND RACING

Jaguar Cars Ltd, after very serious consideration, announce their withdrawal from the field of international racing and other competitive events and state that no official entries or works teams will be entered for events on the 1957 calendar.

The information gained as a result of the highly successful racing programme which the Company has undertaken in the past five years has been of the utmost value, and much of the knowledge derived from racing experience has been applied to the development of the Company's products. Nevertheless, an annual racing programme imposes a very heavy burden on the Technical and Research Branch of the Engineering Division which is already fully extended in implementing plans for the further development of Jaguar cars.

Although withdrawal from direct participation in racing in the immediate future will afford much needed relief to the Technical and Research Branch, development work on competition cars will not be entirely discontinued, but whether the Company will resume its racing activities in 1958, or whether such resumption will be further deferred, must depend on circumstances.

Even though it had taken a private entry to save the day, Le Mans had been won for the fourth time: not only that but, for the first time ever, one marque – Jaguar – had been victorious in the Monte Carlo Rally and the 24-hour marathon of Le Mans in the same year.

Examined in the light of Jaguar's carefully-monitored progress, the timing was right.

Race participation has always been incidental to Jaguar: essential, perhaps, in certain times? – but not *all* the time.

The situation in 1956 was that Jaguar had its new 'compact' in production. Now it was time to get down to the work of producing more cars – and even better ones. Besides, it was time to start work on new models for the future, taking advantage of the racing experience.

While the works team was no more, Lofty England would remain in charge of operating relationships with private owners, through his department – Customer Service – and Bill Heynes's experimental engineers would remain active in competitions, too, particularly on the engine side.

Four specific areas would develop during the next few years, each being covered in later chapters: *Ecurie Ecosse* and other privateers at Le Mans; sports car racing in North America; touring car racing; and the success of the Jaguar XK engine in specialist chassis – particularly the Lister.

There was no doubt that the Jaguar marque had come of age – yet the cars held a special appeal for the true enthusiast, and before the end of 1956 the formation of an independent Jaguar Drivers' Club was approved by Sir William Lyons.

Before moving on into Jaguar's later connections with the world of competition, a chapter should be spent looking at the D-type Jaguar as a production car.

Chapter Seven

Production D-type and XKSS

From the outset, to own a D-type Jaguar was the dream of many a racing driver.

As might be imagined, the situation began with a stream of 'serious' enquiries in 1954 and 1955, petering out as the 1956 season progressed, and ending with a surplus of obsolescent machines in the following winter.

Appendices in this book deal with the early history of the cars, contemporary descriptions of which have also been selected for inclusion.

This chapter covers some of the lesser known aspects of the D-type's life.

With its main engine-carrying frame bolted on to the monocoque – as opposed to the Argon-welded construction of the six original cars – the 1955 D-type lent itself quite readily to a form of 'assembly line' production. After only a few cars had been produced, however, it was apparent that the production and engineering departments would have to share the work of preparing the cars for general sale.

The Jaguar announcement was made well before regular D-type assembly began. It was dated 4 October 1954 and ran as follows:

The Jaguar 'D' type which made its début at the Le Mans Race this year in its memorable duel with the 4·9-litre Ferrari and, later, scored a runaway first and second victory in the sports Car Race at Rheims, is to go into production as a standard competition model and will be exhibited at Earls Court Show this month.

This outstanding car is the direct successor to the famous 'C' type which numbered among its many victories in sports car competition, two Le Mans races, including the sweeping victory of 1953 with 1st, 2nd and 4th places which was won at a record speed of 105·85 mph which speed still remains unbeaten.

The engine of the 'D' type Jaguar, as in the case of the 'C' type engine, is manufactured from identical basic components as the standard XK production engine; crankshaft, cylinder block, connecting rods, timing gear etc., are taken from the production line indiscriminately for the building of the 'D' type engine. In this respect Jaguar is probably unique, but this confidence in the standard product emphasises the quality and accuracy of workmanship which goes into every production XK120 engine.

The 'D' type power unit, which develops 246 bhp at a speed of 5800 rpm, incorporates dry sump lubrication with a built-in oil cooler which enables maximum power output to be maintained for indefinite periods.

The space frame of the 'D' type car is a three-plane tubular truss structure built into a stressed skin unit construction body, a unique Jaguar patented feature.

The 'D' type car also pioneers the introduction of disc brakes as standard equipment. For the past three years, Jaguar have collaborated closely with the Dunlop Company on the development and tests of the disc brakes. The testing which has been carried out, both in international competition and with prototypes on the roads of the world, has established that this brake is the most outstanding advance in brake performance that has been made since the introduction of four-wheel brakes, and the appearance of disc brakes on a production model is an event of the greatest importance.

The Jaguar 'D' type is, undoubtedly, the fastest production car which has ever been offered to the public, and is probably the only production sports car in the world which has ever attained speeds of over 172 mph in international competition. This speed was recorded with a car carrying the standard production type body and full touring equipment required by the regulations for Le Mans. Maximum speeds, considerably higher than this figure can be achieved, in full stripped sprint-racing trim without major modifications to any basic part.

Catalogue artwork actually shows 1954 works car.

Preparing the D-type for series production; Les Ryder and (possibly) Ron Gaudion.

Pre-production car team with Harry Hawkins in the driving seat.

Les Bottrill, who tested the production D-types, is seen here with Jacques Swaters at Le Mans. Bottrill later emigrated to the USA.

For the spring, summer and autumn of 1955, the 'D' production line was situated in the main hall at Jaguar's Allesley, Coventry, works – adjoining the MkVII and XK140 trim and final lines. The central 'tub' was jigged up and the frame and suspension units fitted, turning the whole into a rolling 'chassis' at an early stage. After assembly, the D-type was passed to the experimental department where thorough checks were carried out prior to extended testing at the nearby Motor Industry Research Association (MIRA) establishment. The first 'D' to go through the full 'production' system (XKD 509) was given its first test run – 60 laps (some 200 miles) round the MIRA outer circuit – in July 1955. The first 'line-built' D-type to be despatched to a private customer was XKD 514, in August. This owner, Sir Robert Ropner, used it as a road car well into the 1970s. A most original machine, it has been owned for many years by Ole Sommer, the former Jaguar importer for Denmark.

Of the 67 cars to go through the production system, 42 were sold – as follows: 18 to the USA, 10 in Britain, 3 to Australia, 2 to France, 1 each to Cuba, Finland, New Zealand, Spain, San Salvador, East Africa, Mexico, Belgium and Canada. Of the remaining 25, 9 were either destroyed in the factory fire or dismantled, and 16 fitted out as road cars, as described later.

Although not everyone's idea of a production car, the D-type *was* a serious attempt to produce a 'limited edition' economically – a fact borne out by a nominal, all-in price

The D-type in close-up. (*Courtesy: William Heynes*)

of £3878 and publication of a comprehensive fifty-five page service handbook for owners. The original price, as listed at the 1954 London Show, was even less – at £1895 basic, compared with £2600 for an Aston Martin DB3S. At that time, the price of an XK140 or Mark Seven was £1140 basic (to which £476 tax was added for the British market).

The D-types were meant to be ready for the 1955 season. In fact, few private owners would drive, let alone race, their cars before 1956.

The first highly optimistic sales list – dated February 1955 – suggested seven weeks' (Friday) home deliveries as follows:

Customer	Dealer (Distributor)	Colour
8/4/55		
Ecurie Ecosse	–	–
Ecurie Ecosse	–	–
Ecurie Ecosse	–	–
Col Head	W. M. Couper, St Albans (Henlys)	–
Lord Louth	(St Helier Garages)	BRG
15/4/55		
Alan Brown	Coombs, Guildford (Henlys)	–
Horace Gould	Western Motors, Bristol (Henlys)	BRG
Jack Broadhead	(Henlys, Manchester)	–
22/4/55		
Peter Bell	(Henlys, Manchester)	BRG
Bob Dickson	(Byatt's, Stoke-on-Trent)	BRG
Jack Walton	(Appleyards, Leeds)	Azure Blue
Gillie Tyrer	(Henlys, Manchester)	Pastel Green
Jock McBain	(Rossleigh, Edinburgh)	Scottish Blue

29/4/55		
Anthony Powys-Lybbe	–	–
Bill Cannell	Moore's Brighton (Henlys)	–
Sir Clive Edwards	Charles Fullett, London (Henlys)	–
John Goodhew	(Henlys, London)	BRG
Leslie Johnson	–	–
6/5/55		
Joe Ashmore	(Broad St Motors, B'ham)	Black
Ron Flockhart	David Murray, Edinburgh	–
Geoff Mansell	(Broad St Motors, B'ham)	Pastel Green
Mr Atkins	(Byatt's, Stoke-on-Trent)	–
Noel Cunningham-Reid	(Henlys, London)	BRG
13/5/55		
J Lewis	Imperial, Cheltenham (Henlys)	–
H Webb Motors	R P Powell (Henlys)	BRG
Sir Robert Ropner	(Glover's, Ripon)	Battleship Grey
Dealer Stock	Brooklands of Broad Street (Henlys)	–
Capt. Howey	S. London Motors (Henlys)	BRG
John Young	S. London Motors (Henlys)	–
No date		
Bill Smith	Mann Egerton (Henlys)	–
Tom Meyer	Weybridge Motors (Henlys)	–
Vic Derrington	(Henlys, London)	–

The first to cancel his order because of delivery delays was Sir Clive Edwards. By the end of August, only three production-line D-types had passed muster.

Built into the list were forty-five export orders – some tentative, some not. Among the early hopefuls was Casimiro de Oliveira, who had bought one of the first SS Jaguar 100 sports cars and raced it in Portugal eighteen years earlier. (Indeed, he had been the first Jaguar driver to win a race abroad. *See Vol. 1.*)

Some people cancelled, not just because their cars didn't

materialise on time but because of the price increase, which was probably meant to put off less-serious prospective customers. 'As I am sure you are aware,' William Lyons wrote to one of them, 'the car costs us very much more than the price at which we sell it.'

Alan Currie (of the sales department) advised Lyons that 86 orders had been received by 5 April 1955, the position being:

25 confirmed (including 6 UK)
20 cancelled

5 decision dependent on delivery
3 orders changed to XK140
2 orders changed to Ferrari
31 confirmed.

On 13 April 1955, Jaguar production chief John Silver advised purchase manager Harry Teather that, contrary to previous advice, he felt that the D-type frame and body could be painted in a baked primer on a trestle in the main paint shop prior to assembly. My own recollection is that most production D-types were still in unpainted

Jaguar C-type (XKC 001) as raced in the 1951 TT by Leslie Johnson. (The C-type was Jaguar's first serious competition car, and its story is told in Volume One of this two-book series). Note the Studebaker among the Mark Sevens; Jaguar usually had at least one American car for assessment.

Silverstone test session in 1955, featuring Mike Hawthorn and the new long-nose D-type. With him are (left to right) Les Bottrill, Norman Dewis and Bob Knight. Malcolm Sayer is just visible behind Bottrill.

The first public appearance of the D-type as a works team, Le Mans 1954.

The author with XKC 401, the prototype D-type, at the National Motor Museum at Beaulieu in the early 1970s, shortly after a memorable early-morning drive from Coventry. (Courtesy: Charles Pocklington)

Bob Berry with XKC 403 as rebuilt after the 1955 TT accident and immediately before he wrote it off at Goodwood in 1956, just when he and the car looked set to become the quickest D-type combination in UK national events. (A new car with the same registration number was ready to race in late 1956, in OKV 2's original dark green, and Berry made a brief comeback in it.)

This 1955 long-nose D-type (XKD 507) was prepared by the works for the Briggs Cunningham team, and remained in the fabulous Cunningham collection when its active life came to an end. (Early in 1987 it was announced that the collection had been sold by Cunningham to Miles Collier, and would be transferred in due course from California to Florida.) This picture was taken at Laguna Seca in 1976, when it was given an airing at the 'Tribute to Jaguar' race meeting. Phil Hill (seen here) came out of retirement to drive it. He finished second to British visitor Martin Morris who drove XKC 404, another ex-works car.

Ault & Wyborg's Flag Metallic Blue paint made the *Ecurie Ecosse* Jaguars look stunning. Wilkie Wilkinson mothers one of the wide-screen long-nose cars at Merchiston Mews. *(Courtesy: Graham Gauld)*

The other Scottish team of note in the 1950s was known as the 'Border Reivers', and it gave Jim Clark his first taste of victory with a powerful car – the ex-Murkett D-type (XKD 517). The rural setting for this *Formule Libre* event is Clark's local circuit, Charterhall. The year is 1958. *(Courtesy: Graham Gauld)*

Early hybrids (notably the Cooper and the HWM) gained some success, as did the Tojeiro. This is the third Tojeiro-Jaguar to be built; it was styled by Cavendish Morton, who also influenced Lister. It was leased to *Ecurie Ecosse* for whom Ivor Bueb drove it to fourth place at its début – the 1958 British GP meeting at Silverstone where this picture was taken. *(Courtesy: Graham Gauld)*

Opposite: The 1960 Le Mans programme cover serves to illustrate the definitive Tojeiro-Jaguar and Lister-Jaguar in their final forms, as raced the previous year. No. 8 is a brand new *Ecurie Ecosse* Tojeiro driven by Flockhart/Lawrence; Nos. 1 and 2 are the 1959-model Listers of Bueb/Halford and Hansgen/Blond respectively. Neither the works nor the *Ecurie Ecosse* 3-litre engines – required from 1958 – lasted the race. This time, at last, it was Aston Martin's turn to win, with Salvadori/Shelby (No. 5) first and Frère/Trintignant (No. 6) second. Also seen here is the third-placed Ferrari of Beurlys/Heldé (No. 11) chasing the Calderari/Patthey Aston Martin coupé up the outside. Although slow to start, the Behra/Gurney Ferrari 250TR (No. 12) would lead from the second hour to the seventh, before failing. The Jaguar works still supported Le Mans entrants, and Lofty England, Ted Brookes, and Frank Rainbow were among those present to assist the Lister team in particular – an encounter which would lead Michael McDowel (the 1959 reserve Lister driver) to join the Jaguar company soon afterwards.

Ivor Bueb winning at the Brands Hatch August Bank Holiday meeting, 1958, in the works Lister-Jaguar. Brian Lister's cars were the most successful XK-engined hybrids by far, and were the first 'outsiders' to have works-built-and tested 3.8-litre racing units. *(Courtesy: John Prodger)*

24 Heures du Mans 1960

PRIX DU PROGRAMME : 3,50 N.F.

Like the XK120 before it, the E-type won its first race (the 1961 Oulton Park Spring Cup) – with hindsight, a misleading result. This is the car Graham Hill drove to victory on that occasion, in the colours of Tommy Sopwith's Equipe Endeavour. This picture was taken at Brands Hatch later in the year, by which time Ferrari's 250GT was showing its superiority. *(Courtesy: John Prodger)*

The mid-1960s saw the XK-engined E-type outclassed not only by Ferrari's GTO but by the AC-based, Ford-supported Cobra. Since the January 1963 London Racing Car Show, there had also been a new breed of competition prototype in the form of the Lola GT which would inspire the Ford GT40 and, to some extent, the Jaguar XJ13 project which was to be shelved when Jaguar had other priorities. This picture at the 1964 Bank Holiday Brands Hatch meeting shows how times were changing for 'GT' racing: Jackie Stewart (Coombs E-type) leads Augie Pabst (Mecom Lola GT) through the paddock. Peter Sutcliffe's E-type is just visible on the right. From 1966, it would be necessary only to build 50 (rather than 100) of any GT model, which suited Ferrari and Ford but not Jaguar, who would pull out of active racing involvement altogether. *(Courtesy: John Prodger)*

Mount Panorama, Bathurst, NSW: Nowadays known as the home of the James Hardie 1000km touring car race, this legendary circuit has been in regular use since 1938 when Peter Whitehead won the Australian GP in an ERA. This evocative 1965 picture shows Jane's E-type leading Geoghegan's Lotus Elan across 'the mountain'. Bob Jane's car (also seen, right, in the Bathurst paddock, with Jane's new Mustang) was the only lightweight 'E' to be sold in the Antipodes; it scored a number of wins between 1963 and 1966. In the 1980s, the car was still relatively original, and domiciled in the York Motor Museum, Western Australia.

Below: Having seen the works/Protheroe E-type's bodywork in 1963, Peter Lindner had his lightweight 'E' modified at Browns Lane in a similar, though not identical way for 1964. He was killed at Montlhéry that autumn and the remains of the car were impounded. Eventually, its identity was given to a new car built by Lynx Engineering. This made its bow in the early 1980s; but the roof line was wrong, and the car vanished again for a while. When it re-emerged from the Lynx workshops it looked much more like the original, as created by Malcolm Sayer. It was sold to Germany, and is seen with the evergreen Roger Mac driving, at the 1986 Nürburgring historic race meeting. *(Courtesy: Peter Schack)*

One of the six original competition XK120s was loaned to Clemente Biondetti. Its engine (W 1147) was put into a special chassis, as described in Volume One. At first it had a Ferrari body; for 1952 it had another Italian-built body, based loosely on the then-new Jaguar C-type. (Biondetti had been unable to obtain a C-type from the Jaguar works.) Paolo Dabbeni of Brescia completed the restoration of this historically-important 'Jaguar Biondetti Special' in early 1984, in time to take part in a celebration of the defunct Mille Miglia road race, in which it had run thirty-two years previously. *(Courtesy: Nicholas Storrs)*

Since Volume One was published in 1982, C-types have changed hands, including the 1953 Le Mans winner, XKC 051, brought back to Britain by Duncan Hamilton's son Adrian. Another change of ownership saw XKC 045 joining Jaguar's own collection at Browns Lane. Here Ian Luckett of Jaguar accompanies Tony Brooks in the latter car, during a 1985 cavalcade in Coventry.

Thriving at thirty-three: By far the most consistently active D-type is Martin Morris's OKV3 (XKC 404) which travelled nearly 4000 miles while touring and racing in New Zealand in early 1987 *and* it won a motor race at Pukekohe. Note the passenger's temporary windscreen. *(Courtesy: Martin Morris)*

aluminium when they went on test. Afterwards they were given their primer and final cellulose glaze finish in one of the service department booths. (Standard volume-production Jaguars were by now being treated with synthetic enamel.)

Late in 1954, Arthur Whittaker (the General Manager, and Lyons' deputy since the Swallow Blackpool days) had issued instructions for the provision of 150 sets of parts: '100 models to be produced plus spares and experimental requirements.' There were not too many modifications, once the production prototype specification was confirmed.

On 2 May 1955, Tom Jones ordered some parts changes for the all-synchromesh gearbox, which was prone to seizure. It had been found necessary to revert to Hoffmann roller bearings on the mainshaft in place of needle rollers. By this date the first two gearboxes had been delivered to *Ecurie Ecosse*, and it was noted that theirs could be modified later if necessary.

The first eight 1955 D-types constituted five long-nose cars (XKD 504 to 508) for the works – two being transferred to the Cunningham team – and three short-nose ones (XKD 501 and 502 for Ecurie Ecosse, and XKD 503 for the Belgian team). As indicated earlier, the final testing to a 'system' was not begun, with XKD 509, until July. It was August by the time a regular test schedule was being undertaken by Les Bottrill – a schedule which kept him occupied until Christmas.

Bottrill's 'D' diary began on 14 July with a preliminary check on XKD 509. He found 53 chassis and 15 body items requiring attention, plus six shortages. Next day he took the 1954 prototype (XKC 401) to Lindley – usually

The D-type production line.

145

referred to as MIRA – for unspecified testing. The test record from the following Monday (which covers a period until the end of that year and includes references to cars XKD 509 to XKD 575 inclusive) can be found in Appendix 7.

The test record also includes some interesting pencilled notes relating to the testing of these 67 cars: 2,220 gallons of fuel were used in 203 tests covering 20 461 miles (over 9 mpg). Twenty-four tyres were worn out, and another four part-worn in the exercise. The most-tested car was XKD 525 which covered almost 650 miles in eight test sessions before being despatched to Briggs Cunningham. Other 'problem cars' were XKD 537 (seven tests), 524 and 533 (five tests each).

During the most concentrated test period, Ted Brookes was assigned to the rectification work at Browns Lane. I joined Jaguar at this time: sometimes I 'broke bounds' from the capstan lathes and vertical millers (where new apprentices usually began) to march the length of the works – looking as businesslike as possible – to see the D-types taking shape. Needless to say, their temporary production line was fascinating to factory visitors, too.

Don Saunders, an older apprentice (later to join the service department), made us beginners envious. He had the job of collecting each D-type on completion and driving it over to Lindley for Les Bottrill to test. Later he recalled that he was never once stopped by the police, although he did follow instructions to drive quietly – especially through the centre of Nuneaton, a town which is difficult to avoid *en route*. Nor was there ever, to his knowledge, a complaint – despite frequent use of the same streets. That must be a good sign, in a 170 mph sports-racer. After a while, the routine became fairly straight-forward. Early testing, however, brought to light characteristics which called for action – as in this memo from Phil Weaver to Bill Heynes on 17 August:

Will you please note that further testing has now been carried out at Lindley with the following results.

1. GEARBOX
(a) Oil Leakage.
An extension and rear cover have been modified to provide four extra 2 BA studs disposed on the flange where most leakage has occurred. This has reduced leakage practically to nil.

A further point of leakage has been traced however to the Pesco pump drive gear seal. Although a synthetic rubber seal is called for in the speci. in line with that found necessary, and successful, on our own cars, a leather seal of the type we discarded has been fitted. Since finding this out I understand that the wrong seals have been fitted to all cars now built. These will have to be changed for the correct seal in synthetic rubber (C 9475, speci. A 79, sheet 34 item 14).
(b) Jumping out of gear.
It is understood that the 1955 type interlock, i.e. the type fitted on our own cars, will be standardised for production – this will of course necessitate modification of the lid to prevent overtravel of 1st and 2nd selector rod, caused by indentation of the aluminium boss faces.

2. BRAKES
(a) It is understood that all front disc seals will have to be changed.
(b) Car No. 514 has been equipped with one of this year's front air scoops, fitted in the O/S/F position. Comparative tests of disc temperature have been run in conjunction with Messrs. Dunlop's representatives to determine the extent of modification necessary to lower these to within reasonable limits. From the results it appears that modifications of the bonnet will be required in order to bring the scoops into the air stream.

3. MISFIRING AT PART THROTTLE
Complete elimination of part throttle misfiring has been achieved by modifying the air box lid, so that all three balance orifices now come under the same conditions of pressure. (In the production type air box, modification has been carried out to reduce under-bonnet fouling without reference to engine performance, with a result that the rear carburetter balance was fully enclosed, the centre unit partially enclosed and the front open to normal under bonnet conditions).

Not only has the part throttle misfiring been cured but an improvement has been noted on general all round performance since modifying the air duct lid.

4. BODY SEALING
It is understood that Mr Rippon is carrying out body sealing with an improved compound on a chassis which has not been treated in any way with Bostik.

5. CLUTCH OPERATION
It has been noted on two cars that the screwed taper pins retaining operating lever and fork to the shaft have not been properly tightened. Whilst it is possible to check the lock pin on the outside lever, it is not possible to check and wire lock the pin on the fork as this is inside the bell housing. Tightening can be carried out by removing the starter motor, but wire locking again would be impossible through the small access hole.

In view of this all locking pins will have to be checked and tightened if required.

6. CLUTCH ADAPTOR PLATES
Two gearboxes have been removed, this necessitating removal of clutch from the crankshaft adaptor plate. Whilst carrying out this operation it was seen that both clutch assembly studs and adaptor plates were damaged, this being caused by dimensional interference on the pitch circles of the clutch studs and assembly holes in the adaptor plate. Both adaptor plates were renewed and new clutch assemblies fitted.

The official note from John Silver to all concerned, stating that the original order for 100 complete cars would be reduced to 67, was dated 30 August 1955. The balance of parts or sub-assemblies was to be transferred to the spares department.

In September 1955, mainly for the benefit of USA customers, Ken Bowen of the service department issued a list of suggested spares for D-type users and – rather more expensive – an inventory of special service tools:

	UK retail
Cradle & slings for engine removal	£7 10s. 0d.
Rear hub arresting spanner	£3 10s. 0d.
Rear hub extractor	£6 12s. 4d.
Tie rod inner ball-joint 'C' spanner	£1 9s. 4d.
Tie rod inner ball-joint hexagon spanner	6s. 0d.
Rear hub nut spanner	£3 10s. 8d.
Rear torsion bar lock-nut spanner	£1 6s. 0d.
Suspension setting bars (set)	£2 17s. 4d.
Suspension setting bar pins (set)	18s. 8d.
Axle shaft extractor	£7 10s. 0d.

Early in 1956, the D-type was beginning to become a more familiar sight in the motor-racing world. Some customers mastered the preparation and maintenance (and the handling) right away. Others had problems – notably those in the western United States. John Dugdale, Jaguar's Western Territory manager, sent a memo to his on-the-spot service engineer Kenrick ('Buck') Hickman concerning XKD 522, 527, and 528 which had competed at Palm Springs on 25/26 February, and had caused their drivers – Lozano, Austin, and Woods respectively – to complain about their behaviour. Lozano said 522 was better than when he had first run it in December 1955, and this time came fifth in the main race. The other two did not finish. Austin crashed in practice. Woods retired, in difficulty under braking and on corners, wondering if the shock absorbers had failed. On the same weekend, Dr Hal Fenner of Hobbs, New Mexico, was reported as having won the main race at Mansfield, Louisiana – in a D-type.

So the news was not all bad in the private sector.

Over in Coventry, however, on 8 March 1956, Tom Jones issued a memo: 'D-type – It has now been decided to fit a stronger roll bar to the front suspension . . . also an additional roll bar on the rear, to improve the handling qualities.' This meant Part No. C12196 (formerly XR1153) replacing C9334 at the front, and the addition of C12197 at the rear.

More of a diplomatic problem was created by the evidence of the extra performance provided by the works wide-angle (35/40) cylinder head, which the Cunningham team now possessed but which was not on offer to true privateers. It is interesting to note that Jack Emerson conducted a full-load performance test on a production D-type engine (E2084-9) for Bill Heynes on 27 February 1956. It produced 252·5 bhp at 6000 rpm, which was well up to the standard required.

A visit by Lofty England to California soon afterwards did help: he met the local D-type users, listened to them, and advised them. With familiarity, the D-type would, in due course, produce some satisfactory results in the West.

On 23 April 1956, Claude Baily went on record as saying that 'all unsold D-type cars still at the factory [31] are to be brought up to 1956 standard.' This consisted of the aforementioned roll bar work, fitting dampers with harder settings, and incorporating a filter in the pressure line between the oil cooler and the engine oil gallery; also an alteration to the gearbox layshaft assembly.

Polite correspondence took place at this time with several suppliers – notably Alford & Alder, Girling, and Salisbury Transmissions. Claude Baily requested 'A & A' to redesign the upper ball-joint, which had a habit of tightening up. Heynes expressed grave concern about Salisbury axle shaft failures. His letters to Girling were classics of icy authority. Girling had pointed out that their modified dampers would, 'once again', be supplied without dirt shields, 'owing to the impossibility of providing clearance' when installed. ('No responsibility can be accepted by ourselves for any deterioration of the dampers, directly resulting from the omission of these components.') 'This evasion of responsibility on such a flimsy premise,' retorted Heynes, 'is not in keeping with the Girling tradition.'

As 1956 progressed, with rather more than half of the D-types now operating 'in the field', the responsibilities of having made a classic Le Mans-winning sports-racing car were beginning to weigh heavily. The responsibilities were, of course, accepted – and Lofty England remained the fulcrum for all competition activity (even after the works team's withdrawal from racing was announced). As chief of service, he could make quick decisions relating to the cars and their owners, depending on circumstances. It was the old story, and one as true today as it was then: it is very easy to make sense of a racing policy but it isn't nearly as easy to be positive about a non-racing one. Yet the latter is very often the correct policy, as history has proved.

The XK engine, as developed for racing, would make the D-type competitive for several years; but change takes place quickly in racing and, without a continuous development programme, chassis design becomes dated. Jaguar had done what it set out to do: to produce the regulation number of cars. Some of the 'left-overs' *would* be useful: a third new car for *Ecurie Ecosse* and a replacement for the Belgian team, for example. Most of them sat relatively unprotected in sheds; some were painted and used as dealer showroom display cars following the 1956 Le Mans win – for racing was already overcoming the stigma of the accidents which had spoiled 1955.

The announcement that Jaguar would pull out of racing, in October 1956, was followed on 28 November by the news that 'for the first time in the history of Jaguar, the company is compelled to institute a four-day week'. Having planned a major expansion, Jaguar was now suffering, largely as a long-term result of the Suez crisis and consequent petrol rationing. Fortunately, business picked up again and, by late January, Browns Lane production began soaring to new records.

An oddity: the XKSS
In the interim, not wishing to see them deteriorate through a second winter, nor to be wasteful, Jaguar found a future for its surplus D-types. This press release was dated 21 January 1957:

JAGUAR TO PRODUCE NEW SPORTS-RACING MODEL

Jaguar are to produce a new 2-seater sports-racing car as a result of the increasing demand from America for a type of vehicle equally suitable for normal road use and sports car racing. The new model which, initially, will be for export only, will be based on the already famous Le Mans type Jaguars and will be known as the Jaguar XK 'SS' type.

The new model will depart from the somewhat spartan simplicity of the 'D' type by the incorporation of a full-width orthodox windscreen, folding hood, completely-equipped touring type instrument panel, well-upholstered seating, luggage grid, bumpers and other refinements appropriate to a car intended for fast touring as well as for sports car racing. The car will be fitted with Dunlop disc brakes and the general construction and mechanical specification will follow closely that of the outstandingly successful 'D' type. The new model will be an addition to the Jaguar range and will not supplant any existing models. First deliveries to America are planned to commence in February.

Price in USA. Six thousand nine hundred dollars.

There was less to this announcement than met the eye. Simply, a set of modifications had been devised for the languishing D-types, now over a year old. The division between the seats was cut away and the driver's headrest was removed. There were doors with sidescreens for driver and passenger, but the latter still had to suffer the lack of

Opposite Inset:

The factory fire, February 1957. (*Courtesy: John Silver*)

Left Inset:

This is probably the D-type that had come back for service. (It was replaced by an undamaged one.)

legroom. The XKSS never looked like being acceptable for the 'production', as opposed to 'modified', classes in SCCA (Sports Car Club of America) racing, however, being recognised for what it was – a thinly-disguised D-type, despite the new chassis number.

Sixteen of these 'road-equipped' versions of the 'D' were complete, or in hand, when most of the service department (and the Northern end of the factory, where the D-type production line had once been) were gutted by fire on 12 February 1957. Later, two more D-types would be

Above:

Two D-types that were definitely lost in the 1957 fire at Browns Lane.

converted to full XKSS specification, but they retained their original 'XKD' chassis numbers.

Only one XKSS stayed in Britain initially: John Coombs won his class with it in the Brighton Speed Trials, and the Basil Boothroyd/Russell Brockbank partnership undertook an entertaining road test of it on behalf of *Punch* – discovering, amongst other things, that the passenger compartment was 'gouged out like a small hole in stiff, hot porridge'. Ultimately, this car was converted back into a D-type – as were several others, making the 'real' thing more rare than ever.

Another XKSS went to Hong Kong, and did well in local events – its best successes being victory in the 1959 and 1960 Macau Grands Prix. Two XKSSs went to Canada and achieved considerable success in a country

The Service Department, where some D-types were being converted to XKSS specification at the time of the fire, February 1957. Carrying the broom (*left*) is racing driver Michael Salmon, then a member of the works service department. (*Courtesy: John Silver*)

The flag still flies, February 1957.

US advertisement for the XKSS.

JAGUAR
THE XK-SS TWO-SEATER SUPER-SPORTS

The Jaguar XK-SS is the translation of Jaguar experience in recent competition models into the broader category of the dual-purpose sports-racing car. The XK-SS is a thoroughbred, yet thoroughly roadable machine—a high performance sports-touring car in the tradition of the great continental marques. Unfortunately, due to the recent fire in our Coventry, England, Works, it is available only in very limited quantities. We are proud of the XK-SS because it embodies the race-proved qualities of performance, roadability, reliability and safety that Jaguar believes are as desirable on the highway as they are necessary on the track.

The Jaguar XK-SS: 262 H.P. "XK" engine, 3 Weber dual carburetors, four-wheel Dunlop disc brakes, all-weather top, chrome luggage rack, full touring equipment.

where sports car racing was still in its (comparative) infancy. The other twelve XKSS Jaguars all went to the USA where 'John' Gordon Benett drove XKSS 701 to its first win at Mansfield, Louisiana, in Spring 1957.

Several D-types were in the service department for various reasons at the time of the fire, which incidentally, did much for Jaguar's image – due to the solidarity displayed by the workforce, and the speed with which production was resumed afterwards. The fire also saved the need for complicated explanations (as to why 'production' of the XKSS ceased as suddenly as it had begun). The *absolute* total could never have reached thirty, for the D-type production line and parts sanctions had been cut off long since. Even when it was operating full-time, that line had presented unwanted personnel-problems – inevitable when piecework and more bespoke activities mingle.

Les Bottrill tested these unusual but very exciting cars

and acted as chief inspector, reporting to Lofty England before delivery. Few cars can have been tested as comprehensively, yet awaited sale so long – eventually to achieve true desirability in old age, reaching astonishing prices by the 1980s.

Of the 67 cars built on the production line, 42 were sold as D-types, 9 were burned-out or dismantled, and the other 16 were converted to XKSS spec. as follows:

Below:
The XKSS. Sixteen were completed, and two more D-types were converted later.

Inset:
First race and first win for the XKSS: 'John' Gordon Benett in action at Mansfield, 1957. He turned down the trophy, knowing that the car was not really eligible for SCCA production car racing.

Cross-reference	Despatched (1957)*
XKSS 701, was XKD 555	18 January
XKSS 704, was XKD 563	30 April
XKSS 707, was XKD 564	19 April
XKSS 710, was XKD 568	19 April
XKSS 713, was XKD 569	19 April
XKSS 716, was XKD 575	28 May (Canada)
XKSS 719, was XKD 572	28 May
XKSS 722, was XKD 539	28 May (UK)
XKSS 725, was XKD 562	28 May
XKSS 728, was XKD 547	16 July
XKSS 754, was XKD 542	18 June
XKSS 757, was XKD 559	24 July (Hong Kong)
XKSS 760, was XKD 557	2 September (Canada)
XKSS 763, was XKD 566	19 July
XKSS 766, was XKD 567	16 September
XKSS 769, was XKD 550	19 November

* All despatches were to the USA, except where otherwise stated. Appendix 5 deals in detail with individual cars.

Left:
Benett, the XKSS, and the new 3·4 sedan at Fort Worth dealer showroom opening, Spring 1957.

Left:
Benett, the XKSS, and the new 3·4 sedan at Fort Worth dealer showroom opening, Spring 1957.

The demise of the XKSS went virtually unnoticed, for 1957 was the year of the sensational new 3·4 saloon – soon, of necessity, to be offered with Dunlop disc brakes all round – and the XK150 range of GT cars. More important to *this* story was the continued success of the regular D-type users – notably the Cunningham and *Ecurie Ecosse* teams, discussed in the next chapter – and the birth of the Lister-Jaguar which would keep the XK engine ahead in sprint-type events for sports-racing cars almost to the end of the decade.

Left:
Dealership owner Mr Johnson in XKSS at Fort Worth. Behind the car are his General Manager 'Tad' Maghee, James Stewart (presumably Guest of Honour at the grand opening?), 'John' Benett, and John Dugdale of Jaguar Cars, North America. Note the unsatisfactory fuel-filler position.

The XK150 chassis, introduced in May 1957, brought four-wheel disc brakes to a volume-production model for the first time.

Top:
Norman Dewis demonstrating the XKSS to Prince Philip.

Above: **The Duke of Kent tries the XKSS at MIRA, in the company of Norman Dewis.**

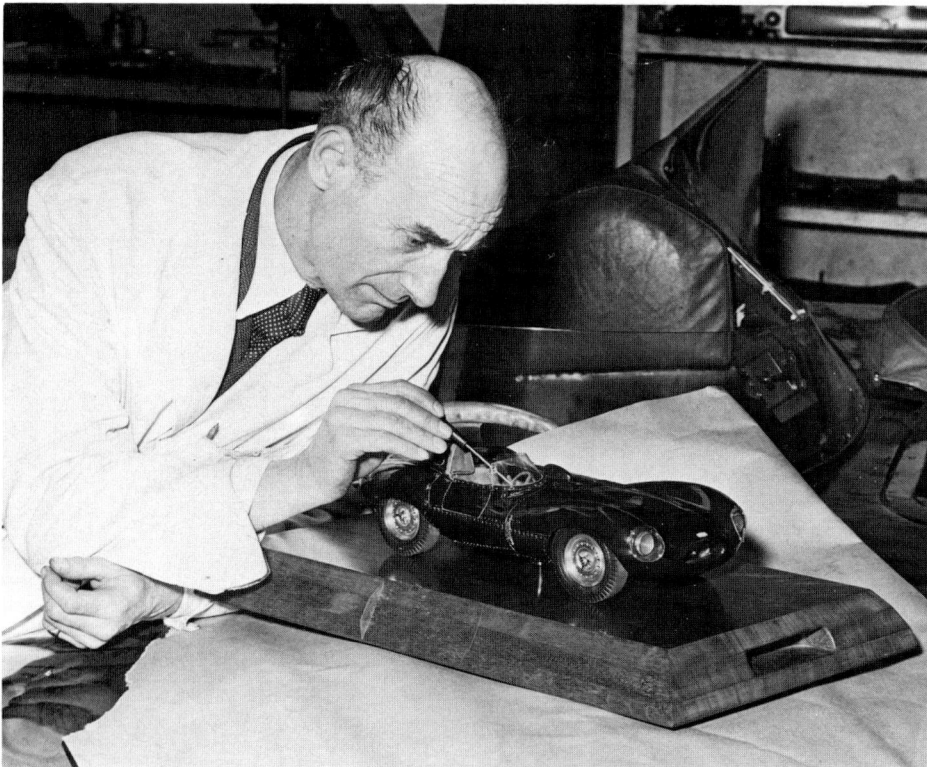

Master modelmaker Rex Hays with the beautiful D-type he created for Prince Charles.

Chapter Eight

D-type ex-works Operations

Those of 'last year's' works D-types that had survived the season, always found their way into good hands. The fate of each car, as far as I can reasonably interpret it, is recorded in Appendix 5. This chapter describes briefly, each of the 'customer teams' and its works relationship.

J. C. Broadhead

Was one of many enthusiasts whose personal motor racing plans were thwarted by the Second World War. Afterwards he took up trials and rally driving himself, and left it to others to race his cars.

The story of how he persuaded Raymond ('Lofty') England to part with one of the 1954 cars is told in the appropriate appendix – by Bob Berry, the Jaguar man who raced privately. After Berry's Goodwood accident in 1956, the numbers 'XKD 403' and 'OKV 2' went on to a new D-type. The remains of the original were believed buried beneath Jack Broadhead's yard. Quite what good they would be to anyone, if unearthed, it is hard to imagine – since the official change of identity had taken place in Coventry thirty years earlier – yet in 1986 it was being said that the search was on in deepest Cheshire. It is amazing, this numbers game, in the world of 'historic' cars. Bob Berry says the interment story is nonsense, anyway.

The new car was raced by Berry and others for several years before Broadhead sold it.

J. Duncan Hamilton

Raced a variety of C-types and D-types privately, most of them ex-works cars rather than new ones.

In 1957 and 1958 he received full works support for his Le Mans efforts with XKD 601, and he could have finished second – maybe even first – in either of those events but for bad luck.

Earlier D-types included in his stable had included 402 and 406.

Of the other 'first-batch' cars, 401 stayed with Jaguar as a show car (Bob Berry drove it out to the Geneva motor show one year) and then spent many years on show at Beaulieu, whence the company borrowed it from time to time – for special events, and as a reminder that it was not a gift. Although not fully appreciative of its own history – what firm is? – Jaguar wisely preserved XKD 605, too. When it came back from the USA it was painted green again and sent to live among the bright red Italian classics of Turin's Biscaretti museum. When Jaguar was revived as an independent company again in the 1980s, arrangements were made to bring it back to Coventry. So Jaguar has two nice originals of its own – one from each end of the D-type spectrum.

On the other hand Adrian Hamilton, having bought XKD 601 back into the family in the 1980s, sent it on its world travels again in 1986. (601 had been rebuilt at the works after father's accident in 1958 and now included bits from 505 and elsewhere – but it was still very much a D-type. To me, it would have been nice to see XKC 051

OKV 2, as refurbished over the winter of 1955, leads Jaguar-powered HWM and Cooper at Goodwood in 1956. (*Courtesy: Bob Berry*)

Jack Broadhead and Bob Berry looking happy at Silverstone, 1956. (*Courtesy: Bob Berry*)

and XKD 601 remain under one roof . . . but: 'business is business'.)

David Murray

Was a staunch ally of Jaguar and, with two Le Mans victories and many more elsewhere, he helped the marque enormously. His *Ecurie Ecosse* team was the product of an idea first voiced at the British Racing Mechanics' Club dinner in November 1951. It came into being on 1 March 1952.

Murray was a chartered accountant and a member of the wine trade. He was a keen amateur racing driver, too, and had close links with the Reg Parnell 'racing car centre' in Derby, where 'Wilkie' Wilkinson was working when Murray asked him to join him in Edinburgh. He realised he was not the best racing driver in the world – and he had several accidents, described in his flippant yet readable book (published in 1962 by Stanley Paul, before all the luck ran out).

The alternative to racing, in his mind, was to create and manage a team of his own: – a 'Scotland Stable' – *Ecurie Ecosse*.

At first, in early 1952, the team consisted of three owners

Left: Above:

OKV 2 became, essentially, a production D-type after Berry's Goodwood accident. These pictures show Peter Blond at Oulton Park and Jack Fairman at Aintree. (*Courtesy: Tom Rowe*)

of Jaguars – Bill Dobson, Sir James Scott-Douglas, and Ian Stewart. The latter's car was painted a beautiful metallic-finish colour – Flag Blue by Ault & Wyborg – and this was to become the team's official colour. 'Wilkie' prepared the cars in a row of garages in Merchiston Mews, Bruntsfield, Edinburgh, Reg Tanner of Esso produced some sponsorship, and David Murray (often assisted by his wife Jenny) ran the team and, somehow, made it work as a business for several years.

The first big victory was in the summer of 1952 when Ian Stewart took his – well *Ecurie Ecosse's* – new C-type (XKC 006) to St Helier for the last-ever Jersey Road Race. This was a satisfying start.

As the team began to make a name for itself, increasing help came from another patriotic Scot, Major E.G. Thomson of Callands who avoided publicity but, as Murray himself wrote, 'helped the team over many a sticky patch'. For 1953 there were two brand new C-types – plus yet another for Jimmy Scott-Douglas, though he had decided to detach himself from regular membership of the team. So well did the cars do, driven mostly by Ian Stewart, Ninian Sanderson and, soon afterwards, Jimmy Stewart, that both Stewarts were given works drives by Jaguar as a result of their natural flair. Moreover, Lyons, Heynes and England were so impressed that it was agreed that all three 1953 works Jaguars should be sold to *Ecurie Ecosse* for the 1954 season.

1954 began with a fairly traumatic trip to Argentina, but then settled down somewhat. Towards the end of the year, this press announcement was proposed by Murray to Rankin:

Mr David Murray, patron of Ecurie Ecosse, *has informed us that arrangements are almost complete for his team to use entirely new Jaguar*

Duncan Hamilton travelled more than most Britishers in his racing days. These pictures of him in OKV 1 were taken at Montlhéry near Paris (where he was successful several times) and at Dakar in 1956, following YPC 614 (XKD 510) driven by Graham Whitehead. (*Courtesy: Duncan Hamilton*)

Originally registered OKV 1 (and later re-registered as such), this ex-works car did return in 1956 to Browns Lane where these pictures were taken. It proved that the cockpit *could* be modified and, to that extent, may have influenced Jaguar when creating the XKSS to relieve the company of surplus D-types. The owner John 'Jumbo' Goddard ran it as 3 APB in the 1956 Brighton Speed Trials

cars in 1955. A close liaison will be in force with the factory, particularly with regard to drivers, and it is anticipated that the nucleus of Scots drivers will remain. It is intended to confine the future activities of the team to international events. The present C-type cars are being sold after a successful season which brought 13 victories at 18 meetings attended.

Rankin replied a week later, asking Murray to hold fire until Lyons was available for comment; but Murray had gone ahead anyway – and in fact, throughout the D-type period, the liaison with Jaguar *would* be closer.

In May 1955, the Scots obtained – brand new – the first two pre-production D-types: XKD 501/502, registered MWS 301/302, which Jimmy Stewart and Desmond Titterington crashed at the Nürburgring, probably due to the nature of the D-type's brakes which had proved troublesome earlier in the month, at Silverstone and Dundrod.

The works long-nose D-types of 1955 and 1956 had full power braking, with assistance to all four wheels. However, the 1954 D-types and the production ones had servo assisted to the rear wheel brakes only. The rear brake servo was introduced to overcome the problems of 'long pedal' due to bending and end-float in the axle shaft, and to try and reduce fluid temperature. Disc brakes for racing were still in their infancy.

The front brakes were operated from the master-cylinder and some braking could be obtained (with a lot of pedal movement) if the servo pump failed. The system did not overcome the problem of 'knock-off' of the front brake pads, due mainly to float in the front hub bearings. Cars with fully assisted braking did not have this problem. The cars which hurtled into the Eifel woodlands almost certainly did. (It should be added that cars with full assistance had NO braking whatsoever if their pump failed.) Jimmy Stewart did one lap of the event – to get Murray his starting money – then retired from racing; his namesake Ian had done so the previous year. From now on, the *Ecurie Ecosse* stars would be Titterington and Sanderson, with Bill Smith contributing at Crimond. The year of 1955 turned into a successful one, once the Scottish team became familiar with the new cars.

A third D-type (XKD 561) was acquired for 1956, when Alan Brown, Ron Flockhart and John Lawrence joined the team. The season didn't start too well, with 'Wilkie' being thrown out of XKD 501 having decided to test it himself at Snetterton, and rolled in the process. He and the car were, by good fortune, back in action within a month. 1956 was to be another good year, with plenty of solid victories against high quality opposition.

In May, Ninian Sanderson (XKD 502) won the production sports car race at Spa-Francorchamps, then he and Flockhart came fourth behind the works Jaguars in the Reims 12-hour – a good disciplined run, and a sample of what was to follow at Le Mans, when the factory cars hit trouble, the same pair – in XKD 501, the very car that 'Wilkie' had rolled – held off top drivers Moss/Collins (Aston Martin) and Gendebien/Trintignant (Ferrari) to take the event of the year to the delight of all and the relief of Jaguar folk in particular.

The only sour note seems to have been struck afterwards, when the combined arrangements for television appearances and a night out in London went awry, and the anticipated camaraderie between *Ecurie Ecosse* and Jaguar people failed to materialise; apparently there was a 'Murray' faction and a 'Hawthorn' faction and Rankin felt bitter that his colleagues should have allowed this to happen. This was natural in the circumstances, for Ernest Rankin, the original head of Jaguar's public relations and advertising, was a thoroughly professional man. It did not take long for him and Murray to bury the hatchet.

For 1957 *Ecurie Ecosse* received their three ex-works cars, XKD 504, 603 and 606. To make space at Merchiston Mews, and to keep the team solvent, XKD 502 and 561 were re-sold, but XKD 501 (the car used at Le Mans) was retained for occasional use and for Major Thomson's collection. After all, the car was his!

The story of 1957 Le Mans is told elsewhere. It was a magnificent 1–2 for Murray's team. With Jaguar no longer racing, the factory attitude was much more relaxed and helpful, and in fact the winning car (XKD 606) was works-prepared and had a works-loaned engine. Flockhart and Bueb won, with Lawrence and Sanderson second, and then, a week later, the team achieved hero status when all three cars (XKD 603, 606 and 504) came 4th, 5th and 6th in the remarkable Monza 500-mile race, described in 'Fearless Jack' Fairman's own words in Appendix 3.

Then it all began to go wrong. Murray was honest afterwards: 'We got a bit big-headed,' he said.

As Graham Gauld – former journalist, and one of the men behind today's rekindling of the *Ecurie Ecosse* spirit – wrote long ago in *The Motor World*: 'The team has been up in the clouds with two wins at Le Mans, and down at the depths.' He put the latter state down to Murray having, 'a too-great faith in Jaguars producing another race car' as well as misreading future trends in the racing game. In fairness, Jaguar probably also had too much

Right:

Le Mans 1957: almost a works team. England, Sayer, and Berry seen in the Hamilton pit. Lawrence, Wilkinson, and Murray of *Ecurie Ecosse* look more independent next door. (*Courtesy: Paul Skilleter*)

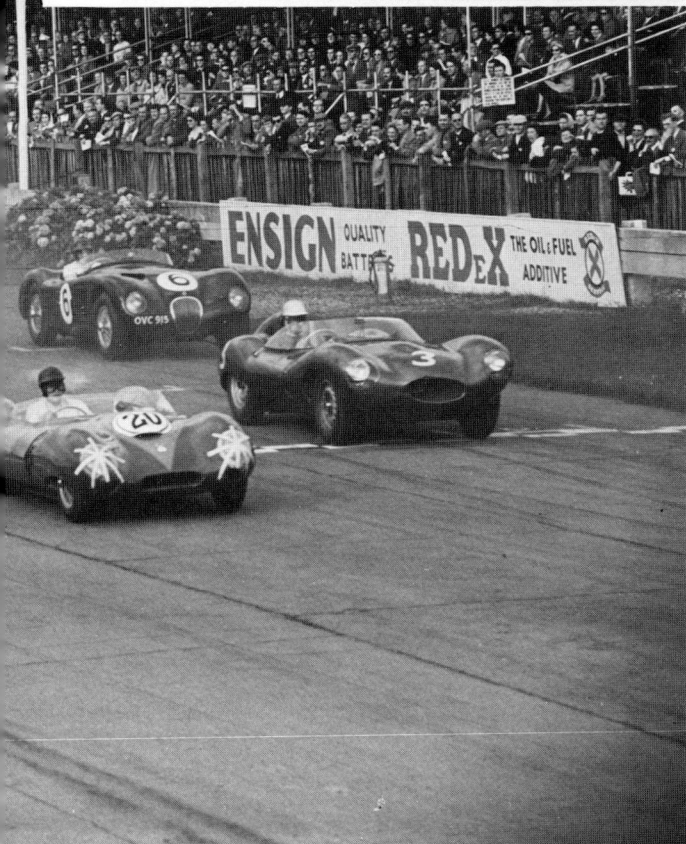

Left:

Archie Scott-Brown (Lister-Jaguar) won this race at Goodwood in September 1957 from Jack Brabham (Tojeiro-Jaguar), Henry Taylor (D-type), Roy Salvadori (Lotus-Climax), and Duncan Hamilton (D-type). The latter surely would have been better placed but for the unseemly move (seen here) which cleared the immediate pit-area rapidly. The chicane suffered, too, as Hamilton strove to catch the leaders. 'Was he mad!' observed Martyn Watkins to *Autosport* readers. (*Courtesy: Autocar*)

David Murray, Sir James Scott-Douglas and Jimmy Stewart in far-off Argentina, 1954. (*Courtesy: J. R. Stewart*)

faith in its own ability to make an effective 3-litre engine as required internationally after 1957.

Besides keeping the D-type available, David Murray tried Lister-Jaguars, and Tojeiro-Jaguar before moving to other types of car; the pace of progress would not wait for the Scots or for Jaguar. In the end, perhaps wisely, *Ecurie Ecosse* would never go the E-type route – lightweight or otherwise. Even a second go at Monza in 1958, with no limits on engine size, failed to produce a very satisfactory result – Bueb (D-type) ninth, and Fairman in a specially-built Lister-Jaguar single-seater eleventh. Masten Gregory – who would hasten *Ecurie Ecosse*'s financial downfall by writing-off several of its cars – retired with a broken fuel line and other problems created by the downforce on the steeply-banked bends of Monza bumpy high-speed course.

There was some more diplomatic letter-writing by Rankin in 1958, following press features building 'Wilkie' Wilkinson into a 'magician' in areas for which he was not responsible: 'Mr Heynes assures me that all development work for *Ecurie Ecosse* which has had successful results has been carried out by us ... Neither Mr Heynes nor indeed anybody, here has anything but the highest-possible regard for Wilkie's capabilities, but it does seem to me that there is some danger of his being built up into some kind of Freddie Dixon legend which has quite definitely left a generation of motorists with the belief that Freddie knew more about developing Rileys than did the people who designed the car.'

David Murray replied apologetically and confidingly: 'From time to time in personal interviews I have stressed the outstanding workmanship of Jaguar ... Unfortunately some reporters have rather fanciful notions about what

Ecurie Ecosse line-up in Merchiston Mews, Edinburgh, with David Murray presiding. *Left to right*: Stan Sproat in XKD 501, Ron Gaudion (newly arrived from Jaguar) in XKD 502, and Sandy Arthur in the team's latest acquisition XKD 561. (*Courtesy: R. Gaudion*)

'Wilkie' Wilkinson at Reims for the 1956 12-hour race.
(*Courtesy: P. Skilleter*)

Above: Below:
Ecurie Ecosse D-type XKD 501 en route to victory at Le Mans in 1956: Flockhart passing the Mulsanne signallers and Sanderson taking over at the pits.
(*Courtesy: Motor*)

Le Mans 1957: the winning D-type (XKD 606) – factory - prepared, Murray-managed.

The 1957 runner-up (XKD 603) photographed at Arnage.

happens at Merchiston Mews and there you have the trouble. I will do everything in my power to ensure that this sort of thing will not be allowed to continue.'

There was not quite the same urgency to apportion responsibility in either direction, once Jaguar and *Ecurie Ecosse* found, separately, that the XK engine in 3-litre form was not providing the necessary reliability for Le Mans.

Besides Wilkie, David Murray's other loyal workers Sandy Arthur and Stan Sproat soldiered on for the team in the dark days of *Ecurie Ecosse*. Ron Gaudion, who had joined from Coventry (where he had worked on the D-type production line and been with the team at Le Mans in 1955), returned home to Australia while the Scots were still on top. There was another outstanding mechanic in Patric Meehan; it should be added that Jenny Murray and Peter Hughes did a fine job, keeping track of the team's progress at Le Mans.

The decline of the Scots team, despite the flashes of brilliance, was sad but inevitable. The old *Ecurie Ecosse*

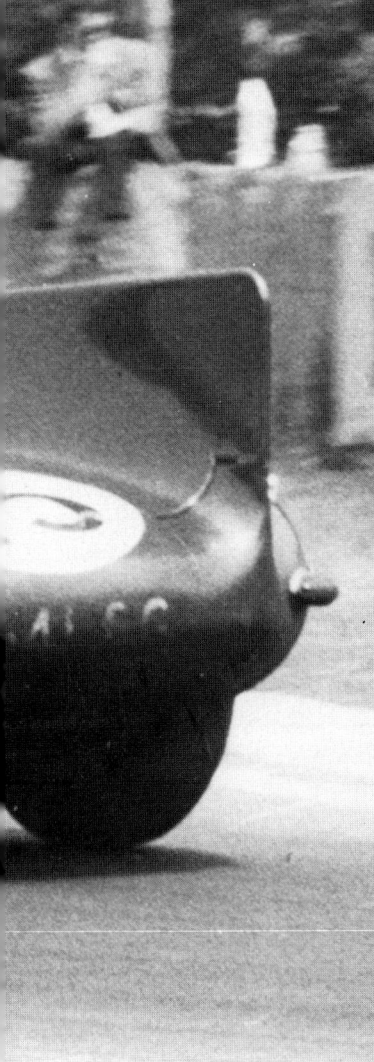

First *and* second at Le Mans in 1957, the two ex-works, long-nose D-types give *Ecurie Ecosse* its finest hour.

and its relationship with Jaguar petered out; but it was good to see the famous name re-emerging with a star performance in Group C2 World Championship racing the mid-1980s. *Ecurie Ecosse* was on top again – without Murray and without Jaguar.

Briggs Cunningham

Was responsible for putting Jaguar on the racing map of America and, for a time, represented Jaguar as a New York area distributor. He was also the guarantee behind the Long Island engineering organisation of Alfred Momo.

Flying, sailing, golfing – they all took the fancy of Cincinatti-born Briggs Swift Cunningham; but it was the sport of motor racing that provided the strongest pull. He was pally with the Collier brothers, founders of the Automobile Racing Club of America in the early nineteen-thirties. In the last pre-war ARCA race (actually held in 1940 at the New York World's Fair) Miles Collier drove Cun-

Flockhart and Bueb try to please all the photographers after their 1957 victory. Murray smiles at left. (Thirty years later, the name of *Ecurie Ecosse* would be associated with success in category 'C2' sports-prototype racing, using Rover rather than Jaguar power.)

ningham's first sports-racing special, the BuMerc – tuned and modified Buick Century with SSK Mercedes body – but crashed due to brake-fade. That race was won by Frank Griswold (Alfa Romeo) who would also win the first important *post*–war American sports car race at Watkins Glen, the runner-up being none other than Briggs Cunningham himself in the impressive but elderly BuMerc. That was in 1948.

From then on, it became increasingly feasible to import new cars, and Briggs Cunningham was first to bring in Ferraris and other exotica. Increasingly, too, he sought the means to quench his thirst to win the 24-hour race at Le Mans with an American car.

In 1950 Briggs Cunningham made his first assault upon Le Mans with two more-or-less standard Cadillacs, one being fitted with a special open body and dubbed *Le Monstre*. Basic reliability overcame weaknesses of trans-

Left:
Jack Fairman's moment of glory as he leads all the Indy cars at Monza in 1957. ('Fearless Jack' wrote an account of this race for the *Jaguar Apprentices' Magazine*. It has been reprinted in Appendix 3.)

Ecurie Ecosse could not repeat its previous performance when, in 1958, the team raced around Monza anti-clockwise for the second year running. Ivor Bueb (seen here) did best of the three entries, coming ninth. (*Courtesy: P. Skilleter*)

Below:
The specially-prepared *Ecurie Ecosse* Lister-Jaguar did not last the pace in 1958. Jack Fairman is seen in the Monza paddock. (*Courtesy: P. Skilleter*)

Ron Flockhart in the *Ecurie Ecosse* car (newly-modified for a final fling at Le Mans), prepares to overtake Mike Salmon in his more normal-looking ex-*Ecurie Ecosse* D-type during the BRDC International Trophy meeting at Silverstone in May 1960. (*Courtesy: P. Skilleter*)

Below:

No half-measures: from 1950 to 1963, Briggs Cunningham (in shirtsleeves) spared no effort to come to Le Mans properly prepared. (*Courtesy: Robert Blake.*)

The Cunningham team, Le Mans 1955 with Cunningham C6R and Jaguar D-type (XKD 507), later acquired from the works. Both cars (the former fitted with a Jaguar XK engine in place of the Offenhauser) were kept for the Briggs Cunningham museum in California. Familiar faces include Stanley Sedgwick who worked with the team and Bob Blake (arms folded) who provided this picture.

mission and braking, and the cars came tenth and eleventh.

One practice incident had involved 'Ted Tappett' (Phil Walters) running into a haycart with *Le Monstre* while out 'demonstrating' to a pretty girl related to a race official. The one-off Grumman-engineered nose had been thoroughly mussed-up. Alec Ulmann was at Le Mans with the Cunningham team; he remembered Bob Blake – an expert in alloy fabrications – and rang Arlington, only to discover that Blake was visiting Northampton. He caught up with him just as he was leaving for a few days at Weston-super-Mare with his English wife. Within moments a deal had been struck and, instead, Bob and

XKD 507, Art Mayhew of the Cunningham team, and a new line in headgear. (*Courtesy: R. Blake*)

SCCA duel of the year, 1955. Phil Hill (Ferrari) and Sherwood Johnston (XKD 507) at the fine new Wisconsin circuit known as Road America. In the end, the Ferrari driver took the chequered flag by about this much, having out-fumbled Johnston into the last corner.

After coming second at Road America, Sherwood Johnson won at Watkins Glen. He is seen here, winning again, this time in the 1955 President's Cup at Hagerstown Air Force Base, Maryland.

Jean Blake were heading for Croydon and a private charter plane to Le Mans. Bob mended the special body in time for the race.

That autumn, he packed up his Arlington business and travelled to Florida to work for Briggs Cunningham full time.

Cunningham had taken over Frick-Tappett Motors of Long Island to form a new company in West Palm Beach. There, for five seasons, a series of American sports, GT, and sports racing cars was produced in Cunningham's own name from 1951 to 1955. In the latter year, Cunningham's financial advisers pointed out that he could not go on running this kind of activity as a tax loss. The Cunningham team went to Le Mans each year, always doing well but never winning. At the end of the road the Frick organisation returned North, while Bob Blake – who had been responsible for the Cunningham sports car bodies – took the opportunity to join Jaguar and settle in England. He would be the company's leading body fabricator for over 25 years, making D-type, E-type, XJ13 and many other prototypes.

Meantime, Cunningham had turned to racing Jaguars, beginning with an arrangement to run XKD 406 at Sebring (1955) for Phil Walters and Mike Hawthorn. They won, after a lap scoring argument.

Then a new long-nose D-type was prepared for Cunningham to run at Le Mans (XKD 507) in conjunction with the works. Unfortunately, it had engine failure. Undeterred, Cunningham had the car shipped to the USA, and Sherwood Johnston scored a second and then two firsts with it before 1955 was out. The second place achieved at the new Elkhart Lake ('Road America') circuit in Wisconsin, was a famous shoot-out with Phil Hill in a Monza Ferrari. Hill led first then Johnston went in front. Johnston led by several lengths as they went into the final lap of this 150-miler. On the very last bend, Hill shot through on the inside when a tougher nut than

'Woody' Johnston would have 'closed the door'. The Ferrari beat the Jaguar to the line by a few feet in a great race. Johnston went on to win at Watkins Glen and Hagerstown.

At the end of the season, two more works cars (XKD 506 and 508) joined the Cunningham team, preparation for which was done by the Momo Corporation.

Alfred Momo was born in Turin in 1895 (making him 12 years older than Cunningham) and had a distinguished background of aero and automobile engineering at home and in the USA where he had settled, finally, in 1924. Until the war, his main involvement was Rolls-Royce. Afterwards he opened his own small car repair shop and Cunningham (on recommendation) brought his Lagonda along. From that point they became friends and, for a time, partners. The Momo Corporation and Cunningham's Jaguar distributorship were, in the late 1950s, side by side in the New York borough of Queens.

By arrangement with Johannes Eerdmans, 'John' Gordon Benett, and his old friend 'Jock' Graham Reid of Jaguar Cars North American Corporation, Lofty England was able to keep in regular touch with the team's doings. In addition, a degree of rapport was established in due course between the Momo Corporation and Jaguar Engineering. (Momo did his own 3·8 conversion ahead of Coventry.)

The Cunningham team started well in 1956, with Johnston (507) winning at Walterboro, North Carolina and Cunningham himself third in his personal car XKD 525. Sebring presented problems for the three team cars, however; and at the 'Mickey Mouse' Cumberland, Maryland, circuit they finished 4th (Fitch, 508), 5th (Benett, 525), 7th (Johnston, 506) and 9th (Cunningham, 507). The winner that day was another Jaguar driver, Walter Hansgen, in XKD 529 – a 'customer' car owned by Boston engineer Tage Hansen. Hansgen looked like beating the Cunningham drivers regularly, so he was brought into the team at the earliest possible moment.

Sherwood Johnston receives the President's Cup from Major-General Griswold, a motive force in the use of US airforce bases to get American sports-car racing going in the early post-war years. (Each year, still, Sebring continues to remind racers of these conditions.)

Hansgen joined for the 1956 Fort Worth, Texas, meeting. This is what Briggs Cunningham wrote to Lofty England immediately afterwards:

Last Sunday, 3rd June, Sherwood and Hansgen took Cars No. 506 and 507 to Texas for the race. There were 2 races; a preliminary 50 mile event, and a final of 100 miles, on an airport. Hansgen won the 50 mile event, Ferrari 3 litre ran 2nd, D Jag (Brero) 3rd, Ferrari 3 litre 4th, Johnston 5th, Ferrari 3·5 litre 6th. This was just a preliminary qualifying race. Car No. 506 used a 3·54 rear-end with ZF diff, Car No. 507 (Hansgen) used a 3·77 with ZF. Johnston changed his ratio from 3·77 to 3·54, as he reached top revs, sooner than the standard engined car. This actually hurt him coming out of the corners in the race, while in the gears. Brero's D used a 3·77 with Hi-Tork diff. He also changed from Firestones to Pirelli tires for the 100 miles. Hansgen on his car won the 50 miles using Pirellis, but had to go to Firestones for the 100 miler, as we had no more Pirellis. The tire wear was very bad, and in the 100 miler, Brero was leading until he went off the course 2 laps from the end, and was penalized 3½ minutes for not returning to the course *where he left it!* This set him back to 6th at the finish. Johnston and Hansgen both blew their left-rear tires on the same lap, two laps from the finish, necessitating pit stops. Tires blew because they wore thru to the tube. Hansgen went from 2nd to 4th, and Johnston from 4th to 3rd. This let the Ferraris into 1st and 2nd, from 3rd and 5th positions. They were using Pirellis. Katskee finished 5th with his D Jag. Both Jags ran O.K, but the tires just didn't last the 100 miles, as they both started on new tires. Brero also used the Hi-Tork diff which seems to be better for acceleration out of corners, and divides the tire wear evenly, which the ZF doesn't do. Sorry we didn't do better in this event, as Brero really should have won, with Hansgen 2nd.

England replied at great length – encouragingly and helpfully. Clearly, from the volume of correspondence at various levels, the exercise was a serious one.

Back at Road America in June, disaster struck the cars – but fortunately not the drivers. Hansgen rolled 506 in practice. Then, in the 150-mile main race, he did the same

Jaguar did not do too well in the 1955 end-of-season Bahamas meeting, although Johnston led the Governor's Trophy race early on; but De Portago spun, trying to take the lead, and took Johnston with him. Johnston (here) took longer to recover, eventually giving best to De Portago and Hill in Ferraris. (*Courtesy: Joel Finn*)

Plenty of watchers as winner Hansgen laps Benett at Cumberland in 1956. Soon Hansgen joined the Cunningham team and became its star driver. (*Courtesy: C. G. Benett*)

again with 508. Johnston had performed similarly a few laps earlier. Briggs Cunningham himself came 8th, in 525; hardly surprising in view of his repeated views of disabled machines! Jaguar honour was carried that day by Lou Brero (509) and Ernie Erickson (503) who came 2nd and 3rd behind Carroll Shelby's 4·4 Ferrari.

Needless to say there was some interruption to the pro-gramme, and Jock Reid was more busy than ever on special spares ordering from Coventry. It was at this stage that two of the long-nose cars acquired their special 'Cun-ningham looks', as explained in this late-season report from 'John' Gordon Benett – the expatriate Jerseyman working for Jaguar USA – to Lofty England, based on information supplied by Cunningham/Momo:

XKD 506 Larger openings in front of bonnet to give more ventilation to the front brakes and adjustable window shade type radiator blind has been fitted to control the water temperature. A standard production 'D' type rear section has been fitted to this car after the accident and has no fin behind the head rest. A roll bar has been installed in the head rest and has proved very satisfactory. This car has the old 'D' type engine out of Chassis No. 507 and the cylinder block has been bored out 170 thousands and special J & E pistons fitted which has raised the compression ratio to approxi-mately 10 : 1. Also, some special cams have been fitted which were made up for us by the Iskenderian Company which provides far better torque st low rpms.

XKD 507 Larger openings in front of bonnet to give more ventilation to the front brakes and adjustable window shade type radiator blind has been fitted to control water temperature. A standard production 'D' type rear section has been fitted to this car after the accident and has no fin behind the head rest. A roll bar has been installed in the head rest and has proved very satisfactory. This car has the new 'D' engine with the 35–40 cylinder head. The block has been bored out 170 thousands and special J & E pistons fitted raising the compresson ratio to approximately 10 : 1. The engine in XKD 507 is the engine which was originally fitted to XKD 508.

XKD 508 This car is still in pieces and has not been rebuilt since it was wrecked at Elkhart Lake. The engine out of XKD 506 has not been touched since it was taken out of XKD 506 after this car was wrecked at Elkhart Lake.

Racing in 1956 in the USA didn't finish up too badly, though. George Constantine (XKD 523?) won the Watkins Glen Grand Prix, Fitch and Cunningham (525) were second by 7 seconds to a Ferrari in the Road America 6-hr, and Hansgen won the Class C (modified) category for the season. He would do so again in 1957 *and* he was voted the SCCA's Driver of the Year.

For 1957, Cunningham had a newer loan car (XKD 605), which brought his team up to strength after Sebring. It was a good year, too, with Walt Hansgen showing the way – winning many events including the Road America 150-mile race (on the same day as Le Mans!) and the Watkins Glen Grand Prix, making it a Jaguar hat trick there.

There would be *some* D-type racing for the team in 1958 but the new Lister-Jaguars were Cunningham's pace-setters. Hansgen and Ed Crawford were the usual drivers, and Hansgen took national titles again in 1958 and 1959.

XKD 506 and 508 were sent back to Browns Lane where they sat around the experimental department area for

Jerseyman 'John' Gordon Benett and D-type at Sebring 1956. (*Courtesy: C. G. Benett*)

Top Right:

'Just about the most complete parts and service unit in the USA' was how *Jaguar Journal* described the Cunningham rig for 1956. Benett, Fitch, Cunningham and Johnston (on steps) are seen here. Engineer Alfredo Momo made the '3·8' version of the XK engine a reality in that year. (*Courtesy: C. G. Benett*)

Another win for Hansgen's Cunningham team D-type at Marlboro', Maryland. Intakes are non-standard; likewise the fin which had to be fitted on to a 'production' D-type tail after a series of accidents which used up the 'works' tail sections.

Above:
Walt Hansgen (D) dives inside Paul O'Shea (300SL) at Road America, Elkhart Lake, Wisconsin, 1957.

scavengers to feed upon. XKD 507 would join the Cunningham collection and XKD 605 came home.

Maseratis and Chevrolets were the main subjects of Cunningham's attention, but he was back with Jaguar, too, with E2A (1960) and works-prepared E-types, one of which gave him and Salvadori fourth place at Le Mans in 1962. His final fling was with three light-weight E-types in 1963. These did not bring him much joy.

In the mid-1960s, Cunningham decided to concentrate on setting up his museum in California, leaving Momo to pursue his business on the East Coast for several more years until the Italian decided to retire too. Many people in America owe Briggs Cunningham a debt of gratitude for the way he developed their businesses, and a general awareness of sports cars throughout the United States. Jaguar owes him much, too.

Above:

Phil Forno, occasional racer of the Cunningham D-types, working on a racing engine at Browns Lane, Coventry, where he was a trainee. (*Courtesy: Len Lucas*)

C. Gordon Benett (who prefers to be called 'John') was the first person to race an XKSS. He won. Benett, a regular Cunningham team member, was a vice-president of Jaguar Cars North America corporation, maintaining close links with Coventry.

1957 Cunningham team line-up. Nos. 61 and 59 are rebuilds of 1955 ex-works long-nose cars. No. 58 is XKD 605, on loan from Coventry. No. 60 is the Cunningham C6R, by now fitted with a Jaguar engine. It was announced in 1987 that the Cunningham Collection, which includes two of these cars would be sold to Miles Collier Jr.

Chapter Nine

E1A & E2A and the Last D-days at Le Mans (1957-60)

Jaguar's announcement of withdrawal in 1956 was followed by a decade of varying involvement in motor racing. At the end of that time, the merger with BMC ensured that no Jaguar competition programme would be embarked upon by an independent Jaguar company until the 1980s – a whole generation away. When Sir William Lyons and Sir George Harriman got together in 1966, little did either man anticipate the nature (let alone the effect) of the monster to be born in 1968, called British Leyland. The XJ13 – Jaguar's only pure-and-simple competition project since the D-type – would be shelved soon afterwards.

Of course, Jaguars never disappeared from the circuits altogether, even at club level. The total obsolescence of current models in the professional categories would virtually coincide with the birth of 'historic' and 'modsports' racing, which are dealt with in Appendix 2. Up to 1964 (with the exception of one year, 1961) Jaguar personnel would continue to attend Le Mans, to assist the XK-engined runners. It had been the race where Jaguar had made its name internationally and the race for which the D-type had been built. There would be other works involvement, too, and this chapter is intended to outline it.

1956/57 was a bad winter for Jaguar on several counts. On 28 November, a press release was issued: 'For the first time in the history of Jaguar, the company is impelled to institute a four-day week', it began. Publicity chief Ernest Rankin went on to explain that Jaguar had built up its facilities to meet expected demand, only to be scuppered by the petrol restrictions (following the Suez crisis) at home and on the Continent.

Within two months (just after the irrelevant XKSS announcement) on 23 January 1957, 'thanks to substantial US orders', Jaguar was able to revert to normal working. With statistics provided by export sales specialist Ben Mason, Rankin prepared an internal analysis of significant post-war sales to the USA. For three years, Jaguar sales there had been constant at around 3500 cars per year. Mercedes-Benz had approached this figure in 1956, having started with about 500 in 1954. Despite Mercedes sales representing less than half Jaguar's over those three years, the growth-rate of the German marque was clear for all to see. Jaguar was Britain's top dollar-earner, but needed to improve its position further. At 5000 units a year, MG was ahead numerically; but Austin-Healey and Triumph sports cars were increasing their market penetration too slowly, with around 2500 US sales a year each, and Porsche was catching up fast. (It is interesting to note that, as BMC and Rootes failed to take advantage of the potential small saloon market, VW had sold a record 45,000 Beetles in the USA in 1956 alone.)

Sir William Lyons – he had been knighted in 1956 – made it clear that, while the export market remained the prime objective, Jaguar's success depended upon a buoyant home market. 'This should not be lost sight of by those with the power to influence selling conditions at home,' said Lyons, as his response to recent tax increases on cars.

Jaguar was preparing to defend its hard-won position,

and by early February some 200 examples of a new, compact high-performance saloon had been shipped across the Atlantic. This model, the 3·4, was to be announced on 26 February, and nothing – nothing whatsoever – was to interfere with its launching.

On the evening of 12 February 1957, some 270 cars and about one third of the main Browns Lane factory building at Allesley, Coventry, were destroyed by fire. In one way this was a disaster; in another it was no bad thing. The speed of recovery, thanks to the co-operation of the workforce and of suppliers, placed Jaguar in an even more favourable light publicly. Long overdue building work was carried out quickly and, despite the disruption, 1957 was to turn out to be another record year with nearly 13,000 Jaguars produced.

During 1953, 1954 and 1955, output had been about 10,000 cars annually. With the advent of the 2.4, the 1956 financial year (ending 31 July) had taken the total past 12 000 units for the first time. From 1958's 17 500 there was a further jump to 20 000 in 1959 and 1960. Then Daimler was acquired and, throughout the decade of the 1960s, close on 25 000 cars became the annual norm – plus, of course, the products of subsidiary companies, for the Jaguar Group's products would then include Daimler bus and coach chassis and military vehicles, Guy trucks and buses, Coventry Climax fork trucks and fire pumps, and Henry Meadows gearboxes by 1965. (Acquisition of Coventry Climax in early 1963 would also mean a new, peripheral involvement in motor-racing: and the return to the Jaguar fold of Walter Hassan, the man responsible for Coventry Climax Grand Prix engines. This subject is beyond the scope of this book; but it is on record that Jaguar did look at the possibility of taking part in Grand Prix racing long before the connection with Coventry Climax. It is also a fact that a Jaguar-Lotus combine was, briefly, on the cards.)

Back in 1957, the chief reason for pulling out of racing as a works team was the time which would be consumed by personnel who should be undertaking other duties contributing to the production of road cars. An exception was the case of Len Hayden, who had joined the company as a racing man in 1953 and would devote most of his time to racing for another season or two. Subsequently, he would be the chief trouble-shooting link between engineering and production – a thankless task, which he would, nevertheless, take very seriously.

Sebring swansong
On 11 March 1957 Lofty England – newly promoted to the position of Service Director – wrote to Len Hayden, c/o the Pan American desk at London Airport North, to mention one or two last-minute ideas about his trip to Sebring – including the request to make a cushion for Ivor Bueb, who always needed one when driving a car prepared in the first place for Mike Hawthorn. The car in question was XKD 605 which had been painted in 'Cunningham' colours and flown out a week earlier together with a number of spares. Its previous engine (E4003-9) had been replaced by a new one – the first works 3·8 – numbered E5001-10. (Alfred Momo had 'invented' the 87mm-bore XK engine which, once found to be reliable, had been

approved and adopted by Browns Lane.)

Sebring 1957 was, in effect, the swansong of the works team: hence the presence of Hawthorn and Bueb in XKD 605, which would stay on in the USA after the race. The set-up there was that Briggs Cunningham and Alfred Momo ran their team in association with the Jaguar Cars North American Corporation whose Service Manager R. Graham ('Jock') Reid provided the main logistical link with Coventry. There had been a series of three accidents at Elkhart Lake the previous autumn, however, and a replacement D-type for the 1957 season was not going to come amiss at the Cunningham camp.

Particular attention had been paid to braking – a critical factor at Sebring, as 1956 had proved – and two complete quick-change brake sets (including new 'long' rear pads) were among the parts sent out to be fitted to the cars being prepared in the Momo Corporation's workshops in Woodside, New York. Amongst the latest features were stops to prevent a piston coming out of its cylinder if a pad should wear out or break up completely. Unfortunately, brake-pipe failure interrupted a fine run by Hawthorn and Bueb who, nevertheless, scored a worthy third behind two works Maseratis: the 4·5 of Fangio/Behra and the 3-litre of Moss/Schell. Another fine drive was that of Walter Hansgen and Russell Boss in a Momo-prepared 3·8 D-type, on Webers, which came fifth behind the Ferrari of Masten Gregory/Lou Brero but ahead of those driven by Collins/Trintignant and de Portago/Musso. Jack Ensley and Pat O'Connor (XKD 553) retired.

The works might be racing (and rallying) no more but the Jaguar name was still making news in sporting circles. In Britain, the new sensation of sports car racing was the Lister-Jaguar, which was to prove the most effective of all the Jaguar-powered sports-racing cars. Assistance from Jaguar in terms of advice and power-unit supply would be commensurate with the results achieved. In British sprint races Archie Scott-Brown swept all before him in 1957 with Brian Lister's new creation.

Birth of the E-type
Work on new sports cars was continuing at Browns Lane. The XK 150, announced in May, had Dunlop disc brakes fitted all-round but, in other ways, was a stop-gap model in the Jaguar range. In the same month, a much more interesting event occurred, in secret. The first E-type prototype ran for the first time. The date was 15 May 1957. As yet un-named, this car was 14 ft 2 in long and 5ft 3in wide and powered by a 2·4-litre XK engine (E1001-8) fitted with twin SU HD8 carburetters. Bill Heynes drove it on its first test: 25 miles on Friday afternoon, 17 May. Sir William then did nine miles in it before it was hidden away for the weekend. Phil Weaver drove it 55 miles on the next Wednesday and then went with Norman Dewis in it to Lindley (MIRA) on Friday, 24 May, to add another 54 miles. It was painted pastel green the following week. I mention these trivia simply to put on record the timing of the true birth of the E-type.

The neat car is described in Paul Skilleter's book *Jaguar Sports Cars*, and does not belong here except in passing. It weighed just under 16 cwt, dry, and was to become known as EIA ('A' referring to the predominance of aluminium in the construction). It was track-tested tentatively on 4 July 1957 by Ivor Bueb and Archie Scott-Brown. Clearly there were thoughts of developing a competition car from it. So far, evidence of a real break with racing was singularly lacking at Jaguar. Indeed, some thought a return in 1958 quite on the cards.

Ecurie Ecosse, strengthened by the use of more ex-works equipment, and the fact that it was no longer competing against a factory team, reached its high-point in 1957. The highlight was a brilliant win at Le Mans where Ferrari, Maserati, and Aston Martin – the latter fresh from a fine Nürburgring victory – provided potentially strong but, in the end, fragile competition.

It was a simply wonderful tonic after the fire at Browns Lane, where the engines for every entrant – and indeed three of the cars complete! – were prepared. In fact, the competition shop looked much as it had done prior to any one of the five previous Le Mans races. (The 1951 cars had been prepared at the old Swallow Road factory, of course.)

The bright yellow 'Belgian' car (XKD 573) had been back once already since finishing fourth at Le Mans in 1956: in August it had needed considerable detail attention prior to a race at Oulton Park. Now it was to be made ready for Le Mans again. A new engine (still numbered E2079-9, however) was fitted, as was a new gearbox. Power on test was 257·2 bhp at 6000 rpm. Another 3·4-litre engine (E2022-9) was prepared for *Los Amigos*, the team with which Henri Peignaux – Jaguar's Lyon agent, and a notable rallyist – was associated. The car (XKD 513) was prepared in France. XKD 603, sold to *Ecurie Ecosse* with 3.4-litre Weber-equipped engine E4007-9 in 1956, was prepared in Edinburgh by 'Wilkie' Wilkinson: not to be confused with W. ('Bill') Wilkinson, the man responsible for all experimental engine build and test work at Browns Lane since Jack Emerson's untimely death.

Bill Wilkinson provided three more engines for Le Mans 1957, all of them to the new '3·75-litre' specification. E5006-9 for Duncan Hamilton (purchaser of XKD 601) showed 288·2 bhp at 5500 rpm on the bench; a similar spare carburetter engine (E5007-9) gave 280 dead. The third of these 87 mm × 106 mm units (E5005-9, developing 297·5 bhp at 5750) was equipped with fuel injection and thus on loan (rather than for sale) to *Ecurie Ecosse*. It was destined to be installed in XKD 606. The second of the Scottish team's newly-acquired '56 ex-works long-nose cars. (*A third car was being prepared for another use – at Monza. It was XKD 504. See Jack Fairman's story in the appendices.*)

XKD 606 – like 573 and 601 – was delivered to the works competition shop in early June. It had been involved in a minor practice crash at Le Mans in 1956, driven by Desmond Titterington, and remained the practice car. Afterwards the superficial damage had been rectified prior to storage and end-of-season sale to *Ecurie Ecosse* – only for Ron Flockhart to shunt it good and proper in practice for the Argentine 1000 km in January. So 606 spent a long period of hospitalisation in the service department at Browns Lane, obtaining a new front frame, nearside suspension, and bonnet assembly before being passed to Phil Weaver's men for its temporary-loan engine, plus all the

usual preparation such as the fitting of a 2.69 to 1 axle ratio and a full check of all electrical equipment. Dunlop vetted the brakes; Jock Thomson stripped and rebuilt the gearbox (in the service department). Nothing was left to chance.

The three cars (XKD 573, 601, and 606) were given the full works treatment and looked like new cars when they signed on at Le Mans. The French car and the other Scottish one looked fine, too, and all five were a credit to Coventry – although only Duncan Hamilton's retained the traditional 'works' dark green paint job.

David and Jenny Murray, with 'Wilkie' Wilkinson, ran the *Ecurie Ecosse* pit. Frank Kennington was to be Hamilton's *Chef d'Équipe*, with personal mechanic Robin Freeman and Len Hayden, the latter on loan from Jaguar, to look after the car. Tony Gaze and Michael Head and their wives joined the Hamilton crew, which was backed strongly by suppliers' representatives; and there, ready to advise and assist was the forgiving 'teacher' – Lofty England. Among the other specialists from Browns Lane was Malcolm Sayer who kept a full record of the strongest Jaguar race since Le Mans 1953. It was just as if nothing had changed!

The story is a familiar one to those steeped in Jaguar lore. It is a story of annihilation.

1957 Le Mans: account closed

Mike Hawthorn (Ferrari) and Stirling Moss (Maserati) battled for the lead early on, followed by their team-mates, but all were in trouble before long. Ivor Bueb handed over to Ron Flockhart and, with only 10 percent of the race run, XKD 606 was establishing itself very firmly in a lead it would not lose. Aston Martin maintained a challenge, but by half-time it was obvious that a Jaguar walkover would occur. Ivor Bueb and Ron Flockhart were leading from Paul Frère and Freddy Rousselle (573), Ninian Sanderson and John Lawrence (603) and Jean Lucas and Jean Brussin (513). Never before had the marque been in such complete command. Only Duncan Hamilton and Masten Gregory (XKD 601) had broken ranks, but they were rushing up through the field and in eleventh place after twelve hours, having lost close on two hours because of electrical trouble and an unusual exhaust problem: due to the ignition slipping, the exhaust had become excessively hot and burnt through; eventually only a major welding operation prevented the passenger compartment from being permanently on fire.

The leading Jaguar ran trouble-free, except for one involuntary stop to change a light bulb. (The other Scottish car *and* Hamilton's had a similar problem – but, apparently, the two 'production' 'Ds' did not.) The winning car stopped ten times – never for longer than two minutes. The last two stops were completed in less than a minute; though *Ecurie Ecosse* was in no hurry by then, the average speed having come down from 118 mph to 114 mph by the end.

That was still a record which would stand until 1961. The other Scottish team car ran almost as regularly, its one unscheduled stop out of ten being early on, to fix a loose plug lead. The *Ecurie Ecosse* mechanics for this epic effort were Sandy Arthur, Stan Sproat, Ron Gaudion (formerly of the Jaguar works team), and Pat Meehan.

The Belgians were unlucky later on, when an ignition fault saw Rousselle working on the car out on the circuit for 55 minutes before he could get back to the pits. Still, fourth place was salvaged, behind the blue *Los Amigos* car which ran steadily, stopping only as scheduled (nine times).

Ron Flockhart cruising home, Le Mans 1957.

After 24 hours, Hamilton and Gregory were back up to sixth, with only Lewis-Evans and Severi (Ferrari) splitting theirs from the other D-types.

These are the essential statistics relating to Britain's most crushing Le Mans victory of all time, based largely on Malcolm Sayer's notes:

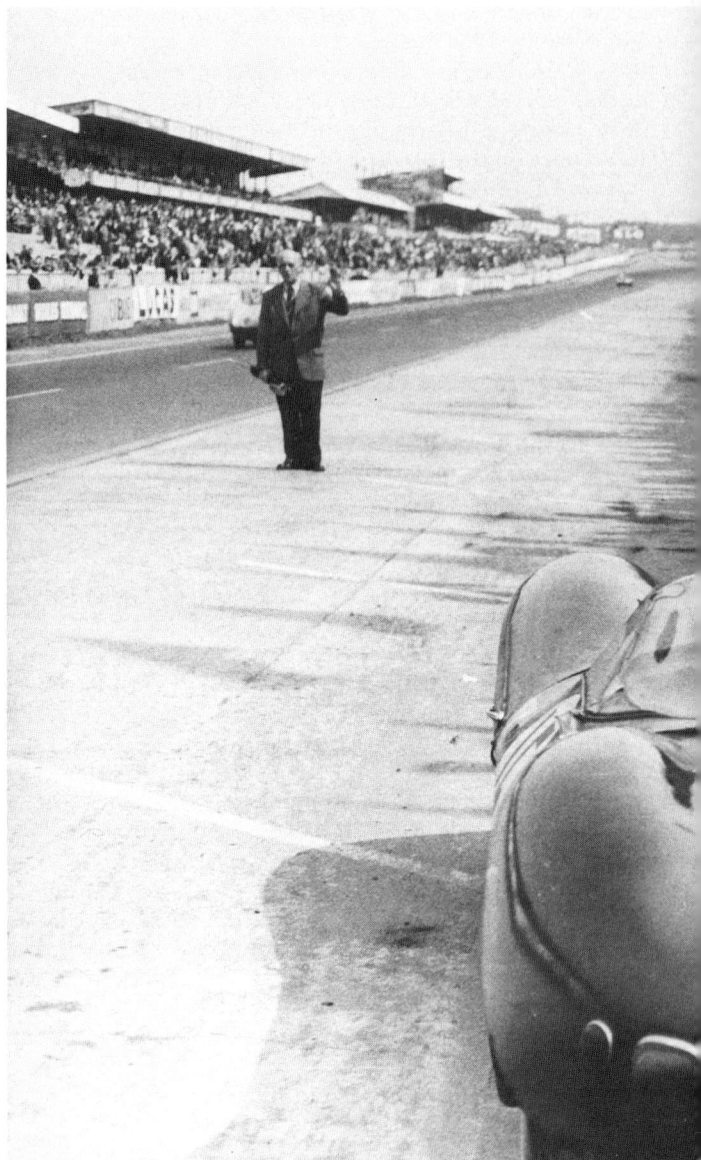

	XKD 606	**XKD 603**	**XKD 513**	**XKD 573**	**XKD 601**
Entered by	Ecurie Ecosse	Ecurie Ecosse	Los Amigos	E. N. Belge	J. D. Hamilton
Year made	1956	1956	1955	1955	1956
Model	ex-works long-nose (works prep.)	ex-works long-nose	'production' model	'production' model (works prep.)	ex-works long-nose (works prep.)
Engine	3·8 (works pi.)	3·4 (Webers)	3·4 (Webers)	3·4 (Webers)	3·8 (Webers)
Race No.	3	15	17	16	4
Total laps	326	318	317	309	297
Fastest lap	4m. 06s. (Bueb)	4m. 11s. (Sand.)	4m. 14s. (Lucas)	4m. 10s. (Rou.)	4m. 08s. (Greg.)
Average lap (excluding stops)	4m. 22s.	4m. 25.5s.	4m. 29s.	4m. 21.5s.	4m. 23s.
Total time at rest	13m. 09s.	15m. 03s.	16m. 13s.	81m. 06s.	126m. 36s.
Drivers:					
start	Bueb	Lawrence	Lucas	Frère	Gregory
finish	Flockhart	Sanderson	Brussin	Rousselle	Hamilton
Final placing	1st	2nd	3rd	4th	6th

Plenty of 'works' faces around when the second-placed D-type leaves the pits. (*Courtesy: P. Skilleter*)

Five Jaguars had started and five had finished. It was, in effect, the final signing-off for the D-type as a World Class competition car. Not for close on thirty years would a Jaguar win a World Championship event again.

Championships had never been Jaguar's goal. To win Le Mans regularly: that had been the aim and the achievement. 1957 was the fifth Jaguar victory at Le Mans, and the third in a row for the D-type. While that purpose-built machine seemed increasingly dated whenever it raced on tight or bumpy circuits, there appeared to be no limit to its capacity to go on doing well at Le Mans – except for one thing: the new regulations for World class sports car racing called for a 3-litre limit and Jaguar's XK engine had not been designed as a 3-litre. It was the start of a new scene, in which the Jaguar car would play only a minor role. Ever since the birth of the Sports Car World Championship in 1953, Jaguar had been one of the top

three scoring manufacturers, despite no attempt being made to go for the points. From 1958 a new name would join that of Ferrari in the leading trio: Porsche would soon be much more than a sports Volkswagen adaptation. In 1957, the watershed year, Maserati were unlucky not to wrest the championship from Ferrari who had dominated it (except for 1955 – 'Mercedes year') from the outset. It was going to take a British company other than Jaguar to topple the house of the Prancing Horse: 1959 would see Aston Martin win the World Sports Car title for the first and only time, and, after years of trying, Le Mans itself.

Below:
'It goes fine when it's not on fire,' Gregory tells England and Hamilton. (*Courtesy: F. R. W. England*)

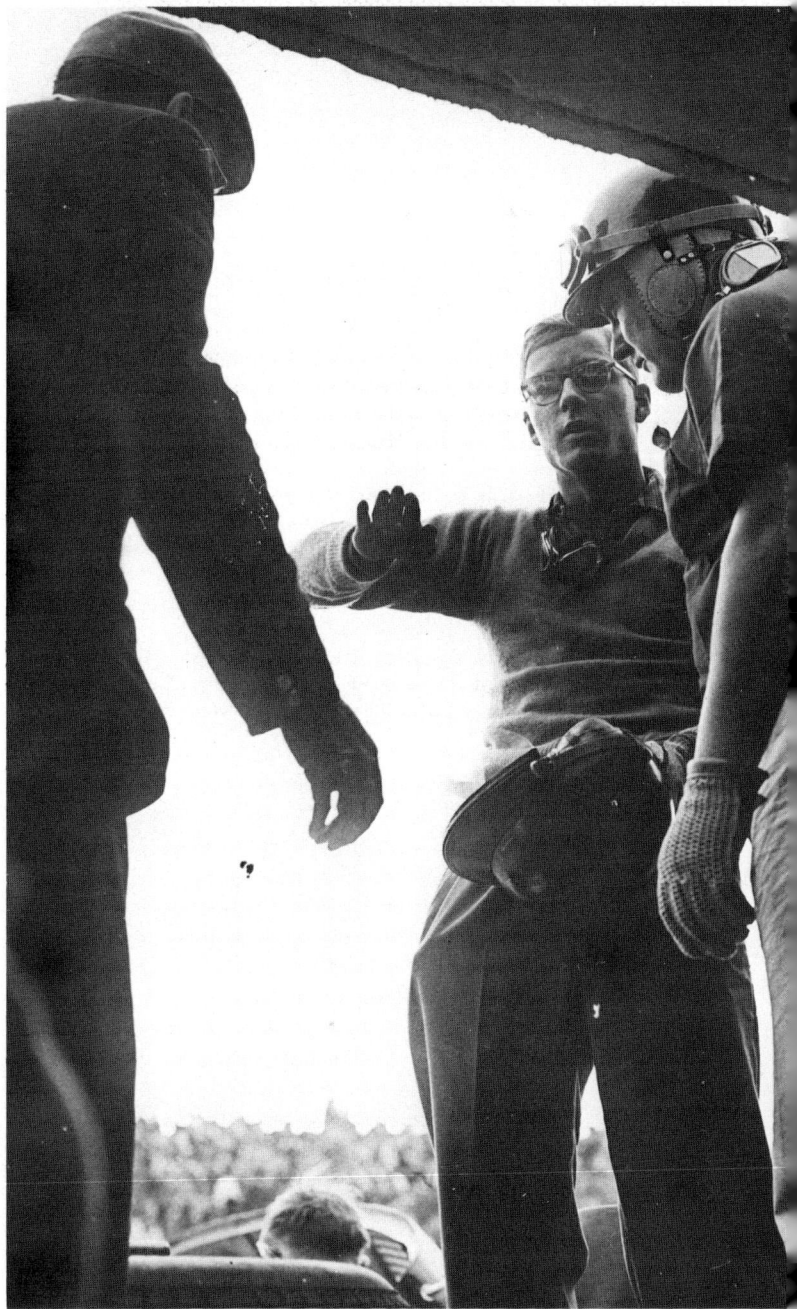

Above:
Masten Gregory in action in the Hamilton Jaguar.

Right:
The second 'Belgian' D-type, XKD 573, finished fourth at Le Mans in 1956 *and* 1957. One intervening event much less to its liking was the 1956 *Daily Herald* International Trophy race, held at Oulton Park in rain so heavy that David Murray decided to withdraw the two D-types he had entered. It became an Aston Martin benefit. Freddy Rousselle, who came eleventh after a few spins, is seen leading Noel Cunningham-Reid (HWM-Jaguar). (*Courtesy: P. Skilleter*)

Below:
The Brussin/Lucas D-type accelerates past the Colas/Kerguen DB3S after Tertre Rouge, Le Mans 1957. The Jaguar was finished third, the Aston Martin eleventh.

Los Amigos delighted with their fine third place, Le Mans 1957. Brussin stands up in the seat. (*Courtesy: Frank Rainbow*)

Jaguar's relationships with privateers led to opportunities to examine other people's racers. With this 'Belgian' Ferrari Testa Rossa on the Browns Lane sports field are Malcolm Sayer, Len Hayden and Phil Weaver. (In 1958, the Belgians also ran a Lister-Jaguar.)

1958 Le Mans: Hamilton unlucky

Largely because of the two successive *Ecurie Ecosse* victories, David Murray continued to pursue an international programme whereas – while the works team had still existed – his team had participated only in selected events abroad. In Edinburgh, 'Wilkie' Wilkinson established a 3-litre configuration, based on the 2.4 block. This 2954cc unit was run on the test bench in Coventry, where Jaguar was developing its own long-stroke 3-litre. Such an engine, fitted with Weber carburetters, recorded 254 bhp at 6300 rpm in December 1957. The compression ratio was 10.25 to 1 and the dimensions of 83 × 92mm gave a displacement of 2986.6cc. This engine was supplied to various customers who needed a 3-litre – but soon it was apparent that none of these adapted units retained the XK's legendary reliability, piston failure being a common occurrence.

Seven 3-litre engines were built for customers' Le Mans entries in 1958. Two were fitted to Lister chassis and the other five to D-types, several of which were prepared at the Browns Lane works. Judging by this extract from a note by Bill Heynes in December 1957 to 'Dear Duncan', it may not have been his intention to become so involved.

I understand from our Service Director that you have now broadcast all the arrangements we have made with you to all the other racing drivers in the country and consequently they are all asking for the same diplomatic privileges that you yourself enjoy, and just what we think about you won't bear printing.

The supply of the 3-litre engine conversion with a 35–40 head is, of course, conditional to having your own engine to convert after we, of course, settle how much this is going to cost you, so you will have to mind your Ps and Qs in future.

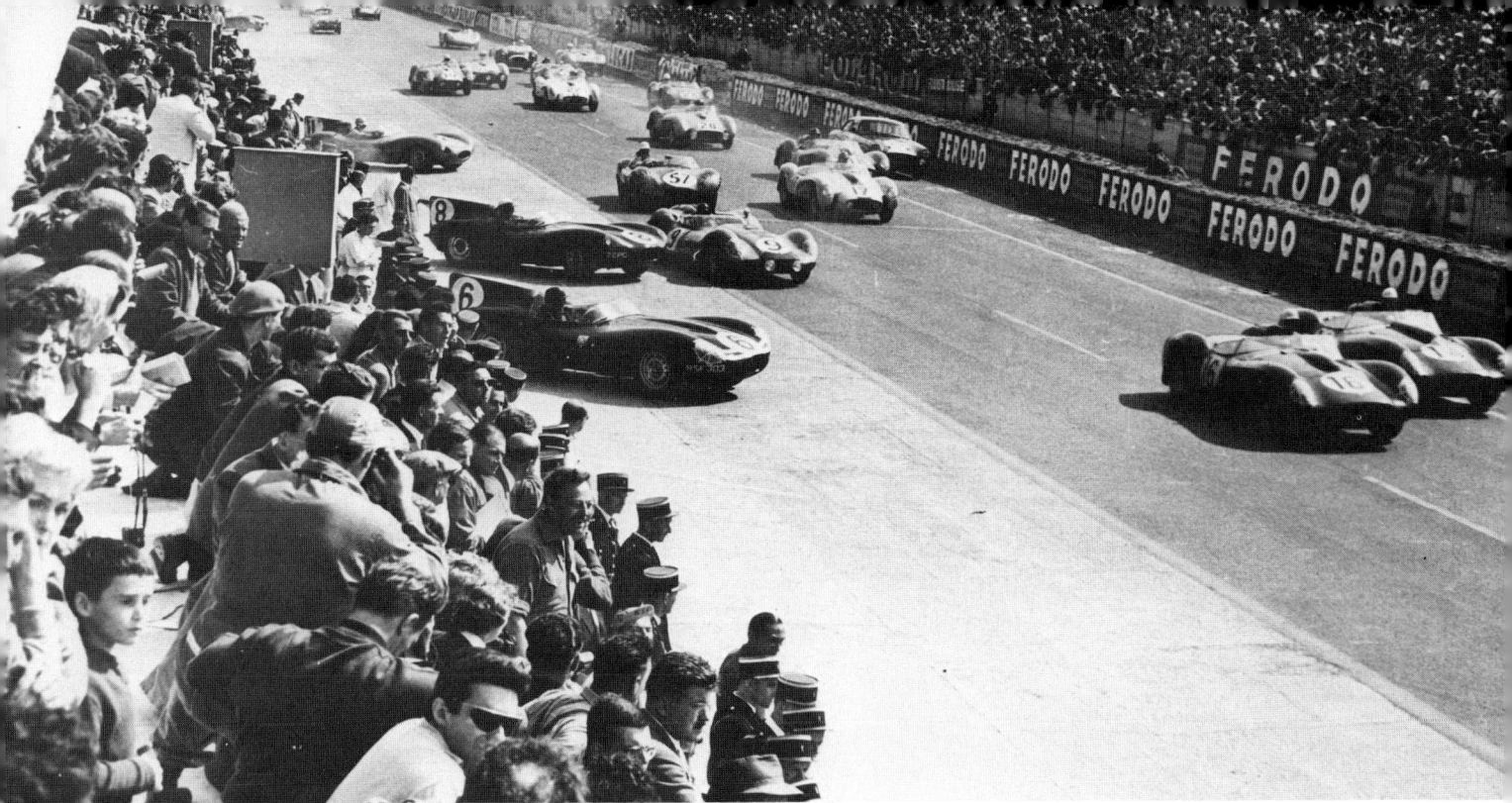

Above:
Duncan Hamilton's D-type hits the new 'Belgian' Lister-Jaguar in 1958, while the D-types of Brussin/Guelfi(11) and Fairman/Gregory(6) are slow off the mark. That year's 3-litre limit brought an end to Jaguar's Le Mans supremacy. (*Courtesy: J. D. Hamilton*)

Left:
Ivor Bueb and Lofty England talk to Jean Brussin at the 1958 Le Mans, before which XKD 513 was thoroughly overhauled at Browns Lane, and fitted with a tail-fin. Frank Rainbow, leaning on the fence, supplied this picture.

Duncan Hamilton's car (XKD 601) underwent complete factory preparation, including the necessary engine change (to EE1202-10) for the 1958 marathon and, with the quick and dependable two-time winner Ivor Bueb co-driving, it looked a certainty for second place. Indeed, the car was leading at midnight while the eventual winner – the Ferrari Testa Rossa of Phil Hill and Olivier Gendebien – was refuelling. It was not long before midday, with nearly 20 hours gone and the Jaguar still pressing the leading Ferrari quite hard, when Hamilton found his chosen path blocked by an almost-stationary car at Arnage during one of a number of cloudbursts. The resultant crash put Hamilton in hospital; the engine was still running well at the time of the incident. Lofty England was there to see that both casualties were well looked-after. The car came back to the works, and a number of items were replaced in the rebuild; this is just one reason for the car's identity problem in modern times, though it remains an authentic vehicle in spirit.

The weather was largely responsible for a number of other accidents, the worst of them claiming the life of Jean Brussin, the owner of the *Los Amigos* D-type (XKD 513), which had been third in 1957. This car had been back to the works for its new engine (EE1208-10) with wide-angle

D-type with hood up – a requirement for 1957, together with more strictly applied Appendix C body and door regulations. (*Courtesy: Paul Skilleter*)

cylinder head – an item it had not had before. When its accident (which also involved Bruce Kessler's Ferrari) took place at Tertre Rouge, the car was misfiring – as it had been in practice – and lying well down the field. This was the only fatality ever to befall a Jaguar driver in the 24-hour race at Le Mans. Maurice Charles crashed his ex-*Ecurie Ecosse* D-type (XKD 502) near White House early on, and had to go to hospital. The two *Ecurie Ecosse* entries retired within the first half-hour, Sanderson going out before Fairman with piston failure depriving (respectively) Lawrence and Gregory of a turn at the wheel.

The Belgians had switched to a new Lister with a works 3-litre engine, which failed in the fourth hour; and, up to then, neither Freddy Rousselle nor Claude Dubois had got it running well – even in practice. Another Lister-Jaguar was left to make history in this miserable race; Bruce Halford and Brian Naylor were running strongly in sixth place at half-time, but then a broken camshaft, a seized gearbox and partial brake failure kept it out of action for a long time. Nevertheless, it *was* running after 24 hours, and was classified fifteenth. The history? Oh yes! This was to be the only 3-litre Jaguar-powered car ever to reach the finish at Le Mans!

1959–60 Le Mans: the last D-days

Four 3-litre cars came to the Sarthe again in 1959 – two works Listers (Bueb/Halford and Hansgen/Blond) and two *Ecurie Ecosse* entries (a Tojeiro for Flockhart and Lawrence and a D-type for Gregory and Ireland) – but no engine lasted even half the distance, although all four cars had reached high positions before retiring. The D-type was the

ex-works car, XKD 603. It was lying second during the fifth and sixth hours, but a warping cylinder head sidelined it in the seventh.

In fact XKD 603 was the last D-type to be works-prepared for Le Mans. It had been brought back to Coventry following a crash in the 1958 Nürburgring 1000km race. Before his accident, blamed on brake lock, Masten Gregory had lapped in 9min. 58sec. – better than any 3.4-litre 'D' had done before, but hardly competitive with Moss's 9min. 43sec. in the winning Aston Martin DBR1. At Browns Lane, just before Le Mans 1958, XKD 603 had been given a new front frame, bonnet, and suspension (apart from the stub axle carriers); also a rear-end rebuild,

Lofty lengthwise. When Pip Shanks lost his Austin-Healey at Woodcote Corner during a 1959 Silverstone club meeting at which Lofty England was officiating, he managed to trap Jaguar's racing supremo in the alcove below the timing box. England reckons he saved Brico's Cecil Winby and Roy Taylor (BOC) but failed to escape the wayward car himself. (*Courtesy: F. R. W. England*)

a new engine (EE1207–10 with 35/40 head) and a complete pre-Le Mans overhaul. Its final visit to the experimental department in Coventry appears to have been just a year later, in May 1959, when its pre-Le Mans preparation schedule again included the installation of a short-stroke 3-litre engine. This necessitated fabrication of new inlet and exhaust manifolds and a new water outlet pipe, all in steel, new engine mountings, new dynamo brackets, pulleys and drive belts, a new rev-counter drive and cable, a new throttle linkage, and alterations to the radiator header tank.

That seems to have been the last time any D-type was readied at Browns Lane for international racing. XKD 603 did pay a final trip to Le Mans in 1960, and once again it behaved well, running fourth for many hours in the hands of Flockhart and Halford, despite the effect of pushing a high windscreen and an ugly hump through the air – these changes being made necessary by new Appendix C regulations. The last D-type ever to race in the 24-hour race ground to a halt shortly before dawn, its crankshaft broken. It would be uncharitable to suggest that this *Ecosse* engine had one of the Laystall crankshafts of which 'Wilkie' Wilkinson was so proud. His view was always that Murray had been talked into using 'works' engines more and more, as they had more power than his variation on

Malcolm Sayer and Derrick White hold a model of E1A.

E1A on the steering pad at MIRA.

the XK theme.

The works *did* have a very powerful 3-litre engine at Le Mans in 1960 – but it was fitted to a development of the D-type that was not a D-type at all.

Hawthorn tests the original 'E'

At first, the Jaguar withdrawal from competition work was temporary. The company was quite open about this. For example, in January 1958, Rankin issued a statement announcing that no fewer than 30 Jaguars had been

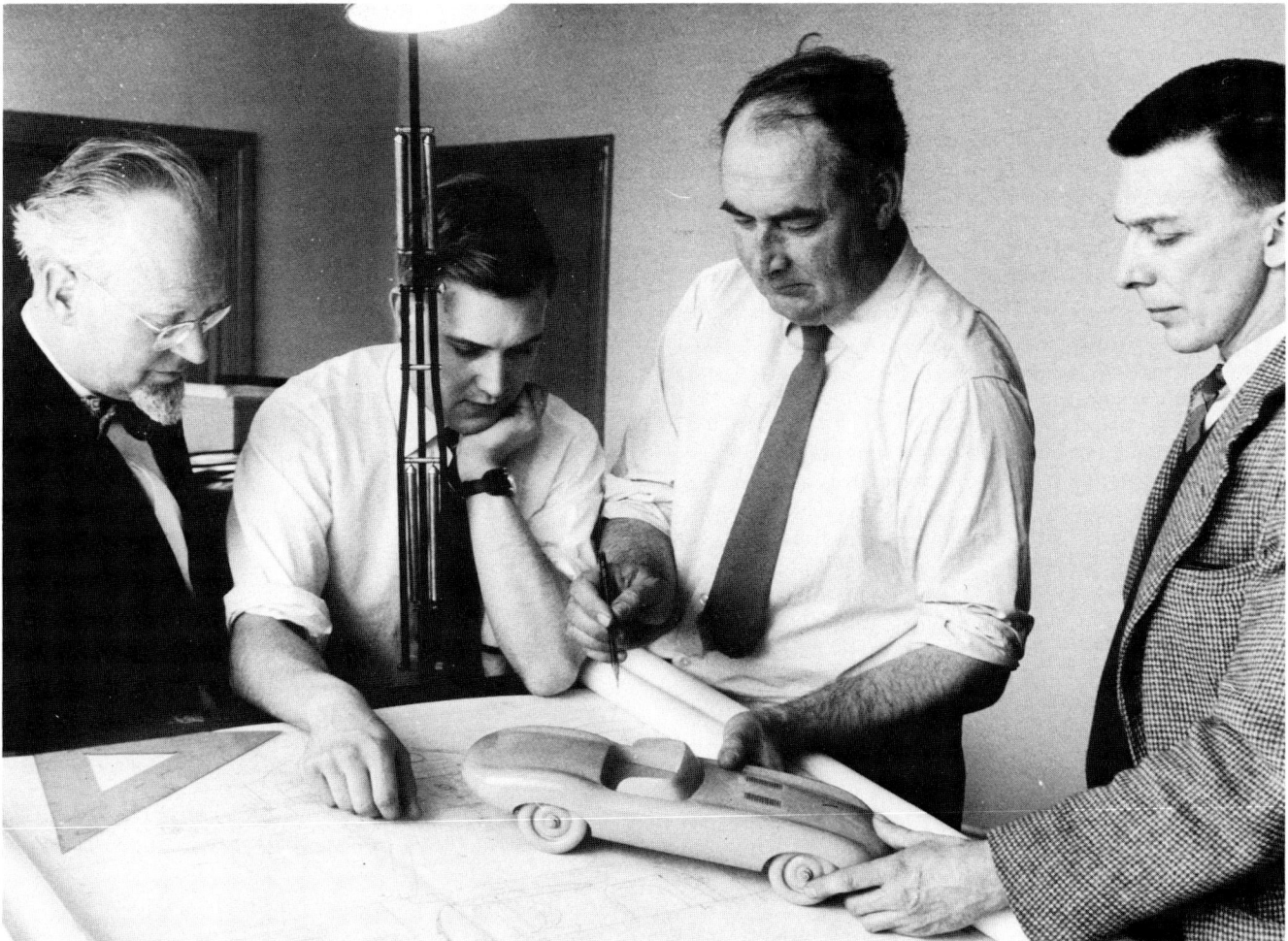

Margaret Jennings in E1A at Brecon.

entered for the Monte Carlo Rally, but that not one of those private entries was 'sponsored in any way' by the company: 'This in no way betokens any lack of interest by the company in the event ... but is simply the result of the company's temporary withdrawal from all forms of competitive motor sport.'

The accent was on the 'temporary'. A similar note was struck prior to Le Mans, also in 1958, when another press release praised the efforts of private entrants and their D-types which 'although they will have been meticulously prepared, this does not alter the fact that they are in effect over three years old.' Rankin emphasised the inconvenience of the 3-litre limit but suggested that the cars were 'still a force to be reckoned with, though they may not start hot favourites'.

For a while, 3-litre versions of the XK engine were believed to have great potential; but their singular lack of success was a great disappointment even to those who may have been cynical about them in the first place.

On the other hand, the light green E-type prototype (which had first run in May 1957, as mentioned earlier) was clearly a 'right first time' concept as a road car, even though it had emerged from a 'racing' design. Now it was covering high mileages. Its independent suspension worked well on the road, and when Bill Heynes lent it to *Motor* editor Christopher Jennings in May 1958, a confidential editorial memorandum followed, describing it as a 'potential world beater'. (That memo and a complete description of the car are to be found in Paul Skilleter's companion volume, *Jaguar Sports Cars*.)

When Jaguar received the car back from Jennings, it was decided to test it at Silverstone again. Indeed it appears to have been track-tested secretly on several occasions. For this purpose, the 2.4-litre engine was replaced by an experimental 3-litre alloy unit. Lofty England succeeded in 'borrowing' his old friend Mike

Hawthorn from Ferrari, and later he sent a memo to Sir William Lyons, with copies to Bill Heynes and Phil Weaver, as follows:

'E' TYPE TESTS – SILVERSTONE, 10 JULY 1958.

Weather: Fine. No wind. Ambient temperature 71°F.
Driver: J. M. Hawthorn.

Car.
Aluminium bodied 'E' type.
3 litre aluminium engine – brake horse power 260 at 6750 R.P.M.
Fuel 100 octane.
Oil Shell X100/30.
Sparking plugs Champion NA12.
Rear Axle ratio 4.09. (No self-locking differential).
Tyres Dunlop R5 Road Racing Speed. Tyre pressures 35 lbs. per square inch front, 40 lbs. per square inch rear.

1.	2 10.5 standing.
2.	1 53.3
3.	1 49.6
4.	1 50.2
5.	1 50.4
6.	1 49.8
7.	1 49.7
8.	1 59.5 stopping.

Rear axle temperature 132°C.
Engine oil temperature 95°C.
Water temperature 65–70°C.
Oil pressure 60 lbs. per square inch.
Maximum R.P.M. on straight 6900.

Driver reports only top and third gears used, engine performance good, handling in corners lacking, due to initial under-steer changing to over-steer, car weaving under heavy braking, severe wheel spin out of corners under power, steering lacks feel.

Caster angle increased by 2° to 4¾° positive. Front wheels changed for wheels having new tyres. Six laps then completed at:-

1.	2 08.6 standing
2.	1 49.0
3.	1 50.8

4.   1 49.1
5.   1 49.5
6.   2 04.0 stopping.

Rear axle temperature 128°C.
Engine oil temperature 85°C.
Water temperature 70°C.
Oil pressure 40 lbs. per square inch.
Maximum R.P.M. on Hangar Straight and Abbey/Woodcote Straight 6900.
Approximate fuel consumption 9 miles per gallon.
Driver reports steering feeling improved with increased center but other comments quoted above apply.

Summary

Prior to commencing tests it was noted that front brake hydraulic flex pipes fouled the wheel rims on full lock and rubber casing of pipes had been cut by wheel rims. Also noted that rear suspension lateral radius rod ball ends still very close to wheels and foul balance weights if fitted on inside of wheel. With steering column and steering wheel raised to give leg room for a tall driver, clearance between wheel rim and windscreen on right-hand side is inadequate. The foot rest for the driver's left foot would be better positioned to allow the driver's leg to be a little more extended when using the rest. The gearbox cowling against which the driver's left leg rests needs heat insulation.

The driver's seat cushion press studs come unfastened when driving the car. Some more secure fastening is required or, preferably, a seat frame with adjustment to suit varying heights of drive, which would be preferable to additional cushions being used. It is also of considerable importance that for future cars we may race the seat cushions are made of water-proof material and that something other than absorbent rubber is used in them, both avoid the driver getting cramp through sitting in a wet seat and to avoid carrying additional weight, the weight of the cushions when fully soaked being something quite fantastic.

The windscreen height at the present time is too low and there is a considerable amount of wind pressure on the driver in the car, due to the low windscreen height plus the absence of side screens. The rev. counter is badly positioned, being blanked out by the driver's left hand when on the steering column, and would be better placed so that it can be seen through the steering wheel, i.e. immediately to the left of the steering column.

It is obvious that to improve lap times the suspension must be stiffened considerably and the roll stiffness sorted out to overcome the change from under-steer to over-steer. It is also obvious that there will be no improvement in lap times at Silverstone until a self-locking differential unit is fitted, together with larger sectioned rear tyres, i.e. larger than the present 600 × 15, and that we might have to consider going up to as much as 700 × 15 if we are going to use the full power of the car on circuits such as Silverstone.

It should also be noted that the air scoop at present fitted for rear axle cooling, which joins up with the brake air scoops, fouls the road under normal touring conditions. While this was not noticed at Silverstone, it would obviously foul on a rough circuit.

The present braking system is obviously not what is required for racing purposes, for which a vacuum servo system is not really ideal.

A five speed gearbox would certainly be advantageous and is really a necessity. I would also suggest it would be of considerable advantage if some form of quick change axle unit could be used, since it would seem that to remove the present differential unit is a major operation, quite apart from changing the gears themselves being a major operation.

I also think it would be worth while either to do away with the steering rack rubber mounting or have very much stiffer mounts.

No doubt it is intended to place the oil tank somewhere other than in the position in which it is now mounted and on the next occasion we carry out some tests I think it would be worth while to load the rear end of the car to the weight which apply if 35 gallons of petrol were being carried in place of the nine gallons, since this might well have some effect on the handling characteristics.

There followed a series of modifications including variations to the roll-centre and the fitting of a 4 HU drive unit with ZF differential (instead of a 3 HU unit). The rear end was strengthened structurally. Notes for the car towards the end of 1958 show that the engine needed developments e.g. 'Engine removed for investigation of loss of oil pressure – crankcase fractured on four main bearing webs.' The last 'Comp. Shop' note says: '1 inch roll bar fitted 3/12/58. Test abandoned because of bad weather'. It is a great pity that Bill Heynes ever ordered this fascinating car to be broken up without its ever being seen in public. He did change his mind, but his orders had been carried out by then. There was a steel prototype, too, but it was meant as a mock-up to test rigidity, although it was driveable.

Jaguar returns – or does it?

The car which appeared at Le Mans in 1960 was E2A – a prototype which *might* have become the definitive new Jaguar competition model. Its original *Autocar* description is included in an appendix. The 'Comp. Shop' notes open with this remark: 'Car commenced building properly Jan. 1st 1960. Car finished build Feb. 27th 1960. First test-run around works Sunday morning Feb. 28th. Mr Heynes drove it up by-pass Feb. 28th. First Lindley test Feb. 29th.'

E2A at Le Mans practice, April 1960, carrying VKV 752, formerly used on E1A.

The engine was EE1301-10 with fuel injection and light alloy block. It was removed on 11 March after gearbox failure at Lindley. Its power was in doubt because it had proved unable to pull a 2.93:1 final drive ratio. Another engine (EE1307-10) with a new type of dry sump was fitted on 1 April. It was removed on the 12th, after the No. 1 connecting rod had failed at Le Mans during tests on the 9th; EE1301-10 was then refitted but it burned its

E2A, unpainted, still had no fin in April 1960 at which time it was geared to do 200 mph at 7000 rpm. Malcolm Sayer later told Roger Woodley that it got up to 6800 rpm on the Mulsanne Straight.

No. 2 piston on test later that month.

The failed gearbox was a 5-speed alloy-case unit. Its top and fourth gear selector retaining pin had broken and the dogs were damaged. It was decided to use a 4-speed synchromesh gearbox thereafter, using D-type bell-housing and release mechanism. The unit gave no trouble during pre-Le Mans testing and a later tendency to jump out of top gear was cured by Jock Thomson re-setting the selector fork on 30 May. New engine and gearbox units were fitted for Le Mans. Between April and June, a new bootlid with fin was made up.

This is how Jaguar explained its position (through a Rankin release, dated 6 April 1960):

JAGUAR DENY RACING COMEBACK

The news that Mr Briggs Cunningham, millionaire American sportsman, had entered two Jaguar cars for this year's Le Mans 24-hours race has given the impression, in some quarters, that this indicates a return of the Jaguar Company to the racing scene. This is incorrect, and the facts behind the Cunningham Le Mans entries can be very simply told.

Mr Cunningham is President of Jaguar of New York Distributors Inc.

E2A, painted in 'Cunningham' colours, at Browns Lane just before the 1960 Le Mans race.

which operates a distributing organisation covering eight of the Eastern States of America, and he is keenly interested in everything appertaining to Jaguar. His other interest is Ocean Yacht Racing, and he skippered the winning American yacht *Columbia* in the America's Cup races in 1958.

He has for several seasons maintained a large Jaguar racing 'stable' in America which has met with considerable success, using such cars as Jaguar 'D' types and Lister-Jaguars.

In addition to the active interest which Mr Cunningham takes in racing in America, he has always been keen on competing in the Le Mans 24 Hour Race and, for several years, ran a team of cars of his own manufacture in this event. The close liaison existing between Jaguar Cars Ltd and Mr Cunningham, coupled with his renewed desire to compete in this year's Le Mans Race, resulted in an agreement by which Jaguar were to prepare a 3 litre car for use by Mr Cunningham. Thus it can be seen that this is a purely private arrangement and does not indicate any intention of Jaguar Cars Ltd to resume sports car racing.

The car itself is not an entirely new design, but is a development based on the 'D' type Jaguar which scored three of the five Jaguar Le Mans victories. It incorporates certain features which have not been previously employed by Jaguar. The power unit is a 3 litre development of the world famous six cylinder XK engine.

As Rankin stated, Cunningham's team had, by then, a long string of successes. These could be traced back to Sebring 1955. Since 1956, Walter Hansgen had been the outstanding American Jaguar driver, often supplying not only overall victory, but useful race reports which were passed on to Lofty England. Hansgen's regular team-mate in the late 1950s was Ed Crawford; but, for Le Mans 1960, England approached Dan Gurney on behalf of Cunningham, and Crawford – who had been nominated to drive with Hansgen initially – was duly peeved.

Hansgen lapped the Sarthe circuit at over 120 mph in April, prior to the engine failure which caused an oil slick on the Mulsanne Straight. The race in June went badly, too, despite a good start by Hansgen. By then the car had been painted in Cunningham's familiar white livery with two blue stripes. Fuel injection pipe failures led to a weak

Ominous puff of smoke at Le Mans, 1960. (*Courtesy: P Skilleter*)

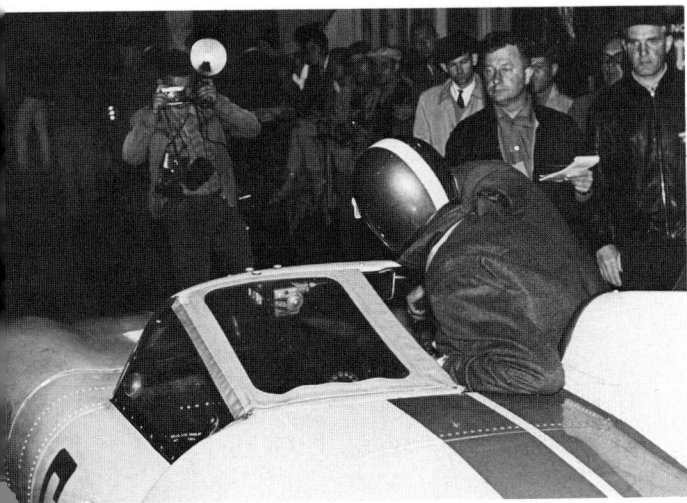

A weary Dan Gurney emerges from E2A. (*Courtesy: P. Skilleter*)

mixture, burned pistons and a blown gasket. In the early hours of Sunday morning, having completed 89 laps (according to Tom Jones's records), the car was pushed round to the paddock. At least Cunningham had the pleasure of seeing one of his new Chevrolet Corvettes finishing eighth.

E2A's outstanding feature was its strait-line speed – Sayer calculating it at over 190 mph on the Mulsanne Straight.

E2A wins one!

In SCCA racing, the Momo-prepared D-types and Lister-Jaguars were able to use the well-proved 3.8-litre engine, and such a unit – EE5028-10 developing 294 bhp at 5500 rpm on triple Webers – was fitted to E2A after Le Mans. This car was generally known as the 'Cunningham E-type' by now; and it *was* loaned to the Cunningham/Momo team for the rest of the season. Its American début was on 27 August 1960, at Bridgehampton, Long Island – not far

Walter Hansgen en route to E2A's only victory: Bridgehampton, Long Island, 1960.

from Alfred Momo's headquarters, where final preparation took place. This included a cutting-down of the high Appendix C windscreen. Hansgen led from the start to finish, followed by Bob Grossman (Lister-Jaguar) and Bill Kimberley (Maserati Tipo 60). There was not much other opposition in this event, which was undertaken mainly to check gear ratios prior to the 500-mile race at Road America (Elkhart Lake, Wisconsin) a fortnight later. There, Hansgen scored a good third place, running on a set of Firestone tyres which lasted the full distance. The only serious problem was the need for high brake pedal pressures. David Causey (Maserati Tipo 61) won from Augie Pabst (Ferrari Testa Rossa). Hansgen could put his wet-weather skill to advantage towards the end but, despite only one fuel stop, he was unable to do anything about the cars ahead of him.

In October, following a Jaguar (NY) press announcement, the Cunningham entourage was in California for the Riverside Grand Prix, in which E2A was driven by Jack Brabham who had just become Formula 1 World Champion for the second year running. The car was just not competitive here, and he had to do well in a consolation race (he came second) in order to qualify for the 200-mile 'Grand Prix' proper. In it, the Australian was tenth, completing 61 laps – one less than the winning Maserati of former D-type driver Bill Krause. Hansgen was able to watch the car's behaviour from Cunningham's Maserati; he noted that Brabham was having to brake very early and that E2A was lifting a wheel and losing traction in the tighter turns. Dennis Shattuck, reporting for *Road & Track* called E2A *Le Monstre II*, because of its ungainly gait.

Bruce McLaren was due to drive E2A in the Pacific GP at Laguna Seca the following week but apparently did not qualify. Stirling Moss's winning Lotus 19, like so many of the new sports cars, had its engine tucked in behind the cockpit. E2A would have been outclassed. "Much too heavy," declared Alfred Momo to *Road & Track*'s Jerry McNamara in a later interview.

E2A was shipped home but was used rarely, although there is still evidence of Maxaret testing. The car was painted dark green and lost its fin. One later purpose was to act as 'decoy' to deceive any prying eyes that might be glimpsing the top-secret XJ13 on test at MIRA from behind the pub at Higham-on-the-Hill. To my knowledge, no XJ13 photographs were published at the time; but then there wasn't the money in photo-scoops in those days.

E2A at Silverstone

1960 was the year in which Sir William Lyons bought-out Daimler, thus acquiring its staff – including the apprentices of course. One of them was David Hobbs, younger son of the Australian Howard Hobbs, already a well-known figure in the motor industry, whose patent manual/automatic transmission (the 'Mechamatic') always seemed on the verge of commercial success. Hobbs had begun racing in 1959 with a Mechamatic Morris Oxford, and in 1960 he was a regular winner in a Mechamatic Jaguar XK140 drophead coupé. Lofty England was always encouraging apprentices in their endeavours and he admired David Hobbs's single-minded approach to motor-racing; it was his sole ambition. 1961 saw the Hobbs career taking a further step forward, with the acquisition of a Lotus Elite (Mechamatic-equipped, of course). Few others had the courage to go it alone in racing in those days, however. When it was decided to compare E2A with the newly-introduced production-series E-type at Silverstone, David Hobbs was chosen to drive it. After several laps the times began to come down respectably and Michael MacDowel – of whom more anon – decided to put out a signal with a time on it. Another apprentice – Richard Hassan (son of the legendary Walter) and then working in Engine Experimental under Bill Wilkinson – was carrying the signalling board to the trackside when it happened. 'I saw the whites of his eyes that day,' he recalled 25 years later.

As was their wont, the small Jaguar group had set up base on the outside of the course, but on the *inside* of the exit from Abbey Curve: there was no bridge for vehicles then. E2A had been powering through quite comfortably, with Hobbs changing up into top gear afterwards. On this particular lap, however, he had decided to get into top before the corner. Somewhere near the apex, E2A took charge and snapped around. It spun towards the Jaguar crew; fortunately all jumped or ran clear, as the car sat, flat-spotted, tinkling, and pointing the wrong way. There were no spare tyres and further tests on them would have been futile. Bob Penney had a puncture on the way home and had to ring Browns Lane for assistance.

Could it be that the inadequate suspension travel, which seemed to affect Brabham at Riverside, had got the better of Hobbs? Just occasionally that excellent Jaguar IRS *can* give you a funny moment on the road if the conditions are right (or rather – wrong).

In the late 1960s Roger Woodley – another Jaguar (ex-) apprentice who was working at Browns Lane – negotiated the purchase of E2A on behalf of his future father-in-law, the collector and photographer Guy Griffiths. Penny Griffiths (Woodley) gave me a memorable high-speed run in it on the long runway of Gaydon, shortly before she took it to the 1970 British Grand Prix at Brands Hatch for a special Jaguar parade – resplendent once again in its 'American' paint job. In 1985 it made its second public appearance, in Britain, when the Woodleys took it to Coventry for a motoring centenary event; and who should be at the wheel? – none other than Sir Jack Brabham himself. Yes, he remembered driving it . . . just about. Not a memorable car, perhaps, but important all the same.

E2A and XJ13 are the two specific links between the D-type era and the modern Jaguar V12 racing prototypes – the American XJR-5/7 and the British XJR-6. The difference is that the car was ALL-Jaguar in those days, from drawing board to chequered flag – or wherever. Moreover, E2A and XJ13 were products of a period of rapid change. Jaguar itself still had racing in its blood – but the adrenalin had gone and, anyway, the regulations and the opposition had moved on a stage. As one-off engineering exercises of the kind at which Jaguar excelled,

Roger Woodley with E2A at Gaydon, prior to its first public appearance in Britain, 1970.

Penny Woodley (née Griffiths) and *Autocar*'s Edward Eves, 1970, at Gaydon air base, the scene (16 years earlier) of the D-type's first test runs.

E2A at Gaydon, 1970, without fin, but still featuring a 3·8-litre engine as fitted for racing in the USA ten years before. (The Woodleys had been considering attempting to reach 200 mph at Belgian speed trials.)

however, E2A and XJ13 are classics. The build quality achieved by Bob Blake and his colleagues was exceptional – indeed, throughout the factory, in the fifties and sixties, there were special skills ready and willing to do special one-off jobs of that kind.

To race or not to race

The Jaguar company was moving ahead so quickly businesswise in the late 1950s and early 1960s that there was little time for the analysis of competition matters. The successes of the 1950–57 period did not provide any real warning of the need to work harder and harder to stay successful. To Bill Heynes, it still seemed feasible to go motor-racing *and* maintain all new-model projects. He had been reluctant to give up racing involvement for any length of time; but when the implications of 1958's 3-litre limit became apparent, he took a more cautious view. In acknowledging the need to keep out of racing then, for example, he had pushed hard for a return in 1959 – but he insisted (in a memo to Sir William, and copied to England), that NO 'intermediate development work' should 'be dished out piecemeal to Ecosse, Lister, Cunningham, or Lotus' –*(hmmm, AW)* – 'either by ourselves or by Weslake'. He also believed that the public announcement – or at least the strong rumour – of a return to racing would add impetus internally. 'The same sense of urgency is never present without a short target date,' he told Sir William, citing Harry Weslake's as an organisation that worked best at the last minute. He made another basic but telling point. 'Dunlops will not develop new tyres until needed. There is sense in this, as tyre development is proceeding very quickly now, and the manufacture of a special tyre that will never be raced is a very expensive experimental exercise.'

Prior to the decision to keep out of racing, Heynes had

Sir William Lyons – who led the cavalcade of Jaguar sports cars at the 1970 British GP meeting – chats to Penny Woodley. (*Courtesy: Guy Griffiths*)

Penny and Roger Woodley in the Brands Hatch cavalcade 1970. *Road & Track* once dubbed this car *Le Monstre II*. Maybe unfairly? (*Courtesy: Guy Griffiths*)

drawn up the following document, headed '1958 Racing – Agenda and Discussion':

1) *Availability of staff to build new cars particularly from the design point of view.*
2) *Interference with current design and development work.*
3) *Value of new racing car in comparison with current production models.*
4) *Possibility of completing the car in time for our next competition season.*

B. *A specification of proposed car will include the following items but it must be remembered that it will be difficult to proceed very far with the design on the car until its known definite whether the competitive limitation is to take place.*

1) *3.4 litre engine 35–40 head petrol injection experiments at present in hand which should give us a further increase in power and we may expect 320. B.H.P.*
2) *Aluminium cylinder blocks are being tried out to reduce weight.*
3) *Experiments with four valve head.*
4) *Independent rear suspension.*
5) *Body shape similar to prototype E-type with improved fairing and larger tail fin.*
6) *Dry weight of existing E-type 15.9 cwt with the 2.4 litre engine; with light alloy block on 3.4 engine this weight would be maintained. Additional lightening on the frame body and front suspension should enable us to get below 15 cwt. If smaller wheels and tyres are used a further ½ cwt can be saved this would give us a car which would certainly last the 24-hour Le Mans race.*
7) *Alternative specification 3 litre car for short circuit work; aluminium block engine, lighter electrical equipment, 15" wheels, reduced fuel tank and battery size, should enable us to reduce the weight of the car still further probably under 14 cwt.*

Even in its lightest form, E2A was not down to 'racing' weight. As for the steel E-type, now well on the way to production: even in the new GT category (as opposed to sports-racing) weight would be the biggest single enemy of a Jaguar racing programme.

Heynes' keenness to race is given credence by various exercises to examine Formula 1. The latest in Cooper and Lotus designs had been studied, and a cockpit mock-up made. In 1960 Bill Heynes was favouring a V8 engine and desmodromic valve-gear. Four-wheel drive was considered and drawn, in conjunction with a V12 – and four-valve heads had been on Claude Baily's drawing board for ages. It may have been the last year of the existing formula but there was no shortage of new ideas at Browns Lane. It would not be long, however, before acquisition of Coventry Climax Engines brought Jaguar into the Formula One arena anyway. This could not help but replace any last vestiges of the idea for a Jaguar Grand Prix car.

The late Jo Siffert joins Penny Woodley in E2A for the Grand Prix drivers' parade lap, Brands Hatch, 1970. Modern Formula 1 seems to have less time for crowd-pleasing touches like this. (*Courtesy: Guy Griffiths*)

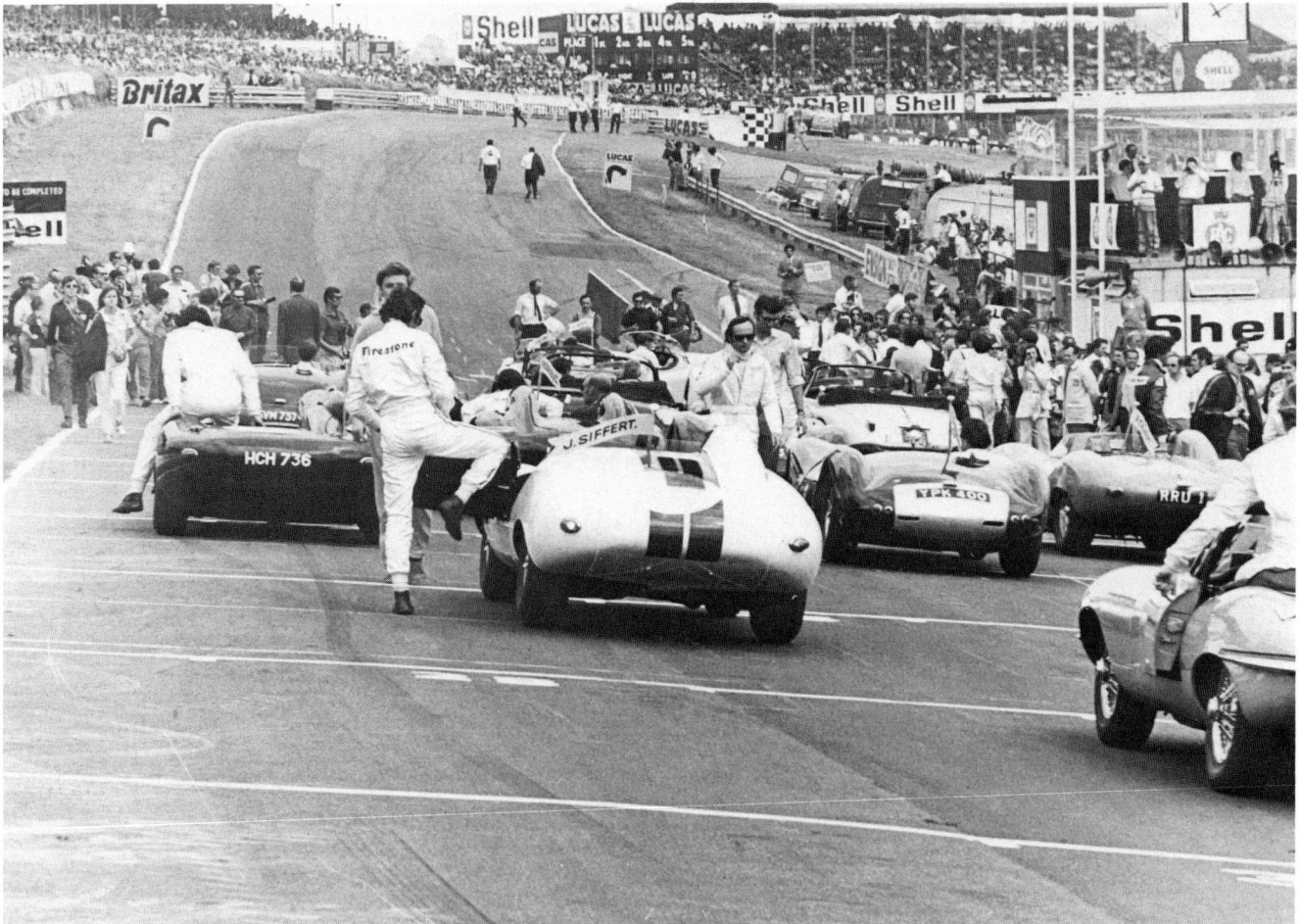

Chapter Ten

The Comp. Shop lives on

The works team had ceased to exist in the winter of 1956/57 but, because of the continuous 'reviewing of the situation' – to race or not to race – a 'Jaguar Competitions Department' continued to exist, well into the 1960s, its original core consisting of Ted Brookes, Gordon Gardner, Len Hayden, Peter Jones, Geoff Joyce, Bob Penney and Joe Sutton. From January 1960 the team was joined by Stan Flello and Cliff Harris – refugees from neighbouring GEC who had moved away, leaving a ready-made office block which was to become Jaguar Engineering HQ and remain so until the late 1980s when Browns Lane ran out of space and acquired a site at Whitley, on the other side of Coventry. Sam Bacon (newly out of his apprenticeship) and George Mason joined the team around that time, too; and when they were not working on favoured customers' cars, there were plenty of other projects – like Maxaret (Dunlop anti-lock braking) development, and prototype work. For example, they carried out Project ZX 530/112 – the fitting of a Daimler SP250 engine into a 'Mark One' 2.4 saloon (chassis number S972046, previously a guinea pig for Dunlop air suspension). They had this car running on 8 November 1960 and developed and tested it over the next sixteen months. The Daimler $2\frac{1}{2}$ litre V8 saloon (using the Mk 2 shell, of course) was announced in the autumn of 1962 and established a special niche for itself in the market. (It also served an important function in softening the blow for traditional Daimler workers and customers. All later Daimlers – unless one counts the limousine differently – have been Jaguars with crinkly grilles.)

Many other people who played a part in Jaguar's competition activities continued to do so behind the scenes, mostly in the engineering and service departments. The latter under England continued to be the 'front-door' for all but the most highly-regarded customers. One very good reason for this arrangement was that the 'Comp. Shop' was at the back of the factory, in the heart of the territory where secret projects lurked. In the late 1950s and early 1960s this meant, among other things, the new E-type and MkX models.

Compacts for competition

Although the main subjects of this book are, essentially, the purpose-built Jaguar competition cars, it would be wrong not to mention the touring and 'GT' models.

From the early 1950s, the big MkVII had proved invincible in touring car racing, although there were occasions in its later life when it had to work hard to keep ahead. The arrival of the compact Jaguar saloons – with the 2.4's announcement in Autumn 1955 – put the marque on top again. The 2.4 itself did well in a number of rallies and races in 1956, but the MkVII was still 'King' with its victories in the 'Monte' and at Silverstone. However, it was the 3.4 which gave Jaguar a big responsibility in providing the customers with the fastest four-door production saloon in the world, as of the spring of 1957. Really, it should have had disc brakes from the outset, such was its performance – and, in early September, it was announced that these would be offered as an option.

Lofty England instigated the publication of 'tuning'

Best touring car performance of the 1956 RAC Rally was put up by Bill Bleakley and Ian Hall in the new 2·4, which finished fourth overall behind the Aston Martin of Lyndon Sims, the XK140 Jaguar of Ian Appleyard, and Dr Spare's Morgan. (*Courtesy: W. D. Bleakley*)

Right:

Lofty England with Duncan Hamilton and Mike Hawthorn who raced 2·4 saloons at Silverstone for the first time in May 1956; but they had to concede victory to their Jaguar team-mate Ivor Bueb who gave the now venerable Mk VII its fifth successive victory in this popular annual event. (*Courtesy: F. R. W. England*)

booklets for the 2.4 and its successors, and kept Bill Heynes informed of race regulations as they became increasingly complex. The *Daily Express* Silverstone meeting had been a Jaguar speciality since the first such event in 1949, always providing the marque with at least one race victory; and, despite the withdrawal from sports car racing in 1957, there was no let-up in the seriousness of Browns Lane's approach to touring car events. Seven weeks beforehand, England sent a memo to Heynes advising him of the modifications permitted for Improved Series Production Touring cars conforming to Appendix J of the FIA Code, Article 263. Even by the standards of Group A since 1982, the modifications permitted then were relatively minor ones. Four cars were prepared for individual entrants, whose names may have prompted Sir William to send England this terse memo on 10 September 1957:

I confirm my wish that you should use every endeavour to prevail upon Hawthorn, Bueb, Hamilton and Archie Scott-Brown to refrain from breaking up their cars against one another.

The race has great prestige importance from our point of view, but little so far as the drivers are concerned.

All these drivers expect our support and preferential treatment, including Archie Scott-Brown for whom we supplied the 3.8 engine [for the Lister

chassis, not *a saloon, A.W.], and we have always been willing to give this. I think, therefore, we are entitled to ask them to co-operate, and ensure that the cars are driven to keep in the lead, not raced against one another.*

I feel very strongly about this. The fact that it is a short race, I believe makes it all the more important.

Businesslike at all times, Lyons was well aware that the new 3.4 must have things all its own way against the likes of Rileys, Austin A105s and Ford Zephyrs; but his message got lost in rubber dust four days later as the four carefree drivers mixed it for their own and the spectators amusement. Hawthorn led throughout, though Scott-Brown was on his tail until Lister's miracle man ran out of brakes (still drums!). Hamilton and Bueb survived to come second and third, giving Jaguar the team prize.

September 1957 *should* have seen the 3.4 score its first win in a truly competitive event – the *Tour de France*

Tommy Sopwith (3·4) leads Mike Hawthorn during their legendary party piece at Silverstone in 1958. (*Courtesy: Robert Trappe*)

Hamilton beats Sopwith at Goodwood in May 1958. With the 3·4-litre engine, the 'compact' Jaguar was in a performance class of its own. (*Courtesy: J. D. Hamilton*)

Automobile. This combination of timed mountain-climbing, circuit racing and rallying was run as two events in one, with separate classifications for Touring and GT cars. For many years these would be dominated by Jaguar and Ferrari respectively. However, disc brakes were still not available and the three competing cars retired. First Consten/Renel led; then Da Silva Ramos/Monnoyeur; then Baillie/Jopp. At Rouen, the British pair had a puncture which pitched their car into the woods where it caught fire – fortunately after the occupants had jumped clear. Da Silva Ramos led again only to retire near the finish, leaving a bevy of Alfa Romeos in charge. In the GT event, Peter and Graham Whitehead were no luckier in their brand-new XK150, despite its disc brakes: a leaking master cylinder could not be repaired and they had to give up. A sad postscript was that, after switching to a 3.4 litre saloon, Peter Whitehead – a passenger at the time – should die in a freak accident while leading the same event a year later. (1958 was another 'Alfa' year, though the Baillie/Jopp 3.4 managed to finish third.) Mike Hawthorn won again at Silverstone in 1958 after a spectacular if contrived duel with Tommy Sopwith. Hawthorn had a special relationship with Jaguar. His first names – John Michael – were the same as those of the Lyons's son, killed in that 1955 road accident, and he may have 'replaced' him in some way. He would attend apprentice events, and became a member of the Jaguar 'family' to such an extent that the whole of Browns Lane seemed stunned on the day – early in 1959, and so soon after he had become World Champion for Ferrari – that Mike Hawthorn, too, died in a road accident.

Right:
Bill Heynes congratulates Donald and Erle Morley at Browns Lane after their 1959 Tulip Rally win. Jaguar treated them to lunch but left it to BMC to reap the rewards of their brilliance subsequently.

Two famous and contrasting cars – Tom Rowe's ex-works Mk VII and Hugh O'Connor Rorke's 3.4 – take Brands Hatch 'the wrong way round' during the 1958 RAC Rally. (*Courtesy: T. H. Rowe*)

The Morleys' victorious 3·4 seen at Zandvoort during the final test of the 1959 Tulip Rally.

In 1959, the 3.4 came into its own, winning not only at Silverstone and in other short races but taking the *Tour de France* (da Silva Ramos/Estager), the Tulip Rally (the Morley brothers) and the Monte Carlo Rally team prize led by Parkes, Howarth, and Senior who came eighth overall. Driving XK140 and 3.4 (and in due course the 3.8 Mk2), 'Bobby' Parkes had taken over as Britain's most distinguished Jaguar user in rallying, following the virtual retirement of Ian Appleyard from the sport.

Bernard Consten was unstoppable in the *Tour de France Automobile*, winning the touring category four years in a row, driving a 3·8 Mk 2 each time. This 1960 Montlhéry grid shot also shows his chief rival José Behra. Visible, too, is the 3·8 of Sir Gawaine Baillie.

The grey cars of John Coombs and the dark blue ones of Tommy Sopwith were deadly rivals during the 3·4/3·8 and early E-type era of touring and GT racing in Britain. The crowds loved it, and Jaguar benefited. This is Brands Hatch.

Opposite Inset:

Bob Jane succeeded David McKay, Bill Pitt and Ron Hodgson as Australia's leading Jaguar driver, dominating the touring scene from 1962 to 1964. Here his 3·8 (increased to 4·1 litres) leads Norman Beechey's Ford Galaxie to win at Sandown Park, Melbourne in 1964.

Britain's most consistently successful Jaguar rally driver (after Ian Appleyard) was 'Bobby' Parkes. Highlight of his career was to win an Alpine Cup in 1960; this picture was taken on Mont Ventoux during the 1962 *Coupe des Alpes*. (*Courtesy: G. H. F. Parkes*)

Special engineering projects were now being instigated for the preparation of 3.4s for racing at home and abroad and the activity escalated when, in October 1959, the 3.8-litre Mk2 was announced with disc brakes as standard. It won almost everything in sight. Cars were prepared for North and South America, Australia and New Zealand, France and Germany. Paul Skilleter's book *Jaguar Saloon Cars* highlights their achievements worldwide. In 1960, there was even a plan to produce a limited-edition GT version, Bill Heynes being keen on making a special production line at the newly acquired Daimler works. The 3.8 remained a tourer.

Bernard Consten (3.8) won the touring category of the Tour de France four times in a row; his third place on the fifth occasion (1964) was a clear indication of Ford's arrival on the touring car scene. A touring car championship of Europe was inaugurated in 1963, and Peter Nöcker was the winner, entered by Jaguar's German importer Peter Lindner, much to Daimler-Benz's chagrin. I always felt that we could have made more publicity out of that particular achievement than we did. The Lindner/Nöcker team did much for Jaguar's sales and reputation in Germany, but was hardly noticed elsewhere. Not

Castrol-sponsored run at Monza in 1963 resulted in four long-distance class records. The works-prepared 3·8 was driven by John Bekaert, Geoff Duke, Andrew Hedges, Peter Lumsden, and Peter Sargent.

until the 1980s would touring car racing begin to attract the attention it deserved.

The battles between the 3.8s of Peter Berry, John Coombs, and Tommy Sopwith continued to enliven the major British race meetings, but the writing was on the wall in 1963 when the Ford Galaxies arrived. People moaned that they had huge roll cages to stop them from warping but Jaguar itself always took the precaution of welding bodies and reinforcing mounting points very carefully when preparing 3.8s.

Down under, Bob Jane was still holding off the opposition in sprint races in the mid-1960s, but could never use his 3.8 – or, rather, '4.1' – in long distance ones like Bathurst because they were for locally-assembled vehicles. Not so in New Zealand, where Ray Archibald and Tony Shelly gave the 3.8 its third and final win in the 6-hour race at Pukekohe near Auckland; the year was 1966, and that was to prove the last significant endurance event ever to be won by a Mk2 Jaguar. 1966 was also the year in

The experienced Eugen Böhringer and his young Mercedes partner Dieter Glemser – closest rivals to the Jaguar drivers in the very first ETC race.

How the touring car championship began: the 1963 6-hr race at the Nürburgring was the first round of the original *Europa-Pokal Für Tourenwagenrennen*. The Lindner/Nöcker Jaguar Mk2 beat the Böhringer/Glemser and Waxenberger/Lang Mercedes-Benz 300 SELs on their home territory by over half a lap, despite a front disc detaching itself towards the end. The handling of the British and German cars was about as contrasting as their looks. Best practice laps were: Jaguar 8 min. 35 sec; Mercedes 8 min. 37 sec.

Peter Nöcker, the first European Touring Car racing champion (1963), with his entrant and regular driving partner (suffering from over-heating!) Peter Lindner, Jaguar's importer for Germany.

Jaguar gave some encouragement to drivers in Australia, where Coventry compacts were the National Championship winners from 1960 to 1963: David McKay, Bill Pitt, and Bob Jane (twice) respectively. Jane – who looked set for the hat-trick when clutch trouble intervened in 1964 – is shown at work at Catalina Park, Katoomba, NSW.

which Jaguar and BMC merged and the pattern of life at Browns Lane began to change.

Jaguar, the supplier

Although the 3-litre rule applied to World Championship sports-car events from 1958, there were still plenty opportunities to race with bigger engines; and, ever since its introduction, the XK engine had appealed to specialist manufacturers and individual 'home-producers' of competition vehicles.

Jaguar was sometimes wary, sometimes helpful, depending on the way a project was being tackled, and how the Jaguar name might benefit from it or otherwise.

There was also the element of enthusiasm. For example, Phil Weaver's personal commitment to adapting Jaguar engines for water-borne vehicles was invaluable to Norman Buckley for his series of record-breaking craft named Miss Windermere. By contrast the four-engined off-shore racing powerboats Tramontana II and Jackie S were spectacular, but rarely came home with the wins which Jaguar needed to stay interested in any branch of the sport.

In the 1970s and 1980s, the V12 Jaguar engine would prove just as effective as the XK unit, when given either of these marine roles. As for Jaguar-powered land machines, there have been dragsters, stock cars, and specials of all kinds – notably emanating from Australia and America but, above all, the UK.

The first XK engine to be sold specifically for fitting to a non-Jaguar chassis had gone to St Helier Garages in 1950 for the use of Jerseyman Frank Le Gallais, who had persuaded Bill Heynes that his LGS hill-climbing special

Christof Von Mayenberg and his very successful record- breaking XK-engined *Mathea VII* at the Wörthersee in the early to mid 1950s.

Above:
Norman Buckley in action with his XK-powered *Miss Windermere III*. (Courtesy: G. Hallawell)

Inset:
Phil Weaver of Jaguar with Norman Buckley after a record run. (Courtesy: C. P. Weaver)

The not-yet-notorious Dr Emil Savundra helps the innocent victims aboard after *Jackie S.* ran amok during the 1963 *Daily Express* Offshore Powerboat Race. (*Courtesy: Daily Express*)

was worthy of attention – maybe because of the Citroën thinking that had gone into its design (Heynes admired Citroën). The mid/rear engined LGS-Jaguar was an effective sprint car, reaching its peak of development in 1957. A noted mainland sprinter of the period was Gordon Parker, whose more orthodox specials – the Jaguara and

Left:
Four XK engines powered *Tramontana II*, seen heading for Bembridge Ledge, 1965. (*Courtesy: Bill Kedge*)

the HK – featured supercharged XK engines.

In racing, HWM were the first 'outsiders' to use a proprietary XK-powered chassis in an international endurance race – the 1953 Reims 12-hour – although Oscar Moore's privately-owned HWM had been raced with a Jaguar engine for nearly two years by then. The first notable success for an HWM-Jaguar came when Lex Davison won the 1954 Australian GP at Southport, Queensland (not far from today's Surfer's Paradise circuit), in his single-seater. Often competitive – as when Abecassis was runner-up to Gonzalez (4.9 Ferrari) at Silverstone in 1954 – the HWM-Jaguar sports cars with their de Dion rear ends proved quite capable of beating the privately-owned D-type Jaguars which began appearing

Phil Weaver with *Tramontana II* photographed at Cowes, 1963, by the author.

Four sets of dials in the cockpit of *Jackie S*, one for each Jaguar engine.

by late 1955. However development became near-static after 1956 when John Heath – partner to George Abecassis at Hersham & Walton Motors – was fatally injured in the Mille Miglia.

Another XK-engined sports-racer of the period, which shared some HWM body design, was Richard Shattock's RGS-Atalanta. It showed flashes of brilliance but only occasionally.

Charles Cooper and his son John were in the motor trade in SW London, too, and their tiny single-seater 500s were forerunners of the cars which Stirling Moss, Jack Brabham and Bruce McLaren would turn into Grand Prix

winners. There were Cooper sports cars, too, and the first XK-engined one looked very purposeful when it made its début in the hands of its owner Peter Whitehead at the 1954 *Daily Express* Silverstone Meeting. He was cautious in this wet race and came ninth. The car had all-independent suspension and outboard disc brakes all-round, and appeared to have potential. It overheated at first, due to an interesting but ineffectual radiator and air intake layout; in reverting to the orthodox the car lost some of the originality of its appearance. The best results Whitehead gained with the prototype T33 Cooper-Jaguar were victories at Snetterton, and in Eire where he won the Wakefield Trophy race on the Curragh road circuit. He sold the car to Cyril Wick who used the car for continental touring as well as racing. Whitehead, meanwhile, brought

Peter Whitehead in the unpainted Cooper-Jaguar, Silverstone, May 1954. (*Courtesy: P. Skilleter*)

a new T38 Cooper-Jaguar for 1955, running it at Le Mans (as he was no longer in the works Jaguar team) only to be flagged-in to retire with an oil leak. He sold it in Australia where it went well in the hands of Alan Jones's father Stan and others. Besides the two Whitehead cars there were four Cooper-Jaguars, all of which showed potential; but the Coopers' hearts were not in them as they were in their new Coventry Climax-engined machines which would help change the face of Formula 1 and sports-racing cars in a relatively short time.

The first Tojeiro-Jaguar was made for the same reason as the first Cooper-Jaguar – because a customer had asked for one. In this case, John Ogier approached John Tojeiro and the car first ran in 1956 with Ogier and Dick Protheroe as the principal drivers. The de Dion rear suspension was not the best of its kind, however, and results were commensurate. The few that were made were very distinctive, good-looking cars. *Ecurie Ecosse* used one from 1958 and acquired another for 1959. Ron Flockhart won a few races for them. The later car was written-off by Masten Gregory who flew out across the Woodcote

Main photograph:
HWM-Jaguar at Brands Hatch in the late 1950s.

Above left:
Richard Shattock had several moments of glory with his RGS Atalanta-Jaguar. Here he follows Mike Hawthorn (D-type), Silverstone May 1955. (*Courtesy: P. Skilleter*)

embankment as the car folded itself up at Goodwood; the event was the 1959 Tourist Trophy and Jim Clark was having a one-off *Ecurie Ecosse* drive. He found the handling weird but he had a sensitive touch and had put the car into quite a strong position when his co-driver lost control. The Jaguar-engined HWM and the Cooper were out of international racing before the 3-litre limit came into force. The later Tojeiro was an occasional victim of the 3-litre Jaguar engine's unreliability, however, and of course this did not help the Royston marque's racing record.

The same could be said of the Lister-Jaguar; but – such was its outstanding record in 3.4 and 3.8 litre forms – its 3-litre manifestation is obscured without difficulty.

John Cooper in the impressive 1954 Cooper-Jaguar, built
for Peter Whitehead.

Right:
Cooper-Jaguar 'Mk II' chassis *en route* to a motor show
(Brussels?), overseen by John Cooper.

Cyril Wick used the ex-Whitehead Cooper-Jaguar for
Continental touring as well as racing.

Above:
The 1955 T38, or Mk II, Cooper-Jaguar takes shape at Coopers Hollyfield Road, Surbiton, premises.

Below:
The characteristic transverse-leaf rear suspension of the 1955 Cooper-Jaguar.

211

Left:
Frank Cantwell's Tojeiro-Jaguar.

Below:
Tojeiro-Jaguar at Silverstone. (*Courtesy: P. Skilleter*)

Gregory shows weird Tojeiro handling.

Right:
Leslie Marr in his Connaught-Jaguar in the 1950s.

Below:
John Harper with the re-created Connaught-Jaguar in the 1980s.

Lister: Best of the Hybrids

The Lister's ascendancy co-incided perfectly with the D-type's obsolesence and Jaguar's withdrawal. Brian Lister was a director of the family engineering company, of which he had been the head for many years. The firm had made some parts for early Tojeiro sports-racing cars, and Lister, already a keen 'club' driver, bought one to replace his Cooper-MG. The next step was to create his own car and he was inspired to do so by his observation of the respective driving and tuning skills of two other Cambridge-based clubmen – Archie Scott-Brown and Don Moore. From 1954 to 1956, the Lister-Bristol and (to a lesser extent) the Lister-Maserati, set UK sports car racing alight, and Lister was about to step into Formula 2 (who knows? – it might have led to F1) when Jaguar announced that it would not be racing a works sports car team anymore. This left both Shell and BP without a major contracted sports car team.

Shell Mex-BP was the joint UK marketing set-up for two major oil companies which, in international terms, were business competitors. Most operations were run separately but one man – Bryan Turle – controlled UK motor sport contracts for both, with a brief to bear in mind the 60/40 (Shell/BP) stake in his firm.

Aston Martin had gone to Esso; and *Ecurie Ecosse* (purchasers of much of the Jaguar equipment) were with Esso already. So Turle felt the need to regain some of the action.

Listers were regular class-winners and, apparently, capable of greater things. Turle's brainwave was to persuade Brian Lister to use Jaguar engines and go for outright victories. Despite the plan to limit World Sports Car championship races to 3 litres from 1958, there were plenty of important events (in the UK and USA especially) for unlimited capacity sports-racing cars. Lister went along with the idea and purchased an engine from Jaguar – a

213

full competition engine, but not one of the new 3.8s. (A Jaguar-engined Lister *did* exist already, incidentally, although customer Norman Hillwood had found Brian Lister reluctant to fit an XK power unit at the time.)

The first 'official' Lister-Jaguar made its début at Snetterton on 31 March 1957, when Archie Scott-Brown put it on pole position for a 15-lap race. He led away in the race-proper but the hydraulic clutch operation failed and left him stranded until Moore and Lister fixed it; after that, Scott-Brown rocketed past the race-leaders to make fastest lap of the day, just for the entertainment. In the same race, Henry Taylor's D-type 'took out' Peter Whitehead's DB3S, and it was Dick Protheroe in the Ogier Tojeiro-Jaguar who won the day from Peter Blond and Max Trimble in D-types. Scott-Brown had made it evident that the Lister-Jaguar was going to be in a class of its own.

I was fortunate enough to see the Lister-Jaguar win its next two major races in April 1957, and the impression it made then is a lasting one. I remember, too, the way in which Archie Scott-Brown – quite unaffected by his short, malformed right hand – threw the de Dion suspended car around with nonchalance, as he pulled clear of Roy Salvadori (Aston Martin DBR1) and the rest in the British Empire Trophy at Oulton Park and soon afterwards in the Sussex Trophy race at Goodwood on the Easter Monday.

The only major modification to this car in its early days was to fit an air-scoop to ventilate the inboard rear disc brakes; otherwise it was right first time. Later in the season

it did not take Lofty England long to say 'yes' to Bryan Turle's request to borrow Len Hayden to accompany Scott-Brown and Lister lad Edwin Barton on a winter tour to New Zealand. Len wrote an article about the trip for the *Jaguar Apprentices Magazine* (of which I was editor). It

Cavendish Morton's impression of the 1958 Lister-Jaguar

Works Lister-Jaguar in Goodwood paddock, Easter 1957.

Brian Lister and Archie Scott-Brown with the original Lister-Jaguar.

opened like this: 'On 3rd January 1958 I boarded a KLM 700 series Viscount on the first stage of a journey to Auckland via the Polar Route. As this route has only recently been inaugurated by Canadian Pacific Airlines, I thought a diary of the flight would be interesting, particularly to those who have not had the good fortune to fly on a trans-continental passenger aircraft of today.' Good fortune! Even today's one-stop flights to the Antipodes – taking around 24 hours' flying time – seem tedious. It took twice as long in those days – much more if you counted the period at rest. The CPA 'plane to which Len switched at Schipol that evening was a DC6B with four Pratt & Whitney 18-cylinder air-cooled engines giving a cruising speed of 300 mph. There were stops-off at Sondreström (Greenland), Vancouver, Honolulu, Canton Island and Fiji. The flying time to Auckland had been just under 47 hours, but arrival (allowing for the international date line, admittedly) was on the morning of 7 January! Len was a seasoned flyer, though.

The Lister-Jaguar did seven New Zealand races – mostly free-formula events – winning two and coming second in two. Brian Lister had met Sir William Lyons at the 1957 motor show. They were very different in most ways; but both men were courteous and businesslike in their manner and recognised these traits when dealing with one another with the result that the car had had a

— CAVENDISH MORTON —

Archie Scott-Brown leads Jack Brabham and the rest at Auckland during a partially-successful New Zealand tour attended by Jaguar's Len Hayden. (*Courtesy: P. Skilleter*)

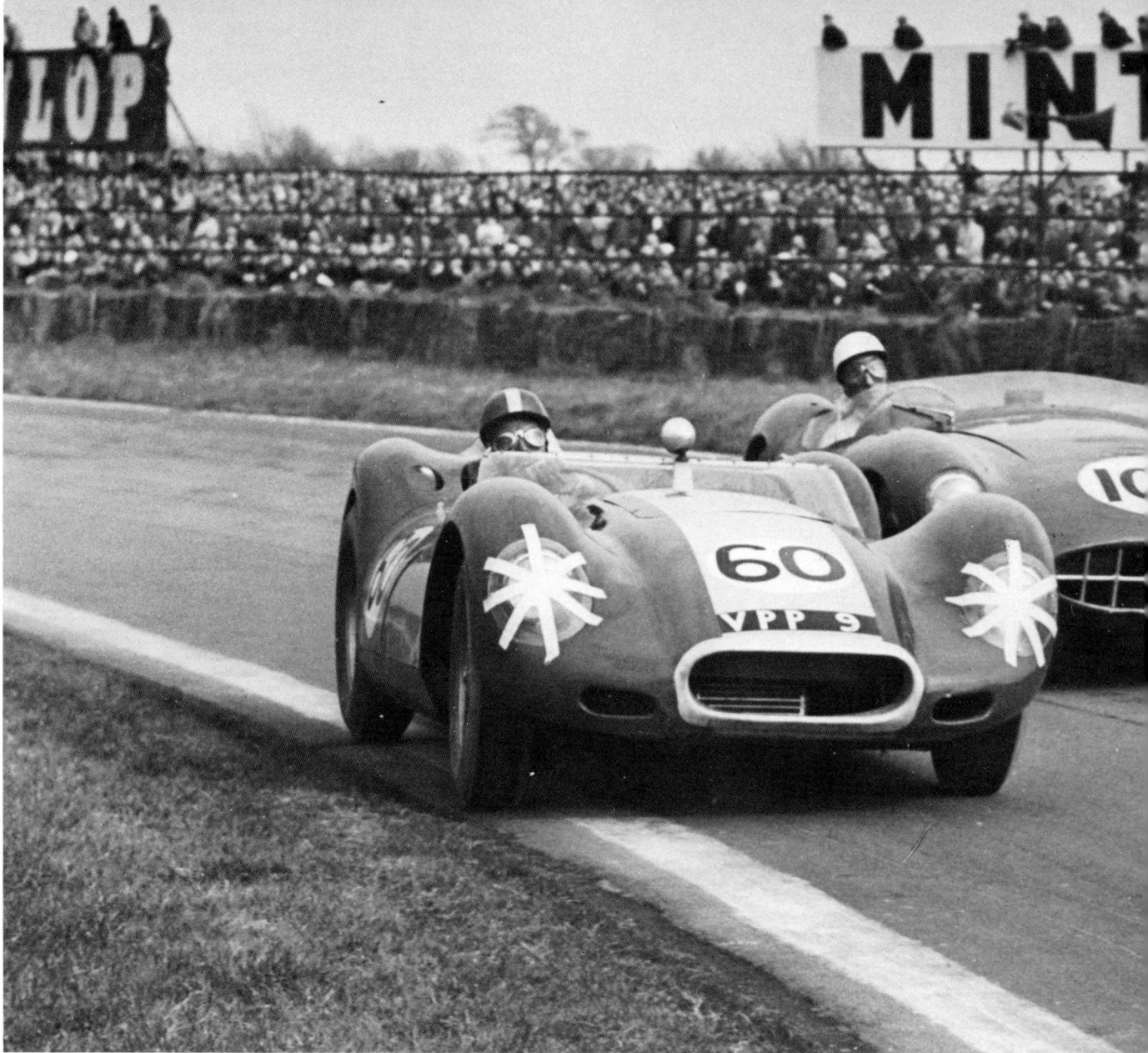

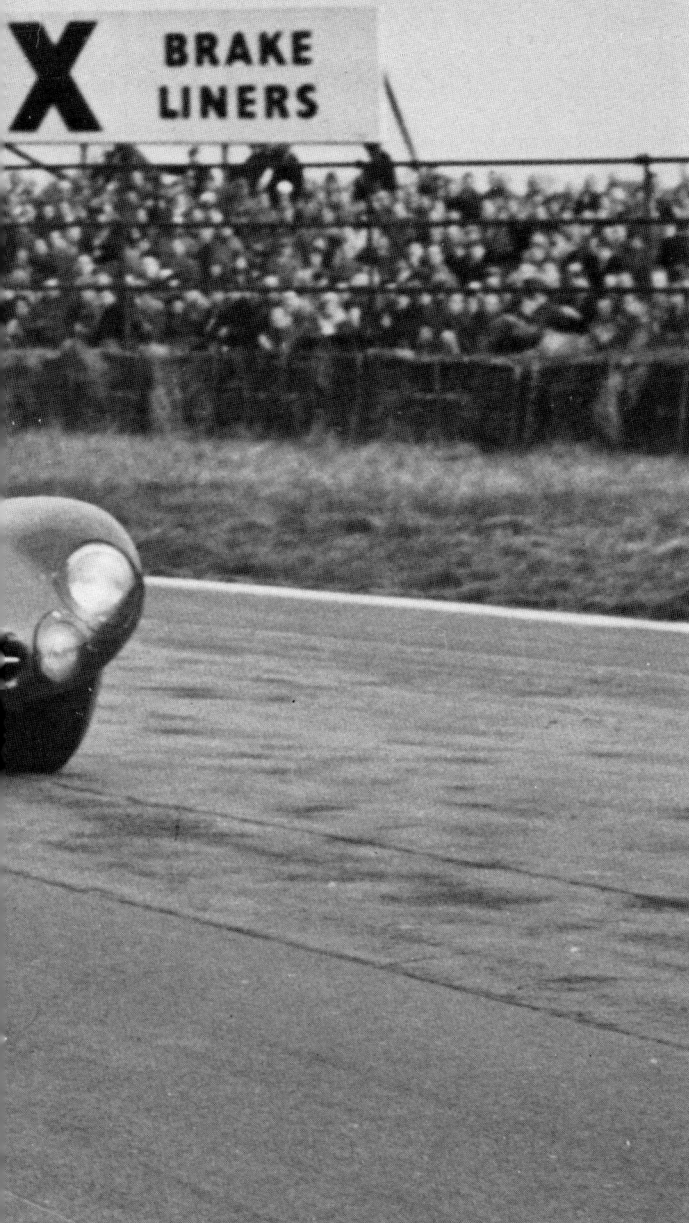

Archie Scott-Brown after finishing second to Masten Gregory, Silverstone, May 1958.

Left:
'Wilkie' brings Gregory's victorious *Ecurie Ecosse* Lister-Jaguar back to the paddock, Silverstone, May 1958.

Main photograph:
Archie Scott-Brown v. Stirling Moss, Easter Goodwood, 1958. (*Courtesy: P. Skilleter*)

3.8-litre engine by the time of its New Zealand tour.

In the middle of 1957, specifically for the British GP meeting at Aintree, the Lister-Jaguar had been modified to meet the Appendix C modifications which were now being insisted upon, and which included the need for a deeper windscreen. For 1958, Brian Lister thought the regulations through, and issued a press release (for publication on or after 15 October 1957) stating his intentions:

THE 1958 LISTER-JAGUAR

This is artist Cavendish Morton's impression of the 1958 Lister-Jaguar. Basically the specification is similar to the 1957 works car which has been driven so successfully this season by Archie Scott-Brown, the main difference being a 10% reduction in frontal area over the 1957 car, (the height of the car has been reduced by 3 ins.) this being achieved partly by the low seating position. The tail, running at the same level as the top of the windscreen, ensures maximum aerodynamic efficiency and has the added advantage of providing extra fuel storage space, (tankage capacity now being 35 gallons). The body conforms to current appendix C specification. Basic price of the complete car is £2750, plus tax. This car offers the best combined price to performance, power to weight, and power to frontal area ratios available anywhere in the world for a sports car.

The 1957 racing season has now ended and out of the 14 races for which they were entered Scott-Brown and the Lister-Jaguar won 11, finished second in one, and had minor mechanical trouble in the other two when in the lead, nevertheless setting up the fastest lap in both races. They have also either equalled or broken the existing unlimited sports car lap record during either the racing or at practice on all circuits where they have appeared.

Any other information required about the latest Lister car may be obtained from Brian Lister (Light Engineering) Ltd., Abbey Road, Cambridge, Tel. Cambridge 55601/2. We welcome your enquiries and interest.

Cavendish Morton had styled the early Tojeiro-Jaguar, too, incidentally.

Among those early enquiries, so welcomed by Brian Lister (who needed to sell cars if he was to stay in the racing game), came one from Briggs Cunningham, who brought Alfred Momo to Cambridge to help him make up his mind. It wasn't difficult. Walt Hansgen and Ed

Stirling Moss wins sports car race at 1958 British GP meeting. (*Courtesy: B.H. Lister*)

Crawford were to dominate SCCA racing with their 3.8 Lister-Jaguars throughout 1958 and 1959. However, the Sebring efforts in those years were not successful for Lister, any more than they were for other 3.0-litre Jaguar engine users.

In Britain, 1958 began with four more wins for Scott-Brown; but at Silverstone in May, Masten Gregory found more speed in the new *Ecurie Ecosse* Lister-Jaguar and pushed him into second place. A fortnight later, Scott-Brown and Gregory confronted one another on the testing Spa-Francorchamps circuit, where the Belgian sports car Grand Prix was held in wet-and-dry weather conditions. The spectacular duo traded the lead until Lister's protégé got into an almighty slide; there was not enough space to correct it and the ensuing crash cost Archie Scott-Brown his life.

Only Lister's newly-won customer commitments kept him in the game; otherwise he would have pulled out. The Lister kept on winning, and for 1959 there was a new shape – by Frank Costin – to be formed, as before, by Charles Williams and Len Pritchard, the panelling specialists. Jaguar continued to be very interested in Lister's activities. For example, Malcolm Sayer would report back to Bill Heynes, whenever he went to a circuit session. This one was on 27 February 1959:

TESTS ON LISTER-JAGUAR   SILVERSTONE

The following points may be of interest:-
1) Best lap times:- Moss (3-litre) 1.45
*   Bueb (3.8-litre) 1.52*

2) These were interim cars, to get the body right for use on the new space-frame car to be introduced this summer. The space frame will weigh 62 lb, a saving of 70 lb.

3) The basic shape of the car is good, although designed purely by eye and without any wind-tunnel work, but so many exits and entries for cooling-air have been added that I think the drag will have increased considerably. Similarly, it has been found that the curved screen offers virtually no protection to the driver, so a perforated perspex plate has been added as shown, which by spoiling the flow reduces the steady blast to a buffetting. This again must greatly increase drag.

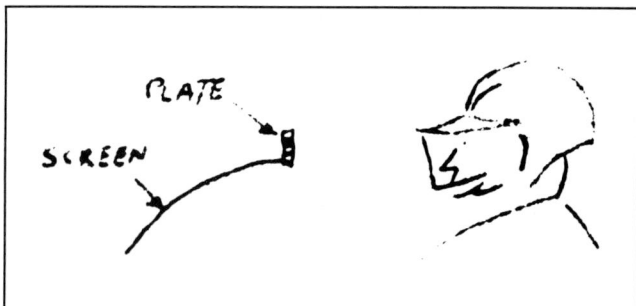

4) Both bonnet and tail are simple skins, having no rigidity once detached. They hook on and are each held by 3 Dzus fasteners. This seems precarious to me, as cracks were already visible round some of the fasteners.

5) As in earlier cars, rear brakes are cooled by a scoop under the car, this scoop fouled the track and came off, and I was told 'They usually did, last year'.

6) At Mr Badger's [of Dunlop] request further holes were cut to cool the rear tyres, but proved too localised so that only the outer half of the tread was cool enough. We left before further tests were made.

7) The 3.8 litre car had only a temporary 5-gal. fuel tank, and a weight of approx. 200 lb was fitted just behind the rear axle.

Top:
Playford coupé body on the last (space-frame) Lister-Jaguar, as raced by Sargent and Lumsden at Le Mans in 1963. (*Courtesy: P. Sargent*)

Stirling Moss and Ivor Bueb proved that it was not *just* the Scott-Brown magic that had made the works Lister-Jaguar so special.

Then, on 23 July 1959, Brian Lister Ltd (the racing had been kept separate from the engineering) made this announcement:

Moss in 1959 Lister-Jaguar at Sebring. (*Courtesy: P. Skilleter*)

Lister-Jaguar coupé raced by Coundley and Fairman at the Nürburgring in 1964, when previous drivers Sargent and Lumsden reverted to their rebodied lightweight E-type. (*Courtesy: P. Skilleter*)

LISTERS WITHDRAWING FROM MOTOR RACING

After six years in the field this company is retiring from active participation in motor racing for at least a year.

During this six year period Lister cars, powered mainly by Bristol and Jaguar engines, have won practically every event of importance in their class at one time or another in this country and the USA.

Last Lister: 1959/60 Frank Costin-designed Lister-Jaguar space-frame car, as converted to coupé by Playfords for Peter Sargent in 1962/63. (*Courtesy: P. Sargent*)

It should not be forgotten that the late Archie Scott-Brown, whose wonderful and courageous driving was an inspiration to all, was at the wheel of our cars for many of these victories.

The main reasons for our decision are:

1. *The incessant changes made to sports car regulations by the C.S.I. leading to unnecessary expense practically every year.*
2. *Competing for drivers with more powerfully backed works teams is making racing uneconomical.*
3. *Motor racing in 1960 is going through a most uncertain stage with the new sports car regulations being applied, with other manufacturers retiring, and with Formula 1 racing in its present form entering its final year.*
4. *The tremendous influx of work into the other departments of our business, and the wish to build up our existing machine shop equipment and capacity. The latter will, of course, enable us to compete even more effectively when we return to motor sport.*

Owners of Lister cars, both in this country and abroad should have no worries concerning spares for their cars, as these will be readily available.

We should like to thank those companies and organisations who have supported us in the past, and hope that when we do return in the future we may look forward to working with those organisations again.

Our last race this year will probably be the Tourist Trophy Meeting at Goodwood on 5 September.

Just after the announcement Ivor Bueb, who had become a regular Lister-Jaguar driver, crashed in a Formula 2 race at Clermont Ferrand and died not long afterwards; and there were other tragedies around that time – Peter Collins, then Mike Hawthorn, then Jean Behra. Racing was going through a bad patch, and Lister – more than most *chefs d'équipe* – was sensitive as well as sensible. In any case, it had to be admitted; the days of the front-engined sports-racer were numbered. He stuck to his guns, and the works Listers were not raced again after the 1959 TT.

The Lister-Jaguar was the most successful Jaguar-powered hybrid of its day, however, and it played a big part in keeping the Jaguar name in the forefront of British sporting achievements.

Chapter Eleven

The Six-Cylinder E-type, and Customer Service

Much could be written about every Jaguar prepared for competition; but the main theme of this book is the *pure* competition car, designed as such. That is something the E-type was not.

While most of the 'front door' competition activity of the early 1960s related to saloons, constant development work on the E-type proceeded in the drawing office and in the experimental/competition workshops. (There was also an unusual customer liaison service, which is described by Michael Macdowel later in the chapter.)

There has been much speculation about the E-type, especially the model known as 'lightweight'. When the early slightly-modified E-type raced and won at Oulton Park and Crystal Palace in early 1961, the Jaguar ambivalence towards motor racing became even stronger. No Jaguar appeared at Le Mans that year, however. (1961 was, in fact, the only year out of fifteen – from 1950 to 1964 inclusive – in which there would be no participating Jaguars.) Nor did any appear at the Goodwood TT – Britain's premier event for the new 'GT' cars. Priority went to the Coombs and Endeavour (Sopwith) teams, which had shown their dominance in saloon car racing; and it was the Coombs car (chassis 850006) which came to Jaguar at the end of the season and became the guinea pig 'lightweight'. Although he had driven the Sopwith car to victory at Oulton Park, Graham Hill became the regular tester and driver of Coombs' machine, registered 4 WPD for 1962. (Previously it was BUY 1.)

The appeal of the new GT World Championship of 1961 must have been one reason for the decision within Jaguar to try and make a competition car of the E-type.

Here was a formula which would permit continued development of the reliable 3.8-litre engine for racing in international events and, in theory, satisfy Jaguar's supporters. (After four years away from racing there was plenty of external pressure, but the volume of resultant hot air within Jaguar was to prove disproportionate.) The E-type *did* look like the D-type and, to some eyes, E2A's good points *did* outweigh its failings as a racing car.

Yet, by comparison, Ferrari were perfectly placed for GT racing. The 250GT was already well-proved. At Le Mans its reliability and speed had given it 3rd, 4th, 5th and 6th places in 1959 (behind the works Aston Martin DBR1 prototypes); in 1960 they achieved 4th through 7th. Ferrari's Scaglietti-bodied 250GT Berlinetta was the epitome of *gran turismo*; no matter that it was harsh and noisy for touring on the road, its performance in competition was grand indeed. And there was more to come from Maranello.

If Jaguar had developed its competition version alongside the production prototypes, and if the roadster-based 'lightweight' E-type had been ready in 1961 instead of two years later, then it might have had more success. As things were, the struggle was a continual one. The accomplished South African engineer Derrick White, who had been with Connaught, was now at Jaguar and he was assigned the work. After Roy Salvadori crashed the Coombs E-type at Goodwood on Easter Monday 1962, it was rebuilt with many non-standard parts, thus beginning the true 'lightweight' gestation stage. Throughout 1962, White, Mac-

E-type evolution. One picture tells the story. This shot of a BBC TV *Wheelbase* scene was taken at Browns Lane in the 1960s. Ron Bromage of the service department's competition 'detachment' is at the wheel of the D-type.

Dowel, Hill and the 'comp. shop' team laboured on the Coombs car and improving it all the time; but, they were rewarded with only a few minor wins. By August, Hill was able to lap Silverstone consistently in 1min. 45sec. thanks to improvements in handling.

Roy Salvadori made up for his Easter transgression, returning to Goodwood to score a very respectable fourth place in the TT with this car. Le Mans 1962 had produced a good result for him too, with a fourth place in the production-type coupé specially prepared with a full-

house dry-sump cast iron block engine at the works for Briggs Cunningham, who co-drove. Shortly before the end, they overtook Peter Lumsden and Peter Sargent in their Playford-prepared E-type (850009) which might have come third overall, but spent the last part of the race restricted to top gear. Lumsden and Sargent were fifth, in the end.

Below: Right:
Jaguar 3·8-litre Mk2 'County' – a one-off estate car owned (but not built) by Jaguar Cars Ltd. It made a useful high-speed tender car for races and rallies. (The author took these pictures during the 1962 *Tour de France Automobile*.)

E-type's race début, Oulton Park, April 1961. Salvadori leads Hill temporarily. They would come third and first for Coombs and Sopwith respectively.

Below:
Second circuit appearance of the E-type: Crystal Palace, May 1961. The Jaguars of Roy Salvadori and Jack Sears would beat the Ferraris of Graham Whitehead and Mike Parkes, the latter failing to finish after several spins.

Below right Inset:
Salvadori wins for John Coombs at Crystal Palace on Whit-Monday, 1961. With two wins in two races, the E-type stood little chance of remaining the simple road car its creators had envisaged.

Above right Inset:
Peco Trophy Race, Brands Hatch, August Bank Holiday 1961. The Ferrari Berlinettas of Moss and Parkes lead the Jaguars of Hill, Salvadori, and McLaren. The final order was Moss 1st, McLaren 2nd, Salvadori 3rd; Hill and Parkes suffered punctures. In practice the Ferrari of Moss (1 m. 52·4s.) had been 1·2 sec. quicker than the fastest Jaguar – the Coombs car driven by Salvadori. The writing was on the wall for the 'production' E-type.

Despite the loan of a works engine the John Coundley/Maurice Charles entry failed early. This fourth/fifth result was an excellent one, otherwise. On the other hand, the two successful Jaguars were beaten by a pair of the very latest GT Ferraris – the 250 GTO model. After the race the Cunningham car sat in Experimental and John Coundley tried to buy it. On learning of this, Cunningham arranged to have it in America, where it raced once or twice. This nice, original, racing E-type was still a feature of the wonderful Cunningham collection in California when these words were written.

The low drag coupé
Begun in 1961, the 'low drag coupé' had the look of a winner. It was presented by Derrick White and Tom Jones to Bill Heynes as a project on 2 January 1962. It was one of a batch of four (or six?) such cars planned, but only it was completed. Its specification included an alloy 3.8 dry-

The 'Coombs car', still with soft-top. Oulton Park, early 1962.

Left:
4 WPD, now with hard-top, Silverstone 1962.

sump fuel injection, 9.5 to 1 engine with squish-crown pistons, lightened flywheel and 35/40 head. A D-type all-synchromesh gearbox was specified, with Plessey brake-boost pump driven off it. The body was described as having 'light gauge steel panels off production tools; L.A. coupé lid riveted on'. Bonnet, doors and seat frames were in alloy, windows in perspex. This was the car (numbered EC1001) whose curvaceous good looks were reminiscent of the D-types: this shape was the trademark of Malcolm Sayer. The special coupé weighed 2188 lb dry, and it was destined to spend a long time in the experimental department workshops, until Dick Protheroe prised it away from Jaguar in 1963, winning a major race with it at Reims almost immediately. (The 1964 fastback coupé

First serious modifications of the 'Coombs' E-type at Browns Lane; boot took fuel tank in well, with spare wheel lying on top.

top for the Lindner E-type was inspired by this car's design.)

The 'Lightweight'

The normal roadster-with-hardtop (an alloy top, not glassfibre as in production) body was retained for the modified Coombs E-type over the winter of 1962/63, when it was rebuilt with extensive use of light alloy – notably in the centre section.

The 1963 competition E-type specification was pre-

PI-type 35/40 cylinder head casting with Webers attached.

Heater hose appears to be in use for this photograph of engine in E-type with dummy of tuned exhaust.

Leicester Jaguar distributor Robin Sturgess was more successful than most of the early 'production' E-type drivers at national level. Here he leads George Pitt (lightweight Aston Martin DB4GT) and Sir Gawaine Baillie (3·8 Jaguar saloon) at the 1962 Oulton Park spring meeting.

Jaguar competition liaison man Mike MacDowel with Graham Hill, who did the most E-type race-development test driving.

David Hobbs in Peter Berry team E-type, Oulton Park, April 1962. (*Courtesy: D. W. Hobbs*)

pared (again by White and Jones) against project number ZP537/50. On 4 February 1963 Roland Abbott, who ran the general office at Browns Lane – and, in retirement would help Sir William Lyons run his farms – issued this memo to the 25 managers and supervisors who would expect to receive such information:

18 SPECIAL G.T. 'E' TYPE CARS

PROJECT NO. ZP 537/50

Will you please note that the 18 special GT 'E' type cars to be built in the Experimental Department and Competition Department have had the following identity numbers allocated:
Engines   EE2001 upwards
Chassis   EC2001 upwards
Bodies   EB2001 upwards

Sixteen days later Abbott sent the same people corrected information under the same heading:

Will you please note that this instruction is now cancelled. It has been decided to allocate identity numbers from the current production 'E' type series: The chassis numbers to be prefixed with an 'S' and the engine numbers to have an 'S' suffix.

Five days later, on 26 February 1963, Lofty England circulated Sir William, Bill Heynes, Bob Berry, Derrick White and Christopher Leaver (MacDowel's successor on competition liaison and administration) with a copy of the RAC's document:

Right:
These two action shots of the Briggs Cunningham/Roy Salvadori works-prepared E-type were taken at Le Mans in 1962 by John Pearson who was present on behalf of the less successful Coundley/Charles entry.

The fourth-placed 1962 Cunningham Le Mans entry, photographed at Browns Lane with stalwart Jaguar 'competition' men Bob Penney and Frank Rainbow.

Below:
The modified Lumsden/Sargent E-type comes fifth at Le Mans in 1962. *Courtesy: P. Sargent*

An early visitor to the sandbank at Mulsanne, the Ferrari 330 GT of Bandini/Parkes is passed by the Bonnier/Gurney Ferrari 250 TR which is about to overtake the Coundley/Charles E-type which was to retire in the fourth hour with engine failure. There had been exasperation even during practice, when the team had difficulty in obtaining the use of a works engine. 'Mr Charles, please put Mr MacDowel down', Lofty had been heard to say in his usual quietly authoritative way.

METHOD OF DEALING WITH HOMOLOGATION OF CARS BY THE FIA IN ACCORDANCE WITH APPENDIX 'J' TO THE INTERNATIONAL SPORTING CODE, dated January 1963.

One of the items confirmed minimum production in a consecutive 12-month period as being 1000 units for saloons and 100 units for GT cars. Another item made it clear that alternative coachwork *could* be declared for GT cars; seen in that context, the Ferrari GTO 'got away with it' as a differently-bodied 250GT, although there was a lot more to it than that. Of course, production E-types were being made, not just in hundreds but in thousands annually by now. The question was: could the specification of Project No. ZP 537/50 be incorporated in the homologation for the E-type? Surely the low drag coupé with its steel centre section was closer to meeting the regulations than a car built in alloy material?

The 18 alloy cars must have represented the reasonable expectation of sales for a stripped-to-the-bone competition car at the time when the project was put in hand. One advantage of the use of production-sequence chassis numbers would have been the opportunity it provided to sell the cars at production prices and related taxes – then add an 'extras' charge to cover costs; and there would be plenty of those. One costly item was the alloy cylinder block; some cars would be switched to cast iron before

their old age. The alloy block, based on the standard-design casting, was not rigid enough; and it presented problems throughout the life of the 'lightweight', especially when the heavy ZF gearbox was attached.

Between them, EC1001 – the 'low drag coupé' – and the 'Coombs' car were the prototypes for the remaining cars. Roger Woodley recalls working in the drawing office under Derrick White and acting as general gopher. It was a cart-before-the-horse job, with drawings and specifications often established from existing one-off parts. The first few cars were done in a great rush, as it had been agreed to supply a car each for Briggs Cunningham and Kjell Qvale in time for Sebring. Only a short time before its 1961 announcement, the production E-type had been given a steel bonnet instead of an alloy one at the instigation of Bob Knight. At one time, glass fibre had been considered; then aluminium. Abbey Panels had made a large quantity of the latter. There was never a shortage, so it seems probable that these were, indeed, adapted for the 'special project' E-types. In the end there were fourteen of them (not counting EC1001, the sole example of the previous project); all are listed in Appendix 9.

Sebring 1963 proved that Ferrari was well and truly in command of sports-prototype *and* GT racing at international level, although the new Qvale-owned Huffaker-prepared lightweight E-type of Ed Leslie and Frank Morrill put in a good steady run to seventh overall after

Peter Chambers, Clive Martin, Ron Bromage, and Brian Jacques in the Monza paddock in 1963 after the Castrol-Jaguar record-breaking run. All worked in the Browns Lane service department. Bromage and Chambers were the department's designated competition specialists.

Dick Protheroe in his 'old' E-type, May 1962.

Right:
Protheroe and EC 1001 at Goodwood in 1964.

Below right:
Ducking for EC 1001 at Oulton Park, administered by David Wansborough during the 1965 TT meeting.

Below:
Silverstone, May 1964. Protheroe (37), Sutcliffe (36) and Mac (38).

Sayer's tail for EC 1001.

A great start for EC 1001 as a competition car: Protheroe at Reims in 1963.

12 hours. Walt Hansgen and Bruce McLaren would have been higher than eighth in the first of the Cunningham lightweights if it had not been for brake trouble. (Cunningham also had his 1962 coupé and a fairly standard roadster on hand, but neither was well placed.)

In Britain, Graham Hill proved the Coombs car in full lightweight guise to be quite a flyer, winning at Snetterton, Goodwood, Silverstone and Mallory Park. Roy Salvadori was sometimes quicker in the Atkins-sponsored car but tended to finish second or third in these UK sprints. He could have won at Silverstone if he had not spun off.

In the Nürburgring 1000 km race, Peter Lindner made a wonderful start (despite not being used to right-hand drive) and led the whole field – prototypes and all – for more than a lap in his brand new car; he was lying fourth (still the GT leader) when the engine failed. British privateers Peter Lumsden and Peter Sargent moved up well after a slow start; then Lumsden crashed after 34 of the 44 laps.

Left Inset:

4 WPD, now the fully-fledged 'lightweight prototype' at Loton Park hill-climb, 1963, driven by Michael MacDowel who had just joined Coombs' staff from Jaguar. (MacDowel perfected this art as a hobby, and would become RAC hill-climb champion twice in the early 1970s)

Right:

Jackie Stewart ('Coombs' E-type) and Roger Mac (ex-Atkins E-type) set off together at Crystal Palace national, 1964.

Below right:

Jackie Stewart wins at Crystal Palace, 1964.

Left:

Hill, Parkes, and Salvadori at Silverstone in 1963. Hill won from Salvadori; Parkes spun off.

Le Mans, 1963

Lindner and his regular co-driver Peter Nöcker were making a determined effort in the first European Touring Challenge (forerunner of today's FIA Touring Car Championship) and did not take the 'E' to Le Mans in 1963: they were busy in the 3.8 Mk2, giving Jaguar its third successive victory in the Nürburgring 6-hour. For Le Mans, Lumsden and Sargent switched to their special Lister-Jaguar coupé, while the Cunningham team arrived with three lightweight E-types, two brand-new. The Lister went out with transmission failure and two of the Jaguars had gearbox trouble. Hansgen/Pabst retired; Salvadori/Richards kept going in the upper gears and then the E-type spun on another car's oil-slick, crashing so heavily that Salvadori, who had not done up his seat-belt, was thrown out through the rear window. Tough as ever, Salvadori – who suffered bad bruising but nothing more – crawled up the bank to safety. The Jaguar was a write-off, structurally.

The remaining car driven by Bob Grossman and the patron himself, looked set for a place in the top six; then in the morning a brake pedal pin broke. Totally brakeless the car charged on through the bales towards Mulsanne. Grossman got the mangled machine back to the pits for a major front-end rebuild. The reward was ninth place. It would be the last 'finish' for a Jaguar at Le Mans until Bob Tullius dragged his crippled XJR-5 across the line 22 years later! Besides the winning, there is ration-free heartache at Le Mans. Needless to say, a Ferrari GTO won the GT category that year; and a new GT car – the Cobra – was noted in seventh place.

In the same month (June 1963) Dick Protheroe finally took delivery of the old 'low drag coupé, EC1001, but beforehand the fuel injection manifold was changed from slide throttle type to butterfly type with $6\frac{1}{4}$-inch trumpets, and the 15/32 inch lift camshafts were replaced by 7/16-inch ones. The Plessey pump was removed and a new non-servo brake system was fitted. Following Grossman's Le Mans fright, a modified brake pedal was fitted to this car and to all 'special project' E-types immediately.

Success at Reims

Protheroe chose wisely if ambitiously for his début with

EC1001, (His previous E-type coupé was now being raced in the UK by a youthful Roger Mac.) There was to be a 25-lap all-comers' race at the French GP meeting: prototypes, sports-racers, GTs – all were invited. Protheroe knew the excellent race record of the C-type and D-type Jaguars at the fast road-circuit of Reims which shared some characteristics with Le Mans. Sure enough, his sleek machine was in its element.

The fastest car – a 4-litre V12 Ferrari prototype driven by Mike Parkes – lapped nearly as quickly as Jim Clark & Co., in practice. It retired early with clutch mechanism failure. Jo Schlesser (uncle of eighties Jaguar driver Jean-

Louis) led next in one of the prototype Aston Martin coupés, but was displaced briefly by Roy Salvadori (Cooper Monaco); both went out with engine failure. Carlo Abate won in a front-engined Ferrari Testa Rossa, but Protheroe held off Bianchi and Noblet in their snapping GTOs by just over a second after more than an hour's racing. So Protheroe was second overall *and* winner of the GT category. Also, he had proved that, given the right circumstances, the right E-type could beat the Ferrari GTO over a reasonable distance. In the TT, however, the GTO held sway again, with Hill and Parkes in Coombs/Maranello Concessionaires' entries taking first and second place, followed by Salvadori (Atkins E), Sears (Coombs E), Piper (GTO) and Protheroe (EC1001).

Jackie Stewart in the 1964 version of the Coombs competition E-type.

Below:
Charles Bridges in his ex-Coombs E-type winning at Snetterton in early 1966. Usually he let Brian Redman do the winning for him.

Above:
Jackie Stewart leads Piper, Sears and Salvadori at Brands Hatch – but there was no holding the Shelby Cobra of Sears. The Jaguar finished second.

1964–a lean year

Derrick White worked hard all winter and got even more performance out of the Coombs E-type, which Jackie Stewart drove occasionally in 1964. Most noteworthy was the drive he put in at Brands Hatch on British GP weekend; he led initially, but he could do nothing about the 4.7-litre AC-based Cobra with which Jack Sears flew that day.

Peter Sutcliffe had crashed his car at Brands Hatch a year earlier, but was the most successful lightweight E-type owner of 1964, winning at Zolder and at Montlhéry. He had a good South African tour, too.

From Jaguar's point of view, however, 1964 was the year in which the marque was overtaken on every side in international racing. The Anglo-American Ford onslaught on saloon car racing had put the 3.8 finally in

second place, and there was no suitable new Jaguar compact even on the horizon. In 'GT' when the Ferrari GTO wasn't winning, the Shelby-developed Cobra was: indeed the Cobra would take the world GT title in both 1964 and 1965. In many races – like Le Mans – to win the GT category did not mean to win outright. Outright victory has always been Jaguar's true aim.

By this time, much of the work on the Coombs car at home circuits was being done by Peter Jones and Peter Wilson; but many of the older team from a decade earlier were still closely involved, including Phil Weaver, Ted Brookes, Bob Penney and Frank Rainbow – and members of the team were often loaned to serious Jaguar competitors.

By now, Briggs Cunningham had finally given up, and the only serious competitor linked really closely to Jaguar was Peter Lindner, the importer for Germany. His car had been modified many times and now sported a 'Sayer' roof similar to that of EC1001. It was a terrible shock when he aquaplaned at high speed in the 1000 km race at

Authentic competition E-type tails: Mike Wright (EC1001) leads Penny Griffiths (Woodley) in the former Atkins car down Shelsley Walsh in 1968, when tyre widths were increasing rapidly. (*Courtesy: Guy Griffiths*)

Alfredo Momo looks at the mess. Two of his Cunningham E-types were out, but one survived to finish ninth at Le Mans in 1963.

Jaguar's Peter Jones works on car No. 15, Le Mans 1963.

Montlhéry at the end of the season. He was thrown clear while the car wrote itself off; he died in hospital soon afterwards. Ferraris dominated, as usual, and Protheroe and Coundley came a subdued seventh, in EC1001.

Le Mans 1964 was the last fling for any Jaguar in the French classic (so it would turn out) for exactly twenty years. It is, I feel, an important bit of history to record the occasion in the words of the late Derrick White. Thus his report to Bill Heynes is included in Appendix 8 (he also sent copies to Sir William, Lofty, Claude Baily, Ted Brookes, George Buck, Norman Dewis, Walter Hassan, Tom Jones, Bob Knight, Christopher Leaver, Harry Mundy, Malcolm Sayer, Phil Weaver and Bill Wilkinson).

Derrick White stayed on for a while at Jaguar, working on the XJ13 project (see next Chapter). Many of his proposals were rejected, especially those related to the front suspension. (Bill Heynes always wanted the XJ13 to have an E-type-related suspension system.) Roy Salvadori was one of the motivators at Cooper by now, and he head-hunted White to be chief engineer. The temptation was

Below:
Briggs Cunningham and Bob Grossman win their class at Le Mans in 1963 and take ninth place overall. The Cunningham cars were using prototypes of Jaguar's new four-speed synchromesh gearbox which would be introduced for production the following year.

great and, after some six years at Browns Lane, he returned to the racing scene. Sadly, Cooper was already going down hill, and the quiet South African moved on to join the Surtees/Honda team for the period 1967/68. In 1969 he joined Spencer King's engineering department at Standard-Triumph, in Coventry; but he did not live to see the development of British Leyland. He was still in his early

project – eventually to become the XJ6/XJ12 in public.

For the record, there is a list of the 15 special-project E-types built, with a few notes on each, in Appendix 9.

Serving the customer

It was a chance meeting at Le Mans in 1959 that led to a change in the organisation of factory-to-customer relation-

Easter Goodwood 1963: Salvadori (Atkins E) and Parkes (Ferrari) lead eventual winner Graham Hill (Coombs E) at the start.

forties in the autumn of 1970 when he was struck down by a very rare and, in his case, fatal brain disease. He was a sad loss to the industry and his quiet intensity did not overshadow his friendly disposition and unbounded enthusiasm. He had a great influence on the production E-type as well as the fast but, inevitably, overweight 'lightweight'. Derrick White was a man of quality. Jaguar was often fortunate in that respect.

At the end of 1964 John Coombs took charge of his car – though little, if any, of his original 1961 purchase remained – for, although several cars remained competitive at national level for a couple of years, the day of the lightweight E-type was done, and Coombs was nothing if not commercial. Interestingly, several lightweight E-types found hill-climbing an ideal niche; but the dubious original homologation meant that they were not always put in the GT or 'production' class. If the light steel (EC1000-series) cars *had* gone ahead quickly in 1961, in parallel with the general introduction of the E-type, there is every reason to suppose that a legal racing E-type could have been a consistent Ferrari-beater through 1962 and 1963 – but Jaguar was no longer set up internally for the pace and style of progress in the racing field, and everyone was looking ahead to the fruition of the exciting new XJ4

Mac leads Sutcliffe at Silverstone, 1964.

238

Two shots of Sutcliffe car when in Bryan Corser's possession, showing effect of rapid increasing in tyre width.

ships on competition matters.

Lofty England was there as usual, giving support to the users of Jaguar engines; Ted Brookes and Frank Rainbow were on hand, too. The story of the meeting was told to me by Michael MacDowel:

After nearly two years in the RAF my old friend Ivor Bueb fixed it for me to be reserve driver for the Lister-Jaguar team at Le Mans in 1959.

The cars were the Frank Costin aerodynamic 3-litre models, built by

Brian Lister who I found to be a most sincere and pleasant person.

Unfortunately Frank Costin had not quite got his calculations correct because at 160 mph on the Mulsanne straight the cars were very 'light' on the front suspension and the tail was very low, causing a lot of angularity to the independent rear axle drive shafts, a power-consuming factor.

Lofty briefed me as well as Brian Lister, and I was permitted to practice in the quiet period before the light failed and, despite the fact that I had not sat in a racing car for two years (and helped by the lack of traffic), my lap times were favourable and I found the car fairly easy to handle, except for the 'lightness' on the Mulsanne high speed kink mentioned earlier.

Ivor Bueb had taken me round the circuit in a road car before practice and pointed out all the land-marks and suggested where to place the car and where to brake etc.

As I came into the pits I engaged bottom gear, but on stopping the engine I tried to select neutral. When struggling to ease the lever out of first, Lofty appeared, peering down into the cockpit and quietly reminded me that Jaguar D-type gearboxes were equipped with a clutch interlock preventing the selection of first gear without depressing the clutch. The famous index finger was extended during the latter lecture and I felt rather deflated!

I had noticed that the heat in the cockpit was considerable, but being a humble reserve driver I said nothing then; but I mentioned it to Ivor Bueb. He had the same opinion and on returning to the garage in Le Mans asked Brian Lister to see if more cooling air could be ducted in.

Frank Costin, being an aerodynamicist, started to work something out involving NACA ducts and low pressure areas but I recall Lofty peering into the car and quietly pointing out that there was a large gap in its bellhousing cover allowing hot air straight from the exhaust manifold to enter the driver's compartment. This was a typical example of Lofty's practical approach to a problem: look for the obvious before you redesign the body!

Regrettably both cars (Ivor Bueb/Bruce Halford and Walt Hansgen/Peter Blond) retired from the race before midnight with blown engines. The 3 litre was never a happy size for the marvellous Jaguar engine. Even so it was a remarkable visit to Le Mans and my meeting with Lofty England was to prove a milestone in my life.

Michael MacDowel competed in speed events over many years in total, although there were long periods when he did not compete at all. The youngest son of a naval surgeon from Sligo, MacDowel was born in Great Yarmouth in 1932 and studied mechanical engineering. From 1951 he

239

Bob Jane in action on Tasmania, 1964. (One of the Longford circuit's two narrow river bridges can be seen.)

Right:
With wider wheels for 1965, Bob Jane leads Ian Geoghegan at Warwick Farm. (*Courtesy: Spencer Martin*)

Opposite right:
Phil Scragg's lightweight E-type at Shelsley Walsh, September 1964.

worked for the Rootes Group distributor in Cheltenham where he met Bueb, and he first raced in 1953 at Thruxton with the ex-Clive Lones Tiger Kitten 500. (A certain John Coombs won the race from Don Truman and Bill Nicholson, later a well-known figure at Jaguar. MacDowel was unplaced, but so was one Ken Tyrrell.) In 1954 he built a Lotus 6 and came second in the 1172 championship which he won the following year in a Lotus 9, taking home the Colin Chapman Trophy. His big success in 1955, however, was to win the 1100 cc class in the last-ever TT to be held at Dundrod, sharing the 'Manx-tailed' works Cooper with Ivor Bueb. For 1956 he built up an 1100 Cooper-Climax himself, and took part in the Rouen sports car race with the works Cooper 1500. His best result for the Cooper team was to finish second in the 1957 Formula 2 Prix de Paris at Montlhéry. He led briefly but team leader Jack Brabham soon showed who was boss. Soon afterwards MacDowel drove in the French GP at Rouen but handed over to Brabham after the latter had damaged his own car; they came seventh. Then he was called up, opting for a three-year short service commission in the RAF's technical branch and motor racing became inpracticable. That invitation to join the Lister team at Le Mans in 1959 had come from his old friend Ivor Bueb, who would be killed at Clermont-Ferrand a few weeks later. Meeting Lofty England at Le Mans prompted MacDowel to write to him and ask for an interview towards the end of his RAF service. He joined Jaguar in July 1960.

At first his main work consisted of customer and dealer relations and technical correspondence. Almost immediately, however, he became Jaguar chief motor sport wallah, organising assistance and service for private

Peter Sargent taking part in a Silverstone club meeting, 1963.

owners. His recollections sum up many aspects of the Jaguar attitude to competition – within the factory and outside – and help paint a personal picture of a fairly small but rapidly-growing car manufacturing business of the early 1960s. I am grateful to Michael MacDowel for supplying the following personal reminiscences:

Very positive support was given by Jaguar Cars Ltd to a number of private people, including John Coombs, Tommy Sopwith, and later Peter Berry.

I quickly became involved with the Competition Shop, which was run by Phil Weaver in Experimental. Bill Heynes was, of course, his direct boss but Lofty had quite a hand in what went on, especially when he became Assistant Managing Director in

Right:
Result of Lumsden's Nürburgring accident, 1963.
(*Courtesy: P. Sargent*)

1961.

All the 'official' *Tour de France* cars were built up by Phil Weaver's department and in 1960 a car was supplied for Bernard Consten via the Paris distributor for Jaguar, Charles Delecroix. The Baillie/Jopp car was also prepared by the 'Comp. Shop'.

I was despatched with Ted Brookes to organise the service points and follow the *Tour de France* in 1960, '61 and '62. They were remarkable times; we used a 3.8 Mk2 saloon in 1960 and 1961 and the one-off 3.8 Mk2 estate car in 1962, as tender vehicles. Michel Cognet, of the Delecroix organisation also accompanied us in 1960, using a Citroën DS estate for the

purpose.

Setting up service points at short notice all over France was quite an ordeal for my indifferent French vocabulary. Following the rally each year meant a lot of driving, we only had a night stop every other night during the 10 day event. The competition cars were incredibly reliable, we never had a major problem and Consten won the category every year I went.

The appearance of the Jaguars always created great excitement for the locals at the Service points. The French had not

forgotten the Le Mans victories, and the name Jaguar was highly regarded. It seems extraordinary in these days that we should have covered such a major event with just one service car, plus the assistance of Dunlop for race tyres at the circuits.

Ted Brookes vowed he would never accompany me after the 1960 event, especially when we blew a rear tyre tread at 100 mph plus on one occasion. He was equally unhappy when I removed most of the exhaust system on our heavily overladen car on a bumpy road in Belgium, at about 6 o'clock one morning. I maintained we had to go quickly between the rendevous points with the competition cars, but I never got the impression he agreed. To his credit he accompanied me in 1961 and 1962; and he still speaks to me.

The factory took the *Tour de France* very seriously. It was a very tough event and I'm sure it helped Continental sales a lot.

When Lofty England was made Assistant Managing Director in March 1961, the Service Division was taken over by Geoff Pindar; I then had the most unusual situation in that I worked for Lofty for competition matters and Geoff Pindar for service. This was further complicated by a number of service-based

competition jobs which were undertaken for a few private owners. Their cars came into the Service department and, whilst I was responsible for sorting out the details and organising special bits and pieces (usually from Engineering), the people who actually did the work came under Bill Norbury, manager of the Customer Service Department.

One quickly had to learn how to be tactful and how to persuade people in Service and Engineering (and Production, if

Bottom:
Peter Lindner (right) and Peter Nöcker collect the new light-weight E-type at Browns Lane 1963.

Two 1964 Goodwood views of Peter Sargent in restyled car.

242

one wanted parts in a hurry) – as well as Spares – to co-operate without actually saying 'Mr England wants this done'!

I had the odd brush with Bob Knight in Experimental who, unlike Phil Weaver, did not always welcome my appearance with a particular problem; but, looking back, I can only say that the co-operation and help everyone gave was incredible,

reflecting the general spirit of comradeship which I found at Jaguar in those days.

I became involved in the E-type in early 1961 and dealt personally with all the people who received early cars. They were the 'chosen few' that Lofty had selected for early delivery and included John Coombs and Tommy Sopwith who raced

The E-types of Lindner and Lumsden were headed by a GTO at the start of the 1963 Nürburgring 1000 km but this aerial view, taken a few seconds later, shows Lindner in the lead – and he was still leading at the end of the lap!

their cars, driven by selected drivers, at the very beginning.

The launch of the E-type was made in Geneva in March 1961 and the publicity was remarkable. It is hard to think of any car making such an impact on the public these days; the E-type was a success overnight and greatly sought-after.

The first race for the E-type was at Oulton Park in April 1961. Roy Salvadori was to drive the Coombs car and Graham Hill the Sopwith car. In practice we had a fuel pick-up problem; a misfire would occur when the tank was about $\frac{1}{4}$ full as the cars came out of tight corners.

We drove (as usual!) both cars back to Browns Lane and worked most of the night in Experimental with Phil Weaver and a couple of chaps. Lofty also appeared and worked with us in his shirt sleeves, practical and positive as ever.

The E-type used an unusual fuel pump which had a small pick up 'well' in the form of a screw-in circular chamber at the base of its tank. It also housed the filter. We increased the depth of this 'well' in an attempt to provide a baffle for the fuel. Unfortunately, although much better, it was not a 100 per cent fix when tested the following day. John Coombs was not best pleased and proceeded to move his car to the far end of the paddock and with his own men modified its system by fitting two conventional SU pumps to replace the one. Much to our embarrassment this worked beautifully for the race! Roy Salvadori led for quite a while but cooked his brakes, leaving Graham Hill to win in the Sopwith car. It was a small but important event for Jaguar: first time out in front of the public with a very standard production car.

Brakes were a great problem with the E-type in the early days, and I did some testing at MIRA in order to give Lofty a report which he could discuss with Bill Heynes.

The Cunningham E-type project for Le Mans in 1962 was a good example of the factory's back-door involvement. This coupé was a slightly modified production example. The car was built-up in Experimental but was fairly standard in that it had the regular four-speed manual box with no synchromesh for bottom gear, and a standard body except for an aluminium bonnet. It had, of course, a very high final drive ratio. I maintained to Bill Heynes that the gearbox would not survive 24 hours of tired drivers double-declutching into first at Mulsanne every lap. He brushed aside my views in his usual quiet manner – and he was to be proved 100 per cent correct.

I *drove* the car on the road to Le Mans. It raced for 24 hours, finished fourth overall and then I drove it back home again. The race drivers were Roy Salvadori and Briggs Cunningham himself. He was a great sportsman and the arrangements for catering had to be seen to be believed. Needless to say, iced Coca Cola was on tap in large quantities throughout. It was at Le Mans that year that I met Stanley Sedgewick. He controlled the lap chart for the team. The standard of the catering I mentioned earlier was reflected in Stanley, being an English gentleman, having a special breakfast served for him: bacon, eggs, toast and real English marmalade, whilst the rest of the crew were tucking in to their waffles and syrup.

Whilst Jaguar was not deadly serious about racing or rallying in those days, Lofty had an uncanny ability to pick out a few people to support, and discreetly give them first-class engineering know-how in areas which, when successful, could only help the Jaguar image; but if unsuccessful, which was rare, the poor publicity could not be laid directly at the factory door. The entrants were, after all, private people who just raced or rallied Jaguar cars. Except for the *Tour de France*, rallying was not of much interest. By the time I arrived, the events were changing in character and the car was not really suitable. We did support Jack Sears and Willy Cave in one RAC Rally, in 1960, but they lost some time in heavy fog on the first night and, whilst they finished fourth it was a large car for that sort of event. (This was

the particular rally which introduced Britishers to the 'special stage'.) The Monte Carlo rally was also not attractive; but we gave advice to a few people and set up some servicing points in co-operation with dealers.

The lightweight E-type was a good example of factory involvement through a private entrant. The Coombs car, finished in the usual Coombs colour of Pearl Grey was always entered by John Coombs Racing. In reality the car *never* went to the Coombs workshops. I drove it to a meeting and returned it to Experimental at the end of the meeting.

All the preparation and modifications were carried out at the works and it was a 'works' car in all but the entrant's name.

The 3.8 Mk2 saloons were a different matter; as I recall it Jaguar supplied the modified parts including seam-welded bodyshells, and Coombs and Sopwith built-up the cars themselves. The engines were built and tested in Experimental.

The private entrants maintained the cars; my job was to go to meetings as the 'factory man' to give advice, or receive abuse which I often did! Actually the abuse was always good natured but I was constantly accused of favouring one or other of the teams. Tommy Sopwith's caravan was always more comfortable than the cab of the Coombs transporter, so I suppose there was something in it.

History will, no doubt, confirm the great success of the 3.8 Mk2 in saloon racing until the Ford Galaxie appeared but the same could *not* be said of the lightweight E.

This, unfortunately, is a little unfair since it was pitted against the 250 GTO Ferrari which was a quite exceptionally advanced car for that time, and is now rightly one of the great classics. The E-type was too narrow-tracked and still too heavy, despite its alloy engine and body panels, but considering it was only a derivative of a highly successful road production car it went remarkably well. No real budget existed for its racing development.

The drivers of those Jaguars which left me with the biggest impression were Graham Hill and Roy Salvadori. Graham was always complaining, bless him, and wanting bigger and bigger anti-roll bars fitted. He could analyse his driving very accurately and could tell the difference a couple of pounds' tyre pressure could give. He often stated, very bluntly, what he wanted done but, even if one could not do anything to help by radical change, he always gave of his best when racing.

Apart from the restrictions of the 'GT' regulations, it was understandable that Engineering did not want to become too involved. Add this to the fact that the era when the drivers requested changes and 'read' their cars was really only just starting. Jaguar traditionally had prepared Le Mans winners by engineering design, and the driver's job was to drive the car and not request any major changes. Consequently Engineering, and paticularly Bill Heynes, did not take too kindly to a driver telling us what he wanted, or thought he wanted.

One example was very vivid for me, and concerns the Coombs E-type. I went tyre-testing at Goodwood with the modified car (which was, at that stage, still pre-'lightweight') since we had noticed very heavy tyre wear in racing. After 13 laps I went off sideways on a very fast kink and ended up in the bank with front and rear damage to the car.

In the moment of adversity John Coombs was very understanding – not the least bit upset as I imagined he would be. We found that the left rear tyre was practically bald, after only 13 laps, and on further investigation found that there were tyre marks on both the front and rear edges of the inner wing panels on both sides of the car. This indicated that the rubber bushes, retaining the rear axle subframe, were allowing too much movement and compliance, thus affecting the road-holding and tyre wear. We got the car back to the factory on a trailer and I had to convince Bill Heynes that we needed stronger rubber blocks

For 1964, the Lindner car acquired a 'Sayer' top not unlike that of EC 1001. For Le Mans (where this picture was taken) the car developed 344 bhp – the highest-known factory test figure.

for racing, whilst at the same time explain the circumstances of the accident which occurred only four days before the next race was due. The car was repaired in time by Phil Weaver's team and this graphic example led to a re-design of the bushes, with a great improvement in performance. I do not think the general call for harder suspension, less compliance in the rear axle location etc., would have occurred if it had not been for the incident.

Returning to the drivers, Roy Salvadori was quite different to Graham. When testing with Roy it did not seem to matter what we changed, he just went grey quicker and quicker as the day went on. Roy would simply adapt to the car and had very little to say regarding the effect of a change. As with Graham, once racing, he gave everything, whatever the problems.

I recall once when Dan Gurney drove the lightweight E at the Silverstone GP meeting and it rained heavily. Because of the conditions he just took it easy in the race; now Graham or Roy would never have done that.

Mike Parkes was another real tryer, and very quick. His feedback was excellent, displaying his high technical qualifications as an engineer as well as a racing driver.

Jack Sears was a man with immaculate style, and manners to match; 'Gentleman Jack' we called him. I saw him drop his standards and get upset only once. His car, a 3.8 Mk2 ran out of fuel at a Snetterton race and he had a real go at the *Chef d'Équipe*, Tommy Sopwith, who took a long time to live that one down.

My time at Jaguar was tremendous, and my admiration for Lofty England as a boss unbounded.

He was hard and demanding and stretched your abilities to the full. However he was always entirely fair and, once you got used to his particular brand of sarcasm, great fun to work for. One of his special attributes was to protect his employees by standing up for them when problems arose. If you were wrong he could cut you to pieces afterwards; but at the time, in front of the customer, he gave his support and never made you feel small.

Jaguar was very autocratic in those days; occasionally you would see Sir William walking through the plant, dressed immaculately, and there was never any doubt who the 'Governor' was.

Sir William had an ingenious telephone system which allowed him to cut into any internal extension at any time. It did not matter who you were talking to: the Chairman had complete priority.

He never addressed anyone, even his Directors, by their Christian name. It all seems unreal by to-day's standards; but we all knew where we stood, and the system worked. One had the impression it was an honour to work at 'The Jaguar'; they did not pay too well even by the standards of the day, but they were successful and the spirit of co-operation and comradeship was very real.

When an offer came from John Coombs to join his company as Service Manager in 1962 I was in a great dilemma, I loved working for Jaguar and had learned a great deal. The lure of a much better salary was strong, but people said that John Coombs was a difficult man to work for. I already knew him well and was not too worried at that aspect. I just felt I was being disloyal to Jaguar (a conceited viewpoint). However, after long

The result of the Lindner tragedy at Montlhéry, Autumn 1964.

discussion with Lofty England, who was fair and practical as usual, I made the break and joined Coombs in October 1962. Strange to relate, and perhaps indicative of the challenge – which is still real, well over 20 years later – I found I was the General Manager when I arrived at Coombs, despite the fact that I had never sold a car in my life.

One final anecdote from my Jaguar days: the occasion was the marque's 25th anniversary and the Jaguar Drivers' Club held a big celebration at Beaulieu. Sir William was the Guest of Honour. One of the events in the 'ring' was a Pit Stop competition and teams were entered by John Coombs Racing, Equipe Endeavour (Tommy Sopwith) and Jaguar Cars. I think these were the only three.

The idea was to drive a car a short distance from Line A, stop in the 'Pit' B, change 2 wheels (using an ordinary garage jack) and one sparking plug and then proceed to Line C. Obviously, the fastest from A to C was the winner.

Our works team was fully rehearsed and prepared by morning practice, but we decided to leave the centre lock wheel nuts very loose since the wheels were unlikely to fall off in the few yards from A to B. The chosen spark plug was not unduly tight, either. We left our car and proceeded to have lunch.

The moment of truth arrived and I drove our car smoothly from Line A to Line B. Under went the jacks, marked so that the pads lined up with the correct part of the underside and we were in business. To my horror I realised great difficulty was being experienced in getting the wheel nuts off! Someone had made an excellent job of banging them well and truly home. It transpired that none other than John Coombs had fixed our car! All this took place under the firm gaze of Sir William and I received a rocket from Lofty afterwards for not watching our car. He was not the least surprised to learn that Coombs was capable of such a trick.

Needless to say when the Coombs car went through its paces the wheel nuts fell off at the first sign of a tap, and when I picked up their discarded spark plug I found it only had 3 threads on it; the remainder had been carefully machined off!

It was a lesson in Gamesmanship. Coombs won the day and

we went home ruefully contemplating our failure, but everyone had a good laugh when the truth was told.

After joining Coombs & Son at Guildford, MacDowel did race occasionally the company's GTO Ferrari, 3.8 Mk2, and lightweight E-type – but when these became obsolete he had no further connection with racing until he went hill-climbing privately with Bob Jennings' E-type (modified at Coombs) in 1967. In 1968, Jennings acquired the ex-Bob Vincent lightweight E, and MacDowel drove it before moving on to single-seaters. His highlight years were 1973 and 1974 when he was RAC hill-climb champion. In 1980 he drove in a couple of County Championship races in a TWR-prepared BMW 323i, for BL had succeeded in parting with the Coombs representation. 'I finished,' he told me, 'but it was quite an eye-opener to watch (or, rather, keep out the way of) the hard-driving tactics of the majority of the drivers.'

John Coombs had moved abroad, happy in the knowledge that his business was in Michael MacDowel's safe hands. In his period at Jaguar, 'Mr Mac' had established a special rapport with the private owner. His successors – first Christopher Leaver then Roger Woodley and finally Chris Butler – maintained it. The competitiveness of the Jaguar declined, however, and when the mergers began – Jaguar with BMC and so on – all Service Department staff concentrated on bread-and-butter work. Soon came the XJ6, which gave the Jaguar marque a quieter, less racy image than any of its forebears. The E-type, too, seemed to go soft, as it went from 3.8 to 4.2 and ultimately to 5.3.

Bill Heynes was still very much in charge of engineering, as Jaguar's vice-chairman. His final fling in the competition field was a magnificent exercise, even though it never raced. Jaguar's last in-house racing car design to reach prototype form, the XJ13, is the subject of the next chapter.

Re-incarnation of the Lindner car by Lynx Engineering, eighteen years later.

Chapter Twelve

The XJ13

On 9 July 1965, a young Jaguar engineer was commissioned by Malcolm Sayer to pay a visit to Silverstone for the Grand Prix practice day. Jaguar and Coventry Climax were now close allies; but it was not to attend Jim Clark's great victory for Lotus in the Grand Prix itself (despite nearly running out of oil) that Michael Kimberley was setting off for the Northamptonshire countryside on a weekday. It was to brush up on the latest in sports-racing car design, just to see what the others were doing.

Unfortunately there wasn't very much for Kimberley to study; the Surtees, McLaren, and Lotus team cars were absent, their entrants having refused the RAC's offered starting money. The 'second-string' entries were basically similar, though.

This was the era of the sports-racing prototypes with their big American engines. Eric Broadley's original Lola GT of two years before had now grown into the Ford GT40, but it had also provided much of the experience that had gone into the Lola T70 which Hugh Dibley now flung round the fast Silverstone circuit in 1 min. 31.6 sec. – this was more than 115 mph, and good enough for a second row position, had the Chevrolet-powered monster been qualifying for the Grand Prix grid.

Next quickest in practice for this somewhat motley 'Senior Service' sports car race was John Coundley's McLaren-Elva-Olds, but it was over three seconds slower.

The V8 Lola and McLaren sports cars would come into their own with the creation of the tailor-made Can-Am Cup from 1966. The third and more famous marque to contend the 1965 Silverstone event was Lotus; but the Lotus 30-Ford V8, unlike its rivals, was to disappear from the scene with a reputation for temperament.

These were the notes Mike Kimberley made in the Silverstone paddock:

*DATA NOTED AT SILVERSTONE
PRACTICE 9th JULY, 1965*

Car No. 26 LOLA – S.M.A.R.T.
Engine capacity 5960 cc.
Radiator – 2 off 18″ × 10″ × 3″ thick (360″² Total Area).
Water pipes $1\frac{5}{8}$″ bore.
Anti-roll bar mounted in D.U. bearings on rear sub-frame with ball joints on end links.
Anti-roll bar dia $\frac{3}{4}$″ (Front and rear).
All front and rear suspension links mounted in solid bushes.
Steering column – single tube with one bush below wheel – adjustment in vertical plane only.
Pedals – pendant type with cable operated throttle.
Engine and transmission unit mounted on rear subframe.
A.C. Remote oil filter.
4–$2\frac{1}{8}$″ O/Dia exhaust pipes branching into one $2\frac{5}{8}$″ O/Dia. through $4\frac{1}{2}$″ O/Dia.
Expansion box into $3\frac{1}{2}$″ O/dia. tailpipe.
Gauge of tailpipe 16 SWG.
Type sizes: – 12.00 × 15 rear. 9.20 × 15 front.
Front brake ducts 5″ dia.
Rear brake ducts $2\frac{1}{2}$″ dia.

'*Not invented here*' *(1)*: **Daimler V8 engine. Peter Westbury proved its effectiveness (lightly supercharged) by using one to become British hill-climb champion of 1963.**

'*Not invented here*' *(2)*: **Coventry Climax V8 racing engine which brought Jim Clark two World Championships after the firm joined the Jaguar Group in early 1963. In the picture: Leonard Lee, Jim Clark, Colin Chapman and Walter Hassan. Hassan had had two stints at Jaguar before; now it was being joked that Sir William had to buy Coventry Climax Engines Ltd to get him back a third time.**

Car No. 12   McLAREN ELVA
              Engine—Oldsmobile 4450 cc.
              Radiator 22″ × 18″ × 3½″ thick (396″² Total
                  Area).
              Water pipes – 1⅜″ dia. bore.
              Anti-roll bar ⅝″ dia. front. $\frac{7}{16}$″ dia rear mounted
                  in D.U. bearings on frame and ball joints on
                  end links.
              All front and rear suspension links mounted in
                  solid bushes.
              Pedals mounted on floor with adjustable ratio,
                  duel brake master cylinders on balance bar.
              Pedal ratio 5.5:1.
              Cable operated throttle.
              Steering column – single tube (non-adju-
                  stable)with ball joint connection to pinion.
              Engine and transmission unit mounted on rear
                  sub-frame.

Car No. 17   LOTUS – FORD
and 21   Engine capacity 4727 cc
              Radiator – 2 off 14″ × 8″ × 4″ thick (224″ Total
                  Area).
              Oil cooler 10″ × 3″ × 1½″ (30″²).
              Water pipes 1½″ bore.
              Anti-roll bar mounted in D.U. bearings on rear
                  sub-frame with ball joints on end links.
              Anti-roll bar dia (rear) ¾″
              Pendant pedals with cable operated throttle.
              Master cylinders incorporating fluid reservoirs.
              Petrol filler cap positioned in front of wind-
                  screen.
              Engine breathers – 2–1¼″ bore pipes.
              Remote oil filter.
              Engine and transmission unit mounted on rear
                  sub-frame.
              All front and rear suspension links mounted in
                  solid bushes.

Next day, Dibley's Lola blew up its engine and Coundley (McLaren) won the 25-lap race easily from Trevor Taylor in Banford's Lotus 30, who spun the difficult machine at least once. Bob Bondurant (Lotus 30) was excluded for a push-start, after working his way up to second place 'on the road'.

A copy of that Kimberley data sheet is the first reference, in the Jaguar experimental department's engine record books, to the interest being shown in going racing with a mid-engined Jaguar. Elsewhere, however, was evidence that a V12 engine had been on the stocks ever since the company's mid-fifties heyday of motor racing. That

project had – until lately – received scant attention. In the summer of 1964, however, things had started to move. The four ohc Jaguar V12 engine was receiving its first tests, and the structure of the competition car itself was advancing, too. (Bill Heynes issued instructions to proceed with a set of body panels on 15 December 1964.)

That autumn saw at least three of the new 4·2-litre MkX (or 'XJ5') Saloons being fitted with roadgoing versions of the four-camshaft V12 engine – and most spectacular was the performance. The engine itself had the project number 'XJ6'. The mid-engined car project was called 'XJ13'. The original idea had been for Jaguar to make its Le Mans comeback with it as early as 1965. Records indicate that

The Lola GT of 1963; it showed the way for the Ford GT 40 and, in a sense, for the XJ13.

serious construction of the XJ13 as a complete car did not begin until June of that year.

In the strange world of Jaguar numbering systems, there was another project number – a very important one. It was 'XJ4', and it was reserved for a new Jaguar saloon. This car would be announced in 1968. Its commercial title was ... XJ6! No wonder confusion occurs from time to time.

In November 1965 Malcolm Sayer and Mike Kimberley advised Claude Baily of the modifications necessary at that point of development to 'facilitate Stage 1 engine installation in XJ13 car'. They listed five times as follows:

1. *Ground Clearance*
   Ground clearance reduced at front of oil sump to 2·75″. This gives only 0·08″ clearance on full bump.
2. *Starter Motor*
   Starter motor cannot be fitted due to reduced flywheel P.C. dia. to give 4″ ground clearance. M418 starter motor (with reduced o/dia) designed for XJ13 fouls on rear scavenge pump and does not allow oil sump to be modified to suit.
3. *Oil Sump*
   Bosses to be provided on sump for:
   a) Engine mountings to oil samp – 4 per side
   b) Bell housing to sump – 2 at rear.
4. *Air Inlet Pipes*
   Rear inlet pipes to be inclined forwards to clear cooling ducts and upwards to give insulation from exhaust pipes.
5. *Cylinder Head Breathers*
   O/S Breather (i.e. 'A' bank) to be deleted to give clearance on driving seat. Can cover connection could be utilised to allow breathing of chain box through N/S (i.e. 'B' bank) breather.

Left:

The GT40 production prototype at Abbey Panels, Coventry, where the XJ13 also took shape.

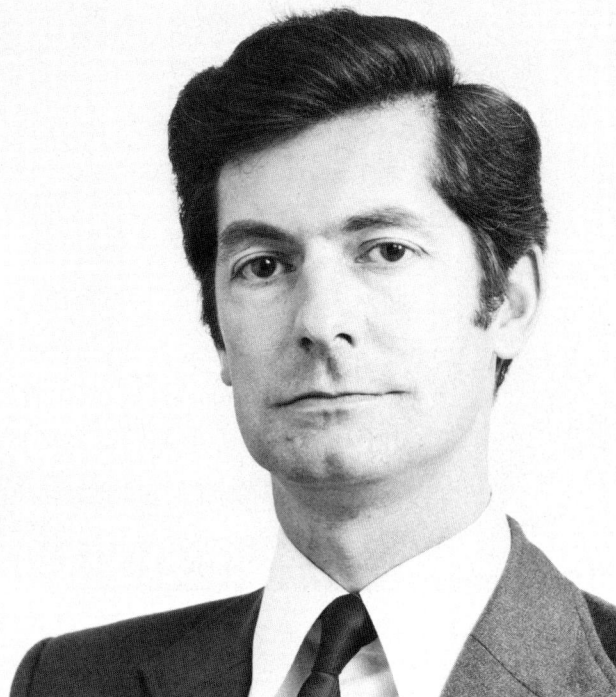

In February 1966, George Buck sent a note to Harry Mundy, the former Coventry Climax engineer who had joined Jaguar (from technical editorship of *Autocar*) in 1964. Buck was concerned enough to copy it to Messrs Heynes, Hassan, Baily and Kimberley. During tests to check the dry-sump (competition) V12 modifications, made to suit installation into the XJ13, he had found pressure problems were letting oil re-enter the engine unfiltered. On 20 April 1966, after further redesign work, Buck was able to compile the following report to Harry Mundy on behalf of Bill Wilkinson, copying it to Heynes, Hassan and Baily.

V-12 COMPETITION ENGINE FOR XJ.13 CAR AUTOMATIC P.I. CONTROL

The No. 1 XJ6 V-12 has been prepared for use in the XJ.13 car with mechanical control of the mixture strength. A cam form has been developed on the test bed which provides a relationship between the throttle opening and fuel delivered.

Details of this cam designated No. 1A are attached hereto; the fuel control characteristic suits the broad engine specification given below:

The performance figures shown, are those obtained using the above control, correct ignition distributors, and the recently modified dry sump. The latter item will be the subject of a separate report. The engine is also fitted with a piston type oil pressure relief valve on the dirty side of the element.

Michael Kimberley was a Jaguar apprentice and then a member of the engineering department. He was closely involved with the XJ13's development and, in his spare time, with the design of national award-winning ploughing equipment. Few Jaguar people were surprised when he reached the top at Lotus.

Below:
Mike Kimberley seen here in apprentice days with colleagues and XK engine. On the right is Phil Forno who later drove for Cunningham. (*Courtesy: Leonard Lucas*)

GENERAL SPECIFICATION

Capacity: 4991 cc (87 mm × 70 mm).
Compression ratio: 10·4:1.
Cylinder heads: Stage 1 – 1⅞″ dia. inlet valve.
Camshafts: ·440″ lift time 40° – 40°.
Intakes: 1⅝″ dia. throttles, 10″ overall length, angled 16° towards vertical.
Ignition: Lucas T. A. L. Master distributor LT. 22355.
Slave distributor LT. 22359.
Static setting: 8° B. T. D. C.
Injection timed: 20° B. T. D. C.
1½″ I.D. × 30″ primary pipes.
1⅞″ I.D. × 31″ tail pipes.
Fuel: Shell 100 octane.

PERFORMANCE AS PREPARED FOR CAR INSTALLATION

R.P.M.	Corrected B.H.P.	B.M.E.P.	Torque	Observed Pt/BHP/Hr
4000	259·5	168·0	340·0	·544
4500	282·2	162·8	330·0	·568
5500	373·5	176·0	359·0	·531
6000	382·5	165·5	335·0	·569
6500	420·0	167·8	340·0	·558
7000	445·0	165·2	334·5	·567
7500	430·0	148·5	300·5	·627

By way of comparison here are the maximum figures in relation to those for a Maserati engine tested by Jaguar Cars Ltd; both units were run with Shell 100 octane fuel:

(Engine)	**Jaguar** (April 1966)	**Maserati** (June 1964)
Type	V-12, 60°	V-8, 90°
Capacity	4991 cc	4990 cc
Bore	87 mm	94 mm
Stroke	70 mm	89 mm
Compression ratio	10·4 to 1	10·0 to 1
Corrected power	445 bhp	429 bhp
at rpm	7000	6000
max. torque	359 lb ft	376 lb ft
at rpm	5500	6000

Later in April a series of fourteen tests was conducted on the competition engine, in various conditions to try to overcome power losses due to oil drag. Maximum power at this time was 460 bhp at 7000 rpm.

The highest figures on record for the XJ6 V12 engine were to be 502 bhp at 7600 rpm and 386 lb ft torque at 6300 rpm.

The early part of 1966 had seen Sayer and Kimberley carry out torsional tests on the XJ13 as a body structure and as a complete vehicle. (It should be remembered that Derrick White had left Jaguar.) Torsional stiffness was worked out as torque per degree of overall twist on the test rig. The car with engine, transmission, sub-frame, and mountings attached came to 4200 lb ft/°, whereas the body structure alone produced 2890 lb ft/°. These figures indicate not only the structural element of the power unit in this car, but also suggest the strength of the whole – a feature that was to be proved unexpectedly five years later.

That spring also saw Dewis, Kimberley and Sayer join forces to supply Heynes with a performance test and technical description of the Ford GT40. Being the detuned version, compared to Ford's Le Mans entries, the car they borrowed was not subjected to full performance tests, but the handling was thought to be 'of sufficiently high standard to warrant a complete analysis of the front and rear suspension geometries, wheel and spring rates, centre of gravity, roll centres, steering geometry, etc.' Interestingly the main dimensions of the GT40 and the XJ13 were within a couple of inches of each other except in the rear overhang.

If international racing was at a turning point, so was Jaguar Cars Ltd itself.

The company now consisted of Jaguar plus four other companies and their subsidiaries: Daimler, Guy, Coventry Climax and Meadows.

Since the takeover of Daimler from the BSA group, annual car production had been averaging over 24 000 units – thanks largely to the extra factory space – and, for the first time since the war, world markets were beginning to be satisfied with their quota of cars.

None of these acquisitions had any great effect upon Jaguar engineering policy. Political, psychological, and practical reasons had combined to prevent Jaguar from making better use of existing Daimler V8 power units than it was doing. On the other hand, the purchase of Coventry Climax Engines Ltd early in 1963 had brought extra strength to Browns Lane – in the form of Walter Hassan (returning to Jaguar for the third time in his career) and his team. Hassan continued to concentrate on Coventry Climax until the end of the Grand Prix season; but early in 1964 he and Bob Berry persuaded Harry Mundy to join Jaguar to develop new engines for regular production.

Bill Heynes was still very much in charge of Jaguar engineering, as he had been for well over thirty years.

In July 1966, Sir William Lyons joined forces with Sir George Harriman, head of the British Motor Corporation. Their two firms were to merge and, although they would retain autonomy to start with, it soon became clear that Jaguar would never be the same again.

Just before the London Motor Show that October three new models were launched – the 420 (based on the S-type, an existing 'compact'), the 420G (virtually a Mk X), and the Sovereign (a Daimler version of the 420). There was now a wide range of saloon models, but nothing *really* new. The 'XJ4' was running late, and would not be seen for another two years. At the press preview of his 1967-model 'interim' saloons, Sir William Lyons commented on the new economic climate: 'The myth of the motor industry as the golden goose of the twentieth century has finally evaporated in the harsh reality of a major recession'.

In retrospect they may not look like hard times! Nevertheless, it is hardly surprising that very little work was done on the XJ13 project in the latter part of 1966.

Then, early on Sunday morning 5 March 1967, a small group of Jaguar men shivered on the tarmac at MIRA – the Motor Industry Research Association's testing facility at Lindley, near Nuneaton. Two days later came the first report on the running of a mid-engined Jaguar. This report, dated 7 March, can be found in Appendix 11.

In the final paragraphs of the report it notes that the test session was discontinued from 'possible big end failure'. In this Mike Kimberley was quite right: big end failure

The XJ13 under construction.

had resulted from oil starvation during those first XJ13 trials. On 20 April 1967, George Buck noted the new modifications carried out to overcome the problem.

G. Buck to H. Mundy.
  c.c. W.M.H., W.T.F.H., C.B., W.E.W. & M.K.

LUBRICATION The internal arrangement of the oil tank has been changed by the Competition Dept., to ensure reliability of oil pick up, improve de-aeration and anti-splash – see Mr Kimberley's report No. 2 dated 7–4–67 for details.

  The relief oil has been directed from its original discharge (into the oil tank), to the pump inlet pipe, thus making the relief recirculatory. This reduces both the volume of oil flow with which the tank has to deal, and any tendency towards aeration due to the relief discharge itself. During bench tests conditions in the relief discharge were found to be neutral i.e., neither pressure or vacuum was exerted on the relief oil.

  The original fabricated steel sump floor has been replaced by a single steel pressing, which should be more mechanically resistant to vibration effects.

  A series of bench tests was carried out using a mock car tank having the latest internal modifications and with the car oil cooler in circuit. Initially, the amount of oil held in the tank was $8\frac{3}{4}$ gallons; this was eventually reduced to $6\frac{1}{4}$ gallons which on the test bench proved adequate, and also avoided flooding the de-aeration baffles. With the latter quantity, tests were carried out with the tank tilted at an angle of 45° in four directions, successively to simulate acceleration, deceleration and c.f. conditions. While these tests could not be expected to exactly reproduce dynamic effects, they at least showed that pick-up and de-aeration were reliable at these altitudes.

BREATHING The excessive blow from the oil tank and engine breathers experienced during the car trials could be accounted for by the condition of the top rings, eight of which were found to be broken when the engine was stripped. We have experimented with additional breathers taken from the front of the cylinder heads, but these have been found unnecessary, and we have finalised the breather system using one breather from the crankcase and twin ones from the camshaft covers joined into a single exit, both leading to the tank de-aerator tower. This arrangement has proved capable of dealing satisfactorily with the engine's needs without oil blow-over.

Installed in the XJ13, the engine output was now showing somewhat changed characteristics with a power of 472 bhp at 7250 rpm but maximum torque of 381 lb ft at the lower speed of 5500 rpm.

Kimberley and his colleagues knew by now that competition car development was proceeding much too quickly for a half-hearted project like the Jaguar to lead to success at Le Mans or in any other race. Just the same, Dewis's Sunday morning tests continued into the summer. After 286 miles on 18 June, the total mileage for the car read 766. At an early stage, Dewis felt the handling becoming less positive, the car more prone to weave, the braking more uneven. All the same, he did see 178 mph on the straight during this run. Unfortunately, oil was leaking from the engine on to the off side rear pads. Moreover Kimberley was annoyed to find that although the brake pads were to specification, all were not from the same batch or even of the same age.

A week earlier, Ford had gained the second (of four) successive outright victories at Le Mans; their 7-litre Mk IV broke the race and lap records with ease. Le Mans weekend had also seen a major decision – to reduce the

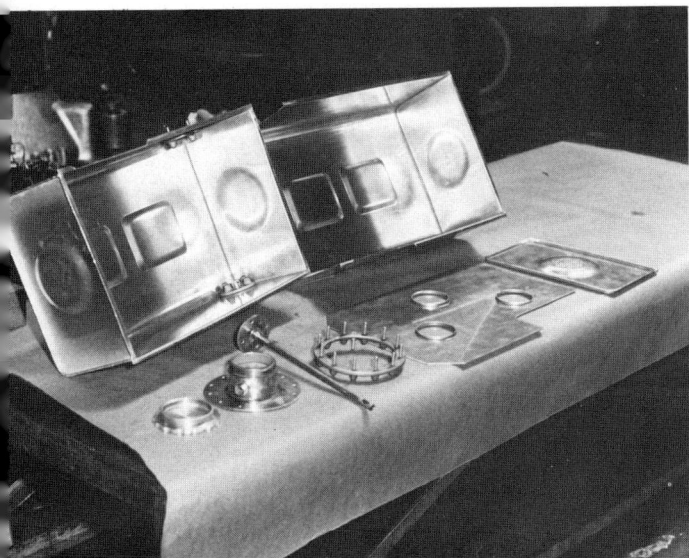

engine capacity permitted for the next year's prototype category to 3 litres maximum (shades of 1958!). Mike Kimberley attended Le Mans 1967 in the company with another former apprentice, David Hobbs, who was driving the ill-starred 5-litre Aston Martin-engined Lola.

Ford had long nursed the dream of becoming leaders in sports car racing and all of a sudden, in 1963, it had turned into a possibility.

5-litre engine installed in the XJ13.

Jaguar V12 5-litre engine (project no. 'XJ6'!). Tom Jones first drew such a unit in 1951.

Russell Brockbank's view. (*Courtesy: Motor*)

"Nobody in the industry can understand how they do it for the money."

A multi-million dollar project had been launched – for 1963 was the year of the brilliant Lola GT, a beautifully clean design from a clean piece of paper. Its designer, Eric Broadley, and in effect his whole Lola company, were seconded to Ford's advanced vehicle operation, and thus was born the 'Ford' GT40.

The Ford onslaught

The years 1964 and 1965 had seen all the Fords fail to finish at Le Mans. Thirteen Fords had started in 1966, and ten had failed – but the others took the top three places, ending Ferrari's six years of supremacy. Now, in 1967, Ford had done it again; so it mattered little to them that the regulations had changed – they would withdraw, having spent their money and proved their point.

Sports and GT cars for Le Mans could, in future, be of 5 litres capacity, however. The standard Ford GT40 being run by private teams had become a regular and reliable race winner. It had the right engine size and it would take victory at Le Mans in 1968 and 1969 on the proved characteristics of good fast driving, experienced pit-work and sheer reliability.

There was no possibility of Jaguar coming up with anything other than a pure prototype, and the 5-litre four ohc engine was to be abandoned anyway.

Walter Hassan had moved offices from Widdrington Road to Browns Lane in 1966. Coventry Climax had an experienced enough engineering team for its fire-pump and fork-truck work, now that the company had pulled out of Grand Prix racing after scoring a record number of Formula 1 wins and four World Championships – two each for Jack Brabham (Cooper) and Jim Clark (Lotus).

First in 1954, then when it was revived seriously nearly ten years later, the Jaguar four-cam V12 engine was influenced by XK racing experience. Bill Heynes acknowledged that he 'always had a feeling that we might one day be asked to return to competition and it was necessary to have a basic power unit that would take care of this contingency'. Thus for a time, there were the road and race versions of the 'XJ6' 5-litre.

Now that Bill Heynes and Claude Baily were nearing retirement, it was natural that Heynes should delegate to his former colleague Walter Hassan, whose own book

Climax in Coventry (MRP, 1975) describes how its author and Harry Mundy thought the four-camshaft 5-litre racing unit with its downdraught inlet parts and Lucas fuel injection:

. . . looked splendid and made a lovely noise, but I think we were all disappointed when we found that it was a struggle to extract more than 500 bhp from it, even in racing trim and with a very short stroke. However, having said this, the engine in a suitably stream-lined car would probably have been quite good enough to propel a winning combination at Le Mans as it stood – the 7-litre Fords won easily in 1966 and 1967 with around 550 bhp and a lot of Climax-like mid-range torque.

This power output was equivalent to 100 bhp per litre – a figure achieved only once previously by Jaguar when they built the very special racing 3-litre XKs for the prototype 'E' Type in 1960 – which was creditable enough. However, over at Coventry Climax we were now accustomed to seeing more than 130 bhp per litre on Grand Prix designs. Even if one had conceded a little power to aid endurance running, say to 120 bhp per litre, this should have resulted in a 5-litre Jaguar producing around 600 bhp, considerably more than was ever achieved by this four-cam engine. There were, in addition, other puzzles. Not only was there a lack of top-end power, there was also a distinct lack of low-speed and mid-range torque.

An engine lacking both top-end power and mid-range torque was not my idea of a potentially successful racing unit. In a way it reminded me of the elegant engine my old boss, W. O. Bentley, designed for Lagonda; his V-12 looked good and sounded splendid, but it suffered the same characteristics as this Jaguar; namely a lack of low-down power.

By the time I became involved in the engine's development, its 'raison d'etre' had changed somewhat from a pure racing to a touring application; consequently, the need for lusty low-speed and mid-range torque had become much more important than top-end power. We also had to make sure that the new engine was quiet and smooth in operation, and that it would satisfy the exhaust emission limitations being imposed all around the world. It was this last requirement which held back production for some time.

Jaguar policy at the time also envisaged two types of engine being evolved from one basic design – hopefully a high-powered sports car version with hemispherical combustion chambers and twin-cam cylinder-heads, and a second version intended to be much cheaper to manufacture, saving money, weight and complication by having single-cam cylinder-heads.

One of several Sayer
models, when mid-
engined road cars
were in the air.

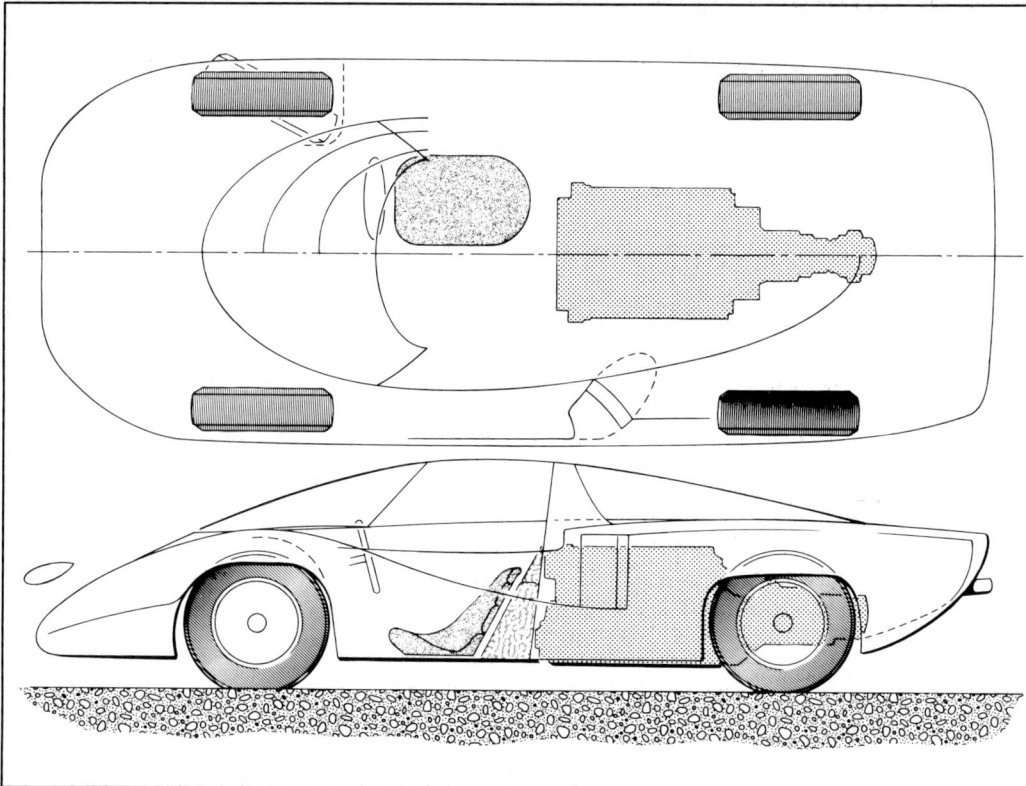

Left:
A **two-view
illustration based on
one of several scale
drawings from
Malcolm Sayer in the
mid-1960s of potential
XJ13 derivatives.**

The real XJ13
at MIRA in early 1971.

Much experimental and test work was carried out, and by the end of it Hassan and Mundy were convinced that – while *all* were in agreement with the smoothness and marketability of a V12 their flat-head engine would be superior for touring car purposes. 'My interpretation,' said Hassan, 'is that a hemispherical head is better when allied to long-stroke layout, and not so good for short-stroke layouts unless sheer maximum speed is required'. He recalled how Sir William Lyons ordered a full report on both lines of development – the Heynes/Baily line and the Hassan/Mundy line – and tested cars with both types of engine. 'At a technical board meeting a vote was taken – and the die was cast in favour of the single-cam type of cylinder heads for production cars. By this time it had also become clear that we could not afford to produce two types of [V12] engine (the extra tooling charges could not be justified), and this led to the demise of the twin-cam cylinder-head'. Incidentally, twenty years later, the 'Hassan/Mundy' engine was being raced (on both sides of the Atlantic) in 6.5-litre form, and was producing close on 110 bhp per litre, in normally aspirated form, in the XJR-6 and XJR-7 prototypes.

Before being put under dustsheets in a corner of the experimental department, the XJ13 paid two more visits to MIRA.

On 2 July 1967, Norman Dewis was still finding that the car lacked positive handling and tended to weave, despite rear suspension alterations between tests. Brake lock, fade, and rear-wheel steer were also experienced. Total mileage at the end of the session was 957 miles.

For the record, included in Appendix 11 is Mike Kimberley's resport of the XJ13's final fling at MIRA, where David Hobbs covered over 200 miles on Sunday, 9 July 1967. Best lap speed around the banked outer circuit for the 1955 D-type is believed to be 67 seconds, or 151·5 mph. The XJ13's 62·8 seconds (161·6 mph) in 1967 was to become an annual entry in the Guinness Book of Records as it represented the highest speed ever recorded for a lap of an enclosed circuit in the UK. The first car to record a higher lap speed is thought to be the TWR Group A XJ-S – eighteen years later! In 1985 Tom Walkinshaw recorded 176·16 mph for a lap of GM's Millbrook track, using (of course) a development of the Hassan/Mundy V12 engine. ...

Besides MIRA, Silverstone was used for XJ13 runs, and Richard Attwood (like David Hobbs, an ex-Jaguar employee) was brought in to try the car and add his wealth of racing experience to that of his former colleague, and that of Norman Dewis who had lived with the XJ13 throughout its frustratingly inconsistent early development programme. The conclusion was inevitable: chassis and tyres for racing were becoming outdated not by the year but by the month. You had to be in a position to run a large full-time department, properly budgeted, or subcontract as Ford had done. As things stood, the XJ13 – and there was and is *only one* car – had run out of time. The car was beautifully built, but its braking and handling needed much more attention, and its weight gave it a performance disadvantage which could not be overcome.

Lofty England and David Hobbs would discuss racing as they drove together from their adjacent homes through the lanes on those quiet early-morning trips to Silverstone or the Lindley (MIRA) proving ground in 1967. Such a project naturally created rumours and, now, motor racing circles hummed for a while, for no test at MIRA or Silverstone could guarantee total privacy Jaguar even with the presence of old E2A as a 'decoy'. England and the rest of the Jaguar team knew that if Jaguar was to go racing it must be with a clean sheet of paper; there was no category for which the XJ13 could ever be used. Out came the dustcovers. The decision was the right one.

Jaguar forsakes mid-engine plans

In parallel, Malcolm Sayer had drawn-up a number of schemes for mid-engined road cars, based on the XJ13 concept; they looked good. But this was also the time of the new US Federal safety laws and, with the proposed crash tests an unknown quantity, Jaguar Engineering took the positive decision to proceed along the traditional front-engine route for production models.

At the beginning of 1968 came the first warnings of the plan to form British Leyland; it was implemented in May. Jaguar was still Jaguar, though, and the announcement of the XJ6 strengthened it for a while. Then Bill Heynes – technical chief since the very first Jaguar of 1935 – retired in 1969. The duties of senior engineering director were shared for a while by Walter Hassan and Robert Knight: an engine man and a chassis man. Mike Kimberley, aged 30, left Jaguar and joined Lotus as Project Engineer in 1969 – believing, rightly, that he would be advancing his career there. Jaguar had taught him plenty, but he wanted more.

There were rumours of a new 'F-type' by now. Indeed the XJ-S Jaguar as we know it was nearly called 'XK-F': but the XJ-S was a long way off, yet the Hassan/Mundy 5·3-litre V12 engine was getting tooled-up in the Radford (Daimler) works. To stay in the consciously sporting car market, it was decided to modify the roadgoing E-type to take the new power unit; at first it was intended to be optional. Shortly before the Series Three E-type's announcement, however, it was decided to make the car in V12 form only.

Anticipating a degree of disappointment, the Company decided to make up for the lack of an entirely new car by presenting to the World the Jaguar that had never been seen before.

The XJ13 was known to only a few people; it had been spared the embarrassment of ever running unprepared at Le Mans, and had lain under wraps for over three years when, in early 1971, it was wheeled out and dusted off. Its engine bore little relationship to the car about to be launched, except that it was a Jaguar creation – *and* it was a V12. That idea itself was something completely new to a generation that had been brought up on the faithful XK six-cylinder.

The Series Three cars were due to make their bow at the 1971 Geneva Show. The plan was to invite members of the press to a quiet out-of-town *Auberge* for a bite of lunch, away from the wearisome footslogging of the exhibition halls. The surprise would be the distant sound of an unfamiliar engine; the sound would grow; then it would burst from the forest in the form of Malcolm Sayer's (and

Norman Dewis ready to go, MIRA, 1971.

Norman Dewis and the film crew get ready for first 'take'.

XJ13 at MIRA.

Derrick White's, and Mike Kimberley's) glorious XJ13 ... the mystery Jaguar. The plan went wrong before it could be implemented.

On 20 January 1971, in order to carry the V12 theme right through the launch programme, a film session was arranged at MIRA. The XJ13 was to be filmed on the banking, to introduce Raymond Baxter, Walter Hassan, and Harry Mundy talking about the new production V12. (In fact, all that went well; the film was 'in the can', and was eventually edited and used.) However, just as Norman Dewis was completing his final lap – going quickly, but never on that day as quickly as he'd gone four years earlier – when something went at the rear: a tyre or a wheel. Whatever it was, it took the car up to the lip of the

banking. There the tension of the retaining fence sprung the car away down, thumping, bumping and rolling across the track to the ploughed infield.

The XJ13 landed on what was left of its wheels. Norman Dewis walked away with a stiff neck. The car looked ruined, at first sight – but it was not. The central structure was still intact. Naturally, though, it was taken back to Browns Lane to stay under wraps for the best part of two more years. Meantime, the Series Three E-type launch was held-over until the end of March 1971, and became a largely American-oriented affair. Sir William went with Harry Mundy to Palm Springs; not only did he introduce the car, he also visited his American colleagues for the last time before his own retirement. (That would take place in 1972, the year of the XJ12.)

When Sir William went, Lofty England took over as chief executive and in due course, as the internal XJ13 furore melted away, he took the decision to investigate a proper rebuild. Abbey Panels still had the formers and soon an impossible-looking task became feasible. The rebuild, carried out under Phil Weaver's supervision mainly by George Mason and Peter Dodd, was expensive;

261

Dewis in action.

but the subsequent publicity for Jaguar design and workmanship was to pay off in the years to come ... years when Jaguar would often need the odd boost to its pride.

Lofty England demonstrated the XJ13 publicly for the first time ever in July 1973, in front of the British Grand Prix crowd at Silverstone. When he retired the following January, it was the end of an era. Any Jaguar competition car would be built as an outside contract. The late 1970s would not be good times for Jaguar. With the 1980s, however, the company would re-emerge again ... and it would have its own, winning, sports car race teams on both sides of the Atlantic.

Right and Below:
Dewis walks up and down to get his bearings after inadvertently demonstrating the roll-over strength of the one-and-only XJ13.

Above left:
The view back to the MIRA banking.

Top and Below:
At first it looks bad ... but a closer look shows that there is hope for a rebuild.

Original body formers (one is in foreground) help ensure a proper rebuild at Abbey Panels.

Right:
The XJ13 back at Browns Lane for completion.

Below and opposite Top:
Restoration complete, 1973.

Below left:
Lofty England invites Ronnie Peterson for a road test, Silverstone, 1973. It was the first time that the car had been seen in public.

Another 1973 demonstration, this time at Shelsley Walsh hill climb. Philip Weaver is in the car; George Mason, Lofty England and Peter Dodd can be seen beyond

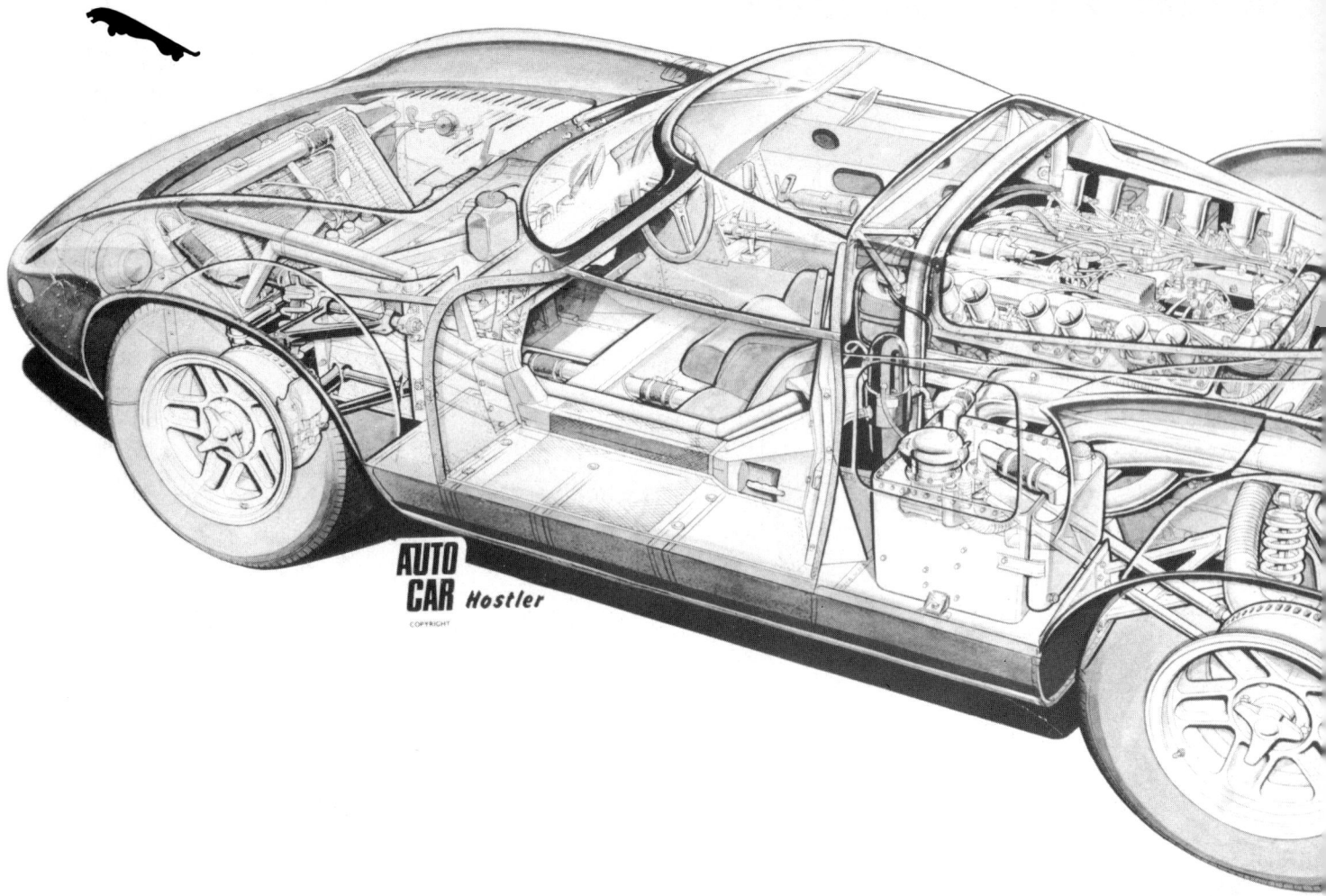

XJ13's engine installation.

Right: **XJ13 rear end detail.**

Cutaway of rebuilt car. (*Courtesy: Autocar*)

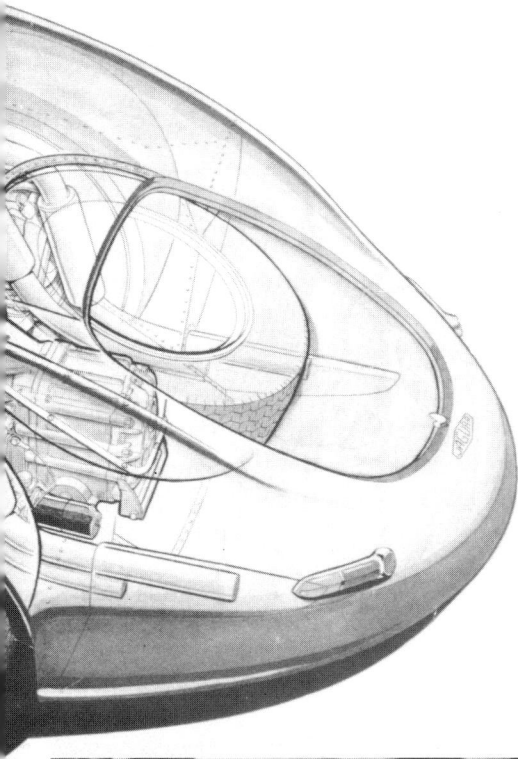

Bob Blake, Jaguar's competition body fabrication expert from 1955 (and subsequently in charge of the styling workshop) with Sayer's XJ13 concept model at a US seminar in 1976.

Chapter Thirteen

BL and Broadspeed

The period during which it was controlled by British Leyland was not a happy one for Jaguar. Fortunately, thinking about it a decade or so later was (to me) akin to remembering an earlier period of 'state' employment: National Service. The similarity was a tendency to remember only the good bits.

BL's best bit was the arrival of Michael Edwardes. This event occurred on 1 November 1977, immediately after he had accepted the chairmanship of British Leyland on condition that he could wield absolute power.

Edwardes would be responsible, more than two years later, for the recruiting of John Egan to rebuild Jaguar as an independent British business enterprise. Meantime, Jaguar's crises of quality, liquidity and identity continued.

The Edwardes appointment coincided with the end of two disastrous seasons of racing which a Browns Lane team – had there been one – would have opposed with vehemence. As it was, Jaguar's engineering chief Bob Knight had concentrated single-handed upon a fight for Jaguar individuality. Knight was the last executive director remaining from the old independent Jaguar company, which had merged with BMC (the British Motor Corporation) back in 1966. British Leyland had been formed in 1968 and, shortly after Sir William Lyons's retirement in 1972, Jaguar autonomy had begun to disappear.

Before his retirement in early 1974, Lofty England had ensured the survival of the XJ13 – for posterity but NOT for development. Jaguar was busy enough, protecting its interests wherever it felt they were threatened by corporate insensitivity. One interest which seemed safe from outside interference was Jaguar's racing heritage.

It is true to say that, in normal circumstances, 1975 *would* have been the right time for a return to competition. The saloon and GT Jaguars had lost their competitive edge at international level a decade earlier, and by now the marque's loyal supporters were lobbying strongly for a race-winning car. However, those who saw the need to save Jaguar from extinction realised that racing must remain a low priority for the time being. In the short term it was essential to maintain economic production volumes and high quality in the XJ range. Lofty England's successor Geoffrey Robinson had achieved the former but not the latter by the end of 1974, when the British Leyland Motor Corporation finally ran out of cash. Donald Stokes' dream for the British motor industry became a lost cause with the publication of the 'Ryder Report' in April 1975. This recipe for nationalisation did not solve the industry's problems, however, and for more than two years a BL division known as Leyland Cars was charged with the impossible task of holding the business together. Despite the good intentions of Leyland Cars chief Derek Whittaker, the famous marques which Stokes had brought together now looked like vanishing one by one; and with them, would go the customers.

Leyland Cars' director of sales and marketing was former Standard–Triumph PR man Keith Hopkins, the force behind Stokes' rise to fame. Towards the end of 1975 BL overlord Alex Park, together with Whittaker and Hopkins, gave official blessing to the ill-starred Broadspeed XJ12 affair.

At the Browns Lane unveiling of the 1976 Broadspeed V12 coupé (*left to right*): Simon Pearson (Leyland Cars PR, Motor Sport Liaison Manager), Derek Bell (driver), Tony Thompson (Chairman of Jaguar 'operating committee'), Richard Seth-Smith (Leyland Cars PR, Product Affairs Manager), and Peter Craig (Director, Browns Lane Plant).

Enthusiasm v Politics

Ralph Broad's enthusiasm for Jaguar lay in his belief that the V12 production engine *could* make a good competition unit. From the time of its announcement he would, in open conversation, bubble over at the thought of developing the new 5·3-litre engine – pooh-poohing the views of those within the company who were circumspect. It was the danger of losing control of Jaguar's engineering policy and operations that made Bob Knight retreat further and further into the shell of Browns Lane. Perhaps retreat is not the best word; rather, he entrenched. If Knight believed then that entrenchment was the only hope for Jaguar, he was to be proved correct. It is my own belief that without Knight's firm stand in 1975, Jaguar would not have remained sufficiently intact to be reconstructed five years later.

Broadspeed Engineering of Southam in Warwickshire was best known for its preparation of Ford cars but had made a recent switch of allegiance to British Leyland – a move originated by Stokes's deputy John Barber shortly before he left (in the wake of Ryder). Broadspeed's almost immediate success in preparing the unlikely Triumph Dolomite Sprint as a national championship winner had done much to enhance Ralph Broad's personal reputation, and strengthened his hand when he raised the subject of Jaguar within BL. In the 'pre-Ryder' period (1974 or early 1975) Broad had approached Geoffrey Robinson about the potential of a V12-powered Jaguar in racing; but Robinson took Knight's counsel and steered clear altogether.

In the double backwash of the 'oil crisis' and 'Ryder' came the announcement of the XJ-S – a characteristic Jaguar design in every respect but its looks. This was the car which (Bob Knight later confirmed to me) BL and Broad *had* planned to race as a touring car. On Jaguar's behalf, Knight was determined that it should not be raced as *anything* by 'outsiders'. Many years had passed since Jaguar itself had been close to the racing game and, in this instance, it was easy to portray the XJ-S as a 2 + 2 rather than a 4-seater even though both cases could be argued. With the failure to ratify the XJ-S for Group 2, it seemed that Knight had achieved his aim. So he was silently aghast when another type of Jaguar was chosen as BL's great white hope for outright victory in Touring Car Championship races. It cannot have helped Knight's particular cause when Bob Tullius used a V12-engined E-type to win a US national championship in the autumn of 1975. Certainly, that success coincided with Broad winning *his* case at last, when Leyland contracted Broadspeed to prepare a Group 2 Jaguar XJ12! Not that there was any reason – other than political – for the XJ12 to be barred from homologation.

When the XJ series was first introduced in 1968 as the ultimate expression of Sir William Lyon's genius, it had marked a change of emphasis. Through the 1960s, the popular compact 3·8-litre Mk 2 had given the marque something of a 'Boy Racer' image in the second-hand car market. With the XJ6 and XJ12, the Jaguar car became an altogether more sophisticated machine of unparalleled refinement. Small wonder, then, that many Jaguar people were appalled by Leyland Cars' decision to take 'their' XJ12 racing. The fact that it was never offered with a manual gearbox was just one reason why the XJ12 simply had not been given earlier consideration (at Browns Lane) as a practical Group 2 racing car. It was too late for Knight to find a way of legislating against the car once

269

The Broadspeed XJ5.3C, as first demonstrated to the press at Silverstone on a mad March day in 1976.

This Gorgon's Curse lurked beneath the Broad bonnet of early 1976. It would be tidied up before long.

BL's intention were known, and by 1976 the Broadspeed XJ12 had become a racing certainty.

The full story of the Broadspeed XJ12 project is covered in the competition section which I contributed for Paul Skilleter's *magnum opus, Jaguar Saloon Cars* (Haynes, 1980). Nevertheless, it is important to cover the major elements here for the sake of completeness.

It was on 23 March 1976 that Derek Whittaker announced that the XJ12 would be taking on the BMWs in Europe 'for exactly the same reasons as we do anything else in our business – to sell more cars and make money'.

There was no major sponsor other than Leyland, since 'Leyland' was the word to be promoted. The effort began full of optimism and Ray Barker, editor of *British Leyland Mirror*, quoted Ralph Broad fulsome statement: 'This is my life's ambition ... to develop and run an outright winner for Great Britain. I'm a great patriot. ... Frankly I am overwhelmed to be bringing Jaguars back into racing. ... These cars are representing not only Leyland but Britain. It is a very, very patriotic exercise.'

No-one could doubt the earnestness of Broad's pronouncements, but his remark about being 'overwhelmed' turned out to be prophetic. Above all, he was overwhelmed by time. What he needed most was at least a full season's development work. BMW and Ford had enormous experience in Group 2 racing; indeed, one version of BMW's CSL was capable of winning in Group 5. Lightness and agility had been built into BMW's coupé, the lines of which were spoiled by the kit of wings and fins which had been homologated for it. Even without such eyecatching aerodynamic aids, the new Broadspeed Jaguar looked brutally purposeful, with its extended wheel-arches and a phalanx of cooling radiators. The two-door bodywork was painted white with blue stripes and still carried the 'XJ12C' badging at the rear. Being out of date, this was changed quickly to 'XJ5.3C'. ('C' stood for coupé.)

Not that Group 2 cars bore much relationship to their road-going counterparts. The BMW CSLs had no trouble in getting down to their top weight limit of 1050 kg, whereas the Jaguar had its own built-in penalty of about 400 kg more. This would be reduced slightly in 1977, but the Jaguar never could be got down to within 100 kg of the 1280 kg *it* was permitted. Indeed, in compensating for component failures, Broadspeed would increase the weight again as the 1977 season progressed. It was to be a vicious circle.

Besides bad weather, the Broadspeed team ran into many other difficulties, the most frequent being oil surge. The first appointment – Salzburgring, Easter 1976 – came and went. So did Mugello, Brno, and the Nürburgring. The 24 hour race at Spa-Francorchamps was missed, too. By August, the XJ12 Group 2 car had not turned a wheel in anger, and fuel was added to this particular fire when it was learned that Group 44's first XJ-S was already racing in North America.

With all the publicity that had been fed to the media, the need for a début in the Tourist Trophy race at Silverstone in September seemed imperative by this stage. One car – two had been promised all season – lapped the fast aerodrome circuit on 'qualifying' tyres in 1 min. 36·72 sec. with Derek Bell at the wheel – nearly two seconds

better than the BMW of champion-elect Pierre Dieudonné. Extra speed was essential, however, because of the Jaguar's need for more frequent pit stops in a long race.

Bell led the race first, then Nilsson (BMW), then Bell again until Lap 9 when tyre wear began to affect the handling. Soon afterwards a tyre began to deflate. Bell noticed this when it was just too late to get into the pit-lane; he had to do another lap, during which the tyre went down completely. Thereafter the car ran spectacularly (but well down the field) until a driveshaft broke and Bell's co-driver David Hobbs watched the wheel rolling by as he parked resignedly on the grass beside Hangar Straight, leaving the race to the BMWs. The Jaguar had completed 38 laps (of 107) in this, its only race of 1976. The autumn and winter were to be fully occupied with development, and then yet more development.

There was no doubt that the Jaguar's presence had brought in the crowds as never before at this particular meeting. This is how Alan Henry summed up the Jaguar's début race in his *Motoring News* report: 'Sunday's performance could well be the tip of the iceberg. BMWs may rule for the time being, but a two-car team of Jaguar XJ coupés could have them well and truly on the run within twelve months and focus a spotlight of racing attention on the ETC [European Touring Car Championship] the like of which it has never enjoyed before.' Regretably, that prophecy was not to be fulfilled. At the time, however, Alex Park and Derek Whittaker led the chorus of optimism which rang out from end to end of the Silverstone grandstands.

No more races were attended that year, but a full two-car ETC programme was promised for 1977. Broadspeed would spend the next six months relatively free from criticism, not being due to present itself again until the opening round of the championship at Monza.

The only other noteworthy British development exercise on works-supplied engines at this period was by the Forward Engineering Company, in the context of water speed records. (Forward boss, Ron Beaty, was a former Jaguar engineer, and he had kept in touch with Browns Lane.)

During that winter Ralph Broad put into effect more development than had been possible during the whole of the previous year. The main reason for this was the appointment by Broad and his chairman John Jackson of a young doctor of engineering with ten years of motor industry experience, named Colin Mynott, as general manager of Broadspeed which was, by now, devoted to BL work almost exclusively. This should have taken off some of the pressure; but, being full of nervous energy anyway, Broad continued to work flat-out as before. Nevertheless, Mynott was a very useful ally and an old friend, having raced a Mini-Cooper against Broad in the formative years of the ETC.

Leyland Cars motor sport liaison man Simon Pearson – who had been closest to Ralph Broad when the plot was being hatched eighteen months earlier – left the corporation in February 1977. His role was not replaced as such. He had been a member of the public relations team. Competitions would now be aligned more directly to BL's marketing organisation. It should be remembered,

Cleaner underbonnet view in late 1976, when Ralph Broad and Andy Rouse attended a Jaguar Drivers' Club event at Browns Lane. They are seen here with JDC Chairman David Harvey (*centre*). The car's livery was somewhat modified already.

however, that almost every organisation within BL at the time was as fluid as the corporation itself. An exception was Jaguar's engineering department, which repelled all potential boarders; this situation helped ensure that (for example) no production Jaguar ever carried any visible Leyland badging – unlike the Broadspeed XJ12 which, for 1977, was treated to a new paint job.

The relationship between Southam and Browns Lane, as directed from the corridors of BL power, was that Knight's department should respond to Broadspeed if need be; but Jaguar itself should not spend time initiating ideas or solutions to problems. The political clout remained, as ever, in Leyland's corporate hands.

The story of 1977
Late March 1977 saw the full potential of the team as the vast new Scammell articulated tractor-unit and semi-trailer manœuvred and unloaded its cargo in the Monza paddock.

Mightily impressive with their wide Speedline 19-inch (as opposed to 16-inch) wheels, the new cars smacked of professionalism. However, the omens began to look bad almost from the start of practice. Broad had extracted the

STAND BY, EVERYBODY. IT'S <u>ANOTHER</u> BRIEF, DEFINITIVE STATEMENT FOR THE MOTORSPORT INFORMATION PACK.

WHEN I SAY OUR MOTORSPORT PROGRAMME IS A CROSS-FERTILISED, DICHOTOMOUS PANACEA, I MEAN IT— AND YOU <u>CAN QUOTE ME ON THAT.</u>

Leyland Cars press officer Glen Hutchinson found some humour in the generally unhappy Leyland-Broadspeed alliance. He has since turned professional in the world of commercial art, and kindly re-drew two of the cartoons specially for this book. They represent the best way in which to recall a strangely unreal period of competition history.

272

During the 'Broadspeed' era, there was a successful project to break international water speed records with the venerable ex-Norman Buckley craft *Miss Windermere V*, powered by a V12 Jaguar engine. Engine preparation was by Ronald Beaty of Forward Engineering, seen here with the boat (and Philip Weaver) at Browns Lane.

Below:

For 1977, the one word 'Leyland' dominated the blue and white Broadspeed coupé, which lapped the new Donington Park circuit at over 90 mph in early 1977 to create an unofficial record.

The No. 2 Broadspeed car did not reach the start line at Monza, 1977, due to engine damage in practice.

necessary 100 bhp per ton – a rule of thumb target power-to-weight ratio necessary for competitiveness in Group 2; but the forces generated in braking and turning-in for the three new Monza chicanes were playing havoc with the supply of oil to the bearings and, remarkably, Broadspeed had brought only one spare engine; John Fitzpatrick and Tim Schenken got it because they blew up first. Derek Bell and Andy Rouse were the unlucky non-starters, (David Hobbs had left the team, following a BMW offer he couldn't refuse.)

Fitzpatrick put the re-engined Jaguar on pole position with a 2 min. 2·94 sec. lap. Alongside him was the Alpina BMW of Dieter Quester (2 min. 3·7 sec.), and the two cars made quite a spectacle as they accelerated hard for the first chicane. Fitzpatrick made it first – and he stayed in front for nearly an hour of the four-hour race. Then, at a scheduled stop, Schenken took over; but he had no chance of recovering the lead, for oil starvation had set in already and he was able to complete only two laps before coasting to retirement.

Although a BMW did win at Monza, the Bavarian marque was in trouble, too. In attendance at Monza was Leyland's new head of competitions, former scribe and rallyist John Davenport, who had just spent a brief sojourn with the RAC, and was something of a specialist in motor sporting law and politics. One of his first tasks was to be Leyland's spokesman on the question of allowing dry-sump lubrication, which was banned at this stage. Visits to the Paris authorities soon made this concession a likely happening, as it was a problem for BMW, Ford, and

everyone else at the faster end of Group 2.

Meantime, the cars came home to Southam for a few more weeks of preparation, under the guidance of David Griffiths. In April, Tim Schenken lapped the brand-new circuit at Donington Park in 1 min. 17.9 sec. (90·45 mph) but this was a PR stunt rather than a test session. Most sessions were at Goodwood or Silverstone, and Bell lost a

Right:
Signed by Broad, Fitzpatrick, Bell, Rouse and Schenken, this fine picture was taken in the village of Bosonohy on Czechoslovakia's Brno road circuit. If any venue suited the powerful Broadspeed cars, this one *should* have done. (*Courtesy: Chris Gross*)

Fitzpatrick leads Quester at Monza, spring 1977.

274

wheel during at least one of them. Shortly afterwards the mighty Scammell transporter was *en route* for Salzburg, where practice for Round 2 of the 1977 European Touring Car Championship seemed to go quite well for the Jaguars. The only chicane at the Salzburgring is not a tight one, and the engines were lasting better. The Jaguars of Bell/Rouse and Schenken/Fitzpatrick were on pole and fourth grid positions; both led, and both retired early with the same problem – failure of the outer driving flange – though neither car actually lost a wheel. Schenken was the first to go, at 11 laps; then Rouse came in not many minutes later with a punctured radiator. His car was then found to have the same problem. 'Faulty components from a new batch' was the official reason for failure.

Since the racing programme had become a fact, rather than a mere plan, it was only natural for Bob Knight and his engineers at Browns Lane to co-operate as best they

Tim Schenken at the Nürburgring Karussel during practice. (*Courtesy: Chris Gross*)

One of the coupés howls along the old straight behind the Nürburgring pits.

could. Tom Jones, chief chassis engineer at Browns Lane and one of Jaguar's longest-serving staffmen, spent more time than most trying to help resolve problems that were not of his own company's making.

There was consternation in May when Leyland announced that the Broadspeed cars would not practice *or* race at Mugello and must come home at once. Jaguar engineering could not or would not give Leyland's policy-makers a firm OK on the driveshafts. Andy Rouse was actually ready and waiting to take them to Italy by air; but they did not materialise. 'What's going on at Leyland?' demanded the *Motoring News* editorial headline, on behalf of its patriotic readership. 'We can understand Leyland's refusal to run the cars as they stood, when they knew a vital component was likely to break. ... What we don't altogether understand is why the newly-designed replacement driveshafts cannot be flown out and track-tested, instead of recalling the whole team back to base. That way the Jaguars could still run at Enna.' But at Enna, a fortnight later, there were no Jaguars. Round 4 of the 1977 ETC championship was yet another BMW walkover.

At Brno on 5 June 1977 the XJ12 racer had its best-yet chance of victory. Here was a true road circuit – long and fast and open and bumpy, with steep gradients which the V12 Jaguar engine could devour ravenously. In practice the Jaguars shone; the slower one was more than six seconds per lap quicker than the best BMW, according to the official grid chart!

The story of the race could make a book in itself. With its long straights, the Brno circuit did not demand dry-sump lubrication quite as urgently as most others. It did demand three-and-a-half hours of hard work from the pit crews, and in terms of driver concentration at least half that time. Each 6·8-mile lap could introduce a new hazard, according to weather and traffic conditions. Each high-speed hazard *could* be a heart-stopper – and so it proved to be for the Jaguar drivers.

For the first time, the two XJ12s shared the front row; and they could not fail to impress – resplendent in red, white and blue and embellished with Leyland-image logos.

Where normally the number plate would be and across the top of the windscreen, was the word 'Leyland' with the infamous 'Flying Whatnot' on the right. (Some said this symbol looked like a swastika which can, of course, represent good luck.) On the left was the new Leyland Motorsport 'helmet', devised by Kevin Best, Christine Dwyer and Alan Zafer – three of the lighthearted marketing folk who helped keep the whole outfit human at this somewhat frantic stage of Leyland history. Another was PR man Glen Hutchinson, an accomplished cartoonist.

And Leyland history *was* made as Derek Bell led John Fitzpatrick through the uphill Farina curve for the first time. (The Farina curve had been so-called after the original world champion had one of his dramatic accidents there.) The two Jaguars pulled away from Dieter Quester's Alpina car and the other BMWs, and made a fine sight as they surged into the pits straight and bellowed away into the village street of Bosonohy for the second time.

Next time around, Fitzpatrick was all alone. The gremlins had stuck again and this time Derek Bell coasted in with a failed camshaft oil-feed. Bell did have another go an hour or so later, but then the car stuck in third gear. The other car led by twelve seconds after five laps and was continuing to pull away from the CSLs when, on Lap 7, Fitzpatrick felt a huge thud which he thought might have been caused by debris – not a nice thing to happen at close-on 175 mph on a country road, even when you have it to yourself. Probably what he had heard was a flailing offside rear tyre ripping through the bodywork. Somehow the crippled car was brought under control and coaxed back to the pits where the best part of half an hour was spent rectifying the mechanical havoc which had been wrought. Afterwards Schenken and Fitzpatrick put in the fastest (unofficial) race laps in 3 min. 31·7 sec. and 3 min. 31·4 sec. respectively before clutch slip set in. They were, eventually, classified as finishers having covered 45 laps – 11 less than the winners, Facetti and Finotto, whose CSL had taken over from the Quester/Walkinshaw car after the latter broke its crankshaft. Leyland's was not the only troubled team in this very hard, fast motor race. Jeremy Walton was more than fair in his *Motoring News* report: 'The Leyland Broadspeed personnel had shown the kind of sheer bloody-minded persistence that must lead to a reward commensurate to the big cat's phenomenal turn of speed. ... Battered but unbowed, the Jaguar was a wonderful addition to the finishers' *parc-fermé*!' Overall placing was sixteenth, and third in class – which meant that only two of the BMW CSLs had survived.

Five weeks later at the Nürburgring, all the problems of the 'Big Cats' (Alan Zafer had made this their semi-official title) seemed to re-emerge in practice, despite a lengthy on-the-spot private test session beforehand. John Davenport had done his stuff and dry sump lubrication was now permitted – but Broadspeed was, ironically, not ready to take advantage of this mid-season relaxation of the rules. Despite constant engine trouble, Fitzpatrick made pole position. Leyland Cars' product marketing director Alan Edis was 'cautiously optimistic' (another term Alan Zafer claims as his own from the contemporary glossary of BL terminology), and felt that it was important to race if the cars could be got to the starting line as 'runners' – Germany being the home of the Jaguars' chief rivals in the marketplace (Mercedes-Benz) and on the race-course (BMW). I was Jaguar's reluctant representative on that occasion, to witness the Broadspeed boys working tirelessly to keep the XJ12 coupés going at

Above and below:

Throughout practice at the Nürburgring, Ralph Broad's team seemed to be removing, repairing and replacing engines without pause. On this occasion, at least, they would glimpse success briefly. (*Courtesy: Chris Gross*)

all. I was of the belief that the cars were stretcher cases yet again and should be treated as such; but I was quite wrong.

The race began with a typical Fitzpatrick flyer; a Group 2 lap record of the old Nürburgring at over 100 mph, from a standing start, *and* it would stand all day long. Hardly had the Jaguar, with its 12-second lead, vanished into the forest on its second lap when the V12 engine (now claiming 570 bhp) failed again. So Tim Schenken missed a drive; Derek Bell and Andy Rouse, however, then put together the best-ever performance by a saloon racing under the Leyland banner. Fifth at the first bend, fourth after one lap, third after two laps, and second after four: that was the story of their softly-catchee-monkey race, as they lapped steadily. With anything like reasonable reliability and luck, this *could* have been a win. I was more than ready to eat my words at this race of attrition, for all the BMW CSLs were in desperate trouble. At 16 laps, however, the surviving Jaguar lost some 10 minutes while one of the radiators was fixed. It was a four-hour race – not the traditional six-hour – and that stop was enough to present victory to Burkhard Bövensiepen's brilliant green BMW, driven by Dieter Quester and (for the final stint) by the magnificent Gunnar Nilsson, lately winner of the Belgian Grand Prix for Lotus yet so soon to die bravely in the face of chronic cancer.

There was distinct relief in the BMW camp, for Bell had brought his times down in those final laps, reducing the deficit from five to two minutes; but Nilsson had kept his 'cool', and nursed the BMW (low on oil pressure) to a victory which would put the European championship within reach of his co-driver Quester. Immediately afterwards, Colin Chapman was telling Nilsson that he would prefer it if he would kindly concentrate upon his Lotus Grand Prix commitments; but the Swede had done what was necessary by then. It was his last victory. So, Bell and Rouse finished a creditable second in Germany. The fact that a Zakspeed Ford Escort came third proved two things: one was that the smaller-engined car was competitive, now that *it* had dry sump lubrication; the other was that the super-tuned BMW CSLs were also unreliable when made to work hard. Even so, in its moment of glory, the Jaguar had been defeated again. You cannot advertise a second placing in isolation. An outright victory – just one – is necessary, if you are going to cash in on your investment. Leyland's Jaguars had come as near as ever they would.

Below and Top Right:
The old Nürburgring as it is remembered. One picture shows Peter Lindner leading Böhringer (Mercedes) and the rest in the very first ETC race (1963) with his 3·8. The other, taken a little further away from the pits, shows one of the very fast BMW CSLs chasing the Bell/Rouse XJ in 1977.

The 24 hours of Francorchamps (at one time under consideration) did not count towards the ETC championship in those days, and the four-week gap between Nürburgring and Zandvoort was used to convert one of the Broadspeed cars to dry-sump lubrication. Browns Lane was not involved directly. Davenport used his contacts – in this case Group 44 – to obtain from the American aerospace industry, oil lines of the strength and diameter to cope with the necessary pressure and flow rate. Bob Tullius and Lanky Foushee had more than three years of Jaguar V12 experience behind them by then; yet Tullius has since spoken of his surprise at the Europeans taking so little advantage of his team's accumulated knowledge. Harry Mundy's antipathy towards developing the V12 for racing was certainly an element here.

Zandvoort was the first circuit where neither Cat could take pole position, mainly because of rain, though the third-on-grid Bell/Rouse wet-sump car did qualify only half a second slower than the fastest BMW – that of series leaders Carlo Facetti and Martino Finotto. Tim Schenken was on the third row, guinea-pig for the new dry-sump system which incorporated twin Cosworth DFV-type scavenge pumps.

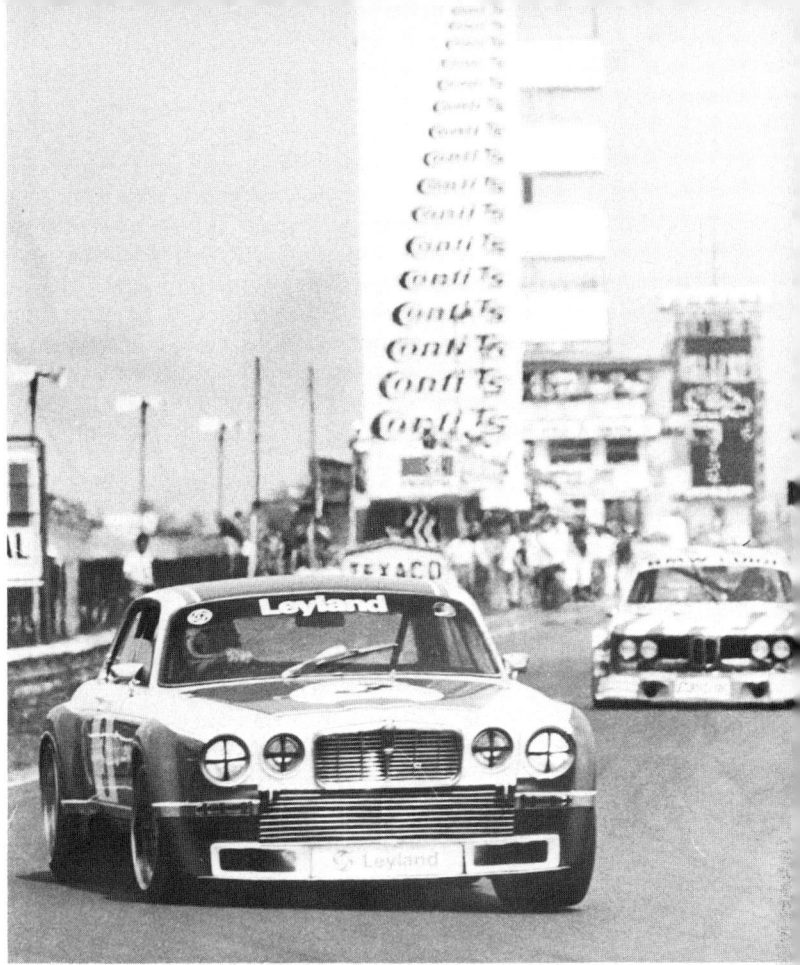

Below:
Broadspeed's finest hour. A fine action shot of the Group 2 car looking its best as Bell and Rouse bring it home second at the Nürburgring in a race of attrition.
(*Courtesy: Chris Gross*)

Andy Rouse dived ahead at the end of Lap 1, and spent the next twenty laps dicing with Quester's partner-for-the-day, local ace Antoine Hezemans. Then Rouse had to stop because of a rear-wheel puncture. Bell continued and ran third until the differential oil pump seized at two-thirds distance; after this was changed it became clear that the crown wheel had stripped.

Schenken made his first stop on Lap 5; scavenge pump drive failures were to blame for this, and for three more long involuntary visits to the pits, where pump couplings were changed each time.

There were not as many championship races in the 1970s as there would be in the 1980s, and another six-week intermission gave the Broadspeed team a chance to gather strength for the XJ12's 'first anniversary appearance' – the 1977 Tourist Trophy race.

By this time, papers were being put through to get the XJ-S homologated after all. Beautiful as the XJ6/XJ12 two-door models were, they were not popular enough in the market place; so there was strong pressure, from those promoting racing within Leyland, to get the newer design developed. The XJ-S was a heavy car too, but it could be made lighter than the present racer.

At a pre-TT Silverstone test session good old Derek Bell was still speaking enthusiastically about the XJ12, despite the weight problem. By this time he was pointing out that the car itself *had* become lighter than before – but that it was back in square one because of the *extra* weight caused by the fitting of stronger driveshafts, bigger wheels and brakes (with water cooling), cooling fans and so on. There was a problem of traction, too. Bell said he could hear the inside rear wheel and the differential scrubbing with each other as the front wheel lifted under power through Abbey Curve at around 145 mph. The car would not change its line easily: nor could it jink around obstacles in the way most saloon racers could by now.

Bell put it in a nutshell when he said that the Group 2 XJ12 was a brutal machine that you had to drive rather than race: 'You have to keep thinking about the car,' he said. 'Now it's even worse ... all the time there's some bloody switch you should be playing with.' The latest item in this category was a pair of fans for the inboard rear brakes, which the driver had to switch on and off.

Derek Bell still felt the car had a future. His attitude was that he was driving for Britain, as well as 'helping to keep a legend alive' – which, of course, was the attitude which *was* keeping Jaguar itself alive (though only just). He and the other drivers – like all good racing men – were interested only in winning. They still believed they could win, too. Bell was saying he would like to carry on with the car in 1978; but things would be different again once the TT was over. . . .

The TT spells 'Finis'

The Jaguars occupied the front row for the 107-lap (500 km) classic at Silverstone, and the cheers filled the grand-stands as Schenken led from Rouse and Quester first time around. Schenken lost control momentarily at Copse Corner, resuming in third place only to have a front hub failure which took him off-course at Becketts. Rouse and Quester battled on, until the Jaguar – just ahead – came in for its first stop. Bell drove from Lap 39 to Lap 75. The Alpina car, driven from mid-race by Tom Walkinshaw, led the Jaguar of Rouse by about 22 seconds as the latter began his second heroic stint.

Weather was dull, with occasional rain. There was tenseness everywhere as the gap narrowed at a rate which made victory seem possible. Then it rained harder. With nine laps still to go, and Walkinshaw visible in the distance, Rouse lost the Jaguar in the biggest possible way; though car and driver were little more than shaken, nothing could be done to make the car mobile again that day. Even so, Rouse and Bell were credited with fourth place, behind the three BMWs of Quester/Walkinshaw, Joosen/Grano, and Dieudonné/Xhenceval – the latter pair being penalised one minute (and therefore one place) for missing out the Woodcote chicane to avoid an inadvertent 'moment' early on. This would have a bearing on the outcome of the drivers' championship later on.

Andy Rouse and Tim Schenken lead Dieter Quester in the Alpina BMW, Silverstone, September 1977.

Schenken spins away his lead at Silverstone. This car went off-course for good later on.

Derek Bell working hard at Silverstone, where a win might – just might – have reprieved the project which Ralph Broad still believed could succeed. Unfortunately, Andy Rouse was to crash this car in a vain chase of the champion's BMW.

What I remember most about that day is the feeling of suspended animation in the BL enclosure as the Walkinshaw V. Rouse duel unfolded. I was watching with John Fitzpatrick at that certain moment when the rain got worse and it became clear that unless Walkinshaw made a gross error Rouse would not catch him. There were those present – like the drivers (they had shown great

esprit de corps as well as exceptional bravery throughout a troubled summer) – who believed that a win at Silverstone could have tipped the balance. Just one victory would have meant so much to everyone – and would mean so much to historians too. The fact remains that a secret decision was ratified on Monday 26 September 1977, with a message issued by Leyland: 'The company will continue with its motor racing activities, although the racing Jaguar will not figure in future racing plans. . . .'

There was an element of sportsmanship to the end. Rather than pull out late, the team took part in the Zolder race. One car led and both retired – this time for good.

It was a sad time for Ralph Broad. There had been the tragedy of his daughter's death in a road accident; and his own health demanded a change of air and environment.

To the end he believed he was on the verge of having a winner. He and Colin Mynott were convinced that a redesign of the XJ12's rear suspension and drive-line – as allowed by the Group 2 regulations – would have seen to that. It was also his belief that Knight had persuaded Whittaker not to allow such a major modification to take place. If that was so, then it was all part of Knight's ultimately successful plan to protect Jaguar from BL and extinction.

Aside from the progress being made by Andy Rouse, there was little to interest Ralph Broad on the motor racing front, now his dream for Jaguar had evaporated. He and his partner John Jackson sold out to John Handley.

Ralph and Jean Broad emigrated to Portimão, and began a new life; but he did not become inactive – he couldn't have done that. He went into the business of wood-burning stoves; the business grew, and in the mid-1980s the Broads' son joined them in it. If the Leyland hierarchy of the time learned anything from the whole costly exercise, it was that the name Jaguar still meant something to the fans; though all the goodwill in the World could not produce a victory for BL's 'Big Cats'.

It was a time of change. Soon after Michael Edwardes' arrival to run BL, Bob Knight was made Managing Director of Jaguar Cars. From then on Jaguar remained in limbo until the spring of 1980, when it was given proper company status under John Egan. It should never have lost it.

Touring car racing had not reached the commercial peak then. There was not the variety of opposition, or the Worldwide publicity potential. The introduction of Group A racing in 1982, however, was to put touring cars on a higher plain altogether. The man who saw how Jaguar could fit into the new scheme of things was, ironically, the man who had kept Jaguar out of the headlines at Silverstone in 1977. . . . Tom Walkinshaw. He has made amends a hundredfold. The TWR story is told in the next chapter but one. Meantime, the Jaguar V12 engine was beginning to come into its own in America's own special brand of national sports car racing, under the Group 44 banner. Europe in 1977 looked like this. (With hindsight it is not as bad as it looks, for those Broadspeed monsters delighted the hopeful fans while they were running.)

1977 Group 2 European Touring Car Championship

	1st	2nd	Jaguar Performance
Mar, Round 1, Monza	Facetti/Finotto/Grano (Ex-Luigi BMW)	Merzario/Bigliazzi (Alfa Romeo CTV)	DNF
April, Round 2, Salzburg	Quester/Nilsson (Alpina BMW)	Finotto/Joosen (Luigi BMW)	DNF
May, Round 3, Mugello	Dieudonné/Xhenceval (Luigi BMW)	Facetti/Finotto (Imberti BMW)	DNS
May, Round 4, Enna	Facetti/Finotto (Imberti BMW)	Dieudonné/Xhenceval (Luigi BMW)	DNS
June, Round 5, Brno	Facetti/Finotto (Imberti BMW)	Dieudonné/Xhenceval (Luigi BMW)	16th
July, Round 6, Nürburg	Quester/Nilsson (Alpina BMW)	**Bell/Rouse (Broadspeed Jaguar)**	2nd
Aug, Round 7, Zandvoort	Quester/Hezemans (Alpina BMW)	Dieudonné/Xhenceval/Joosen (Luigi BMW)	DNF
Sept, Round 8, Silverstone	Quester/Walkinshaw (Alpina BMW)	Joosen/Grano (Luigi BMW)	4th (DNF)
Sept, Round 9, Zolder	Quester/Neve (Alpina BMW)	Dieudonné/Xhenceval (Luigi BMW)	DNF
Oct, Round 10, Jarama	Joosen/Grano (Luigi BMW)	Dieudonné/Xhenceval (Luigi BMW)	DNS
Oct, Round 11, Estoril	Facetti/Finotto (Imberti BMW)	Quester/Grano (Alpina BMW)	DNS
Oct, Round 12, Ricard	(Cancelled: Lack of Entries)		

Champion Driver: Dieter Quester (Austria) 125 points.
Runners-up: Carlo Facetti (Italy), Pierre Dieudonné (Belgium) and Jean Xhenceval (Belgium) 119 points

BMW = 3·2-litre BMW CSL, 330–340 bhp.

Jaguar = 5·4-litre Broadspeed XJ5.3C, 550–580 bhp.

DNF = Did Not Finish

DNS = Did Not Start

Chapter Fourteen

Racing Revival, USA

By the beginning of the 1970s, the original Jaguar import organisation in North America had disappeared. British Leyland had been created in 1968, coinciding almost exactly with the launching of the XJ6 saloon. This car was to prove the most significant single retainer of Jaguar's identity throughout a decade in which every other BL member marque would lose its distinctive character and indeed its soul. The retirement of Jo Eerdmans in April 1970 was the turning point.

Johannes Eerdmans had gained his early business experience with the Phillips Electrical organisation back home in Holland. Later he had run the Formica division of De la Rue in Britain; then William Lyons invited him to organise a Jaguar Cars North American Corporation (later Jaguar Cars Inc.) in the winter of 1952–53. This timing had coincided with the Browns Lane, Coventry, factory getting into full swing, and with the introduction of automatic transmission for Jaguar's MkVII saloon. With success at Le Mans making Jaguar a world name for the first time, this was the ideal time to build up the market upon which Jaguar was so dependent. This appointment had not pleased the existing distributors – namely Max Hoffman in the East and Charles Hornburg in the West – but it had kept Jaguar strong, *and* under control, in tough territory. Eerdmans had introduced the XJ6 to America, and would return in an honorary capacity to assist in the launching of the V12-engined E-type at Palm Springs in 1971. This occasion also marked the last visit to the USA by Sir William as head of Jaguar Cars Ltd (accompanied by Harry Mundy).

The V12 E-type was very much an interim model which had to survive a period in which motoring for pleasure was seen in many quarters as anti-social. Moreover, the E-type concept – considered a classic one now – was seen as old fashioned and unergonomic, with the shadow of the 'F-type' constantly looming. The 'F-type' or (misnamed) 'XK-F' would become the XJ-S, but not until the 1976 model year. Meantime the E-type continued to sell, but with increasing difficulty – especially after the demise of the 2 + 2 coupé towards the end of 1973, leaving only the long-wheelbase roadster on offer.

No-one in Coventry had considered the V12 E-type a serious competition car from the works point of view. Jaguar's engineering division was hanging on to its independence staunchly, despite the recent retirements of Bill Heynes (1969) and Walter Hassan (1972). Heynes's XJ13 had given warning of the possibilities of corporate decision makers dabbling in homespun projects. Their successor, Bob Knight, entrenched. His engineering department would keep the dormant Jaguar heart beating until the great re-awakening of the 1980s. One thing this meant was no official participation in competitions. (This policy did not prevent British Leyland from embarking upon a brief and abortive racing programme of its own in 1976–77 using the XJ12 as a basis and employing Ralph Broad as the outside contractor. The episode is described in Chapter 13.)

Those responsible for the individual products were, of course, thrown together as members of the new corporation, under Sir Donald Stokes. In 1968 he had said that

Graham Whitehead (*left*) with Sir William Lyons and Jaguar power-unit engineer Harry Mundy at the 1971 American launch of the V12 engine, the latter being eyed longingly by Whitehead's deputy in charge of US operations, fellow-Briton Mike Dale. Jaguar Cars Ltd still existed as a company, though already within British Leyland; but by the end of 1972 (the year of Sir William's retirement) its identity was being eroded. Dale, himself a successful SCCA race driver, would be responsible for Jaguar's return to US racing with the V12 E-type in 1974, thus playing his part in keeping the marque alive – even under a BL banner.

the Specialist Car Division of British Leyland (Triumph, Rover, and Jaguar) would 'remain as separate entities and be given every encouragement to develop their own character car'; it would not stay that way, and the results of his efforts to unite the British motor industry would bring economic catastrophe.

In North America, Jaguar Cars Inc. had become the Jaguar Division of British Leyland Motors Inc., and its headquarters transferred across the River Hudson from Manhattan's East 57th Street to new premises in Leonia, New Jersey, a few minutes west of the George Washington Bridge.

President of the new company was an Englishman,

Graham Wright Whitehead (no relation of the racing Whiteheads), who had started out in the motor industry immediately after the Second World War as a Wolseley apprentice, and had travelled the world for Nuffield and the British Motor Corporation before setting down roots in the USA. Among his six vice-presidents were Jock Reid (in charge of car service for the new group but soon to retire), Mike Dale (Austin and MG sales), and Bruce McWilliams (Triumph and Rover sales). In October 1969 Tony Thompson (Jaguar's US sales chief) left the company and Dale (34) was given that additional responsibility.

Michael Harrington Dale, a Britisher, had been a BMC

First major V12 Jaguar race victory in the USA was by this E-type on 11 August 1974 at Seattle. Preparation was by Joe Huffaker; the driver was Lee Mueller. On the Seattle straight, this 'B-production' car was timed at 178 mph.

Below:
Joe Huffaker, ace tuner from San Rafael, California, had plenty of experience with the six-cylinder E-type before the V12 version came along.

Below centre:
Lee Mueller scored three victories in 1974 and four in 1975 to become Northern Pacific SCCA divisional champion, driving the Huffaker Engineering B-production V12 Jaguar E-type.

man throughout his career, apart from a spell in the Royal Air Force. A former athlete of international standing, his competitive nature not only attracted him to the USA but gave motor racing a special appeal for him. He had raced Minis in South America as 'Eduardo Harrington' after a local newspaper had got his name wrong. (He had dropped 'Dale' from his entry form for reasons of identity.) From 1968 to 1975 he raced in the USA, and was 1973 H-production champion with an Austin-Healey Sprite.

One by one, the British marques would fade from the American scene but, despite years of frustration (when policy was being dictated in London rather than Coven-

Below right:
The winning smile of Robert Tullius.

Bob Tullius began winning sprint trophies around 1955 with this Pine Alley Racing Assoc. Buick, photographed at a New York drag strip.

Tullius's former partner, engineer, and occasional co-driver Brian Fuerstenau was invaluable to the development of Group 44 as a smart and professional racing team, and was still involved as a freelance consultant in the 1980s.

try), Whitehead and Dale overcame all the odds. This tenacity would result in their becoming Jaguar's two top executives for North America in the headier days of the mid to late 1980s. There can be no doubt that it was Mike Dale's own enthusiasm which brought Jaguar back into racing in the USA at a most unexpected time.

There were two catalysts. One of these was the desperate need to promote E-type sales; the other was the existence of two ready-made racing teams in the USA.

Although not a true successor to the E-type – there *could* never be one – the XJ-S was intended to fulfil that role to some extent. The idea of an exciting new Jaguar was being discussed in detail in *Car* and other international magazines as early as 1972, with artists' impressions of the XJ-S and – before very much longer – pictures of the real thing. So the vital need was to liven up the E-type's image in the USA, where sales of the Great British Sports Car – the MG, the Healey, the Triumph, the Jaguar – were lagging badly, as emission controls sapped their performance. 'Gas guzzler' it might be, but the V12 was the key to the charisma which so many Jaguar lovers felt had been lost. To them, Jaguar's name had been built upon winning great rallies and races; and on representing a 'different', individual organisation. Now it seemed so impersonal; and anyway, how long was it since a Jaguar had won a big race?

Group 44's background

To go racing at national level was more rewarding in North America than elsewhere; and in many ways this applies today – not just through television coverage but through gate-money and sponsorship. One of the first people to commercialise the essentially amateur world of SCCA production sports car racing, back in 1961, was a determined, crewcut Kodak salesman called Robert Tullius. He had proved his Triumph TR3 (being bought on the never-never after an initial deposit of two hundred dollars) to be quicker than two sponsored TR4s, and on the strength of this he had pushed Mike Cook and Fred Gamble of Standard-Triumph, New York, into talking to

287

The Group 44 and Huffaker E-types line up behind the official pace car for the 1974 B-production final at Road Atlanta. Mueller punctured and Tullius finished second.

him. His persuasiveness did not have any immediate effect but after some more racing (and after coralling S-T president Martin Tustin in the foyer as he was leaving the office one evening), Tullius scored his first goal: he obtained a brand new TR4 to which he transferred his best TR3 tweaks. After one early smash-up, Tullius went from strength to strength, winning the SCCA's E-production championship for four years in a row and, in partnership with Brian Fuerstenau, he formed an image-conscious business called Group 44 Inc. (44 was Tullius regular race number). Tullius's approach was not always popular with other racers in those days; but racing did go the commercial way, as he knew it must, and the true amateurs became thinner on the ground. By the end of the decade, Virginia-based New Yorker Bob Tullius had established Group 44 as an immaculately turned-out team known to every motoring buff in North America as a regular race winner. The shining whiteness of transporter and cars were the hallmarks of Tullius and his main sponsor, Quaker State Oil. Here was a clean and tidy outfit, thoroughly professional in its presentation, ready to produce results for the potential customer. Mike Dale had watched Group 44's progress; when he got the go-ahead to race the V12 E-type (largely through the efforts of Bob Berry, by now working for BL International in London) there was no doubt who would be chosen to run the show on the East Coast.

The goal was to get nationwide coverage, and to ensure defeat for the all-conquering Chevrolet Corvettes which were dominating Class B races. The Sports Car Club of America ran regional races; and the best of the regional racers went to Road Atlanta at the season's end in search of the national title. So Whitehead and Dale decided to put a similar promotional effort into a West Coast E-type. If two cars made it to the Georgia finals, then the chance of taking the National Championship would be doubled.

Joe Huffaker returns

Selection of a West Coast team was, again, a straightforward one. Joe Huffaker of San Rafael (half an hour north of the Golden Gate Bridge) had a fine reputation as an engine builder and race preparation specialist – from Indy cars to MGs. He knew his Jaguars, too. Almost as soon as the six-cylinder E-type arrived in California Huffaker had set upon it, and produced a raceworthy car. The first car was written off by Frank Morrill in 1962, but another Huffaker E-type had been campaigned by Merle Brennan who won 39 races (from 42 starts) between 1963 and 1965.

Top and bottom insets:

The 'West' and 'East' cars enjoyed a full and successful season in 1975 – the final year for E-type sales. Both had distinctive flat wind-deflectors. The Huffaker car had a less obtrusive roll-over bar and retained its front bumper and overriders. The Group 44 car featured an air dam.

In those days, Huffaker had been Kjell Qvale's competitions manager at British Motor Car Distributors, San Francisco. He had prepared a Lister-Jaguar and the lightweight E which Qvale had entered for the Sebring 12-hour race. Since then, he had built and tuned XK engines for various customers, while continuing to make MGs his speciality. His company, Huffaker Engineering Inc., was already contracted to prepare an MGB for British Leyland when their request to examine the V12 E-type (and its potential opposition) came his way.

Back in Coventry, nothing could have been further from the management's mind than motor racing. The former service and racing manager, Lofty England, retired as Chairman early in 1974. Geoffrey Robinson, the new BL-appointed chief executive, had more than enough to contend with as he worked on the combined deficiencies of quality and quantity. *His* hours were numbered, anyway, as nationalisation was imminent for BL and therefore Jaguar. So the Leonia management was on its own as it embarked upon America's first 'official' Jaguar racing programme for many years.

It was well into 1974 by the time the programme got the final go-ahead. The decision was precipitated, finally, by the somewhat unexpected requirement to market the E-type for another full season. Despite the fact production was petering out in Coventry, there were still hundreds of the spectacular V12 sports cars to be shifted from the showrooms.

Huffaker Engineering and Group 44 compared notes as they went along but were essentially independent of each other, and set things up in their individual ways. The outcome was that the Huffaker car produced more power, whereas the Tullius machine could claim the edge on braking and handling. SCCA 'production' regulations were more liberal than the equivalent in Europe; but they were more stringent than those for Group 2 – the category into which BL/Broadspeed would soon be launching themselves (and the XJ12C) so disastrously. So, for example, the basic quadruple Stromberg emission carburetters had to be retained, despite the progress with fuel injection in Coventry; by 1975, however, the Tullius car was able to show 425 bhp and the Huffaker one a best bench figure of 460 bhp.

Tullius's V12 E-type racer

This is how Paul Brand (Group 44's public relation man) described the modifications and preparation which took place between May and August 1974:

Preparation of the Group 44 V-12 Jaguar has been due mainly to the labors of two men – project engineer Brian Fuerstenau and crew chief Lawton Foushee. Conservatively, three to four thousand man-hours have gone into building and preparing the Jaguar to date, and the car is still in an early stage of development.

What does it take to build the Jaguar into a competitive race car? Fuerstenau explained the basic philosophy followed in building the car: 'We decided to be ultra-conservative because of the rush to complete the car in time to qualify it for the run-offs while at the same time maintaining three other cars and racing two out of every three weekends. Unless a component or system was entirely unsuitable for racing, we decided to leave it stock.

Development of the first engine was undertaken with the idea of looking

for reliability first and then horsepower. The engine is a 60–degree overhead cam V-12 with aluminium pan, block, and heads, and is fitted with four 1¾ in. Stromberg sidedraft carburetors and single distributor with solid state ignition. They started by porting and polishing the cylinder heads and installing heavy duty valve springs. New cams were engineered for the V-12's specific requirements, and were reground on the stock billets.

The block is fitted with cast iron, slip-in liners, and in order to hone them to the proper clearances, Fuerstenau fabricated a special jig to hold the liners because, once out of the block, they proved to be very flexible. 'We had to build the jig because you could deflect the liner two or three thousandths of an inch just by squeezing it in your hand.'

The seven main bearing crankshaft was left completely stock, including the factory balancing which proved quite accurate. To save weight and ensure uniformity Fuerstenau lightened and balanced the connecting rods. He installed special pistons and rings that brought the compression ratio up to 11.0 to 1.

The majority of efforts with the engine went into building an oil system that would guarantee a continuous flow of oil under the heavy braking and cornering loads generated on the race track. A 360-degree swinging oil pick-up was built (but modified later) with a series of baffles to try to hold the oil in the center of the pan. The pick-up swivels on a ball bearing and oil seal, which is pressure fed from the oil pump to make it as frictionless as possible.

The stock flywheel pressure plate and driven disc were replaced by an aluminium flywheel and heavy duty clutch assembly. The only modification to the transmission, which looks strong enough to handle a pair of V-12s, was to fabricate a shorter shift lever.

The headers and exhaust pipes were fabricated from scratch by installing a dummy engine in the Jaguar chassis, and welding up the headers piece by piece to fit them in and around the tubular front frame. Several of the twelve pipes are assembled with slip joints for ease of removal. The six pipes for each bank of cylinders come out below the rocker panel and join into twin collectors that run half-way along the door before joining into a single pipe which ends in front of the rear tire.

Because SCCA rules do not allow a change in carburetion, Fuerstenau was limited to modifying and re-jetting the stock Strombergs. To insure a strong spark at high RPM, he adapted a capacitive discharge system to the stock coil and distributor.

Will the engine deliver enough horsepower to be competitive with the Corvettes? He thinks it will. 'At this early stage of development, I would guess that we're getting somewhere around 400 HP at 7500 RPM, and with continued development, we might look for as much as 450.'

While Fuerstenau was building the first engine, Foushee was preparing the chassis. The first project, as with all Group 44 cars, was to completely strip the car. Besides the drive train and suspension, all of the interior trim, insulation, and undercoating was removed and the entire chassis cleaned and given a coat of paint.

Except for fitting Delrin bushings to reduce flex and increase reliability, Foushee left the front suspension components and geometry stock, including the ventilated disc brakes. He added a 1 in. adjustable sway bar mounted on solid bushings; this is extremely complex because of the route it follows through the engine compartment. The front torsion bars were replaced by a heavier set with a 30 per cent higher spring rate, and double adjustable aluminium shocks were installed.

The Jaguar rear suspension is somewhat similar to that of the Corvette in that the half-shaft serves as the upper control arm. But instead of the transverse leaf spring, the Jaguar has two coil spring/shock absorber units on each side. Foushee shortened the stock springs to lower the ride height and increase the spring rate, put a pair of double adjustable aluminium shocks under each side, and added a 5/8 in. adjustable sway bar. He replaced the solid rotor brakes with optional ventilated rotor discs and calipers that are standard equipment on the front. For strength the original trailing arm with rubber bushings were discarded in favor of new heim-joined steel arms.

The standard vacuum assisted brake system was retained, but to obtain the desirable front to rear brake ratio, Foushee installed a variable proportioning valve and Velvetouch brake pads.

The boost system, run off the engine's intake manifold vacuum, was modified to incorporate the hydraulic clutch system so that the brakes and clutch are vacuum assisted to ease pedal effort. The entire package, including a vacuum tank and hydraulic cylinders, is neatly mounted in the floorwell of the passenger compartment.

In addition, Foushee kept the standard power steering unit with the only modification being a larger diameter pulley on the pump to keep from turning it at too many RPM.

For cooling, the mammoth Jaguar radiator was retained, and an oversize aircraft oil cooler was built into the right front headlight opening. Because of the large quantity of oil in the engine and cooler, twin filters were plumbed into the system.

Foushee welded up the roll bar, and flaired the fenders to cover the 15 × 8 Minilites with 23 × 10.5 × 15 Goodyears in the front, and 24.5 × 10 × 15s in the rear. The front fenders were just stretched a bit, but Foushee had to cut off the rear fenders and weld on handformed steel flairs.

Fuerstenau fitted an aerodynamic windscreen and built a new dash incorporating a tachometer with rev limiter (set at 7700 RPM), water temperature, oil pressure, fuel pressure, and two oil temperature gauges, one into, and one out of the cooler. Foushee installed a racing seat with five point restraint system and mounted a tiny 10 in. diameter racing wheel to the standard, adjustable steering column.

By early July, the Jaguar was ready for testing, but the first session lasted just two laps before a problem with the oil system showed up. Fuerstenau went back to the shop, did some rethinking, and came up with a mark two version of the oil system with a new set of baffles and a new oil pick-up that swings 120 degrees side to side, rather than a full 360 degrees. After the second test session, he built a new exhaust system incorporating two megaphones on each side instead of the single straight pipe.

Because the inboard rear brakes were overheating, and in turn causing the differential to cook, Foushee designed a special air duct fitted to the underside of the car to force air to the rear brakes, and installed a differential cooler mounted in the left front headlight opening.

By the third outing, the Jaguar was running quite well, and turning lap times consistently under the B-Production record at Summit Point. For the fourth session, minor chassis adjustments were made to improve the handling, and the car was run for a full thirty minutes at speed to simulate a race. Everything worked, the car went extremely fast, and the only problem encountered was excessive tire wear. The cantilevered Goodyears, originally designed for the Porsche Carreras, seemed too soft for the 2800 lb. Jaguar and lasted only 40–50 minutes at racing speeds.

All the work was kept secret, and it was not until August that the two cars made their simultaneous but separate débuts. Bob Tullius raced the white car with the front spoiler and the impressive rollover bar at Watkins Glen. Having qualified second quickest, he led the field until the gear lever broke and he had to retire three laps from home.

First victory goes to Mueller
On the very same day, 11 August 1974, the Huffaker car scored a runaway victory at Seattle, an auspicious start to the modern era of Jaguar in racing: that is to say, the era in which outside contractors are employed to promote marque names. The driver was Lee Mueller, and the car looked extra-sleek, its BBS three-piece cast-magnesium wheels, its neat rollover bar, its retention of front bumpers and over-riders, and its magnificent silver-finish paint job.

Although only a few more races remained, Mueller and Tullius took them by storm. Mueller won again on 18 and 25 August at Ontario, California, and at Portland, Oregon; but at Sears Point, California, in September, a Mustang side-swiped the Huffaker Jaguar and bent it sufficiently to affect the handling and steering – which

meant Mueller had to rest content with second place. Otherwise the car gave no trouble, and only after those first four races was the engine taken out for examination and preparation for Road Atlanta. 'The motor has been a real joy to work on,' declared Joe Huffaker at the time.

Meanwhile, Bob Tullius was having an even longer run of success. On four successive weekends, from 18 August to 8 September, his E-type swept to victory at Summit Point (W. Virginia), Gainesville (Florida), Bryar (New Hampshire), and Nelson Ledges (Ohio). A fortnight later he did it again at Bridgehampton (New York).

These results ensured that Mueller and Tullius were respective 1974 B-Production regional champions for the Northern Pacific and North Eastern states; they also meant that the two Jaguars would appear at Road Atlanta for the grand finale on 3 November.

It was an exciting race, too. Mueller was out of luck, his car going off-course and suffering a flat tyre; but Tullius battled throughout with defending champion Bill Jobe, only to lose by less than a second. This was the fourteenth of seventeen National B-Production titles to go to a Corvette.

On the slowing-down laps Tullius fumed at himself; quite apart from an increasing braking problem, he had felt that he had allowed himself to get 'uptight' because he had so wanted to beat that Chevrolet. Now he vowed that his 5·3 litres of Jaguar E-type would defeat 5·7 litres of Stingray – next time.

During the winter of 1974–75, Group 44 moved from Falls Church 10-or-so miles west to Herndon, Virginia, not far from Washington's Dulles Airport. The team needed extra space if it was to develop, for there were still commitments to run MG and Triumph cars as well as the Jaguar in SCCA races. The new premises gave 8000 square feet as opposed to 2000 square feet and, in a typically publicity-conscious action, Bob Tullius was able to have the access road named 'Victory Drive' which gave Group 44 a nice new address, too. Goodyear tyres, Quaker State Oil, and BL continued to back this professional outfit which always presented itself – and therefore its sponsors – so well. Bob Tullius, already something of a legend, was about to move on to even greater things; but, before that, he had a particular score to settle.

The two E-types had an even more successful year in 1975. Tullius opened the account with a victory at St Louis, Missouri on 17 May. Lee Mueller won at Portland, Oregon, on 15 June and then, a week later, Tullius was first at Summit Point, West Virginia. Group 44 scored two more mid-west firsts in July, at Brainerd, Minnesota, and Nelson Ledges, Ohio. Mueller responded by taking the chequered flag at Westwood, British Columbia, and again at Portland in August. On 29 August Tullius was the winner at Lime Rock, Connecticut; his sixth win of the year was at Indianapolis Raceway Park on 20 September. A week earlier, Mueller had been the victor at Phoenix, Arizona. With ten wins between them, the two E-types were certain qualifiers for the final shoot-out, for the second year running.

Even at this stage it was felt that the Corvette's V8 engine was producing more power in SCCA racing than the Jaguar V12; and both Jaguar teams found that the long-wheelbase Series Three E-type, with its relatively

Both cars made the SCCA Road Atlanta finals in 1975 for the second year running. Car No. 12, featuring BBS wheels, would have made a great race of it but for a fractured differential carrier (probably caused by a practice spin) leading to final drive seizure moments after these pictures were taken. The comparison shots of the Group 44 car – which won the race to make Tullius B-production National Champion – illustrate several differences between the cars, including the use of Minilite wheels.

narrow track, kept reminding them that it had *not* been created with racing in mind. Joe Huffaker: '... compared to the Corvettes, I feel that our Jaguar handles better on fast, sweeping turns – and as well as the good Corvettes on tighter turns or series of turns where the high polar moment causes the V12 Jaguar to resist quick changes in direction. The V12's brakes are adequate on all but the toughest tracks; and, in this case the high polar moment helps stabilise the car under hard braking. It will definitely outstop the Corvettes. We have sufficient power to out-accelerate them, too, but due to the long wheelbase and the narrow-rim wheels we suffer from wheelspin.' The latter led to the use of higher-than-normal differential ratios for the Huffaker/Mueller car and may, in turn, have contributed to its second failure at Road Atlanta, where the 1975 finals were held on 2 November.

Up to this time, the V12 engine had performed 'flaw-lessly'; Huffaker's heavy breathing had resulted in a best test-bench power output figure of 460 bhp (to the 500-plus bhp of some Corvette claims). During qualifying, however, Mueller went into an enormous high-speed spin on his own oil when a connecting-rod bolt sheared. Huffaker's theory was that, besides flat-spotting all the tyres, the E-type had suffered some invisible rear end damage.

Tullius is champion
Lee Mueller did not get far in the 1975 National B-pro-duction final. He had made best practice time – 91·76 seconds to Tullius's 92·33 – but, on his way round to take up pole position the differential carrier fractured. This allowed the ring-gear to 'climb', resulting in a shearing of the attachment bolts and a complete lock-up of the rear end.

Tullius, like Mueller, had been runner-up in his regional championship this year, and so he had qualified for the final, too. Until the Mueller car had ground to a halt at Turn 5, there had been the fine sight of two E-types following the pace-car (an XJ-S driven by Phil Hill). Now Tullius must fight alone for the Jaguar cause.

This time there was no mistake. Tullius paced himself to a comfortable victory, completing the 18-lap race with a margin of 29·7 seconds over Ray Anton, whose thundering Corvette was separated from its brothers by the third-placed Porsche Carrera of Howard Meister. Tullius also put up the fastest lap in 93·90 seconds, representing 96·61 mph for this undulating, swooping and very testing 2·53-mile circuit.

Lord Stokes was present for this big meeting, during which the six-cylinder E-type of Ohio dealers, Gran Turismo Jaguar (driven by Roger Bighouse), also per-formed with credit, coming fifth in the C-production final despite a spin. (This car would reach *its* pinnacle of achievement five years later.) In fact, the days of Donald Stokes as founder-boss of British Leyland had just ended, following the Ryder report and nationalisation; but his presence as Honorary President indicated clearly that the SCCA production car championships were not quite as amateur as they had set out to be. This final meeting was publicised heavily as the Champion Spark Plug Road Racing Classic; such had been the case increasingly, since the meeting had been evolved to produce 'instant' cham-

pions. Bob Tullius's four championships for Triumph, back in the 1960s, had been won on aggregate per-formances; now he had become champion through winning the final race. His fifth national championship was also Group 44's thirteenth. For Tullius it was the most important single result to date in an impressive racing career – especially so, since the Chevrolet/Jaguar/Porsche confrontation had made Class B the fastest production car race category. (In Class A the bigger-engined Corvettes were relatively unchallenged, and therefore less developed.)

While this success was a highlight for Bob Tullius the racing driver, the achievements of Group 44 in the latter part of 1975 had tended to be overshadowed by the XJ-S's arrival in the marketplace, as if to emphasise the E's obsolescence. Even before the Georgia final, it was announced that it was to be the last 'official' appearance of the V12 E-type in racing. This would prove not to be strictly correct. Following his win at Road Atlanta, Tullius was given an indication that Group 44 might continue to race Jaguar cars – but to what extent? No-one yet knew.

In Coventry, Jaguar was anxious to distance itself from motor racing, despite the studies that were being carried out behind the scenes. The politics of keeping the engin-eering department intact was sapping quite enough of its personnel's energy. Although there was some com-munication across the Atlantic, Group 44 was virtually on its own when it came to preparing an XJ-S for racing.

1976 turned out to be an 'interim' year, but a very busy one as Group 44 was preparing and racing not only Jaguars for Tullius to drive , but an MG Midget, an MGB, and a Triumph TR7 for John Kelly, Brian Fuerstenau, and John McComb respectively. They did not win any championships to add to the team's tally of thirteen national titles since 1962, but they *did* take 29 victories from 45 starts. Four of these were achieved by Tullius in Jaguars.

As the XJ-S was not going to be fully prepared until well into the season, Tullius reasoned that it was worth racing the 'old' E-type since it was still competitive and could put him in a good position to qualify for road Atlanta to defend his B-production title. Relatively little publicity was given to the three E-type victories Tullius gained in 1976.

As a lighthearted interlude, the two E-types were given a final pensioning-off party at Laguna Seca on 28 August 1976, watched by new BL chief, Alex Park. This took the form of a duel between the Huffaker and Group 44 cars at Laguna Seca, California, as part of the third annual Monterey Historic Automobile Races programme which, on this occasion, carried a 'Tribute to Jaguar' theme. Martin Morris, Phil Hill, and Stephen Griswold drove D-types to 1st, 2nd, and 3rd places in the excellent 1948–56 feature race, but the match race came to nothing when the Tullius E-type punctured a front tyre and Mueller won as he liked.

That California meeting made a happy swansong for the V12 E-type racers, with many Jaguar enthusiasts present. In the USA, as in Europe, the 1970s saw a great strengthening of the Jaguar club movement – surely a measure of the strong and widely-held sentiment that the marque should not be allowed to die. Soon afterwards, with 22 race victories between them, the E-types were sold – Huffaker's remaining in the USA and Group 44's returning home. The latter move was quite an unusual one for those days. Former army man Charles Maple was responsible for the deal which brought the white roadster back to Coventry. He was the BL director responsible for getting to grips with BL Cars' production quality, and recognised the historical importance of the car when he saw it during a visit stateside. I can recall that a memo kept doing the rounds of BL corridors until the top brass realised how petty it would be NOT to find a budget to bring back the car which, perhaps, can now be described as 'XJR-1'.

Jaguar engineer Peter Taylor, who had raced his own V12 E-type in the UK, demonstrated the Group 44 E-type at Donington Park and Mallory Park race circuits on Jaguar club occasions, but, essentially, the Group 44 E-type is now in honorable retirement. its chassis number, for the record, is 1S24250.

In retrospect, it seems a little surprising that America did not discover the E-type's potential earlier than it did. The answer is two-fold. Firstly, it is arguable that Jaguars were, until the time of the fuel crisis, selling quite well enough without the need to go racing. The second factor is that until Mike Dale became responsible for selling and servicing all BL cars, no-one in British Leyland Motor Inc. had had the special blend of experience, enthusiasm, and authority that is essential in the modern world of motor racing.

If it had not been for Mike Dale – whose dream is, still, to see a Jaguar win again at Le Mans – it is quite possible that Jaguar Cars Ltd would not have put its name to the marque's new international racing projects, which were to prove so rewarding from 1982 onwards.

Introducing the 'S' to racing
A standard white-painted Jaguar XJ-S coupé, chassis number 2W51120, purred quietly into the hospital-clean Herndon workshop of Group 44 Inc. in February 1976. Within days it was stripped of its sophisticated road equipment by Lawton Foushee and his crew – a prelude to its being turned into the first effective racing XJ-S anywhere.

It was not easy to concentrate on this work alone, however, because British Leyland was making full use of Group 44's race car preparation to keep the names of MG and Triumph alive and kicking in the USA. In the early part of the season Bob Tullius maintained his chances of keeping the B-production title by racing the 'old' E-type, but as an outdated model its successes were not valued highly by British Leyland despite the car's clear capability of winning the title for Tullius again. In any case, Mike Dale wanted to see Jaguar move on to higher things. Nineteen seventy-six was going to be a testing year in more ways than one: testing for the whole Jaguar organisation which, for the time being, was without a chief executive. (There was supposed to be an Operating Committee but it was never permitted to operate.) Engineering director Bob Knight was making quite sure that Browns Lane would not go motor racing as long as Jaguar was unable to control its own destiny. Racing, in Jaguar terms, was done for business reasons if it was done at all. No longer was it easy to relate competition-type innovations to future road-car technology – it had become too specialised a game for that. Even so, as recorded in Chapter 15, several racing-orientated engineering exercises were undertaken by Knight's department in the mid-to-late 1970s.

The works had no XJ-S racing experience to draw upon. So, 1976 was very much a year of testing for Group 44 and its XJ-S.

It was also a year of transition for US sports car racing regulations, with the SCCA running Trans-Am championships for manufacturers as well as drivers, in two categories. Category 2 contained such esoteric equipment as the Porche turbos and the Chevrolet Monzas. Category 1 included more standard vehicles like the Chevrolet Corvette, the Porsche 911S, and, of course, the Jaguar XJ-S. There was plenty of scope for reasonable modification, even in Category 1, however. Ten-inch wheel rims and extended wheel-arches were permitted; suspension and brakes could be improved accordingly; and there was free breathing for the engine. Brian Fuerstenau – Bob Tullius's partner when Group 44 was formed back in the 1960s and by now thrice champion in SCCA racing himself – was the chief engine builder. A studious and intellectual soul, Fuerstenau avoided modifying the heart of the engine. He considered the Jaguar's V12's crankshaft and connecting rods more than adequate for racing. What he did was to fit six double-choke Weber 441DF carburetters and a manifold of the type then being made up in Britain for Ron Beaty's Forward Engineering Company by Mangoletsi. Forward had began tuning the V12 engine almost as soon as it had come on the market, and Beaty recalls that his first customer for his Weber conversion was Hugh Hunter, a well-known and successful sports car driver in the immediate pre- and post-war periods. Hunter had wanted his 1974 V12 E-type road car to do a genuine 150 mph, and with Beaty's conversion this requirement was more than met. In 1975, Forward Engineering had supplied a bored-out super-tuned race-prepared V12 E-type to Glen Bunch of Newport News, Virginia, for his use in the newly-created IMSA Camel GT race series. It was natural, therefore, that Jaguar engineers should point Bob Tullius in the direction of their former colleague, Beaty, in expectation of a performance that would be needed to propel Group 44's XJ-S as quickly as the E-type which had a smaller frontal area and was, of course, lighter. Fuel injection – newly introduced for the XJ12 and the XJ-S road cars – was considered but rejected by Group 44 at this stage.

The most important engine modification, designed by Fuerstenau, was the use of dry-sump lubrication. There would be long-distance events now (the Group 44 E-type had had to compete only in relatively short races), and so reliability was more important than sheer power. Nevertheless, at an early stage, a power output of 475 bhp at 7600 rpm was being quoted, and *Road & Track* magazine recorded a 0–100 mph time of 10·3 seconds during a track test with Tullius.

Suspension, steering, and brakes were adapations from the road car. For example, rear (Girling) discs were kept inboard, although the units were the larger ones usually fitted in front. Even larger (Lockheed) discs with eight-piston calipers were installed at the front of this competition car.

Having begun to amass SCCA points with the E-type, Tullius presented the XJ-S as a racer for the first time at Watkins Glen in July 1976, when the World Championship of Makes entry list included (incidentally) a BMW CSL for John Fitzpatrick, Brian Redman, and Tom Walkinshaw – all to become Jaguar drivers later on. Tullius was fast in practice but weather conditions were blamed for his decision not to race at 'The Glen' that

siasm for motor racing but would not be drawn into discussing the BL Motor Sport programme in depth. Walton did put it to *MN*'s readers that, 'there is a very much brighter side to Leyland's competition plans ... It is called Group 44 and it operates Leyland sports cars ... With Bob Tullius as number one driver and Quaker State Oil as co-sponsors, this neat team aggressively defends British honour in the World's best market for sports cars.'

Park told Walton: 'The Group 44 team is economically efficient and successful, and we gain good feedback from them ... A first-class investment.' As if in response, Bob

Final competitive event for the two American Series Three V12 E-types, at Laguna Seca in August 1976, was this East v. West match race which Mueller won after Tullius suffered a puncture. The Huffaker car was later sold privately.

weekend. So, it was not until 22 August 1976, at Mosport, that the Group 44 XJ-S made its début. Here Tullius qualified quickest and led Category 1 until the oil temperature began to soar. He eased off, therefore, and settled for fourth in category, and tenth overall.

This may not have been a brilliant beginning, but Group 44 had stolen a march on the BL/Broadspeed team, whose XJ12 had not yet started a race, despite hopeful pronouncements since early in the year. So the Americans' effort began to take the limelight – and some of it was reflected across the Atlantic. This was, no doubt, helped by the presence of BL's Chief Executive, Alex Park, at Laguna Seca's 'Tribute to Jaguar' race meeting a week after Mosport.

In that week's issue of *Motoring News* (dated 26 August 1976) Alex Park had been interviewed by Jeremy Walton, mainly on the depressing subject of British Leyland's troubled sales figures. He did admit to a lifelong enthu-

Jaguar engineer Peter Taylor demonstrates the ex-Tullius E-type at the new Donington Park circuit in 1977.

The first Group 44 XJ-S, as raced by Tullius at Mosport Park, Ontario, in late 1976, when 475 bhp (using six Weber carburetters) was being claimed for its dry-sump V12 engines.

Tullius took the XJ-S to Lime Rock, Connecticut, soon afterwards and made best practice time. He went on to win his race at this SCCA national meeting. Now the XJ-S was on its way as a competition car.

Failure of an experimental oil pump drive at Indianapolis Raceway Park meant another non-start but, towards the end of the year, the SCCA finals began to loom ahead. With that Lime Rock win to add to the three earlier ones with the E-type, Tullius now had enough points to go back to Road Atlanta and try to retain his B-production crown – though quite how the Group 44 XJ-S in its modified form got in as a 'production' car it is hard to tell. However, the arguments about its eligibility were

forgotten after an uncharacteristically wayward performance. Tullius took pole position; but on the first corner he found himself short of tarmac and the XJ-S dropped to twelfth place in the resultant drama. For eight laps it gobbled up the Corvettes and Porsches but then disappeared for a second time, having set a new class lap record in 92·069 seconds. A carburetter leak on to the exhaust led to an underbonnet fire. It was quickly doused but Tullius's chance to take another national title was blown. Chevrolet was in control once more; but Group 44 was about to take on the Corvettes in a more advanced category.

To complete 1976, Tullius took the Jaguar XJ-S to

Bob Tullius in action with the first racing XJ-S, 1976.

Daytona for the season's last IMSA Camel GT race but retired with cockpit overheating, having run fourth. He had learned in that short season enough for Mike Dale to declare: 'Group 44 has amply demonstrated its professional racing capability but we could not make a commitment until we had a car which would be competitive in a 'pro' series . . . the car can be a winner, and we expect its success to benefit all our cars in terms of sales promotion. That, of course, is why we are in racing.'

Dale added that Huffaker Engineering would continue to campaign a Triumph TR7 and an MGB in SCCA national racing. Although it was not forsaking SCCA

production racing completely, Group 44 was now committed to becoming the first team in the world to go title-hunting with the XJ-S – fully five years before the great Group A assault in Europe by Tom Walkinshaw Racing. The Trans Am series was the obvious next step, Dale opined, and the XJ-S was ready to provide victory in Category 1. How right he was – and at what a crucial time for Jaguar.

One particular characteristic made the XJ-S a more 'natural' racer than the Series Three long-wheelbase E-type, and that was its aerodynamic integrity. Tullius said he thought all the talk of wind-tunnel testing had been half 'bull' and half dreaming. '... but now I'm a believer,' he added. 'At Daytona I could drive up and down the banking at 180 mph quite effortlessly.'

A special attraction of the SCCA's 1977 Trans-Am professional race championship was the clear separation of Categories 1 and 2, from the point of view of scoring. Basically, the Trans Am Category 1 rules were similar to those for B-production. To provide more spectacle, the SCCA permitted big weight reductions and body modifications – to improve aerodynamics still further and to accommodate wider-rimmed wheels. For 1977, the Group 44 XJ-S began to look as impressively fierce as a Camaro in full battle order, and power was now up to over 500 bhp, thanks to the engine development programme carried out during the winter by Brian Fuerstenau, while 'Lanky' Foushee (winner of the 1976 S-K Mechanic of the year award) masterminded a complete rebuild of the car itself.

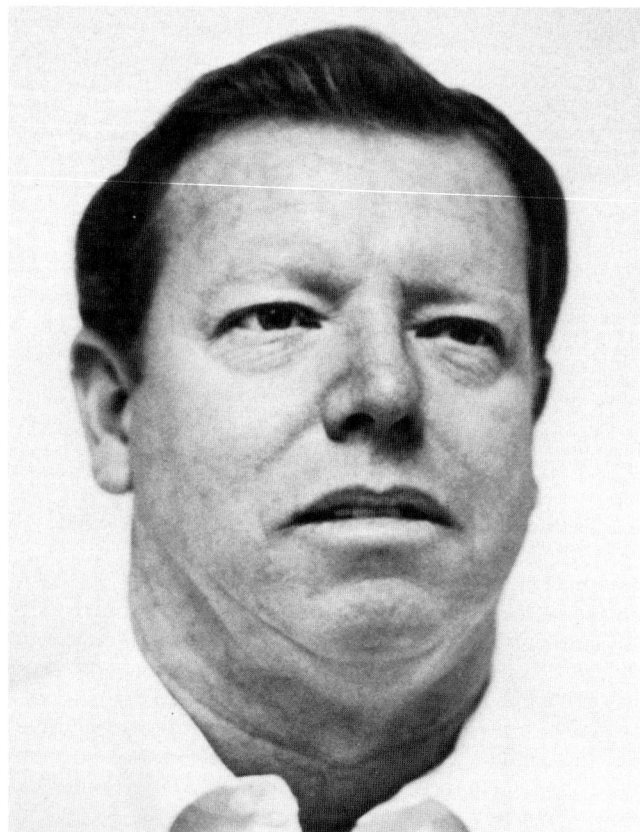

Crew chief Lawton ('Lanky') Foushee, Bob Tullius's 'right hand' since before Group 44's E-type era.

'Thundering Elegance'

For the New York Auto Expo in the spring of Silver Jubilee year, Graham Whitehead and Mike Dale produced a very Special XJ-S, the Jubilee Jaguar. Their colleague Bruce McWilliams (who was, by then, in charge of BL product planning and legislation in the USA) had got together with none other than Albrecht Goertz whose styling of the BMW 507 is still regarded as an artistic triumph, and who had conceived the format of Nissan's Datsun Z-series – the world's biggest-selling sports car. Goertz had, in fact, admired the E-type Jaguar which had helped inspire the 'Z' car. His task with the XJ-S was limited, in that the existing shape could not be altered; but this colour-

Group 44 XJ-S in 1977 'Trans Am' guise.

co-ordinated show-model did illustrate how the XJ-S could be made more elegant and attractive inside and out, and so paved the way for the works-introduced improvements to the model in the 1980s. From late 1977 the advertising theme for the XJ-S in North America became 'Thundering Elegance', with the two words suitably linked to two pictures – one depicting the dramatic looking Trans-Am

Bob Tullius takes over from Brian Fuerstenau at Watkins Glen during the 1977 6-hour race – the XJ-S's first endurance event.

Group 44's main rivals in 1977 were Corvettes, Camaros, and Porsches – but occasionally another highly-competitive Jaguar would appear …

… the six-cylinder E-type prepared by Gran Turismo Jaguar of Eastlake Ohio, which laid claim to be the 'winningest' Jaguar of them all.

machine, the other the sleek, silent road car. It was important to maintain the luxury image of the latter while portraying a high-performance, new look to the marque. It was good advertising at a time when Jaguar most needed it for, without proper leadership at Browns Lane, product quality (as opposed to engineering quality) was at a low ebb, despite the untiring efforts of plant director Peter Craig (who was to die suddenly in early 1977) and his colleagues.

Trans Am 1977

The Group 44 XJ-S was now on course for two outstanding seasons of Trans Am racing, beginning in May 1977 at Kent Raceway near Seattle in Washington State. The following comments on the ten 1977 races are by Bob Tullius:

299

Round One, Seattle, 29 May: Outqualified by David Mock's Chevrolet Corvette, but in Sunday practice faster due to new tyres. Race run in rain. *Result: 1st.*

Round Two, Westwood, BC, 5 June: Fastest practice and race laps. Car ran perfectly. *Result: 1st.*

Round Three, Portland, Oregon, 12 June: Fastest race lap. Leading when third gear failed. Retired. *Result: 19th.*

Round Four, Nelson Ledges, Ohio, 26 June: Fastest practice and race lap. Leading with three laps to go when 'space age' ignition component failed. Retired. *Result: 8th.*

Round Five, Watkins Glen, NY, 10 July: Fastest practice lap. RH Front wheel failed. Replaced wheel and brake caliper in 13 minutes; changed battery later. Fuerstenau co-drove in this 6-hour race. *Result: 4th.*

Round 6, Hallett, Oklahoma, 31 July: Fastest practice and race laps. Tight course and great heat. Tough race with John Bauer (Porsche) until the latter slowed with heat exhaustion. *Result: 1st.*

Round Seven, Brainerd, Minnesota, 14 August: Fastest race lap. Piston ring broke when leading. Pit-stop near end. ('I thought Brian was waving me in when in fact he was waving me on. My fault.') *Result: 2nd.*

Round Eight, Mosport, Ontario, 21 August: Fastest practice lap after frantic rush from Brainerd. Co-driver Brian did a superb job and crew ran flawless pit stops in this 6-hour race. *Result: 1st.*

Round Nine, Road America, Wisconsin 3/4 Sept.: Fastest practice lap. Two races. Broke front caliper in Saturday race (retired, classed 31st). Came from 42nd on grid to win on Sunday, taking lead in drivers' championship. *Result: 1st.*

Round Ten, St Jovite, nr Montreal, 11 Sept.: Fastest practice lap, and 1st in preliminary race after close battle with Tom Bagley's Corvette. Led main race but eased off (with unidentified vibration) just enough to stave off closest rival John Bauer (Porsche) and thus clinch the drivers title. *Result: 3rd.*

With five victories from ten meetings, Tullius had won the Trans Am Championship in Category 1; but insufficient points prevented the manufacturers' title going to Jaguar. Victory in Category 1 races represented 4th, 5th, or 6th place against Category 2 machinery; but this fact does not detract from the achievement on paper. The Mosport six-hour had been the first major long-distance Jaguar race success anywhere in the world for over a decade.

A late-season appearance in the IMSA Daytona finale was followed by a winter of hard work, the main aim being to bring the XJ-S nearer to the 2860 lb (1300 kg) minimum weight allowed. The 1976/77 car (chassis number 2W51120) was modified, and a completely new one (numbered 44-1) was built up from scratch at Group 44 headquarters, the latter being the regular race car for the new season.

Trans Am 1978

By now, BL's abortive assault on European racing had ended without a single victory and new broom Michael Edwardes was sweeping clean. An even more decisive Trans Am title in 1978 would not come amiss. After an initial spate of bad luck, everything began to fall into place. The ten 1978 Category 1 Trans Am meetings went like this:

Round 1, Sears Point, California, May 1978
Tullius gets involved with other people's accidents; car damaged and time lost. Result: *9th.*

Round 2, Westwood, B.C., 4 June
Brake overheated. Result: *2nd.*

Round 3, Portland, Oregon, 11 June
Further niggling problems. Result: *3rd.*

Round 4, St Jovite, near Montreal, 25 June
First victory of the year. Result: *1st.*

Round 5, Watkins Glen, NY, 8 July
Fuerstenau co-drives with Tullius again in this six-hour marathon which was stopped and re-started due to torrential rain. Despite damaging its nose in an early contretemps at the chicane, the Jaguar comes home 7th overall in a field dominated by Group Five Porsches. Result: *1st.*

Round 6, Mosport, 20 August
Tullius looks unassailable in drivers' championship, and comes 5th in overall classification. Result: *1st.*

Round 7, Brainerd, 13 August
Yet another Category 1 victory. Result: *1st.*

Round 8, Road America, 4 September
Tullius retains his Trans Am drivers' title. Result: *1st.*

Round 9, Laguna Seca, California, 8 October
Tullius is backed by Fuerstenau (driving the 'old' car) as Manufacturers' title becomes a probability. Fuerstenau is 3rd, as Tullius wins. Result: *1st.*

Round 10, Mexico City, 5 November
Tullius (again with the backing of Fuerstenau in the other car) scores his seventh win in succession (equalling a record set by the late Mark Donohue). Manufacturers' title confirmed. Result: *1st.*

This final event was called the *Copa Mexico Trans-Am* and was held at the Ricardo Rodriguez Autodrome in front of a large crowd. Fuerstenau spun on oil and damaged a wheel; then a stub axle broke, probably as a result of the earlier accident, yet he was still classified eighth in class. Category 2 and overall winner was Ludwig Heimrath (Porsche 935); but in sixth place, clearly ahead in Category 1, came Tullius to retain his title. Victory over Chevrolet in the 'makes' championship was a special bonus this time. 'Of all our victories this has to be the most memorable,' said Tullius. 'To achieve it with the Jaguar name behind us is the dream of a lifetime.'

Jaguar now needed all the goodwill it could get, for it was about to enter an even more gloomy period (in the production and quality senses), with all models difficult to obtain – especially the new Series Three XJ saloons, announced in the spring of 1979 – *and* suffering from problems arising largely out of a decision to change the painting processes.

In 1979 and 1980 Jaguar Rover Triumph – a new and temporary form of BL 'specialist car division' – proved as inoperable as BL itself, and it was not beyond the bounds of possibility that Jaguar might be allowed to close down. Fortunately, (Sir) Michael Edwardes realised that Jaguars were unique cars – and that they were uniquely desirable whenever they were well-assembled and reliable. He knew that a management team must be put together, and that Jaguar might then be able to fight its own battle – *and*

Tullius takes the chequered flag in the 1977 Molson Trans Am race.

Despite this crunch ...

Left:
... Bob Tullius and Brian Fuerstenau won their Trans Am category at Watkins Glen, 1978.

Below left:
Towards the end of the 1978 season, Group 44 ran two XJ-Ss to strengthen its grip on the manufacturers' championship. Tullius is seen in the newer car at Laguna Seca ...

Below:
... where Brian Fuerstenau (No. 4) drove Tullius's 1977 Trans Am title-winning XJ-S.

Top:
On the starting grid for the 1978 Mexico City Trans Am final.

Above left:
Fuerstenau leads Tullius in the 1978 final – the *Copa Mexico Trans Am*.

Left:
Tullius ahead of Fuerstenau at the *Autodromo Ricardo Rodriguez*, Mexico City, 1978.

Above:
Bob Tullius, 1978 SCCA Trans Am Category 1 champion, in Mexico with his partner Brian Fuerstenau who helped him in his successful bid to take the manufacturers' title for Jaguar, too.

recover its pride.

Group 44 did continue to race Triumphs in 1979 and 1980, but – after another sortie to Daytona – the two Jaguar XJ-Ss were put under dustsheets.

During 1979 and 1980, however, the Jaguar name was not allowed to be forgotten around the North American circuits.

Freddy holds the fort

For several years Frederick Baker, an Englishman living in the USA, had been driving an elderly six-cylinder E-type in SCCA C-production races. This machine was owned and developed by Gran Turismo Jaguar, an official Jaguar dealership run by Lou Fidanza and Steve Tanski in the Ohio town of Eastlake. Its ever-increasing competitiveness was a source of considerable annoyance to the opposition – the more so because, since the E-type was obsolete, little direct publicity could be gained by Jaguar through promoting it. Jaguar Rover Triumph Inc. (the new name of British Leyland Motors Inc.) was, understandably, less than smitten by the idea of promoting a model of Jaguar that was no longer being made – especially as it was in direct competition with the Triumph V8 on the circuits. The Gran Turismo Jaguar team was very much on its own; yet it produced results.

Throughout 1979, Freddy Baker dominated his regional events, taking three victories and two runner-up spots – performances good enough to assure him a place in the national finals at Road Atlanta. There he qualified fourth on the grid with a time of 92·178 seconds – not far short of Tullius' personal best with the Group 44 XJ-S (set

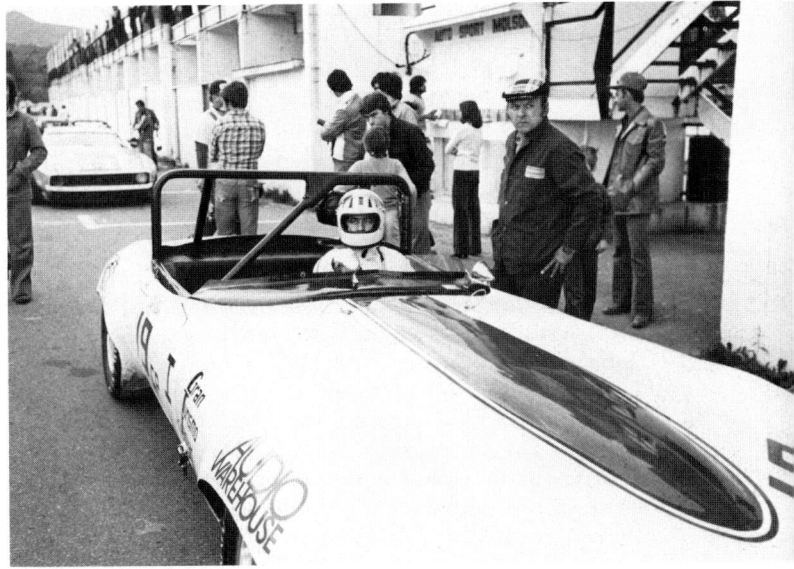

Britisher Fred Baker, who would become SCCA C-production national champion and Jaguar Driver of the Year in 1980. He was still racing this old E-type occasionally in the mid-1980s.

during the 1976 B-production final: 92·069 seconds). In the race-proper brake fade and an excursion dropped Baker's E-type from an early third to sixth at the finish. Film star Paul Newman's Datsun 280Z was the winner.

The year of 1980 brought Gran Turismo Jaguar the championship towards which the small team had laboured so hard – and which it so richly deserved. Freddy Baker won five races between May and July: three at the team's home circuit, Nelson Ledges, Ohio, and one each at the Mid-Ohio and Indianapolis Raceway Park tracks. Main opposition came from well-financed Datsun 280ZX, Mazda RX7, and Triumph V8 entries.

The aged Jaguar was rested through August and September, while more power – to well over 300 bhp – was extracted from its engine, which could now rev past 7000 rpm in reasonable safety. Only by reading the regulations to the letter could Fidanza put the E-type on a par with the opposition; and it is to his credit that no protest – and there were plenty – ever held up. As underdogs, the Eastlake team-members came to the 1980 Road Atlanta finals with nothing to lose, plus a wealth of popular support.

Datsun 'Z' cars had won the last ten annual SCCA C-production championships, so Freddy Baker's best practice lap of 90·769 seconds was calculated to cause some unrest. No Jaguar of any kind had ever circulated Road Atlanta as quickly as this. Two of the 'Z' cars and a

Jaguar Journal cover records Freddy Baker's superb victory in the SCCA C-production national final at Road Atlanta, 1980, when the Gran Turismo Jaguar E-type defeated all the Datsuns and V8 Triumphs. The E-type's dents were caused by early attempts to knock it out of contention. Runner-up was the 'Z-car' of Paul Newman who had avoided the rough stuff. Soon afterwards, John Egan presented Baker with Jaguar's Driver of the Year award for this great performance.

TR8 got below 92 seconds, however, to emphasise that C-production had overtaken B-production for speed and competitiveness. Indeed, there were (by all accounts) remarkably open warnings that the Datsun delegation might stop at nothing to make sure of an eleventh straight victory for the Japanese GT car which – ironically – had been inspired to a large degree by the design of the E-type Jaguar. It was even reported that one driver wore a badge marked 'Designated Hitter' the day before the race.

On the C-production grid for the 1980 Road Atlanta final were nineteen cars: nine Datsuns, four V8 Triumphs, two Mazda RX7s, two Porsche 914/6s, a Lotus Elan, and, in pole position, the white-and-blue Jaguar.

At the end of the pace lap, the Designated Hitter (the experienced Datsun driver, Jim Fitzgerald) appeared to steer his Datsun into the Jaguar while the Starter's flag was still up. Baker managed to keep the car under control, but he missed a gear-change and the Datsun ZX of Logan Blackburn got by. The Jaguar driver was not going to accept that situation; at Turn 3 the now-dented E-type dived inside Blackburn's ZX and passed it on the grass. Fitzgerald's car once again became an obstacle but, after further contact between it and the Jaguar, Baker was able to accelerate clear before the end of Lap 1. A final tap on the door occurred on Lap 2, Turn 3 – but the Jaguar led for the rest of the 18-lap race. Baker set a new class record in 90·766 seconds (nearly 100 mph average) on Lap 4 and extended his lead until half-distance. Behind him, Ken Slagle (Triumph V8) moved up to second place, only to be knocked off-course by Blackburn's ZX. The final order was the Jaguar by 6·9 seconds from defending champion Paul Newman's ZX and the similar cars of Bob Leitzinger, Logan Blackburn and Jim Fitzgerald. The latter was disqualified for his hit-and-run tactics, however, and this let the surviving Huffaker-prepared Triumphs of Lee Mueller and Bruce Qvale up to a respectable fifth and sixth; but they were the only other runners not to be lapped.

There was natural glee in the Gran Turismo Jaguar camp, for the phlegmatic Baker had come out of the battle as a true David among the Goliaths. Jaguar Rover Triumph Inc. hid its chagrin over the accident to Slagle (who had remained virtually uninjured as the Triumph wrote itself off around him), and issued a press release eulogising the winner's performance – a performance which Coventry would recognise several weeks later when John Egan presented Freddy Baker with the 1980 Jaguar Driver of the Year award in Chicago. Baker's was the first SCCA national title to be won in a six-cylinder Jaguar since Merle Brennan's achievement back in 1964. It must be added that Baker's average speed (98·087 mph) was, like the lap record, well up on Bob Tullius's winning figures with the twelve-cylinder car just five years earlier.

The degree of pique displayed by the losers did their image in race circles little good. Andy Schupack, PR Account Executive for Nissan USA, made it quite clear that the SCCA production classes had become as commercial as any other branch of motor racing. Schupak told writer Lori Toepel afterwards:

Auto racing is a business, and the sponsor needs to use it to sell its product. The C-production race is, along with every other race, a promotional campaign. Pioneer Car Stereo, Budweiser, Kendall Oil, Canon, and Datsun all use the exposure gained by racing to sell their products. If it wasn't for money put into the SCCA from these and other companies, Fred Baker wouldn't have had an event to run in. Even JRT [Jaguar Rover Triumph] don't sponsor Baker because they cannot merchandise a car they don't make and sell anymore. If Lou and Freddy want to attract a good sponsor, they need to get a current car they can merchandise.

These words were hard but, essentially, true. Fidanza, Baker and the team continued to do well, attracting support from individuals and small companies who admired their style and attitude; but the regulations were tightened-up for 1981, and so 1980 was to remain their highlight year. No matter what is said about racing an obsolete car, there is no doubt that (afterwards) the Gran Turismo Jaguar effort was recognised in Leonia and in Coventry as a valuable piece of continuity in the resurgence of the Jaguar marque in motor sport.

One up on 'Vanishing Point'
An even quieter public reception was accorded by Jaguar people for another amazing performance at that period. In 1979 Dave Heinz of Florida and Dave Yarborough of South Carolina drove across the USA from Darien, Connecticut, to Redondo Beach, California, to win the contest known as the 'Cannonball Sea to Shining Sea Memorial Trophy Dash' – a highly irregular event, held irregularly. Their unobtrusive, black automatic XJ-S took 32 hours and 51 minutes for the journey; the second-placed Mercedes-Benz 300SEL 6·9 took just eight minutes longer. The Jaguar's average speed worked out at over 87 mph. Grand touring, indeed.

Jaguar Rover Triumph Inc. was well on the way to becoming Jaguar Cars Inc. – a title all Jaguar enthusiasts would be pleased to see revived, though it did not augur well for the identity of the other two great names. In 1980, Bob Tullius was giving serious consideration to pulling out of big-time racing and (maybe) turning Group 44 into some kind of historic car emporium. Group 44 had done much for Triumph in the marque's last days as a sports car; now it was, in effect, Jaguar or nothing – and at first it looked like nothing. Soon, however, John Egan had got Jaguar out of its immediate troubles and was able to consider new subjects; motor racing was one of them.

Brian Fuerstenau stopped racing in 1979, to concentrate on Group 44 technical developments – something he would continue to do in the 1980s, as a freelance engineering consultant, rather than a full-time partner. Number Two driver in the Group 44 team was now the Scots-born Canadian-resident Bill Adam, who had shared some IMSA GTO long-distance class wins in 1980 with Tullius in the obsolescent Triumph TR8.

A third season for the XJ-S
On 17 March 1981, Graham Whitehead announced the return of Group 44 to Trans Am racing with a Jaguar XJ-S. No longer was it a matter of chasing a category win; outright victory was now a possibility and this fact helped Egan and Whitehead to give Tullius the go-ahead, albeit

With the revival of Jaguar Cars Ltd, Group 44 was able to race with the marque once again. These pictures show the NASCAR-type tubular-framed Group 44 XJ-S lookalike taking shape in early 1981. Note Frankland quick-change rear end and inboard discs.

well into the race-preparation season. Trans Am rules now permitted a complete change of structure, and accordingly Lanky Foushee built a sturdy tubular frame around which to attach lightweight XJ-S body panels. The 525 bhp engine was placed $7\frac{1}{2}$ inches further back than normal. Another feature was a Frankland NASCAR-type quick-change differential unit.

Foushee was the one full-time member of Group 44 to have stayed on, apart from Tullius himself; such was the certainty that Group 44 would be wound up. Now, however, Group 44 was beginning to recruit new blood once more; for this was not to be just another isolated racing season, it was the start of something really big.

The 1981 CRC Chemicals Trans Am Championship was a nine-race series starting on 17 May, and the new Washington-built XJ-S went to every event. Instead of 'British Leyland', there was now just one word emblazoned across the windscreen: 'Jaguar'.

Round 1, Charlotte, N. Carolina
There were many problems in practice, and Tullius qualified half-way down the field. In the 100-mile race he moved up to third and was right on the tail of Eppie Wietzes's Corvette when the chequered flag fell. Overall winner George Follimer (Camaro) was penalised 15 seconds for an overtaking infringement and relegated to fourth behind Doc Bundy in a Holbert Racing Porsche Carrera. So Wietzes was first and Tullius was second, a prophetic result – and a very satisfying one.

Round 2, Portland, Oregon
Here Tullius turned the tables, pipping Wietzes for the chequered flag for the 1981 Jaguar's first victory.

Round 3, Lime rock, Connecticut
Electrics failed with six laps to go when running second. Winner: Greg Pickett (Corvette).

Round 4, Road America, Wisconsin
Another electrical fault had Tullius coasting to a halt when second. This time he effected a repair; the engine fired again and he drove hard to the finish – but had lost too much time for a placing. Winner: Monte Shelton (Porsche).

Round Five, Brainerd, Minnesota
Tullius beat Wietzes again. (Jaguar's second victory.)

Round 6, Trois Rivières, Quebec
Jaguar ran second until the timing chain failed. Wietzes extended his championship lead by winning.

Round 7, Mosport Park, Ontario
The series leader suffered an engine failure at this, his home circuit. Tullius scored his third victory, closely followed at the flag by Doc Bundy (Porsche turbo).

Round 8, Laguna Sea, California
George Follmer (Camaro) won; Wietzes clinched the title by coming third; John Bauer, defending champion, wrote off his

'Lanky' Foushee (*right*) and the 1981 top-category Trans Am Jaguar.

Porsche but not himself; Tullius had gearbox selection trouble and fell back to fifth at the finish.

Round 9, Sears Point, California

Tullius looked set for another good finish – maybe even a win? – when a gearbox seal failed. He retired as gears became difficult to engage. Winner: Tom Gloy (Mustang).

So Bob Tullius did not win the championship, but he was a strong runner-up – and he had the bonus of winning more races than anyone else. As Graham Whitehead had said when announcing the programme back in March: 'Winning in a category or class is fine; but winning overall is easier to merchandise ... more

emphatic.'

So, 1981 was a rewarding year. Tullius (Jaguar) took three wins; Trans Am winner Wietzes (Chevrolet) won twice; and the other four races went to Shelton (Porsche), Gloy (Ford), Pickett, and Follmer (Chevrolets). After three seasons of racing with the Jaguar XJ-S – 1977, 1978, and 1981 – Tullius had taken part in 29 Trans Am races and won no fewer than 15 of them. 1981 was also the year in which Bob Tullius became the first recipient of the Sir William Lyons International Jaguar Trophy. This award – conceived by John Steen of Atlanta and a group of dedicated enthusiasts, and

Purposeful look to the first version of the 1981 Group 44 XJ-S, proudly proclaiming 'Jaguar' for the first time since Tullius began racing with the marque.

subsequently 'adopted' by Jaguar Cars Ltd – seeks to honour outstanding contributions to the evolution or success of Jaguar. Sir William himself took an active part in promoting the new award and, as honorary chairman of the selection committee, had no hesitation in ratifying Tullius as the winner; for the American's racing successes on Jaguar's behalf had come at a time when Coventry most needed a morale-boost. Now, Jaguar was in a position to make its own policy decisions. One of these decisions was: to go motor racing at international level.

Jaguar returns – officially!

Soon after the appointment of John Egan as chief executive in Coventry, three key men met to discuss the future of Jaguar racing. Mike Dale and Bob Tullius had been the lead players in the story so far. The third man was Lee Dykstra.

Dykstra had been designing and building competition cars for close on twenty years, working with General Motors and with Ford at different times. His own business, known as Special Chassis Inc., was based at Grand Rapids

in his home state of Michigan. From 1976 he had been responsible for the successful Chevrolet Monza raced in the Camel GT and Can-Am series by Al Holbert.

All three men had watched the progress of the Camel GT series in particular. IMSA had been built from scratch by the enterprising John Bishop.

Formerly an industrial designer, John Bishop had been an SCCA (Sports Car Club of America) director. He had left because of a disagreement over race championship administration and formed IMSA (International Motor Sports Association) in 1969. What he wanted was to create a top-class series of races in which domestic and foreign cars – or combinations of both – could compete on even terms. The series began in 1971, and since 1972 the R J Reynolds Co. has sponsored it strongly to publicise its famous 'Camel' brand of cigarettes. Up to 1978, it was chiefly a battle between Porsche and Chevrolet, with occasional Ford and BMW intervention. In 1980, for the first time, Porsche 935s won each of the fourteen rounds, and Britain's John Fitzpatrick was the champion.

For 1981, the fastest (Camel GT) category was given a new set of regulations, and variety immediately returned. Another great British driver, Brian Redman, began the season with a win for Porsche (with World Endurance champion-elect Bob Garretson and Bobby Rahal) in the Daytona 24-hour marathon which starts the IMSA season off. By May, he had at his disposal a new Lola-Chevrolet and this gave him five more wins before the season was out.

Two views of the tube-frame XJ-S shared by Bill Adam and Tullius in action at Daytona in early 1982. There was a deal for Gordon Smiley to race it – still as No. 44 with Intermedics sponsorship in 1982. Smiley's death (at the wheel of another car) brought that project to an untimely end.

Even omitting his early-season Porsche points, Redman would have been the 1981 champion. A new era had begun. (Incidentally, in January 1982, 44-year-old Brian Redman announced his retirement from racing!)

Throughout IMSA's growing up year, many specialists were at work, creating new designs. Even in the early months of 1981, the first Dykstra drawings of an exciting new shape were being shown, surreptitiously, to trusted allies by a newly-motivated Bob Tullius. Later in the year, the rebuilt team moved away from Washington to new headquarters in Winchester, Virginia, where – once again – Tullius was quick to reflect his aspirations in his postal address: 'Group 44 Inc., Victory Lane'. (The large new premises were to be used not only for workshops but as a warehouse, for Tullius had built up a Kendall/Quaker State oil distribution company and, at that stage, still

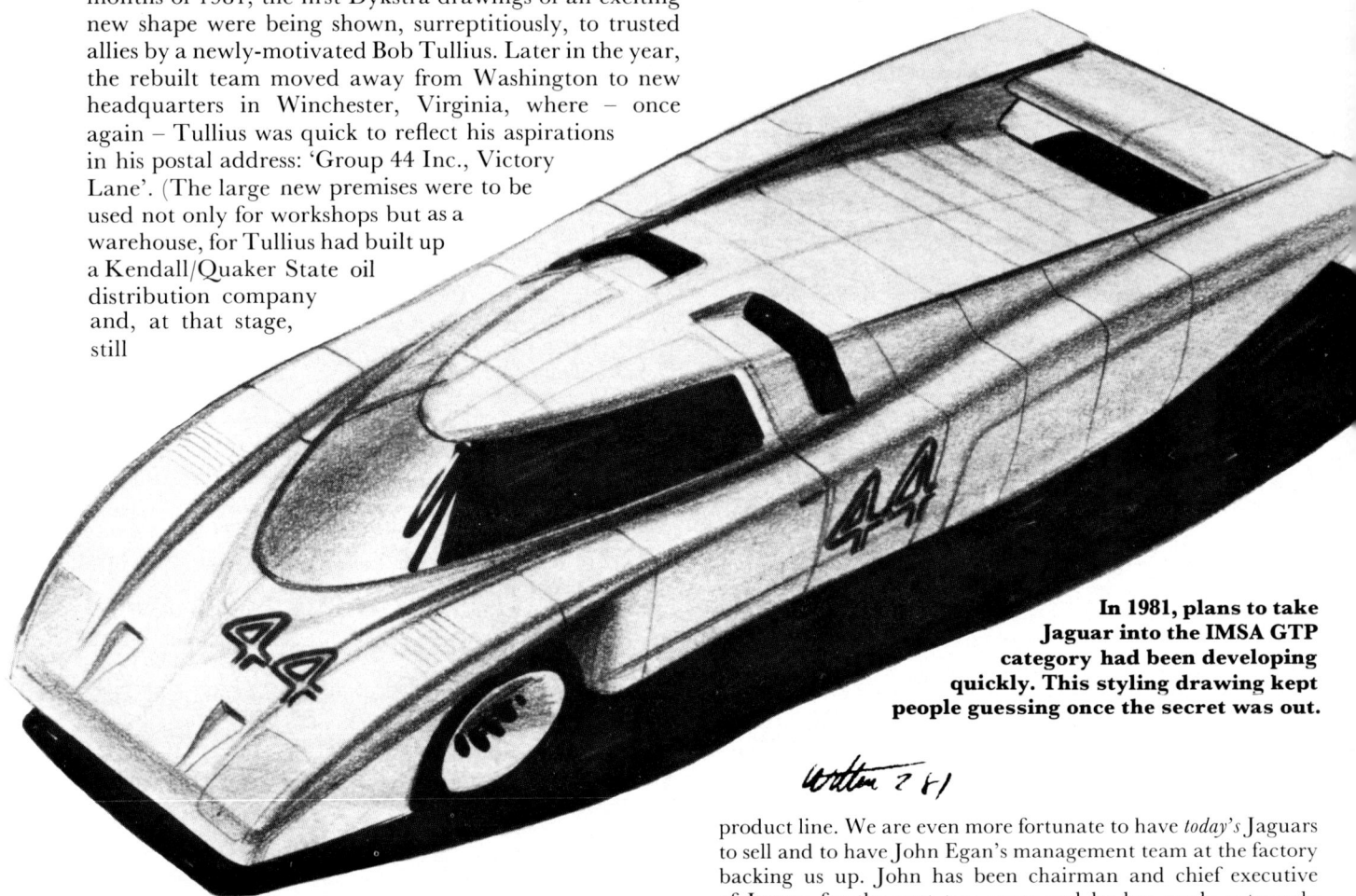

In 1981, plans to take Jaguar into the IMSA GTP category had been developing quickly. This styling drawing kept people guessing once the secret was out.

received some backing – as he had done for many years – from Quaker State. This company, Skyline Oil Inc., was managed by former Jaguar apprentice David Sunter.)

At a press conference on 6 January 1982 Graham Whitehead, head of the Leonia company which would soon be renamed Jaguar Cars Inc., ended months of rumour and speculation. Not only was this a new era for racing; it was a new era for Jaguar's involvement in it, an era which is continuing as this book is written. Whitehead thanked IMSA for having 'kindly provided us with a tailor-made series to win races in'. He went on to say:

Most of you are aware that we have had our problems, first with the loss of MG from our product line in 1980, then the loss of Triumph sports cars and the withdrawal of Rover from this market in 1980. In a two-year period, we have gone from being a leading marketer of sports cars plus luxury sedans to a one-marque luxury car specialist and we had to reduce the company by half to stay in business. However while doing this we have been able to retain our Jaguar dealer organization and provide parts and service back-up for the discontinued sports cars and Rover.

Not only that but we kept selling and, in the midst of the reorganization, our 1981 Jaguar retail sales have exceeded 1980 by 55 per cent. At the rate we have been selling the last few months, and the way January is shaping up, I believe we'll double Jaguar sales in 1982.

We have always been happy to have Jaguar as part of our product line. We are even more fortunate to have *today's* Jaguars to sell and to have John Egan's management team at the factory backing us up. John has been chairman and chief executive of Jaguar for the past two years and he has made extremely satisfactory advances in both production volume and quality control. Just at the time that we have to depend on Jaguar as our sole product line, we are getting the best-designed, best-engineered and best-finished cars we have ever had, and getting them in the quantities we need!

Some of this is due to better communications between our company and the factory. We are now directly responsible to Jaguar and I am going on the Jaguar Cars board of directors later this month. We are now building a team of Jaguar engineers resident in this country who will be working closely with our own staff on product development, government liaison and field service problems. In short, the United States is recognized by Jaguar for what it is ... the largest potential market for Jaguar products in the world. Our moves are their moves, and our input is acknowledged as essential to the future success of the company.

Despite all of these positive statements, can a company which has just undergone a major reorganization and size reduction afford to be involved in an expensive professional racing program in a highly competitive class in which we will be relative newcomers? Well, of course, the answer is that we can hardly afford *not* to. Few luxury cars are sold without some emphasis on performance and Jaguar's reputation rests firmly on its history of racing success.

Then it was the turn of Whitehead's deputy, Mike Dale, to step forward. He reminded his audience of his organisation's deep involvement in racing in the United States, and spoke of its views on continued participation:

We have had a long-term commitment to exposing our products in this demanding arena which can sometimes expose your weaknesses as well as your strengths. That, of course, is one of auto racing's major benefits to a marketing program. The people that you're selling to can see it for what it is. It's honest, competitive and can provide a manufacturer with an image which cannot be gained, practically, in any other way.

It's a marketing tool. It's quite different to television, magazine, radio and newspapers but it's still a marketing tool. In fact, it has some unique properties.

One: It has great integrity. It's not like advertising where the public perception is that you're going to exploit only the strengths of your product. In racing, your success, or otherwise, can be clearly seen by the marketplace and there is nothing you can do to fix the results!

Two: If you're successful it can give you an image which cannot be earned in any other way. It not only gives you the opportunity of selling more of your product but will increase its perceived value to the customer.

Three: The costs, while astronomical from some points of view, look quite reasonable when you compare them with 30 seconds of television, bought in prime-time. It's quite easy to spend a hundred and thirty thousand dollars for that 30 seconds and spend another hundred thousand preparing the TV spot. It takes no effort to spend a million dollars in prime TV in one evening and, while this could be extremely effective for Chevrolet, it is not anywhere near as efficient for a highly specialized low-volume product such as Jaguar.

For a manufacturer of speciality vehicles looking to improve its image, racing has, therefore, considerable attraction. It is particularly so for Jaguar, with its reputation for highly desirable cars of questionable reliability and erratic quality control.

With the arrival of John Egan as the Chairman of Jaguar, that reputation is no longer deserved. The situation is improving so rapidly that one of our main marketing tasks is to find some speedy way of getting an improved quality message to the consumer. Long distance racing provides that opportunity, particularly as Jaguar has a heritage of success in that area.

The IMSA long-distance races provide a spectacular showcase for a manufacturer to show the durability of its products. That is why we have chosen to build a GTP car that can use Jaguar's basic engine line so that we can relate our, anticipated, success to the products we sell.

As this is a new and highly competitive area for us, 1982 will be a development year. We expect to compete in approximately eight races, all of them long distance, and we shall start with Sebring if we feel the car is ready. There will be no championship bid. We will select the events which best suit our needs in evaluating the car.

We have chosen a well-proven combination in Group 44 and Lee Dykstra to undertake this project on our behalf. Those of you who are closely involved in long distance racing know that proper planning and team work are essential to consistent success, and one might say that Group 44 have been preparing themselves for a long time for such an effort.

The successful long distance race car is essentially a *durable* fast moving system rather than the ultimate race car used in sprint racing. Those of you who have had direct contact with Group 44 know how well organized they are as a team and know that they build durable cars.

If you study the results of the Trans-Am racing in 1981, you will see again and again that Group 44 qualified well but not at the front. In the race they went consistently as fast as they qualified and won because the other competitors could not sustain their qualifying speeds. In long distance racing, this, of course, is exactly what is needed.

In Lee Dykstra we have a designer who has already proved that he can design cars that are as quick as Porsche. He hardly needs any other qualifications!

We think the combination of Group 44, Lee Dykstra, and Jaguar engines will provide us with a formidable entry in what we see as long-term commitment to endurance racing.

The new car was not given a name immediately. This is how Leonia press chief Mike Cook worded the press release, dated 7 January 1982, which heralded the first full-scale racing programme to be undertaken as an official Jaguar exercise for more than 25 years:

JAGUAR IMSA GTP COUPE ANNOUNCED

A new ground effects Jaguar V12-powered IMSA GTP coupe, designed by Lee Dykstra, will be campaigned by Group 44 in 1982 with Bob Tullius driving, it has been announced by Jaguar Rover Triumph Inc., principal sponsor of Group 44.

Providing wind tunnel and track testing are successful, the car will compete in a selected group of events and is intended to make its debut at the Sebring 12-Hour March 19–20.

A tentative schedule will be announced after Sebring.

The prototype car will be developed during 1982 as part of a long-term program which will emphasize endurance races, according to Michael H. Dale, JRT vice president for sales and service. 'The goal of the program is to demonstrate the quality of Jaguar engineering and provide the company with a powerful marketing tool,' Dale stated.

The venture is an American one. Its sponsors are JRT and Quaker State Oil. Dykstra designed the car in his Special Chassis Inc. shop in Grand Rapids, Mich. The body work is being done by Diversified Fiberglass in Detroit. The chassis and suspension are being fabricated at the new Group 44 facility in Winchester, Va., and engine preparation and final assembly will also be done there.

Dykstra and Tullius met in the late 60's when Dykstra was project engineer of the Ford Motor Company's Trans-Am racing team and Tullius was driving a Dodge Dart in the series.

They went their separate ways in the racing world. Dykstra moved on to IMSA GT cars and then ground effects Can Am cars. After a stint as an SCCA National racer, Tullius returned to the Trans-Am and won back-to-back championships driving a Jaguar V12 XJ-S.

The Jaguar GTP project began early in 1981. Dykstra said: 'JRT was interested in a car that would put the Jaguar name in the forefront of long-distance racing as it was in the 1950s with the Le Mans winning C-types and D-types. They were also convinced that GTP was the way to go in terms of excitement.'

JRT officials, Dykstra and Tullius all said they are delighted by IMSA's recent announcement of an endurance race schedule within the framework of the Camel GT series. 'The IMSA long-distance races will provide us with a spectacular showcase to prove Jaguar reliability, said JRT's Dale. 'When you are successful in that kind of racing you create a quality image that can not be earned in any other way.'

For Tullius, the Jaguar GTP car is a dream come true. 'It looks like we've got a chance to win in the most prestigious class of all,' he said.

Canadian Bill Adam will co-drive with Tullius at Sebring. They last paired in the 1980 IMSA season, driving a Triumph TR8 in GTO. They won the Sebring endurance race in GTO that year finishing sixth overall. Adam has 10 years driving experience.

Tullius said the Group 44 team is definitely ready for GTP competition. 'We've come a long way since the TR3 days.' He views Sebring as a severe test for the new car. 'It is a car killer. If the Jaguar does well there, we'll know that we've got a strong and very fast car capable of winning anywhere.' Tullius anticipates a top speed of 230–240 mph.

The first XJR-5's structure is aligned, April 1982.

The new car will be powered by essentially the same 525 horsepower V12 engine that Group 44 used in their 1981 Trans-Am Jaguar XJ-S. Its displacement is 5.3 liters (326 c.i.) and it is fueled by six Weber carburetors. The body will be semi-monocoque fiberglass. The chassis will have an aluminium honeycomb floor with steel bulkheads. Dykstra wind-tunnel tested the design using a quarter-scale model.

Comparing the new Jaguar to the 1981 IMSA GTP championship-winning Lola, Dykstra and Tullius say that it will be more straightforward and simpler, and better, they add.

Since there was no car – only a quarter-scale clay model – to show in January 1982, it is not surprising that the new 'American Jaguar' did not make it to Sebring: nor to any of the other early races in the IMSA Camel programme.

XJR-5 becomes a rolling chassis, May 1982. ('XJR-4', in Intermedics livery, is visible at the far end of Group 44's pristine workshop.)

Specifications

Type:	Two-seat, mid-engined ground effects racing car designed for IMSA GTP.	
Engine:	60 degree V-12 water-cooled aluminium block and heads	
	Displacement	5343 cc (326 cubic inches)
	Horsepower	525 horsepower
	Carburetion	6 Weber 44 IDA
	Valve Gear	Chain-driven single overhead cam
Clutch:	3-plate Borg & Beck	
Steering:	Schroeder rack and pinion	
Body:	Semi monocoque. Fiberglass panels.	
Chassis:	Aluminium honeycomb floor, steel bulkheads.	
Wheels, tires, brakes:	Jongbloed wheels.	
	rear:	14 × 16 in.
	front:	12 × 16 in.
	Goodyear tires	
	rear:	27 × 14 × 16 in.
	front:	23.5 × 11.5 × 16 in.
	Lockheed discs, outboard mounted, air cooled.	
	rear:	1-1/4 × 13 in.
	front:	1-3/8 × 13 in.
Dimensions:	Wheelbase	108.5 in.
	Overall length	187 in.
	Width	78 in.
	Height	41 in.
	Ground Clearance	3 in.
	Front track	66 in.
	Rear track	62 in.

By May, a test programme had been worked out through July, leading to the expectation of a début at Watkins Glen on 1 August. The car's name had been established by now: 'XJR-5'.

The familiar and successful tube-frame Jaguar XJ-S – team build number 4 (or 'XJR-4'?) – might well have enjoyed another season of Trans-Am racing. Lanky Foushee was to fit a Borg Warner T-10 gearbox but, in other respects, the car would be as it had been in 1981. Then, on 15 May, came tragedy. It was the first day of Indianapolis qualifying and, as he was about to make an official run, Gordon Smiley died in a high-speed accident. The Texas-based driver, popular and successful on both sides of the Atlantic, probably never knew anything about it – so sudden was the dive his March Indycar took into the concrete wall at Turn 3. Smiley had impressed Tullius on many occasions – not least for his Camaro driving in

XJR-5 as raced in 1982–3, wearing the traditional Tullius 'Quaker State' insignia.

'Lanky' Foushee and Jeffrey Eischen assemble the prototype XJR-5, May 1982.

Canadian Bill Adam, Tullius's first XJR-5 co-driver, shared victory at Road Atlanta, Mosport, and Lime Rock in 1983.

Doc Bundy replaced Bill Adam for the latter part of 1983, when he and Tullius scored at Pocono.

some of the later Trans-Am races of 1981 – and a deal had been struck whereby Intermedics Inc., would sponsor him in the Group 44 XJ-S. With Smiley's death, all thought of running the Trans-Am Jaguar were shelved. (Tullius, Adam, and Smiley had had a troubled run with it in the 1982 Daytona 24-hour race. It was the Group 44 XJ-S's last appearance.)

XJR-5 on test

The XJR-5 continued to take shape in Group 44's Winchester 'factory', and had its first track tests on 21 and 25 June at the local circuit, Summit Point Raceway. It was not the first mid-engined car to be called 'Jaguar'. There had been the XJ13, of course; *and* there had been the 1973 paper-only feasibility study, dreamed up by *Autocar* technical editor Geoffrey Howard and staff artist Vic Berris – a road-going supercar called the GTR V12, incorporating a Jaguar engine.

At a time when sports-racing cars tended to be singularly ugly, and often badly finished, the Dykstra/Foushee prototype of 1982 was delightfully different, beautifully made, and turned out in the typically immaculate white-and-green livery that made members of other teams comment rudely (but, in fact, enviously) on Group 44's disciplined approach. Tullius is, among his talents, a marketing man. He guards Group 44's independence by

treating all his sponsors as customers. This might seem obvious: but how many other racing car builders make such a point of presenting a product so smart and eye-catching, and keeping it that way? Not many.

The XJR-5 was distinctive, viewed from any angle. It did not resemble any road-going Jaguar, of course; but that matter was dealt with logically. The works logo lettering, with the dropped 'J', was applied in large letters on the sides and on the shapely nose of this exciting débutante.

July 7 to 9 1982 were spent at Road Atlanta, where lap times of around 82 seconds made favourable comparisons with those recorded at the most recent IMSA race meeting there. Naturally, there were lessons to be learned; but no major adjustments or alterations were necessary. The performance of the stressed, dry-sumped Jaguar V12 – soon bored out from 326 to 331 cubic inches displacement – was good, although the Crane cams presented more conservative profiles than their Trans Am predecessors. Compression ratio was 12·6 to 1. With more and more applications of 'adjustable' turbocharged engines, the big normally-aspirated V12 was not expected to produce the best lap speeds; on the other hand, the V12 engine was only about 40 lb heavier than that of the contemporary racing Chevrolet V8. With the emphasis on endurance, the American Jaguar effort is more concerned with race results rather than records. In Jaguar's Le Mans heydays, consistent lap speeds were more important than quick ones. At Leonia and Winchester, Le Mans was – naturally enough – the ultimate but unspoken goal. As it was, Tullius did observe at the time that there were 'a few compromises' because 'we wanted a car eligible to compete in both Group C and IMSA GTP'. Steve Nickless, interviewing Tullius for *On Track* magazine, considered this idea a 'public relations mystery', once the Group 44 chief had steered him away from the subject of Le Mans. 'The project has the blessing of the Jaguar factory,' Tullius told him, 'but it is strictly an American effort, and therefore IMSA's programme is the most sensible for us.'

Before leaving Georgia, on 10 July, the XJR-5 visited Lockheed's Marietta wind-tunnel where it proved ground-effective. Indeed, this exercise was a complete vindication for the aerodynamic calculations which Dykstra had calculated. With the wings set for high speeds, a drag coefficient of 0·38 was recorded.

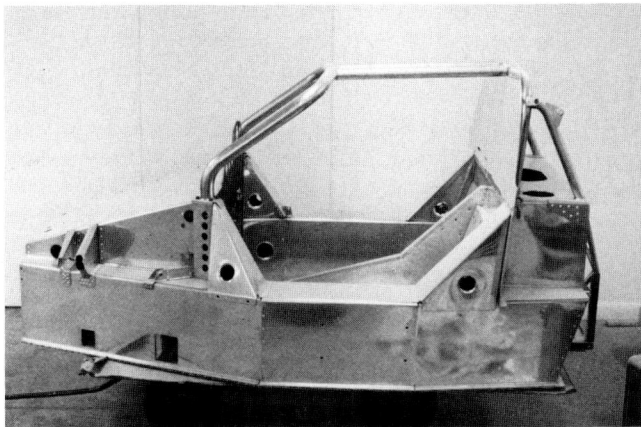

Safety cell: the strength of the XJR-5/7 cockpit proved invaluable on several occasions, in the rough-and-tumble of IMSA racing.

At the end of July, the Group 44 team was making its way to Road America, the famous circuit near Elkhart Lake, Wisconsin. Soon afterwards Mike Cook issued a press release on behalf of Dale, confirming that the XJR-5 would now make its race début in the 500-mile race at Road America on 22 August 1982.

Jaguar's own interest in the project was emphasised by the presence at pre-race testing of the head of vehicle engineering in Coventry, Jim Randle (Bob Knight CBE had retired in 1980). John Egan came for the race itself.

Thirteen of the eighteen IMSA GTP rounds had taken place so far. John Paul Jr (Porsche 935 and Lola-Chevrolet) had already established a handsome points lead, and was well on the way to taking the championship in which he had been runner-up to Redman in 1981. In second place by the end of 1982 would be the Interscope Lola-Chevrolet driver Ted Field.

A class-winning début

It was John Fitzpatrick, the 1980 champion, who won the fourteenth round of the 1982 IMSA Camel GT series, helped by fellow Midlander David Hobbs. The XJR-5 made a copybook start to its career. It ran consistently, made its four scheduled pit-stops efficiently (each stop

taking less than a minute), and the V12 Jaguar engine sang a healthy song throughout.

Bob Tullius came from the fourth row of the grid to run fifth before handing over to Bill Adam after 28 laps; third place was assured when the Lola T600-Chevrolet of Ted Field and Danny Ongais blew up after lapping fastest of all. The official result of the XJR-5's first-ever race was as follows:

Road America 500-mile race

IMSA Camel GT Championship
Round 14 (22 August 1982)

1st J Fitzpatrick/D Hobbs (Porsche 935 turbo) 125 laps (105·922 mph)
2nd J Paul Jr/M de Narvaez (Porsche 935 turbo) 124 laps
3rd *R Tullius/W Adam (XJR-5 Jaguar V12)* 123 laps
4th J Adams/C Cord (Lola T600-Chevrolet) 122 laps
5th D Cowart/K Miller (March 82G-BMW) 119 laps
6th R Lanier/M Hinze (March 82G-Chevrolet) 119 laps

Porsche 935 turbos filled the next three places, down to ninth; but it was the new American Jaguar, No. 44, which caught the imagination. The presence of certain marques in motor racing adds a special lustre. Just when the progress of IMSA Camel GT racing had begun to lack fizz, Group 44 had added a new sparkle to the scene. It would not be very long before there was even more variety.

In finishing third at Road America, the XJR-5 had also won the GTP category: a happy début but one that would not be repeated in the six-hour race at Mid-Ohio a fortnight later. Tullius damaged the car badly against a sand-bank in practice. As a result, Road Atlanta – a mere week away – was missed, too.

There remained only Rounds 17 and 18, Pocono and Daytona; and they brought little joy. On Mount Pocono the XJR-5 had to come in for a new nosepiece and a suspension check after it had hit a spinning Rondeau early on. The car had caught up respectably when Tullius handed over to Adam, who got as high as third; then an engine vibration made retirement inevitable. Bearing failure was blamed.

Tullius was no luckier when he took time off for a trip to Australia in October, when he shared the wheel of John Goss's XJ-S in the James Hardie 1000 km race at Bathurst until hub failure intervened.

1982's IMSA finale was the Daytona 3-hour race (really a practice run for January's 24-hour grind), but again racing luck took over. Tullius was in third place when a soft tyre – maybe the result of hitting debris – took him into the wall at high speed.

Group 44 looked on the bright side. With each rebuild came the opportunity to fabricate lighter components: weight was an enemy.

Rumours were rife. 'I know there's a lot of speculation about Le Mans, but it is just that – speculation. No decisions have been made on taking the XJR-5 outside the US, because it is essential that we get the car reasonably well developed before even raising such a possibility.' Those were the words of Mike Dale at the end of a year in which an all-time record number of Jaguars – more than ten thousand – had been sold in the USA. Less than three years had passed since Jaguar itself had looked doomed. While racing meant a lot to him and to his company, one of his theories was that 'good management means not biting off more than you can chew'. Although the pressure was now upon him to 'keep the sales situation moving along', and despite the setbacks caused by two major crashes (without serious injury to Tullius, thanks largely to Dykstra's sturdy alloy and steel tub), Dale still made the time to keep in constant touch with Tullius and Dykstra. Their dream was, naturally, to bring the name of Jaguar back to Le Mans.

Dale was a cautious statesman: 'I shall be surprised if we do not win a major race in the US before 1983 is out,' he told me by letter. In fact, as a first full season with a brand new design (and running only one car per race) 1983 was to be an outstanding year for the XJR-5.

Motoring writer Patrick Bedard joined Adam and Tullius for the 24 hours of Daytona. After some front-running there was a delay when a thread came cross-threaded during a wheelchange. Then, at around the five-hour mark, Tullius hit a barrier and was out with broken suspension.

A new 300-mile street race, the first Miami Grand Prix, with plenty of prize money and television coverage, gave the XJR-5 its first finish of the year, but not in the truest sense, since the positions at 50 miles had to stand when torrential rain made driving conditions impossible. Championship points were awarded, however, and Tullius was placed fifth.

The month of March saw action in the most traditional of North America's long-distance sports car races – the Sebring 12-hour, held on the notoriously rough runways of an old Florida aerodrome where a Jaguar had won outright in 1955. Could history repeat itself?

With more power and torque, the 6-litre V12 engine came into its own and the XJR-5 was second in practice. From the front row of the grid Tullius (driving first) and Adam ran at the head of the field, swopping the lead with Haywood and Holbert (Porsche 935 turbo). During the fifth hour, Tullius noticed overheating and came in to discover a blown cylinder head gasket. This was changed, but a brief return to the race revealed much more serious damage. However, the performance brought renewed optimism as the IMSA circus headed for Road Atlanta. On the other hand, it meant that *any* thought of taking the car to Le Mans in 1983 could be forgotten now.

Jaguaring through Georgia

The 500 km of Road Atlanta – Round 4 of the championship – took place on 10 April in mixed weather conditions. Not only were there unscheduled switches from dry to wet tyres and back again, but there were several damaging altercations with other cars. With five of the 124 laps to go, a car swerved into the XJR-5 damaging the left side to the extent that it caused a water leak. If the race had been much longer, another stop would have been needed. As it was, Tullius nursed it to its first victory. Tullius and Adam finished 18 seconds ahead of circuit owner Bill Whittington and Emory Donaldson in a March 83G-Chevrolet. They had covered 124 laps, to the 122 of third place-men Sarel van der Merwe and Gianpiero

Moretti (Porsche 935 turbo).

Successive weekend races were then held in California – at Riverside and Laguna Seca. Adam skidded on oil and couldn't restart, when running fourth after two (of six) hours at Riverside; this race was marred by Rolf Stommelen's death. In the 100-miler at Laguna Seca, Tullius was runner-up to series leader Al Holbert.

Except at Daytona and Sebring (where he shared Bruce Leven's Porsche 935) Holbert had, so far, driven a March 83G-Chevrolet. For Round Seven at Charlotte, North Carolina, the American engine was replaced by a single-turbo Porsche flat-six in one of Robin Herd's March 83G chassis, and Holbert gave the new car a first-time-out win, assisted by Jim Trueman. This was lucky as the car *and* the drivers were suffering from overheating. Tullius and Adam had the race in their pocket but a variety of incidents made it necessary to fit no fewer than three new noses to the XJR-5, which still came third.

A fortnight later, on Memorial Day, Tullius and Adam scored their second victory, this time at Lime Rock, Connecticut. This race took the form of three one-hour races. However, at Mid-Ohio, although Tullius recorded fastest lap of the 500-mile race, the XJR-5 failed to finish; an opportunity lost, since the near-invincible Holbert was away in France, winning at Le Mans with a Porsche 956. Likewise at mid-season Daytona, neither driver added to his points tally because neither was present: Holbert was said to be resolving the March-Porsche heat problem, while Tullius was paying an unexpected visit to the UK.

Bell tests XJR-5 at Silverstone

On Tuesday, 28 June 1983, the XJR-5 paid its first visit to a British circuit. Derek Bell's lap times were not recorded but some of his comments were! 'The engine is fantastic,' he advised a *Daily Express* reporter.

'I have raced against it in the United States and it has gradually improved and improved. The car is very nice to drive,' Bell told Russell Bray of the *Birmingham Post*, adding politely that details of his evaluation were for Jaguar people and not for anyone else. Bell had won at Silverstone with a Porsche 956 Group C car only a few weeks earlier, so comparison was not too difficult for him.

John Egan, Jim Randle, and Tom Walkinshaw were at Silverstone that day. Jaguar had hired the Porsche driver for his very great experience in both American and European racing. Bell made quite a telling point for *Motoring News*: 'No, of course Porsche didn't mind my driving it. I asked their permission but they saw the test as encouragement to other manufacturers to enter the World Endurance Championship.'

The break in continuity appeared to throw the Group 44 team out of gear, and the XJR-5 was in trouble again. Returning to America for the July rounds at Brainerd, Sears Point, and Portland Tullius could pick up only a few points each time; Holbert, on the other hand, won these three events. It is interesting to note that the XJR-5 had made fastest practice lap at both Californian events before gaskets started blowing again.

Two cars were taken to Mosport for the 6-hour Labatt's Grand Prix on the tricky Canadian circuit (at which, incidentally, the British XJR-6 would make its début just two years later).

Mosport had been good to Group 44 in the past; and so it would be, once more – now that Foushee had cured the gasket trouble, by discontinuing their use altogether. In practice, Holbert (77·190 sec.) and Tullius (77·619 sec.) shared the front of the grid, and although Tullius jumped ahead initially the battle seesawed. The XJR-5 had a fuel consumption advantage while Holbert's turbocharged car was having to be driven hard. The co-drivers took over and Adam was about half a lap ahead of Trueman when the latter's turbocharger cracked and had to be changed; the March-Porsche lost more than 20 laps.

It was in this race that the consistently fast driver Hurley Haywood (Porsche 935) crashed so heavily that he would be hobbling around on crutches long after his return to racing in 1984.

After this great victory, it was reported that Group 44 would pull out racing for the rest of the season. *Motoring News* opined that: 'One chassis will now remain in the USA for test and development purposes but the other one is due to be freighted to England and Tom Walkinshaw Racing, where it will provide the basis for a Le Mans effort next year.' Whatever the actual intention, events were to prove this prophetic remark premature.

Indeed, Group 44 did absent itself from Road America in late August, when the remarkable new *front*-engined GTP Ford Mustang scored its one big win.

Jim Randle, Derek Bell, and Bob Tullius: Silverstone 1983. (*Courtesy: Maurice Rowe*, Motor)

One mystery at this time was the sudden dropping of Bill Adam, who had backed up Tullius admirably, from the Group 44 team. He was replaced by Harry ('Doc') Bundy who had fallen out with the Whittington brothers (owners of Road Atlanta where he had worked as head instructor). Adam later went on record as saying: 'I left because of a personality conflict with Bob.'

Classic D-type (supplied by John Pearson) greets the 'American Jaguar' on its 1983 visit to Silverstone. John Egan (*dark suit*) was on hand, too. (*Courtesy: Maurice Rowe*, Motor)

Jim Randle and 'Lanky' Foushee in consultation at Silverstone. (*Courtesy: Maurice Rowe*, **Motor**)

Derek Bell tries the XJR-5 at Silverstone in June 1983, giving rise to justified press speculation as to Jaguar's Le Mans plans. (*Courtesy: Maurice Rowe*, **Motor**)

Fourth win for the XJR-5

In a late change-of-mind, Group 44 turned up for the September 500-miler at Pocono, Pennsylvania. There were two good reasons for doing so: Mount Pocono is within an easy day's drive of both Leonia, New Jersey and Winchester, Virginia; and (perhaps more important) Bob Tullius, although placed second in the IMSA Camel GT points chase, was still vulnerable to attack from Holbert's long-distance partner Jim Trueman, as well as from the consistently well-placed Bob Akin (updated Porsche 935).

It was to be a scintillating end to Tullius's first full IMSA GTP season. Fastest in practice, he led initially only to be passed by Holbert; but he reeled him in and the XJR-5 was ten seconds ahead by Lap 30. Soon afterwards, Tullius came into the pits with tyre damage after being forced off course by a slowcoach. Bundy took over and led again from Lap 46. On Lap 50, Holbert's co-driver-for-the-day Dennis Aase spun off and stalled when, apparently, the throttle stuck open. Such was Bundy's lead that he could hand the car back to Tullius with a comfortable lead over van der Merwe and Moretti in a Porsche 935.

This fourth win consolidated Tullius's position as runner-up in the championship, which Al Holbert brought

Above: Top Right: Right:
The men behind the XJR-5: Mike Dale, Lee Dykstra, Bob Tullius and Lawton ('Lanky') Foushee.

to a stylish conclusion when he won again at Daytona in November – by which time Group 44 was immersed in testing and overcoming the season's problems. These been related mainly to gaskets (cured for Mosport) and suspension. The seventeen races had produced 5 wins for the March-Porsche, 4 each for Jaguar and Porsche, 3 for the March-Chevrolet, and 1 for the turbo Mustang GTP cars – as follows:

Daytona I	Porsche 935	Foyt/Wollek/Ballot-Léna/Henn
Miami	March-Chevrolet	A. Holbert
Sebring	Porsche 934	Baker/Mullen/Nierop
Road Atlanta	*Jaguar XJR-5*	R. Tullius/W. Adam
Riverside	Porsche 935	Fitzpatrick/Hobbs/Bell
Laguna Seca	March-Chevrolet	A. Holbert
Charlotte	March-Porsche	A. Holbert/J. Trueman

Lime Rock	*Jaguar XJR-5*	R. Tullius/W. Adam
Mid-Ohio	March-Chevrolet	Rahal/Bundy/Trueman
Daytona II	Porsche 935	A. J. Foyt/H. Haywood
Brainerd	March-Porsche	A. Holbert/J. Trueman
Sears Point	March-Porsche	A. Holbert/J. Trueman
Portland	March-Porsche	A. Holbert
Mosport	*Jaguar XJR-5*	R. Tullius/W. Adam
Road America	Mustang GTP	K. Ludwig/T. Coconis
Pocono	*Jaguar XJR-5*	R. Tullius/H. Bundy
Daytona III	March-Porsche	A. Holbert/J. Trueman

Jaguar was placed second to Porsche among the engine manufacturers and to March in the chassis makers' championship. The top ten drivers scored their points as follows in the 1983 Camel GT championship:

	Points	Overall best results		
Al Holbert	204	7 wins	1 second	1 third
Bob Tullius	*121*	4 wins	1 second	1 third
Jim Trueman	113	5 wins	1 second	0 thirds
Bob Akin	113	0 wins	4 seconds	1 third
John O'Steen	95	0 wins	4 seconds	1 third
Bill Adam	*78*	3 wins	0 seconds	1 third
Kenper Miller	73	0 wins	3 seconds	0 thirds
David Cowart	73	0 wins	3 seconds	0 thirds
Hurley Haywood	71	1 win	0 seconds	1 third
Doc Bundy	*62*	2 wins	0 scconds	0 thirds

One of the big differences between IMSA GTP and Group C racing was, the totally different approaches by the respective sanctioning organisations to the continuous problems of world-class 'sports car' racing (or whatever term might be most appropriate). By now Porsche had renewed its periodic stranglehold on WEC racing (with the 956) despite the introduction of complex fuel-consumption regulations. On the other hand IMSA's sliding scales of weight to engine capacity and power were leading to more variety and more competition on the Camel GT race grids; and in North America there were more races, varying from 100 miles to 24 hours. The money, the spectacular attendance, and the publicity (including wide television coverage) were taking IMSA ahead in general appeal. The Jaguar involvement had been a big influence. Then came the news that there would be a new Porsche designed specially for IMSA use. This was, perhaps, the turning point in the acceptance of the Camel GT series. The Porsche 956 did not qualify because of its twin-turbo engine and an IMSA regulation forbidding a driver's feet to protrude beyond the front axle line. From it, however, the new Porsche 962 was created for the 1984 season. It was to put a completely new complexion on the American series, though not immediately.

Of the British chassis-makers, March was still well ahead of Lola in producing effective IMSA cars which could take a variety of engine makes and types. Ford's amazing 'mid-front'-engined Mustang GTP – essentially a Zakspeed Capri – had also shown promise but poor reliability; so the portents for the 1984 season were indicating a three-way fight between March (with various engine options), Porsche (with the 'American' 935 and the 962) and the updated Jaguar XJR-5 – about to be run as a *two-car* team. So many improvements had been made that the

Visiting Jaguar engineer, David Scholes, with Group 44 at Miami, 1984.

1984 cars were completely new.

Here it should be said that the construction of the modern racing car does not lend itself to the provision of a continuous history. For this reason, and because Jaguar's IMSA Camel and World Sports Car race programmes were still active when this book was written, I have made no attempt to provide individual histories for each car. The Coventry-built C-types and D-types were constructed as entities by the Jaguar company itself, and I have listed them individually because (up to a point) their histories are identifiable. In the twenty-first century – when the XJR-5 and *its* successors *will* be 'history', too – I only hope that all of us will have a more precise sense of what is of 'historic' value (and how to identify it) than we seem to possess today. This little hobby-horse is pursued in the D-type appendix.

Brian Redman, and a two-car team
The year 1984 began fairly well. John Egan and Jim Randle were the key Coventry men to fly to Florida where the big news was the presence in the Group 44 team of Lancastrian Brian Redman. (How many times *had* he retired?). Forty-six isn't by any means an exceptional age for a long-distance driver, and the popular 1981 IMSA GT champion had so much to offer in terms of skill, experience and – above all – a record of winning, that it would be difficult to imagine a greater asset. Patrick Bedard, who had driven the XJR-5 at Daytona in 1983, was Tullius's choice to complete a regular foursome for 1984.

Two extra drivers were drafted in for Daytona – the

first and longest race of the IMSA year. Bill Adam made a return for this one event, to drive with Bedard and Redman. David Hobbs (who had raced a Jaguar in Florida 22 years earlier) was to share the wheel with Tullius and Bundy.

The biggest difference between the two XJR-5s was that one was now fitted with Lucas electronic fuel injection.

A sole works Porsche 962 did make its début in the hands of Mario and Michael Andretti who served notice on the opposition with a practice lap time nearly 2 seconds up on that of the March-Porsche, with the best Jaguar (the Tullius car) almost another second behind. It was said that the crowd exceeded 60,000. The XJR-5s were well-placed on rows two and three of the 82-car grid.

From the start No. 44 ran a steady third behind the Porsche 962 which was battling with the (ex-Holbert) March-Porsche driven by the South African Sarel van der Merwe and now sponsored by a swimming pool cleaning company called 'Kreepy Krauly'. The turbocharged Porsche engine was more thirsty than the Jaguar V12, and Bundy put No. 44 ahead, as the XJR-5 could cover much more ground (in hard-driving circumstances) between pitstops. Adam was well-placed, too, in No. 04 which featured Lucas electronic fuel injection whereas No. 44 still had the traditional Weber carburetter set-up.

Thrown auxiliary drive belts were to become the main cause of Jaguar delays – and all attempts to find a regular cure during the race were to no avail. Even so, Tullius, Hobbs, and Bundy came home third, behind the March 83G-Porsche of van der Merwe and his compatriots Graham Duxbury and Tony Martin. The Andrettis retired in the night, the new Porsche's terminal trouble being a broken camshaft; but the 'old' 935 of Bell, Foyt, and Wollek took over second place from the XJR-5 (No. 44) during one of four alternator belt changes. Car No. 04 needed a water pump replacement (amongst other things) but Redman did record fastest lap during one of its catching-up periods; it was classed twenty-fourth among the 32 finishers, despite spending nearly four hours at rest.

First and second in Miami GP

The problems were not fundamental and the possibility of a visit to Le Mans was not being ruled out. Le Mans would become a commitment after the Miami Grand Prix, three weeks later.

Miami was to prove the high point of the XJR-5's life as a competition car. The street race was held in fair weather this time and television rights were sold worldwide; Leonia PR man Mike Cook calculated that as many

High point of 1984: the XJR-5 wins the Miami Grand Prix.

Brian Redman, out of retirement for the nth time, with Doc Bundy on the winners' rostrum at Miami, 1984.

as four hundred million viewers in forty countries COULD watch the race. The commercial benefits of racing became clear when the helicopter-mounted camera zoomed in on to the two distinctive Jaguars as the gleaming white projectiles cruised along Biscayne Boulevard with the race under their complete control, while the voice-over observed: 'they really do look superb'. Jaguar's new standing was emphasised during the early battle with the Mustang turbo GTP car, when the commentator (referring to Ford and Jaguar) spoke of 'two of the biggest names in the industry' fighting it out.

At the start, Brian Redman had dived from Row 2 to take the lead from Klaus Ludwig (Mustang) and Tony Garcia in a 5·8-litre March 83G-Chevrolet. Redman held off Ludwig until the German snatched the lead on Lap 28; but he snatched it back two laps later. The course was very twisty and bumpy (including two railway crossings), and many cars suffered. The Mustang was one of them and was withdrawn after it was forced to come into the pits with suspension damage. Redman then led until Lap 53, when he stopped and handed over to Bundy. Tullius led briefly at this point until his pitstop. Jaguar fans, glued to their television sets, breathed in sharply as Bedard accelerated No. 04 away from the pits, nearly swiping No. 44 in which Bundy happened to be passing – a heart-stopping moment with, fortunately, no after-effects.

Former World Grand Prix Champion Emerson Fittipaldi charged up the field, having replaced Garcia in the March, but his race ended with a broken half-shaft. The same fate befell the Holbert/Hobbs Porsche 935 – another

Still on crutches from a racing accident, Hurley Haywood joined the Group 44 team in mid-1984.

From 1974, Robert Tullius and his 'Group 44' organisation were Jaguar's leading ambassadors on the circuits of North America, keeping the marque identified in its most important export market while BL threatened its whole future. In 1975, when this picture was taken, Tullius would become SCCA National B-production champion with his V12 E-type, seen here alongside Jeff Jones' McLaren at flag station No. 10, Lime Rock, during the pace lap of the Labor Day National race meeting. Behind them in a very mixed field are Bob Sharp (Datsun 240Z) and Sam Feinstein (Cobra). Tullius would lead from the second lap to mid-race, and run second to Jones thereafter, despite having virtually no braking effect. (Courtesy: Karen Miller)

The Huffaker-prepared V12 E-type of Lee Mueller (No. 12) and the Group 44 car scored many outright wins in 1974 and 1975. Their active lives ended with a demonstration 'match race' at Laguna Seca in 1976 when this picture was taken. Tullius had a puncture, and gave the race to Mueller. The silver car stayed in the USA, but the white one would spend its retirement years in Britain.

Left: Trans Am regulations permitted Bob Tullius to create, in effect, a 'silhouette' XJ-S. In 1981 he won three races and came second in the championship. In practice at Lime Rock that year the car tangled with another that had spun, suffering the front-end damage shown here whilst damage is being assessed and with the front sub-frame removed. The car could be dismantled within half an hour, and in this case it was repaired and racing next day. *(Courtesy: Karen Miller)*

Late 1981 and early 1982 saw the Tullius XJ-S further modified. Note the immaculate transporter, with Quaker State and Jaguar Rover Triumph sponsorship. Very soon, the latter would become 'Jaguar Cars Inc'.

Road America, near Elkhart Lake, Wisconsin, August 1982: Début of the XJR-5 – all-American, apart from its Jaguar V12 engine. John and Julia Egan were on hand to give Coventry's seal of approval to the new IMSA GTP initiative. *Above:* a snappy pitstop as the XJR-5 heads for third place in its first race ever.

A pensive Bob Tullius with the XJR-5 at Pocono, September 1982. A Lee Dykstra design, the XJR-5 shows that a GTP car can be both functional and distinctive. GM folk helped create the shape. *(Courtesy: Karen Miller)*

XJR-5s at Le Mans, 1985, lined up in the old way. The race begins with a rolling start, these days, however.

Regular Group 44 team drivers for 1985/6 were Chip Robinson (left), Hurley Haywood, Bob Tullius, and Brian Redman, seen here just before the start of the 1985 Le Mans 24-hour race in which Tullius would bring car No. 44 home in thirteenth place: the first Jaguar 'finish' at the Sarthe for 22 years.

The New European Touring Car Championship challenger from Tom Walkinshaw, the Jaguar XJ-S, practising at Donington prior to the 1982 season. The marque's return to this type of racing coincided with the start of the new 'Group A' formula.

Pitstop at the high-speed Brno road circuit in 1983. Up to 90,000 spectators filled the enclosures and the pit-lane! Tom Walkinshaw scored a personal hat-trick for Jaguar, winning here in 1982, 1983, and 1984. It seemed that this, the last of the great European road circuits, would not be used from 1987.

There was a third livery and a third regular TWR team car for 1984, the year in which Walkinshaw won the European championship. However, this particular race, at the Salzburgring, was won by his loyal team-mates Win Percy and 'Chuck Nicholson'. By now, the Rovers and Volvos were becoming competitive, but it can be seen that the BMWs remained the Jaguars' leading adversaries. *(Courtesy: Helmut Krackowizer)*

BATHURST 1985: Having conquered Europe, Tom Walkinshaw took his team to the other great bastion of touring car racing, Australia, sponsored by the Jaguar importer to take part in the 1000km race at Mount Panorama, perhaps the last of the great road circuits, and certainly one of the most challenging anywhere. Practising in this shot (taken by the author from above 'The Dipper') is the car that would win the great event driven by Armin Hahne and local hero revived, John Goss.

There was another XJ-S at Bathurst in 1985, acquitting itself well in the hands of Garry Wilmington and Peter Janson, to finish fourteenth overall. Here it approaches McPhillamy Park at the top of 'the mountain' during practice for the ultimate in touring car contests.

While Walkinshaw no longer ran a full season's XJ-S racing programme after 1984, he retained a strong Jaguar connection in creating a Group C car. In the winter of 1984/5, he also arranged to install an experimental 48-valve Jaguar V12 engine in an XJR-5, as seen here, thus creating much speculation as to his plans. It was the ordinary (24-valve sohc) V12 which was to be developed for his own car, the XJR-6, and was still Allan Scott's choice in 1987 for the XJR-8.

Proud father: Tom Walkinshaw and his 'baby', the XJR-6, shortly before the 1986 Silverstone 1000km race.

The Cheever/Warwick XJR-6 passes the Jaguar fire-tender at the Woodcote chicane at Silverstone in 1986, en route for the marque's first WSC race victory since Le Mans 1957.

victim of one of the 'level' crossings. Daytona visitors van der Merwe and Martin were affected (as Holbert had been in 1983) by the heat in the March-Porsche's cockpit and were content to finish 9th, with four Lolas (a good day for Lola), a Porsche and the two Jaguars ahead of them. The final order was:

1984 Budweiser Miami Grand Prix. 3 hours duration

1st	*Redman/Bundy*	*(XJR-5 Jaguar)*	118 laps
2nd	*Tullius/Bedard*	*(XJR-5 Jaguar)*	118 laps
3rd	Morton/Lobenberg	(Lola T600-Chevrolet)	117 laps
4th	Wollek/Foyt	(Porsche 935 turbo)	115 laps

Bob Tullius, who put in the fastest lap of the race at 79·095 mph, was jubilant. He described the Jaguars as 'perfect' and their success as 'the thrill of a lifetime'; and he paid tribute to Lanky Foushee, his assistant Jeffrey Eischen, and the whole team. The winners averaged 72·623 mph – a reflection of the nature of the downtown circuit which had twelve distinct corners per 1·85-mile lap.

Sebring four weeks later was approached with confidence and with Group 44 drivers Bundy and Tullius occupying 1st and 2nd places in the IMSA table. Redman was fastest in practice; Bedard took the first stint, but the engine died; 1½ hours were lost tracing and repairing an obscure ignition fault. Redman broke the race-lap record at 122·563 mph as he and Bedard brought No. 04 up from forty-sixth to eleventh at the finish. Tullius and Bundy led for most of the first three hours but spent the latter part of the race trying to identify a bad misfire. Only after the car had expired on the course was the fault traced to a broken timing-chain tensioning spring. The fact that No. 04 ran strongly through to the 12-hour mark helped sustain spirits. Winners were Hans Heyer (soon to join the European Jaguar team), Stefan Johannsson and Mauricio de Narvaez in that long-distance workhorse, the Porsche 935.

Redman and Bundy: league leaders

The Whittington brothers' March-Chevrolets wrapped up first and second places in the 500 km race at the track they owned – Road Atlanta, Georgia – after the Mustang failed again. Tullius and Bundy went well until the latter had an accident which dropped them to the tail of the field. Redman and Bedard, on the other hand, came a respectable third. The points situation looked very rosy at this stage; with four rounds gone, Redman was at the top of the list, followed by Bundy who, incidentally, put up fastest lap in the race at Road Atlanta in 78·830 seconds (more than 115 mph average) – quite a difference from the 90 sec. times of the SCCA Jaguars a few years earlier.

It was now April and the decision to take two XJR-5s to Le Mans was made public before the month was out. The announcement was made in Coventry, but a 'pre-run' for Le Mans was to take place at Pocono. This decision meant that, logistically, Group 44 should miss out Rounds 5 to 9 inclusive. Certainly, Riverside (5) and Laguna Seca (6) were just too far to go with so little time in hand. Lime Rock (8) and Mid-Ohio (9) clashed with the shipping schedule. Naturally those who appreciated IMSA races, for any reason, did not like the idea of losing Group 44 for so long. The response was to take a couple of 'old' XJR-5s to Charlotte for Round 7 on 20 May, when Tullius/Bundy and Redman/Bedard came second and third

Doc Bundy puts the power down through the 'Devil's Elbow' during practice for the 1984 Pocono race, in which he and Tullius brought the XJR-5 home second to the Holbert/Bell turbocharged Porsche 962. (Courtesy: Karen Miller)

respectively. Shortly afterwards, Bedard was injured during the Indianapolis 500-mile race and his place in the Group 44 team was taken by Hurley Haywood, who was driving regularly again although his foot (damaged at Mosport in 1983) had not yet healed up. Doc Bundy had hurt his ribs in a testing accident and wasn't comfortable at the wheel, so there was a feeling that Group 44 had a monopoly on walking wounded.

The cars failed to finish at Le Mans, but their performance impressed everyone.

Somehow or other, victory eluded the team, although there were four more seconds and two more thirds. So near, and yet so far. The mid-year diversion may have been part of the reason; but there were two others, more positive: one was the rise from relative obscurity of 30-year-old Randy Lanier who, with the Whittington brothers' help, had become a regular winner with a pair of 5·8-litre March 84G-Chevrolets sponsored by Apache power boats. The team name was an impressive one: 'Blue Thunder'.

The second new force was the very strong partnership of Derek Bell with Al Holbert in a Löwenbrau-sponsored Porsche 962, which had not started winning until mid-season but was now doing so regularly.

The XJR-5 was far from outclassed but was being worked harder than ever and some problems would not go away – like regular ring-and-pinion failure in the Hewland gearbox which seemed a 'marginal' item for the V12 engine, now it was developing around 600 bhp.

The Kreepy Krauly team continued to do well and Sarel van der Merwe ended the season quite high up the points table; he would have been higher but for the loss of two cars by fire.

Again there were seventeen races. Eight of them were won by March-Chevrolets, six by Porsches, two by March-Porsche, and one by the XJR-5 Jaguar. For a team that had worked so hard, and from which so much had been expected, Group 44 had a right to feel some disappointment. But for 'racing luck' – and the break for Le Mans – there could have been three or four wins. The cars were smart and well-driven, and the exposure of the name Jaguar in a good light was beyond doubt.

John Bishop, the father of IMSA, was pleased with 1984, mainly because he had achieved his object of running a series in which the regulations gave a fair chance of victory to domestic and foreign engines. With nine European and eight American power units sharing the winnings, the balance could not have been better. These are the details:

Daytona I	March-Porsche	van der Merwe/
		Duxbury/Martin
Miami GP	Jaguar XJR-5	B. Redman/H. Bundy
Sebring	Porsche 935	Heyer/Johansson/de
		Narvaez
Road Atlanta	March-Chevrolet	Don. Whittington
Riverside	March-Chevrolet	R. Lanier/W. Whittington
Laguna Seca	March-Chevrolet	R. Lanier
Charlotte	March-Chevrolet	R. Lanier/W. Whittington
Lime Rock	March-Porsche	S. van der Merwe
Mid-Ohio	Porsche 962	A. Holbert/D. Bell
Watkins Glen I	Porsche 962	A. Holbert/D. Bell
Portland	March-Chevrolet	R. Lanier/W. Whittington

Coffee break time in the Group 44 workshop at Winchester, Virginia. Team chief Tullius is on the left.

Sears Point	MArch-Chevrolet	W. Whittington
Road America	Porsche 962	A. Holbert/D. Bell
Pocono	Porsche 962	A. Holbert/D. Bell
Michigan	March-Chevrolet	R. Lanier/W. Whittington
Watkins Glen II	March-Chevrolet	R. Lanier/D. Whittington
Daytona II	Porsche 962	A. Holbert/D. Bell

This time Jaguar had to accept third place in the chassis and engine manufacturers' championships, Porsche being runner-up in both categories.

In drivers' championship, the four regular Jaguar men finished in the top ten, although Haywood earned some of his points in other makes. His predecessor, Pat Bedard, was placed sixteenth. These were 1984's top points scorers:

Drivers

Randy Lanier	189
Bill Whittington	168
Derek Bell	164
Al Holbert	136
Sarel van der Merwe	105
Brian Redman	97
Doc Bundy	94
Bob Tullius	74
Kenper Miller	70
Hurley Haywood	68

Manufacturers

Chassis		Engine	
March	263	Chevrolet	248
Porsche	224	Porsche	246
Jaguar	144	Jaguar	144
Argo	68	Ford-Cosworth	75
Lola	62	Mazda	53
Momo	42	Buick	32

One of the XJR-5s was brought to Britain in October, to be displayed in the motor show at Birmingham's National Exhibition Centre. Afterwards it was taken to the workshops of Tom Walkinshaw Racing and tried out, briefly with a 48-valve version of the V12 engine.

1985: a year of toil

Group 44 beavered its way through 1985. Top placings were frequent and once again the drivers were ranked high in the end-of-season table, with Hurley Haywood only just failing to take second place from Derek Bell, once again Al Holbert's Porsche partner. It was, without question, Holbert's year.

Doc Bundy had left Group 44 to join Ford, whose so-called Mustang GTP was being replaced by the 'mid-rear'-engined Mustang Probe. He was replaced in the Group 44 team by Chip Robinson, a relative youngster

want of you is very reasonable, especially when you consider everything Group 44 does. Everybody tries to compare Group 44 with other teams in IMSA; but there can be no comparison, because of the scope of what they're trying to do: designing cars, developing engines, *and* racing two cars.

The strong character of the 1985 Group 44 driver line-up would be emphasised a year later when they were still together: four Davids, still in the camp of sports car racing's Goliath – Porsche.

Robinson had made a very reasonable point. The

Official Hal Crocker photograph of the team drivers, Daytona, February 1985, shows Brian Redman, 'Chip' Robinson, Mike Dale, Bob Tullius and Hurley Haywood. (Robinson was Bundy's replacement.)

fresh from a fine season of Super Vee racing and now ready to take his career a stage further. Intelligent, quiet, and orderly, Robinson appeared to have no difficulty in accepting Group 44 team discipline.

Back in 1983, Bill Adam had left Bob Tullius's employment because: 'I didn't agree with all of his ideas as to how a racing team should operate.'

Following his own arrival in the team, Chip Robinson said to the same reporter (Tom Ford of the *Tampa Tribune*):

I've always admired Jaguar as an outsider. The cars are immaculate and the team has such a strong presence.... What they

Porsche 962 had made its bow in 1984. At least six were competing regularly in 1985 and, for 1986's opening round, nine would be turning up! Against such resources the self-contained Group 44 Jaguar team, using a maximum of two cars per race, seventeen weekends a year, must operate efficiently to produce any kind of reasonable result. 1985 did, in fact, product good results for Jaguar's banner wavers in America.

In terms of reliability the Jaguars had the measure of the Porsches. Looking at the first four cars to finish in each of 1985's IMSA GTP races, it is clear that Jaguar had far out-stripped every other rival of Porsche. The cars which filled the top four places in the seventeen races, that year, did so in these quantities:

Porsche 962   44 times

Jaguar	18 times
Ford 'Probe'	3 times
March-Chevrolet	twice
Alba-Ford	once

That gives a much more balanced impression of 1985 than Porsche's sixteen victories to Jaguar's single one. Often, the margin of victory was very small; but there was the constant frustration for the Jaguar drivers of trying to match the magic of the turbo's mighty boost which Porsche men could apply at will.

Bob Tullius was very fortunate not to be hurt badly at Daytona in 1985's opening round. The XJR-5 hit some rubbish, throwing a tyre which damaged the bodywork; this led to a puncture of the oil tank. Tullius coolly slowed the car, passing a group of fire marshals, but not realising he needed their services. The car was well alight when it came to a halt with Tullius unable to open the door. His only burns, however, occurred when he removed his gloves to get his helmet off and breathe some fresh air. The door was beginning to melt by the time he got out. Up to that time No. 44, co-driven by Haywood and Redman, had been running well – mostly second to Holbert but sometimes leading. 'Rookie' Robinson was joined by two old hands at the endurance racing game – Jim Adams and Claude Ballot-Léna – in the '04' car which lost its oil pressure, and was brought to a halt rather than risk a costly seizure.

Donington Park, early 1985. Painted in TWR's colours this XJR-5 had been displayed at the 1984 Birmingham motor show and now gave the misleading impression that a British-run Le Mans team might be imminent. (*Courtesy: Paul Boothroyd*, Autosport)

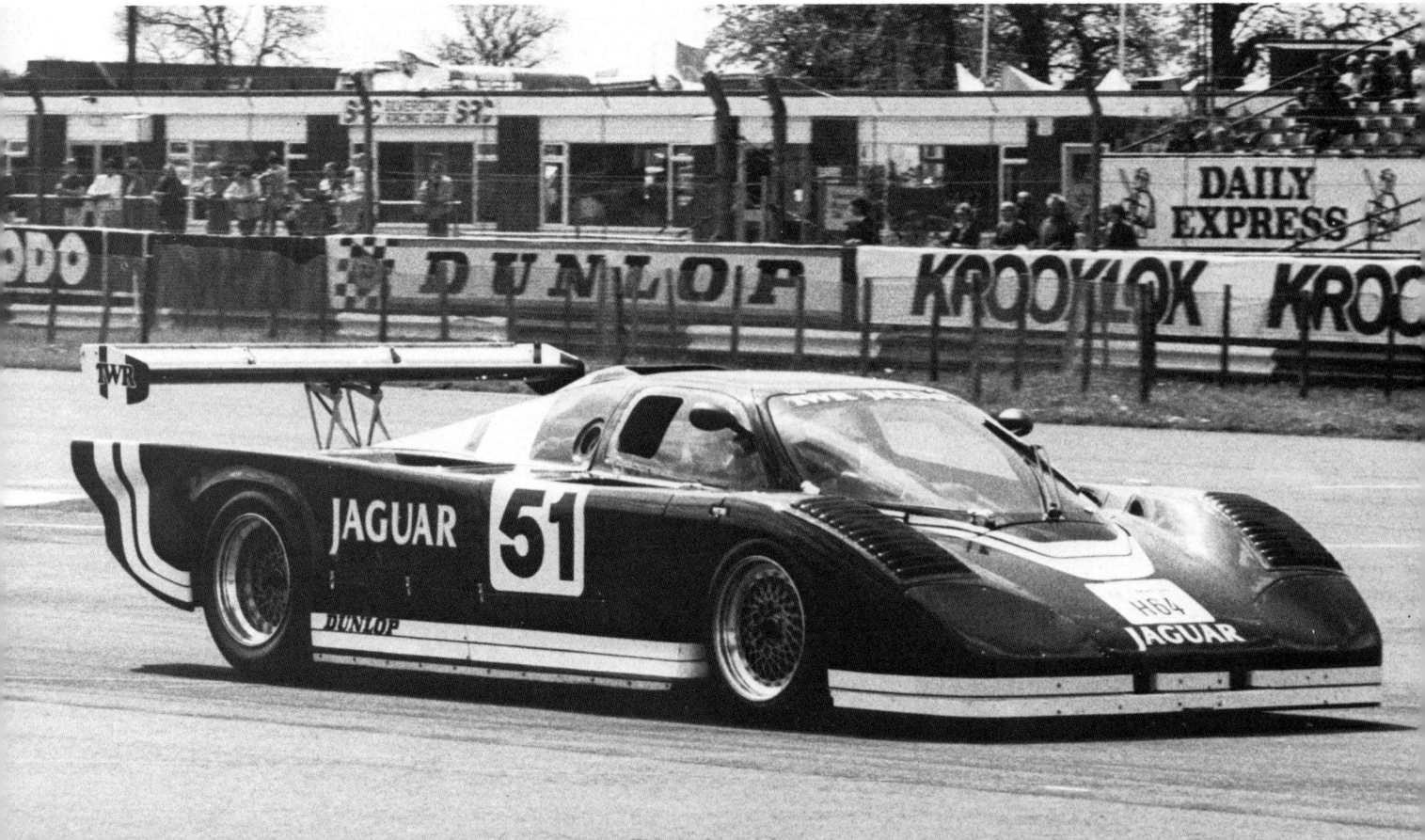

this tough 12-hour race since the 1950s. This time the
Tullius/Robinson combination scored.

Victory again at Road Atlanta
Mike Dale had declared his hand in January. He wanted
Group 44 to return to Le Mans. If he had any opposition,
it dematerialised on 15 April when the Road Atlanta 500
was run. This course had witnessed some wonderful and
often unexpected Jaguar victories in the past. Now it was
to provide Group 44 with its best day of the year.

Two years earlier, the XJR-5 had scored its first victory
on this scenic, undulating circuit near Braselton, Georgia.

Holbert, as ever America's leading Porsche man,
decided to run solo. He took pole position and led the
race; but Road Atlanta is not an easy course on which to
overtake or be overtaken without co-operation, and IMSA
grids mean big fields and widely differing lap speeds.
Holbert could not avoid a slower car, lost time in the pits
for repairs, and recovered to finish a commendable fifth.
(Tullius had a similar but less time-wasting experience
when a Chevrolet turned across *his* bows at the Esses.)
Before the race, Holbert had described Haywood/Redman
as: '. . . the best driver pairing here. Given the right break
they can run the race on one stop. I'll have to be careful
if I'm going to manage with two.'
'We're capable of winning,' said Redman in another

**Final victory for the XJR-5, by Haywood and Redman,
at Road Atlanta, Georgia in 1985.**

Left:
**The dark green XJR-5 (with 'TWR Jaguar' on the
windscreen) also made an early 1985 appearance at
Silverstone. In 1986 it even spent a brief period at
Heathrow Airport for the opening of Terminal Four,
painted in Silk Cut livery! – NOT conducive to good
British-American relations. Afterwards it was
resprayed *à la* Group 44 and put on show in Coventry.
(Courtesy: Jeff Bloxham, Autosport)**

Something that impressed everyone was the effectiveness of the winter's rear suspension modifications
which – Redman was sure – made the XJR-5 the best-
handling car in GTP racing. Jaguar Cars Inc., now
claimed 625 bhp – a useful increase for the well-developed
V12 engine.

Qualifying sessions for the Miami GP went well. The
latest March 85G-Chevrolets flattered only to deceive;
likewise the same chassis, powered by the McLaren-
developed Buick unit, which Bill Adam and John Paul Jr
were driving. The race was hectic but Haywood and
Robinson survived the shunts and bumps of the temporary
street circuit (including an onslaught on '04' from the victorious Porsche, which did not improve some TV viewers'
opinion of Derek Bell's driving) and came fourth. The '44'
car suffered a jammed gearbox, thanks to a broken selector
fork.

At Sebring, another fourth was Jaguar's best result in

Although outpaced and outnumbered, the Group 44 XJR-5s always gave the Porsches a fight. Here the Redman/Haywood car outbrakes the Halsmer/Morton 962 at Turn 7, Lime Rock, May 1985. (*Courtesy: Karen Miller*)

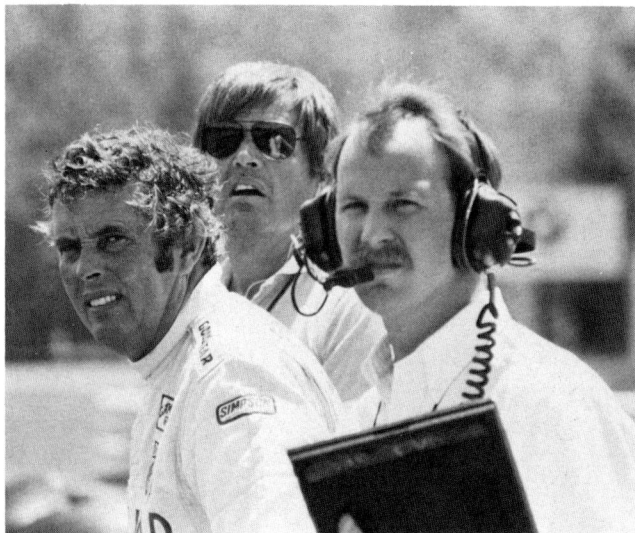

Grant Weaver, the man responsible for the '04' car, shows less worry than Redman or Dykstra in the Lime Rock pit-lane, 1985. (*Courtesy: Karen Miller*)

interview, 'but just look how many Porsche 962s there are now. The Jaguar is feeling better than ever. It's just a matter of time . . .'

Soon after making those remarks, and with a cheerful Hurley Haywood alongside, Brian Redman was savouring his second big win for Jaguar. It meant even more to Haywood, who hadn't had a win since 1983, before his accident. They had come from the second row of the grid, and Tullius/Robinson (third row start) came through to make it a Jaguar 1-2, with four of the usually invincible

Porsche 962s and three March-Chevrolets filling the next seven places. An 'old' Lola T600-Chevrolet was tenth. Former champion John Paul Jr (second in qualifying and fastest race lap) failed to finish with the turbocharged March 85G-Buick again. Perhaps *its* day would come? Today was Jaguar's day.

Later in the month Jaguar Cars Ltd announced that its Le Mans plans featured two Group 44 entries. The difference this year was a determination by Group 44 not to miss any IMSA races (because of Le Mans) if at all possible. There were enough cars, two being prepared specially for Le Mans. The pressures on the whole team, to keep two projects on the boil until June, made the early part of 1985 one of the most difficult periods in Group 44's history. It was made no easier for Bob Tullius when the provisional Le Mans entry list showed three Jaguar reservations in addition to his own. These entries would not be taken up, however. Jaguar honour at Le Mans would rest, once again, on American shoulders.

Meantime, the Group 44 team pushed on with its US programme. Another win was on the cards at Riverside, until Redman was punted-off from behind. Tullius/Robinson were third here and then second at Laguna Seca; third at Laguna Seca were Redman and Haywood, who went on to take second place at Charlotte and Lime Rock. They could have won both! At Charlotte something went wrong with the final pit-stop, which followed a spectacular display of car control on the banking by Brian Redman. He was leading the race when he came in; but then (for no explained reason) Hurley Haywood's safety harness would not do up and a whole lap was lost. At Lime Rock, they were again leading when oil from another car obscured forward version. A stop to clear the screen lost them the race.

Because Le Mans was only a week away, just one car was sent to Lexington for the Mid-Ohio race. It was the half-way point in the 1985 IMSA GTP championship and, with three victories already, Holbert was charging ahead with 114 points; but the consistent Robinson was running second with 78 and not far behind him (fourth) was Haywood on 72. Since it was now clearly a points chase to keep Porsche drivers at bay, the logical pairing for Mid-Ohio was Haywood/Robinson, and they produced a gallant third.

As recorded further on, Le Mans produced a finisher for Jaguar for the first time in twenty-two years, thanks to Bob Tullius.

In the first post-le Mans race, at Watkins Glen in July, both cars were troubled by the bumps and a variety of 'engine management' gremlins. Tullius/Robinson had alternator failure. Redman/Haywood made it to fourth place here – and again in the heat of Portland, Oregon, later in the month. Tullius/Robinson, second at Portland, showed yet again that Group 44 *could* out-race every Porsche 962 user except the Holbert-Löwenbrau team which now had a second, brand new, 962 and was beginning to steamroller the series – to the extent that John Bishop was already looking for ways of restoring a balance for 1986. The Holbert Porsche was only ten seconds ahead of the Jaguar at the finish of 'GI Joe's Gran Prix' (as the Portland was called). Holbert had everything under control in the race but had not been without his practice problems – mostly because of the pop-off valve sticking

open and consequent loss of turbo boost.

Holbert was also concerned about what he called his arm wrestling with John Bishop over the whole Porsche position in the Camel GT series. Tullius was, naturally, doing his own version of the same thing, arguing that IMSA's regulations gave too much advantage to the turbocharged Porsches. This was how Steve Duin (of *The Oregonian*) reported the situation on 28 July 1985:

Since 1980, Bishop has maintained competitiveness in the Camel GT series with the same engine displacement/weight formula. Knowing that Bishop is considering some fine-tuning of the rules, Holbert said: 'I'm trying to keep him busy enough so that he doesn't have time to daydream. He's trying to create some incentive for the normally-aspirated guys, make them a little lighter. Every time I turn around he has a new idea.'

The Group 44 Jaguar team believes advances in turbocharger technology have upset IMSA's formula. 'There's no question that this has leaped ahead faster than anything else,' said Brian Redman. In 1981 (Redman said) he read IMSA's GTP rules and built a Lola T600 to take advantage of them. 'We decided

First appearance of the modified car, known as the XJR-7 was at Daytona in December 1985, Bob Tullius prepares to go aboard; his car chief, Brian Krem, stands by.

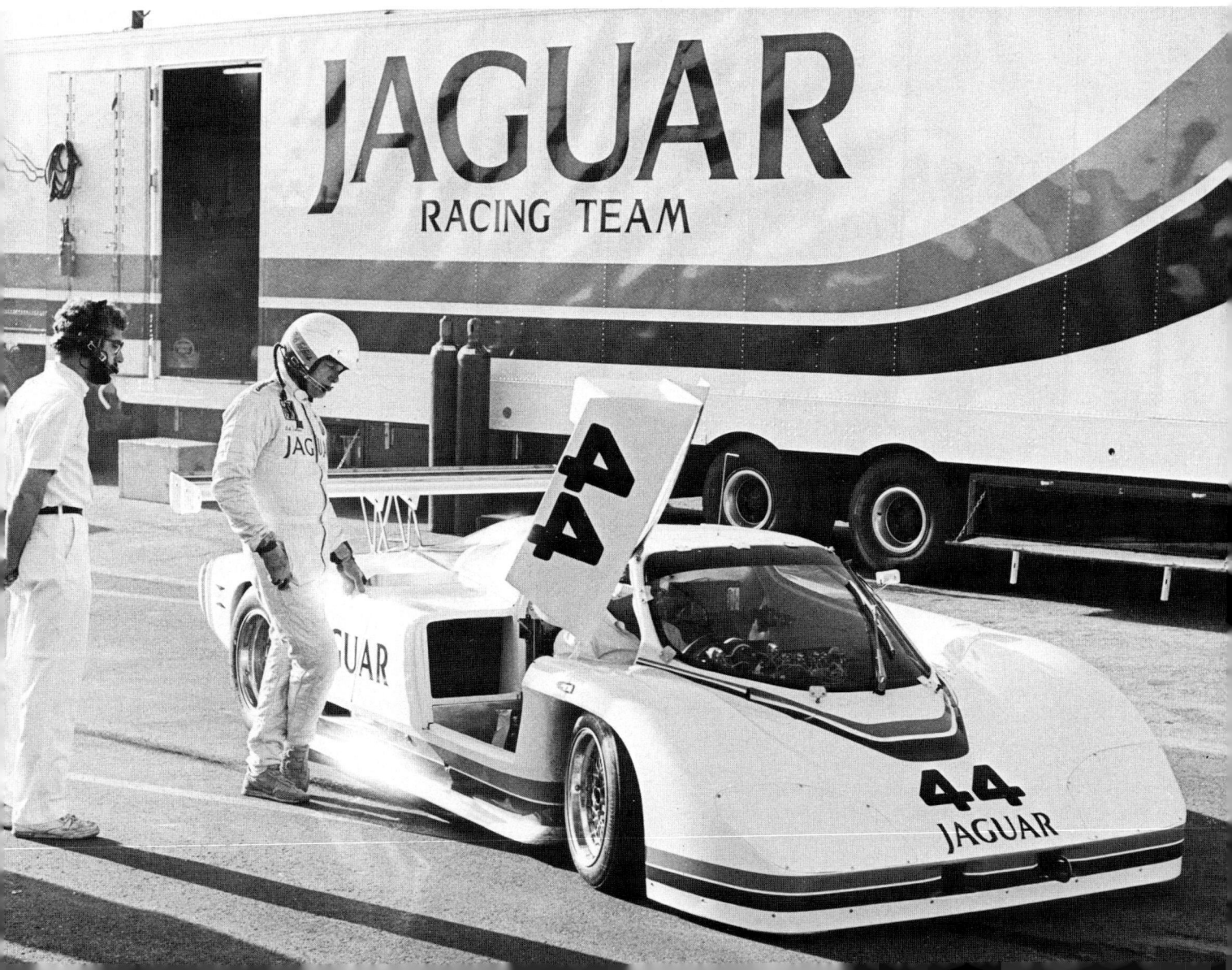

the Chevy V8 could beat the Porsche 935 turbos, which had lost only one race in four years.' [*Redman became champion with that car.*]

Yet Porsche recovered. 'Porsche will always recover,' Redman said. 'Porsche has forgotten more about racing than most manufacturers ever knew. They are racing bred. The whole factory has been oriented towards racing for twenty years.'

Redman's comment, far from being defeatist, was simple historically-proved fact. Indeed it was a way of paying Jaguar a compliment. Every race success for Jaguar was, and is, achieved with products based on equipment which was not, in its original form, designed with competition work in mind. The bulky stock-block Jaguar V12 engine is a particularly good example.

Transmission failure sidelined both XJR-5s at Sears Point and car No. 44 at Road America where No. 04 was heading for second place when a water hose blew: an incident which dropped Redman/Haywood to eighth.

The press-box practice notes at Pocono in September told an increasingly familiar story. 'We're about 20 mph slower down the straights,' said Redman. Haywood commented: 'We're just so out-gunned; but the cars are working good. We'll be all right in the race.' Tullius retired with a broken engine, but Haywood/Robinson claimed second place – 4 seconds down on Holbert/Bell after nearly three hours, having led for half the race. Holbert simply added boost towards the end, to reel in Robinson who won praise all round for a mature and very fast drive for which he won the Norelco 'driver of the day' trophy.

Haywood v. Holbert duel
The second Watkins Glen meeting brought Redman/Haywood another third place; the other pair came sixth. Neither car starred in the Columbus, Ohio, street race; but the seventeenth and final round at Daytona on 1 December saw the character of the 1985 season encapsulated in one almighty battle between Holbert/Bell and Haywood/Redman. In fairness, it must be said that Holbert had put one car into the lead, then hopped into another and did the same; but this was a demonstration. Holbert had already clinched the title and didn't need the points. Bell was away at Selangor, so Holbert's co-driver for this his ninth victory of the year was Al Holbert Jr. The final hour saw a magnificent duel between an inspired Haywood and Holbert the opportunist. He took advantage of a race incident to put some slower cars between him and Haywood, who lost by less than 10 seconds after 3 hours of racing. In the duel, the race-lap record for the Daytona speedway-cum-road circuit fell to Haywood at an average speed of 124·374 mph – a celebratory note on which to sing the XJR-5's swansong, for it was to be the car's last race.

XJR-7 makes it bow
Since early in the season, there had been hints that the XJR-5 might be replaced by a similar, yet different variation on Dykstra's original theme. The XJR-7 was announced in November 1985 and made its race début at Daytona on 1 December driven by Tullius ('chief's privilege', he called it) and Chip Robinson who lost two

laps due to a spin which cost him a place in the drivers' championship by allowing Pete Halsmer (Porsche) through to third place; the XJR-7 was fourth.

In the final analysis the leading drivers of 1985's IMSA GTP category were:

1st	Al Holbert (USA)	Porsche 962
2nd	Derek Bell (GB)	Porsche 962
3rd	*Hurley Haywood (USA)*	*Jaguar*
4th	Pete Halsmer (USA)	Porsche 962
5th	*Chip Robinson (USA)*	*Jaguar*
6th	Drake Olson (USA)	Porsche 962
7th	*Brian Redman (GB)*	*Jaguar*
8th	Bob Wollek (F)	Porsche 962
9th	*Bob Tullius (USA)*	*Jaguar*
10th	Jim Busby (USA)	Porsche 962

Only the V12 Jaguars had been able to present any effective defence against the Porsche onslaught.

In three seasons – 1983, 1984, 1985 – the XJR-5 had won 6 races outright, been runner-up 14 times, besides taking a dozen thirds. But for a little more luck, and the

Points	1sts	2nds	3rds	4ths
218	9	2	0	1
154	6	2	0	0
149	1	4	3	3
138	1	0	4	5
137	0	4	2	4
117	3	0	3	1
112	1	3	2	2
105	3	3	1	0
100	0	3	1	3
98	0	2	3	0

effect of two sorties to Le Mans in 1984 and 1985 (covered in a later chapter), the team's record of victories assuredly would have been higher – and Jaguar in America (as in Britain) is in no two minds about the fact that WINNING counts for more than any other achievement.

Jaguar's approach to racing changed radically in 1985. The XJR-5 (in minds of interested parties at Browns Lane, as opposed to Kidlington) had begun the year as the potential basis for a Group C as well as an IMSA GTP car. After all, it had been in the minds of Dale, Dykstra, and Tullius since the car was first conceived, NOT to race in America only but to bring Jaguar back to Le Mans. Not entirely rewarding, those two sorties did at least produce the first Jaguar finish at Le Mans for 22 years.

XJR-5 and XJR-7 together at Daytona, final IMSA race meeting of 1985. During the year, Group 44 took eighteen top-four finishes; but just one of them was a victory.

Detail features of the 1986 XJR-7 at its Daytona début, December 1985. (*Courtesy: Karen Miller*)

By then, however, it was already clear that another avenue had been opened up in Britain, and soon TWR's Group C car – the XJR-6 – was racing tentatively, as the XJR-5 had done exactly three years earlier.

So it was that XJR-7 evolved strictly as a GTP car, taking advantage of the detail changes in IMSA's rules for 1986. Not all the anticipated changes, notably to the transmission specification, could be incorporated right away, and the early races of 1986 were troublesome ones; but hopes were high as the season developed.

Dykstra leaves Jaguar

A worrying feature early in 1986 was the departure of Lee Dykstra in, apparently, somewhat acrimonious circumstances. 'It's surprising he stayed as long as he did,' observed one Jaguar man, typifying the reaction. So Group 44 was without a full-time design engineer – normally an essential ingredient of modern motor racing. It is all the more creditable that the team was able to remain competitive at most circuits *and* finish the season on a high note.

The Daytona 24-hour race saw Ballot-Léna assist Robinson and Tullius in a troubled drive to sixth place, but at Sebring – the notorious car-killer – both XJR-7s retired. There were fourths at Miami and at Road Atlanta. The latter event, in April, marked an engine capacity increase to 6·5 litres for the XJR-7. A testing accident at Charlotte and a spectacular roll (instigated unintentionally by two other competitors) at Riverside, left the team somewhat short of equipment but did not damage Chip Robinson, the driver on both occasions – a tribute to the XJR-7's construction. There was only one car available for the sixth IMSA event of the year at Laguna Seca on 4 May, but Haywood and Robinson took it to an encouragingly close second place.

Returning east, Group 44 missed the Charlotte race, and concentrated upon rebuilding the two wrecks, incorporating detail improvements. Best mid-summer result was a third for Haywood and Redman at Palm Beach, where the latter was elbowed out of the lead on the last corner with a certain lack of ceremony. A feature of this street-race meeting was an historic event organised by former Jaguar Driver of the Year Graig Hinton; it was a reminder of the sports car race held at Palm Beach Shores, Florida, on 3 January 1950, when the Jaguar XK120 had made its overseas racing début. One of the participants was Walter Hill, owner of the ex-works XK120 which Leslie Johnson had raced in the 1950 event. (The Palm Beach Shores race was covered fully in Vol. 1. This reminder also gives me the chance to confirm that the caption on Page 86 of that book was right, but the text below it wrong; the chassis number of the car raced by Johnson was 6700001. Apologies for the discrepancy. *AW*.)

Victory came close yet remained elusive during the second, late-summer sortie to the west coast where Robinson and Tullius repeated their 1985 result in the quaintly-titled 'GI Joe's Gran Prix' on the Portland International Raceway. They finished second, beaten only by the 1985 IMSA GTP champion (and 1986 champion-elect) Al Holbert, whose Porsche 962 continued to set the standard for all Porsches in the series. A week later, on 3 August, Haywood and Redman came third at Sears Point; Robinson suffered from heat exhaustion here. Later in the month mechanical gremlins returned at Elkhart Lake (Road America), but Haywood and Redman scored a fifth at Watkins Glen and a third at Columbus to put Haywood, up, temporarily, into fifth position in the drivers' standings.

The toughest season so far for Group 44 was drawing to a close. Even without interruption for Le Mans (except for Haywood and Robinson, on loan to TWR), 1986 had been a year of unremitting labour for the Virginia team – now overshadowed to some extent by the Walkinshaw operation, which was not only racing for Jaguar but selling its showroom product. (October 1986 was the month in which the new Jaguar XJ40 range was being toasted in Britain; but it would not be sold in America until well into 1987.) If the factory had distanced itself from Group 44 slightly during season, Jaguar Cars Inc. certainly had not. In addition to promoting further record sales, Graham Whitehead and Mike Dale had maintained strong support for Tullius and his entourage, knowing full-well that their very presence added to Jaguar's reputation. There was the loyalty element, too, for Tullius and Jaguar had been associated for more than a dozen years; his independence of approach and almost West Point presentation were legendary. He had produced at least one major victory a year for the marque (apart from 1979 and 1980, when he reverted briefly to Triumph), and that was all he needed now.

Grand finale of the 1986 IMSA Camel GT season was to be Round 17, the 3-hour Eastern Airlines event at Daytona – the traditional end-of-season race often used for refamiliarisation, since this was also the location of the following season's opening battle. The combined high-speed banking and tight infield twists made this a circuit for cars with all-round ability, and an opportunity for the XJR-7 to prove itself a winner within a year of its début at the same Florida track.

There had been several occasions when the XJR-7 appeared to be about to grab victory from the still-dominant Porsche 962s; but the cards had been stacked the

Chip Robinson and veteran Claude Ballot-Léna wait hopefully at Sebring, 1986, when neither XJR-7 finished the race.

Right:
Group 44's Jaguar V12 engine incorporated a number of US-conceived modifications. This Lovell photograph was taken at Daytona in early 1986.

wrong way. Although more consistent than the new challengers – GM's Lola-Corvette, Ford's Zakspeed-Probe, and McLaren North America's March-BMW, all of them turbocharged – the XJR-7 had not done what each of *them* had done at least once; it had not been first past the chequered flag.

Yet Group 44 had not been standing still; far from it! Mike Dale had set up a US-based engine-development and component manufacturing facility, and this was now beginning to prove itself in terms of improved economy and power. The 6·5-litre engine was now developing a claimed 703 bhp at 7250 rpm, and problems could be overcome more quickly than had been possible when Transatlantic advice and parts had been the norm. With consistent availability of adequate power, the XJR-7 had added to its store of built-in qualities. At 2080 lb dry, it was still considerably heavier than its European Group C counterpart, the XJR-6; but it also retained and improved upon its known trackworthiness. As Brian Redman had said to me early in the season (just before the car's designer resigned): 'Lee Dykstra has provided us with the best-stopping and best-handling cars in GTP racing.' It was as simple as that. If there was an Achilles Heel now, it was in the transmission.

Tullius and Robinson win the 1986 final

Many pundits, the unbelievers who had come to think only in turbo terms, gave little thought to the Jaguars at Daytona. Others, who had noted Group 44's increasing confidence on fuel consumption, saw the team's chances in a more optimistic light, even after the cars qualified sixth and thirteenth on a strong grid; for the team's speedy

pitwork was demonstrably the best. Key factor was the XJR-7 drivers' ability to run for three hours in the knowledge that each car would have to stop only twice.

So it was that Redman – thirteenth on the grid, but fourth *and* on the pace after half an hour – swept into the lead shortly before handing over to Haywood. Nor was Tullius far behind when he came in for a lightning pit-stop, at which Robinson took over. For most of the race, from then on, the distinctive white XJR-7s ran first and second, with Robinson leading briefly as Haywood passed 04's helm to Redman again. Robinson spun harmlessly on his worn tyres just prior to his second stop.

It was not to be an untroubled day, however, for Tullius felt his throttle sticking and promptly ran off-course; Lanky Foushee's '44' crew under Brian Krem fitted a new nose and tyres in double-quick time and sent Tullius on his way in fourth place. Then, with little more than half-an-hour to go, Redman slowed suddenly and trickled into the pits for good, 04's crankshaft broken. Some development *was* still needed. This let the March-BMW of Jaguar 'old boy' David Hobbs and former GP star John Watson go ahead; but Watson ran out of fuel (he had been due for another stop but not quite so soon), and Tullius passed him to run second, duly catching the Dyson Porsche (which required a late fuel top-up) and winning gleefully by more than a minute.

So, like the XJR-5 and XJR-6, the XJR-7 did prove itself a winner within a year of its début. With the benefit of hindsight it is easy to add that it could well have done so earlier, on more than one occasion. This was the top-

334

six order in that great IMSA final:

Daytona 3-hour race, 26 October 1986
1st *Jaguar XJR-7* of Group 44 team, Bob Tullius/Chip Robinson (113·98 mph),
2nd Porsche 962 of Dyson Racing, Price Cobb/Rob Dyson,
3rd Porsche 962, Busby & Goodrich, Darin Brassfield/John Morton,
4th Porsche 962, Akin & Coca Cola, James Weaver/Bob Akin,
5th Porsche 962, Joest & Blaupunkt, Bob Wollek/Paulo

Barilla/'John Winter',
6th Porsche 962, Holbert & Löwenbrau, Al Holbert/Derek Bell.

A Jaguar one-two would have been a perfect ending, but there were plenty rewards to be shared out just the same. Chip Robinson was elevated to fifth place in the drivers' championship, behind Holbert, Cobb, Bell, and Brassfield respectively. Next came Dyson, Wollek, Akin, and Morton.

It was a special day for the ageless autocrat, Bob Tullius, for he was presented with the Norelco Cup – the 'driver-of-the-day' award. There was an implication in his post-race speech that he might not be doing quite so much

Cockpit, centre-section, and rear suspension assembly of XJR-7 photographed at Winchester, Va., in March 1986. (*Courtesy: Bill Mather*)

st oil cap led to unsightly smears on the normally-spotless Tullius/Robinson XJR-7 at Miami, 1986.

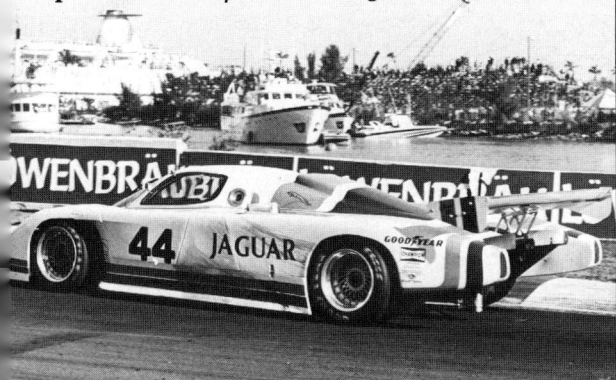

racing in the future. Such a thought was not unreasonable, for Tullius had first raced a 1937 Ford on a New York short track as long ago as 1953. In his youth, Bob Tullius had been a seller of Verifax copiers, so there was an element of nostalgia when car No. 44's fitters, under Brian Krem, won the Kodak Copiers IMSA top pit-crew award for 1986. At every meeting, the teams would compete for this prize. The exercise was to change all four tyres, refuel, and switch drivers as quickly as possible, the winners being the men with the best overall time at the end of the year.

A Grumman amphibian flies by, while the Group 44 cars are attended during 1986 Miami practice. Lee Dykstra, designer of the XJR-5 and the XJR-7, had now severed his connection with Bob Tullius. The absence of a technical supremo was to be reflected in some race results – but the XJR-7 would prove itself a winner before the season was out!

XJR-7s in their tent at Sebring, 1986. Air-intake splitters are new, identifying, features. (*Courtesy: Karen Miller*)

The No. 04 crew was well-placed, too, re-emphasising the strong element of team discipline for which Group 44 was renowned. These were the final placings:

Kodak Copiers
IMSA Top Pit Crew Award, 1986

1st	*Jaguar*, Group 44, car no. 44
2nd	Porsche, Busby team, car no. 67
3rd	BMW, N. American M team, car no. 19
4th	Corvette, Hendrick team, car no. 52
5th	*Jaguar*, Group 44, car no. 04
6th	Porsche, Bayside team, car no. 85

For Jaguar, too, there was satisfaction. True, on force of numbers the Porsches had triumphed again; but the General Motors, Ford, and BMW-powered opposition was beaten soundly, taking 1986 as a whole. This is how the provisional points looked at the year's end:

IMSA Camel GT Championship (manufacturers), 1986

Position	Engine	pts	Chassis	pts
1st	Porsche 3·2T	309	Porsche	309

2nd	*Jaguar 6·5*	155	*Jaguar (Group 44)*	155
3rd	Chevrolet 3·5T	89	Chevrolet (Lola)	88
4th	Buick 3·5T	64	Hawk (March)	61
5th	Ford 2·1T	57	Ford Probe	59
6th	BMW 2·1T	52	BMW (March)	52

It had been a costly period; but it had been a time of high profit making for Jaguar Cars Inc. Now it was time to take stock and one thing was clear: for years Group 44 had placed the name of Jaguar prominently on its cars.

Right:
Group 44's XJR-7s and Jim Busby's Porsche 962s in the pit-lane at Lime Rock, where these detail shots were taken of the rear suspension, front-mounted oil-coolers, and latest water radiator position (one each side). Sam Headley is seen at work in one of these mid-1986 pictures. (*Courtesy: Karen Miller*)

Below:
Modern history: With the introduction of the XJR-7, the XJR-5 became a museum piece. First private custodian was the great enthusiast Walter Hill, seen pondering his latest responsibility – XJR-5/001 – which was delivered to his Florida base in March 1986. (*Courtesy: Richard Lovell*)

More names would be needed in the future; sponsorship of a major kind would be required if Jaguar Cars Inc. was to maintain a full two-car IMSA programme.

1987: A Limited Programme

Despite being an interim year for Jaguar in North American racing, 1987 was not without its successes for the single-entry XJR-7 which Group 44 ran in selected events scoring two victories, plus a fourth and a fifth by the middle of the year. The victories were achieved by Hurley Haywood/John Morton at Riverside and Palm Beach; on both occasions it was a close-run thing between them and champion-to-be Chip Robinson who had now joined the Holbert Porsche team. At Palm Beach in June, the XJR-7 appeared thanks to a local sponsor. It was to prove the ninth and final IMSA victory for a Group 44 car on behalf of Jaguar.

Bob Tullius did not race much in 1987; he was creating new plans for his team, in view of the changes which he knew were to be made. He did drive with Morton at Watkins Glen in July, when the XJR-7 had a troubled run; but they finished the race. It was the last *official* appearance of Group 44 for Jaguar, and the team was cheered to the echo. In twelve seasons of racing with Jaguar's V12 engine, the American team had played a significant part in the Coventry marque's survival – and *re*vival. So it was only right that the team should complete 1987 in a blaze of glory, taking part in the final IMSA race at Del Mar, California, in October sponsored by a Jaguar dealer. The XJR-7 finished tenth, Morton and Haywood taking eight and ninth places in the year's points standings (aided by several non-Jaguar drives). The blaze of glory came from Lanky Foushee and his men taking the Kodak Copiers pit-work prize for the second year running. It made a neat ending to a memorable chapter.

One of Britain's greatest-ever sports car drivers, Brian Redman, with his team-mate Chip Robinson, photographed by Team Unicorn Inc. at the 1986 final.

The winning team: Car No. 44's crew won the 1986 Kodak Copiers award for the year's best pit-work, which helped the XJR-7 take the final at Daytona, where this picture was taken by Team Unicorn Inc. This success would be repeated in 1987.

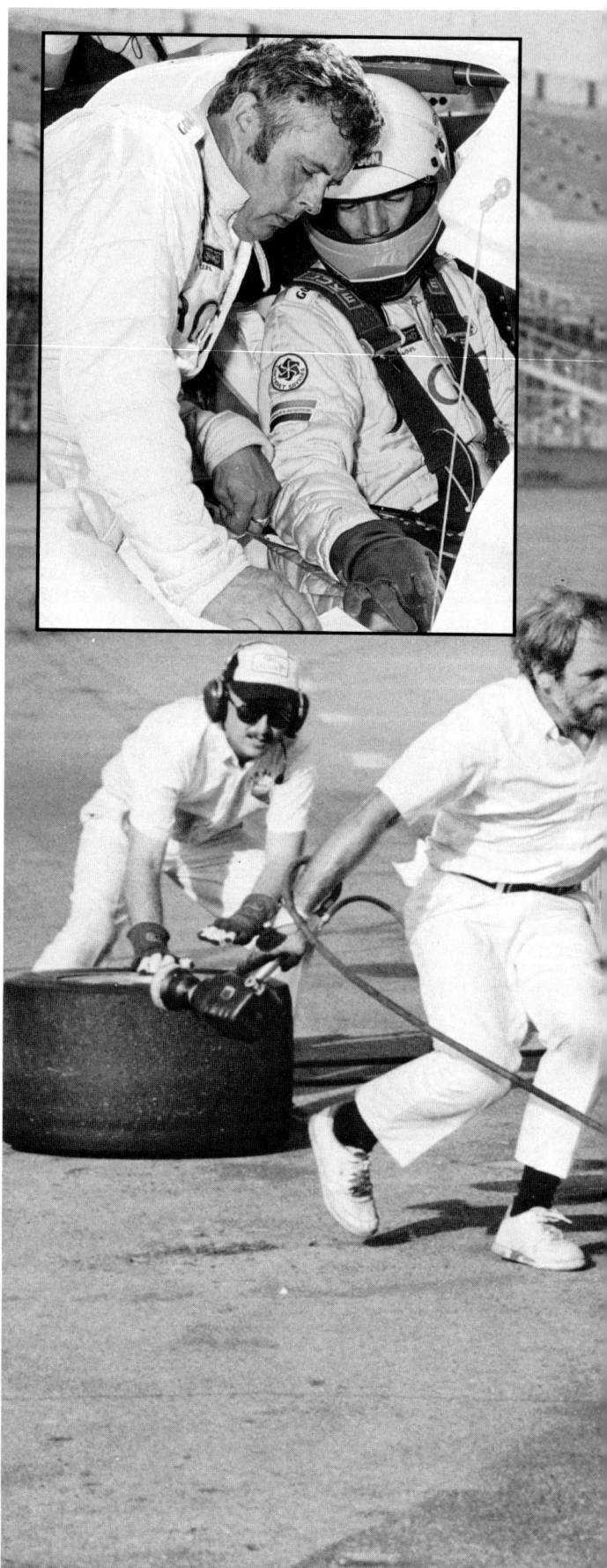

Capping a racing career that had already spanned more than thirty-three years, Bob Tullius heads for victory at Daytona, October 1986, in the three-hour IMSA final. This Unicorn picture was taken on the tricky infield section.

Bob Tullius and Chip Robinson, winners of the Eastern Airlines Trophy, Daytona, pictured by Team Unicorn for Jaguar Cars Inc. – truly a grand finale to 1986.

National Speed Sport News front page headline for 29 October 1986 placed Group 44's achievement at Daytona above the news that Alain Prost had retained his World Championship in Adelaide! – a measure of the significance to American sports enthusiasts of this result, and of the benefit of racing to Jaguar in its biggest export market. Picture shows the Redman/Haywood XJR-7 leading from that of ultimate winners Tullius/Robinson.

Imsa Latest

Quite early in 1987, it was announced that Tom Walkinshaw's TWR organisation would take over from Bob Tullius's Group 44 at the start of the 1988 season. Guy Edwards, who had masterminded the Silk Cut deal for Jaguar, introduced Castrol's American company as a full-scale sponsor for TWR's IMSA offensive. This enabled TWR to set up a US base run by Tony Dowe, with Ian Reed as chief engineer. These two Englishmen had plenty of US racing experience, and were now responsible to Roger Silman, the TWR director of racing. Cars and engines were to be supplied from Kidlington. The 1988 6-litre Jaguar-powered XJR-9 is seen *(below)* in its IMSA livery. The TWR sports-car story is told between Pages 398 and 427.

Joyous victory lap at Palm Beach for the Haywood/Morton XJR-7 in June 1987. This was the third win for the XJR-7 and the ninth for a Group 44 Jaguar in five years of IMSA GTP racing. But the team knew already that Jaguar was turning elsewhere for 1988 ...... That's motor racing, as they say. (*Courtesy Graig Hinton for Racal-Milgo*)

344

Chapter Fifteen

The Works, the XJ-S and Walkinshaw

When I began working on this history of works involvement in motor-racing, the name Jaguar had been missing from world-class racing for many years.

In the USA Bob Tullius had begun winning for the BL import organisation with a much-modified XJ-S, as described in the previous chapter. In Europe and elsewhere, Jaguar engines were still doing well in historic car racing, as well as in such minority activities as water speed record-breaking and tractor pulling; but that was about all.

Jaguar's own priorities were: to survive and to make money. Neither looked likely as the new decade (the 1980s) got under way. The company's destiny still lay in the hands of Sir Michael Edwardes. Racing could not have been further from the minds of Jaguar's engineers. Although hardly involved themselves, they were still smarting from the costly failure of the 1976–77 BL-Broadspeed debacle which could not help reflecting badly on the marque at a time when Jaguar customers were having their problems, too.

It is true that there had been several secret, desultory projects which showed that Bob Knight wanted to know about modern motor racing. As early as May 1976, Peter Gebbels had prepared a Group 5 XJ-S proposal. That autumn, development engineer Malcolm Oliver – later XJ40 project manager – compiled a data sheet on the XJ-S's aero-dynamics and arranged a series of wind-tunnel tests at MIRA using four different wing configurations on one of the red launch cars, JVC 482N. During 1977 Jaguar made further XJ-S investigations, trying a variety of aero-

dynamic aids; the main problem was to try to reduce excessive front-end lift. There was considerable work on the reduction of fluid operating temperatures – one of Broadspeed's constant headaches with the XJ12C that year. Abbey Panels became involved with major modifications to the body structure and indeed a complete build programme for one car was issued by Malcolm Oliver on 20 July 1977, this being sent to Bob Knight with copies to Tom Jones and David Fielden. The ground rules were spelled out thus: 'For the purposes of this assessment, it has been assumed that the vehicle will be built to as competitive a standard as possible without the use of "exotic" materials.'

At another stage Oliver opined: 'In view of the problems and experiences of the Group 2 two-door, it would seem that two sets of all stressed components would be required.'

There were studies of specifications and analyses of power-to-weight ratio in competitive cars, which led Jaguar to speculate that a Group 5 racing XJ-S should not weigh more than 1155 kg – a tall order to say the least.

Records show that 360 man-days were expended on the in-house XJ-S racing project, including 32 drawing office hours shared by Peter Gebbels, Ray Kitchen and Ted Laban. Numerous components were drawn and fabricated before the exercise was dropped. The timing co-incided more-or-less with BL's canning of the Broadspeed racing programme (late 1977) and Bob Knight's elevation (early 1978) to the post of Managing Director of 'Jaguar Cars' – a title suggesting a step in the right direction for the organisation and for him. Knight chose to take early retirement just over two years later, following the appointment of John Egan to chair Jaguar Cars Limited. There were no Browns Lane-originated race-car engineering exercises after that. Group 2 and Group 5 specifications were going 'over the top' and racing was dominated by single makes – BMW and Porsche respectively. There was no money with which to create a Jaguar budget and there was a general loss of interest in the categories in anticipation of new regulations: Groups A, B, and C.

At least, some of the Jaguar work would prove helpful to John McCormack and, later, John Goss, both Australian.

What was particularly clear was the fact that motor racing, more than ever before, was an activity which needed total vigilance, constant updating of information, and involvement of the complete technology – from optimum design to team management and race tactics.

Jaguar is staffed not just by specialist tradesmen, technicians or managers but – almost across the spectrum – by enthusiasts for the motor car itself. The character of the company and its products today demonstrates this feature very well. Enthusiasm, however, is not enough to qualify anyone to go motor racing seriously. Those involved in the original Jaguar race programme – and some were still working at Browns Lane in the 1980s – know better than anyone that motor racing has led to a completely new and specialised industry. The 1950s had been the time of opportunity; Jaguar had seized it. In the 1960s, Ford had shown the way, by investing millions in external technology. Jaguar dipped its toe with the XJ13, but that was all. And in the 1970s, while many people still hoped for a return, it became clearer all the time that Jaguar would be lucky if it stayed in business at all, let alone if it chanced its arm in motor racing: Hence the secret, low-key nature of its own racing studies, and the anguish over the BL-Broadspeed affair.

The Walkinshaw Story

Jaguar in the 1970s was battling to maintain its quality standards, and it was failing. At the heart of the problem lay the events surrounding the nationalisation of British Leyland. Matters came to a head with the Government's 'Ryder' investigation of 1974.

In that year a 27-year-old Ford race development engineer-driver came to Browns Lane to collect his father's new car. Campbell Ritchie, newly out of his apprenticeship, was detailed by his boss (Home Sales Manager, Patrick Smart) to attend to him and was suitably embarrassed when – within moments of acquaintance – the Series Two XJ was discovered to have a seized steering wheel adjustment collar and inoperative wipers. (It was, of course, raining hard that day.) The faults were dealt with – but the seeds of doubt had been sown, and niggling faults continued to plague the car. Disillusioned the customer, so far a confirmed Jaguar man, sold it a year or so later. By then, his son was establishing his career as a racing driver and as an independent businessman. Tom Walkinshaw was on his way to the top.

Tom Walkinshaw comes from Prestonpans, just east of Edinburgh, where he first worked in the family's market

Britain's Group A challenger in Europe, Tom Walkinshaw, with Paul Davis in 1982. (*Courtesy: Vladimir Havranek*)

Walkinshaw at the wheel of the Group A Jaguar XJ-S V12 touring coupe, practising for its first UK race at Donington Park, 1982.

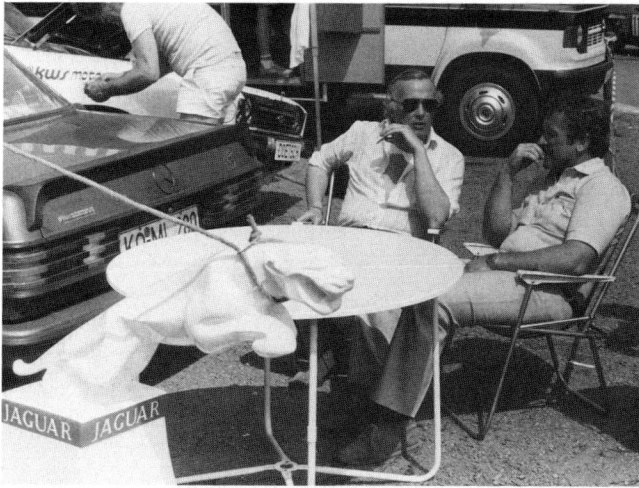

pionship in the same (Formula Ford) category with a Hawke in 1969. He 'emigrated' to Hertford, working for David Lazenby (the Hawke's manufacturer) by day and on his own car in the evenings. Soon he progressed into

Unleashing the Jaguar: Tom Walkinshaw and 'Chuck Nicholson' at Brno on the eve of the XJ-S's first ETC race victory. (*Courtesy: Vladimir Havranek*)

'Chuck Nicholson' confers with Tom Walkinshaw in the Brno pits during practice. (*Courtesy: Vladimir Havranek*)

gardening business, earning himself a Mini van for his seventeenth birthday. That was the Mini-Cooper era, and as an enthusiast (he even recalls tuning-in to Raymond Baxter reporting on the early Jaguar victories at Le Mans!) Walkinshaw took little time to find and fit a more suitable engine, thanks to the proximity of Seton Mains Garage – the headquarters of Bill Borrowman's Mini-Cooper S racing team.

Walkinshaw proved a canny operator in the soft fruit trade and saved enough money to buy himself an MG Midget which he raced for the first time, aged 19, at his local circuit, Ingliston, in April 1966. A decade later he would score his first World class victory; but there was to be a long uphill struggle first.

A racing Singer 'Shammy' preceded Walkinshaw's single-seater period which began in 1968 with a Lotus 51, tuned by Stan Sproat who (with Sandy Arthur and Ron Gaudion) had been responsible for preparing the *Ecurie Ecosse* Jaguar D-types of old. He won the Scottish cham-

Formula 3 with March Engineering with whom he signed a test/drive contract towards the end of 1970. A broken leg hindered progress for a while. In any case, single-seaters did not produce much success for the ambitious Scot, and when Ford offered him a contract he saw it as an opportunity to learn from the 'big boys'. His arrival on the touring car scene coincided with a time of intense rivalry between Ford and BMW, and both marques gained from his increasing skill as a driver. His aggression was coupled to a mechanical sympathy and physical strength which suited him for long-distance racing. These characteristics shot him into the headlines in 1976 when he and John Fitzpatrick won the World Championship six-hour race at Silverstone by a matter of metres. (Their be-winged BMW CSL 'Batmobile' was running Group 5 trim.) Later that year, Walkinshaw acquired a BMW 528 to gain his first-hand experience of modification for production car racing. In 1977, with Dieter Quester, he won the Group 2 Tourist Trophy in an Alpina CSL, depriving

347

Main photograph:
**High-speed crocodile led by Walkinshaw (Jaguar) and
ETC champion Helmut Kelleners (BMW) through the
village of Bosonohy on Lap 1 of 1982 Brno GP. (*Courtesy:
Jos Reinhard*)**

Inset left:
**'Chuck Nicholson' at Veselka, en route to victory with
the lone Motul-sponsored Jaguar, Brno 1982. (*Courtesy:
Jos Reinhard*)**

Inset right:
**'Chuck Nicholson' and Tom Walkinshaw on the first
step of Jaguar's ladder of success in Europe – the Brno
podium, June 1982. (*Courtesy: Jiri Drtil*)**

BL-Broadspeed of any chance of a last-minute reprieve for
the XJ12 – and was by then well advanced in building up
his own empire, TWR, which has continued to grow and
thrive on a variety of motor industry and racing-related
agencies and contracts ever since he acquired his first
industrial site at Kidlington, Oxford, at the beginning of
1978.

A new touring car formula

It was in 1981 that Tom Walkinshaw made his approach
to Jaguar. The timing could not have been better. Two
important factors coincided for him. The first factor was
a new racing category suitable for the XJ-S, Jaguar's
impressive if not stylish roadgoing coupé. Examination of
the new FIA Group A regulations, due to be introduced for
the 1982 European Touring Car Championship, suggested
that the potential was there. Walkinshaw could see that
Group A touring cars for racing were going to *look* like the
road cars from which they were derived. 'Complete wheels
(wheel = flange + rim + tyre) are free, provided that they

**First visit by the TWR-Motul XJ-S to the Nürburgring
in July 1982 – the final year for the complete, original
circuit.**

**The XJ-S crosses the bridge before the pits during the
1982 Nürburgring 6-hour race.**

may be housed within the original bodywork; this means
the upper part of the wheel rim, flange, and tyre flank
located vertically over the wheel hub centre must be
covered by the bodywork, when measured vertically.'
That regulation meant an end to the vast wheel-arch
extensions which had become commonplace in the various
'modified saloon' formulas; yet within the wheel-arch there
was freedom to fit the 13-inch wide tyres permitted for
over-5-litre cars.

One fly in the ointment was a fuel tank capacity limitation of 120 litres – applicable to *all* cars of over 2·5 litres
cylinder capacity. Minimum race distance was specified
as 500 km. (some organisers would choose to run the
optional 3½-hour timed event), and it became clear that
in a race not complicated by excessive tyre wear or other
problems, a 5.3-litre Jaguar was going to have to make at
least two stops whereas any BMW (for example) should
manage on one. It was an ingredient which would make
for some exciting motor racing.

Braking and transmission systems were unrestricted;
TWR would specify special AP disc with four-pot calipers
(the rear ones moved outboard), an AP clutch, and five-
speed Getrag manual gearbox – although Jaguar's tough
old four-speed would be used in early races.

The engine could be modified extensively but there were
restrictions on inlet and exhaust valve-lift dimensions and
on fuel feed; the latter had to be 'the original system' –
meaning Lucas petrol injection, although some very early
testing was done using a Forward Engineering power

The XJ-S performance provided the TWR-Motul team with every reason to cheer. (It was Jaguar's first victory in this gruelling event for nearly two decades.)

Paul Davis and the wheel that *could* have cost TWR dearly at the Nürburgring.

unit with Weber carburetters. (Ron Beaty of Forward Engineering also provided some engine test facilities before TWR acquired their own.)

There was another element that helped Walkinshaw 'think Jaguar' for Group A, to the surprise of others in the racing game: as well as for tyre and fuel tank dimensions, there was a third sliding scale applicable to weight. For Group A, cars of over 5 litres engine capacity had a minimum weight limit of 1400 kg. The limit for a BMW 528i was 1035 kg and for a BMW 635 CSi (as approved from 1983) was 1185 kg. – a big advantage for the Bavarian marque in one sense, yet not *un*favourable to Jaguar in that it seemed likely that the XJ-S could be got down to the minimum weight; and so it would prove.

By the skin of its upholstery, the XJ-S *could* be judged as meeting the official definition of 'a touring car of four seats minimum'; *and* it managed to meet the basic homologation requirement of at least 5000 cars 'manufactured in twelve consecutive months'. This was achieved on a 'component' basis, for Jaguar production was still recovering from the pre-Egan era. After all, the 5000 figure was an arbitrary one; there was little doubt that the XJ-S did come within the true spirit of the Group A concept. (The 5000-a-year requirement was to be surpassed with ease during the TWR Jaguar's three outstanding seasons of racing in Europe.) And so, to the second factor that made Walkinshaw's timing so perfect: the positive reaction of Jaguar itself.

Tom Walkinshaw, Phil Ebberson, Allan Scott, 'Chuck Nicholson' and Kevin Lee celebrate in Germany.

Ever since his own bad experience at Jaguar in 1974, Walkinshaw had had little reason to return. Things were different, though. Not only was there now a Jaguar capable of winning races at international level; there was leadership at Browns Lane itself – people who could (and might) talk business.

Since April 1980, the improvements at Jaguar – in morale and motivation – had happened because of the presence of John Egan. He and his team had trimmed the workforce, increased productivity, and appeased the customer. 'Jaguar' was Jaguar Cars Ltd once more and, by the time Tom Walkinshaw was ready for his first official visit to Browns Lane in seven years, the two life-saving investments had been promised by BL's board – those for the alloy-block AJ6 engine and the long-promised new car, codenamed XJ40.

John Egan's message to Tom Walkinshaw was: Let's see what you can do. Egan knew that his responsibility for the name Jaguar demanded that he should at least consider a return to winning important motor races – somehow, sometime. He had reprieved Group 44 and given the go-ahead for the IMSA project that was to become the XJR-5. Until they met Tom Walkinshaw and heard his proposals, however, neither John Egan nor Jim Randle had any reason to believe that there was a worthwhile international race category in which a Jaguar *production model* could shine.

The European Touring Car Championship would go Group A for 1982 and Walkinshaw convinced the Jaguar men of his seriousness when he agreed with their policy: to provide some facilities and technical assistance but to distance themselves, while they watched. They knew from his past record that he was good; and already in 1981, they had observed his adaptability – for he was already experienced in preparing and running BMWs, Mazdas and Rovers for racing by then.

For his smart black Jaguar XJ-S, Walkinshaw obtained major sponsorship from the Continent, by becoming UK distributor for the French Motul Oil company, not that much Motul got sold in Britain – but of course, because this was a European championship, it was a sensible deal. (TWR's later Bastos Cigarettes contract on behalf of Rover showed similar marketing acumen.) Subsidiary sponsorship came from Akai audio. Whatever Jaguar may have provided – like the permanent relinquishing of cars and parts – the information was not made public.

The Tom Walkinshaw racing policy is, in several ways, similar to Ralph Broad's. A decade later, Walkinshaw was able to recall the 1976/77 XJ12 racing effort with some sympathy: 'It *could* have been done,' he insisted, 'but they went and changed the basic car so much, they lost their datum points. They lost their way. But they needn't have done.' Of course, the regulations were the real culprits. Not everyone had believed that the XJ12C could make

BMW kings Dieter Quester (*right*), Hans-Joachim Stuck, and Umberto Grano leave Tom Walkinshaw to soak the photographers. Nürburgring, July 1982.

Two Jaguars ran in the 1982 Belgian 24-hour race. Both were to be eliminated by accidents.

Inset Left:
Originally a Forward Engineering unit, this TWR-developed Jaguar V12 engine ('Old Faithful') brought the XJ-S its early successes. (*Courtesy: Bob Constanduros*)

Inset Right:
Testing the regulations: TWR's automatic jacking units aroused the scrutineers' interest during 1982. (*Courtesy: Bob Constanduros*)

Chief mechanic Kevin Lee is nearest camera in this 1982 TT start-line shot of the winning Jaguar.

it; that, perhaps, was the main barrier afterwards. Tom Walkinshaw saw racing from an entrant's point of view in much the same light as Broad did: regulations are there to be made as elastic as possible. The German magazine *Auto Motor und Sport* tried putting pressure on Walkinshaw in an interview, in 1983; they reported one of his responses thus: 'My business is to build successful racing cars and I can assure you that no-one wears a totally white or totally

Runners-up in the 1982 Silverstone TT were Pierre Dieudonné and Peter Lovett in this TWR-Motul XJ-S.

black hat in this sport. If it's black, there are protests at every race. If it's white, you won't win. Therefore, you have to keep somewhere in between. All the successful people in this sport wear grey hats.'

The Walkinshaw policy, like the Broad policy, ensures regular victory and continual progress. It doesn't win you popularity but it wins you respect. That *Auto Motor und Sport* feature (published in TWR's second season of XJ-S racing – when regular winning had begun) accused TWR of cheating at BMW's expense. Afterwards, in its issue of 7 September 1983, it played fair enough by publishing a response from the highly respected former champion BMW driver, Hubert Hahne: 'Don't forget the important part of your magazine's title: "Sport". You have pilloried

the Jaguar with'out troubling to investigate or comment on what their opposition is up to. ... An article such as yours could be written by anyone "in the know" at BMW, Ford, or a number of other makes.'

Back in 1982, however, the Jaguar's presence had been welcomed, since it looked like bringing ETC racing back to life without posing a threat to BMW – yet.

The new Jaguar company was still without its own, separate marketing or public relations departments initially, and so it was via BL Motorsport (later an Austin Rover Group function) that the first rumours emerged. This was not illogical since its director, John Davenport, had been largely responsible for his company's decision to turn to TWR to make the Rover SD1 an effective competition car. Davenport's remark to his employers of yore, *Motoring News*, at New Year 1982, added to the speculation. The news item began: 'Jaguar to return to the European Touring Car Championship? Don't laugh: it may well be true!' In the second paragraph, Davenport was quoted as saying that 'the engine is too big for British Group A' (top limit, $3\frac{1}{2}$ litres); the inference drawn was that it *wasn't* too big for European Group A. No connection with TWR was suggested, however; but other teams were hinted at.

In *Motoring News* a week later (14 January 1982), it was clear that Tom Walkinshaw had been doing some more teasing: 'Although the details of last week's Jaguar XJ-S story were a little wide of the mark, we were at least right about the project's existence. However, the car is not destined for European Group A as we suggested, but for the Bathurst touring car classic in Australia.... Wal-

First and second, in the TT, the two Jaguars take the Woodcote chicane together.

Tom Walkinshaw and 'Chuck Nicholson are joined by Division One winners Bob Meacham (*right*) and Bill Pinckney (VW) for their lap of honour after the 1982 TT. (*Courtesy: Graig Hinton*)

kinshaw tells us that the car is about two months away from completion, and that it will be tested in this country prior to its despatch overseas.' (Incidentally, there was plenty Jaguar news that week. Over the page, the American GTP Jaguar, later named XJR-5, was announced – officially.) The story led to continued, and by no means unfounded, implications of further TWR Rover activity and eight weeks passed before the cat was, truly, out of the bag. In the second week of March, TWR made its own announcement; there was no mention of Jaguar Cars Ltd.

Sponsored by the French Motul company, TWR would race one XJ-S in Europe initially, driven by Walkinshaw and 'Chuck Nicholson' who had been planning to run a Group A Jaguar of his own but, having mentioned it to Walkinshaw when racing Mazdas with him, was happy to change his mind. A second car would join the team for the Belgian 24-hour race, as would Jeff Allam, Pierre Dieudonné, and Peter Lovett. The season was about to start, and Tom Walkinshaw had achieved his aim: to keep the opposition guessing as long as possible. When he did make his announcement, the idea of a racing Jaguar XJ-S was no longer such a laughing matter.

The first season started shakily but ended confidently, with Walkinshaw winning only a minor (Belgian national) event at Zolder in the spring. The first championship race victories were at two of Europe's most testing circuits – Brno and the old Nürburgring – in high summer. Despite continued teething troubles, Walkinshaw and 'Nicholson' overcame the odds and, suddenly, the XJ-S was a serious contender. The win in Germany's six-hour marathon – a regular Jaguar success around two decades earlier – did much to boost Browns Lane's still-tarnished image in the land of the BMW, the Mercedes-Benz, and the Porsche. The failure of both Jaguars in the 24 hours of Francorchamps at the end of July was the salutory lesson that can be learned by the best of teams, just when it has tasted success for the first time. (That was the first time out for TWR/Motul/Akai as a two-car team.)

There followed a welcome six-week respite, in which many lessons were learned and Rounds 10 and 11 of the 1982 European championship – at Silverstone and Zolder – gave the Jaguars the front row of the grid and first and second past the chequered flag on both occasions. It was just a pity that Jaguar's own low-key involvement, and the fact that ETC racing had not yet caught on generally, should lead to so few people actually turning out to witness that historic victory at Silverstone.

The following is the 1982 Jaguar race record in a nutshell:

March 1982, Monza
Walkinshaw and 'Nicholson' shared the front row with reigning champions Kelleners and Grano who made best practice time. Jaguar led until near half-distance when Walkinshaw went over a chicane and damaged the underside, leading to retirement. BMWs prepared by ace Swiss tuner Rüdi Eggenberger came first and second (Kelleners/Grano and Vanoli/Calderari).

March 1982, Vallelunga
On this tight, twisting Roman circuit,. Walkinshaw/'Nicholson' finished third.

April 1982, Zolder
Belgian National (non-ETC) event won by Walkinshaw.

April 1982, Donington
Jaguar holed its radiator when leading. Kelleners/Grano (BMW) scored their third successive ETC victory.

May 1982, Mugello
Having ducked out of Round 4, at far away Enna, Walkinshaw returned to ETC racing for Round 5 in the hills north of Florence, gaining pole versus the usual opposition of BMW 528i and Chevrolet Camaro. Walkinshaw/Dieudonné started well but retired due to valve spring failure. (Cosworth would supply the solution.) Five wins in a row virtually guaranteed Kelleners and Grano another ETC title.

'Chuck Nicholson' takes the '83-livery XJ-S through a slippery Becketts Corner during pre-season Silverstone testing.

Tom Walkinshaw (*centre*) demonstrates the factory's involvement to the press by sitting between Jaguar directors (*left to right*) Jim Randle, John Egan, Neil Johnson and David Boole, Waldorf Hotel, Aldwych, London, March 1983.

June 1982, Brno
This was a tactical victory by Walkinshaw and 'Nicholson', the latter staying on slick tyres in a damp spell and overcoming an alarming throttle-response problem to give the Jaguar its first ETC win. Their biggest challenge, the Czech-driven Hartge-prepared BMW of Zdenek Vojtech and Bretislav Enge, crashed trying to catch up. The Jaguar's 'race' engine proved unsatisfactory in practice, so the original V12 'nail' was refitted for this race . . . and it would be used several more times!

June 1982, Zeltweg
This was Vojtech's biggest triumph to date. In pouring rain, and partnered by the late Jo Gartner, he won by just over a minute from Tom Walkinshaw who had driven single-handed. The Scot had started from pole but lost time due to windscreen wiper failure, of all things.

July 1982, Nürburgring
The most significant Jaguar touring car victory for nearly two decades, this one was achieved against BMW in BMW's own country, and the Münich factory had decided to call on extra forces in the form of a specially-prepared BMW 528i for Hans-Joachim Stuck and Dieter Quester. Despite a puncture, Walkinshaw and 'Nicholson' finished ahead of them. The ultra-reliable team of Kelleners/Grano confirmed their championship form by coming third in this six-hour event.

July–August, Francorchamps
The classic 24-hour race in the Ardennes saw two Jaguars appear for the first time. The Walkinshaw/'Nicholson'/Percy car, with its new Getrag five-speed gearbox, took pole position and an all-too-brief lead in pouring rain, for which its Dunlop tyres were ill-suited. Both it, and the Dieudonné/Allam/Lovett car, which qualified seventh, switched to Pirelli tyres in a frantic effort to stay competitive, but both retired after night-time crashes. The BMW of Armin Hahne, Hans Heyer, and Eddie Joosen took first place.

September 1982, Silverstone
A 1–2 demonstration by Walkinshaw/'Nicholson' and Allam/Lovett gave the Jaguar marque its first major home win for many years – and its first TT victory since 1951! An ultra-fast Rover could have been a threat had it not run out of fuel. Kelleners and Grano came third in the consistent Eggenberger BMW entered by BMW Italia. No-one took very much notice of a turbocharged débutant – a Volvo which retired after only a few laps.

September 1982, Zolder
Another 1–2 for the Jaguars, Walkinshaw/'Nicholson' leading Allam/Dieudonné, with the BMW of champions Kelleners and Grano third. Both cars had the five-speed Getrag gearbox by now. As at Silverstone, the two Jaguars occupied the front row of the grid.

Controversial 'duct' for XJ-S oil coolers was called an 'aerodynamic device' by the opposition; but TWR was to use this unsightly appendage throughout 1983. Nearest camera in this Monza practice shot is the Schnitzer BMW 635CSi of Thierry Boutsen, one of a number of top-line drivers retained by BMW Motorsport.

So it was that in addition to its early-season victory in Belgium, the Group A Jaguar won four ETC races: Brno, Nürburgring, Silverstone, and Zolder. The successes came too late for Walkinshaw to have a chance of winning the European title but, in the end, only one BMW crew (Kelleners/Grano) remained ahead of him. The Jaguar team had contested ten of the eleven races, Walkinshaw winning four (with Nicholson), coming second once (on his own), third once, and retiring four times. Moreover, in the last three races a second car had appeared and it was the runner-up two occasions. The only real mystery retirement was at Mugello, where valve spring failure was

The as-yet unfamiliar sight of a Jaguar pace-car ...

... and Jaguar top brass, including John Egan and Jim Randle whose obvious concern towards the end of the race was more than justified. (Monza 1983)

The Dieudonné/Calderari car, which ran second initially, gobbles up small fry in Monza's irritatingly tight chicane. It would retire with engine damage soon after its first scheduled pit-stop.

attributed to the great heat generated by the restricted exhaust passages demanded by the regulations. The only major argument with officialdom was related to the built-in air-jacking mechanism; at Donington its use had been forbidden but as the season wore on, it became an increasingly acceptable system if operated with an external compressed air supply.

Group A's first season had shown the potential, and it had begun to produce a flicker of interest around the motor industry. The only big disadvantage of the scoring was in the manufacturers' section, where points were awarded for performance *in class* – which meant that the winner of a poorly-supported or uncompetitive class was likely to be the champion manufacturer; Alfa Romeo would win the makers' title regularly because of the GTV6's almost total domination of the 1.6 to 2.5 litre category. To win outright meant nothing.

On the other hand, back in 1963 when the series had begun, there was only one ETC championship – the one for drivers. This still existed, and took into account overall results as well as class performance and made fairly sure that the winner would be the driver (or pair of drivers) who combined the highest overall placings with a good finishing record.

The only thing lacking, for most of 1982, was a true *market* competitor for the Jaguar XJ-S. The Group A BMW 528i had been a worthy opponent but it was not the kind of car an XJ-S owner would be likely to see as an equivalent model; the BMW 635 CSi coupé was a more obvious model and in the autumn of 1982 Dieter Stappert, competition chief of BMW Motorsport GmbH, announced that production had increased sufficiently for hom-

In his final stint at Monza, 'Nicholson' almost caught Quester despite a bonnet that tried to blind him under braking. Had the Jaguar overtaken the BMW, Walkinshaw would have been champion at the season's end. The ifs and buts of motor racing are endless.

ologation to be sought in time for the 1983 racing season.

Unlike Jaguar, BMW was so racing-orientated that it could arrange to build batches of bodies and farm them out to specialists of its own choice for blueprint construction of cars to Group A regulations. It is difficult to imagine a similar situation originating in Coventry; but perhaps time will change that?

Stappert spoke of his company's interpretation of the rules about fuel feed, and how the FIA had confirmed that if a production car's petrol injection equipment was

electronically-operated, then mechanical operation was unacceptable for Group A. This undoubtedly referred to the first appearance of a V8-engined Rover in Group A. If Brian Muir and Win Percy had not retired from the TT, out of fuel, more might have been said at the time. Potentially a straight-forward formula, Group A was already showing that it could be the scene of many a wrangle – just like almost every other form of motoring competition!

Jaguar comes into the open

From Jaguar's point of view, the promise of a direct confrontation between the XJ-S and the 635 CSi was very attractive. Jaguar's own new sales and marketing operation had been directed since December 1981 by ex-army

TWR's Hugo Tippet, who handled timekeeping throughout 1983, photographed at Vallelunga.

Martin Brundle, Pierre Dieudonné, and Paul Davis at Vallelunga, where Brundle had to forego his first TWR team drive after the team chief switched cars.

officer and former BL executive Neil Johnson, to meet 1982's correctly forecast turnaround in production volumes and manufacturing quality. For 1983, it was announced that the emphasis would change. While Motul would still be a sponsor, the two-car TWR Jaguar team would be run as an official company effort, with Johnson the budget holder.

The press release from Browns Lane was dated 4 March 1983 – the day of Jaguar's first-ever full-scale racing press conference, held at the Aldwych Waldorf Hotel on Fleet Street's doorstep. John Egan, Neil Johnson, Jim Randle and David Boole (Director of Public Affairs for the re-formed Jaguar company) joined Tom Walkinshaw and members of the TWR racing team for the announcement.

'We watched and encouraged Tom Walkinshaw and his team last year when they scored four ETC victories in their first season with the XJ-S. This year they will receive our formal support,' announced Egan, and he went on:

Jaguar's image owes much to the racing programme it undertook in the 'fifties and early 'sixties. In those days racing cars were directly related to the subsequent generation of road cars.

We believe that our ETC involvement will assist in our plans for sales growth in Continental Europe, particularly Germany which is the home of one of our major competitors. One of these, BMW, has dominated ETC racing in recent years and we know they have been working hard throughout the winter to prepare new cars for this season. Our two Jaguars will be trying hard to win!

Whatever the outcome I am sure that this year's ETC races will provide more spectator interest and will be a shot in the arm for European motorsport.

The TWR Motul Jaguar team at a Donington Park practice session, not attended by driver Pierre Dieudonné or fitter Gary Davies. Those present were (*left to right*) Keith Partridge, Clive Parker, John Fitzpatrick, Kevin Lee, Colin Marriott, 'Chuck Nicholson', Allan Scott, Tom Walkinshaw, Enzo Calderari, Martin Brundle, David Roberts, Charles Bamber, Phil Ebberson, Rolf Steur, Sharon 'Nicholson' (pit signaller), Paul Davis (team manager), Peter Battam (Jaguar marketing), and Hugo Tippet (timekeeper).

Jim Randle added to the rationale of using the experience of independent specialists:

Never since Jaguar stopped racing have we given up the idea of returning, but times and conditions change and no matter how interested you are in the sport, you cannot start 'cold' in racing and expect immediately to be successful.

The new regulations called Group A mean that there is an international category in Europe for cars bearing a close relationship to those the customer can go out and buy for everyday use.

Jaguar's 'big rig', complete with mobile showroom and turntable, makes its debút at Donington, 1983.

One of the great features is that the general exterior shape cannot be altered, so the cars being raced don't look like freaks. Even so, we have not been blind to the need to take full advantage of the best possible experience at our disposal – and no British-based team has more experience in ETC racing than Tom Walkinshaw Racing.

The form of racing is very important to us too. As Tom has said many times, we don't attend simply to pick up points in a championship. We come to demonstrate the quality and reliability of the product and above all, of course, we come to do a good job every time we race. Long-distance endurance racing is Jaguar's traditional platform. It proves so much more than a 'sprint' event.

The XJ-S on show at the Waldorf was finished in a new livery, predominantly white with dark green – simple, distinctive, and clean.

It looked rather less clean when it stood in the pit lane at Monza just a fortnight later.

Not seen either at the London launch or in the action pictures taken during Silverstone testing was a cooling duct for the rear axle oil-coolers, which *could* have been taken to be an 'enveloping aerodynamic structure' – a feature specifically barred by the regulations. *Motoring News* reported BMW people describing the feature as 'controversial or even illegal', but Walkinshaw stuck to his guns and retained the unsightly duct for the whole season.

The big difference for the Scot, now, was the need for him to fit in diplomatic visits to the Jaguar importer's enclosure behind the paddock to meet customers and press – not exactly his scene.

BMW were well-organised at Monza, with ten of the newly-homologated 3.5-litre coupés from a variety of teams and sponsors from Belgium, Czechoslovakia, France, Germany, Italy and Switzerland. With around 400 bhp at their command, the V12-engined Jaguars had no trouble in making the front-row positions. Memories of the Broadspeed team's agony here six years earlier seemed thoroughly erased as Walkinshaw led Dieudonné away from the scrapping BMWs, watched by (amongst others) John Egan, Jim Randle, and Neil Johnson. Shortly after taking over from Dieudonné, however, new team member Enzo Calderari from Switzerland came into the pits to retire – engine failure being blamed at the time on poor fuel. The race still seemed to be in Jaguar's pocket when, to the consternation of 'Nicholson' in particular, a securing pin pulled out, permitting the bonnet to flap. One pit-stop did not do the job and there was an uncharac-

The fateful pitstop, featuring the worried faces of Keith Partridge, Colin Marriott and Rolf Steur. Shortly after this picture was taken, 'Nicholson' was told to get going. He ran out of fuel.

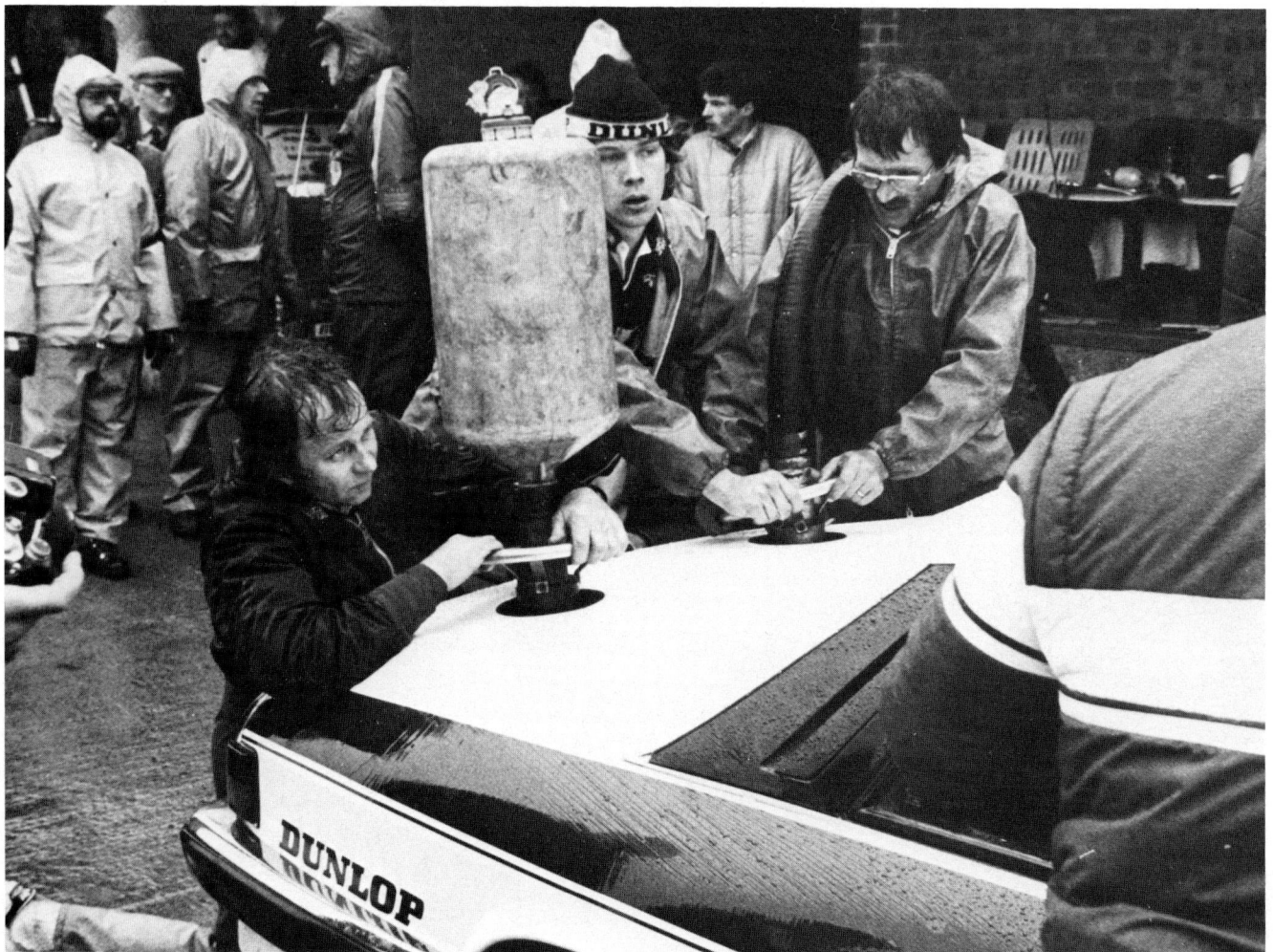

The winning Jaguar at Donington Park, where it rained constantly. (*Courtesy: Martin Collyer*)

Inset:
Martin Brundle is greeted by a delighted John Egan after achieving what had appeared an impossible task – winning with ...

... a brilliant demonstration of car control.

teristic TWR flap as a simple commodity – sticky tape – was sought frantically. A second stop partially resolved the problem and 'Nicholson' tore after the three Alpina-engined BMWs now ahead of him in the form of the works car of Thierry Boutsen, the Juma entry of Armin Hahne, and Dieter Quester's Schnitzer-prepared machine. He caught two of them, and was in sight of the Austrian former champion when the chequered flag fell. The once-pristine Walkinshaw/'Nicholson' XJ-S lost by $3\frac{1}{2}$ seconds after more than three hours of racing. The frustration would have been even worse if anyone could have predicted that those $3\frac{1}{2}$ seconds were to make all the difference between Quester or Walkinshaw becoming European champion twelve races later.

At the 'mickey mouse' Vallelunga circuit three weeks later, the Jaguar and (quicker) BMW times were much closer. BMW brought in Manfred Winkelhock to boost Quester's title chances. He put in a 'flyer' at the end of practice and even Tom Walkinshaw couldn't beat his time, so the Jaguars were second and third on the grid.

Walkinshaw led easily again, and was over 10 seconds ahead when, inexplicably, one of his brand-new composite wheels broke at the bolts, pitching his Jaguar into the barriers. Despite damaging his hand (the steering wheel smashed into it) TWR's team leader managed to get his car back to the pits for a new wheel and some metal-bashing; then he charged into the race.

Meantime, 'Chuck Nicholson' had been holding third place behind Winkelhock; this of course became second until the Jaguar driver was passed by reigning ETC champion Helmut Kelleners. After 'Nicholson's' pit-stop, Dieudonné brought the No. 2 XJ-S up from sixth to fourth

Dunlop engineer Bill Mack and technician John Clifford checking tyres beside the lake of Pergusa.

place. Calderari, replacing Walkinshaw, had done only a few laps when Winkelhock's BMW came into contact with the rear bumper of the No. 1 Jaguar, which spun into the undergrowth and out of the race at high speed.

When Dieudonné came in, Walkinshaw took over from

Tom Walkinshaw takes the chequered flag for his first win of 1983 – Round 4 at Pergusa.

him to bring the surviving XJ-S home in third place – unable to claim championship points, since he had switched cars.

New to the Jaguar team for the Donington 500 in May were veteran John Fitzpatrick and rising star Martin Brundle. The Jaguars were on the front row as persistent rain fell. Except in such extreme conditions, soft Dunlops would have heated-up too quickly to be a serious proposition for race use – but Walkinshaw used them this time to leave the field well behind initially, while Fitzpatrick with a harder compound held off the pack with difficulty. Eventually the quicker BMWs got past, but he pressed on strongly despite a harmless spin.

Walkinshaw's first stop went wrong – insufficient fuel being added – with the result that 'Chuck Nicholson', fending off would-be helpers, had to push the car to the pits, a feat made easier by the favourable incline.

With the leading Jaguar suddenly out of contention BMW once again seemed to have the race sewn up. Calderari did a fine mid-race spell after Fitzpatrick; then came the drive of the day. Brundle, who had not raced the XJ-S before (he had been due to drive at Vallelunga, but had only practised) took over. The rain which had been falling all day got heavier, and Brundle had the right tyres. Suddenly, from the order of a lap adrift, the gap between the Jaguar and the leading BMW – Quester's again! – was seen to be lessening. Two seconds a lap, then four, and so on. Brundle was throwing the XJ-S through the corners in beautifully controlled slides – and so was Walkinshaw, for he was back in the race, making up what places he could. The Jaguar drivers were revelling in the conditions, and Walkinshaw was able to pass Quester and make him drive in the Jaguar's ball of blinding spray. Responding to the encouraging signals he was getting, Brundle applied the power and the opposite lock, and with 12 laps to go, amid cheers, made his way to the front. There was nothing Quester could do about it, try as he might, and the Austrian lost the race by 20 seconds in an enthralling contest, marred by an abortive protest from a BMW 'consortium' over a pace-car period during which the winning car had made a pit-stop.

At last, on 15 May, Walkinshaw and 'Nicholson' scored *their* first win of the season, at the hot bowl of Pergusa, close to the Sicilian hilltop town of Enna; but Calderari retired the second car with zero oil pressure. A week later, after a lengthy trek north to Mugello, Walkinshaw and Fitzpatrick had to be content with third place; they would have been second but for a late stop for fuel – their car running rich and thirstily. Calderari/Nicholson had a puncture; then went out altogether with a broken pulley tensioner – a recurring problem.

A second win at Brno put Walkinshaw one point ahead of Quester with six races gone. Calderari and Dieudonné were comfortably second until a rear-end breakage made their car almost unsteerable for the last two laps, during which the Belgian-driven XJ-S was overtaken by four of the BMWs.

The Oesterreichring provided the team with its first 1–2 result of 1983. Martin Brundle was free of single-seater commitments, and shared Walkinshaw's victory in the shadow of protest and counter-protest on eligibility

grounds. (It was the rejection of Schnitzer's protest here that probably led to the aforementioned *Auto, Motor und Sport* anti-TWR article.)

The Jaguar company hosted a major promotion at the Nürburgring for the last-ever international 6-hour race on the grand old *Nordschleife* circuit. Germany was the home of Jaguar's rival manufacturers, and it was important to rebuild the marque's reputation there. Neil Johnson had just announced the plan to form a new import company, Jaguar Deutschland GmbH, and Tom Walkinshaw was leading Dieter Quester in the championship by 30 points. There was confidence in the air; but in fact it was mid-season crisis time. John Fitzpatrick left the team after an argument, while the Jaguars – when driven hard – were finding the unyielding Nürburgring more of a test than ever. Both cars came to rest out on the circuit, one with clutch failure, the other with an ignition fault which gave Walkinshaw a cockpit full of smoke. (He had led for an hour and made fastest lap time, switching to the second car when 'Nicholson' had failed to return.) 'It's all the flying over brows of the hills. The car takes off and the wheels spin free. When you land, the tyres grip and it puts a tremendous shock through the transmission,' explained Walkinshaw to the *Coventry Evening Telegraph*'s Keith Read – one of a number of journalists who had come specially to see a Jaguar win. It was Quester's crucial race, however. With Winkelhock to share the wheel of the BMW, he took maximum points to close-in on Walkinshaw in their title chase.

Only a week after the Nürburgring race, the 3½-hour event in the hills behind Salzburg presented grave scheduling problems to the Jaguar preparers. Tom Walkinshaw therefore took the decision to leave one car in his Kidlington workshops for rebuilding prior to the forthcoming Belgian 24-hour race.

The Jaguar went beautifully, and was aided by the speed of two lightening pit-stops which drew applause from those watching. It was a scorcher of a day, and keeping an eye on mechanical temperatures was a major occupation. Vojtech's was the quickest BMW in practice and the race, and led briefly while the Jaguar was making its first scheduled stop; then it was sidelined by serious engine trouble.

Jaguar now had five wins to BMW's four: but things would go very wrong in the last three rounds. The Belgian 24-hour race looked promising. Win Percy was seconded into the team once again and followed Walkinshaw in the opening laps, taking the lead when 'the boss' suffered a puncture. Then Percy, suffering from the heat, slowed and came in to hand over to Calderari. Walkinshaw and Dieudonné (who had shared victory in a Mazda two years earlier) lost time changing the propeller shaft which had thrown its balance weight, and finally retired with differential failure. Percy, Calderari, and Brundle kept their car going through the night; but in the morning Brundle experienced a massive engine failure and it was all over.

Because of the importance of Germany to Jaguar, two TWR cars were entered for the non-championship Group A race at Hockenheim during the German GP meeting. Walkinshaw had a puncture on the first lap, but Enzo Calderari won with ease from Klaus Niedzwiedz (Zakspeed Ford Mustang). Zdenek Vojtech had defied a general boycott by the leading BMW teams who were still being encouraged to treat the Jaguars as 'illegal'. Unfortunately, Vojtech's car spun off and, when another BMW came a distant third, it would have been natural for the casual spectator to presume that their home teams might have been chicken.

End-of-season blues

Quester was now leading Walkinshaw by a short head – yet in theory the odds were still in the latter's favour during the six-week lead-in to Rounds 11 and 12, and on the day of the TT until the drizzle set in. Dieudonné had to come straight into the pit after the warming-up lap, another belt-tensioner broken at the cost of two race laps. Meanwhile 'Nicholson' led from pole position, but only momentarily; Dunlop simply could not produce a suitable tyre for these race conditions and, despite a tyre change, the Lincolnshire man spun out of the chicane and into the catch fencing as he tried to use the 'wet' line. Walkinshaw, having hedged his bets by not driving first, took over from Dieudonné; but nothing would make the car go quicker, and all the Scot could do was keep trying, and be grateful that one of his other team's cars was winning for the Austin Rover Group at BMW's expense. Sir William Lyons – just turned 82 years old – and John Egan were among the many interested parties who found it difficult to accept why ninth place was the best a Jaguar could do.

Even then, it seemed reasonable that Walkinshaw could be champion. All he had to do was to finish fourth *and* ahead of Quester at Zolder, and the title would be his! Win Percy was back in the team for the final race and, having disposed of Grano, he led until sidelined by clutch failure due to gearbox trouble. Brundle was having difficulty with *his* gearchange, losing a couple of laps; but then the car motored well, with Percy and Walkinshaw having a stint each. All they could show for it was eighth place, whereas, thanks largely to the brilliance of his co-driver Hans-Joachim Stuck, Quester came fourth to clinch the European title.

There was a nice touch at the end of a great season, tainted only by the accusation and counter-accusations of BMW and TWR. Tom Walkinshaw was seen to congratulate Quester, the man who had helped him beat the Broadspeed Jaguars six years earlier. The Austrian is said to have replied that he was sorry about his rival's late-season misfortunes, but: 'only a little bit'.

So the 1983 season ended with Quester first, then Walkinshaw followed quite closely by the perennial Kelleners/Grano combination. BMW had won six ETC races to Jaguar's five; disappointing, maybe, but the season-long battle had revived interest in touring car racing to an unprecedented level and that would do everyone good. This was the story of those top men of 1983:

Monza (20/3/83) 500 km

1st	BMW	D. Quester/C. Rossi
2nd	Jaguar	T. Walkinshaw/'C. Nicholson'
3rd	BMW	H. Heyer/A. Hahne
6th	BMW	H. Kelleners/U. Grano

The winning car at Brno, where Walkinshaw took the lead in the ETC series. This picture was taken at Veselka, the village at the end of the longest straight where ...

Vallelunga (10/4/83) 500 km

1st	BMW	H. Kelleners/U. Grano
2nd	BMW	D. Quester/M. Winkelhock
3rd	Jaguar	'C. Nicholson'/P. Dieudonné/T. Walkinshaw

Donington (1/5/83) 500 km

1st	Jaguar	J. Fitzpatrick/E. Calderari/M. Brundle
2nd	BMW	D. Quester/H. Heyer
3rd	BMW	H. Stuck/U. Grano
5th	Jaguar	T. Walkinshaw/'C. Nicholson'
(DNF)	BMW	H. Kellener/U. Grano

Pergusa (15/5/83) 500 km

1st	Jaguar	T. Walkinshaw/'C. Nicholson'
2nd	BMW	H. Kelleners/U. Grano
3rd	BMW	M. Vanoli/R. Hollinger
20th	BMW	D. Quester/H. Heyer

Mugello (22/5/83) 500 km

1st	BMW	H. Kelleners/U. Grano
2nd	BMW	Z. Vojtech/B. Enge
3rd	Jaguar	T. Walkinshaw/J. Fitzpatrick
5th	BMW	D. Quester/H. Heyer

Brno (12/6/83) 3½ hours

1st	Jaguar	T. Walkinshaw/'C. Nicholson'
2nd	BMW	D. Quester/H. Heyer
3rd	BMW	H. Stuck/W. Brun
(DNF)	BMW	H. Kelleners/U. Grano

Zeltweg (26/6/83) 3½ hours

1st	Jaguar	T. Walkinshaw/M. Brundle
2nd	Jaguar	P. Dieudonné/E. Calderari
3rd	BMW	H. Stuck/W. Brun
(DNF)	BMW	D. Quester/M. Winkelhock
(DNF)	BMW	H. Kelleners/U. Grano

… it is easy to run short of brakes, as Dieter Quester (BMW 635CSi) discovered during practice.

Nürburgring (10/7/83) 6 hours

1st	BMW	D. Quester/M. Winkelhock
2nd	BMW	H. Kelleners/U. Grano
3rd	BMW	M. Vanoli/C. Danner
(DNF)	Jaguar	T. Walkinshaw (both cars)

Salzburgring (17/7/83) 3½ hours

1st	Jaguar	T. Walkinshaw/'C. Nicholson'
2nd	BMW	H. Stuck/W. Brun
3rd	BMW	D. Quester/M. Winkelhock
4th	BMW	H. Kelleners/U. Grano

Spa-Francorchamps (30–31/7/83) 24 hours

1st	BMW	T. Tassin/H. Heyer/A. Hahne
2nd	BMW	D. Quester/M. Winkelhock/C. Rossi
3rd	Rover	J. Allam/P. Lovett/S. Soper
(DNF)	Jaguar	T. Walkinshaw/P. Dieudonné
(DNF)	BMW	H. Kelleners/U. Grano/J. Cecotto

Silverstone (11/9/83) 500 km

1st	Rover	S. Soper/R. Metge
2nd	BMW	J. Palmer/J. Weaver
3rd	BMW	Z. Vojtech/B. Enge
5th	BMW	D. Quester/H. Heyer
6th	BMW	H. Kelleners/U. Grano
9th	Jaguar	T. Walkinshaw/P. Dieudonné

Zolder (25/9/83) 3½ hours

1st	BMW	H. Kelleners/U. Grano
2nd	BMW	M. Duez/M. de Deyne
3rd	BMW	M. Delcourt/'Davit'/G. Trigaux
4th	BMW	D. Quester/H. Stuck
8th	Jaguar	T. Walkinshaw/M. Brundle/W. Percy

Having finished third in 1982 and second in 1983, there was only one 1984 goal for Tom Walkinshaw, but there were several winter developments before he was ready for Jaguar to announce what form the TWR challenge would

The winning Jaguar of Walkinshaw/Brundle at the Österreichring, near Zeltweg, June 1983. (*Courtesy: IRP*)

take. Bathurst remained nothing more than a red herring – so far.

During 1983, heat had continued to be the main enemy, and the water and oil radiators had undergone a number of moves, always keenly watched by the opposition. There were some cockpit changes for comfort and convenience. The smart new colour scheme – still green-and-white, but now essentially green – featured the names of the major sponsors, Jaguar Cars Ltd and Motul Oil, although the latter now took a low-key role.

The other major visual change was in the wheels, increased to 17 inches diameter and of clean appearance. These 'Speedline' wheels had a 13-inch rim width as per-

Zeltweg 1983 (*left to right*): Walter Brun and Hans-Joachim Stuck (third for BMW) with Martin Brundle, Tom Walkinshaw, Enzo Calderari and Pierre Dieudonné. (*Courtesy: IRP*)

The Dieudonné/Calderari XJ-S makes an unscheduled stop in the temporary pit-lane which enabled the *Nordschleife* to be used in 1983 when the *Neue Nürburgring* was being built. Neither Jaguar would finish in this, the last 6-hour touring car race to be held where the very first ETC event had been held just twenty years earlier.

Walkinshaw leads the field away from the temporary startline at the Nürburgring – as used in 1983 while the new circuit was being constructed.

Below:
Only one Jaguar at Salzburg where Walkinshaw pulls away from Vojtech (Hartge-BMW) – his closest rival that day.

mitted by the Group A regulations. The official 'Brief Specification' was as follows:

Group A Jaguar XJ-S, prepared and managed by TWR for Jaguar Cars Ltd

ENGINE	*60 degree V12, front-mounted, water-cooled.*
	Bore: 90mm (3.54 in) Stroke: 70mm (2.76 in) 5343cc (326.1 cu in)
	Single Camshaft for each cylinder bank, chain-driven.
	Electronic fuel injection
	400 bhp approx
	Max Torque: 350 lb ft, at 5000 rpm.
	Compression ratio: 12 to 1.
TRANSMISSION:	*Rear Wheel drive*
	AP clutch
	Getrag 5-speed gearbox
	Ratios: Top: direct
	4th: 1.147 to 1
	3rd: 1.355 to 1
	2nd: 1.681 to 1
	1st: 2.337 to 1
	Final drive: Salisbury limited-slip
	Ratios: 'High': 3.07 to 1
	(Two 'lower' ratios available, as permitted by Group A regulations)
SUSPENSION:	*All-independent, fully rose-jointed, Bilstein telescopic dampers*
BRAKES:	*All-disc, outboard-mounted 13-inch racing discs (by AP), with 4-pot calipers*
	Pad material: Ferodo DS11
WHEELS & TYRES:	*Speedline centrelock*
	Diameter: 17 ins
	Rim width: 13 inc
EQUIPMENT: includes:	*12 volt ignition system with –*
	Lucas racing loom
	25 ACR alternator
	VDO instruments
	Williams seatbelts
	Recaro seats
	AP air jacking
	120 litre bag fuel tank
	2 Lucas HP fuel pumps
	'Relumit' fuel filler systems
WEIGHT:	*1400 kg plus (regular model 1750 kg plus)*

The leading BMW teams were back in force. Rüdi Eggenberger (for BMW Italia) stepped up his effort; the fast and reliable Helmut Kelleners was to be partnered by the mercurial Granfranco Brancatelli who was taking a step up after two spectacular seasons contributing to Alfa Romeo's class domination. The second car would be driven by Siegfried Müller Jr, and Umberto Grano.

The Schnitzer team – closest of all to Münich – paired Dieter Quester with the ultra-quick Hans-Joachim Stuck

and brought in two young lions Gerhard Berger and Roberto Ravaglia.

Another German tuner, Herbert Hartge, was close to BMW, too, and was now associated with Würth International as well as Czechoslovakian entrepreneur Vaclav Bervid.

The Belgian Bastos cigarette company continued to sponsor the BMW prepared by Julien Mampaey ('Juma') for selected events leading up to the Francorchamps 24-hour race in which Juma cars had been successful in 1982 and 1983. And there were others ready to show that the BMW 635CSi could remain the 'winningest' car in Group A – for there were new threats besides Jaguar. Volvo's 240 Turbo had been homologated with new performance equipment since the 1983 TT and was suddenly a serious threat.

In Britain, somewhat amazingly, TWR had obtained a contract to run at least two Vitesses for the Austin Rover Group whose Mark Snowden declared commitment to 'winning in Europe'; amazing to me, at least, since another branch of TWR, across the road at Kidlington, was just as committed to doing the same thing on Jaguar's behalf! It would make an interesting fight, for Volvo and Rover were aimed at a particular category of the market; while the BMW 635CSi and the Jaguar XJ-S vied for a totally different sector. In fact, 1984 would turn into another Jaguar v. BMW duel, with Volvo finding reliable form only late in the season and the Rovers never quite in the hunt, except at the new Nürburgring.

Three-car team for 1984

The Jaguar announcement was made on 26 March, when the news was that there would be *three* cars and that former champion Hans Heyer (41) would be Walkinshaw's driving partner. He had not only helped Quester to win the 1983 title but he had also won the Francorchamps 24-hour race – the most important single event in the ETC calendar. Another anticipated catch from the BMW pool of top rank drivers was Zdenek Vojtech who tested the Jaguar at Silverstone only to be offered a BMW retainer that he could hardly refuse; he would regret his decision, for the Hartge BMWs were in for a rotten year.

However, Win Percy was to become a regular Jaguar man with 'Nicholson' as his usual deputy. Easily underrated, because racing to him was a hobby, 'Chuck Nicholson' did a lot for team spirit at bad moments. He had already contributed personally to seven of Walkinshaw's victories.

Enzo Calderari was re-enlisted but Pierre Dieudonné had left to join the Belgian Volvo team; so the Swiss would share the third car with Martin Brundle (when ETC did not clash with the young star's first season of Grand Prix racing) or.... ? Well, it was a case of wait-and-see at first.

To win the first race of the year must be good for morale. Three times – in 1977, 1982 and 1983 – hopes of a Jaguar victory in the opening ETC round at Monza had been dashed. With a three-car team, surely 1984 would be TWR's year?

There was a bigger TWR entourage than ever. Since the Group A project began, there has been a considerable staff turnover, too. Yet certain right-hand men remained

The 1983 advantage continues to disappear with Dieudonné's bonnet up as the Silverstone grid is cleared. Kevin Lee has a quick word with 'Nicholson' as he dashes back to the TWR pit in readiness to provide car number seven with a new belt-tensioner.

Right:
Newcomer to the TWR Jaguar team for 1984 – Hans Heyer of Germany, a former ETC champion.

Below:
'Nicholson' leads briefly at the start of the 1983 TT. He was to 'lose' the Jaguar later, as he accelerated out of the Woodcote chicane.

Zdenck Vojtech of Czechoslovakia put in some pre-season laps with the XJ-S at Silverstone before being retained for 1984 by BMW.

BMW would be competitive again in 1984, despite stronger Jaguar, Rover and Volvo teams. The 'X-ray' artwork identifies this 635CSi at Monza as the Stuck/Quester car.

Martin Brundle and Roger Silman at Monza, 1984.

Above Right:
Jaguar's new racing liaison engineer, Ron Elkins, at Monza (with TWR's Paul Davis).

Inset Below:
A simpler 'duct' was used at Monza, but revised rear-end cooling would permit its removal altogether for most of 1984.

Below:
A fine start for the Jaguars at Monza, where Walkinshaw would win (at the third attempt with Jaguar), helped by his new driving partner Hans Heyer. (*Courtesy: Jos Reinhard*)

with TWR's Jaguar racing programme throughout its first five seasons. Obviously, it is not possible to give credit to everyone who played a part, for there were so many comings and goings. Back in late 1981, however, when Tom Walkinshaw was working out his first Group A XJ-S weight reductions and redesigns – on what was a 6,000-mile unsold sub-standard works reject – the strip-down was done by Paul Davis and Kevin Lee. They went on to become team manager and chief mechanic respectively for TWR's Jaguar racing operations. Edward Hinckley was the engineer responsible for the design and drawing-office work (joined later by Russell Sharp), and remained close to all aspects of TWR racing, in a variety of roles. Of all Walkinshaw's 'officers' (the boss himself is often referred to as 'Major Tom' by the Continental press), the quiet, humorous Hinckley gives the impression of being a staunch ally yet an independent spirit. It is difficult to imagine him not being able to take on any role in the team should the need arise. Likewise, Allan Scott was principle power unit development engineer from the outset, using the experience of Forward Engineering, Group 44, Broadspeed and, of course, Jaguar itself, and adding his own original thinking and vast accumulation of knowledge to adapt the big V12 engine for long-distance Group A racing.

The first official TWR Motul Jaguar team of 1983 is seen (photographed at Donington Park) on a previous page in this chapter. For 1984, Kevin Lee, assisted by Andrew Smart, was to look after the Walkinshaw/Heyer car; Colin Marriott and Gary Davies the Percy/'Nicholson' car; and James McCreadie and David Roberts the car for Calderari and 'X'. Other pit crew and transportation regulars included Ian ('Blue') Dorward, Stuart Redman, Loubor Schiller, Keith Partridge, and John Spears.

Paul Davis had joined TWR from the garage trade at the beginning of 1979, having served his apprenticeship as a civilian with the Royal Electrical and Mechanical Engineers. The son of an RAC scrutineer, Davis had taken part in rallies and auto tests for which he had built his own specials. His responsibilities had, naturally, increased over the years, and for 1984 he had the 'gopher' services of Graham Hall. There was also a significant restructuring of the whole racing organisation, with the arrival of Roger Silman.

Born in 1945 and educated at Witney, Roger Silman had served an engineering apprenticeship at Pressed Steel Fisher, Oxford. Determined to make a career in motor racing, he applied for a fabricator's job with Len Terry of Lotus and Eagle fame in 1967 and got it. After two very enjoyable years the Poole, Dorset, operation failed, much to Silman's disappointment.

He stuck to his plan, however, and joined Surtees Racing for whom Terry had just designed the TS5; John Surtees was not an easy man for creative people to work with, and the stay was brief. March Engineering was a much more positive step, and brought him the job of chief fabricator in 1971.

Silman spent 1972–75 with the new Shadow F1 team, learning the racing side as second mechanic to George Follmer, then first mechanic to Peter Revson, Brian

Jean-Louis Schlesser at Vallelunga, where he joined the TWR Jaguar squad briefly.

Redman and Tom Pryce. He also worked on the project to fit Matra's V12 engine, before returning to March as Bruno Giacomelli's Formula 3 mechanic. This led to Formula 2 management and an approach from Alex Hawkridge to set up business systems for the new Toleman team, then sharing premises with TWR at Kidlington. Walkinshaw watched the team advance quickly to take the European F2 title for 1980, thanks largely to the stability of its management. When things went less well (after entering the F1 arena) the vast majority of the original staff saw the job through, despite countless disappointments. Roger Silman is as proud of this as any of his achievements. His acceptance of Walkinshaw's invitation to join TWR in January 1984 had a great bearing on the success that has come Jaguar's way seen then.

Another new face was that of Ronald Elkins, formerly of BL Motorsport, but from 1984 appointed as the Coventry-based motor racing representative of Jaguar itself, with links to Jaguar Cars Inc. and Group 44 as well as to TWR. Later in the year, Ron Elkins would be joined by former

Tom Walkinshaw swoops into the cutting on opposite lock as he fights for grip (and his habitual pole position) at Vallelunga.

Below:

The stands were almost empty as the miserable Vallelunga race came to an end with a most unusual-looking BMW taking the chequered flag.

Left:

A closer look reveals the extent of the damage to the Cudini/Snobeck Juma-prepared BMW at Vallelunga. The Jaguars did not have a very good day, but at least they remained intact.

Bottom:

By now very much involved in the modification of road cars, Tom Walkinshaw displayed some of his new TWR Jaguar Sport XJ-Ss during the 1984 Donington 500 meeting.

A regular member of the 1984 team, Winston Percy drove regularly with 'Chuck Nicholson'. Their first victory together was at Donington Park shortly before this picture was taken.

Jaguar apprentice Peter Dodd in the works engineering/racing liaison office, through which any related component purchases or experimental facilities were channelled. (Dodd had worked under Phil Weaver and Ted Brookes in the last days of Jaguar's old competition shop, and later on the installation of the V12 engine into its first production structure – the E-type. He and George Mason had done much of the rebuilding and subsequent maintaining of the XJ13; and he had stayed on with Jaguar engineering throughout the gloomy days of the late 1970s.)

At last – a win at Monza!

At Monza in 1984, the overall impression was that Tom Walkinshaw Racing Ltd had joined the big league.

Race day at the traditional Monza opening round dawned dubiously and, sure enough, it rained for most of the event which proved close and exciting; but relatively few Italian enthusiasts came to see it, and the great grandstand was sparsely populated.

The Brundle/Calderari car lost three laps with radiator damage after leading, and went on to make fastest race lap en route to thirteenth place. The Percy/'Nicholson' car shed a couple of belts and, as these take so long to change, it was withdrawn. Although Thomas Lindström (Volvo turbo) and Helmut Kelleners (BMW) led for a while, Walkinshaw had every intention of winning the Monza 500 at this, his third, attempt with the Jaguar. Co-driver Heyer had just taken the lead when he came in to the pits for the second scheduled stop, and Walkinshaw's 'power-boat' display as he accelerated up the pit-line to start his final stint showed sheer determination. Sure enough, with 12 laps still to go, Walkinshaw sliced past Kelleners and went on to win by 7 seconds.

It was a very wet spring in Italy and the umbrellas were out again in force at Vallelunga a week later. Correct tyre choice was vital. Walkinshaw on 'intermediates' was soon passed by Percy on 'wets' but Calderari spun into the sand and lost three laps early on. Varying between drizzle and heavy rain, the conditions meant three to four stops – often

Pergusa 1984 witnessed the first ETC Jaguar 1-2-3 result. Note the bug deflectors. (*Courtesy: Alan Hodge*)

for a purely speculative tyre change under constantly grey skies. The battle towards the end of the race lay between the Stuck/Quester and Cudini/Snobeck BMWs and the Jaguar of Win Percy and Jean-Louis Schlesser (the latter on loan from Rover). Percy was holding off Stuck when the Jaguar ran out of battery charge due to a thrown belt. There was much pushing and shoving among the BMWs, and one of them actually landed on the roof of the car that went on to win – looking as though it had begun a journey through the crusher. Walkinshaw and Heyer kept their XJ-S on course to finish third despite the wrong initial tyre choice, while 'Nicholson' helped Calderari climb back up to eighth place.

There followed a magnificent mid-season run of five Jaguar wins in a row; but it was not all plain sailing. At Donington, the first dry race, wheel breakages and related brake trouble interfered with the team's progress. Nevertheless, all three cars finished in the top ten with Winston Percy and 'Chuck Nicholson' overcoming adversity to win outright; Calderari/Schlesser were fifth and Walkinshaw/Heyer ninth – the latter pair retaining (by a single point!) the championship lead they had held from the start of the season and would not now relinquish.

At Pergusa, Martin Brundle was fastest in practice and the race. Swarms of insects conspired to blind the drivers. The Jaguars came 1, 2, 3, followed by the BMWs of Kelleners/Brancatelli and Stuck/Quester.

Czechoslovakia saw a repeat performance, despite odd bothers for all. Walkinshaw/Heyer had a caliper problem but it did not prevent the TWR chief from scoring a remarkable hat-trick of victories in Brno's Grand Prix.

Right:
Win Percy's punctured rear tyre is smoking, but he reaches his pit quickly thanks to the Dunlop 'Denloc' bead-locking system. Brno, 1984.

Below:
The Jaguars set off towards Bosonohy as they were destined to finish the 1984 Brno GP – 1st, 2nd and 3rd.

Percy did the best part of a lap with a rear wheel punctured, after which he was full of praise for performance of Dunlop's new Denloc bead system. He and 'Nicholson' were second; Calderari finished third instead of second, brandishing a broken gear lever. His co-driver was young David Sears, whose father raced many a Jaguar in his day; Sears would stay with the team for the rest of the season, but at the Oesterreichring he was out of luck when a well-used engine lost its oil pressure, and the formation was broken. All the same, Jaguars came first and second again – and so it was two weeks later at the Salzburgring, only on that occasion it was Walkinshaw/Heyer who had to give up when an intermittent misfire led to an explosive transmission failure, with bits of casting landing on the track.

The brand new Nürburgring saw the Jaguars take up their now-regular 1–2–3 grid positions in front of John Egan and a whole host of company and trade folk. The circuit was tight, the day was hot, and soon trouble was in the air. Had Walkinshaw smelt it? He chose not to drive initially. Heyer led, only to come in after three laps with a belt thrown. (After a long interval, Sears took this car out for a few laps, only to return to the pits with a water leak.) Win Percy and Ulf Granberg diced for the lead until the latter's Volvo stopped for turbo attention; Percy handed over to Calderari who got up to a strong second place, nicely ahead of his race schedule, when there was an internal electrical storm so sudden that the Swiss driver had difficulty in getting out of the way of the cars behind, his race over.

Below:
New boy David Sears at Veselka village. Note clean under-body at rear.

Right:
The team greets Tom – Brno 1984.

Meanwhile, at an early stage, Heyer had forfeited his chance to score points by transferring to the 'Nicholson' car. It kept the Jaguar flag flying – though a long stop to deal with a displaced caliper piston put it out of contention for victory. Naturally, Walkinshaw took over for the final driving session, gaining 10 points for fifth place – thus ending the day with a 10-point advantage over Heyer. A Jaguar, a Volvo, or a Rover could so easily have won but it was the trusty Eggenberger BMW that scored this time.

Jaguar wins Belgian 24-hour

If the *Neue Nürburgring* is a great leveller – as practice and race had shown – the circuit of Francorchamps in the Ardennes is one that separates the weak from the strong, especially when it comes to the ETC's showcase, the 24-hour race. As with Le Mans, however, 'racing luck' takes its fair toll, too.

Everyone wants to win Les 24 Heures de Francorchamps, but it has been a BMW stronghold in modern times, reflecting the Bavarian marque's constant association with the racing scene. Tom Walkinshaw, helped by Belgian journalist-racer Pierre Dieudonné, broke the mould in 1981 to win with a rotary-engined Mazda RX7; but his first two Jaguar onslaughts had not been so successful; BMW seemed to be in charge again. Clearly, 1984 *must* be the year of the Jaguar – for the XJ-S was reaching the end of its Group A development yet at the same time new opposition was promised and, in some cases, beginning to make its presence felt.

In a carefully-planned assault, Walkinshaw decided to concentrate on a two-car entry – one for himself, Heyer and Percy; the other for Calderari, Sears, and the experienced Belgian Teddy Pilette.

It was a drizzly start, with Walkinshaw leading Calderari away from the front rank, hotly pursued by the ever-spectacular Hans-Joachim Stuck (Schnitzer BMW)

who took the lead in Lap 3. The pace was far too hot. 'To finish first – first you must finish'; that was a good old David Murray chestnut, and it fitted TWR's tactics perfectly. The Jaguars dropped back, allowing others less-cautious to set the pace. For a brief period Rovers, ideally shod for the conditions, held the top three positions; then their troubles began. In the evening, the circuit dried perceptibly, only to be soaked again as darkness fell. There were incidents galore, including a spin by Calderari in a momentary lapse of attention towards the end of his second stint. He managed to creep back to the pits but the barriers had caused a lot of damage and the Jaguar team's attention was turned totally to the keeping the other car in the lead, which it regained on Lap 74.

Team managers past and present: Lofty England meets Paul Davis at the Salzburgrung, 1984.

The night of fog and rain brought out the pace cars four times, and on two occasions the lone Jaguar lost its advantage by the way in which it was held back in relation to the opposition. Walkinshaw knew that his car could now keep pace in the wet (despite stops every hour or so); he knew that he had two of the most trustworthy co-drivers in the business; and he knew that a fine day was forecast for the Sunday. His race plan was restored, just after half-time, due to the fact that the leading BMWs of Cudini and Quester ran off the road briefly, suffering time penalties at least as stiff as Walkinshaw's pace-car delays.

Before 9am, the clouds had peeled away to reveal the promised sunshine and a very grubby but healthy Jaguar leading easily. A three-lap 'cushion' was maintained during those last eight hours, permitting methodical pit work and making a late puncture a mere formality to rectify.

It was a copybook performance. The TWR team had given Jaguar its greatest-ever touring car race victory – in the very week that queues were forming to buy shares in the Jaguar company, freed at last from its BL bondage.

It was as well, however, that Walkinshaw and Heyer had amassed a healthy advantage after nine races, for the last three of the season – as in 1983 – would not go their way. In the TT at Silverstone TWR did, in fact, fall victim of its own policy which, with spontaneous decision-making, would have given the Jaguar marque its eighth ETC victory of the year. The race began in the dry, with Walkinshaw, Percy and Calderari pulling away from the field comfortably. All three cars made their first scheduled stops, climbing back to run comfortably in leading positions by the half-way mark, in the order Heyer, 'Nicholson', Sears, with the single-stop BMWs making, or about to make, their pit call.

Suddenly the heavens opened, and the deluge, distinctly localised at first, turned Silverstone into a skating rink. Woodcote Corner was the worst place. Heyer got through, having decided he could not make it into the pit-lane safely. 'Nicholson' radioed to his pit, explaining how the conditions were changing by the second; he got no reply which meant 'stay out'.

Sears did make straight for his pit, to be waved away again. A wall of water under the *Daily Express* bridge then sent Sears spinning, but he recovered without hitting anything, and made for the pits again. Meantime Heyer had come in, but Jaguar's race was effectively lost already. 'Nicholson' never got back; he was not alone in spinning into the catch-fencing at Woodcote, wedged and immobilised. At least no-one was badly hurt, although several drivers were bruised as others' cars ran into theirs. Newly-shod, with the boss fuming at the wheel, the leading car had to wait at the pit-lane exit while the pace car crept around for a full lap and now it was no longer leading, for the two top BMWs had taken on fuel and 'wet' tyres, and were now well ahead of the two surviving Jaguars. Worse, the pause may have let in the rain; whatever the reason, Walkinshaw's car never ran cleanly again – though the Scot still drove at a pace which could have brought him victory. With the circuit drying it looked distinctly possible, as he disposed of Quester and chased Brancatelli. Then on the hundredth lap (of 107), the 'V10' engine

would take no more, and Walkinshaw coasted to a rest.

Calderari fought well, but there was just too much leeway to make up; he and Sears should have won the TT instead of coming second but for that wrong decision in the pits, and a good proportion of the many Jaguar supporters went away mystified that such an opportunity to win on home ground had been thrown away.

Added to this disappointment was the fact that Walkinshaw could not yet claim the European title for certain, since the ever-present Kelleners and Brancatelli had closed the gap yet again. Still it was nearly in the bag, and a steady run by 'Major Tom' made sure that the Silverstone story was not repeated at Zolder.

There *was* a similarity, though, in the ferocity of the Belgian mid-race storm which led to nasty accidents for the BMWs of Gerhard Berger and Lucien Guitteny. A more minor incident led to the disappearance of Kelleners, and so Walkinshaw (who had waited in the pits to take over the healthiest car) could drop back from a mighty battle between Stuck and Granberg. Walkinshaw came third, the new champion, and was followed home by Percy who had transferred to the Calderari car after his new machine (shared with Nicholson) overheated.

Although no-one was very keen to prolong the season, most of the top teams trekked south for the late-October Mugello fixture. Here Martin Brundle made a brief reappearance (he had been injured earlier in a GP practice accident), and came fifth with the help of Calderari and Sears. Walkinshaw (suspension damage) and Percy (puncture) withdrew after running first and second as usual. Outgoing champion Quester spun off, so his regular 1984 co-driver Stuck switched to the other Schnitzer BMW and promptly scored a well-deserved and long-awaited victory.

Despite many problems and lost opportunities, the TWR Jaguar team had done what it had set out to do: to outpoint BMW in the over 2.5-litre class of the manufacturers' championship to take the drivers' title. With seven wins to BMW's four and Volvo's one, really there was no doubt that TWR had done a wonderfully pro-

First and second at Salzburgring 1984. (*From right*)**: Win Percy, 'Chuck Nicholson', David Sears, and Enzo Calderari.**

David Sears and his father Jack – a former Jaguar race (and rally) driver – meet at the *Neue Nürburgring*.

fessional job which no other team could have expected to emulate – for there had been a clear pattern in 1983, repeated in 1984, which showed that although they were faster than the opposition everywhere, the heavy XJ-Ss needed to consolidate their success on the fast, open circuits like Pergusa, Brno, and the Oesterreichring in order to stay with the hungry pack on tight courses.

Walkinshaw (181 points) and Heyer (171) finished fairly well clear of Rinaldo Drovandi (157) – a regular class-winner for Alfa Romeo. Then came Kelleners, Brancatelli (151) and Stuck (146). The latter's end-of-season win put him one point ahead of Percy who deserved better.

Constant class wins put Alfa Romeo at the top of the manufacturers' table with maximum points (180), followed by Jaguar (167) and BMW (152). These were the top placings in each ETC race of 1984:

Monza (1/4/84) *500 km*

1st	Jaguar	T. Walkinshaw/H. Heyer
2nd	BMW	H. Kelleners/G. Brancatelli
3rd	BMW	M. Sourd/R. Dorchy

Vallelunga (8/4/84) *500 km*

1st	BMW	A. Cudini/D. Snobeck
2nd	BMW	H.J. Stuck/D. Quester
3rd	Jaguar	T. Walkinshaw/H. Heyer

Donington (29/4/84) *500 km*

1st	Jaguar	W. Percy/'C. Nicholson'
2nd	BMW	V. Woodman/J. Weaver
3rd	BMW	H. Stuck/D. Quester

The regular 1984 TWR Jaguar team – 'Nicholson', Heyer, Walkinshaw, Percy, Calderari, and Sears – at the *Neue Nürburgring*. (*Courtesy: Neville Marriner*, Daily Mail)

TWR JAGUAR
JAGUAR
Racing
MOTUL

FEN
römer
26
MOTUL
19
TWR JAGUAR
JAGUAR
3 JAGUAR
5 JAGUAR
DUNLOP
MOTUL

Inset:

Practising pad changes at the *Neue Nürburgring*. Paul Davis is foreground. (*Courtesy: Neville Marriner,* Daily Mail)

First-ever ETC race at the *Neue Nürburgring*. All the Jaguars would have problems, and BMW scored a home win. The shortened *Nordschleife* can be seen in the background. (*Courtesy: Neville Marriner,* Daily Mail)

Pergusa (13/5/84) *500 km*
1st   Jaguar   E. Calderari/M. Brundle
2nd   Jaguar   T. Walkinshaw/H. Heyer
3rd   Jaguar   W. Percy/'C. Nicholson'

Brno (10/6/84) $3\frac{1}{2}$ *hours*
1st   Jaguar   T. Walkinshaw/H. Heyer
2nd   Jaguar   W. Percy/'C. Nicholson'
3rd   Jaguar   E. Calderari/D. Sears

Zeltweg (17/6/84) $3\frac{1}{2}$ *hours*
1st   Jaguar   T. Walkinshaw/H. Heyer
2nd   Jaguar   W. Percy/'C. Nicholson'
3rd   BMW   U. Grano/S. Müller, Jr

Salzburgring (1/7/84) $3\frac{1}{2}$ *hours*
1st   Jaguar   W. Percy/'C. Nicholson'
2nd   Jaguar   E. Calderari/D. Sears
3rd   BMW   H. Kelleners/G. Brancatelli

Neue Nürburgring (8/7/84) *500 km*
1st   BMW   H. Kelleners/G. Brancatelli
2nd   Rover   J. Allam/M. Duez
3rd   BMW   A. Cudini/J. Gärtner

Spa-Francorchamps (28–29/7/84) *24 hours*
1st   Jaguar   T. Walkinshaw/H. Heyer/W. Percy
2nd   BMW   A. Cudini/D. Snobeck/T. Tassin
3rd   BMW   H. Stuck/D. Quester/J. Weaver

Silverstone (9/9/84) *500 km*
1st   BMW   H. Kelleners/G. Brancatelli
2nd   Jaguar   E. Calderari/D. Sears
3rd   BMW   H. Stuck/D. Quester

Zolder (23/9/84) $3\frac{1}{2}$ *hours*
1st   Volvo   U. Granberg/R. Kvist
2nd   BMW   H. Stuck/D. Quester
3rd   Jaguar   T. Walkinshaw/H. Heyer

Mugello (21/10/84) $3\frac{1}{2}$ *hours*
1st   BMW   H. Stuck/R. Ravaglia
2nd   Volvo   U. Granberg/G. Elgh
3rd   Volvo   T. Lindström/A. Olofsson

Enlisted for a one-off drive in his homeland's 24-hour race – Teddy Pilette of Belgium.

Win Percy in the winning car at Spa-Francorchamps.

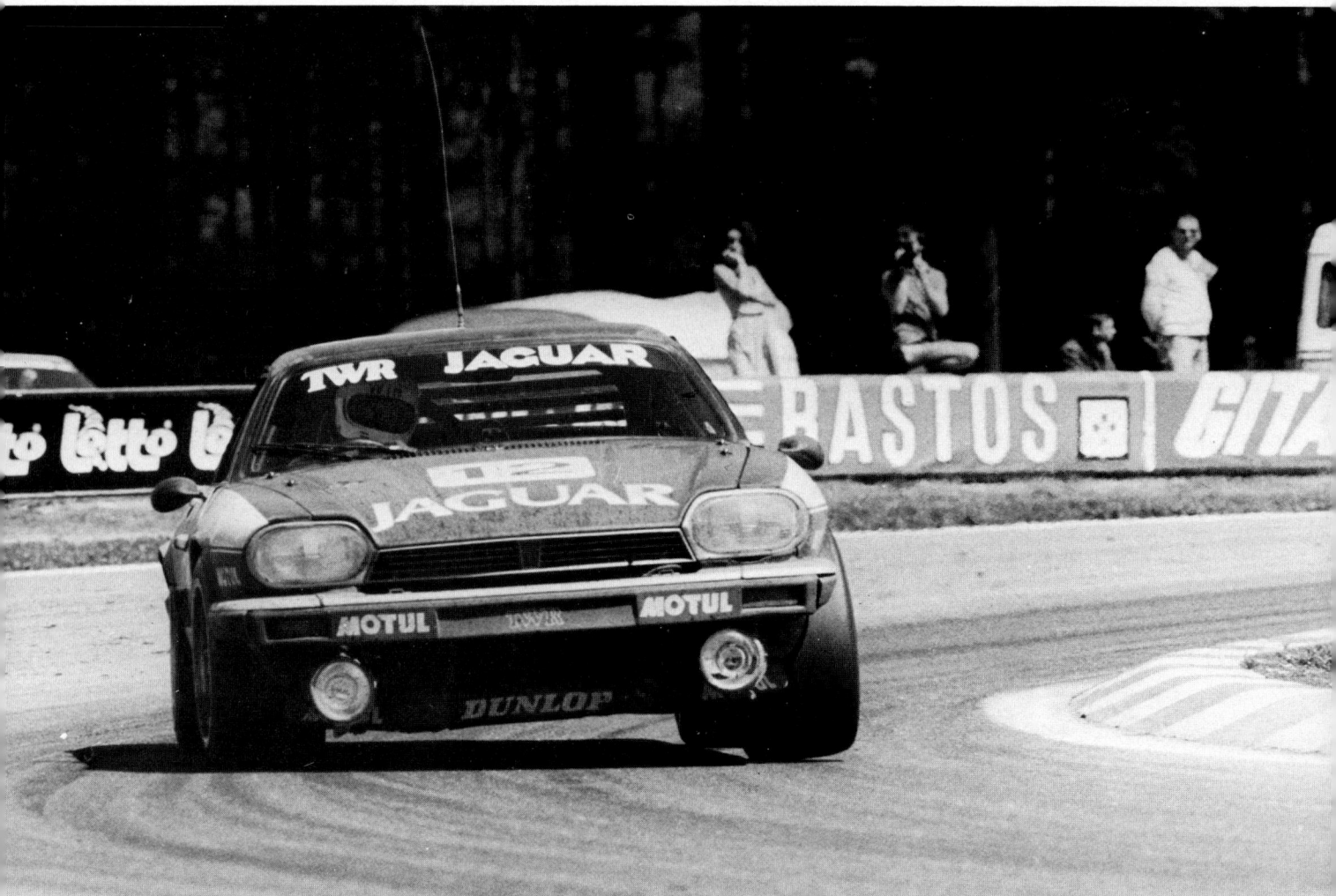

Tom Walkinshaw had established himself as the leading driver in Group A racing, with twelve wins to his credit in three seasons during which he had worked his way to the forefront. This table indicates his progress and that of his chief rival Helmut Kelleners of Germany, who decided to retire from racing at the end of the 1984 ETC season:

European Touring Car Championship Races

Championship position					
1982					
1st =	Helmut Kelleners/Umberto Grano	BMW	5 wins	0 seconds	4 thirds
3rd	Tom Walkinshaw	Jaguar	4 wins	1 second	1 third
1983					
1st	Dieter Quester	BMW	2 wins	4 seconds	1 third
2nd	Tom Walkinshaw	Jaguar	4 wins	1 second	1 third
3rd =	Helmut Kelleners/Umberto Grano	BMW	3 wins	2 seconds	0 thirds
1984					
1st	Tom Walkinshaw	Jaguar	4 wins	1 second	2 thirds
2nd	Hans Heyer	Jaguar	4 wins	1 second	2 thirds
3rd	Rinaldo Drovandi	Alfa Romeo	(six class wins)		
4th =	Helmut Kelleners/Gianfranco Brancatelli	BMW	2 wins	1 second	1 third
6th	Hans-Joachim Stuck	BMW	1 win	2 seconds	3 thirds

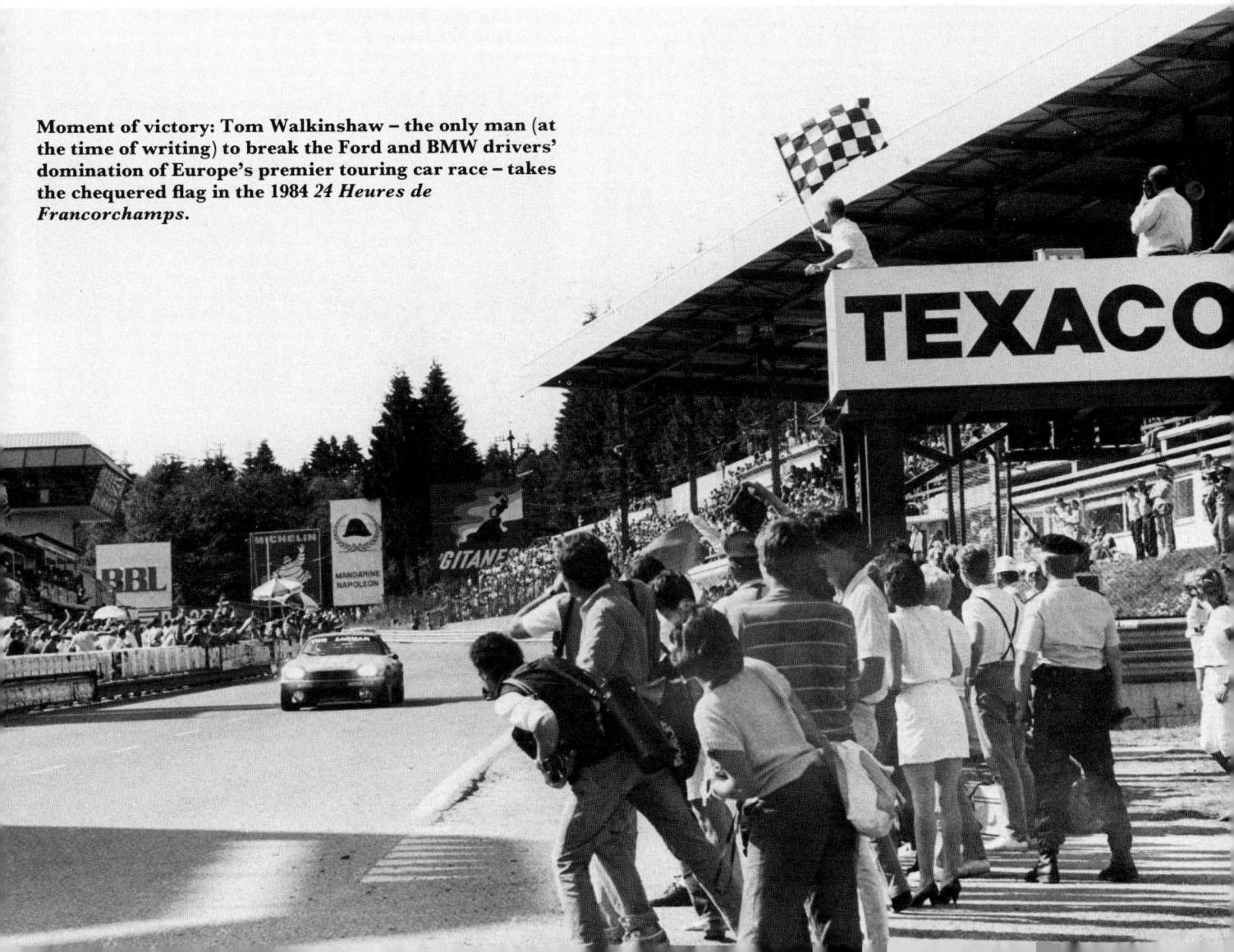

Moment of victory: Tom Walkinshaw – the only man (at the time of writing) to break the Ford and BMW drivers' domination of Europe's premier touring car race – takes the chequered flag in the 1984 *24 Heures de Francorchamps*.

But the season was not quite over for the racing XJ-S.

Of all Asian motoring events, the November meeting at Macau is the longest-established and one of the most commercial – especially among the vying tobacco magnates. The 95-mile touring car 'Grand Prix' of Macau is a favourite second feature event, and in 1984 attracted two Marlboro-liveried Schnitzer BMW 635CSi coupés and two TWR Jaguars repainted equally hurriedly in the black and gold colours of John Player Specials. The balance of the pack was made up largely of oriental machines, one of which had an accident which caused the race to be stopped and restarted. It didn't make any difference: Walkinshaw won with Heyer at his heels. Just over a minute behind came Stuck. Quester was fourth in the other Schnitzer BMW. The only other serious challenger, Kent Baigent (BMW 635CSi) retired. It seemed a long way to go, but it was good for TWR in territory where brand-selling means big money. The JPS cigarette had just been introduced to Chinese territory, so presumably the Jaguar's success made this one-off deal worthwhile for the sponsor.

Below:
The weather changes and the worry sets in – on the faces of John Egan, Jaguar PR chief David Boole ...

Top:
... , Jim Randle, Bill Mack, Allan Scott, and Paul Davis.

Left:
Win Percy, Tom Walkinshaw, and Hans Heyer celebrate the culmination of TWR's endeavours for Jaguar in touring car racing. Spa-Francorchamps, 1984.

Bottom:
Before the storm. The Jaguars start the 1984 TT with a sense of purpose.

Left:
Jaguar's 1984 TT story is summed up in the rescue of the 'Nicholson' car from the Woodcote tangle on a beautiful sunny evening.

Below:
Helmut Kelleners, former champion, celebrated his impending retirement with a great Silverstone win for BMW Italia, assisted by Gianfranco Brancatelli.

Bottom:
The black JPS TWR Jaguars in the Macau paddock.

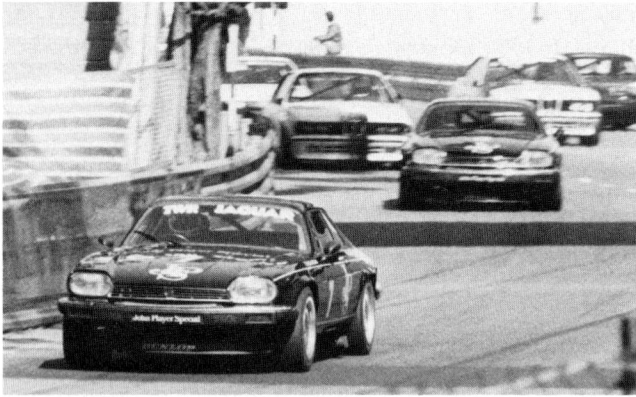

Walkinshaw and Heyer lead Stuck and Quester – two John Player Jaguars versus two Marlboro BMWs – and that was the order in which they finished the Macau touring car event which rounded-off 1984 – a great year for Jaguar in racing.

Below:
1985–86 saw ETC Champion Tom Walkinshaw turn to sports car racing with Jaguar but concentrating on Rover in touring car racing. He did not forget the XJ-S, however, and took this one to Millbrook for a special purpose in the summer of 1985. (*Courtesy: Andrew Yeadon,* Autocar)

XJ-S Group A underbonnet, 1985. (*Courtesy: Andrew Yeadon*, Autocar)

XJ-S Group A rear suspension assembly. (*Courtesy: Andrew Yeadon*, Autocar)

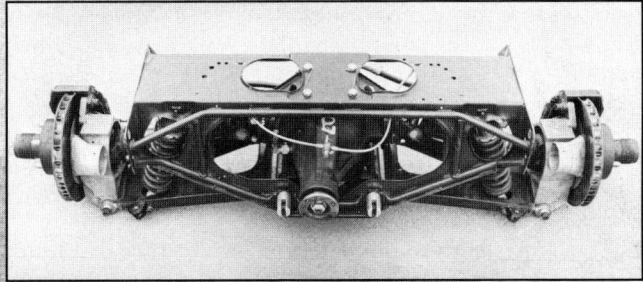

GM's Millbrook, Bedfordshire, test track was lapped by Walkinshaw at 176·16 mph in 1985 – surely a UK enclosed-circuit speed record? – certainly for a Group A car, carrying a passenger! (*Courtesy: Andrew Yeadon*, Autocar)

Below:
TWR Jaguar driven by Tom Walkinshaw with *Autocar*'s Michael Scarlett as observer achieving 0–100 mph in 9·8 sec. and 0–150 mph in 21·5 sec. despite using a 3·07 to 1 final drive ratio. Millbrook, 1985. (*Courtesy: Andrew Yeadon*, Autocar)

XJ-S Group A cockpit. (*Courtesy: Andrew Yeadon*, Autocar)

The challenge of Bathurst

Now that Walkinshaw had proved the Jaguar a winner, it seemed likely that TWR would continue to race the XJ-S for Jaguar in selected races; but this made less sense when it became apparent that the TWR Rovers – which had had a poor year in Europe and an argumentative one in Britain – were to get priority.

As 1985 progressed, though, the name of Bathurst kept recurring – and each time the subject came up it seemed less like the red herring it had been when Group A Jaguars had been discussed in the first place.

The James Hardie 1000 km touring car race at Mount Panorama, Bathurst, New South Wales – then the most publicised motoring event south of the equator – had been run to Australian formulas for modified touring cars up to and including 1984. Ten years earlier, by winning it *and* the Australian Grand Prix, an earnest and talented Tasmanian called John Goss had been elevated to the motoring peerage 'down under'; unfortunately, Goss had not been able to come anywhere near repeating his outstanding 1974 double. He had first raced a Holden in Tasmania in the early 1960s; then he had moved to Sydney and, thanks to a Ford dealer there, drove Australian Falcons in the legendary Bathurst race every year from 1969 to 1979. But, even with Henri Pescarolo on hand to help, his brilliant 1974 success (achieved with Kevin Bartlett as co-driver) was never repeated, and Goss began to take the brickbats of the kick-em-when-they're-down Australian press. He went into yacht brokerage, but did not leave racing alone, and 1980 marked the start of his optimistic XJ-S effort. Three times his Jaguars started – at Mount Panorama in 1980 (with Ron Gillard), 1981 (with Barry Seton), and 1982 (with Bob Tullius) – but despite all the encouragement of Jaguar and his own accumulated experience, Goss could not get up to the pace or finish. In 1983 he did not take part but he did come to Europe and watched TWR perform.

Touring car racing is very important in Australia, and the progress of ETCC racing under Group A was being followed avidly. In 1984, the Bathurst race was to include a Group A category with a view to making it universal for 1985. Tom Walkinshaw provided a couple of works Vitesses for the importers, Jaguar Rover Australia (JRA), and accepted a ride in John Goss's XJ-S. This meant Goss would have the benefit of three years of TWR experience in XJ-S preparation and race management, at the cost of a lot of JRA's money. Walkinshaw reached 170 mph on the notorious Conrod Straight and his best practice lap time was 2 min. 16.09 sec. – seventh quickest. Peter Brock's V8 Holden Commodore, the (almost) inevitable race winner, did a best pre-race lap of 2 min. 14.03 sec.

When Walkinshaw let in the clutch on raceday, however, the weeks of preparation came to naught. The only thing that moved was the clutch centre; the car stayed put. Despite Walkinshaw's raised arm there were too many bullets and too much muck for the Camaro driven by John Tesoriero to avoid hitting the XJ-S. As he watched the restart, Walkinshaw vowed that he would be back and show those Aussies what he could do.

So, while ETC '85 became a running battle between the TWR Rovers and the Volvo turbos, a small TWR

A true road circuit: Mount Panorama, Bathurst, New South Wales. Designed as a 'scenic drive', it has witnessed car and motorcycle racing since 1938. This photograph shows a helmetless Peter Whitehead (later to become the first man to bring a Jaguar to victory at Le Mans) winning the Australian GP on Easter Monday, 1938. The loose surface and lack of spectator protection are evident as the ERA (R10B) drives down the 'mountain'.

gang under 'Blue' Dorward was quietly fettling three XJ-Ss in a corner of the Jaguar workshop at Kidlington. There was circuit testing of the usual kind; and of an unusual kind, too. For an *Autocar* stunt, and with technical editor Michael Scarlett alongside as witness, Tom Walkinshaw took an XJ-S around GM's dished track at Millbrook, Bedfordshire, at an average speed of 176.16 mph – an all-time (if unofficial) closed circuit record for the UK. By then it was mid-summer, 1985; time to send the Jaguars south.

If it seemed risky to be racing three cars that had not raced for more than ten months, the TWR team didn't show it. 'Blue' Dorward assembled a mixed UK/Aussie crew in JRA's Sydney workshops well in advance. The people who did have to move fast were the administrators: the men who would organise the running of the pit. A small team of anchor men – led by Eddie Hinckley and Andy Morrison, in between crucial ETC rounds for the Rovers – would fly out to Sydney to provide these services. Then, there were the drivers.

The lead car would be driven by Walkinshaw and Percy – the latter being his regular Rover co-driver in Europe and a behind-the-scenes visitor to Bathurst in 1984, although he did not drive there then. Rover ace Jeff Allam, racing a Jaguar for the first time in three years, would share with Australia's Ron Dickson, eleven times a 'mountain man' in the past. Then there was Armin Hahne,

Touring car racing has always been popular in Australia, and Mount Panorama has seen its share of excitement – as in this shot of Ron Hodgson (3·8 MK.2), Bill Pitt (3·4) and Ian Geoghegan (3·4) taking Hell Corner in some kind of formation, in 1961. The first four Australian touring car champions (1960–63) were Jaguar drivers – David McKay, Bill Pitt and, twice, Bob Jane. (*Courtesy: Ron Hodgson, 3rd in 1960 and 1961 ATC championships*)

twice a Francorchamps winner for Juma-BMW, and (with Allam) Group A victor in the Rover at Bathurst in 1984 – providing some consolation for Walkinshaw that year! Hahne's co-driver was not only a promise kept but a show of TW's faith. That faith was not misplaced. John Goss was back!

With 16 ETC wins and three non-championship events to their credit, TWR were set on scoring their twentieth Jaguar victory in Mount Panorama's first all-Group A marathon. A number of Australians, mostly driving BMW, Holden, Mustang, or Volvo were equally determined to prevent a pommy team getting anywhere at all.

Three hours' drive west of Sydney, across the Great Dividing Range, the remarkable circuit is 3.84 miles around and was intended originally to be a 'scenic drive' to attract tourism and please the populace. It was built by the unemployed at a cost of £30,000 and provided spectacular views over Bathurst – one of Australia's earliest inland communities. But it was to be used for another purpose, too. On 1 April 1938 the *Western Times* of New South Wales published an aerial photograph together with the announcement that the Australian Grand Prix would be run at Mount Panorama on Easter Monday.

In fact, the very first races on the new circuit were for motorcycles. These took place on Easter Saturday with honours in the 500 and 350 cc TT's going to Norton riders Tobin and Sherrin respectively, averaging something over 60 mph. Next day, 17 April, a young Englishman, Peter

Jaguar, Chevrolet, and Toyota block the Bathurst track to cause a re-start after the 1984 starting collision. Walkinshaw vowed that a Jaguar would come back and win.

John Goss tried unsuccessfully to win at Bathurst with his own XJ-S most years between 1980 and 1986. This picture shows his co-driver, Bob Tullius, in the 1982 event. A bonnet pin pulled out later.

Whitehead, took his single-seat ERA *voiturette* around the steep, twisting, dusty track at close on 70 mph – by far the quickest practice lap for the first-ever car race at Mount Panorama.

On Easter Monday, 18 April 1938, Peter Whitehead had to start from scratch, but had no difficulty in winning from a field of production cars and specials. The black 1½-litre supercharged ERA (R10B) completed the 38 laps (147.23 miles) in 2 hr. 36 min. 50 sec., with a best race lap time of 3 min. 22.4 sec., to take victory by more than ten minutes.

'I think it is a really fine track,' Whitehead told the *Western Times* reporter afterwards. 'It has fast and slow corners, and a long straight that enables a car to make up lost time'. He added that the course was comparable with any he knew, and commented that when tar paving was carried out it would be difficult to better it. 'Some nasty bumps appeared on the road down the mount towards the latter part of the race but these were not hard to negotiate'. During the race his windscreen was broken by a stone. Whitehead who drove without a helmet, made one pitstop for fuel, oil, water, and a dusting-down.

Later in the week it was reported that Sydney Traffic Court had charged Whitehead with speeding on the Parramatta Road back in February but, following his Australian Grand Prix victory, he was discharged with a reprimand as a first offender.

As recorded earlier, Peter Whitehead was to become famous in the postwar era as the first man to race the works C-type and D-type Jaguars to victory, at Le Mans in 1951 and at Reims in 1954.

The 1985 James Hardie 1000 got under way with no immediate drama. Tom Walkinshaw (with a superb qualifying lap of 2 min. 18.82 sec.) shared the front row with Jeff Allam (2 min. 19.91 sec.). Goss was on the third row.

Walkinshaw and Allam got away in unison but the latter's car faltered on the approach to the first bend, the ninety-degree left-hander known as Hell Corner, to be swamped by the Commodore of Allan Grice and the Volvo of Robbie Francevic. The slight mêlée allowed Dick Johnson's Mustang through on the tail of the Walkinshaw car for the long drag up Mountain Straight as Allam began a quick recovery from fifth; but Dickson was to be denied a drive. After only three laps, Allam dropped from second place with a sick engine. Allan Scott, recognised among all the tappet chatter the symptom of a damaged valve – probably caused by the inhalation of a piece of headlamp glass, shattered by contact with the Grice Commodore. This freak cause for retirement was classed, simply, as 'racing luck' of the kind which emphasises the value of having a three-car team in a tough race like the Hardie 1000.

The two remaining TWR cars took command of the race as John Goss moved up to second after half-an-hour's motoring, hindered for him only when a Commodore – Grice's again! – slowed dramatically just in front of the Jaguar with a broken distributor, slightly crumpling the TWR car's nose. About eighty minutes into the race, on successive laps, the Jaguars made their first pit-stops. Percy

The remarkable 3·84-mile Mount Panorama course, with a height variation of over 500 ft between the pits and McPhillamy Park. Also shown are the twenty-seven camera locations used by Channel 7 in 1985. The spectacular worldwide coverage was a factor in the proposal for a World Touring Car Championship.

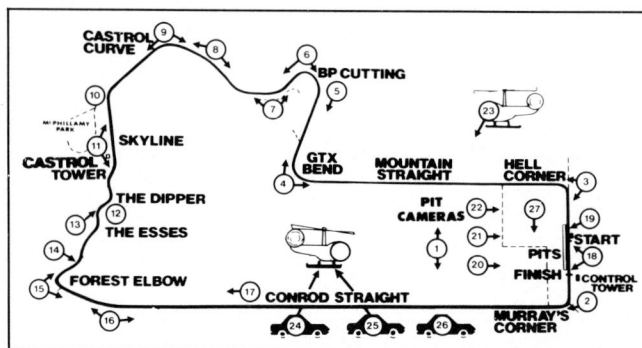

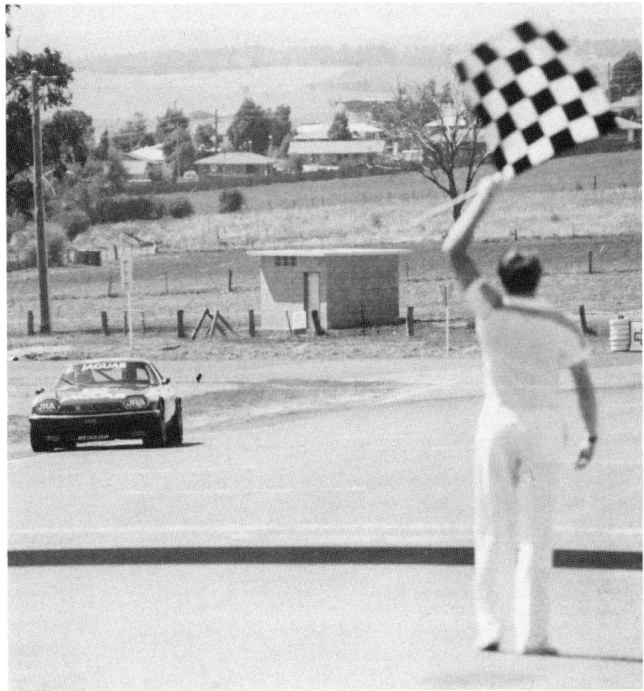

Hardies's Heroes. **Part of the Bathurst spectacle is the 'top-ten run-off' for final selection of grid positions. In 1985 three Jaguars, three Holdens, two BMWs, a Ford (Mustang) and a Volvo shared the honours.**

Tom Walkinshaw accelerates out of Murray's Corner at the end of his 'Hardie's Heroes' lap, which gave him pole position at Bathurst.

took over from TW, and Hahne from Goss. They had lost the lead, but in a very short time the Jaguars were running first and second again. The second stops came after a similar interval and took longer because of scheduled brake-pad changes; Hahne mentioned to Goss that he was having trouble with a collapsing seat squab, which was later 'shored up'. At the third pit-stops the clockwork efficiency of the JRA/TWR team was maintained, although Percy extended his lead over Hahne who was grappling with a deteriorating seat back.

Shortly before the fourth and final scheduled stop, Win Percy came past, slightly overdue, indicating that he was coming in next time around. Something – probably a stone – had severely damaged one of the low-mounted oil coolers. A brief stop to nip the pipe, and let Walkinshaw take over, was not the full answer. The Scot, wreathed in oil-smoke, had to return to the pits again, there to lose three laps while a complete new oil cooler was fitted. In the final hour, Walkinshaw put on one of his demonstrations by charging up from seventh to third place, separated from the leader by only one BMW – a Schnitzer car sponsored by Australia's erstwhile Jaguar champion Bob Jane, and driven by Roberto Ravaglia and Johnny Cecotto.

For much of the race, the Jaguars were shadowed by Bathurst's most famous winner, Peter Brock, whose 5-litre V8 Holden was co-driven by David Oxton; but Brock clattered to a halt at his pit three laps from home, a timing chain gone. Volvo and Mustang had ceased to pose a serious challenge. As in Europe, the constant BMW barrage was the Jaguar's greatest threat in the end.

It is history that John Goss made good on 6 October 1985. Like his co-driver, Armin Hahne, he had concentrated on keeping the car mechanically healthy and on the pace, while grappling with the forces which are normally the work of an ordinary inanimate part of a motor car – the driver's seat. He completed the 163 laps

Last-minute discussion between Win Percy and Tom Walkinshaw, shortly before the Australian 1000 km race which they were to control for so long.

with a comfortable lead over the Schnitzer BMW, and met a rapturous welcome. 'You have to keep pinching yourself when something like this happens,' he said.

This was how the battle ended:

1st	Jaguar XJ-S	John Goss/Armin Hahne	6 hr. 41 min. 30.19 sec.
2nd	BMW 635CSi	Roberto Ravaglia/Johnny Cecotto	(47.7 sec. behind)
3rd	Jaguar XJ-S	Tom Walkinshaw/Win Percy	Three laps behind winner
4th	BMW 635CSi	Jim Richards/Tony Longhurst	Three laps behind winner
5th	BMW 635CSi	Kent Baigent/Neil Lowe	Four laps behind winner
6th	BMW 635CSi	Jim Keogh/Garry Rogers	Four laps behind winner

There *was* another Jaguar at the finish, too. After a steady mid-field run, Garry Willmington and Peter Janson came fourteenth. Their privately-entered XJ-S covered 150 laps (to the winner's 163).

To win the Belgian 24-hour race *and* the Australian 1000 km is to prove you are the world leader in touring car racing – and TWR had done it for Jaguar. Although he was about to lose his crown in Europe – where Volvo were stretching the rules further than he was with his Bastos/works Rovers – Tom Walkinshaw was still king of Group A.

In 1986, the final year of the Jaguar's Group A homologation, TWR stayed with Rover in Europe and Win Percy was set to be rewarded for his years of *esprit de corps* by becoming (provisional) champion. In Kidlington, 'Blue' Dorward was mothering the Jaguars, and throughout the spring it looked as if two of them *would* be returning to Mount Panorama for the 1000 km race in October.

Summer 1986 saw Win Percy spend three days testing. Little had changed for the XJ-S which was in its ultimate Group A form already, with well over 450 bhp now on tap. Much attention had been paid to protection of vulnerable areas. There was no intention of letting foreign bodies hinder progress this time. Roll stiffness was improved, and Percy recorded a best lap of approximately 1 min. 35.8 sec. for the Silverstone long circuit on race rubber, plus 'consistent low thirty-sixes'. These compared very favourably with Walkinshaw's 1984 qualifying and race lap records of 1 min. 34.58 sec. and 1 min. 38.78 sec., neither

of which had been beaten in 1985. The XJ-S was still competitive, and Walkinshaw made no secret of the fact that his chief remaining personal ambition as a driver was to beat the Aussies in their biggest event. One car had been converted to left-hand driving position, to suit the fast left-hand bends at the top of the 'mountain'.

Then, in early August, Walkinshaw pulled the plug. The deal did not meet his requirements. In Australia, the dollar was going through a bad patch and there was natural uncertainty about the future of Jaguar Rover Australia, which was about to be reorganised privately; and it was with Sydney rather than Coventry that TWR had to negotiate. Garry Willmington and late-entrant

Privateer Garry Willmington's XJ-S which came fourteenth at Bathurst in 1985, with Peter Janson co-driving.

Bathurst 1985, Lap 2. The V12 Jaguars of Walkinshaw and Allam lead from the V8 Holden of Grice (whose day would come, one year later).

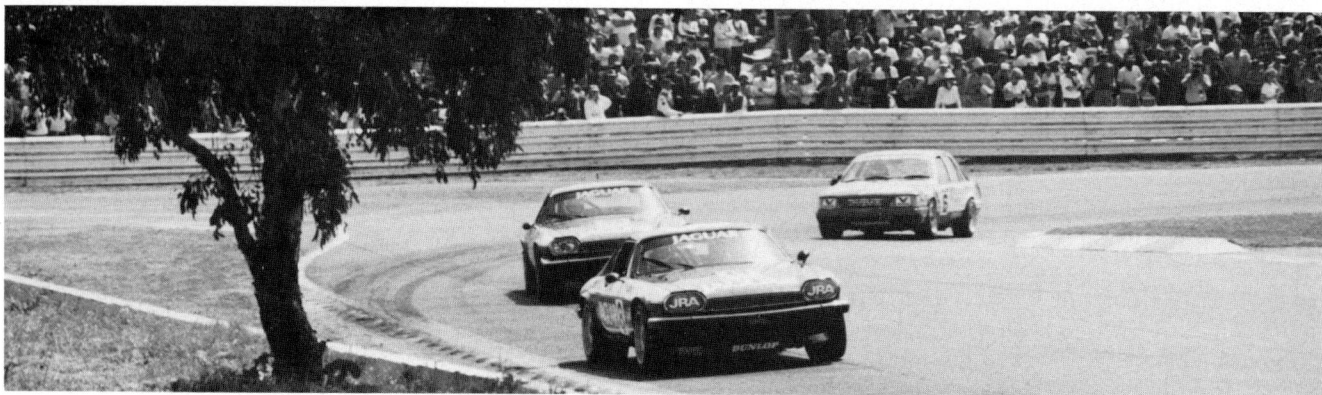

John Goss took their own XJ-Ss to Mount Panorama in October 1986; but neither looked like winners, and Australian tradition was restored when a GM-H Commodore took the chequered flag.

It looked as if the XJ-S's serious racing career was over. With twenty Group A victories in Europe, Asia, and Australasia, the TWR cars had done much to restore confidence in the Jaguar marque.

One car had been sold to collector Campbell McLaren; Tom Walkinshaw remained custodian of the others, their work apparently over, their destiny unknown ... for they were his cars, *not* Jaguar's. TWR was spreading its wings with Jaguar. 'TWR Jaguar Sport' had been created in early 1984, and well publicised with a special display of customized Jaguars at the Brussels motor show.

In early 1985 the relationship with Jaguar became closer with the opening of a TWR distributorship in Leamington Spa, exclusively for the Jaguar and Daimler marques. Another TWR Jaguar franchise at Rye Hill – within a mile of Jaguar's Browns Lane, Coventry, headquarters – was opened in 1986 to coincide with the announcement of the new XJ6 and its derivatives on 8 October. Known until that date by the code name 'XJ40', this super-saloon was the subject of a TWR Jaguar Sport cosmetic extras package only two days later. Walkinshaw was living up to his name for opportunism, by taking full advantage of his special bond with Jaguar as the marque continued its climb to the top of the industrial tree again.

There were accolades galore for the new saloon, reflecting great credit on the Jaguar engineering team, and in particular their chief – Jim Randle. On the day he received the Guild of Motoring Writers' UDT Top Car award in London in November 1986, Randle made it very clear that the XJ40 was NOT a potential Group A race car as far as he was concerned – a sound policy from a public relations or a marketing view, too, one would have thought.

Japan in 1986; NZ in 1987

But the XJ-S was a different matter, and in fact the TWR-prepared cars had not vanished for ever after all. In a new deal with the Auckland-based Strathmore publishing and investment group (closely associated with the planned WTCC race series), Walkinshaw had 'his' car converted back to right-hand controls and had both dark-green coupés shipped to Japan for the five-hour Group A race at Fuji on 9 November 1986. It seemed a brave act: to expect these machines, unraced for well over a year, to produce results at their first reappearance, and at a relatively unfamiliar circuit. On the other hand it had been a similar situation at Mount Panorama in 1985, so why not prove these old favourites competitive yet again?

The Fuji International Speedway's sweeping bends and long straight suited the Jaguars well, although the circuit itself did not provide very good adhesion. This affected all competitors; no other car could match the XJ-S on maximum speed, however. There had been an opportunity, only a few weeks earlier, for the likes of Walkinshaw and the Dunlop tyre technicians to examine the state of the circuit during the Group C race meeting; so it was not as a total newcomer that the boss succeeded in choosing the best selection of the tyres available to him to obtain his customary pole position. Armin Hahne put the other Jaguar in third place on the grid, pipped only by an artificially-boosted Mitsubishi. The Japanese car could not stay with the early leaders, however, as the race got under way.

Walkinshaw led Hahne initially, with Brock and Grice (Holdens) and Cecotto (Volvo) fighting for third. But the

A down-field Holden Commodore gets between the Jaguars of Goss (first) and Walkinshaw (third) as Australia's 1000km touring car classic comes to an end. The winner's crumpled nose resulted from the sudden failure of Grice's Holden in front of it, early on.

Bathurst winner,
Armin Hahne of
Germany.

Jaguar team leader was back in the pits after only six laps with the recurrence of a loss of oil pressure which had been noted – too late for an engine change – during the pre-race warm-up. His co-driver, Win Percy, 1986's uncrowned king of Group A in Europe, was going to remain a spectator today.

Cecotto disposed of the Australians and, at 25 laps, overtook Hahne shortly before the Jaguar's first scheduled stop. The great and popular former Formula One champion, New Zealander Denny Hulme, who had raced Jaguars occasionally in the 1960s, took over from Hahne and passed everyone except Anders Olofsson who was Cecotto's co-driver in the leading RAS-prepared Volvo turbo. Walkinshaw drove the surviving XJ-S from Lap 61 to Lap 85; then the unusual failure of the differential brought him slowly to retire for the second time in one race. This and trouble for the Holdens promoted Emanuele Pirro and Charlie O'Brien (Schnitzer-Siddle BMW 635CSi, sponsored by Bob Jane) to second place behind the Volvo which was able to score a clear victory at the end of a very foggy year for the Swedish marque. (In Europe the TWR Rovers and the Schnitzer BMWs had shared most of 1986s honours, while the RAS Volvo team suffered several disqualifications for alleged rule-breaking – a clear reminder of Tom Walkinshaw's quoted comments on black, white and grey hats.)

There were two schools of thought as far as Jaguar was concerned, in the winter of 1986–87. The year 1986 had been the final one of eligibility for the XJ-S in its existing form, and there were those who felt that it had proved itself sufficiently in Group A: that the job had been done. Others considered it worth examining the possibility of adapting the car for new homologation; this would mean achieving a minimum dimension for rear seat depth that involved costly modification. (Other makers, including Jaguar's rival BMW, had work to do, too – but probably not so much.) Would it be worth the expense? – that was the question. In the event, the answer was an unsurprising NO.

Because of the Jaguars' popularity with racegoers and fans worldwide, however, New Zealand's Group A race organisers decided to allow a month's extension of Group A homologation for the outdated TWR cars, which were shipped from Japan in late 1986.

Above Left:
Co-winner John Goss with 'Blue' Dorward (*left*) who was in charge of Jaguar team preparation and Jaguar PR chief for Australia John Crawford during a serious moment in the pits, Bathurst, 1985

Above Right:
The Strathmore-sponsored TWR-Jaguar in the pits during practice at Fuji, 1986. (*Courtesy: Ian Norris*)

A strong finish

On 25 January 1987, two Jaguars took part in the Wellington 4-hour race driven by Walkinshaw/Percy and Hahne/Hulme. They were competitive, but tyre trouble led to Hahne hitting the barriers and the team leaders losing time. Percy retired just before the end, apparently with the same trouble as at Fuji – differential failure. Walkinshaw then flew back to Britain, and only one Jaguar lined-up for the very last Group A appearance of the TWR XJ-S on 1 February 1987 at Pukekohe (scene of the last great endurance race victory for the Mark 2 3.8, back in 1966). Hulme was snatched up by Larry Perkins (Holden Commodore), and they won the 500-km event; but Win Percy and Armin Hahne in the lone XJ-S finished a close second. It was not the same as winning, but it was an impressive end to the first five years of Group A, in which TWR Jaguars had won twenty races all told.

By this time, TWR was well into Group C on Jaguar's behalf. That is the subject of the next chapter.

New Zealand 1987: The TWR XJ-S team was sponsored by the Strathmore Group for its last two races, at Wellington (here) and Pukekohe. (*Courtesy: Martin Stewart TVNZ*)

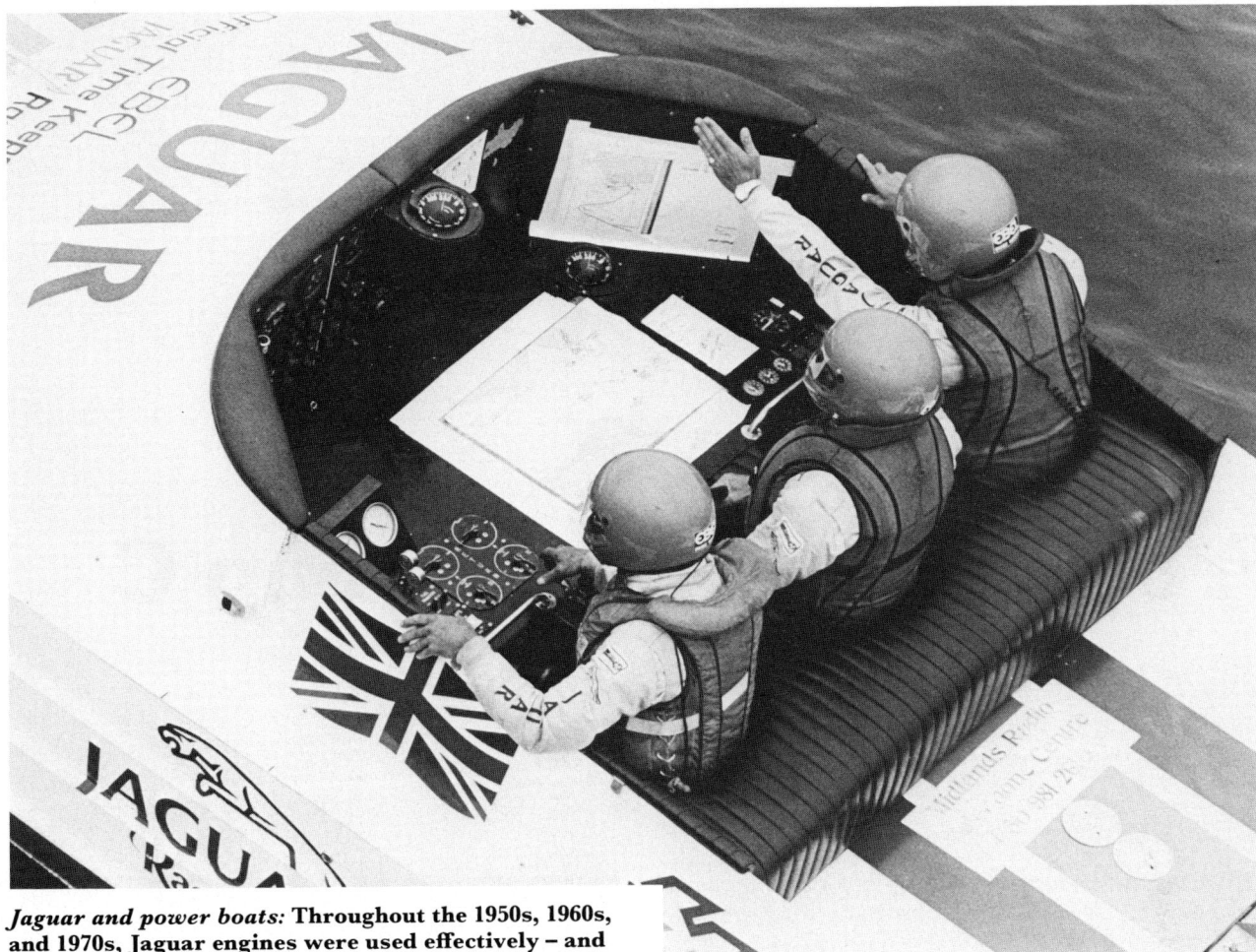

Jaguar and power boats: Throughout the 1950s, 1960s, and 1970s, Jaguar engines were used effectively – and with some factory encouragement – in record-breaking and off-shore racing craft. This occurred again in the 1980s, when there was a direct link between the new Jaguar company's marketing operation and the power-boat fraternity – in particular Bill Bonner and Colin Gervaise-Brazier. There was an engineering link, too, mainly in connection with transmission research. Marinisation and turbocharging of Jaguar V12 engines were essentially independent of Jaguar – indeed, the first, stillborn, project was done without any reference to Coventry – but there *was* works co-operation when Bonner took on the highly-specialised role of development engineer in this field. Bonner's own Cougar catamaran, *Supercat*, crewed by Barry Simpson, Grant Wilson and Bonner himself, won several events including the 1984 Brixham Bay race.

More successful, however, was Guernseyman Brazier's Don Shead-designed monohull *Goldrush* – later re-named *The Legend* to match Jaguar's marketing campaign 'The Legend Grows' – which ran with twin Garrett-turbocharged Jaguar V12 engines. Crewed by David Hagan, Jim Booker, and Brazier, it won the 1983 and 1984 Fowey off-shore races, plus the Guernsey and London-Calais-London events in 1984. Despite structural and transmission troubles, Brazier's craft succeeded in winning several of the daily stages in the 1984 Round Britain race including the circuit of the Isle of Man. From 1985, Jaguar sponsorship of this activity was reduced.

These fine action pictures of *The Legend* are by courtesy of Colin Taylor (the close-up) and Richard Bailey.

Chapter Sixteen

From Group A to Group C

I t is never satisfactory to report upon something that is incomplete, especially in a book that is attempting to record history.

As this book was, finally, closing for press (and, sometimes, it seemed it would never happen) the Silk Cut Jaguar Team had completed only one of three contracted seasons of motor racing. So, the complete story will have to be written another time.

What *can* be reported here is that the name Jaguar did return to Le Mans-type racing, and that in May 1986 a V12 Jaguar-engined car took an historic victory against the might of Porsche in the 1000 km World sports car championship race at Silverstone – Jaguar's home circuit, where history had been made so many times before.

Group 44 paves the way at Le Mans
The sequence of events started in the middle of 1984. The mainstay of Jaguar's return to racing in Europe was the Group A XJ-S, though there were other sporting angles. For example, Jaguar's marketing services department was deeply involved with the use of V12 engines in off-shore power-boating, and Jaguar engineering played a part in establishing a good transmission system. That project was partially successful, and some races were won; but there is no doubt in anyone's mind that a water-borne craft was never actually a Jaguar, whatever the inscription upon it. Works assistance – largely a marketing exercise – was curtailed in 1986. This did not mean that the marine use of Jaguar power units was being overlooked indefinitely.

By contrast, Group 44 and Jaguar Cars Inc., had proved

that, apart from its power unit, a motor car did not have to originate from Browns Lane to be acceptable as a member of the Jaguar family. The XJR-5, as recorded earlier, scored six very important wins and many high placings in American IMSA GTP racing. It also gave the Jaguar marque its first Le Mans representation for exactly twenty years.

Mike Dale's dream for Jaguar – to bring the name back to Le Mans – came true in 1984, when Group 44 broke into its mid-season IMSA programme to conduct a full 24-hour test at Pocono (attended by Jim Randle) and then bring two cars to Europe with official blessing from a very low-profile Coventry management.

The XJR-5s looked marvellous, in Group 44's traditional white and two-tone green, with no vulgar advertising. They were the bright stars, bringing the race to life. The IMSA weight limit of 950 kg was complied with, and so the cars were, literally, in a class of their own. Bob Tullius, Brian Redman and Harry ('Doc') Bundy shared car No. 44, Redman recording 3 min. 35.33 sec. in practice (fourteenth overall) – eighteen seconds down on Bob Wollek's super-boost Lancia turbo time but well up among the flotilla of Porsche 956s. The second car of John Watson, Claude Ballot-Léna and (replacing Indy-injured Pat Bedard) Tony Adamowicz, was four seconds down on that of their team-mates over the eight-and-a-bit miles.

First publicity shots of XJR-6 (early 1985) showed this model.

Insets:
Martin Brundle and Mike Thackwell testing at Donington Park at the beginning of July 1985, when the XJR-6 still had a number of basic problems, particularly in relation to understeer.

First official declaration of Group C intent by Tom Walkinshaw was this *Autosport* page on 11 July 1985, which included a mis-naming of Jaguar Cars Ltd (or Jaguar plc).

Briefly, Bob Tullius *did* lead the race – and did the Britishers cheer? But it was a matter of taking shortlived advantage of the pit-stop schedule.

Still, at half-distance, the XJR-5s were sixth and seventh and – in reasonable anticipation of Lancia's problems ahead – fourth and fifth looked a good possibility. After all, the last good Le Mans result (in 1962) had been fourth and fifth! But, No. 40 lost time with a broken throttle linkage; then, shortly before 6 am, Adamowicz went off-course at Tertre Rouge, probably after a tyre went down. The accident damaged the oil reservoir, and so, despite getting to the pits unaided, No. 40's race was over. Then No. 44 stripped a gear and lost three-quarters of an hour; but it kept going and at the 18-hour mark it was eighth and still well able to improve its position; but then the gearbox began to seize again, possibly due to debris, and it was withdrawn with only a few hours to go. Even so, reaction to the Jaguar return had been much more favourable than the failure of either car to finish might suggest.

TWR goes Group C

On the very same day, Tom Walkinshaw and Hans Heyer (who had flown back to Austria from Lancia duties at Le Mans) made winning with the XJ-S at Zeltweg look as easy as falling off a log.

Shortly afterwards, Tom Walkinshaw was talking to Tony Southgate and before long TWR was thinking Group C seriously. Jaguar Cars Ltd was about to return to the stock market. It was big news, and TWR helped the shareholders' euphoria with its wonderful XJ-S win in

Mosport, 11 August 1985, and Martin Brundle makes history by putting the XJR-6 into the lead at the start of its very first race. (*Courtesy: Castrol*)

Top:
Brundle's XJR-6 holds off the works Porsches during the early laps at Mosport. After this car retired, Brundle would share the wheel of the surviving Jaguar.

Heroes of the XJR-6 début at Mosport – Jean-Louis Schlesser of France, NZ-born Australian Mike Thackwell, and East Anglian Martin Brundle, who brought car No. 52 home third behind the works Porsches.

the Belgian 24-hour touring car race. The new Walkinshaw-Southgate co-operation could have involved a different engine; but Jaguar was on top of the world, and a Jaguar it would be. The new Group C car was on the stocks by the end of the year; but the public accepted a different story. Even in March 1985, when Le Mans entries had to be reserved, the much rumoured TWR cars were referred to in 'XJR-5' terms. There were lengthy tests in mainly bad conditions at Donington and then at Silverstone, with Martin Brundle driving, although Stefan Johansson was on hand on the second occasion. And the car? – it *was* an XJR-5 which had been displayed at the National Exhibition Centre during the 1984 motor show, and had then been earmarked for Kidlington where it was repainted dark green. A 48-valve version of the Jaguar V12 was tried in this car but rejected for immediate development on the grounds of thirst, complexity (which Walkinshaw likes to avoid) and weight, with insufficient power increase.

That XJR-5 was later restored to Group 44 colours. (A year or so later, it would be on show in London Airport's new fourth terminal *in Silk Cut colours* – hardly conducive to any *entente cordiale* with Virginia.)

The TWR XJR-5 test programme may have been good practice for a team new to Group C; but it was very much a red herring, and only when Le Mans entries closed did the realisation of Tom Walkinshaw's actual intentions become general.

But the XJR-6 would not be ready after all, and the 1985 Le Mans Jaguar effort was, once again, in American hands. The XJR-5 had been doing well at home – especially for Brian Redman and Hurley Haywood, recent winners at Road Atlanta and runners-up in the Charlotte and Lime Rock IMSA events; and behind Bob Tullius's show of caution ('We learned a lot last year; now we're coming back for further education') there seemed to be

plenty of well-justified optimism, despite a fuel consumption restriction to 2,100 litres. Engine settings, related to those regulations, provided less reliability (due to detonation) and meant lower power when the time came. In fact, it was a drive-line failure just too late to permit a dive for the pit-lane – that put out car No. 40 driven by Jim Adams, who had joined the Haywood/Redman partnership for this event. Adams had to abandon it at half-time, with lights on for safety, as it could not be moved clear of the circuit; when it was mobilised, the battery wouldn't turn the engine.

No. 44 (Tullius/Robinson/Ballot-Léna) struggled on, finally being forced to run on eleven cylinders only, due to valve failure; it spent a long time in the pits, while the cylinder was isolated, but was still running at the end. Tullius was cheered to the echo by the many enthusiasts who had watched the Group 44 team under Lanky Foushee working away, never giving up. The reward was thirteenth overall: fractionally quicker than the best previous Jaguar speed (1957) and, more noteworthy, the first Jaguar finish at Le Mans for 22 years. Victory in the IMSA GTP class at Le Mans was a nice token of achievement and

Finishing third at its very first race appearance, the XJR-6 photographed for Jaguar by Malcolm Bryan at Mosport, 11 August 1985. (The XJR-6 had a habit of shedding rear wheel spats.)

gave the disappointed party something for the record book. But, in the end, the fuel comsumption rules worked against Group 44 this time.

As Group 44 returned to the USA, TWR was completing construction of the first XJR-6 – a name which surprised many people and, not unnaturally, upset Tullius who had devised the 'XJR-5' title – on the basis that it was the fifth Group 44 Jaguar project – and had gained approval for it. XJR-6 was a completely different design, and nothing to do with Group 44, who would have to skip to 'XJR-7' for a new title.

It wasn't just this that caused something of a rift, but the fact that Group 44 – longing for a third crack at Le Mans – would soon be competing with TWR for Jaguar's favours. It didn't seem to make sense until Jaguar clarified the position. In 1986, the two official teams would operate quite separately, for the time being – Group 44 in the USA and TWR elsewhere. This seemed hard on the American team, after two serious Le Mans bids; but with so much Jaguar money at stake, no-one could be blamed for the decision. Even so, it might have been worth remembering that the most prolific Le Mans winners – Porsche and Ferrari – usually achieved history from a broadly-based entry, and the favourites were not always the victors. (These words are written before the 1987 race.)

Background to the XJR-6

The XJR-6 was taking shape, and was completed at the end of June. There was a test run at Snetterton followed by another at Donington on 8 July 1985, with Tony Southgate on hand. A new era was beginning for Jaguar: it had commissioned a world-class sports-racer, and now this was a reality – in double-quick time, thanks to TWR and Southgate.

Tony Southgate, born in 1940, served his engineering design apprenticeship with Dowty Group subsidiary, Designex Ltd, in his home city, Coventry. His hobby then was the design and construction of '750' formula cars. In early 1962 he joined Eric Broadley at Bromley, Kent, where he worked on the F1 and FJ Lolas and, significantly, on the V8-powered Lola GT, from which the Ford GT40 would emerge.

After a brief spell with Brabham, where he wasn't very happy, he returned to Lola (now Slough based) in 1965. He remained assistant designer until the chief designer's job came his way at Dan Gurney's Eagle headquarters in California. This led to the top design job at BRM during the company's last successful period, 1969 to 1971.

In 1972, Southgate designed the first Shadow DN1 GP

Brundle prepares to take over from Thackwell at Spa-Francorchamps, 1 September 1985. The 'TWR' lettering has been moved from the windscreen to bonnet-top for the XJR-6's first European event.

Yet another aerodynamic feature was used for the front end of the XJR-6 at Brands Hatch for Shell Gemini 1000 in September 1985. Neither of the Jaguars (seen here at Stirling's Bend) was destined to finish the race. Castrol and Dunlop were given more prominent advertising for this event.

Inset right:
In the 1985 WSC final at Selangor, Malaysia Jan Lammers was running strongly in No. 52 until a tyre exploded and took the car off-course.

Top Insets far right:
The heat and humidity of Selangor were almost too much to bear in the confines of Group C cockpits, and the Jaguar drivers had to stop after less than an hour – which meant a six-stint drive for Mike Thackwell and, pictured here Jan Lammers, and Denmark's John Nielsen (shown resting beside a strategic electric fan).

Lower Inset far right:
There was a new central air-intake for car No. 51 at Selangor.

car for a new team organised by Don Nichols. A 15-month spell under contract to Lotus (1976–77) was followed by a return to Shadow – shortly before it folded – then periods with Arrows and Theodore where, in 1982, Southgate had the pleasure of working with a small and happy team 'for the first time in many years'. This period found him working with former colleague and expert fabricator John Thompson, and in due course they formed ART (Auto Racing Technology Ltd). Ford and Osella were the main customers initially. His design for the Ford rally car, the RS200, in prototype form and for production, was a new departure for Southgate. Then, in 1984, came the approach from Tom Walkinshaw, who offered him a free hand in designing a Group C car. He accepted the work (with ART doing the fabricating) and the XJR-6 concept was born.

Southgate retained his independence, and the project's management from the TWR end was assigned to Roger Silman, whose brief included engineering liaison with his former colleague – for Silman had been fabricator and mechanic for Shadow when Southgate was there.

Paul Davis made a move from Group A to Group C at the outset – an obvious transfer, since there was now no regular XJ-S programme; Kevin Lee made the transition at the same time.

The Group C XJR-6 was potentially lighter than the

Below:

A revived Lammers is ready to take over from Nielsen at Selangor, as Dunlop's Bill Mack keeps an eye on the final tyre-change from the pit-lane.

Right:

Selangor, WSC 800 km final, 1 December 1985: Jan Lammers brings the XJR-6 home second. This Malcolm Bryan picture captures the moment. On the right is Gianfranco Brancatelli.

IMSA XJR-5 prototype, having a carbon-fibre rather than aluminium monocoque as well as Kevlar plus carbon fibre ground effect bodywork. From the outset, the dry-sump V12 engine would have the Lucas Micos electronic system of 'management', which Group 44 had already

Silk Cut Jaguar Team director Roger Silman and chief mechanic Kevin Lee in a moment of repose during XJR-6 testing at Donington Park. Lee had also worked on the ETC Jaguars from 1982.

Bottom left:
Tony Southgate, who designed the XJR-6 in a very short time thanks to a background of more than twenty years of racing car engineering experience – and in particular the experience of developing the 1983 Ford C100 ground-effect car.

Bottom middle:
Paul Davis, one of TWR's longer-serving members, managed the XJ-S Group A team from 1982 to 1984 before switching to the XJR-6 project.

Bottom right:
Roger Putnam, Director of Jaguar Daimler Sales and Marketing – the function responsible for Jaguar's side of the racing budget. Putnam moved to the expanding Coventry company in 1982 after 15 years with Lotus, and was promoted when Neil Johnson returned to a Military career in 1986.

First public appearance of the XJR-6 in its Silk Cut livery was at Monza in April 1986.

The 6·3-litre XJR-6 'second series' cars of
Cheever/Warwick (51) and Schlesser/Brancatelli (52,
being chased by the Mass/Wollek Porsche) racing, for
the first time in 1986, at Monza.

adopted; TWR was also investigating its own Zytek
system. The Jaguar engine's basic reliability had been
proved, of course, but race development can highlight
potential problems, and in this case valve springs and
piston circlips were among the early culprits.

In contrast to the XJR-5, the prototype XJR-6 was
crudely finished, and on those early test sessions the doors
had to be taped up to make sure they didn't fly open.
Serious handling problems persisted, too. There was under-
steer galore and this was probably the main reason for a
late decision to withdraw from a Hockenheim race scheduled for 14 July – less than a week after the Donington
tests – to the chagrin of *Jaguar Deutschland GmbH*, who had
laid on a major promotion for the supposed début. It
seemed unfortunate that Jaguar Cars Ltd – owners of the
XJR-6s (unlike the 'works' Group A XJ-Ss which, it
turned out, belonged to TWR) – were not given a proper
opportunity to warn their enthusiastic German importers
that their customers would be disappointed. Apart from
this hiccup, the TWR Jaguar arrival on the Group C scene
was as positive as it was welcome. As in Group A three

years earlier, the presence of Jaguar was going to turn
Group C into a much more interesting and competitive
series. The speed with which Southgate and TWR
developed the XJR-6 was quite amazing.

The XJR-6's début took place in the Budweiser 1000
km on 11 August 1985 at Mosport, Canada: Round 6 of
the world series. Two cars were ready and they looked
very much tidier, despite a variety of front end wings and
suspension resettings. Martin Brundle and Mike
Thackwell, who had done most testing, were soon putting
up competitive times on the tricky circuit near Oshawa,
Ontario, and there was general delight when Brundle
recorded 1 min. 12.602 secs. – third fastest of all, beaten
only by the works Porsche 962Cs. Hans-Joachim Stuck's
spectacular 1 min. 09.775 sec. was quite unbeatable by
anyone: the stuff of heroes.

The second of the challengers was well-placed, too,
Jean-Louis Schlesser recording 1 min. 14.782 sec. with his
untried car – fifth on a grid of fourteen cars; but it must
be added that only four of the Porsches were of the 956/962
variety. Big radiators and heavy-duty steel suspension
components helped keep the XJR-6's weight up around
the 900 kg mark at this early stage of its development.
Cunning design around the bulkhead helped reduce the
apparent size of the 6·3-litre V12 engine, and the car was
amazingly compact. Castrol had provided some spon-

At some circuits the Silk Cut wording had to be deleted, although the 'fag packet' look remained. This is the Cheever/Warwick car, photographed by the author at Stowe Corner as it speeds to its historic Silverstone victory, May 1986.

sorship but the dark green and white cars were carrying the word JAGUAR in large letters where a major backer would have put his name – which was reasonable, for no-one had ever seen a Jaguar look quite like this before.

It was a wonderful start for Martin Brundle who anticipated the starter's flag better than anyone else to swoop through from Row 2 and take the lead from Ickx and Stuck in the Rothmans Porsches; and the Jaguar stayed ahead until Lap 10 when Stuck went past. Ickx did the same thing a lap later and, shortly after this, Brundle swept into the pits with a front wheel bearing ruined – a function of the car's prodigious downforce. The car was wheeled away – a lesson duly learned. Schlesser was going well but handed over car No. 52 to Thackwell and Brundle for the remainder of the race, his own nominated co-pilot

Hans Heyer, standing down. Despite several lengthy stops including a twelve-minuter to deal with a leaking brake caliper, the car was still running at the finish, if roughly. Brundle getting it back up to third place by the time the two works Porsches had completed their 1000 km. It was a fine result for the record book, and provided the team with essential experience of the kind no amount of pre-race testing can offer.

Round Seven on 1 September was the Spa-Francorchamps 1000 km – shortened to about 850 km on the day, by mutual consent, following the death of the reigning champion, Porsche driver Stefan Bellof. (Like fellow German Manfred Winkelhock, who had succumbed to his injuries after a Mosport crash, Bellof was an extremely fast driver whose natural enthusiasm to do well got the better of him.) Here TWR faced a much stronger field including eight fast Porsches and two *very* fast Lancias. The Jaguars

The second-placed Porsche (less Rothmans advertising) driven at Silverstone by WSC champions – reigning and elect – Derek Bell and Hans-Joachim Stuck.

qualified eighth (Brundle) and eleventh (Schlesser).

In the race, Schlesser ran twelfth, last of the (so to speak) 'first division' runners, troubled by inconsistent handling, blamed on the differential. His co-driver Heyer had a go, only to corroborate that the car was behaving too waywardly to continue. Meanwhile, Brundle was making up in skill what his car lacked – turbo boost on the demanding circuit. He and Thackwell, the impressive young New Zealander, came fifth, behind a Lancia, Porsche, Porsche, Lancia sandwich. It was a sad day, though, and soon afterwards Ken Tyrrell (Brundle's and Bellof's Formula 1 team boss) made it clear that he wanted Brundle to forsake sports-prototypes and give his full attention to Grand Prix racing. This was a blow to Walkinshaw. On the other hand, he had already signed-on Alan Jones for the Shell Gemini 1000 km race at Brands Hatch (21 September) as an extra man. Thackwell had a clashing commitment, and so Jan Lammers became the second new face in the Brands Hatch squad, where the XJR-6s qualified fifth and sixth. It wasn't an auspicious British début, however. Jones retired early when the throttle stuck open and the engine broke, thus depriving Schlesser of a drive. Both Jones and Lammers stopped early for wheel changes, due to thrown balance weights and tyres moving on their rims. Lammers/Heyer looked like coming fifth when, before half-time, the Dutchman crawled in; the engine had swallowed something it couldn't digest.

On 6 October 1985, while Tom Walkinshaw and the Jaguar XJ-Ss were making their mighty comeback in Australia, Roger Silman, Tony Southgate, Paul Davis and the XJR-6 team were in Japan for the Fuji 1000 km race where the pairings were due to be Thackwell with his Danish F3000 colleague John Nielsen, and Heyer with fiery TWR-Rover regular Steve Soper. The Jaguars had

This turbocharged Sauber-Mercedes, sponsored (like some of the races) by Kouros, finished sixth at Silverstone and would go on to take its first-ever victory at the Nürburgring in August.

engine trouble in practice – one with a failed piston circlip and the other with slipped camshaft timing. Bent valves were the consequence for both.

Japan was catching the edge of a typhoon, and the race day rain was incessant. The top runners decided that serious racing was impossible and they withdrew. The cars were shipped to Malaysia and the drivers went home.

There followed an eight-week gap to an exciting finale at the Shah Alam circuit near Kuala Lumpur, on 1 December. The Selangor 800 km race was run in unprecedented conditions of heat with humidity. The Jaguars were fourth and fifth on the grid, and closer to the leaders than ever. Thackwell led momentarily from the second row, then the order became: two Porsches (Mass, Stuck) followed by two Jaguars (Thackwell, Lammers). Then Stuck spun and the Jaguars lay second and third, with Lammers passing Thackwell. A stripped rear tread sent Lammers off-course on Lap 19 and his car stuck in soft ground; so, no drive for TWR recruit Granfranco Brancatelli, the man who had just wrested the European touring car title from Tom Walkinshaw.

Thackwell handed over to Nielsen, their car having suffered from a mild coming-together with a Porsche. Lammers was given the final stint, as he had proved so quick (and able to cope with the temperature and humidity). Rain and a suitable set of tyres helped Lammers to get on to the same lap as winners Ickx and Mass; second place for the XJR-6 was, of course, its best race of 1985. Stuck and Bell won the championship for Rothmans Porsche; but the seventh place in the World Group C teams championship was not bad in view of the late start. Southgate found the drivers impressed with the ground effect and resulting roadholding, but there were some definite areas which justified the creation of an XJR-6 'Mk2' with lightened carbon fibre chassis and new materials to help get body weight down. Allan Scott had already pared a lot of weight from the engine and given it more power. A new fuel system was designed to pick up the last drop of fuel, so necessary for 'economy' racing,

and the rear suspension and anti-roll bar were redesigned. Now the team was ready to tackle Porsche.

Silk Cut sponsorship

Even before the end of 1985, word of a cigarette deal was getting around, though Jaguar would, no doubt, have been happier if the conjectured British Caledonian tie-up had worked.

The year of 1986 marked the start of a three-year contract between Jaguar and Gallaher International. The purpose was to contest races in the (re-named) World Sportscar Championship with Group C prototypes built and managed by TWR, but using the title: Silk Cut Jaguar Racing Team.

Of the eight drivers who had tried the cars in 1985, only Jean-Louis Schlesser and Gianfranco Brancatelli were retained for the new season (although Derek Daly did have a test drive at Estoril). The selection was logical, for both would be available to help TWR in its Group A Rover effort which really did need to succeed in 1986.

During the winter, the politics of Formula 1 as usual took priority over all other racing politics but, in due course, the story was out: Eddie Cheever and Derek Warwick were to lead the Silk Cut Jaguar Team.

This chapter ends with a resume of the 1986 season, in which the XJR-6 proved that a well-designed car could, in many circumstances, use a 6·5-litre Jaguar V12 24-valve normally-aspirated engine just as effectively (in long or short races) as the most sophisticated turbocharged opposition.

What was remarkable was the way in which the XJR-6 became so competitive so soon. There were good days and bad days, of course. At Monza in April, fuel pick-up problems plagued the revised, lightened cars. It was a one-stop, two-driver 225-mile event in which Klaus Ludwig (Joest Porsche 956) and Hans-Joachim Stuck (Rothmans Porsche 962) – two of the world's greatest drivers in this category – led Cheever and Schlesser (Silk Cut Jaguars) until pit-stop time: both Jaguars felt as if they were running

out of fuel, however, and came in early. Warwick retired on Lap 48 with drive-line failure when set to finish third. Then Brancatelli's engine died on the sixty-second of 63 laps. It was in fact a pick-up problem rather than a shortage and, as this was a sports car race and not a Grand Prix, the Jaguar was not credited with third place as it did not cross the finish line after the winning Porsche of champions Bell and Stuck. Fuel feed was to prove the crucial element in a dramatic championship.

XJR-6 wins at home

Truly, history was made on 5 May 1986 when, for the first time since Le Mans 1957, a Jaguar won a World Championship endurance sports car race. There was a good entry for the 1000 km race at Silverstone, scene of so many Jaguar victories of old – including fourteen real 'First Division' runners: a works Lancia, a Sauber-Mercedes, and no fewer than ten examples of the ubiquitous Porsche 956/962.

Initially, Alessandro Nannini (Martini Lancia) led from Warwick (Silk Cut Jaguar) who had dived through from the second row to elbow his way past Derek Bell in the No.1 Rothmans Porsche. Likewise, Schlesser soon had the other Jaguar circulating behind Warwick's, once he had disposed of Jo Gartner, Derek Bell, and the other Porsche drivers.

For the first half (106 laps) of the race, it was a straight fight between Lancia and the two Jaguars, Nannini/de Cesaris trading the lead with Warwick/Cheever. Schlesser, close behind in third place, came in early, the gear linkage having pulled out; this was the first of the stops which hindered progress for him and Brancatelli. The No.2 Rothmans (works) Porsche of Mass/Wollek had retired earlier with final-drive failure, it was Lancia's turn for trouble: over an hour was lost in the pits while a fuel-pressure problem was resolved. Up to this point the fastest

Pace-setter at Silverstone, where it broke the lap record, the Martini Lancia lost a lot of time in the pits.

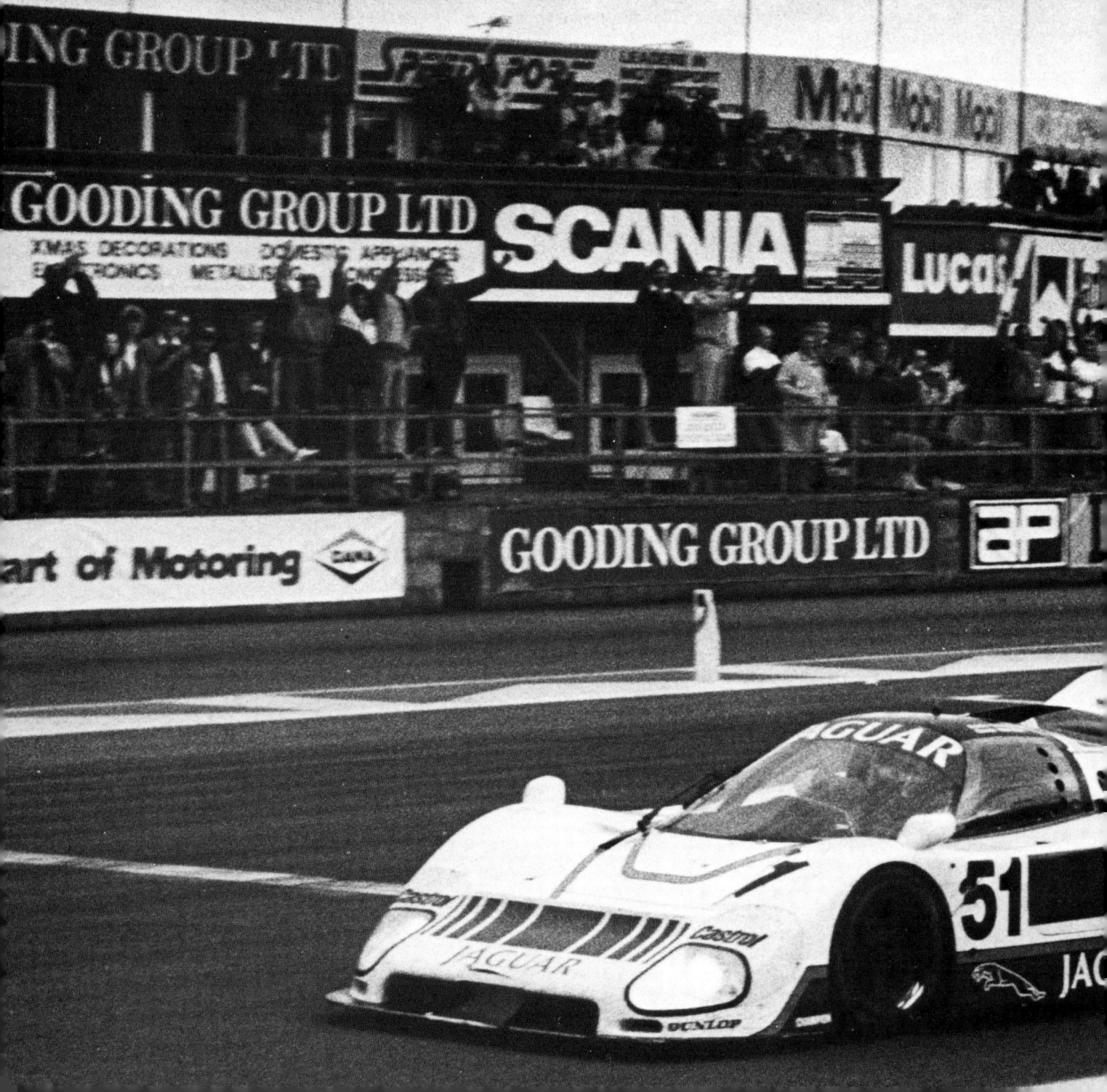

Inset far left:
Will he? Won't he? Tom Walkinshaw and Roger Silman wait for the chequered flag as Eddie Cheever reels off the final laps. Silverstone, May 1986. According to Tom Walkinshaw later in the season, this was the first occasion on which his team ran 6·5-litre power units.

Main photograph:
The first and seventh placed XJR-6s receive a tumultuous reception as they cross the finishing line at Silverstone and ...

Inset middle:
... a few seconds later from Derek Warwick and Tom Walkinshaw who leapt on to the tarmac from their pit-signalling platform as Cheever swept past on his slowing-down lap.

Inset left:
Eddie Cheever and Derek Warwick build up the champagne pressure (to give Tom Walkinshaw a taste of his own medicine) after their history-making Silverstone victory.

race laps had been recorded by the Lancia in 1 min. 15.22 sec. and the two Jaguars: 1 min. 15.57 sec. and 1 min. 15.64 sec. respectively for cars 51 and 52. Sportingly, instead of putting the car away, Lancia sent out Andrea de Cesaris to thrill the crowds with a new sports-prototype lap record of 1 min. 13.95 sec.; but by then the leading XJR-6 was cruising for home.

The V12 Jaguar engines (up from 6·3 litres to 6·5 litres) continued to run sweetly and economically enough to prevent worry about running out of fuel. With Le Mans in the offing, it was hard not to notice the reliability shown by the Porsches, only one of which failed to finish. The No.1 works 962 of Hans-Joachim Stuck and Derek Bell, with the former driving, struggled home after its new PDK transmission gave trouble not far from the finish, thus securing second place. So the 1985 champions extended their points lead, first established at Monza.

Eddie Cheever and Derek Warwick celebrated by unleashing their champagne on Tom Walkinshaw, who was just about all-in (having commuted between the UK and Italy twice over the weekend, in order to drive a Group A Rover at Misano) and past caring anyway. John Egan joined them on their lap of honour. The top twelve finishers finishing in this historic event were:

Le Mans practice day confabulation between Walkinshaw, Warwick and Silman. (*Courtesy: Ian Norris*)

			(Laps)
1st Jaguar XJR-6	Warwick/Cheever		212
2nd Porsche 962	Stuck/Bell		210
3rd Porsche 962	Gartner/Needell		207
4th Porsche 956	Weaver/Niedzwiedz		206
5th Porsche 956	de Villota/Velez		206
6th Porsche 956	Follmer/Barilla/Morton		205
7th Jaguar XJR-6	Schlesser/Brancatelli		204
8th Sauber-Mercedes	Thackwell/Pescarolo/Nielsen		203
9th Porsche 956	Brun/Jelinski		203
10th Porsche 962	Larrauri/Pereja		203
11th Porsche 962	Boutsen/Sigala		200
12th Porsche 956	Laessig/Ballabio/Wood		195

On 31 May 1986 it was TWR's turn to form up behind the pace car at Le Mans, to challenge the all-powerful

Pit scenes at Silverstone and Le Mans show wing and tail changes being tried out for the French 24-hour classic.

Porsches; and there was no real fuel problem – 2550 litres allowed this time.

Group 44 was staying at home with mixed feelings. The American team had problems of its own, for designer Lee Dykstra had handed-in his notice to Jaguar Cars Inc.; what had once seemed a solid working relationship between Tullius and Dykstra was no more. The XJR-7 was going through some traumatic times in its first season of development to match the new opposition promised from Ford, General Motors, and BMW in IMSA racing. In its three full seasons of racing, the XJR-5 had not failed to win at least one major IMSA GTP race. Victory for the new XJR-7 – even in 6.5-litre form, as first used at Road Atlanta in April – was proving thoroughly elusive.

One link with Le Mans *was* retained, however, in the loan of Hurley Haywood and Brian Redman for the Silk Cut Jaguar Team. They were to drive Car No. 52 (Chassis 1/86) with Hans Heyer. Car No. 51 (2/86) was destined for Cheever, Warwick, and Schlesser; No. 53 (3/85) was to be shared between Brancatelli, Percy, and Hahne – the latter being a last-minute substitute for F3000 star Ivan Capelli, who had to withdraw because of a clash of spon-

Aerodynamic experiments on test at Le Mans practice day, 9 May 1986. (*Courtesy: Ian Norris*)

sors' interests. Both Armin Hahne and Win Percy had won classic endurance races with the Group A XJ-S, so Le Mans type racing wasn't a surprise to them, even if the 230 mph XJR-6 was. They adapted well, Hahne simply requesting radio silence from his pit while he got on with learning a new craft.

It's about 9 am and, with a hard night's work behind him, Kevin Lee wears an expression that tells it all. The last surviving Jaguar suffered a rear tyre blowout when running second, causing sufficient rear-end damage to make repairs (within the regulations) impossible.

Left:
The Stuck/Bell/Holbert Porsche cruises to victory, Le Mans 1986. (*Courtesy: Carl Williams*)

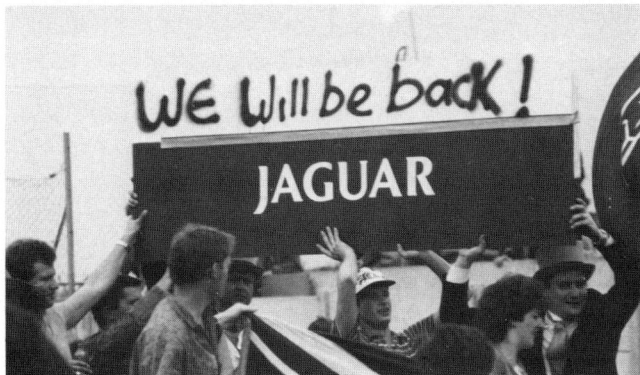

Below Left:
British fans carry away the defiant message left by the TWR team when the last XJR-6 retired. Le Mans, 1986. (*Courtesy: Carl Williams*)

Soon to be knighted, honorary starter John Egan sent the runners on their way. In the early laps Warwick ran second to Ludwig in the Joest Porsche; the other two Jaguars were well-placed, too. All three cars would withdraw however. First to go was No. 52, apparently out of fuel on the fifty-fourth lap; Heyer couldn't get it back to the pits. Haywood then joined No. 53 for a spell; but in the early hours of Sunday morning (1 June) Percy had the task of bringing it to a safe halt when drive-line failure occurred at speed during its 155th lap.

This left No.51 still running second overall to the Porsche of ultimate winners, Bell, Stuck and Holbert, after 16 hours of racing; Schlesser was at the wheel shortly after 8.30 am when a rear tyre blew out with such force that it wrecked the rear of the car; but no repair could be made which did not infringe the rules about what may be replaced. Schlesser, like Percy, was lucky as well as skilled to avoid solid objects while bringing his stricken car to

Above:
Derek Warwick running sixth early in the Norisring race. He came third in the end.

Left:
The XJR-6s of Cheever, Warwick and Schlesser set off in 3rd, 6th and 8th places as the pace car pulls in at the start of Germany's Norisring 'sprint'.

Inset Left:
Cheever, a close second at the Norisring, is seen against a back-ground of Hitler's podium in this fine Malcolm Bryan photograph.

rest. The last XJR-6 had to abandon the great marathon after 239 laps. In the empty Jaguar pits was a message of defiance as the Porsches cruised home unopposed: 'We'll be back'; and as a PS for the benefit of the huge crowd of fans on the terraces across the road: 'Thanks for coming'.

Aside from the harsh circumstances of the failures, Le Mans 1986 proved to TWR that it had the basis of a Le Mans winner another year; it also proved the successful race development of the Jaguar V12 engine.

The team was now up to strength, with a large full-time staff under the overall management of Roger Silman. Day to day running of the TWR workshop and XJR-6 preparation was in the hands of Paul Davis and Alastair McQueen. Kevin Lee was in charge of the race mechanics. They were Nick Caceres, Gary Davies, and Phil Walters (no – not the American driver) for 3/85; they had 3/86 after Le Mans. Jeff Wilson, John Simmonds, and Dave Griffiths looked after 1/86; and Clive Parker, Rod Benoist, and Alva Claxton were responsible for 2/86.

The Silk Cut Jaguar Team was close-knit, well-drilled. Tom Walkinshaw had developed the ability to run a happy operation, and seemed personally unconcerned by the removal of the TWR insignia from the cars. His empire was big, and growing rapidly. The majority of his time might be taken up by motor racing and related matters, but his businesses were much more diverse.

Stuck and Cheever on the front row at Brands Hatch, 1986, with Warwick looking to drive between them.

Insets left and right:
The Jaguars of Cheever/Brancatelli (51) and Warwick/Schlesser (53) at Brands Hatch.

Silk Cut cigarettes were promoted in a distant, detached fashion; everything to do with smoking was put before the public eye more obliquely as attitudes changed. Motor racing provided a vehicle for this kind of promotion. It didn't seem to matter that the words 'Silk Cut' had to be removed for some races – as did 'Rothmans' from the works Porsches – for the XJR-6 did still manage to look a little like a mobile cigarette packet. How much did this matter to Jaguar itself? – the answer is: probably very little, for the romance had gone out of motor racing, compared with the marque's great Le Mans era of the 1950s, when other things were at stake. Then, the very name of Jaguar was relatively new – in need of recognition, which a few classic events and a limited choice of media were able to provide to an amazing degree. Jaguar became a household name. Then, having become a successful independent industrial group, it was sold, ground down and, finally, reconstituted as Jaguar Cars Ltd – an old name in a totally new and unfamiliar world, as far as competition motoring was concerned.

The days of Italian Racing Red still existed as an exception to prove Ferrari's rule – but the days of British Racing Green and German Racing Silver were long gone, from a practical point of view. (I am not referring to the superb use Mercedes-Benz makes of history, through its artefacts and the chance it gives the likes of Fangio, Lang, or Moss to drive them on special occasions. Others can learn much from Stuttgart.)

If anyone wants to emulate Porsche now, they have to look at what Porsche has done. No-one could quite do the same thing as Porsche: it is too late; Porsche never stopped racing and its experience is therefore complete and unbroken. As long as Porsche sustains Weissach, it can be expected to come up with the innovation and the technology to restore its superiority, should an opponent succeed in breaking into its special preserve – world-class sports car racing – as Jaguar and Mercedes did in 1986.

And what of the sponsorship itself? Again, it is necessary to look at Porsche, who carried the names of Gulf, Martini, and Rothmans successively. If Jaguar continued to do well, and to generate good publicity, it seemed likely that new sponsorship from some other source would be forthcoming for 1989 – assuming that Gallaher International did not renew, or that Jaguar did not wish to continue racing. In the old days, there was engineering spin-off; the chestnut of the disc brake tells it all. Today the relationship between the sports-racing and production car is not so easy to find; there may be helpful ideas in matters of advanced electronics, for example, but 1980s Group C cars and road cars are further apart than their ancestors were.

In going with TWR and Silk Cut, Jaguar made it clear that its modern racing programme is strictly promotional. As long as there is a Jaguar production engine that can, potentially, power a car to victory, Jaguar seems certain not to renounce all forms of racing in the foreseeable future. Unless your name is Porsche, however, there are times when – sponsorship or no – there may be a need to look at the scene to be sure that the lure does not become

How to lose a race and – in this case – a championship. Derek Warwick digs out at Jerez, August 1986.

obsessive. It *can* be much more difficult to stop a good thing than to start it. Many a company has succumbed to the obsession of racing; Porsche alone has managed to make it part of its *raison d'être*.

On the other hand, racing's decision-makers can assist manufacturers to make *their* correct decisions. Sports-prototype race regulations have been fluid for generations. Few years pass without a major upheaval to threaten the continuity of this branch of the sport – and so it was again in 1986 when, without consulting the participants, FISA sought sweeping changes for 1988. So, although the Silk Cut Jaguar Team was preparing for a full season's racing in 1987, a question mark hung over the third contracted year, 1988. Fortunately the situation was looking more stable by 1987.

Meantime, 1986 continued to provide a fascinating battle between drivers, marques and teams.

Four weeks after Le Mans, on 29 June, three XJR-6s were raced at the *Nuernberg Stadion*. The Norisring 180 km. 'sprint' race *was* won by a Porsche – the Joest 956 driven by Klaus Ludwig – but the Jaguars of Cheever and Warwick were strong finishers in second and third places. Their team-mate Jean-Louis Schlesser had a less happy race – losing twelve laps with a jammed throttle. He did finish, in seventeenth position.

Great things were expected at Brands Hatch in late July, when the 1000 km race was held in overcast conditions. It was surprisingly poorly organised as regards the handling of pace-car periods. Another surprise was the apparent pique of Derek Warwick who had found himself behind Eddie Cheever on points in the drivers' championship

after Norisring. The two Silk Cut Jaguars were driven by Cheever/Brancatelli and Warwick/Schlesser – second and third respectively in practice, but sixth and fourth in the race itself. Warwick and Schlesser led for many laps during the first half, but fuel filter blockage caused misfiring and unscheduled stops while Cheever had trouble with a faulty hub bearing. It was another field day for the Porsches, with Wollek/Barilla winning from Bell/Stuck/Ludwig. Bell and Stuck therefore extended their championship lead but Warwick was now in third place.

A galaxy of stars went to Jerez for Round 6 of the drivers' championship – the 360 km Trofeo Silk Cut – with the intention of driving Jaguars, but not all of them got the chance.

There were fewer Porsches than usual, and hopes for a Jaguar victory were again high, for XJR-6s were 2nd, 3rd and 4th on the grid, thanks to Jean-Louis Schlesser, Eddie Cheever and Derek Warwick respectively.

Brancatelli (Schlesser's co-driver) made a good start from the front row, as did Warwick from the next one – but when they reached the first corner Warwick turned across from the outside and slammed his team-mate broadside. Cheever, just behind, could not help ramming Brancatelli; both came into the pits, Cheever having to stay longer to tape up the bodywork; and both were destined to retire with drive-shaft failure before their co-drivers – Schlesser and Brundle (on one-off secondment from Ken

Pit-stop at Spa-Francorchamps for the car that so nearly won with Kevin Lee standing bravely on the stop-line as usual.

Tyrrell) – could take over. Meanwhile, embarrassed and angry with himself, Warwick was losing more than two laps, scrabbling around in the gravel trap on the outside of the corner where he had made his uncharacteristic error – an error which, as it would turn out, was going to cost him a championship that was there for the taking. Not that anyone realised this at the time, however. The Warwick/Lammers car came back up through the field to take third place behind two Porsches entered by Walter Brun of Switzerland; but it was of little consolation to anyone – except the Brun team.

Three weeks later, on 24 August, fog and rain played havoc with the Nürburgring round of the World Championship – to the extent that several drivers (notably the brave Hans-Joachim Stuck) were lucky to avoid serious injury after a badly handled pace-car incident which caused the event to be stopped and restarted. Warwick had partially written-off an XJR-6 in practice, which left Brancatelli and Heyer without a drive; and Cheever spun-off in the first part of the race to retire with transmission failure; so his co-driver Schlesser was out of luck again.

Warwick and Lammers had a comfortable lead in the restarted race, but then a camshaft oil-pipe failed and Lammers had to stop at the pits. Stangely, he was sent out again with the pipe sealed off. The engine seized completely, out on the course, almost at once. This turn of events left the way clear for the Sauber-Mercedes of Pescarolo and Thackwell to bring a new make into the winner's circle – as TWR had done at Silverstone.

The race of the year!
The last European Group C race of 1986 took place at Spa-Francorchamps on 14 September. It was, simply, the race of the year – a 1000 km battle between the Porsches of Stuck/Bell and Boutsen/Jelinski and the Warwick/Lammers Jaguar. Boutsen's Brun Porsche was running out of petrol at the very end, and Warwick's XJR-6 looked as though it would accelerate past it to the chequered flag; but when Warwick needed the V12's legendery throttle-response it wasn't there; he, too, was short of fuel. He was less than a second behind at the finishing line; he was also a little closer to the championship leaders, who came third. The championship points at this stage were: Bell/Stuck 82, Warwick 69. Still, only a misfortune for the works Porsche drivers could prevent them retaining their title. The Cheever/Schlesser Jaguar was fifth in Belgium after two punctures.

With no late-season events fixed, Japan's Fuji 1000 km on 5 October was to be the 1986 WSC final. In the interim, Eddie Cheever won the final round of the German championship on the *Neue Nürburgring*, just beating Stuck and Ludwig in Porsches to give TWR a timely boost.

Each race of 1986 is worth a story of its own, and Fuji is no exception.

The Rothmans Porsche 962C of Stuck and Bell had a puncture as it touched another car; later a drive shaft broke and the reigning champions were out of contention – although they soldiered on to finish twenty-fifth.

Meanwhile, Lammers had wheel bearing failure on one of two Jaguars. The car continued, after repairs, driven also by Schlesser and Brancatelli who had gear selection trouble; this trio came seventeenth. Because he had had a fairly troublefree first double-stint it was Cheever who handed over to the waiting Warwick – the man who needed the points. Once Bell and Stuck were out of the top placings, he had only to finish second and he and his team would be World Champions – and this looked a racing certainty until racing luck took over. A piece of

Above:

Eddie Cheever gives the Jaguar team a boost, winning the non-championship race at the Nürburgring in September 1986.

Left:

Warwick just fails to catch Boutsen as the flag falls to mark the end of the 1986 Spa-Francorchamps 1000 km race. (On the right is the Ecosse-Rover with which the reorganised *Ecurie Ecosse* team would win the 1986 'C2' World title.)

thrown tyre-tread happened to knock off the master switch and Cheever took some time to locate the freak fault. Later on in the race, more time was lost when Warwick came in with a misfire; it was only a loose wire, but it was enough to keep the Jaguar down in third place.

There was much confusion at the time, because it was announced initially that Cheever and Warwick were *2nd* – and, therefore, Warwick and the Silk Cut Jaguar Team appeared to be the World Champions! – but few serious lap-scorers believed it. Some time later the first three Fuji finishers were announced:

1st	Ghinzani/Barilla	(Joest Porsche 956)
2nd	Jelinski/Dickens	(Brun Porsche 956)
3rd	Cheever/Warwick	(TWR Jaguar XJR-6)

The Brazilian star, Raul Boesel: World Champion for Jaguar in 1987, and co-winner of five of the season's ten races.

The TWR Jaguar pit-crew with the 6.9-litre Jaguar XJR-8 which won the 1987 Spa-Francorchamps 1000 km race to clinch the drivers' as well as the teams championship – Jaguar's first-ever World titles. On the left is Paul Davis who, in 1988, would move to TWR's new Jaguar road-car project after six seasons managing the racing Jaguars. Next to him are Allan Scott, Roger Silman, and Tony Southgate – engineer, team director, and designer respectively. Also in the picture are Alastair McQueen, Eddie Hinckley (Tom Walkinshaw's first staffman, back in 1978), Kevin Lee, and most of the other members of this closely-knit group.

It was a truly grand finale for the 'old' Porsche 956, since its time had run out; it would no longer be eligible to race in the World Championship.

After the 'growing pains' of its first full season, the Silk Cut Jaguar Team had not really expected either title – but Roger Silman and his team were looking forward more than ever to proving they could do it in 1987.

The provisional order at the end of 1986 looked like this (Derek Bell being very annoyed about a tie-break which prevented his sharing the title with Stuck for a second time):

Driver's Championship, 1986	points
1st Derek Bell (Porsche)	82
2nd Hans-Joachim Stuck (Porsche)	82
3rd Derek Warwick (Jaguar)	81
4th Frank Jelinski (Porsche)	74
5th Eddie Cheever (Jaguar)	61

Teams Championship	
1st Brun Porsche	52
2nd Joest Porsche	48
3rd {Silk Cut Jaguar / Rothmans Porsche}	47 / 47
5th Fitzpatrick Porsche (Danone)	30
6th Kouros Sauber-Mercedes	29

Jaguar's full WSC achievements of 1987 are set out in detail in *Jaguar – World Champions*, also by this author, published early in 1988 by G. T. Foulis & Co. Indeed, at the time of writing, it looked as if 1988 would merit a book

of its own, too. The Silk Cut Jaguar Team looked strong enough to defend its World titles, while the Castrol-backed Jaguars seemed set to present a major challenge in the IMSA GTP series. 'The task we have undertaken is a tough one', said Sir John Egan at his Jaguar Racing press conference on 14 January 1988, 'but neither I nor anyone else involved in our racing teams would have it any other way. If it's not difficult, it's not worth winning.'

As this revised edition went to press in early 1988, TWR was on the crest of a wave. Tom Walkinshaw had just held a big party at Kidlington to celebrate the ten years since he and Eddie Hinckley had got down on their knees to scrub the floor of the first TWR industrial unit. Now TWR was more than three-hundred strong with diverse businesses and no fewer than seven factory units on what amounted to a major industrial complex. Latest project was the setting up of a special Jaguar road-car project department, run by Paul Davis into whose shoes Kevin Lee was stepping on the racing side.

The other celebration on that cheerful evening was the winning of Jaguar's first-ever World Championships (final results of which are shown opposite). For 1987, the XJR-6 had been redesignated XJR-8. Southgate had increased the downforce and reduced the weight, while Scott and his engineers had found more power with reliability in the Jaguar V12 engine, by now displacing about 6.9 litres. Eddie Cheever had stayed on with the team, and Jan Lammers had rejoined it. They were joined by Raul Boesel and John Watson; John Nielsen was Cheever's stand-in (and very effective, too) when the American was racing in

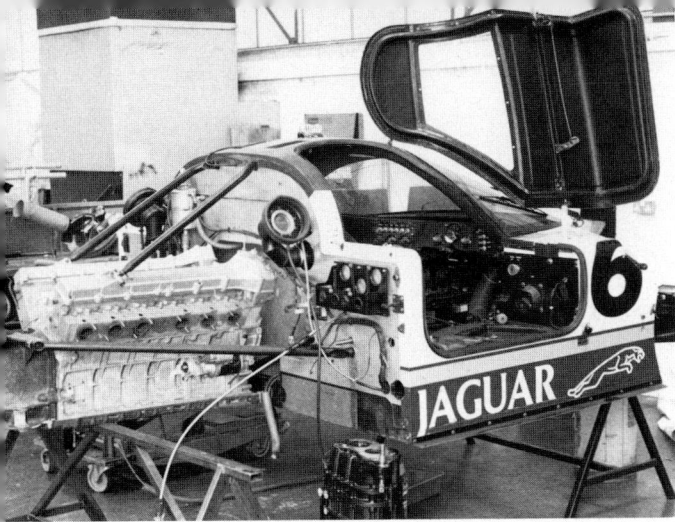

Composite structure of the XJR-8, showing the location and fitting of the Jaguar V12 engine. The 1988 XJR-9 Group C and IMSA structures would be different in detail but similar in principle.

Formula One, and Martin Brundle and Johnny Dumfries played a part in that season of success towards the end. The XJR-8 won eight of the ten World sports-prototype events, missing out only at Le Mans (the only big disappointment) and Norisring. These were the Group C championship race winners of 1987:

Jarama	Lammers/Watson	Jaguar XJR-8
Jerez	Cheever/Boesel	Jaguar XJR-8
Monza	Lammers/Watson	Jaguar XJR-8
Silverstone	Cheever/Boesel	Jaguar XJR-8
Le Mans	Bell/Stuck/Holbert	Porsche 962C
Norisring	Baldi/Palmer	Porsche 962C
Brands Hatch	Boesel/Nielsen	Jaguar XJR-8
Nürburgring	Cheever/Boesel	Jaguar XJR-8
Francorchamps	Brudle/Boesel/Dumfries	Jaguar XJR-8
Fuji	Lammers/Watson	Jaguar XJR-8

This historic season brought Jaguar not only the Teams Championship but the top four places in the drivers' table, as follows:

1988 XJR-9, as depicted in the pre-season press release, proudly carrying 'Number One' in recognition of Jaguar's 1987 World titles. 'Castrol' is also given new prominence. (The IMSA version is depicted on Page 344, and the 1987 World Championship winning XJR-8 is shown in action on Page 6.)

World Sports-Prototype Championship, 1987

		points.
1st	Silk Cut Jaguar Team, UK	178
2nd	Brun Motorsport, Switzerland	94
3rd	Porsche AG, Germany	74
4th	Joest Racing, Germany	63
5th	Britten-Lloyd Racing, UK	58
6th	Kremer Porsche, Germany	41

1st	Raul Boesel, Brazil	Jaguar	127
2nd	Jan Lammers, Netherlands	Jaguar	102
	John Watson, UK		
4th	Eddie Cheever, USA	Jaguar	100
5th	Derek Bell, UK	Porsche	99
6th	Hans-Joachim Stuck, Germany	Porsche	99

During 1987, it was announced that TWR would take over from Group 44 in the USA, and run Jaguar's IMSA race programme from 1988 (*see small picture on Page 344*). This was not just a matter of sponsorship, which *had* been proving hard to get at the right level in America, but a reflection of Jaguar's esteem for Walkinshaw's ability to win regularly. By the end of 1987, TWR had won thirty races outright for Jaguar – an average of five victories per year. Moreover, it made sense to base both programmes on one design, now that Group C and IMSA were really drawing closer in concept.

Appendix One

The Works Drivers

This appendix gives a brief profile of the people who drove the works D-type or factory-built prototypes. Drivers of the 1980s were selected by their Jaguar-contracted team boss, NOT by Jaguar itself: that is to say by either *Bob Tullius* or *Tom Walkinshaw* (see their entries). Although contracted by *John Coombs* – NOT by the works – *Graham Hill* deserves special mention, for he was of particular help to engineer *Derrick White* in developing the E-type for racing between 1961 and 1964. *Jackie Stewart* tested and raced the same car in 1964; he and *Jim Clark* (who had raced a D-type successfully and by now had a connection with Jaguar through its subsidiary company Coventry Climax) also had tentative talks about driving the XJ13 which, at one stage, was being scheduled to run at Le Mans.

Richard Attwood, who tested the XJ13, began racing with a Triumph TR3 when he was a Jaguar apprentice. He went on to single-seaters and won the 1963 Monaco Junior Grand Prix in a Lola. Shortly afterwards, with David Hobbs, he drove the new mid-engined GT Lola which inspired Ford's GT40 which he also drove on many occasions. He drove Ferraris, too.

The son of Jaguar's Wolverhampton agent could be relied upon to maintain the strictest security when – after he had left the company – he was invited by Lofty England to test the XJ13 at Silverstone in 1967. If the project had not been abandoned, his findings would have had more significance today. At the time, his experience of big sports cars was invaluable, and he was able to indicate what (and how much) development would be needed to be competitive with the new generation of Le Mans cars.

Dick Attwood's greatest achievements were at Le Mans (first and second in 1970 and 1971 with the Porsche 917) and Monaco in 1968 when his BRM was second in the Formula 1 Grand Prix. He was still racing from time-to-time in historic-car events in the 1980s.

Dick Attwood meets BRM saviour Sir Alfred Owen at Goodwood, Easter 1964.

Donald Beauman was selected to drive the works long-nose D-type in the 1955 season, having impressed Lofty England by his consistency and attitude during winter tests. Beauman, a London hotelier, had been in 500cc racing from 1950; he had acquired the ex-Hawthorn TT Riley for 1953. His 1954 successes were in an Aston Martin DB3 and a Connaught single-seater, both owned by Sir Jeremy Boles. He was well-placed at Le Mans in 1955 when his D-type became stuck in the sand. Shortly afterwards he was killed (driving the Connaught in Ireland) and so his racing career never did get off the ground properly.

Derek Bell – Britain's leading sports car driver of the 1980s – is associated with Porsche. His long career began in 1964 with a Lotus 7. He was a member of the BL-Broadspeed team which worked so hard for so little reward – in terms of results, if not of cash – to make a racer of the XJ12. (He and Andy Rouse gave it its best result – second – at the Nürburgring in 1977.)

Bell is included here because he was asked to go to Silverstone to assess the Group 44 Jaguar XJR-5 in 1983, when it was flown over from the USA specially, so that its Le Mans potential might be assessed by John Egan and Jim Randle of Jaguar. Apparently, Porsche were quite pleased to release Bell for the day; after all, they were in need of some worthwhile opposition. Two years later they got it. Bell continued to race Porsches and his best-ever season in 1985 when he shared the World Championship for Group C drivers with Hans-Joachim Stuck; he was also runner-up to his other co-driver Al Holbert, in the IMSA Camel GTP series. (The success was repeated in 1986, but only just!)

Below:
Bob Berry and Lofty England on automatic pilot towards the end of another Le Mans.

Below Right:
Bob Berry with Duncan Hamilton.

Robert Emanuel Berry is a borderline case for this section, too, but he *was* an official reserve driver for Le Mans (although never called upon), having recorded good times in winter testing. As he was a company man, all Berry's Le Mans races were to be viewed from the pit-counter – as a worker. He had helped in the pits in 1951 when, as a student, he gave up his university studies to join Jaguar. His experiences with a privately-owned D-type are included in Appendix 3.

Bob Berry became head of Jaguar advertising and public relations shortly before the merger with BMC. He rejoined Jaguar briefly from BL in 1980, but left again to pursue his career in the import and retail motor businesses.

(Sir) John Arthur 'Jack' Brabham had just become World Champion for the second time when Jaguar's North American importers arranged a one-off drive for him in E2A at Riverside in 1960. He was tenth, and very uncomplimentary about the car; but he did drive it again 25 years later, in a Coventry cavalcade to mark the centenary of motoring.

Jack Brabham at Browns Lane in the early 1970s, visiting his old friends Walter Hassan (*centre*) and Harry Mundy formerly of Coventry Climax, suppliers of the power units which had brought him his first two World Championships in Formula 1.

Ivor Leon Bueb was a mellow but mighty fine driver who was selected for the 1955 works team and promptly won at Le Mans with Mike Hawthorn, rising to the tragic occasion brilliantly. They were the fastest pair again in 1956 but lost time until an injection pipe leak was located; they still came sixth. Bueb shared the winning factory-prepared car again with Ron Flockhart in 1957 for *Ecurie Ecosse*.

In 1956, he managed to hold off the opposition in the Silverstone touring car race with the obsolescent MkVII, and shared victory with naughty Duncan Hamilton in that year's Reims 12-hour race. His part in Jaguar's success extended to the 3.4 saloon and the works Lister-Jaguar.

The death of this popular Cheltenham-based Londoner (in 1959, in a Cooper F2 at Clermont-Ferrand) was a blow to the sport.

Briggs Cunningham tested a works D-type in Florida in early 1955, prior to forming his own team. This was the prelude to a long association with Jaguar, described elsewhere in this book.

Ivor Bueb, one of the most successful of Jaguar drivers, on his way to victory in the 1956 Reims 12-hour race. This particular D-type is retained at the Jaguar works.

Above: **Ivor Bueb.**

Right:
Briggs Cunningham trying the works D-type in Florida, early 1955. He would run a Jaguar team himself soon afterwards.

Top right:
Briggs Cunningham (*centre*), John Gordon Benett, and Alfred Momo (in cap) at Le Mans during the Cunningham sports-car era.

Top left:
Briggs and Lofty at Le Mans.

Bottom left:
Briggs Cunningham retained the ex-works car, XKD 507, for his Californian motor museum. Here he demonstrates it in 1976, at Laguna Seca circuit, where he allowed Phil Hill to race it. (Hill came second to Martin Morris, whose car is visible in this picture.)

Bottom right:
Norman Dewis (*centre*), Bob Berry (*right*) and Tony Rolt give Bill Heynes their undivided attention.

Norman Dewis drove in the 1955 works team at Le Mans and looked set for a good result when his race partner, Don Beauman, went into the sand and couldn't get going again.

Dewis had done some racing-for-fun while working at Lea-Francis, and before joining Jaguar as chief experimental department test engineer. One of his first assignments on arrival had been to accompany Stirling Moss on the 1952 Mille Miglia – an event covered in detail in Vol. 1. He was reserve driver at Le Mans several times but 1955 was the only occasion on which he did more than practise there. He must have done more high-speed laps of MIRA than any other driver. In 1955, with Bob Berry he finished fifth in the Goodwood 9-hour race, in the ex-works D-type then owned by Jack Broadhead. He retired from Browns Lane in 1985.

Jack Fairman (with Desmond Titterington), Reims 1956.

John Eric George Fairman had driven for Jaguar at Le Mans in 1951, and won himself a late place in the team again for 1956. With Desmond Titterington, he finished third at Reims in 1956; but at Le Mans, with Paul Frère spinning in front of him, he went into the bank: thus confining the racing history of his brand new car, XKD 602, to just over one lap. After the works withdrawal, 'Fearless Jack' Fairman drove for Jack Broadhead and *Ecurie Ecosse* – and, when XK power was finally overshadowed, he drove for the works Aston Martin team. His greatest-ever drive was at Monza in 1957 (see Appendix 3).

Paul Frère of Belgium was always a Jaguar enthusiast and persuaded his father to buy an SS Jaguar in the 1930s. A scholarly and multi-lingual engineer, Paul Frère first raced in the Spa-Francorchamps 24-hour race of 1948, sharing his MG PB with Jacques Swaters; they finished fourth in class. Eight years later, he drove a works 2.4 to victory in a touring car race at the same demanding circuit – though not over the same distance.

He drove works D-types at Nürburgring, Reims and Le Mans in 1956, crashing twice but finishing second (with Hawthorn) at Reims. He made up for his Le Mans misdemeanor the following year, taking fourth place (with Freddy Rousselle) in a D-type entered by his national Belgian racing team. He was fourth again in 1958 for Porsche and second in 1959 for Aston Martin. Finally in 1960, at the eighth attempt, Frère was victorious at Le Mans: this time in a Ferrari, with his fellow-countryman Olivier Gendebien co-driving.

As a writer, Paul Frère has stayed close to motor-racing,

Top:
Paul Frère at the end of the 1956 Reims 12-hour race.

Above:
The ageless Paul Frère.

and is well-qualified to comment upon it. His logical and straightforward account of the disaster at Le Mans in 1955 – when he and Peter Collins were second in an Aston Martin – is historically important, and is included in Chapter 4 with his kind permission.

432

Duncan Hamilton (*sipping*) and Tony Rolt, rueful runners-up at Le Mans in 1954. Frank Rainbow is on the left, Bob Penney on the right.

Walt Hansgen and E2A at Bridgehampton in 1960 with Dolores Damergy, then editor of *Jaguar Journal* (the US Jaguar clubs' magazine). Momo and Benett are on the left.

Mike Hawthorn at Reims in 1956. (England omnipresent beyond.)

Daniel Sexton Gurney was not a works driver as such; but it was Lofty England who arranged for him to join Walter Hansgen for E2A's début at Le Mans in 1960, although it was Cunningham's 'show'. Dan Gurney also drove the Coombs lightweight E-type at Silverstone, but the weather was bad and he didn't have his heart in the job. He was, of course, one of the big names of Grand Prix, sports car, and Indy racing; his Jaguar involvement was incidental and brief.

James Duncan Hamilton, one of racing's larger-than-life personalities, joined the Jaguar team in 1952 and co-drove regularly with Tony Rolt. Having won Le Mans in 1953, they very nearly did it again in 1954 – the year the D-type made its bow, and the year it RAINED. (They came a close second to the Gonzalez/Trintignant Ferrari). His last works drive for Jaguar was with Ivor Bueb at Reims in 1956 – the famous occasion when he got 'sacked for winning', as he saw it.

Hamilton then cocked a snook at Jaguar by driving for Ferrari, but at the end of the season he had made his peace with Coventry and was allowed to purchase one of the last batch of D-types. He had full works assistance for Le Mans in 1957, finishing sixth (with Gregory) after an irritating problem with an overheating exhaust.

1958 was his last Le Mans; he crashed his D-type when secure in second place, due to an obstruction, in pouring rain. He raced only a few more times after coming out of hospital.

Duncan Hamilton raced Jaguars of his own when not driving works cars, and he brought publicity for the marque by his performances at lesser-known circuits.

Walter Hansgen, a quiet American, was the best of the regular Stateside Jaguar drivers. He qualifies for this section because he drove E2A at Le Mans in 1960, in 3-litre form, then, shortly afterwards, using a 3.8-litre engine, he gave this Jaguar prototype its one and only race victory – at Bridgehampton, Long Island. He had raced Jaguars from 1951, and Briggs Cunningham took him into his team of long-nose D-types when its drivers were being beaten by this New Jerseyman using what was basically a production D-type. As a member of the team, Hansgen wrote regular and useful race reports which were fed back to Coventry via Jaguar Cars Inc., NY.

Cunningham had disbanded his team when, in 1966, Walt Hansgen died following a practice accident at Le Mans while driving a 7-litre MkII Ford.

John Michael Hawthorn had the same given names as the Lyons's late son, and was about the same age. He had a special relationship with Lofty England, too, perhaps akin to that of Jim Clark with Colin Chapman a few years later.

Mike Hawthorn would have had his first Jaguar drive in 1952, but for circumstances described in Vol. 1. It was not until 1955 that he joined the team, winning at Sebring and Le Mans – the year of the accident, after which some sections of the press put great pressure upon him, trying to attribute blame. The sequence of pictures, showing the accident from just beyond the 'kink' on the outside of

At a Jaguar apprentices' function in the winter of 1956–57, guest speaker Mike Hawthorn receives his famous four-spoke D-type steering wheel from Lofty England as a memento. (Jaguar's first sports-car racing programme was at an end, but Hawthorn would continue to race saloons.)

Miss Universe (Marlene Schmidt of Stuttgart) chats up a youthful David Hobbs at the first Daytona 3-hour sports/GT race meeting, February 1962. Dan Gurney won the race in a Lotus 19; Hobbs was forced to retire Peter Berry's misfiring E-type after hitting the wall.

the course (see Chapter 4) was all anybody needed to exonerate him totally; but it took time. His superb drive in the TT at Dundrod later that year was testimony to his buoyant disposition. He continued to drive Jaguar saloons in 1957/8. He became Formula 1 World Champion for Ferrari in 1958, then announced his retirement; but in 1959 this great character crashed his 3.4 on the Guildford by-pass. He was not yet 30 when he died.

David Wishart Hobbs ex-Jaguar/Daimler apprentice, was called back by the company on several occasions to drive the XJ13, both at MIRA and Silverstone. His 160 + mph lap of the Lindley track remained in *The Guinness Book of Records* for many years, and is thought to have been the lap record for any circuit in the UK until 1985, when Tom Walkinshaw lapped Millbrook at well over 170 mph in a TWR Jaguar XJ-S. (Earlier, Hobbs had tested E2A, too, at Silverstone.)

David Hobbs is the only man actually to have raced in both the Broadspeed XJ12 and the Group 44 XJR-5. He lost a wheel with the former: but with the latter he helped Bob Tullius and Doc Bundy take third place in the 1984 24-hour race at Daytona – where he had first raced an E-type 22 years earlier. He just went on and on racing, and winning – mainly in the USA, though he regarded Warwickshire as 'home'.

Michael MacDowel became Jaguar's competitions manager, in effect if not in title, when Lofty England moved into Jaguar's hierarchy. A vastly underrated driver, he tested racing E-types occasionally. His impressions of Jaguar's approach to competitions in the early 1960s are featured in Chapter 11.

Bruce McLaren, runner-up in that year's F1 World Championship, was contracted to drive E2A in the 1960 Pacific Grand Prix at Laguna Seca, but the car just wasn't

David Hobbs in the Peter Berry E-type at Druid's Corner, Oulton Park April 1962. (Hobbs's previous racing experience had always involved his father's patent 'Mechamatic' transmission – fitted to a Morris Oxford in 1959, a Jaguar XK140 in 1960, and a Lotus Elite in 1961.)

competitive and was sent back to Britain soon afterwards. He is included here 'for the record'. The young New Zealander also drove E-types on both sides of the Atlantic, for himself, for Peter Berry, and for Briggs Cunningham.

Stirling Moss is still a legend. He led the Jaguar team, up to and including 1954. That year, the new D-type did not provide him with much luck, though he was the pacesetter, as always; and at the end of the season he had little choice but to leave the Jaguar team, as Mercedes-Benz were offering him a combined sports and GP contract which was far too good an opportunity to miss.

A.P.R. (Tony) Rolt was Duncan Hamilton's regular partner; they took second place in that epic 1954 Le Mans race, having won together the year before. He retired from racing in 1955.

Above:
Walter Hassan tops up Hobbs's glass at a Jaguar apprentices' dinner.

Inset:
David Hobbs with the XJ13 at Silverstone in 1973, just after its complete rebuild.

Stirling Moss at the D-type's public début, Le Mans, 1954.

Michael MacDowel (*right*) receives a special prize from his former Jaguar colleague Bob Berry at the Loton Park national hill-climb, 1963. He had just won his class with the lightweight E-type owned by his new boss, John Coombs. (A decade later MacDowel would become hill-climb champion of Great Britain.)

Tony Rolt contemplates the new D-type at Le Mans in the spring of 1954.

Archie Scott-Brown was 1957's sensation at the wheel of the new Lister-Jaguar, and could well have been in the works Jaguar team had it not been disbanded. As it was he drove E1A (with Ivor Bueb) at its first Silverstone circuit test on 4 July 1957, when it was still thought that the company would return to racing in 1958.

435

Ian Stewart, who gave up racing in 1954.

Archie Scott-Brown, who tested the experimental car, 'E1A', at Silverstone in 1957.

Ian Stewart came from Perthshire. He had a polished driving style, and was one of the original *Ecurie Ecosse* drivers in 1952. He secured a Jaguar works Le Mans drive in 1952 and 1953. He was to have driven again in 1954 but a crash in the Argentine (in an *Ecosse* C-type) hastened his decision to retire, for a variety of reasons – including getting married and business – but not because he didn't want to race. Up to that time he had been seen as a great driver in the making.

James Stewart is no relation of Ian Stewart; he is Jackie's elder brother. Their father had a Jaguar agency at Bowling, near Dumbarton.

Jimmy Stewart used to get time off from National Service to race, and he proved to be the star of the *Ecurie Ecosse* team by 1954.

Stylish Jimmy Stewart's fine C-type performances for *Ecurie Ecosse* – like this one at Goodwood in 1954 – led to invitations to drive for the Aston Martin and Jaguar works teams.

An early-1960s shot of Jimmy and Jackie Stewart at Ingliston, where they were demonstrating *Ecurie Ecosse* steeds of different generations. Jackie drove the mid-engined Tojeiro-Buick – a pioneering design, but not a successful one. Jimmy was re-united with XKD 501, the 1956 Le Mans winner (the very car which he had crashed at the Nürburgring in 1955, when he decided to give up racing). The brothers' racing careers did not overlap at all.

He passed his works driver test at Silverstone and was selected by Lofty England to join the 1955 factory team. He was second to Mike Hawthorn in the Silverstone touring car race, both driving MkVIIs in May; but the same month saw him crash the new *Ecurie Ecosse* D-type, twice. The second time, it damaged the arm he had hurt in an Aston Martin accident a year before. More relevant to his subsequent decision to retire was that he knew how his mother hated his racing. His ebullient driving style was missed, but his decision to quit proved irrevocable.

Desmond Titterington will be remembered for his wonderful drive, backing up that of team leader Mike Hawthorn, in the lone works Jaguar pitted against a full team of Mercedes-Benz 300SLRs at Dundrod in 1955. The Ulsterman's prowess did not bring him any victories in works cars but he won a number of races for *Ecurie Ecosse*. He drove for Mercedes-Benz in the 1955 Targa Florio but gave up racing after 1956, though he continued to enjoy rallying.

Desmond Titterington, photographed at his works team Silverstone test session.

Robert Tullius came from Rochester, New York, but for most of his racing years – since the early 1960s – he has been based in Virginia. He built up his Group 44 team around the TR Triumphs and won a number of national titles. In the BL days, he established the V12 E-type as an SCCA championship winner; then he did the same with the XJ-S.

Together with Michael Dale (V-P of Jaguar Cars Inc.) and designer Lee Dykstra, Bob Tullius created an Amer-

437

Bob Tullius at the 1984 British motor show with Neil Johnson, then Jaguar's sales and marketing chief. Tullius's regular XJR-5/7 drivers included Bill Adam, 'Doc' Bundy, Hurley Haywood, 'Chip' Robinson and Britain's Brian Redman. (Haywood and Redman were also seconded to the TWR Silk Cut XJR-6 team for Le Mans in 1986.) Tullius and Jaguar parted company in 1987.

Tom Walkinshaw, 1984 Touring Car Champion and architect of Jaguar's racing successes east of the Atlantic since 1982. In 1988 he was given responsibility for Jaguars worldwide racing programmes.

ican Jaguar – the mid-engined XJR-5 – for IMSA racing. It won six times and placed well in many more between 1983 and 1985. The team also appeared, and ran with honour, at Le Mans in 1984 and 1985. For 1986 a further development, the XJR-7 was raced by Group 44, the officially-contracted team in the USA (with Bob Tullius as its head) responsible to Jaguar Cars Inc., New Jersey. With Robinson co-driving, Tullius gave the XJR-7 its first victory, at Daytona, Florida.

Group 44 drivers, 1974–1987: Bill Adam, Tony Adamowicz, Jim Adams, Claude Ballot-Léna, Patrick Bedard, 'Doc' Bundy, Brian Fuerstenau, Hurley Haywood, David Hobbs, John Morton, Brian Redman, Chip Robinson, Bob Tullius, and John Watson.

Tom Walkinshaw is the independent chief of the TWR group of operations, based at Kidlington near Oxford. He began racing in Scotland in 1966. Twenty years later he was running the team which gave Jaguar its first victory in the World Sports Car Championship event. He did not drive the Southgate-designed cars in races himself, but he continued to exhibit his talent in touring car racing. From 1982, he had prepared and driven XJ-S Group A touring cars with ever-increasing Jaguar support. By the end of 1985 there had been twenty outright victories, culminating in the James Hardie 1000 km race at Bathurst. Walkinshaw himself was Europe's Touring Car Champion of 1984. TWR's Silk Cut race programme was still in full swing when this edition went to press, by which time Walkinshaw had begun several other Jaguar-orientated businesses.

TWR Jaguar drivers, 1982–1987: Jeff Allam, Raul Boesel, Gianfranco Brancatelli, Martin Brundle, Enzo Calderari, Eddie Cheever, Ron Dickson, Pierre Dieudonné, Johnny Dumfries, John Fitzpatrick, John Goss, Armin Hahne, Hurley Haywood, Hans Heyer, Denny Hulme, Alan Jones, Jan Lammers, Peter Lovett, 'Chuck Nicholson',

John Nielsen, Winston Percy, Brian Redman, David Sears, Jean Louis Schlesser, Mike Thackwell, Tom Walkinshaw, Derek Warwick and John Watson.

Peter Walker who had raced the XK120 in its first event, back in 1949, was still driving with flair in 1954, when he continued as Stirling Moss's regular partner; but he took umbrage at being asked to take part in a driver test session and forfeited his place in the 1955 team. So after one season with the D-type, he moved to Aston Martin, but retired from racing following an accident at Le Mans in 1956. He died in 1984, aged 70.

Peter Walker.

Philip Walters was paired with Mike Hawthorn in the winning D-type – a works car on loan to Briggs Cunningham – at Sebring in 1955. He had been a partner (with William Frick) in Frick-Tappett Motors of Long Island, who had prepared the first Cunningham Le Mans Cadillac entries in 1950. Formerly a track racer calling himself 'Ted Tappett', Phil Walters often drove Cunningham cars, and that Jaguar drive was a nice way to round-off a successful career.

Kenneth Wharton was an all-rounder: good at trials driving, hill-climbing, auto tests, rallies and – not least – as a fast and courageous racing driver. He and Peter Whitehead gave the D-type its first victory at Reims in 1954, but he wasn't invited back for 1955 because William Lyons felt he had 'joined the opposition' when he became involved in a Daimler competition programme. He was invited back for Le Mans 1956, but never got a drive because Fairman crashed 'his' car.

The talented Midlander was one of the few drivers to tame the V16 BRM – but it was a Ferrari that got away from him, then killed him, when he was leading a sports car race in New Zealand early in 1957.

Peter Whitehead was more philosophical than Peter Walker at the end of 1954, when younger drivers were being asked to show their talent alongside the oldsters. Whitehead – who had given the C-type and the D-type their very first wins – was in the Antipodes for the winter and, anyway, he always had cars of his own to race.

In 1954 he commissioned the first Cooper-Jaguar, and he raced another in 1955; later he had an XK150 and a Lister-Jaguar, so he had not forsaken the marque. Indeed, his extremely unlucky death as passenger during the 1958 *Tour de France* was in a 3.4 saloon.

Below left:
Due to poor race administration, Phil Walters (*right*) and Mike Hawthorn were still not confirmed as winners of the 1955 Sebring 12-hour endurance race when this picture was taken. In due course, it was announced that their Jaguar D-type had won at record speed.

Below middle:
Ken Wharton – one of motor sport's greatest all-rounders.

Below right:
The late Peter Whitehead who served the Jaguar works team so well, but was dropped at the end of 1954.

Ken Wharton and Peter Whitehead at the prizegiving, after driving the D-type to its first-ever victory – the 1954 Reims 12-hour race.

Below:
Ken Wharton and Joe Wright (the man behind the general automotive use of disc brakes) fly to France in the Dunlop company plane.

Appendix Two

Privateers at home and abroad

The British Isles

Privately-owned Jaguar competition models had begun to make their mark on the British racing scene with Ian Stewart's victory in the Jersey Road Race in July 1952 the first for a non-works C-type Jaguar on British soil. *Ecurie Ecosse* was in its first season, and Stewart's success led to a team of four C-types for 1953, the XK120 already beginning to show its weight and age.

Leading winners for the Scottish team in 1953 were the unrelated Ian and Jimmy Stewart. Ian Stewart was so good that he was already a member of the Jaguar works team; Jimmy was about to be offered a place. The other

most successful C-type privateers in British national events were Michael Head and Jim Swift.

Fastest XK120 (*non*-C-type) in the land was the ex-works car of Hugh Howorth. The concept of Oscar Moor's HWM-Jaguar – so fast in 1952 and still a winner in 1953 –

The first-known mid-engined chassis to be Jaguar-powered was this one, the LGS, created by Frank Le Gallais of Jersey in the late 1940s. With an XK unit – one of the very first to be sold for non-Jaguar purposes – this remarkable vehicle held the Bouley Bay (Jersey) and Val des Terres (Guernsey) hill-climb records in the mid 1950s. (*Courtesy: F. Le Gallais*)

Other Channel Island specials followed Le Gallais principles. In the 1980s Guernseyman Peter Clarke (No. 9) and Roger King (No. 76) enjoyed hill-climbing and sand racing with their XK-engined machines. (*Courtesy: P. Clarke*)

had caught the imagination of the partnership of George Abecassis and John Heath, and before the 1953 season was out, the HWM works had a regular winner in its all-enveloping new Jaguar-powered sports car.

1954.

No D-types were sold privately this year and, while *Ecurie Ecosse* flourished, it was Duncan Hamilton in his ex-works car who outshone all other C-type drivers in the early part of the year with a moral victory in the British Empire Trophy race at Oulton Park and a remarkable win in the first-ever car race on Liverpool's Aintree circuit, alongside the Grand National course, in teeming rain.

Ecurie Ecosse's star this year was Jimmy Stewart, his namesake having retired from racing. Other notable winners in the Scottish team's C-types were 'guest' driver Roy Salvadori and new star Desmond Titterington.

Michael Head continued to score frequently through steady, competent driving. There were some new privateers on the home front, most notable being Berwyn Baxter and John Keeling in two 'old' *Ecurie Ecosse* C-types which were now replaced by 1953 ex-works lightweight cars. Joe Kelly raced his C-type spectacularly and with abandon on both sides of the Irish sea without scoring a major win.

One driver to put an old cat among the C-type pigeons was Jaguar's young publicity assistant, Bob Berry, who had acquired one of only three one-piece alloy XK120-shaped bodies. Then he got former Jaguar racing mechanic John Lea to make an XK120 that was even more special than Howorth's, and capable of embarrassing potentially quicker and certainly more expensive machinery throughout the season. (*Berry's own description of how this car was prepared can be found in Appendix 3 to the first book in this two-volume series.*)

One of Bob Berry's finest moments of 1954 was when he stormed through the field with the XK120 to come second on handicap in Ireland's O'Boyle Trophy race. Run concurrently was the Wakefield Trophy race (non-handicap, *Formule Libre*) in which an unfamiliar car had its big win of the season. This was the Jaguar-engined Cooper T33 commissioned by Jaguar works driver Peter Whitehead for his own use. In this event – the last ever held at The Curragh, because of a serious accident – the C-types of Hamilton and Kelly dead-heated behind Whitehead. That must have been a stirring sight.

Whitehead's Irish victory followed an equally convincing performance at Snetterton where he had beaten Head (C-type) and Berry (XK120 special) easily.

For the HWM-Jaguar, second place behind Gonzalez's 4·9 Ferrari at the Silverstone International Trophy meeting represented Abecassis's drive-of-the-year while another special builder, Dick Shattock, won a short second-feature race at Aintree's August international with his Jaguar-powered RGS-Atalanta.

In the sprint world Philip Scragg (Alta-Jaguar), Frank Le Gallais (LGS-Jaguar) were regular class-winners.

1955.

Production of the D-type for customers began this year – a tragic year for sports car racing, with the disaster of Le Mans followed by another in the Tourist Trophy.

Before any deliveries had been made, however, one of the 1954 works cars had been released to private hands XKC 402 went to works driver Duncan Hamilton for his own use, to replace his C-type (XKC 038) which he had sold to Dan Margulies. Hamilton collected the car from the works in February, drove it in several North African events, and shipped it home just in time for the first UK International meeting of the year, the British Empire Trophy at Oulton Park. The first race in Britain for a privately-owned D-type Jaguar was, therefore, Heat 2 of the 1955 Empire Trophy, in which Hamilton's car came second to Mike Sparken's 3-litre Ferrari. These two car/driver combinations finished in the same order at the Goodwood Easter meeting a week later.

The first D-types to be sold new were pre-production

(XKD 501 and 502) for *Ecurie Ecosse*, in time for the traditional Silverstone May meeting. Jimmy Stewart crashed one in practice but Desmond Titterington came sixth in the sports car race with the other before taking a fine win at Dundrod.

The second works D-type to be sold was purchased by Jack Broadhead for Bob Berry to drive. (Berry's own story of this car, XKC 403, is told in Appendix 3.) Having started 1955 successfully with his now-legendary giant-killing XK 120 special, Berry raced the D-type for the first time at Goodwood on Whit-Monday, 30 May 1955, twice finishing second to Hamilton in his sister car.

By now, Hamilton had acquired a second D-type of his own, XKC 406, which he lent to Michael Head and George Abecassis.

Two more D-types – XKD 511 for Ian Baillie and XKD 517 for Gillie Tyrer and Alex McMillan – reached their owners just in time for a spot of racing before the season ended. McMillan scored three firsts at the North Staffs MC meeting on 8 October, Silverstone's last date of the season.

C-types continued to do well in club events. Dan Margulies (XKC 038), Dick Protheroe (XKC 021) and Gillie

The obsolete C-type was still highly competitive at club level – when in capable hands. This car (XKC 049, with newly applied XK120 windscreen) is seen circuit racing and hill-climbing in 1955, driven by the versatile Gillie Tyrer. Later that year, Archie Scott-Brown won a race at Brands Hatch with this car, on behalf of its next owner, Louis Manduca.

Tyrer (XKC 049) scored well; and Archie Scott-Brown showed his wizardry with a first and a second at Brands Hatch in XKC 049 after it had been bought by Louis Manduca in late 1955. But it was newcomer Bill Smith who set the circuits alight with his handling of the 1953 Le Mans-winning car (XKC 051) and caught Lofty England's eye.

Bob Berry's two firsts, a third, and best lap of the day (78·89 mph) with the lightened special at Oulton Park on 21 May marked the end of an era for his modified XK 120.

This was not by any means, however, the end for the first of the Jaguar twin-cam sports cars. In July, Michael Heather's XK 120 won the Munster 100 handicap race on the Carrigohane road circuit just outside Cork, while in Scotland a youthful Michael Salmon was already making a name for himself with his smartly turned-out fawn roadster, PCR 379.

One announcement of particular interest to Salmon, and the other users of generally outclassed series-production sports cars, appeared in *Autosport* on 14 October. Having encouraged 500 cc racing in its early days, editor Gregor Grant, was now championing a new championship for *sports* cars, to begin in 1956.

Jaguar-engined competition cars continued to proliferate.

Bertie Bradnack and Jack Walton acquired T33 Cooper–Jaguars but never came to terms with them. Cyril

Dan Margulies (XKC 038) on his way to sixth place at 1955's main Ibsley race meeting.

Wick did very well with the original ex-Whitehead car, apart from a trip up the bank at Goodwood. Peter Whitehead himself now had the new and more mundane-looking Cooper 'Mark Two', thus retaining Jaguar power though no longer in the works team. A second Cooper–Jaguar 'Mark Two' was bought by Tommy Sopwith, but its most competitive result was when Reg Partell brought it home third at Snetterton behind Hamilton and Abecassis in the former's two ex-works D-types. Mostly Abecassis drove the HWM–Jaguar. While the Cooper–Jaguar never quite 'made it' in racing, the Coventry-powered HWM certainly did – despite the 1955 season starting badly – and Abecassis finished a winner again at Castle Combe in the autumn with the 'second series' HWM–Jaguar.

Hill-climber and sprinter Phil Scragg continued to do well on the hills, sometimes with his own HWM–Jaguar and sometimes a works one.

1956.

Although the Climax-engined Coopers and Lotuses were heralding a new period in which small light cars would out-perform the big ones on the tighter circuits, a well-driven D-type could still show them a clean pair of Dunlops. Several more private D-types were appearing, but only Berry, Hamilton, and the faster *Ecurie Ecosse* drivers – Flockhart, Sanderson and Titterington seemed able to get the best out of them on UK courses. Preparation and closeness of works advice may have had something to do with it, but the right kind of driver ability had a lot to do with it, too. For example, at the national Whit-Saturday

Snetterton meeting of 1956, Archie Scott-Brown and John Lawrence in C-types outran Ian Baillie (D-type). Scott-Brown (XKC 049) did, in fact, lose that race when a plug-lead detached itself – but it did emphasise the difference between those prepared to wrestle with their cars and those daunted by them.

May 1956 also saw the birth of a new circuit at Kirkby Mallory in Leicestershire. At that Mallory Park opening meeting, the 1953 Le Mans-winning C-type reappeared in the hands of Yorkshireman Geoffrey Allison its new owner, following the untimely death of Bill Smith. Allison won the over-2·7-litre sports car event from M. L. Mees in the ex-Bradnack 'Mark One' Cooper-Jaguar at the day's highest race-speed; the famous C-type also set best lap-time of the day.

Alex McMillan had already forsaken his D-type for a more wieldy Elva-Climax at this meeting; later he became a Cooper-Climax man.

One driver who made quite a success of his promotion from C-type to D-type this year was Peter Blond. Michael Head, having made that move the year before, was continuing to display an excellent combination of skill with restraint – for he was no youngster – in his handling of a 'Mark Two' Cooper-Jaguar, which proved well able to

hold off most 'club' Aston Martin DB3Ss, D-types, and C-types. During the year Cyril Wick's ex-Whitehead Cooper-Jaguar was sold to Richard Steed. Whitehead sold his second Cooper-Jaguar 'down under' and for the first time in five years did not have regular XK power for his motor-racing; his new sports car this year was a Maserati.

The HWM-Jaguar continued to improve and stay competitive, being among the fastest sports cars at national level, with Noel Cunningham-Reid's fine driving supplementing that of George Abecassis. The original HWM-Jaguar was now based in Scotland, in the hands of capable hill-climb specialist Ray Fielding.

A new special in 1956 was the Tojeiro-Jaguar, commissioned by XK120 driver John Ogier, but usually raced

Even by the mid-1950s, the smaller, mid-engined sports-racer was making its presence felt. This is the start of the 1956 Eastern Counties 100 at Snetterton. *Left to right,* **on the front row, are Noel Cunningham-Reid (HWM-Jaguar), Les Leston (Cooper-Coventry Climax), John Ogier (Tojeiro-Jaguar) and Peter Blond (D-type Jaguar). Leston 'pushed' the leading HWM driver into making a mistake, and won from Blond. The Tojeiro retired with steering failure.** (*Courtesy: P. Skilleter*)

by Dick Protheroe who scored a convincing win with it at Crystal Palace in August.

The first *Autosport* champion was Ken Rudd (AC–Bristol). John Dalton was runner-up in his very special Austin-Healey 100S with disc brakes, winning the over-2½-litre class from David Shale in a similar car and XK120 driver Michael Salmon who was now working in Jaguar's service department.

Left:
Michael Salmon at Brunton hill-climb in 1956.

Above:
Raymond Playford in his ex-Moss XK 120 coupé at a Goodwood BARC members meeting in 1956 – the year in which Playford founded the Jaguar Drivers' Club with (reluctant) works approval.

1957.

As Jaguar itself withdrew from sports car racing, a dynamic combination came on the British scene in the form of Archie Scott-Brown and the Lister–Jaguar which, in effect, rendered *all* other XK-powered vehicles obsolete.

Duncan Hamilton continued to race his own Jaguars successfully, and the best of the newcomers to the D-type was East Anglian Henry Taylor who drove the Murkett Brothers' ex-McMillan car (XKD 517) to victory at Snetterton in July. Runner-up was the best of the year's C-type drivers, John Bekaert, who handled the (now) somewhat scruffy ex-Johnson car, XKC 008 with tremendous fire.

Up to now, serious saloon car racing had been confined, largely, to the International Trophy meeting at Silverstone. Every year from 1952 to 1956 the big Jaguar Mk VII had won – though it had been a close-run thing last time. 1957 saw a change in the face of saloon car racing with the introduction of the compact '3·4', which was to form the basis for another five year period of Jaguar domination in which the opportunities to see touring cars in battle became ever greater. After Mike Hawthorn's win at Silverstone, the 3·4 began its life on the national scene with Tommy Sopwith and his friend Sir Gawaine Baillie taking first and second on Boxing Day at Brands Hatch.

1958.

On 5 April 1958, at the former air base of Full Sutton, near York, the British Racing and Sports Car Club held a race meeting that went almost unheeded at the time. It was, however, the day upon which a future World Champion first raced a competition car; not only did J. Clark win two races that day, but he became first man to lap an unbanked British circuit at over 100 mph with a sports car – namely, the D-type Jaguar. Jim Clark was to win twelve times in all in the former Murkett car (XKD 517) before the season was through; but his wins were at such minor meetings that only in retrospect is their merit fully appreciated.

Duncan Hamilton was as energetic as ever with his D-types; but this was his last season, not just because of his Le Mans accident but because of 1958's series of tragedies which included the deaths of Archie Scott-Brown, Peter

The XK140 and XK150 were not ideally suited to serious competition work, but they gave their owners a bit of pleasure. These shots show Duncan Hamilton making a rare appearance in his XK140 (AMOC Silverstone) in May 1958; and the XK150 of Rosemary Massey (later Mrs E. R. Protheroe), seen talking to another Jaguar driver, Eunice Griffin, at a sprint meeting of the same era.

Two stalwart officials of the JDC's early years were Eric Brown (*nearest camera*) and Albert Powell, shown sprinting their XK120s at Wellesbourne in 1958.

Saloons at Oulton Park, 1958: Tom Rowe in the ex-works Mk VII at Cascades; and Bob Berry in his lightened Mk VII (an ex-works special) chasing Bobby Parkes (3·4) through Old Hall corner.

Collins, Peter Whitehead, and Stuart Lewis-Evans. With Peter Blond co-driving, Hamilton came sixth in the TT at Goodwood in September, then hung up his famous red crash helmet. Bob Berry had given up driving the Broadhead D-type in 1957; now various drivers of varying skills were given a chance to drive it. Cyclist Reg Harris managed to show just how difficult a car the D-type could be, and soon returned (most successfully) to pedal power. Berry had now bought his special lightweight Mk VII saloon and was embarrassing potentially faster rivals with it.

Although also driving HWMs, Peter Blond continued to drive D-types with skill; but *the* man of the year on the club scene was indisputably John Bekaert who had moved up from the C-type to one of the works HWM–Jaguars when Abecassis put them both on the market at the end of 1957. (The other went to Roy Bloxham who promptly crashed it.) One of Bekaert's best wins was at Snetterton in August where he beat two of the year's top 'C' men: Michael Salmon (XKC 011) and Peter Sargent (XKC 038).

Saloon car racing took a step forward with the introduction by the BRSCC of a national championship. Fastest car/driver combination of the year was the Jaguar 3·4 of Tommy Sopwith who finished the season tying with Jack Sears, a regular class-winner with his Austin A105. For a special 'run-off', they were lent two Riley 1·5s. Sopwith won the first match race by 2·2 seconds: then they swopped cars for five more laps which Sears completed just over 4 seconds the quicker thus becoming champion by less than two seconds!

Few D-types were effective at top level by now, though *Ecurie Ecosse* occasionally brought one out to supplement its heavy Lister and Tojeiro programme.

Stars of the UK year, once again, were John Bekaert and Jim Clark, now both in Lister–Jaguars, the latter winning eleven times in the ex-Halford car which had been bought by Ian Scott-Watson for the Border Reivers team, to replace to D-type.

Cooper and Lotus sports cars had now 'grown-up' and not even Ivor Bueb in the works Lister–Jaguar could take them on. It was another sad year, with Mike Hawthorn's death early on, and then Ivor Bueb's in July. Bueb wasn't driving a Lister at the time, but the news led Brian Lister to accelerate his plan to pull out of racing altogether.

Production sports car racing was still not Jaguar's natural territory as long as the quicker Ace–Bristols and Austin–Healeys were around. In any case the *Autosport* championship continued to exclude C-types and D-types, whereas the Austin–Healey 100S was amongst several even rarer models that were considered fair game. Dick Protheroe had run the ex-Dalton 100S in the 1958 championship, and won his class despite losing his lead in the final – the Snetterton 3-hour race – when a stub axle broke. For 1959, Protheroe – who had now left the RAF and was running his own motor business – resurrected his old XK120 which stormed through the season consuming brake drums and much of the opposition. With the 1959 3-hour final nearly over, Protheroe was thundering along in a remarkable second place, headed only by Jim Clark in the Border Reivers Lotus Elite, when fading brakes prevented his Jaguar avoiding the tail of an MG which had appeared unexpectedly in its path. After a lengthy pit-stop, the damaged car continued, to finish fifth in the race, third in the championship, and first in class: an outstanding performance for such an aged machine and a highlight of a lean season for Jaguar enthusiasts.

1960.

With the 'E-type' still an open secret, and new categories such as Marque and ModSports as yet not established, the Jaguar club racer was still relying largely on the Lister.

John Bekaert again drove Derek Wilkinson's ex-Whitehead 3·8-litre Lister–Jaguar to some excellent wins, starting with the March meeting at Snetterton where it beat Michael Salmon's ex-works ex-*Ecurie Ecosse* D-type (XKD 504), and Gerald Ashmore's production model (XKD 510) in the over-3-litre class. They were all beaten over the line by the nimble Lotus XV-Climax 2-litre of Michael Taylor and Tony Marsh's new Cooper–Monaco which made best lap at 92·55 mph, compared with Bekaert's 91·52 mph.

Grand Touring events were becoming popular now, and there was one at this meeting. Russ Taylor led off in the former Protheroe XK 120 but was passed by Graham Warner's Lotus Elite and then rolled in spectacular fashion. (This car, GPN 635, was to survive harsh treatment from later owners, too.) The final order was: Warner (Elite), Foster (MGA twin-cam), G. Baillie (Elite), Staples (AC–Bristol) and Parker (Jaguar XK 150S). Don Parker's fifth placed car had the new triple-SU 'gold-top' XK

engine that would power the E-type a year later. Meantime, in the XK 150, Jaguar's road sports car had become less gainly for circuit use. Excellent as a road car, this model was rarely seen racing. One XK 140, however, was creating much interest in 1960, driven by the younger son of Howard Hobbs, whose 'Mechamatic' automatic transmission was interesting the motor industry. David Hobbs was a Daimler apprentice and, by adoption, about to become a Jaguar one; so it was appropriate that he should graduate from Morris Oxford to XK 140 to demonstrate his father's invention. This he did to good effect, winning several GT events before rolling the car at Oulton Park and moving on to a 'Mechamatic' Elite.

By now the 3·8 Mark Two had reached 'Division One' of saloon car racing. The 3·4 in its (retrospective) 'Mark 1' form continued to flourish, however, driven to most effect by Bill Aston, Albert Powell, and Peter Sargent.

Daimler apprentice David Hobbs scored four wins in 1960 with this 'Mechamatic'-equipped XK 140. On this occasion (NSCC, Silverstone) he was runner-up in the 'series production' car race to Chris Ashmore (Austin-Healey).

1961.

This year marked the first appearance of the E-type Jaguar. After the early success of the cars owned by Tommy Sopwith, John Coombs, and Peter Berry the first E-types to win at 'national' or 'club' level were those of Peter Sargent, Robin Sturgess and Jack Lambert.

The *Autosport* championship now admitted a wider variety of machinery. No Jaguars had starred in the 1960 table, but this year Michael Salmon showed what his D-type could do, winning the end-of-season 3-hour race at a canter from Ian Baillie's Aston Martin DBR1 and Peter Sargent's new E-type. Salmon was runner-up to John Sutton (Marcos) in the championship itself.

There were still Listers on the circuits, notably those of Bill de Selincourt and Gordon Lee. From 1960, hill-climber Phil Scragg had stayed with Jaguar engines, but moved from HWM to Lister chassis.

Sprinter Gordon Parker realised a personal ambition by taking best (car) time of the day at Brighton, covering the standing-start kilometre in 24·63 seconds with his supercharged HK–Jaguar special which had replaced his earlier creations – the Jaguette and Jaguara.

The club year ended on a high note with wins for Gordon Lee (ex-Border Reivers Lister–Jaguar) and Peter Sargent (3·4 saloon) at the first BRDC Clubman's Championship for which the full Silverstone Grand Prix circuit was obtained. Always a Jaguar circuit, this fast course was lapped by Dick Protheroe's 'new' XK 120 (CUT 6) at 90·84 mph – a speed equalled by the E-type of Robin Sturgess – but none of the E-types could do anything about the flying XK120. Final order in this GT race was: 1st, Graham Warner (Chequered Flag Lotus Elite); 2nd Dick Protheroe (Jaguar XK120); 3rd, Robin Sturgess (Jaguar E-type); 4th David Hobbs ('Mechamatic' Lotus Elite).

1962.

The year opened well in March with a win at Oulton Park for Bill de Selincourt's Lister–Jaguar, and one each for Peter Sargent (3·4) and Robin Sturgess (E-type). The next day at Snetterton Sturgess, whose family business was Jaguar distribution for Leicestershire, had changed his 1961 roadster for the fastback coupé which had taken somewhat longer to get into production in Coventry. Second to Sturgess was Ken Baker (in the roadster which was to be *the* most successful club-racing E-type of the

year), just ahead of David Hobbs in the 'Mechamatic' Elite.

Second to Roy Pierpoint (Lotus–Climax) in the sports-car race at that BRSCC Snetterton meeting was Peter Sutcliffe, the new owner of XKD 504. (Mike Salmon had replaced it with an Aston Martin DB4GTZ about which no-one in Coventry could complain, for Salmon had now left the Jaguar company.)

Soon E-types were becoming familiar and the XKs rarities around the circuits. It was Dick Protheroe who showed the clubmen the way, however, by recognising the problems of racing a road car and meeting them with ingenuity. His best win with the first of his distinctive E-types came at the AMOC Martini meeting at Silverstone in July, when he defeated Mike Salmon in the Zagato-bodied Aston Martin to win the GT race.

The six-year-old Jaguar Drivers' club was developing well and fielded two teams for the 750 MC's annual 6-hour relay at Silverstone; they came first and third, split by the Morgans. The winners were club chairman Eric Brown (3·8 XK120 modified), Peter Dodd (3·8 Mk2), Les Fowler (XK120). Don Smith (3·8 XK150S), Peter Woodroffe (3·8 Mk2), and Richard Wrottesley (Lister–Jaguar, ex-Gordon Lee). The variety was continued in the third-place team of Ken Baker (E-type), John Coundley (Lister–Jaguar), Malcolm Delingpole (E-type, ex-Sopwith), Lord Denbigh (E-type), Jack Lambert (E-type), and Keith Schellenberg (3·8 C-type XK 053).

On the hills, Philip Scragg changed from Lister–Jaguar to E-type and went on winning.

Ken Baker's E-type ended the year nicely with a victory over Salmon's Aston Martin and a new GT lap record at Brands Hatch on Boxing Day.

This XK 150, seen at Brafield in 1962, was quite successful in stock car racing.

1963.

Racing opened in early March at Snetterton, where Ken Baker continued his winning ways, leaving the Lotus Elites well behind – a prelude to another good season for Baker's E-type.

Later in the month, at the same venue, came Britain's first International meeting of the year at which Graham Hill produced the first victory for the E-type in its full 'lightweight' guise. The weather was diabolical, yet somehow Peter Sutcliffe's D-type worked its way up to fifth position before spinning into the bank. Another car to appear to be a write-off was Dick Protheroe's new coupé which lost third place in like manner. This was Protheroe's second E-type, an un-numbered car built from a bare shell. It was soon rebuilt and racing again, being taken over by a promising newcomer, Roger Mac, when Protheroe acquired yet another E-type (the 'low drag' car). Other new names at club level were those of John Dean and Brian Waddilove (E-types). Notable XK runners included Warren Pearce (XK150) and Rhoddy Harvey-Bailey whose XK120 had started life with Clemente Biondetti (*as recorded in detail in Vol. 1*). Peter Sutcliffe acquired a lightweight E-type and defeated Ken Baker with it at Snetterton in July.

On the more open circuits, the 3·8 could still hold its own but, more and more, the Fords – large and small – were showing every sign of 'taking over' saloon car racing.

While Coventry Climax was at the height of success in racing, an earlier Jaguar acquisition – Daimler was making news. Peter Westbury's hill-climb championship winning car, the Felday, used a supercharged 2½-litre Daimler engine. Daimler's V8s were never exploited as they might have been, though the SP250 sports car (originally known as the Dart) was light enough to be competitive in some classes. Dick Crosfield and Trevor Crisp were leading contenders with these strangely uncharacteristic but very sporting Daimlers. Crisp, who won the last Goodwood race of the year with his SP250, was with Jaguar Cars Ltd then; in 1980 he succeeded Harry Mundy as Jaguar's senior power unit engineer.

While Ken Baker and Roger Mac were dominating club GT races in the South and Midlands respectively, another E-type driver was being noticed in Northern England and in Scotland – his name: Jackie Stewart. His elder brother, Jimmy had been *Ecurie Ecosse*'s up-and-coming star driver ten years earlier. Now young Jackie was on the brink of an even more meteoric racing career.

Best Jaguar team result in the Silverstone six-hour relay race was third. At Oulton Park in late September, a Red Rose Motors team of 3·8 litre saloons won the five-hour event, the drivers being John Adams, Charles Bridges, Michael MacDowel and Jackie Stewart. Fifth in this interesting and well-handicapped event came a team which included the well-driven D-types of Gerald Ashmore (XKD 510), Bill Rigg (XKSS 722) and Peter Skidmore (XKD 406).

At Brands Hatch on Boxing Day, Ken Baker (E-type) and Dick Stoop (Porsche) spun away their chances, giving victory to John Dean in *his* E-type.

Mallory Park had a Boxing Day meeting, too. Just beaten on the last lap of the GT race here (by Malcolm

Wayne's Elva) was the spectacularly-driven E-type coupé of David Cunningham. This car was painted in White and Blue in honour of its owner's unrelated American namesake; it was in fact the original Protheroe E-type.

1964.

Early season winners were John Dean and David Cunningham, while Rob Beck was soon doing well with a very special Protheroe-prepared XK120.

Roger Mac's brilliance was reflected in his acquisition of the former Atkins E-type, the first 'lightweight' to appear regularly in club racing. Jackie Stewart (Coombs LWE) beat Mac at Crystal Palace however.

The Brighton Speed Trials provided some interesting comparisons between Jaguar competition models. Mrs Patricia Coundley took her long-nose D-type through the standing-start Kilometre in 24·47 seconds – quicker than Jack Playford in the Sargent lightweight E-type (25·25) and Tom Gibson's 3·8 litre C-type (25·30). David Beckett and Ken Wilson (3·8 Lister–Jaguars) got below 25 seconds but were slower than Pat Coundley.

Ferraris and Cobras were beginning to make their presence felt in club racing, but in hill-climbs Philip Scragg and his lightweight E-type (LWE) dominated the sports touring GT classes; his new record time of 37·35 seconds at Shelsley Walsh was better, even, than any of the sports-racers at that August meeting.

Saloon Jaguars were beginning to have a lean time, but

Robin Beck leads Jackie Stewart – the eventual winner in Eric Brown's silver XK 120 drophead – away from the start of a 1964 JDC Crystal Palace race.

the Red Rose Team of 3·8 Mk2s did well in the Oulton Park 5-hour relay once again, though with their handicap the Jaguars came second to the Minis.

1965.

Peter Lumsden won the fastest race of the day at a Goodwood 'clubbie' early in the season, the LWE averaging 93·51 mph to beat the Cobras of John Sparrow and Neil Dangerfield.

Up north, a new name – Brian Redman – had a brilliant season with Red Rose Motors' latest acquisition, the former Coombs lightweight E-type, sweeping all before him at Oulton Park and elsewhere. At Silverstone, he was beaten by Ron Fry (250 LM); but it says much for Redman that he kept the Ferrari in sight at the BRDC Clubman's meeting. Redman's 1965 record was that one second, one retirement, and thirteen wins!

Peter Mould was not in the same class as a driver, but he did have the odd win in the ex-Atkins LWE.

Of the 'non-lightweight' E-types, tuning specialist Warren Pearce's was most consistent in the south, John Cuff's in the north.

A shopping 4·2-litre E-type made a good impression in the Guards 1000 experimental long-distance endurance race for production cars but was only third at the end, due to pad wear and consequently long pit-stops. None of the E-types was prepared for such a long race, which is why they all lost.

For the third year running, Jaguars (E-types this time), did well in the Oulton Park 5-hour relay. Red Rose Motors chief Charles Bridges shared this victory with Brian Redman, Richard Bond, and John Cuff.

Rhoddy Harvey-Bailey was still doing well with the old

XK120 and later in the season was given the occasional drive in Robert Gordon's ex-Protheroe fastback LWE special.

1966.

Philip Scragg was awarded an OBE in the New Year honours list *not* for hill-climbing so well for so long, but for exporting man-made fibre.

Brian Redman having moved to faster formulas, Charles Bridges of Red Rose Motors did most of the driving of the ex-Coombs LWE himself this year, starting with a convincing win at Snetterton in March. At Oulton Park on Easter Saturday Bridges won two races, second place both times going to none other than Brian Redman who borrowed John Cuff's E-type (a coupé with some LW components) for another Jaguar fling. John Scott-Davies rolled the special-bodied ex-Lumsden LWE on the second lap of his first race with it, but two days later he was racing it again. In fact, he came second at that Easter Monday Silverstone meeting behind Harvey-Bailey who was using the former Protheroe 'low drag' car. Bob Vincent was the year's other LWE star driver in club GT racing.

Non-LWE drivers were now able to modify their ordinary E-types considerably for the Marque category. John Quick, Warren Pearce, Tony Shaw, Tony Knight, and Jack Hayden (Len Hayden's brother) were all winners but there was a definite turning point in mid-season, when Keith Holland (E-type) beat Gerry Marshall (TVR) and John Quick (E-type). All of a sudden Holland became the E-man to beat; his car, formerly Tony Knight's, was owned by Alastair Crawford. Once again there was a long-distance race at Brands Hatch and once again a Jaguar led. Jack Oliver did the first 3-hour stint, and was ahead of all the Cobras, GT40s, and LMs when the owner Ken Baker took over and promptly spun into the bank. Bob Bondurant and David Piper (Cobra) won.

The 3·8 saloon was by no means finished as a saloon racer, and Albert Betts and Maurice Runham often managed to hold off the majority of Anglias and other such wolves in sheep's clothing.

While there were opportunities to race historic single-seaters, obsolete sports cars of the post-war era were being ignored or just forgotten – at least, so it seemed to some people, including arch-enthusiast and photographer Guy Griffiths. Having acquired a C-type (XKC 011) of his own, he found that there was no organisation for the owners of similar vehicles. Helped by his daughter Penny – the keen sprinter of a Jaguar-powered Healey Silverstone – he created the 'Griffiths Formula'. The 'Formula' was intended to encourage the preservation and use of competition sports cars of the 1945 to 1955 era (the latter date being movable, to bring in newer cars as they too, became obsolete).It was not meant to be taken *too* seriously.

The first race in the name of the Griffiths Formula took place at the Frazer Nash and Porsche Owners Club's Castle Combe race meeting on 14 May 1966 – the very day on which Jack Brabham won the first 3-litre Formula 1 race to be held at Silverstone. To minimise formalities it was arranged, via Betty Haig, for the Griffiths Formula to function under the auspices of the Frazer Nash Car Club. The promotions committee represented the interests of Allard, Aston Martin, Healey, Ferrari, HRG, Porsche, and Jaguar owners, although other marques were made welcome individually.

Hard-driving Northern collector Neil Corner won that Castle Combe race with ease in his long-nose D-type (XKD 504) from a rather thin field; but it was a start.

1967.

As from the spring of 1967 the 'Griffiths Formula for Historic Sports Cars' was run simply as a register, with an open-ended list of eligible cars of a type 'not catered for by any other club'.

The TT race was now for touring cars only. Although it was now part of the European Touring Challenge, it had lost much of its aura as Britain's longest-established motor race. (It would find it again.)

It was thus something of a coup for the historic sports car movement – still being eschewed by the Vintage Sports Car Club – when the RAC granted the Griffiths Formula Register not only a parade but a race of its own in support of the once-classic Tourist Trophy at Oulton Park in May. The Register's secretary Penny Griffiths took part with her father's D-type (XKD 511), and the competition secretary Jeremy Broad brought his early Cooper–Jaguar. Star of the parade, however, was the rarely-seen D-type XKD 501, *Ecurie Ecosse*'s first Le Mans winner, dem-

Start of the 'Griffiths' historic movement – at the TT meeting, Oulton Park, in May 1967. Winner Neil Corner is flanked by Peter Skidmore (33) and Rupert Glydon (Aston Martin).

Above:

John Harper (Cooper-Jaguar) leads Peter Skidmore (D-type) and David Cottingham in the ex-Bob Berry lightweight XK 120 in a miserable 'Griffiths' race, Silverstone, October 1967. (*Courtesy: P. Skilleter*)

Michael Wright with the ex-works low-drag E-type at Weston-super-Mare speed trials, 1967. (*Courtesy: P. & R. Woodley*)

onstrated (in the absence of Ninian Sanderson) by Graham Birrell.

The race itself was an easy victory for Neil Corner (XKD 504) followed by Rupert Glydon (Aston Martin DB3S) and John Harper in the ex-Sopwith Cooper–Jaguar which he shared with John McCartney–Filgate. Peter Skidmore came fourth, ahead of 'Dickie' Bird whose Le Mans AC Ace overtook the DB3S of Clive Aston on the last lap.

Several other race organisers listed classes for Griffiths registered cars, mostly at Castle Combe in the south and Croft in the north. Leading Jaguar drivers were Corner, McGrath and Skidmore, the latter driving smoothly to beat the spectacular Glydon twice at the Wiltshire circuit. At the end of the season Glydon switched to the ex-works, ex-Hamilton C-type, XKC 038, in search of more power.

Already the seriousness with which owners were tackling their racing was beginning to worry Guy Griffiths – but it is no easy thing to control the degree or type of enthusiasm in *any* area of competition. The 'formula' he created would not remain 'Griffiths' for long. Money and politics now made the scene a fast-changing one. This also meant that thousands of people could now watch and hear those great sports cars in action at national and international meetings once again. The wheel had turned full circle. . . .

Meantime, back in the 'modern' world of 1967, Keith Holland was again the leading E-type driver. It was a highly competitive year in which John Lewis, Warren Pearce and John Quick, were all fighting hard, too. Jack Hayden, Edward Nelson, Tony Shaw, and Henryc Synowiec were winners, too. (Nelson's car was entered by the just-widowed Rosemary Protheroe.)

The LWEs were being seen more in sprints and hill-climbs than in races. Farmer-turned-Jaguar-tuner Michael Wright now had the 'low drag' car and was a regular class winner. His time of 36·13 seconds at Shelsley Walsh was a class record which looked even more impressive when compared with Tony Marsh's new outright record of 31·23, set at the same (June) meeting with the Marsh–GM special. Another LWE hill-climber was Penny Woodley (*née* Griffiths) with the smart ex-Atkins car, which always retained its general slim-line looks in this era when tyre widths were increasing so rapidly in many branches of the sport; described in *Motoring News* as a 'consistently fast driver of this powerful car' she, too, was to prove capable of sub-37-second times at Shelsley Walsh.

On the circuits, Bob Vincent's LWE won the over-2·5-litre class in the *Motoring News* GT championship.

1968.
ProdSports, ModSports, Special Sports – the category changes were endless, and it is certainly not an object of this book to analyse the development of club racing formulas.

The fact remains that the advent of the wide tyre gave an excellent opportunity for 'modified standard' (as opposed to the sophisticated lightweight) Jaguar E-types to win races in an unsophisticated way and yet provide great entertainment. Keith Holland moved away from large sports cars, and the single-driver domination of the previous season was now replaced by a group of talented

Roger Woodley races for a forgotten utensil as his wife-to-be – Penny Griffiths, wearing 'Santa Pod' insignia – gets aboard the ex-Atkins lightweight E-type during a sunny SUNBAC meeting at Silverstone, 1968. (*Courtesy: Guy Griffiths*)

and experienced drivers spearheaded by the trio of John Lewis, Warren Pearce, and John Quick. Their E-types rampaged around the circuits, being likened by at least one reporter to a herd of bull-elephants. Only on tight, wet tracks could the faster 'Spridgets' and the Austin-Healey 3000s of John Chatham, Stuart Hands or John Gott get anywhere near the galumphing Jaguars. Newer to the E-type scene were Rob Schroeder and Alistair Cowin. The latter put his cat among the pigeons when he gave Tony Lanfranchi a drive at Brands Hatch in July. (Perhaps he wanted to see just how fast his car could be driven, for he had been beaten there by Quick, Schroeder, and Pearce the month before.) Again Quick and Schroeder got away first. It was wet, and Lanfranchi harrassed Schroeder into crashing; then he 'nudged' Quick who promptly spun. Lanfranchi won from a recovered but angry Quick. Things could certainly be tough, even when it was meant to be racing for fun.

John Filbee, Michael Loveday, Tony Shaw, Henryc Synowiec, John Wilson and Edward Worswick were all E-type winners in 1968. Worswick's coupé was the former John Cuff car. The amazing 3·8 engined 'Mark 1' saloon of Albert Betts showed *it* could still win, too. 'Coventry should give him a medal,' declared *Motoring New*'s Ted Wilkinson, after Betts had taken yet another victory *and* fastest lap at Snetterton in July.

1969.
Having seen the old year out with a Boxing Day win, John Quick returned to Brands Hatch to win again at Easter, from Michael Franey in the Ex-John Wilson E-type. Quick's car was supposedly giving a full 300 bhp, so it is not surprising that his race average exceeded the Prod Sports lap record. (He set a new one for the long circuit at 89·33 mph). Soon afterwards, in Quick's absence, Franey won a race on the Brands Hatch short circuit, creating a ProdSports lap record of 80·87 mph. Still in the month of

Modified six-cylinder E-types were always popular club race cars. Two of the most successful were those of John Quick (101, Brands Hatch, 1969); and John Harper (149, Silverstone 1971).

April, however, Quick came back to beat Franey and push the lap record up to 81·76 mph. Among the familiar 'E-men' still going strong this season were John Burbidge, John Filbee, Warren Pearce, Tony Shaw and Edward Worswick.

Shelsley Walsh, the hill-climbers mecca, saw Michael Wright in the 'low drag' E-type snatch the class record from John Macklin (Cobra) with a time of 35·58 seconds in June, improving to 35·34 in July. Other good times were put up by Peter Skidmore's D-type (40·38) and Penny Woodley's E-type (38·11) – the latter being a modified standard coupé, her valuable LWE now being used more rarely. Indeed, by this time, it was unusual to see an LWE in the cut-and-thrust of racing. In its day 'light-weight' may have been presented in Coventry as an E-type in very general terms, whereas it was now recognised as an historic model of highly individual character.

Races for obsolete cars were not yet generally run at international meetings, but Shell's Bob Gathercole did organise a significant event at the 1969 British Grand Prix, with an 'Historic and Post-Historic' parade in which the Jaguar marque was well-represented.

Another sign of the times was the presence of John Harper's 3·8-litre XK120, and at the Jaguar Drivers Club's Bank Holiday meeting it showed its dual role by coming second to Neil Corner's D-type in the 'pre-1961' sports car race, ahead of Brian Croot's Allard–Jaguar (née Sphinx), and then going on to win the ProdSports race from the Austin-Healey 3000s of John Gott and Peter Smith, and the MGB of former Jaguar man Bill Nicholson of motor cycling fame. Harper had been racing Jaguar-powered cars for several years already; and he was still racing them in the 1980s.

The late sixties and early seventies saw considerable D-type revitalisation, as these Crystal Palace pictures illustrate. Michael McGrath and Peter Skidmore leading Brian Croot's ex-Sopwith Jaguar-powered Allard-based Sphinx in 1969. The 1970 startline shot shows more real D-types about to do battle, winner was Neil Corner (107) from Willie Green in the ex-Skidmore car (105) newly acquired by Bamford via Hexagon and Measham. Peter Brown (108) spun off in the other Bamford D-type, letting Martin Morris up to third in the Melville-Smith car (109). (*Courtesy: P. Skilleter*)

The 1970s and 1980s.

The 1970s heralded more changes in club racing.

Liberal ModSports regulations permitted even wilder interpretations and a feature of the new decade was the regular appearance of John N. Pearson's XK120 beating the E-types soundly. This XK120 was in fact so much modified that only the shape of its glass-fibre shell ensured recognition of how it started life. John Harper's driving of the Forward Enterprises E–type in 1971/2 showed that Jaguar was still the leading marque in ModSports racing; but as the seventies progressed, so did the speed of the Porsche Carrera, the Lotus Elan and other nimbler, more modern cars.

A little bit of history was made on 25 April 1971 when, within a month of the public announcement, the V12-engined E-type Series Three won its class in its first competitive event, the Lothian Car Club's hill-climb at Doune, near Stirling. The driver was former Jaguar apprentice Tom Sleigh whose new coupé – could it have been the

'demonstrator' from Rossleigh, the family motor business? – had its throttle come adrift on the first run. On his second class-winning, run Sleigh flew up the tight course luridly. 'It still sends shivers down the spine,' wrote *Motoring News*'s Scottish correspondent Ross Finlay reporting on the performance.

On the whole, however, the V12 E-type did not become a competition car east of the Atlantic. The notable exceptions were the 2 + 2 coupés of Guy Bedington and Peter Taylor. These were vastly different cars. Bedington's was a full ModSports machine with Tecalemit–Jackson fuel injection; though very fast, it never quite made the grade against such opposition as the aforementioned Pearson XK120 special. Jaguar engineer Taylor drove his virtually unmodified Series Three in the 1974 production sports car championship and won.

It was on the historic front, however, that Jaguar was to be prominent throughout the seventies and by the end of the decade, there were championships galore.

It all began to become large-scale when the JCB excavator company decided to sponsor a championship for the Historic Sports Car Club from 1971. Anthony Bamford was the instigator, and he was joined, subsequently, by another enthusiastic collector, the late Nigel Moores. The series was effectively revived in 1978, after a lull, by the Lloyds and Scottish finance group. Drivers of Jaguar D-

types and Lister–Jaguars won their classes regularly.

As had often happened in the past, the less pecunious enthusiasts were finding themselves left out. The answer? – more championships!

Significant to Jaguar owners were the 'Thoroughbred Sports' and 'Classic Saloon' series from the mid-seventies.

The first thoroughbred sports championship (sponsored by Charles Spreckley in 1974) brought out some fine not-*too*-modified XK120s. John Harper won his class on equal points with championship winner Reg Woodcock (Triumph TR2) who won again in 1975 – still virtually unassailable within his class. Different sponsors kept the idea alive, notably the Aston Martin Owners Club. A star driver in the late seventies was David Preece in the XK120 prepared by Messrs Oldham and Crowther.

The 'Classic Saloons' movement was carefully conceived to keep out the 3·4 Jaguar which had so dominated saloon racing from 1957. The founders were Jaguar MkVII enthusiasts Peter Deffee and John James. First Bob Meacham, then Bill Pinckney, and later Roger Andreason ensured that most victories went to Jaguar, their 2·4s often being chased hard by Lancias (in the early days, from 1975), and subsequently by Ford Zephyrs – with Graig Hinton towering spectacularly over them with his MkVII, a regular class winner.

In 1974 the Coventry company's own increasing loss of identity led some rebels to try and find ways of keeping

The Two Pearsons – Stars of Silverstone. In 1970 John N. Pearson was lapping the Silverstone club circuit in 1 min. 4.2 sec. with his plastic-bodied XK 120 – probably the fastest modified sports car of its type – seen here passing the late Frank Eaton's XK 150. The other John Pearson – proprietor of a restoration workshop at Whittlebury within earshot of Silverstone – leads fellow-specialist John Harper in a 1975 Thoroughbred Sports Car race. The term 'thoroughbred' indicated an attempt to restore some degree of authenticity to the race specification of historic production cars. Harper, driving the LHD Forward Engineering prepared XK 120, won Jaguar's first Driver of the Year award in 1974. (*Courtesy: P. Skilleter*)

Keeping historic wheels turning: Paul Kelly (of Nigel Moores's Longbacon Engineering), John Pearson of Whittlebury (*in jacket*), and one of the Moores D-types. (*Courtesy: Paul Skilleter*)

'Jaguar' alive – for they felt that every aspect of the firm, even down to its name, was under threat of extinction.

The Jaguars Drivers Club, led by Peter Sargent and David Harvey, responded by using every opportunity to make BL's policy-makers aware of just how strongly Jaguar owners felt about the individuality of 'their' marque.

At Browns Lane, it was decided: another way of showing that a heart still beats within would be to create a 'Jaguar Driver of the Year' award. Up to 1974 it would almost-certainly have been an E-type driver: or either of the two John Pearsons, of metal and plastic XK120 fame. In any case, most of these champions have been drivers of one or another type of 'historic' Jaguar.

Drivers of the Year so far have been as follows:

1974. **John Harper** was the first winner of the award, for his superb driving of XK120 and Lister–Jaguar.

V12 extremes of 1974: Guy Bedington tests the new wheels and tyres of his highly-modified fuel-injected V12 E-type at Woodcote Corner, Silverstone; Jaguar engineer Peter Taylor at Brands Hatch, on his way to becoming production sports car champion in his Series Three coupé.

1975. **David Ham,** who first made his name as an Aston Martin man, had begun racing back in 1960 with a Singer Le Mans. Now he was driving very quickly indeed in his Lister–Jaguar, maintained by Lister engineers Colin Crisp and George Tyrrell, with power unit preparation – like Harper's cars – by Ron Beaty of Forward Engineering.

1976. **Graig Hinton.** Not only did Hinton win his class with the Mk VII; he ran several cars in the new 'Classic Saloon' series under the lengthy banner of 'Lord Bradford's Weston Park Racing Team', sometimes encouraging journalists to race one of the cars, thus giving good publicity to the Formula.

1977. **Bill Pinckney** returned to racing after an absence of fifteen years. Back in 1961 he had co-driven with David Hobbs (Lotus) to a class-win at the Nürburgring. Now, in 1977, his 2·4 Jaguar dominated classic saloon car racing.

Below left:
The Jaguar Driver of the Year award can go to users of any Jaguar-*powered* vehicle. David Ham (Lister-Jaguar) was the 1975 winner.

Below:
1977 Jaguar Driver of the Year Bill Pinckney (2·4) receives his trophy from Jaguar's honorary president, the late Sir William Lyons.

Above:
Martin Morris (1978 Driver of the Year) wins Monaco historic race five years later. (*Courtesy: Autocar*)

Opposite top:
John Harper (*left*) with the Connaught-Jaguar which brought him his second 'Driver' title in 1982.

Opposite bottom:
Neil Johnson of Jaguar with Roger Mac (1981 Driver of the Year) and the John Lewis E-type at Hockenheim, 1983. (*Courtesy: J. Lewis*)

1978. **Martin Morris** had been doing great things with his rebuilt D-type (XKC 404) for many years, and occasionally with his C-type (XKC 052), too. Now it seemed an appropriate time to recognise his efforts.

1979. **Michael Bowler,** first editor of *Thoroughbred and Classic Cars*, won the FIA (European) historic championship with his Lister–Jaguar, maintained by Jim and Tim Abbott of Weedon. The 3·8-litre engine, which Bowler used again with similar success in 1980 and 1981, was prepared by Forward Engineering.

1980. **Fred Baker** is an Englishman resident in the USA. His driving of Ohio-based Gran Turismo Jaguar's old six cylinder E-type brought him a US National class championship.

1981. **Roger Mac** was the winner of Grovewood's top award, as up-and-coming driver of 1964. His experience then included ex-Protheroe and Atkins lightweight E-types. Soon afterwards he had two bad single-seater accidents in quick succession and gave up racing. In 1981 he returned to dominate and win his class in the new 'post-historic' sports car series, driving John Lewis's re-created E-type, and was still driving Jaguars several years later.

1982. **John Harper** won the award for the second time, for his superb handling of the born-again ex-Leslie Marr Connaught–Jaguar. (This was to be the final Lloyds' and Scottish championship year.)

1983. **Ron Lea,** who had been very active on the organisational side, too, had a very good racing year with his V12 E-type 2+2 and took the title for his overall accomplishments.

1984. **Bob Smiley,** a giant-killing SCCA driver with his XK140 (fatally injured while working under another car in 1986), was the second US-based winner of the Jaguar Driver of the Year award.

1985. **Stephen Langton** (Lister–Jaguar) was the posthumous winner. He had died in one of the last races of the season, while racing his Connaught.

462

1986. **Mark Trenoweth** of Queensland took the award south of the equator for the first time as a result of his outstanding performances in Australia with the ex-John McCormack XJ-S 'silhouette' car.

Club racing continued to flourish, although there was less chance than ever to see (for example) D-types racing. It was a great pity that nothing seemed to be happening to permit similar cars (built correctly, using genuine parts where possible, but without identity numbers) to go racing. Apparently, the originals were too valuable to race anymore. One-make, one-type, and inter-marque championships kept the interest in older cars alive and, for 1987, the Historic Sports Car Club and the publication *Classic and Sportscar* were planning a new championship designed to appeal to the owners of genuine road-going sports cars, which looked promising for E-type owners.

It is, unfortunately, impossible to pay tribute by name to the scores of other people who have spent their money, time, energy, skill and patience to help keep Jaguars and other Jaguar-engined marques to the fore in club racing – nor to all those who have used Jaguar power for sand-racing, stock-car racing, tractor-pulling, power-boating, aviating and in fact almost every form of motoring competition. Mind you, many of them have had occasion to pay tribute to Jaguar, too – and thank goodness a Jaguar company exists once again to respond.

Racing Around the World

The pictures on the following pages have been selected to show Jaguar power in a variety of racing situations all around the globe.

Below:
Probably the winner of more sprint awards with the same car – close on 500! – than anyone, veteran Herbert Shepherd was still competing in his ex-Scragg 4·2-litre E-type in 1986. This picture was taken at Curborough near his home town, Stafford.

Bottom:
The E-type remained the most raceable Jaguar sports car for the eighties. Here the JDC's team (less Mike Tye) is seen after winning the 1986 inter-marque championship against Porsche, Aston Martin, and AC Cobra teams. No wonder Chris Shipton, Ron Lea, Martin Wheatley, David Moore and Malcolm Hamilton look happy. (*Courtesy: Alan Hewitt*)

XKs around the World

Many great drivers have cut their teeth on Jaguars, including Volvo's 1958 European rally champion, Gunnar Andersson, seen competing in a Swedish speed event with his XK 120 a few years earlier.

Left:

Early in 1954, a crew led by Queensland distributor 'Geordie' Anderson won the 24-hour race at Mount Druitt, Sydney, in her XK 120 coupé. Not long afterwards she did this to it during practice for the Australian GP meeting at Southport, Queensland – fortunately, not doing herself too much harm. (The Grand Prix itself was won by Lex Davison's Jaguar-powered HWM single-seater.)

Bob O'Brien, chairman of Florida's Carteret Bank (sponsor of historic car racing), competes in the February 1987 Miami 'vintage' race in his 1953 XK 120 fixed-head coupe. (*Courtesy: Graig Hinton*)

Above:
Purchased by Walter Hill of Florida from the estate of the late Charles Rainville, this XK 120 (chassis 670001) was driven by Peter Walker at Silverstone in 1949 and Leslie Johnson at Palm Beach Shores in January 1950. (*See vol. I.*) Here Hill takes part in a less serious historic event in 1986 – at Palm Beach, once more! (*Courtesy: G. Hinton*)

Left and opposite Top:
1984 Jaguar Driver of the Year the late Robert Smiley with his wife Marie at their Northport, NY, home. He had reached the culmination of many competitive years with a flag-to-flag victory at Bridgehampton in his XK 140. Shortly afterwards, a deer leapt into the cockpit of his Lola at the same circuit and Smiley was badly hurt. He recovered but did not race the Jaguar again. In 1986, fate struck an even worse blow when the Lola crushed him while he was working under it at home. The action picture of Bob Smiley and his 'old green monster' (as he called this racing Jaguar) was taken at Pocono in 1982. (*Courtesy: K. Miller*)

Right:
Two unusual XK 150 pictures: the coupé of Jean-Claude Cohade winning the 1958 wet weather *Grand Prix de Staouéli, Algeria*, for GT cars ... and a rare XK 150S roadster laying the dust in an Austrian rally.

466

Inset Above:
Mrs Pat Coundley (D-type) taking part in Belgium's 'national day of records', May 1964.

Above:
There is a long history of Jaguars and Jaguar-powered specials in Australia, and it is well covered in the written works of Les Hughes of Queensland and Terry McGrath of Western Australia. This picture was taken in 1960 at the marvellous Mount Panorama circuit, Bathurst, NSW, where the Jaguar marque would score its greatest Antipodean victory a quarter of a century later. In 1960, there were several races on the first weekend of October, one of them being won by Bill Pitt in a 3·4 saloon. The sports car race (shown here) was won by Frank Matich (Lotus XV-Climax) from Doug Chivas in the Leaton Motors Jaguar D-type, chassis number XKD 526. Other D-types were driven by Jack Murray (XKD 532) and David Finch (XKD 520), but third place went to John Ampt (ex-Whitehead/Jones/Phillips Cooper-Jaguar) seen here at the end of the notorious Conrod Straight, holding off Bob Jane (Maserati 300S).

Opposite Top:
In the USA, it was common practice to try and keep the D-type competitive into the 1960s by replacing its XK engine with a GM V8 unit. This is a typical installation. There were very few note-worthy successes.

Right:
Tribute to the 'D' has been paid in many places and in many ways. These 'bargain' Jaguar-powered Specials provided Tasmanian racegoers with highly entertaining racing during the 1970s, driven by David Dungey (*left*) and Tom Hey of Hobart.

E-types in the USA

Opposite page top:
Most successful SCCA Jaguar racer of the sixties was Merle Brennan whose Huffaker-prepared E-type won 39 races out of 41. It is seen here in the hands of Clint Wells, on parade at Laguna Seca in 1976. (*Courtesy: P. Ryan*)

Opposite page bottom:
Glenn Bunch of Newport News, Virginia, raced this UK-built V12 E-type in the USA. Forward Engineering fitted it with a six-carburetter 5·8-litre engine developing a claimed 410bhp – recalled as being sufficient for John Harper to lap the Silverstone outer circuit in about 1min. 38 sec. on the day this picture was taken.

Left:
Ron Beaty of Forward Engineering working on another V12 E-type with (Weber) breathing apparatus similar to that fitted to Glenn Bunch's car.

Below:
Bob Millstein bought this early E-type as a $300 wreck in 1974, rebuilt it as a road-going racer, and took it to events in North-Eastern USA. The car performed especially well at the VSCCA hill-climbs at Mount Equinox, Vermont (where this picture was taken), finishing second overall in 1984, beaten only by a Cooper. (*Courtesy: K. Miller*)

Below and top far left:
Prepared by Gran Turismo Jaguar of Eastlake, Ohio, this E-type is by far the most competitive XK-engined Jaguar of modern times. Its driver, Englishman Freddy Baker, was Jaguar's 1980 Driver of the Year, following his national SCCA championship victory against the cream of modern C-production sports cars. The pictures were taken at Mid-Ohio in 1979 during and after one of Baker's record-breaking drives. (*Courtesy: P. Lane, Jr*)

Centre top:
One of his arch-rivals from the Nissan camp, actor Paul Newman, congratulates Freddy Baker after another victory for the Jaguar driver in 1982. (*Courtesy: R. Snelbaker*)

Top right:
This XJ-S, bought by Bob How in the UK in the late 1970s, began a trend for this model in Australian touring car racing. (*Courtesy: Les Hughes*)

Above and below:
Jaguar's own wind-tunnel research from the mid-1970s was made available to John Goss whose Australian XJ-S racer first appeared in 1980 and received some backing from Leyland Australia (later called Jaguar Rover Australia). Despite further help from Group 44 and TWR, the car was not as successful as expected. However, Goss did take victory at Bathurst for the TWR team when Group A came to Australia in 1985; he entered on his own again in 1986, but did not achieve the same lap speeds or reliability.

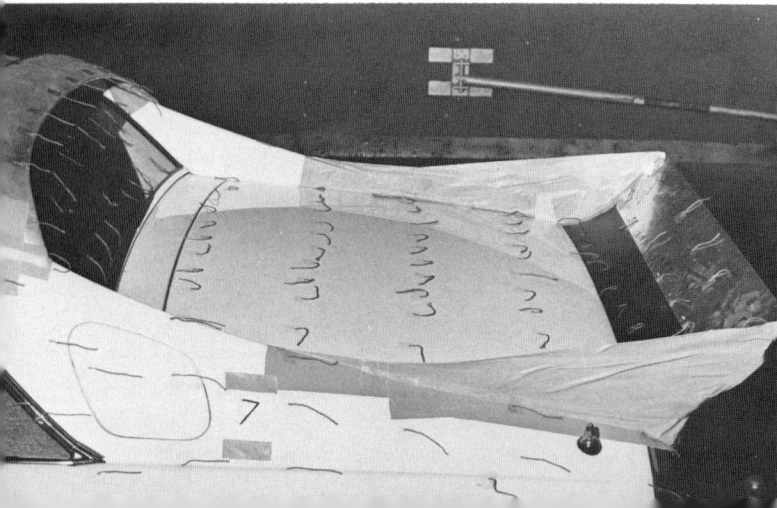

Above and below:

Another Australian with very definite plans was John McCormack, whose programme fell apart after he was injured badly in a road accident. He visited Coventry under the aegis of Leyland Australia in early 1980, and built this very professional XJ-S to Australia's 'GT' formula. After his recovery (later that year), McCormack prepared the car for other drivers including Colin Bond and Alfie Costanzo, but they were never successful. The car and some spares were sold to Brisbane enthusiast Mark Trenoweth, who continued to develop the car with McCormack's help. Trenoweth did better and better and was declared 1986 Jaguar Driver of the Year. These photographs, by courtesy of Les Hughes, show McCormack at work and Constanzo at Calder in 1981.

Appendix Three

Personal Experience

As was done in Volume 1, I have selected here contemporary stories by the drivers themselves. Bob Berry and Jack Fairman were kind enough to write them specially for the apprentices magazine, of which I was editor at the time. A.W.

'Private Owner – 1955/56'
by R. E. Berry (reprinted from the *Jaguar Apprentices' Magazine*)

On the Jaguar stand at Earls Court in 1954 there was shown for the first time a certain motor car of small aspect and considerable power, examples of which had finished second at Le Mans and first at Reims, besides a less profitable outing in the Tourist Trophy. All this had not gone unnoticed by a certain Lancashireman involved in the running of several extensive businesses – scrapmetal, haulage contracting, coach operator and garage proprietor – to name but a few. Thus endowed with a sufficiency of worldly wealth J. C. Broadhead had, for a few years past, bought Jaguars and Frazer Nash cars and loaned them out to promising local drivers. In this way, maintains 'J.C.', you get all the fun of racing without the dangers involved – quite apart from the fact that he is rather too large to fit comfortably into a D-type – a danger that is rapidly overtaking one of his drivers.

Knowing Jack Broadhead but vaguely, I was not unduly surprised to see him inspecting the show D-type and holding an earnest conversation with one of the taller members of the Jaguar staff who is principally concerned with competition matters. The conversation went something like this:

Broadhead: (after close inspection of car). Ee, that looks a right good 'un.

England: Yes, they go very well a big improvement on the earlier cars.

Broadhead: Sithee lad, I should like one of them. How much? Thee can have a cheque now. No messing about, I want it quick for next year.

England: Well it's a bit difficult Jack. We have started to make a few but I don't know when you will get one as they are mostly intended for the States.

Broadhead: ... the States, what about one of them old ones from last season? We could do one of them up quite easily and I could pick it up next week. No messing about now, let's get cracking.

England: Steady on. Leave it with me and I'll see what can be done.

Jack Broadhead's conversation with me was also rather brief:

Broadhead: Sithee lad, I'm getting one of them new things – a D-type.

Berry: Really?

Broadhead: Aye, wouldst thee like to drive it?

Berry: Yes, but I've not much experience.

Broadhead: No matter – tha'll learn. That's that settled then!

Lunch completed, 'J.C.' returned to Manchester, and I to the Exhibition feeling quite pleased with life.

Further negotiations resulted in a promise that we could have one of the light alloy frame cars after the Silverstone Meeting, 1955; 'our' car OKV 2 being driven there by Tony Rolt. The race was spent in an agony of suspense in case Rolt should damage the car but we need not have worried for, after leading

476

Watched by his fiancée Avril, Bob Berry settles into 'his' D-type for the first time at the BRDC Silverstone meeting in May 1955 when Tony Rolt drove it for the works, immediately prior to its sale to John Broadhead.

the field for a few laps, he gradually dropped back, the car appearing to be rather out of breath. A week later, in exchange for a piece of paper produced by a well-known bank, OKV 2 joined the *Ecurie* Broadhead.

John Lea, who had done such a magnificent job on the XK120 (*see Vol. 1*), agreed to look after the car and his first job was to find the lost power. As we wanted to run the car in the Johnson Trophy Race on Whit-Monday, there was no time to take the head off so, apart from a general check-over, the car went to Goodwood in the same condition as at Silverstone. Duncan Hamilton turned up with the sister car OKV 1 and won both the Johnson Trophy and the main sports car race. OKV 2 finished second in both events.

After the race we went 'power searching' and removed the cylinder head from the 'D'. This showed signs of much hard work, the valve seats in particular being really worn and pitted. We knew the cylinder head on the XK120 to be a good one, so the heads were changed over whilst the 'D' camshafts were retained as being superior to those in the XK120. The oil tank, cooler, pipes etc., were removed and cleaned out and the amount of foreign matter that came out had to be seen to be believed. There was no oil filter fitted at this stage so the oil had to be kept very clean or else the bearings suffered. Despite every precaution this proved impossible and we used a lot of bearings during 1955.

With the different head, the car seemed to go very much better and we ran it at Aintree, Goodwood and Oulton with reasonable success, finishing either third or fifth – depending on who were driving the Aston Martins. During this period I was learning to drive the 'D' which, although having a performance of the same order as my XK, had vastly different handling characteristics – chief amongst these being a very powerful under-steer. This under-steer made the car very stable and safe on the straights and fast corners but very unwieldy on slow to medium-fast corners. As most of the British circuits consist of the latter type of corner, we were at a marked disadvantage when competing with the products of Feltham, which handled well on slow/medium corners. The D-type's speed superiority in the straight line merely helped to keep the opposition in sight.

By mid-June we decided to attempt a Continental event and, as we received an invitation to compete in the Portuguese Grand Prix for which a suitably large bag of gold was offered, we decided to undertake the journey. In addition, the Oporto circuit

Berry (XKC 403) and Sanderson (XKD 501) duelled at Aintree during the 1955 British GP meeting until Berry, pre-occupied by problems, took an excursion from which he recovered to finish seventh in the sports-car race

appeared to suit the D-type. By this time we had acquired a transporter in the shape of a Leyland diesel bus, which had been neatly converted to its new role, and which, when fitted with a high rear axle ratio, was capable of cruising in the 60s with no trouble at all. However, an accident, when on loan, rendered it non-standard and, as it could not be repaired in time, another vehicle very much sub-standard, was pressed into service. This vehicle expired at Tours. The 'D' was, therefore, unloaded, filled with the spares we had brought, and at 5 am the following morning was headed south towards Bordeaux, Spain and all points west.

Almost exactly twenty hours and 980 miles later a very travel-stained 'D' roared into the main square of Oporto, having travelled virtually non-stop across Portugal, Spain and three-quarters of France at an overall average of nearly 50 miles per hour and a fuel consumption figure in excess of 30 miles per gallon.

The only part of the car to suffer was the front sump oil seal, which started to leak – a leak that proved to be incurable due to distortion of the seal housing. In the race we had to stop for oil ten laps from the end, with the result that we dropped from a potential third place to an insignificant fifth. Nevertheless, it was a most enjoyable race, run in fine weather on a true road circuit and the prize money, even for fifth place, paid all the bills for our stay in Oporto! The enthusiasm of the crowd, the indefinable 'atmosphere' of a Continental circuit, the fine weather, magnificent scenery, and unusual food are the chief memories of a very hectic ten days.

In strong contrast was our next venue – Aintree – a circuit which I heartily dislike, and I don't mind admitting that I am always delighted when I see the chequered flag for the end of any race there. This dislike of the circuit was reflected in relatively poor practice times, and in addition, the car was decidedly 'off colour'. The weather for both practice and the race was far from ideal – being very hot and without a breath of wind, with the result that it played havoc with the cars. OKV 2, tired after its efforts in the Portuguese race the week before, showed its displeasure by producing a very high water temperature and an all-time low on the oil pressure gauge. As a final gesture most of the oil from the engine found its way into the cockpit and onto me, so the end of the practice found the car in a very rebellious mood with its driver hot, tired, dirty and very dispirited.

The race was no picnic. In a blazing sun, which was to cause so much trouble to competitors in the Grand Prix, the thirty or so cars for the Sports Car Race left the line in a blare of sound and a haze of exhaust smoke. By the end of lap one, Hawthorn (Jaguar) led, trying all he knew to hold-off the three Astons, myself and Sanderson having a private race in that order. By lap three the oil pressure was down to 25–30 lbs (as opposed to 60–80) and the water temperature crept steadily round the dial. By the end of lap five, all the power in OKV 2 had vanished and Sanderson was breathing down my neck. Preoccupied with the troubles besetting the car, I nearly forgot to turn the wheel to round a corner, finally did it badly and promptly spun off. Next lap, angry at my own stupidity and rather frightened, I signalled to the pit that I wanted to stop. But Jack was having none of it – his large frame stood out uncompromisingly from the rest of the people in the pit area – I had to go on. For the first time in my life I was delighted when the race ended.

The following week, the engine was removed from the car and stripped completely. The internal condition of the engine left no doubt as to where the power had gone. The big end bearings were virtually non-existent, the mains were badly pitted and the crankshaft scored to the point of being unusable. However, the engine was reassembled with new material and we were once more ready for the fray.

After one or two minor meetings our next event was the 250-mile International Sports Car Race at Oulton Park. This circuit is one that I really enjoy, being a true road circuit, even if it is not particularly suitable for a 'D' type. Unfortunately I was unable to get away for practice and so we started well back on the grid – a decided disadvantage at Oulton – and especially so in this race, which had attracted a big field of Ferraris, Maseratis and other quick machinery. It took an awfully long time to thread a path through slower cars which were better placed on the grid and it was really a case of pressing on in the hope of catching up with the leaders. Bright spots were a battle with Louis Rosier and his 750.S 3-litre Ferrari – both of which were right on form – and then, towards the end of the race, another duel with Masten Gregory with a similar car to Rosier's. Gregory, a very likeable American, was on a barn-storming motor racing tour of Europe with a Works-sponsored Ferrari and I had struck up a friendship with him in Oporto. We both meant business, but were not above exchanging well-known International signs when one gained some advantage over the other. Altogether a most enjoyable race, even if Gregory and I only finished fourth and fifth. The race was won by Parnell (Aston) with Hawthorn second and Collins third (Ferrari and Aston).

From Oulton Park we went to Goodwood for the Nine-Hour Race. Here we were joined by Norman Dewis, who shared the driving with me. Norman, despite being a newcomer to motor racing at Goodwood, soon showed his ability and in a few laps was returning lap times as good as any we had achieved. The race itself was uneventful. The car ran faultlessly – a tribute to the careful preparation of John Lea and also Bob Penney, who had joined the team for this race and the Tourist Trophy. Jack Broadhead was particularly keen that above all else the car should finish and the result was that we went rather too slowly during the first half of the race. We also, to some extent, under-estimated the speed at which the race would be run and therefore had to motor rather quickly in the closing stages in order to establish a reasonable finishing place – namely fifth. Although we committed several tactical errors, it was a very enjoyable event, and one which I would like to see run every year.

Our last race of the year was the Tourist Trophy Race. After Goodwood the bearings were in need of attention so the engine was stripped and rebuilt. Having a preference for 'road type' circuits, I was looking forward to this event, especially as there was a large Continental entry of Works Ferraris, Maseratis and Mercedes Benz, plus the British contingent of Jaguars, Aston Martins, Cooper-Jaguar, etc. Teamed with Ninian Sanderson for this race, I felt that provided we lasted the distance, we would finish well up amongst the leaders. In practice, the car went magnificently, but being new to the circuit, I found it difficult to memorise the corners and practise at the same time. However, after a great many laps of the circuit during non-practice hours in a TR2 lent to me by Desmond Titterington, I felt confident and practice lap times decreased considerably. Sanderson also returned similar times.

Race day dawned windy and dry but with more than a hint of rain in the sky. With the largest capacity cars at the head of the line for the Le Mans start, Hawthorn held No. 1 on the grid with OKV 2 'next-door'. At the fall of the flag we made a reasonably quick start and were lying third at the end of the first lap. The order remained the same on the second – Moss and Hawthorn out on their own – the rest trying to keep up. Unfortunately I clipped the bank at Tornagrough, which is a double 'S' bend, and very tight. The blow was not very great – it did not even deflect the car – but it was sufficient to damage the front offside tyre which started to deflate. Threequarters of a mile later I slowed right down as the car was handling most peculiarly and entering the left hand Quarry Bend the tyre deflated completely. Unsteerable the car mounted the grass bank on the right of the road and slid easily over the top and down into the field beyond. The only difficulty was that the field was about twelve feet below the level of the road, which fact nearly gave the driver heart failure. However, the car remained upright and the rest of the race was observed from the pits. The most unfortunate person in this episode at Dundrod was poor Ninian Sanderson who did not get a drive.

After the race the car was rebuilt at the Works and we competed in one or two other minor events, having something of a field-day in the final meeting of the season at Oulton Park.

As a result of what we learnt during 1955, a number of modifications were put in hand.

For 1956, *Equipe* Broadhead had, as before, the 'D' type – old faithful – OKV 2 and, in addition one of the latest Cooper–Nortons to be driven by Derek Strange. The Cooper, run completely independently from the 'D' was to have a mixed season, going extremely quickly one meeting, only to give endless trouble at the next. Despite a prodigious amount of work by the mechanic looking after the car, the maintenance and tuning of the Norton engine proved rather too big a task and it is now looked after by Francis Beart. I have never driven it for the simple reason that the bodywork is about two sizes too small – and, once in, I find it nearly impossible to get out again!

The winter of 1955/1956 was spent in a state of semi-hibernation during which period OKV 2 was completely overhauled. In addition, a stiffer anti-roll bar was fitted to the front suspension, and a completely new anti-roll bar assembly incorporated into the rear suspension. This, though rather crude in its method of operation, functioned extremely well, and the result was a car which handled very much better, especially on slow corners.

During this period, Jack Broadhead produced the latest version of his 'J.C.B.' – a trials special with which he had competed with considerable success in 'mud plugging' events the previous year, finishing runner-up to the champion in the BTDA Trials Championship. Being short of a passenger of one or two occasions Jack tried, with considerable persistence, to enveigle either Derek Strange or myself to accompany him on one of his hair-raising trials escapades. I strongly suspect that a secondary reason was to get some of his own back for our misdeeds during the racing season. I remained adamant – I just was not going and Jack could play in his mudbath by himself. Derek on the other hand eventually succumbed and the two set off for Yorkshire where the trial was to be held. The journey was uneventful apart from the fact that they were stopped by the police for doing 60 mph in the Zephyr – with a trailer carrying the special hooked on behind! For Derek the trial was one long succession of letting the tyres down before a hill, only to blow them up again a few hundred yards further on when that hill had been negotiated. During the lunch interval it poured with rain and Derek was given instructions to bounce for all he was worth – in addition, of course, to letting the tyres down and blowing them up again. For Derek, this was too much. At the start of the first hill, 14 stone of Strange was poised about 18 inches off the seat and at the fall of the flag he descended at maximum velocity. At the moment of impact between Strange and seat, Jack let in the clutch and there was a resounding crack. The axle casing had had enough also, and the rear wheels demonstrated a prodigious amount of camber. It must be recorded that the 'special' *had* moved – downwards, and further into the mud. After that we had no further invitations to passenger the boss!

But to revert to the 'D'. This season, which was to end so abruptly, opened auspiciously enough with a visit to Goodwood for the Easter Monday meeting. This is always a most enjoyable event and we regard it rather as a holiday, with some motor racing as the main feature. Practice went off without incident, but it was very obvious that everyone was going very much quicker than the previous year. Salvadori with the Gilby Engin-

eering Aston Martin (a Works-sponsored car) was fastest, with Abecassis (HWM) and me within a second of the Aston's lap time. However, Moss had been nominated as reserve for the car and it was no surprise to see him at the wheel when we lined up on the grid. Needless to say Moss won; Abecassis finished second, with 'D' and me third. It was not until we returned to Goodwood for the Whitsuntide meeting that we learnt that OKV 2 had also set up a new class record for sports cars! What we did know was that our lap times were consistently two or three seconds faster than the *best* we had achieved the previous year – and quite a few of the opposition were doing the same.

The same state of affairs existed at the next venue – Oulton Park – where the 'circus' again gathered to dispute the British Empire Trophy. Previously the handicapping had favoured the smaller cars, despite the fact that they were also the fastest cars on this circuit, but this year the big boys gave every indication of being as fast as, if not faster than, their rivals, and the handicapping was much more realistic. To add to the fun, Swiss motor cycling champion Musy arrived with one of the latest 300S 3-litre Maseratis. Again practice times were very much better than the previous year and a good race seemed a certainty. All the large cars were in heat three and we were in 'pole' position on the second row. After a first-class start OKV 2 emerged from the mêlée unscathed and with a slight lead over Flockhart (*Ecurie Ecosse* D-type) and Musy. This lead increased slightly for a few laps until Flockhart and Musy became engaged in a monumental struggle. First Flockhart scrambled past with Musy hard on his tail and I tried to hold Musy off to give Flockhart a chance to get away. But Musy was not to be denied, and setting up a new sports car lap record, he slipped by at Old Hall corner, caught Flockhart and won the heat. The final was dull by contrast, the smaller cars winning with something in hand despite the increased speed of the big cars. Flockhart won the class, and OKV 2 finished second – Musy paying for his enthusiasm with a seriously deranged engine, which left a lot of oil on the track and Musy a spectator.

The next event was at the *Daily Express* Silverstone meeting, and here I beat both Musy and Flockhart, we having taken advantage of a first-lap accident which did away with much of the faster opposition. [See main text.] OKV 2 came third overall, behind the Aston Martins of Salvadori and Moss. From Silverstone we moved on to Goodwood for the Whitsun meeting and, had we known it, the last race in which we were to compete for a long time. The big races – for sports cars and Formule Libre machines – had attracted a very strong entry: *Ecurie Ecosse* with three cars, driven by Titterington, Flockhart, Sanderson; H.W.M. with two cars, Tojeiro with one car, plus a number of privately owned D-types, Cooper–Jaguar and the rest. In our

Main photograph overleaf:
Bob Berry's car, rebuilt and painted light green, follows Stirling Moss's winning Aston Martin way from the start at Goodwood, Easter Monday 1956. Berry would finish third, just behind George Abecassis (HWM-Jaguar No 57); Alan Brown (Jaguar No 54) would be fourth, ahead of Noel Cunningham-Reid (HWM-Jaguar, No 58). The D-types of Flockhart (55), Hamilton (51) and Dennis (52, at back of grid) would not finish, the latter suffering a fatal accident – probably due to incorrect gear selection. A works D-type was entered for Hawthorn but did not materialise.

Inset overleaf:
OKV 2 – in effect a brand-new 'production' D-type – gives Bob Berry his final (and first post-accident) victory of 1956, at Oulton Park. This was the last event covered in Berry's article for the *Jaguar Apprentices' Magazine*.

Broadhead had the 'new' OKV 2 fitted with a full-width windscreen for 1957. Here Berry wins again at the October (Lancs & Cheshire CC) Oulton Park meeting that year; he made best sports car lap time of the day. Berry would return and win at this meeting yet again in 1958, but by then he was wielding his mighty Mk VII.

Tom Rowe – race and rallyman with an ex-works Mk VII – at the wheel of the D-type. He acted as the Broadhead team's manager. Thirty years on, he was still taking an active interest in racing, as secretary of the Jaguar Drivers' Club's competition committee.

first race for sports cars, OKV 2 occupied pole position on the grid by reason of making fastest lap in practice. A good start and OKV 2 went into the lead at the first bend, a lead which it retained to the end and won by 23 seconds. The Whitsun 100 Trophy Race for *Formule Libre* cars brought a flock of 1500 cc Lotus cars into the fray. Chapman (Lotus) held pole position, with Hawthorn (Lotus), Flockhart and myself (Jaguar) also on the front row. I established a very slight lead over Flockhart, Hawthorn and Chapman, all four cars being literally nose to tail. By the start of lap three OKV 2 had a lead of about two cars' length over Flockhart who, like the rest of us, was trying all he knew. I for one, motoring on the limit, felt that something was bound to happen, and at Fordwater in the second or so it takes to negotiate that bend flat out, realised I had crossed that thin line between safety and total disaster, that the error was irretrievable and an accident inevitable. There followed a mercifully brief period – a kaleidoscope of trees and sky and earth, above all the never to be forgotten sound of the D-type pounding itself to destruction – the calming voice of a doctor and the sweet oblivion of a morphia injection.

After six weeks I was allowed to leave hospital and go home – on condition that I remained there for three more but a visit to the British Grand Prix proved irresistible. After that a speedy return to work was not difficult to negotiate.

By September, the car and I had recovered sufficiently to attempt to find the answer to the question of whether I could still drive the D-type in a race. We therefore entered for the September Goodwood meeting – the last major event of the year at that circuit. Unfortunately, practising being on a Friday, and therefore out of the question, we had to forego that much-needed luxury and my re-introduction to the circuit was, therefore, in the race itself. As a result, we started on the rear row of a grid containing twenty-seven cars, and as confidence increased so the lap times improved. To my great delight we put in several laps at the end within a second of our previous best times. Nevertheless we finished no higher than sixth.

From Goodwood to Snetterton for a twenty-five lap Sports Car Race. Not having raced on this circuit since the XK days it was almost a new experience for me. I was surprised by the bumpy and slippery surface, and in addition it rained. The race itself was a small car benefit, the 'D' finishing fifth, only an HWM of the big car class being in a higher position.

The season ended with another visit to Oulton Park for the

second Lancashire & Cheshire Car Club meeting.

Here, OKV 2 won the scratch race and finished third, fourth and sixth, in three handicap races.

On the whole, an expensive and rather unfortunate season, yet I feel it could have been very much worse!

Robert Berry – Jaguar executive. **Given a simple option by his 'headmaster', Sir William Lyons, Berry switched back from international to club racing on recovering from his severe accident in 1956 and concentrated on his career with Jaguar. He went on to become director of publicity (in succession to Ernest Rankin) shortly before the formation of British Leyland, into which he was drawn. He returned from BL to Jaguar briefly in 1980 (John Egan's inaugural year) before joining Alfa Romeo and subsequently taking charge of a Jaguar distributorship. Jaguar has a magnetic effect on most people involved in the marque.**

(*Author's note*): OKV 2's second rebuild, in the summer of 1956, was more like a transference of its good mechanical parts into a production-type vehicle structure; this explains why the car is so unlike the other surviving examples of the 1954 D-type.

Bob Berry received an ultimatum from Sir William Lyons; as an employee, he didn't want to write about it at the time. Basically, he could work for Jaguar or pursue his racing career. (Berry was considered one of Britain's best up-and-coming drivers but too many long-weekends to practise, plus the long absence in 1956, forced him to make his choice. He chose to reduce his racing activities. He drove the Broadhead D-type in the odd sprint in 1957; he also took part in club events with a Ford Anglia, a TR2, and – a real dark horse – an ex-works alloy-bodied experimental Jaguar Mk VII.)

The race of 'The Two Worlds'

The following account, by Jack Fairman, of the Jaguar team's effort in the 1957 Monza 500 mile is reproduced directly from the pages of the *Jaguar Apprentices' Magazine* of May 1958.

THE MONZA 500 MILE RACE

by

Jack Fairman

I EXPECT every keen type who keeps himself informed about Jaguar racing activities will remember August, 1952. An XK120 fixed-head coupé, in practically standard road trim, staggered the world at that time by motoring round the famous Montlhèry circuit near Paris for seven days and seven nights. A distance of 16,851 miles was covered. The average speed, including all stops for refuelling, was 100.31 m.p.h. Four world and five international records were broken. Although over five years have elapsed, these records still stand. By the way, I wonder how many of the above-mentioned Jaguar fans realise the fact that, apart from the out-and-out land speed record held by the Napier Railton, Jaguar is the *only* British car that can claim to hold a *world* record since the war, irrespective of class or category ?

By now you are probably wondering what all that has to do with Monza—" The Race of the Two Worlds "—where ten U.S.A. cars of the Indianapolis type were to race against the best ten of Europe. Well, in company with Stirling Moss and Leslie Johnson, I was privileged to be one of the drivers in the Montlhèry affair. During a whole week of high speed motoring on a steeply banked and bumpy track, one naturally learns quite a lot about the special technique required. That is the main reason why David Murray asked me to drive when he thought about entering for Monza.

I must confess that the news was received with rather mixed feelings on my part. Most people know all about the so called " boycott " by various drivers and the very strong opinions voiced by some of the Continental Press about the highly dangerous nature of such a race, so I won't repeat the arguments for and against that were bandied about. The most worrying part was the vivid picture painted by many experts about the inevitable result of tyre trouble at the speeds involved.

Tyres v. Heat.

A point usually not realised by the man in the street, is that at 160 m.p.h. on a steeply banked track centrifugal force has the effect of increasing the weight of a car by a substantial amount. This is one reason why much bigger tyres are desirable. To make this clearer by using an extreme analogy, you obviously don't try to run a three-ton truck on Austin Seven tyres. Again, the greater the diameter of the tyre the less times it revolves per mile, so that the casing actually flexes a smaller number of times per mile, and thus less heat is generated. And heat is the great enemy. The strength of rubber decreases rapidly as the heat increases. If a critical temperature is reached, centrifugal force at high speed can result in a complete tread being thrown off. This I can assure you is anything but amusing for the driver. I had already experienced high speed tyre trouble on two occasions. The first was when a rear tyre burst at 115 m.p.h. on the Jaguar at Montlhèry. The second was in 1956 during the Italian Grand Prix at Monza when I threw a front tread from the Connaught at 130 m.p.h. So, knowing that in the 500 mile affair the speed might be in the region of 170 m.p.h., perhaps you will understand why I said earlier that I had mixed feelings about the race !

However, in order to gain some data for Dunlops, and to see how a "D" type would behave on the Monza banking, I went over some weeks before the race with the legendary "Wilkie" Wilkinson. At this stage I should make it clear that only the banked part of the track was to be used. It is 2.64 miles to the lap and consists of two level straights jointed by two steeply banked semi-circles. I cannot remember how high the banking is, but it is much too steep for any normal man to be able to clamber to the top. Some parts of the banking are extremely bumpy and at high speed the car receives a fearful pounding. In the motoring magazines some of you will have seen photographs of cars at various circuits with a caption underneath which says : " Note the calm and relaxed attitude of the driver." I can assure you that at Monza all that goes by the board as the driver is far too busy hanging on to the wheel and bracing himself for the bumps to be either calm or relaxed.

Vic Barlow of Dunlop was present with his various charts and instruments. Up to this point I had been under the impression that we were to have special big tyres. However, owing to the short notice Dunlops had no time to produce specials. In any case there was no room under the "D" type sports two-seater bodywork for bigger wheels. So we had to use the standard road racing 6.50 × 16. All Dunlop's could do was to buff the treads down to about half the usual thickness, in order to reduce the effect of centrifugal force.

After a few practice laps I stopped so that the tyres could be checked for temperature, then covered a few more at a higher speed and stopped again. The speed was gradually increased until Barlow amiably announced that tyre temperatures had reached danger point. Sure enough, about three laps later just as I was approaching the banking at about 165 m.p.h.

the entire right-hand back tread came off with a noise like a 6in. shell, making a nice mess of the bodywork in the process. I was, of course, half expecting this. My previous two experiences of high speed tyre trouble had taught me that one must not panic and shove the brakes on immediately, but concentrate on coping with the inevitable weaving, and lose speed gradually. Wilkie had walked round the banking in order to cast an expert eye on the car's handling as it went round. Oddly enough I came to rest just where he was standing. All he wanted to know was why the heck did I have to throw a tread just when he had walked a mile under a scorching sun to watch me. When we got back to the pits all Barlow had to say was that at least we now knew what our maximum safe speed was ! I cannot repeat the words of the mechanic who went to retrieve the tread which was lying on the track like a snake as he found out too late that it was extremely hot.

Anyway, after consultation by 'phone with David Murray in Edinburgh, it was decided to enter three cars for the race, although it was to be held only a week after Le Mans, and various modifications, such as tyre cooling ducts, would have to be incorporated.

The American Approach

Now a few words about the American cars and their basic differences from the European. Firstly, some of them had tyres as big as 8.00 × 20 compared to our 6.50 × 16 ! Firestones, of course, have specialised in these giants for years. Secondly, although the classic Indianapolis 500 ranks on the International Calendar and counts in the World Championship, the Americans do not stick to the International formula for G.P. cars, which, as you know, limits engine size to 750 c.c. supercharged or 2.5 litres unsupercharged. Their formula is 2.8 litres s/c and 4.2 u/s. As they are also allowed to run on " dope " they obviously produce a lot more power than the Jaguar's 3.8 litre which is built to run on standard petrol as stipulated for sports car events. Some of the Americans were quoting as much as 550 h.p. Next, the U.S.A. cars are designed and built for one thing—track racing.

As Indianapolis is an anti-clockwise track, the cars are built with offset engines, offset transmission and sometimes even an oil tank slung outside to help the car round the continual left-hand bends. They do not have to worry much about brakes as they are not a major factor at Indianapolis. The four bends there do not call for changing down, so the race is run in top gear. Therefore, they only have two gears in the box, the lower one being merely to get it moving. Even then some of the cars are still difficult to get away so they have a rolling start at Indianapolis. All the cars line up in rows of three according to their practice times, and do one lap behind a pace car, holding their grid positions. On reaching the start line the pace car pulls to one side and the race is on.

Now Monza has a very fine road circuit. This, added to the banked circuit gives a total lap of over six miles, and I think the original idea was that the Two Worlds 500 miles should be run over the full circuit. But the U.S.A. cars, even if they could slow down for the bends, would not be very happy on the right-hand ones, and even if they did get round them satisfactorily they would not be able to accelerate away again because of the two-speed box. To sum this up, many people would describe the American cars as freaks. Anyway, it was decided in the end to use the banked track only and to run the race anti-clockwise as a complete copy of Indianapolis. The Jaguars were designed and built as fully equipped sports two-seaters, which can be started on the starter and driven round the town for shopping. You can perhaps understand why so many people thought we were mad to enter.

The time finally came for Ecurie Ecosse to assemble at Monza.

The team was completed by two of the regular drivers, Ninian Sanderson and John Lawrence. Ninian and I were to drive the 3.4's and John was given the 3.8. Vic Barlow of Dunlops was on parade again and we had very strict instructions that our lap speeds would be governed by him and increased or decreased according to the temperature, that being the critical factor.

I have competed in most of the big international races in Europe, but I found the atmosphere of this one was quite new. I have met most types of Americans, but these Indianapolis professionals and their supporters struck me as being a race apart, extremely keen and efficient people who lived and dreamed track racing to the exclusion of everything else.

MONZA 500-MILE RACE, 1957. Ecurie Ecosse prepares for battle.

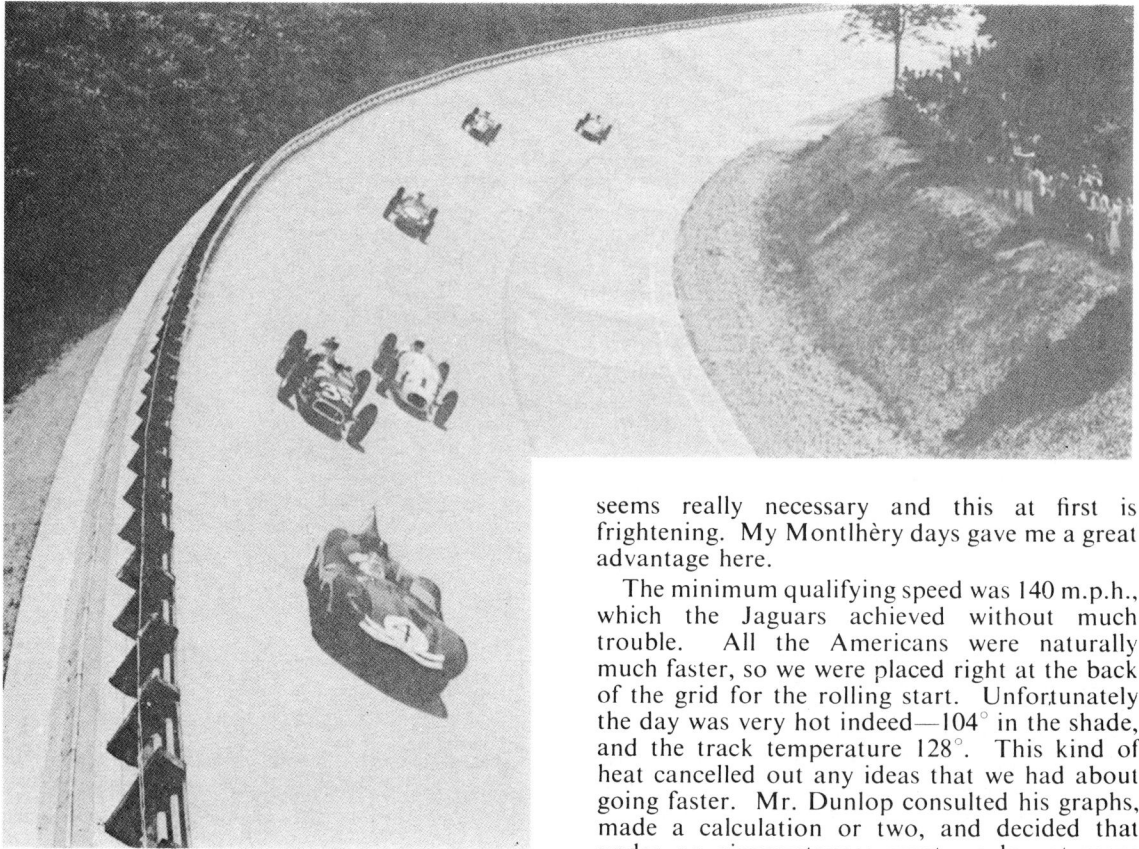

"... a moment that I shall remember for some time."
(No. 35—Sachs, No. 1—Bryan)

As we were the only European drivers there, they made a tremendous fuss of us. They could not have been more friendly or helpful although some of them were a little worried about the Jags getting in their way !

After practice some of them were also worried about the appalling bumps and the effect on their dampers. One driver was even more worried after discussing matters with Sanderson. Ninian assured him that we did not bother about dampers here—Monza was so smooth compared with Le Mans, that our Mr. Wilkinson had removed them all to save weight !

Sanderson and Lawrence had never driven on a banking before and it naturally took them a little time to settle down. Acquiring the correct technique is not easy. The first time you try it you think it is horrible. The tendency is usually to drive too low as you are automatically scared of getting too high and motoring smartly over the top. The best technique is difficult to explain, but with a Jaguar it means going higher than

seems really necessary and this at first is frightening. My Montlhèry days gave me a great advantage here.

The minimum qualifying speed was 140 m.p.h., which the Jaguars achieved without much trouble. All the Americans were naturally much faster, so we were placed right at the back of the grid for the rolling start. Unfortunately the day was very hot indeed—104° in the shade, and the track temperature 128°. This kind of heat cancelled out any ideas that we had about going faster. Mr. Dunlop consulted his graphs, made a calculation or two, and decided that under no circumstances must we lap at more than 150 m.p.h. or off would come the treads.

It had been originally intended to run the 500 miles straight off, but owing to the agitation about tyre dangers, the organisers decided to split it into three sessions of 166 miles, with about an hour's pause between for checking the cars.

A Good Start

The paced lap for the rolling start was led by Luigi Villoresi in an Alfa-Romeo convertible at about 75 m.p.h. The cars followed him round two by two, maintaining their grid positions, with me, feeling a bit of a Charlie, right at the tail of the queue. We were, of course, pulling a pretty high axle ratio, and I had already decided to make full use of the four-speed box. As the flag fell I snicked into second and gave it the gun, fairly leaping by two or three cars in the process. In third, with the Jaguar engine really beginning to bite, I sailed past about four more. The Americans, of course, were handicapped by the two-speed boxes, but surprisingly enough none of them seemed to have given a thought to the possibility of the "D" type using its gears. As we approached the banking after the pits, I was catching up fast behind a gaggle of highly-coloured cars. By now, of course, we were in top and really travelling. I was just about to ease off to avoid creasing an American tail when the two cars in front suddenly parted, so I was able to keep my foot down and nip between them. Now only two were left in front, travelling abreast, and although they were beginning to motor I had enough way on to go to the top of the banking and fairly rocket past on the outside, to take the lead.

In the Lead

Although I had no intention of trailing round at the tail end, I had certainly never expected to find myself in front. Anyway, I knew the tyres would not heat up to danger point in one lap, so I thought I would make the most of the opportunity and go flat out until Dunlops waved me down. For the remainder of the lap I was rather busy looking where I was going and not bothering much about the pack behind. On leaving the banking at the end of the first lap a quick glance in my mirror showed nothing but bare concrete, which was astonishing. For a ghastly moment I thought there had been a false start and that I was the only idiot pressing on. Anyway, as nobody waved a red flag, I kept going.

The beginning of the next banking was now approaching at around 170 m.p.h. at about 30°. As it is desirable to go on to it at the right spot, my attention was too fully occupied to worry about false starts or Americans. However, my mild surprise at leading the field was, according to eye witnesses afterwards, nothing to compare with the utter incredulity of the Italians in the stands and the Americans in the pits. Apparently quite a few were speechless as they had been laying bets on whether Jimmy Bryan in the Dean Van Lines would be leading Troy Ruttman on the John Zink Special, or Tony Bettenhausen on the Nova Special. The last thing they had expected was to see a shiny blue Jaguar, with no advertisements on its sides, come sweeping into view at the very top of the banking, all on its own, about 150 yards ahead of the next car and going like a dingbat. I must say it was a moment that I shall remember for some time.

At the end of the second lap I still led the pack off the banking, but by this time the U.S.A. motors were really wound up, and they started to roar past on the level. And there was David Murray (and Mr. Dunlop) looking very agitated and making unmistakable signs to ease off, so I settled down to lapping at steady 153-155 m.p.h.

I maintained my high line at the top of the banking. Quite a few people criticised this at the time, especially those who were seeing their first

race of this type. Some of them told me that they were genuinely frightened that I was doing it for effect, or to play to the gallery, and that I would inevitably overdo it and disappear over the top. However, there were some very good reasons for it. Firstly, Vic (Dunlop) Barlow insisted that I should keep as high as possible. The reason is that if you drive too low at high speed, the car tries to drift upwards. This causes side scrub, which in turn means more wear and more heat. Going high reduces both these dangerous factors. Secondly, it wasn't quite so bumpy at the top, which gave the car a better chance of surviving the fearful hammering it was getting. Thirdly, it had been agreed with the Americans before the start that I was going to keep well up, so that when they wanted to overtake there would be plenty of room below.

One American reporter, who asked why I thought it necessary to drive at the top, was told that the chief reason was on account of it being so much cooler up there. To my astonishment he evidently believed this, for he wrote it all down in his notebook.

Ninian's orders were to keep to a more comfortable speed and make sure of at least one

. . . **They started to roar past on the level."**
(*No. 12—O'Connor, No. 1—Bryan*)

Jaguar finishing, so it wasn't long before I lapped him. I caught Lawrence up shortly afterwards just as he was approaching the banking. He was surprised to see how high I was going and his Scottish reaction was : " If that blankety-blank Sassenach can drive up there, then so can I ! " So he followed me round and found to his surprise that it was easier, and his lap speeds increased immediately.

The rest of the race was largely a matter of keeping going. I was unable to repeat my lead-snatching on the other two heats because the Americans are not slow on the uptake. They took good care to talk the driver of the pace car into going faster, and they were also carefully bunched together, so that overtaking was next to impossible. More and more American cars suffered from split tanks, broken damper brackets, broken engine bearers, cracked frames, etc. In the hour's interval between heats some of them got out the welding plant and performed a major rebuild. The three Jaguars continued to circulate at their prescribed speeds, and had nothing done at all between heats. Had it not been so hot, Dunlops would have allowed us to go faster, but, of course, for all we know, the extra speed might have shaken something loose.

A Satisfactory Result

We finally finished 4th, 5th and 6th after a completely trouble-free run. It was generally agreed by the Americans that had the 500 miles been run straight off, as originally intended, we might have won, because some of the Indianapolis cars only finished as a result of some comprehensive overhauling between the heats.

Driving in the terrific heat, plus the pounding made it hard work, but it was worth it as the impression made on the Americans by the performance of the three Jaguars was tremendous. They all made a big fuss of everybody in Ecurie Ecosse, and of anybody else who even looked like a Scot. I think the American and Italian newspapermen took more photographs of the Jaguars than of Jimmy Bryan's winning car ! I was filled with admiration for the way the cars stood the test, especially as they were far from new and two of them had finished at Le Mans only a week before. I do not think that anybody who has not driven at Monza can have any notion at all of the battering effect of that banking on a car. It proved beyond any doubt the absolute soundness of the original design. After all, an average speed of 150 m.p.h. for 500 miles is not exactly hanging about. Actually it is an unofficial record as our speed was higher than any other European car in any race, over any distance, since the war.

I cannot close without expressing admiration for the courage of David Murray in going ahead

The author, with Ninian Sanderson and John Lawrence, just after the race.

with his plans in the face of all the people who thought he was crazy, and for the ability of Wilkie and his boys in screwing the cars together so that they didn't fall apart.

Finally I think the most amazing thing was the way the normal road racing standard sized Dunlop tyres successfully stood up to a job for which they were never designed.

Here are the full results of the race :—

	DRIVER		CAR		LAPS
1.	Jim Bryan	..	Dean Van Lines Spl.		189
2.	Troy Ruttman		John Zink Spl.	..	187
3.	John Parsons		Agajanian Spl.	..	182
4.	Jack Fairman		Jaguar	.. ..	177
5.	John Lawrence	..	Jaguar	.. ..	171
6.	Ninian Sanderson		Jaguar	.. ..	159
7.	Ray Crawford	..	Mirror Glaze Spl.	..	117
8.	Eddie Sachs		Jim Robbins Spl.	..	107
9.	Andy Linden		McNamara Spl.	..	91
10.	Pat O'Connor		Sumar Spl.	..	90
11.	Bob Veith ..	..	Bob Estes Spl.	..	55
12.	Tony Bettenhausen		Novi Spl.	..	45
—	Paul Russo	..	Novi Spl.	..	Did not start
—	Jean Behra	..	Maserati	..	Did not start
—	Jean Lucas	..	Ferrari	..	Did not start

Appendix Four

Contemporary Reports

This book's starting point coincides with the first pinnacle in Jaguar racing history.

In the three Le Mans 24-hour races, from 1951 to 1953, Jaguar had won and lost and won again, following a learning curve which had an almost-inevitable dip in the middle. The works C-types (XKC 051, 052 and 053) had put in a copybook performance in the Great Race. For 1954 they were sold to *Ecurie Ecosse* who campaigned them to good effect, mainly in the UK, where home enthusiasts could see these fine cars in action before they became completely obsolete. (Incidentally, soon after *Vol. 1* was published, XKC 051 was brought back to Britain from California for restoration and rebodying on behalf of Adrian Hamilton and his father, Duncan, who – with Tony Rolt – had driven it to victory at Le Mans in 1953.)

Item 1. Those three cars represented the ultimate development of the C-type series, and Laurence Pomeroy's analysis of them for *The Motor* seems an appropriate opening to this appendix.

Item 2. Now for the D-type itself. The 'Jaguar prototype', referred to at the beginning of *The Motor's* May 1954 one-page announcement, is the XK 120C Mk II which appeared at Silverstone, Reims, and Le Mans test sessions in early 1954, before being scrapped. It will be noted that the 'D-type' name had not yet been applied. Internally, the D-type was still the XK 120C Mk IV.

Item 3. By the time of its first full feature (3 September 1954) *The Autocar* was able to call the new car the 'D-type' officially.

Item 4. October 1954 saw the publication of a four-sided D-type folder, with a Roy Nockolds drawing on the front. The information inside was sketchy, so that the description was equally applicable to the existing works cars and to the simpler cars then being planned for production in 1955. The artwork

opposite the 'specification' page is based on a photograph of a 1954 car taken at the broad expanse of MIRA to accentuate the 'light lines'. The back cover (not worth reproducing here) simply bore the Jaguar 'wings' and the imprint of W. W. Curtis Ltd., who did much of Jaguar's printing.

Item 5. This June 1955 description from *The Motor* covers the definitive 'production' D-type design, and the latest long-nose work car derived from it – the ultimate expression of Jaguar's purpose-building for Le Mans.

Item 6. Taken from *The Autocar* Le Mans preview of 1956, this page describes and illustrates how Jaguar got round the full-width screen regulation. (The removable panel, representing a nearside 'door', is clearly visible. On the same page, a diagram of the start/finish area shows the realignment of the pits straight to eliminate the infamous kink so obvious in the pictures of the 1955 accident).

Item 7. Robert Neil, editor of *Auto Course*, visited the D-type production line and included some of Malcolm Sayer's sketches for this seven-page feature.

Item 8. This one-pager from *The Motor* was just about the level of publicity Jaguar needed for its 'new' XKSS model, which was its solution to the problem of how to dispose of unsold D-types. A factory fire (within a fortnight after this item appeared) was a useful peg upon which to hang the discontinuation of the XKSS later on.

Item 9. Although Jaguar had disbanded its own team, it continued to support racing long afterwards, particularly in respect of engine preparation. This page from *The Autocar* of 26 July 1957 illustrates the works-loaned 297 bhp engine (E5005-9) which had just been removed from XKD 606 which had won

Le Mans and, a week later, had come fifth in the Monza 500-mile race. In the picture, upper left, are Bill Wilkinson (who had taken over from the late Jack Emerson) and engine tester Brian Walker.

Item 10. These handwritten notes are from Phil Weaver's Competition Shop notebook, kindly loaned by Ted Brookes, relating to XKD 606 and Le Mans 1957. Each works-prepared D-type was written-up in this way. (It can be seen that the car, which had been damaged earlier in the season, was repaired and prepared for Le Mans 1957 at Browns Lane.) The resultant victory for *Ecurie Ecosse* was, however, masterminded by that very independent operator, David Murray, and his team. Although the notes say '3·75 litres', the 87 mm x 107 mm version of the XK engine worked out at 3781 cc.

Item 11. The XK-engined hybrids did much to back up Jaguar's own racing effort. One in particular – the Lister-Jaguar – was an outstanding sprint-race car, which came on the international scene just as the D-type was bowing out. Indeed the Cunningham/Jaguar-associated Momo team ran Listers very effectively in the USA between 1958 and 1960. This is *The Motor*'s description of the classic 'knobbly' Lister.

Item 12. Although it ran in Cunningham colours, E2A was the last works competition car to race in the 24-hour race at Le Mans. This race-week feature was published in *The Autocar* on 24 June 1960.

Item 13. Also in that issue of *The Autocar* (24 June 1960) was a full Le Mans preview. These extracts show the *Ecurie Ecosse* entry with its high screen and large 'luggage boot' demanded by the latest regulations. David Murray's records (not always accurate) don't agree with the comment about the car's identity in *The Autocar*; but even in this weird form, the old D-type (XKD 606) was to be a leading runner until it retired. It was the last time for any D-type in a 24-hour; in fact there would be no Jaguars of any kind at Le Mans the next year. There was no separate E2A section in the preview, but it will be noted from the entry list reproduced, that the entrant was 'Jaguar New York'.

THE 1953 LE MANS JAGUAR

An Analytical Description of a Record-breaking Car

by Laurence Pomeroy, F.R.S.A., M.S.A.E.

A DESCRIPTION of the Jaguar XK120 C in its latest form would be inadequate if it did not deal with the performance of the car relative to the 1951 prototype (which also won at Le Mans) and also in comparison with other vehicles in this year's race.

The reason for this is that although the latest type shows a gain in lap speed of 8.4%, and of average speed through the race of 13.2%, compared with the 1951 model which it so closely resembles, there is no evidence of any substantial difference in maximum speed as a result of changes made during this period.

During the 1953 event a large number of time records were made with an Omega Time Recorder over a flying km. on one of the fastest parts of the Mulsanne straight. These show that the speeds of the three cars entered by the works vary between 132.76 m.p.h. and 148.83 m.p.h., whereas the privately owned model driven by Laurent and de Tornaco which was virtually unchanged from the 1951 specification varied between 133.39 and 143.49 m.p.h.

SPEEDS OF JAGUAR CARS LE MANS 1953

Drivers	Number of timings	Fastest recorded 1 km speed (m.p.h.)	Running* time	Slowest recorded 1 km speed (m.p.h.)	Running* time
Moss/Walker	32	147.46	14h. 27m.	139.64	22h. 30m.
Rolt/Hamilton	44	148.83	3h. 25m.	132.76	5h. 20m.
Whitehead/Stewart	21	146.19	4 h.12m.	138.86	21h. 25m.
Laurent/de Tornaco	23	143.59	3h. 30m.	133.39	22h. 30m.

*After start at 16 hrs. on 13-6-53.

A further point of interest in this connection is that the standard car submitted for *The Motor* road test averaged 143.71 m.p.h. with a best time of 144.4 m.p.h., figures which closely correspond with those obtained by the privately-owned model shown in the table.

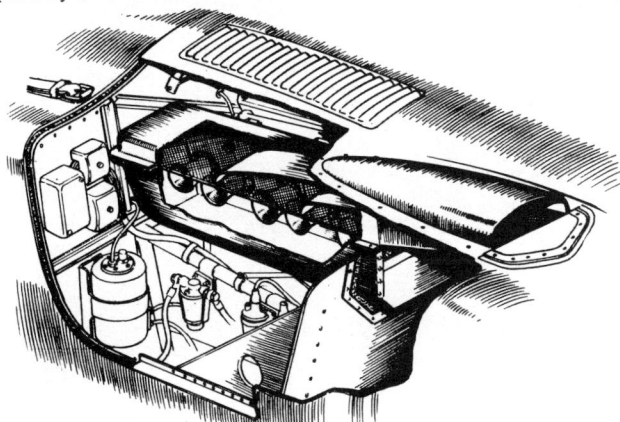

SPLITTING THE STREAM.—The six choke tubes of the three Weber carburetters draw air from a distributor box which is in turn supplied from a scoop on the bonnet top, the air being guided into three separate channels as shown here.

A further analysis of time sheets kindly supplied by Brandt Frères (the Paris representatives of the Omega Co.) shows that the mean of the flying km. speeds for the three team Jaguars was considerably below that of some of their rivals. Set out in order of velocity we have:—3.6-litre Alfa Romeo (Sanesi-Carini) average of 4 timings, 150.88 m.p.h.; 5.4-litre Cunningham (Fitch-Walters) average of 57 timings, 150.37 m.p.h.; 4.5-litre Ferrari (Ascari-Villoresi) average of 3 timings, 149.87 m.p.h.; 3.5-litre Jaguar (Moss-Walker) average of 32 timings, 145.26 m.p.h.; 3.5-litre Jaguar (Rolt-Hamilton) average of 44 timings, 143.09 m.p.h.; 3.5-litre Jaguar (Whitehead-Stewart) average of 21 timings, 142.3 m.p.h.

It is evident that neither the big gains in circuit speed as compared with 1951, nor victory in the 1953 Le Mans race itself, can be accounted for by maximum speed. The superiority of the 1953 cars must therefore reside in superior cornering power or in acceleration positive, negative, or both.

Overriding all performance factors is the paramount necessity for complete reliability which was demonstrated this year by the fact that the four cars entered completed an aggregate of 9,873.6 miles at a mean average speed of 102.85 with only one mechanical incident, which was the clogging and subsequent removal of the fuel filter on the car of Stirling Moss.

Let us now consider in detail the 1953 models, taking into particular account the manner in which they differ from the preceding production models.

Examining firstly the power unit, the most noticeable external change has been the apparent addition of one carburetter, making three instruments in place of two. The modification is, however, more far-reaching than this in that each of the new Weber carburetters embodies two choke tubes which enjoy a common float and throttle spindle. There are therefore six jet, choke and throttle assemblies or one for each cylinder, and in consequence 25 b.h.p. has been added to the engine output at 4,000 r.p.m. and the power curve reaches its peak at 4,500 r.p.m., remaining substantially flat up to some 5,200 r.p.m. This big change offered the opportunity of reducing engine speed and lowering the inertia forces, or alternatively improving the top-gear acceleration from 100 m.p.h. onwards. It is interesting to note that the car which came in fourth had a lower gear than the models which took first and second positions, the differences being between 25.67 m.p.h. at 1,000 r.p.m. and 29.1 m.p.h. at 1,000 r.p.m.

Maximum engine output is approximately 220 b.h.p. at 5,200 r.p.m. and various detail changes are incorporated to ensure reliability at much higher r.p.m. such as might momentarily be realized in the indirect gears. One of the most important of these was the use of Dykes pressure rings in the top grooves of the piston.

These components have been evolved as a consequence of the intensive research work carried out by Prof. Dykes at the Motor Industry Research Association, and they are manufactured by Bricovmo, Ltd. Of "L" section, the rings are very fragile and are made in a centrifugally-cast material heat-treated to give a tensile strength of 30 tons per sq. in., together with high elasticity and excellent wear resistance.

They fulfilled entirely their duty of preventing blow-by of gas into the crankcase which is a difficult problem to solve using normal rings of comparatively large diameter having considerable inertia effects at high engine speeds.

It is no secret that the retirement of all three works Jaguar cars in the 1952 Le Mans race was caused by defects in the water circulation which were independent of the alteration of the front air intake on the bodies. In the past year, therefore, a great deal of attention has been given to re-design of the water-pump rotor in order to ensure freedom from cavitation at over 5,000 r.p.m. The radiator and header tank are now in the conventional position but the radiator cores themselves are developed by Marston and built in light alloy. This not only effected a very useful saving in weight (the new radiator weighs only 15 lb. complete) but also gives a 30% better water flow for a given pressure difference.

Reverting to the engine itself, the damper is made in steel so as to be free from the possibility of bursting, even

The 1953 Le Mans Jaguar - - - - - -

if the crankshaft should go up to 8,000 r.p.m.—an astonishing figure which has in several instances been reached by engines of this type. The valve gear appears fully able to withstand such abnormal, if momentary, loadings, and it is interesting to note that the Weller tensioner used on the Le Mans cars had a hard chrome face. This was a successful experiment as shown by the condition of the dismantled components in the winning engine. Observation of these also disclosed that the main bearings were almost (but not quite) unmarked and that the piston heads were almost (but again, not quite) equally coated to demonstrate equal mixture and burning speed. All the connecting rods on the winning engine were crack-tested after the race and shown to be in 100% sound condition, and measurement on the crankpins and journals showed that any dimensional changes were less than the limits laid down for a new shaft.

At least three "winners" at Le Mans have been put out of the race by electrical failure particularly dynamo break-downs, notably Caracciola's Mercedes-Benz in 1930, E. R. Hall's Ferrari in 1951, and Kling's Mercedes-Benz in 1952. To avoid the possibility of this affliction visiting the Jaguar cars of 1953, great care was taken by Lucas with the whole electrical installation and at the same time the opportunity offered by the special conditions of running was taken to reduce weight as far as possible.

The special conditions are that the lights are needed for no more than eight hours; that rate of charge at low r.p.m. is of no importance; and that there will

PRINCIPAL CHANGES.—This drawing shows the main modifications embodied in the 1953 Le Mans Jaguar car which are: Dunlop disc brakes actuated through a Girling servo mechanism having an oil reservoir ahead of the pedals; three double-choke horizontal Weber carburetters; a Marston light-alloy radiator; I.C.I. 50-gallon flexible fuel tank; lightweight Lucas battery, and modified rear axle assembly embodying a Panhard rod.

- - - - - - - - - - **Contd.**

FATTENING THE CURVE.—The use of individual choke and jet assemblies for each inlet port resulted in a big increase in power between 4,000 and 5,000 r.p.m., making possible improved performance with higher gear ratios and reduced inertia loads.

be no demand on the starter or the battery for the heavy electrical discharges needed with a cold start. As against these simplifications of the electrical duties there are the complications that the dynamo must run reliably at high engine speed, that the starter must turn the engine at high r.p.m. (so as to clear rich mixture which may collect in the manifolding as the result of big jets and choke tubes) and the lights must give the best possible length of beam.

In the ignition system the principal change is that the engine is running almost entirely under full throttle and within a restricted range of r.p.m. and for this reason the Jaguars used standard coils and equally standard distributors except that the vacuum-operated timing control was removed.

The dynamo was driven at 0.9 times engine speed or a maximum of about 5,000 r.p.m., had a yoke diameter of only 3.9 in. against the 4.5 in. of the standard instrument, but at the higher operating speeds the output was 23 amp. Fullest possible use was made of this output by a current

voltage regulator which is not in general production.

The starting requirements were met by substituting for the $4\frac{1}{2}$ in.-diameter standard motor a $4\frac{1}{4}$ in.-diameter instrument to which aluminium end covers were fitted. With a hot engine this actually increased the cranking speed.

The headlamps were designed especially for Le Mans requirements and were approved by the organizers. The lens and reflector are built up into one unit as is standard Lucas practice and a yellow three-pin pre-focussed bulb was used.

The study of weight reduction in detail is shown by the use of light-alloy cable in place of the normal copper core

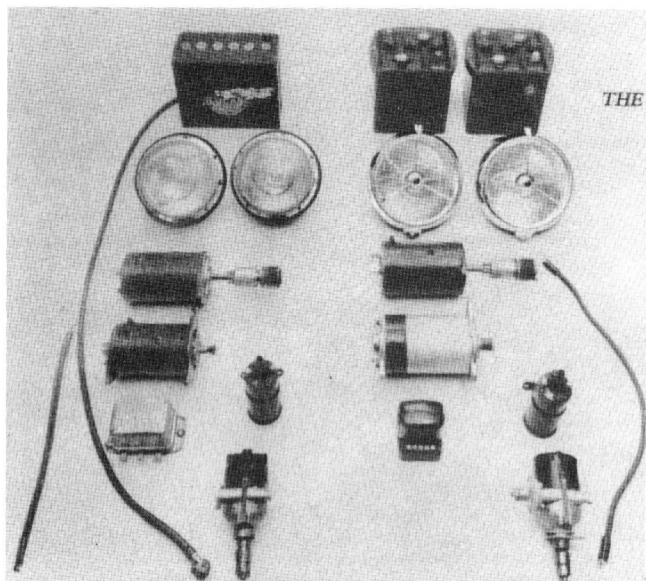

LIGHTWEIGHT EFFICIENCY.—The Lucas electrical equipment fitted to the Le Mans car, is shown on the left-hand side, contrasted with the components employed on the standard model. To improvements in headlight beam and hot-starting cranking speed was added a weight saving of over 50 lb.

The 1953 Le Mans Jaguar   -   -   -   -

tral housing so as to avoid any possibility of their turning under severe torque effects.

The 1953 cars show a reduction in weight of about 120 lb. over their predecessors and this saving arises from three main sources, in addition to the electrical system and the light alloy radiator, which have already been mentioned. The use of 18-gauge tubing in the frame structure had been called for in the original design but for various reasons the 1951 team cars and the subsequent batch of 50 production models were built with 16-gauge tubes. The thinner walls for 1953 reduces the weight somewhat without altering the diameter or layout of the frame tubing and without incurring greater stresses than had been contemplated originally.

A major saving in weight and the elimination of an important source of trouble on racing cars follows the substitution of a flexible fuel tank for the metal type normally employed. The tanks used at Le Mans arrived at the works in a flat parcel and consist of a flexible bag containing a central baffle, the whole being suspended from multiple points attached to the tail section of the car. The wide distribution of load eliminates all mounting problems, and the flexibility of the bag makes it impervious to any slight frame distortion and leak-proof in the most severe conditions. Made by Imperial Chemical Industries the Jaguar tank carries 50 gallons of fuel and has a weight of 11 lb. In other words, the tank weight is under 4 oz. per gallon.

In the race the cars carried at most 40 gallons and the average fuel consumption was 9 m.p.g., being increased by 45% as compared with 13.5 m.p.g. in the 1951 race. As, however, the final average was 13% higher and this percentage demands a power increase of 44% even under level speed straight ahead running, the step-up in gross consumption was the absolute minimum and considerably less than normally consistent with such an increase in circuit speed.

The matters so far dealt with show how the 1953 Le Mans version of the XK120C model was endowed with reliability together with a useful increment of acceleration derived from reduction in laden weight of about 5% and an increase in engine torque in the middle part of the range of between 15 and 20%. No major changes were made to the suspension and steering gear but a very large fraction of the improved overall performance resulted from a radical change in brake design.

but the biggest single item of weight saving was in the battery, the two 6-volt 64-amp.hr. batteries used in 1951 being replaced by a 37-amp.hr. unit using light alloys. Although this type has a restricted life which would make it unsuitable for use on normal production cars, it offers ample capacity and reliability for Le Mans needs and as shown in the table the weight saving effected in the electrical side of the Le Mans Jaguar cars in the course of three years amounts to over 53 lb., or a reduction of some 45%.

WEIGHT COMPARISONS OF ELECTRICAL EQUIPMENT FOR JAGUAR LE MANS CARS OF 1950 AND 1953

Unit	XK120STD	Weight	XK120C 1953 Le Mans	Weight
Dynamo	C.4522462	18.25 lb.	END.2085	12.75 lb.
	Max. output 22 amps.		Max. output 23 amps.	
Starter	M.45G. 26062	21.00 lb.	END.2086	16.00 lb.
Control box	RB.106. 37139	1.25 lb.	RB320	1.50 lb.
Battery	Two 6 volt units	72.00 lb.	One 12 volt unit	32.00 lb.
	Cap. 64 amp. hrs.		Cap. 37 amp. hrs.	
Headlamps	PF.770	6.00 lb. ea.	LREF.700.	3.50 lb. ea.
	Total	118.50 lb.	Total	65.75 lb.
Cables	Tinned copper	3.2 oz. per ft.	Aluminium	2.2 oz. per ft.

Experience over the past two years has shown that a 10-in. diameter clutch is on the limit of safety at the engine speeds which the Jaguar design makes possible, and this fact led to the choice of a multi-plate Borg and Beck clutch with a diameter of 7¼ in. Although undoubtedly noisier, and perhaps somewhat rougher in take-up, than the normal single-plate type this installation proved completely reliable, and from the viewpoints of centrifugal loadings and of unit loadings on the clutch faces is much more lowly stressed than the type which it replaces.

The remainder of the transmission is virtually identical with the production models. The rear axle is tied to a Panhard rod to raise the roll centre from 5 in. to 11 in. and to improve transverse stability, but after Mille Miglia experience the axle tubes were pegged as well as welded into the cen-

EXPERIENCE TEACHES.—An improved location for the rear axle tubes, and a single torque arm on the offside of the car in conjunction with a transverse Panhard rod, represent modifications to the rear axle assembly incorporated as the direct result of racing experience.

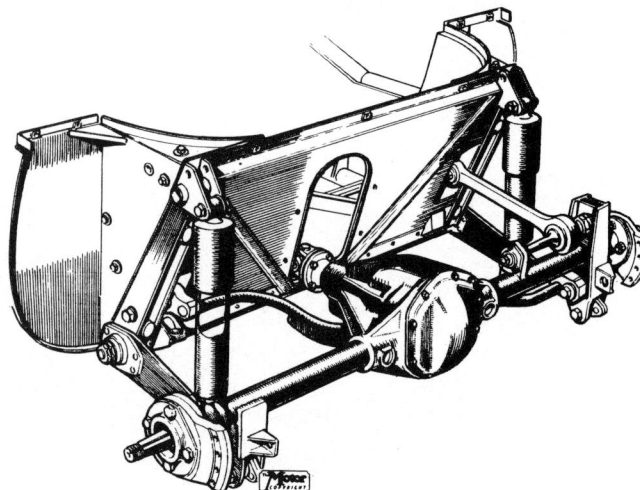

- - - - - - - - - - - - Contd.

It is not too much to say that the successful adoption of the disc-type brake was just as much a turning point in the design of high-speed automobiles as was the use of four-wheel brakes by four differing manufacturers in the 1914 French Grand Prix. In the ensuing 39 years the internal expanding drum-type brake has been considerably improved, but it has not kept pace with increasing demands arising from higher speeds, less body drag and improved suspension systems which permit high rates of negative acceleration without loss of steering control.

In a 24-hour race the problem of sustained braking performance presents peculiar difficulties and it has become axiomatic that on cars capable of 150 m.p.h. and weighing one ton or more, drum brakes must be used with discretion if they are to retain stopping power throughout the full race distance.

Theoretically, a disc brake has a number of advantages. The friction material is fully exposed to the air and is thus well cooled, and the disc that is gripped by the friction pads does not expand or distort whatever temperature it reaches. In practice a number of difficult problems have arisen and it is only recently that they have been overcome. This has been due in large part to intensive development work carried on by the Jaguar Co. in collaboration with the Dunlop Rim and Wheel Co., Ltd., and Girling, Ltd.

The exposed friction pads on a disc brake can perform

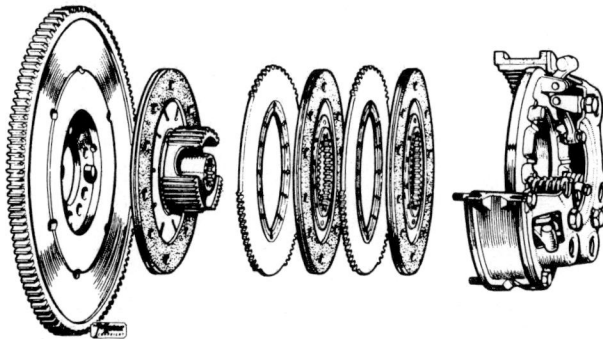

REDUCING g.—With 25% less diameter compensated for by three plates and centrifugally assisted loading, the Borg and Beck clutch has a big safety factor at modern high crankshaft speeds.

about ten times as much work per unit area as a lining within a brake drum, but the total area is limited, in the case of the Jaguar, to around one-third of the normal. There is, therefore, a higher rate of wear. The pads can be made much thicker than ordinary friction linings to compensate for this, but in a given period of time there will still be an increase in pedal travel equivalent to the greater rate of wear.

The disc-type brake has no servo effect (it derives much of its stability from this very fact) and thus if high pedal pressures are to be avoided the driver must have a considerable mechanical advantage in relation to the brake mechanism. This again calls for a long pedal travel.

Finally, owing to clearances in the hub bearings and possible distortion when cornering, the disc itself does not rotate in a constant plane and angular displacement pushes the pads back in their housings when the brakes are not in use. There are thus three separate, if inter-

SAVING 125 h.p.—The decisiveness and sustained efficiency of the Dunlop disc-type brakes (shown here in their latest form) can be shown to be the equivalent of an additional 125 h.p. at the flywheel

related, reasons why disc brakes require a long pedal travel, or frequent adjustment. Both are undesirable features in a high-speed car.

The introduction of an hydraulic servo motor of Girling design has eliminated this problem on the Jaguar by reducing the pedal travel to two inches. A pump driven from the back of the propeller shaft maintains a pressure of 30 lb./sq. in. in a light alloy reservoir, and a movement within the dual pistoned master cylinder discloses a port which permits the pressure oil to supplement the effort of the driver to both front and rear brake assemblies. Should the oil supply fail the driver retains full physical control over the front brake mechanism.

As can be seen from an illustration, a light alloy carrier supports a total of 12 friction pads per wheel at the front (six on each side of the disc) and eight at the back, this reflecting the weight transferred from the rear to the front of the car during the braking act.

The considerable heat input from the hard chromium-plated steel disc to the friction pads when braking is segregated by a steel spacer which breaks the heat path between the pads and the fluid in the wheel cylinders, the latter being in a housing separated from the pads, as shown in a drawing.

In practice for the Le Mans race the Jaguar drivers were able to develop negative acceleration approaching 1g. from 150 m.p.h., and during the race they were able to gain as much as 100 yards at full speed over cars equipped with conventional braking systems. Moreover, although the brakes were fully employed throughout the 24 hours there was no deterioration in their stopping power, and the brake pads had useful life at the end of the race amounting to at least a further six hours of running.

There is no question that of all the new features in the 1953 120C Jaguar the employment of the Girling-operated Dunlop disc brakes was the most decisive on the occasion for which the cars were built, and the most important in the long-term development of the high-speed automobile. Taken in conjunction with the many other improvements effected in the past two years they provide an object lesson in how to improve average speeds within a given framework of engine power and maximum speed, for it can be computed that the benefits obtained by the changes in chassis design were equal to the installation of an engine developing 350 b.h.p. The whole story of this car shows, indeed, convincing proof of Capt. Ferber's "Inventer n'est Rien; Construire c'est Peu: Essayer c'est Tout."

JAGUAR
for Le Mans

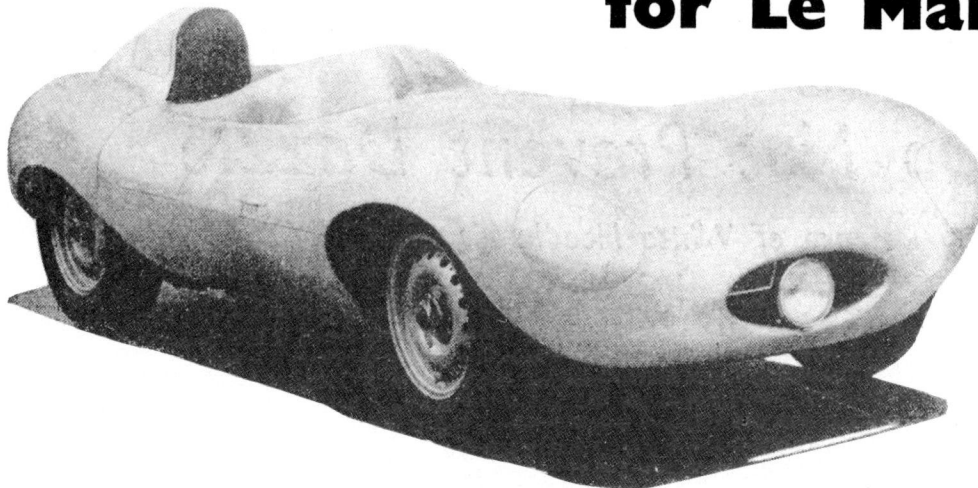

Improved Streamlining — Unitary Construction—Small Frontal Area— More Power—Less Weight

LAST October, it will be recalled, a Jaguar prototype competition model was timed over a measured mile of the Jabbeke road, in Belgium, at a mean speed of 178.383 m.p.h. This car, it can now be revealed, was a prototype of the models which will run this year at Le Mans. The new cars are lower, shorter, lighter and more powerful than the models which were placed first, second and fourth in last year's race, when the winner averaged the record speed of 105.85 m.p.h.

The latest type is the result of 18 months' development work and an example was, in fact, ready for last year's race, the decision not to run it being on the grounds that the design was not then regarded as sufficiently developed.

Outstanding amongst its features of technical interest is a form of unitary construction which is entirely novel and the subject of a patent. Full details cannot be revealed at this stage, but it may be said that the whole structure is carried out in magnesium alloy and

embodies stressed-skin principles, with a fabrication of rectangular-section tubes to support the front nacelle. As before, the entire tail unit, including the large, flexible petrol tank, forms a detachable unit to give access to the rear axle and suspension.

Attention has been paid, both in the mechanical layout of the components and in the shape of the exterior, to reducing frontal area and improving the aerodynamic qualities. To this end, the wheelbase has been reduced by 6 in. to 7 ft. 6 in., with a reduction of 3 in. in overall length to 12 ft. 10 in., whilst the track has been narrowed 1 in. at the front and 2 in. at the rear to give crab-tracked dimensions of 4 ft. 2 in. and 4 ft. 1 in. respectively.

A notable point is the shape of the body sides which follow the "disco-volante" pattern so that, although the overall width (at 5 ft. 5½ in.) is actually 1 in. greater, the effective cross-sectioned area is reduced. Excluding the windscreen and fairing behind the driver's head (a new feature in itself),

the already low overall height has been reduced by 2 in. to 2 ft. 8 in. At the same time, ground clearance has been increased to 7 in. under the flat bottom of the body, to which as much attention has been given as to the streamlining of the upper portions of the structure.

Whilst the wheels remain exposed to avoid pit-work complications and to provide adequate cooling for tyres and brakes, a suggestion of enclosure is noticeable in the way the body contours overlap the upper portions of the wheels. Instead of the so-called aero screen used last year, a wrap-round form of Perspex wind deflector is now employed. The large fuel tank filler cap is located within the fairing behind the driver to avoid an unnecessary protrusion elsewhere; the filler is enclosed by a snap-open panel. In the development of these aerodynamic improvements, wind-tunnel tests with a scale model have played a prominent part.

The engine is a further-developed edition of the well-tried six-cylinder twin-overhead-camshaft XK120C unit and the power has been increased by some 30 b.h.p. to an output of the order of 250 b.h.p., this figure being obtained without any increase in peak r.p.m. A notable feature, used for the first time by Jaguar is dry-sump lubrication aided by an oil cooler.

As before, three twin-choke Weber carburetters are used and receive a ducted supply of fresh air; in this case, however, air is taken from the front opening through which the radiator also receives its supply. To provide clearance for the carburetter intakes without increasing the bonnet height, the entire power unit is canted at 8 deg.

Dunlop disc brakes, which proved such a potent feature last year, are again used and incorporate minor improvements, but a notable innovation is the use of aluminium-alloy wheels of pierced-disc formation in place of the wire type; they are of the knock-on pattern with three-ear caps. Suspension closely follows that of the latest C-type cars with wishbones and longitudinal torsion bars at the front and transverse torsion bars at the rear, the axle in this case being controlled by a pair of links of equal length on each side and located laterally by a Panhard rod.

Except for the inclusion of Ken Wharton in the team in place of Ian Stewart (who has retired from racing for business reasons), the drivers will be as before, the pairs for this year's race being A. P. R. Rolt and Duncan Hamilton (last year's winners), Stirling Moss and Peter Walker, and Peter Whitehead and Ken Wharton.

Replacing the aero screen is a wrap-around transparent wind deflector, while a trap-door in the streamlined head-rest conceals the large fuel filler.

INTERESTING COMPETITION CARS

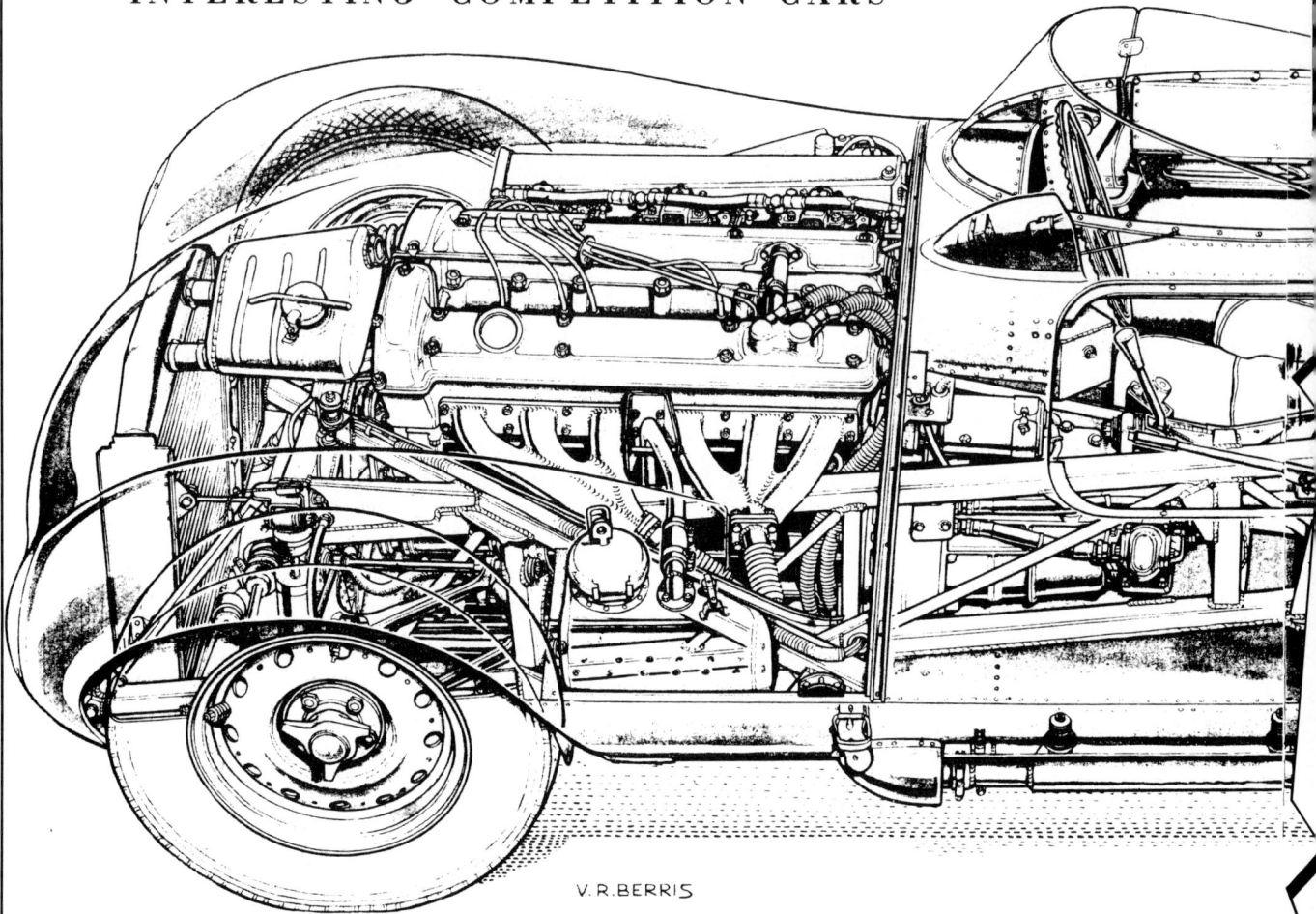

V. R. BERRIS

THE D-TYPE

MONOCOQUE CONSTRUCTION REPLACES

ON the two recent occasions when it has appeared in public, the new competition Jaguar has been extremely successful. At Le Mans in June it gained second and fourth placings, beaten only by the Ferrari powered by a 4,954 c.c. engine, while, soon afterwards at Rheims, it gained the first two places in the 12-hour Sports Car Race. The race averages were 105 m.p.h. at Le Mans (the winning Ferrari recorded 105.1 m.p.h.), and 104.55 m.p.h. at Rheims. So much for its performance, but what of the car itself?

How does it compare with previous competition Jaguars; for example, the cars that gained first, second and fourth positions in the Le Mans 24-hour Race of 1953? The current car is in the direct line of descent from previous models, although there are a number of important differences, outlined in the brief description in *The Autocar* of May 7, 1954.

There are at least two ways of improving a given car's performance: by obtaining greater power from the engine, and by reducing the resistance to motion. The first method increases the amount of work required from the mechanical components; the second can make their task less severe—both approaches have been exploited in the D-type Jaguar.

The C-type Jaguar was built around a tubular frame, the main frame members taking the stresses, while the body panels played a relatively small part in providing structural rigidity. For the D-type, the design of the chassis has been completely revised; there is no separate chassis as such, but the car is built around what may be called a centre-section of monocoque construction and immense strength. This provides a very rigid structure and also results in a useful weight reduction.

The Main Structure

To obtain a clear picture of how the body structure is designed, it is perhaps easiest to consider it as three sections; the centre portion, forming the basis of the structure; the front section, integral with the centre section and housing the engine and front suspension; and the tail assembly (containing the fuel tanks and spare wheel), which is bolted to the centre section.

The centre section consists of an elliptically shaped tube in which are cut suitable openings for the driver and passenger. Below the major axis of the ellipse, extra stiffening is provided by massive L-section pressings, riveted to the main section so that they form, in effect, two tubular members, approximately triangular in cross-section. Both ends of the centre assembly are enclosed by diaphragms which form the front and rear bulkheads.

At the front, a large box-section member is provided above the major axis of the ellipse by the use of two diaphragms and a lower closing plate. In the front bulkhead a central opening houses the transmission and provides additional space for the driver's legs.

The rear bulkhead requires only a small opening, for the propeller-shaft. The good torsional rigidity and beam strength of the centre section is also increased by four tubular members which extend diagonally forward and are welded to the front cross-member. These tubes embrace the complete power unit, while further stiffening is provided by two additional square-section tubes which

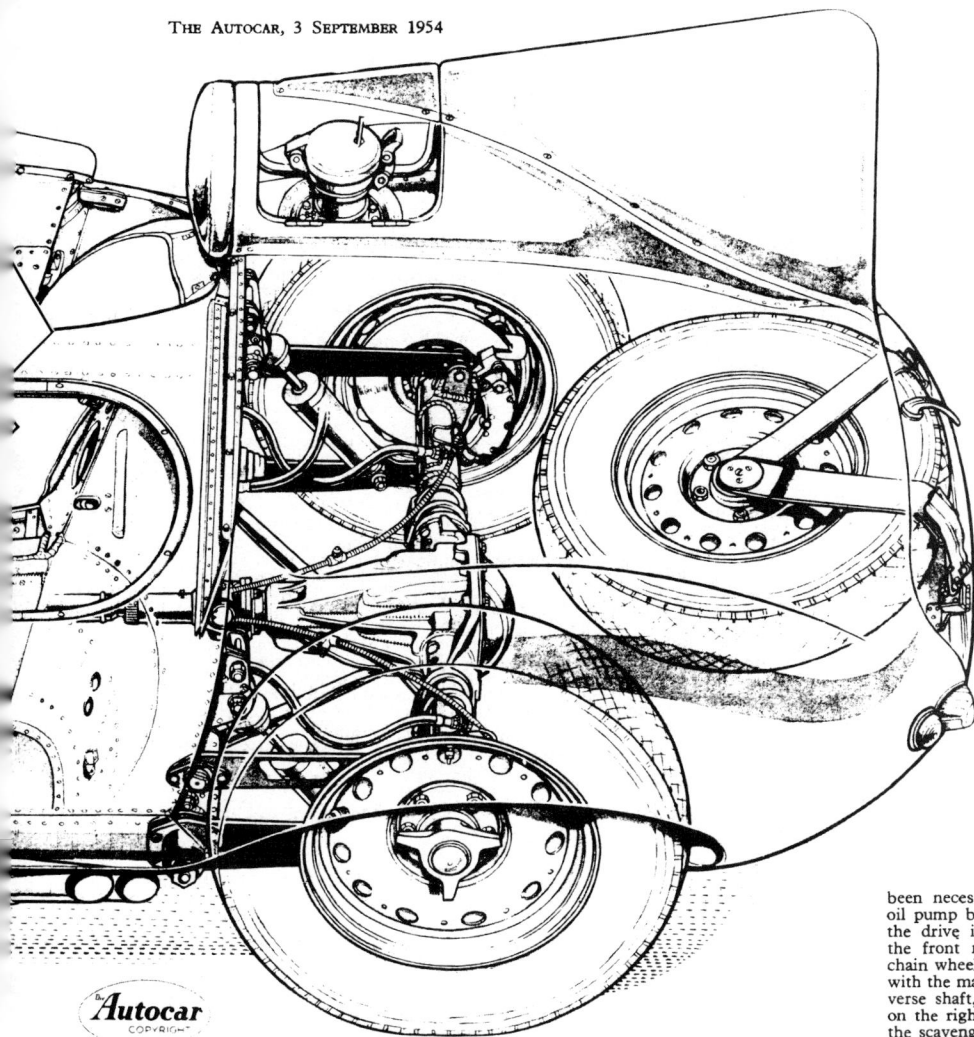

This drawing of the D-type Jaguar shows the layout of the major components together with the main structural members.

JAGUAR

TUBULAR FRAME

run forward diagonally from the front of the bulkhead to meet in the centre of the front cross-member frame. They pass over, and are welded to, the two upper main frame tubes. The whole of the body structure is riveted and arc welded from magnesium alloy, the skin being of 18 gauge material.

Two transverse box-section members are secured to the rear diaphragm, and to these are attached massive vertical assemblies, each of two vertical plates riveted to a channel-section spacer, the whole forming box-section members housing the bearings of the trailing-link rear suspension.

The rear section of the body, which does not carry the main loads, is attached to the centre section by bolts around the periphery of the ellipse, while four additional bolts secure the rear assembly frame members to the rear suspension housing assemblies.

Although the D-type Jaguar is a completely new car, as many standard components as possible are utilized. For

example, although the power unit has dry sump lubrication and develops more power than the standard XK 120 power unit, standard production castings are used for both block and cylinder head—a fact which speaks well for the basic design and layout of the engine and demonstrates to the owner of the normal production machine that his power unit is by no means operating near to the bone!

Developments in the XK 120 engine were outlined in some detail in the April 24, 1953, issue of The Autocar. It is, therefore, intended to explain quite briefly some of the subsequent modifications. All details of modifications are not at present available, for, with any competition machine, detailed development continues until it is superseded by a later model.

Engine Details

A single iron casting forms the cylinder block and crankcase, and the bores (which are relatively long, with a bore to stroke ratio of 0.778 to 1), are machined direct in the casting. The general layout of the crankcase is simple, and there is ample structural rigidity, produced by the internal webbing and the arrangement of the housings for the seven main bearings. The crankshaft and big-end bearings are of indium-coated lead-bronze bearings,

and the shaft itself is of EN16 steel.

The engine has no flywheel, but there is a substantial crankshaft torsional vibration damper at the front, and flywheel effect is produced by the mass of the triple dry-plate clutch and its housing, together with the starter ring which is pressed on the clutch assembly centre section.

The most noticeable difference in the appearance of the engine is caused by the change from wet to dry sump lubrication, made to reduce the height of the engine, the sump height having been halved. This not only enables the bonnet line to be lowered considerably without adversely affecting ground clearance, but also lowers the centre of gravity of one of the major masses.

It has, of course, been necessary to provide an additional oil pump but, as on the standard engine, the drive is taken from a gear between the front main bearing and the timing chain wheel. The crankshaft gear engages with the mating gear which drives a transverse shaft, operating the pressure pump on the right-hand side of the engine and the scavenge pump on the left-hand side.

Oil from the tank is drawn by the pressure pump and directed to the bottom of the oil cooler. Forced through the cooler, it passes along an external pipe to the crankcase where it lubricates the bearings via internal drillings in the normal way. Falling to the base of the sump, the oil is returned to the tank by a dual scavenge pump. It is, of course, necessary to make provision for rapid return of the oil to the tank to prevent build-up of lubricant at the base of the engine, and it must also be remembered that oil produces more resistance than air to crankshaft webs rotating at high speed.

With dry sump lubrication, one of the main problems is to prevent aeration of the lubricant, and on the Jaguar engine this has been accomplished by baffles inside the oil tank, with a breather pipe from the top of the tank connected to the crankcase.

As with the production engine, a light alloy cylinder head is used, with valve seat inserts for both inlet and exhaust valves. It has hemispherical combustion chambers and inclined valves, and the engine operates on a compression ratio of 9 to 1. To aid installation, the engine is inclined in the chassis at an angle of 8 deg to the left when viewed from the cockpit. The barrels of the three double-choke Weber carburettors are set at a similar angle to the vertical centre line of the engine, so that they are truly horizontal when the unit is installed. Six

Both oil and coolant radiators are of light alloy and produced by Marston Excelsior. The radiator system is pressurized to 4lb per sq in by means of a valve unit mounted in the back of the tank.

A conventional fuel system is used, but an unusual feature is the use of flexible tanks, supported in light alloy boxes. To obtain the desired range between refuelling stops, two tanks are used. Twin petrol pumps, placed behind the rear diaphragm, connect to a common delivery pipe to the carburettors.

Power is transmitted from the engine via the triple-plate clutch to the four-speed synchromesh gear box. The main clutch body contains three sets of internal splines equally spaced around its bore, mating with the external splines on the two intermediate driving plates. The rear clutch driven plate is attached to a centrepiece which is internally splined to mate with the gear box input shaft, and contains three sets of external splines carrying the first and second driven plates.

The pressure plate assembly, bolted to the rear, contains six springs together with the toggle levers, which are operated by the ball-bearing thrust withdrawal mechanism. The actual clutch operation is hydraulic by a Girling unit. Radial holes are drilled in the clutch body, to assist cooling and allow lining dust to escape. The complete clutch assembly is housed in a conventional bell housing, with an opening at the back for the starter motor, which is above the transmission on the engine centre line.

Single helical gears are used in the gear box and special close ratios have been chosen. The gears are selected by a short change lever conveniently placed

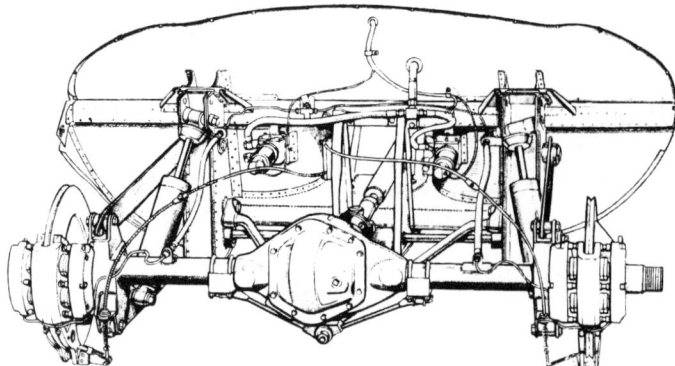

The rear suspension is by means of trailing links and a one-piece torsion bar which is anchored at the centre. Note the disc brakes and additional caliper hand brakes at each end of the axle.

tubular intake ducts are attached to the carburettor intake flanges, and connected by a large-diameter balance tube, the side walls of the intake tubes being cross-drilled at the appropriate points.

An intake duct in the bonnet conveys air from the radiator grille to an open-ended box which, surrounding the carburettor intakes, eliminates the need for pressure balancing pipes to the float chambers. The two three-branch, welded exhaust manifolds direct the gases via two short, flexible pipes into the two main outlet pipes. Just before the pipes terminate in front of the left-hand-side rear wheel, they are enclosed in a sheet-metal cover somewhat similar to a small silencer, which, in conjunction with drilled holes in

the inner walls of the pipes, forms an effective expansion chamber and provides substantial mounting points for securing to the main body structure.

An orthodox arrangement of engine cooling is adopted, but to enable the bonnet height to be kept low a separate light alloy radiator header tank is placed between the front of the engine and the radiator. After passing through the head the coolant is conveyed to the tank which contains outlet pipes at each side, with a central, longitudinal baffle. The intake pipe discharges the coolant near the centre in order to feed both outlets equally and to prevent ineffective cooling that might be caused by the coolant being directed to one side of the radiator.

THE D-TYPE

With the bonnet open the engine and front suspension are very accessible. The oil tank is carried just behind the left front wheel, while the small battery is placed in a similar position behind the right wheel. The large pipe running from the oil tank between the two exhaust manifolds is a breather which is connected to the engine.

The D-type engine can be distinguished by the very shallow sump used in conjunction with the dry sump lubrication system. The torsional vibration damper can be seen at the front of the engine behind the dynamo and water pump driving belts.

vide bearing housings for the trailing-link units. The top links are 16in long and of flat steel plate of approximately $2 \times \frac{1}{4}$in section. Rubber bushes are used for both the inner and the outer bearings. Metal bushes used for the lower bearings are $1\frac{1}{4}$in diameter, and are lubricated by grease nipples. Steel plates are also used for the lower links, and these have a similar centre distance to those above, so that a true parallelogram is formed.

To provide attachment of the lower links to the torsion bars, bearing units are riveted to the inner ends of the lower links; these are also bored to provide clearance for the torsion bar, and contain a larger diameter outer ring which is internally splined. The ends of the torsion bar, also splined, are of a much smaller diameter, so that, to connect the torsion bar to the rear links, rings are used which are externally splined to mate with the lower links and internally splined to connect with the torsion bar.

The single torsion bar used for the rear suspension has an enlarged centre section which is attached to a reaction plate bolted to the centre of the main body structure and containing arms which pass on each

just aft of the gear box unit. A small, flexible breather pipe extends forward and upward to the front of the main bulkhead.

From the rear of the gear box, a short Hardy Spicer propeller shaft continues the drive to the Salisbury rear axle. Except for a change in ratio and modified length of the axle tubes, this unit is similar to that fitted in the production XK. It has a hypoid final drive with a ratio of 2.79 to 1 and, with the tyres

JAGUAR .. continued

used at Le Mans, this gives a speed of 183 m.p.h. at 6,000 r.p.m. engine speed.

The front suspension is by upper and lower wishbones and longitudinal torsion bars. The inner fulcrum bearings are in line with the longitudinal centre line of the chassis, and rubber bushes form both upper and lower bearings; the front bushes are conical, while the rear ones are parallel. The upper wishbone—a one-piece forging—contains the ball housing at its outer end to permit the required movement for suspension and steering, while at the inner end there are two split bosses with pinch bolts.

The front boss is threaded internally, while a smaller diameter, plain section is provided for the rear one, the shaft which forms the top wishbone inner fulcrum having screwed and plain portions to mate

with the wishbone. These two portions are concentric with the axis of the shaft, but the portions which pivot in the rubber bushes are eccentric, and the combined effect of the screw thread and eccentricity enables the wheel caster and camber to be adjusted after assembly.

With a number of torsion bar front suspensions, the bar supporting the weight of the car is concentric with the lower pivot point, but in the Jaguar layout, the front member of the lower wishbone assembly extends from its fulcrum point towards the centre of the car, forming a splined attachment for the bar which runs at an angle of $2\frac{1}{2}$ deg to the centre line of the car. This enables the bar to be changed without disturbing the main suspension components, but it also means that the suspension characteristics are modified slightly by the combined effects of bending and torsion. To adjust the height of the car, a vernier arrangement of splines is provided.

Rack and Pinion Steering

The steering arms, extending in front of the wheel centre line, are linked to the rack and pinion steering unit, which is placed fairly high in front of the main cross-member assembly. There is a universal joint in the steering column.

At the rear, the suspension consists of a live axle, trailing arms and a torsion bar. Two massive, box-section members attached to the main body structure pro-

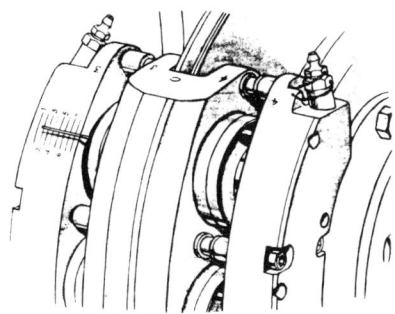

To enable the rate of wear of the brake friction pads to be determined during a race, a small visual indicator is provided with a pointer which lines up with a series of marks engraved on one of the caliper housings.

side of the propeller-shaft. The effective length from the reaction point to the splines is 20in. Under cornering conditions, the plates forming the suspension links are in torsion, increasing the roll stiffness of the car and necessitating the use of material for the links which will permit some flexibility.

To provide transverse location of the axle unit, an open A bracket is pivoted to the main structural members, the bearings being slightly forward of the link bearing line, while the apex of the A

How the tubular frame members are united with the rear diaphragm plate. To provide extra clearance for the driver, a small diameter tube is used in place of a large square section one for the top right-hand member.

This sketch gives a diagrammatic representation of the main members which form the structure of the car; this complete magnesium-alloy structure has been carefully stressed to provide maximum rigidity with very light weight.

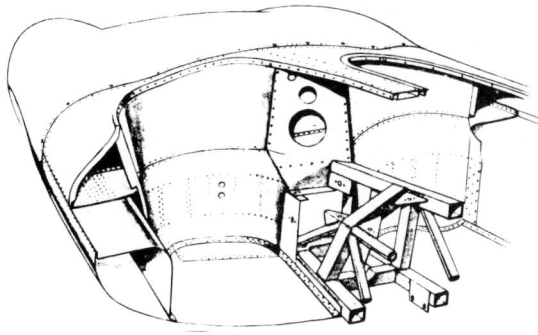

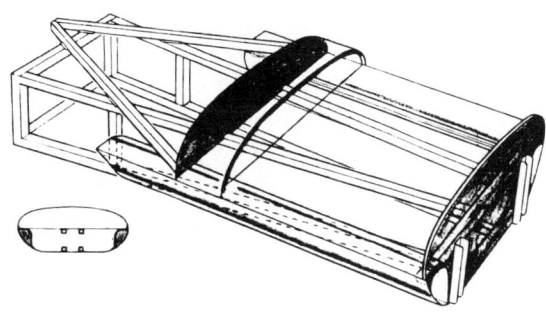

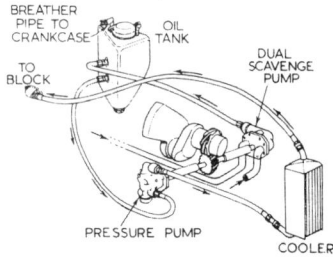

Engine lubrication: A cross shaft, gear driven from the front end of the crankshaft, provides the drive for the pressure and scavenge pumps.

attached to the lower link and bracketed to the main body structure. Built-in bump stops in the dampers consist of large rubber pads placed around the main damper spindle, which contact with the top of the main damper casing, while hydraulic rebound stops are also incorporated.

It was emphasized previously that one of the methods used to improve the performance of the new D-type car was to reduce wind resistance. When the drag of a car is reduced, so that it requires a relatively small b.h.p. to propel it at a high speed, it also requires extremely good brakes, since the retarding effect of air resistance has been reduced. As on last

caliper, machined from medium carbon steel, attached to a suitable flange on the front or rear suspension in the same way as the brake back plate is fixed on a drum-brake system. Bores in this caliper provide housings for the brake pads—which are circular blocks of brake lining material—so that torque reaction is taken by the caliper housing.

To eliminate the effect of disc distortion which might arise through deflection of the rear axle half-shafts when cornering, the rear brake pads are placed symmetrically about the horizontal axis of the wheel centre line. The brake discs are of mild steel, which is hard chromium plated to reduce the rate of wear.

THE D-TYPE

To transmit the drive a neat and compact triple plate clutch is used, and the two intermediate driving plates are splined into the centre portion of the clutch housing.

terminates in a bearing which is secured by a bracket to the axle tubes, serving not only to provide transverse location but also to determine the height of the rear roll centre.

The suspension is damped by CDR 4½ type Girling telescopic dampers. At the front these are attached to the upper section of the front cross member at the top and the lower wishbone at the bottom, while the rear dampers are inclined transversely to clear the upper suspension links, the damper itself being

year's cars, Dunlop disc brakes are fitted to all four wheels. They have 12½in diameter discs and three pairs of pads are used at the front, and two at the rear, to provide the required braking distribution. All the pads are 2¹³⁄₁₆in diameter, so that the total friction lining area for the foot brake is 45 sq in front and 30 sq in rear. To improve the brake life, the volume of the friction material has been increased by approximately 20 per cent since last year.

Structurally, the brakes consist of a

Under very arduous conditions, the temperature rise in and around the caliper area might cause the brake fluid to boil. To provide adequate cooling, the brake-operating cylinders—one for each pad, twenty cylinders therefore, being required —are arranged in the form of light alloy blocks, attached to the calipers by bolts and distance pieces to provide adequate air space. The outer end of each piston has a spherical seating so that slight tilting of the brake pad does not produce severe side loading on the piston. A normal type of rubber diaphragm seal is fitted towards the outer end of the piston to prevent foreign matter from reaching the cylinder bores. Drillings in the light alloy block take the supply pipes, while nipples are provided at convenient points to enable the system to be bled.

Automatic Adjustment

It is necessary to reduce to a minimum the movement required to bring the brake pads into contact with the disc, but at the same time to ensure that the pads are not rubbing when the brakes are not applied. If an unnecessarily large clearance were provided between pad and disc there would be an excessively long pedal movement before the brakes came into operation, owing to the large number of operating cylinders that are employed in this system.

To overcome this difficulty an ingenious system of retraction and automatic adjustment is provided to maintain

Left: Air scoops form part of the unsprung mass on the front suspension, and direct air over the front brake discs.

The front torsion bars are attached to an extension on the front portion of the lower wishbone, which is continued in past the fulcrum point.

7

only 0.010in to 0.015in clearance between the pad and the disc when the brakes are in the off position.

To apply the brakes, a dual hydraulic system is provided, with servo assistance by a Plessey pump driven, from the back end of the gear box, whenever the propeller-shaft is rotating. A simple hydraulic layout is used to operate the front brakes which, if necessary, can be applied without assistance from the servo, in the event of a failure occurring in the servo circuit.

With the servo in operation, the fluid is pumped from the header tank into the rear of the master cylinder, through four cross drillings into the hollow centre-

JAGUAR .. continued

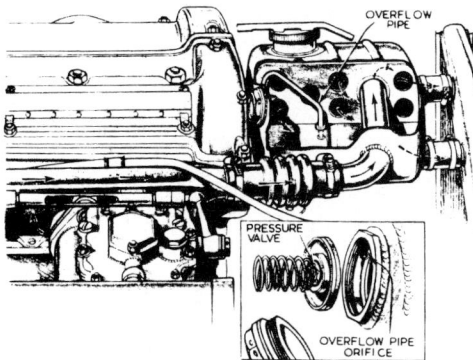

A baffle plate is fitted halfway across the radiator header tank to distribute the flow through both sides of the film block. The overflow pipe from the pressure valve runs out through the base of the header tank.

section of the rear portion of the piston, and out into another pipe which returns to the header tank. Whenever the car is in forward motion the fluid circulates in this way.

When the brakes are applied, the rear piston is forced against the main piston, applying the front brakes, and at the same time preventing the fluid from the servo pump returning to the header tank. The line pressure from the servo pump increases, and as this pipe is connected to the rear brakes they also are applied, and at the same time the build-up in servo pressure exerts a force on the back

The layout of the pistons in the brake master cylinder. An hydraulic servo is used.

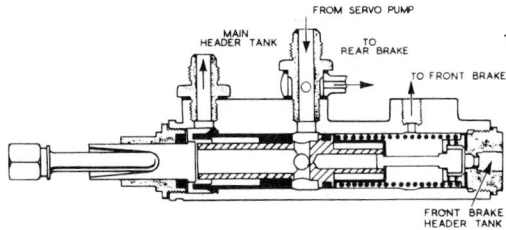

of the master cylinder piston which applies the front brakes.

Although it is necessary for the driver's foot to close the valve which increases the line pressure, the area so covered is much less than the area of the front brake master cylinder piston, and it is this difference which determines the servo ratio.

As the servo pump is driven from the output side of the propeller-shaft, it will be rotated in reverse whenever the car moves backward, and, unless precautions were taken, this might cause air to be drawn into the system.

A valve box is fitted between the input and output pipes from the pump, with a non-return valve so placed that pressure in the suction side of the pump causes the valve to open, providing a short open circuit between inlet and outlet sides of the pump. Two separate sets of mechanically operated calipers with triangular friction linings, fitted below the main hydraulically operated units on the rear brakes, are operated by a single cable connected to the handbrake lever by a pulley compensating mechanism.

To reduce weight, perforated disc light alloy wheels are used. They have a centre-lock fixing but, in place of the splined hub often used on a conventional centre-lock wheel, the wheel disc is attached to a steel centre portion by five bolts which have domed heads. These locate in holes drilled in the back flange of the hub and transmit drive or braking torque.

The cockpit is well laid out and is free from unnecessary equipment. It contains three instruments—a tachometer with an additional hand to record the maximum speed which the engine attains, an oil pressure gauge and a water temperature gauge. The steering wheel is adjustable and held on its splined column by a screwed clamp. In true racing tradition it has light alloy spokes and a neat wooden rim.

The curved plastic windscreen sweeps well round the sides of the cockpit, and the rear part of the body has a head rest just in front of the fuel filler cap and, to improve the direction stability under adverse wind

The fuel is carried in two flexible tanks which are neatly fitted into light alloy boxes in the tail of the car.

conditions, particularly at speeds of over 150 m.p.h., a tail fin which neatly blends into the driver's head rest.

SPECIFICATION

Engine.—6-cyl. 83 × 106 mm, 3,442 c.c. Compression ratio 9 to 1. 250 b.h.p. at 6,000 r.p.m. Maximum torque 242 lb ft at 4,000 r.p.m. Seven-bearing crankshaft. Hemispherical combustion chambers. Overhead valves operated by twin overhead camshafts.

Clutch.—Three plates, six springs. Hydraulically operated, ball-bearing withdrawal mechanism.

Gear Box.—Ratios: Top 2.79; third 3.57; second 4.58; first 5.98 to 1. Reverse 6.1 to 1.

Final Drive.—Hypoid bevel, ratio 2.79 to 1 (14:39). Two-pinion differential.

Suspension.—Front, independent, wishbone and torsion bars. Rear, trailing link and torsion bar. Suspension rate (at the wheel) front, 120 lb per in; rear, 120 lb per in.

Brakes.—Dunlop disc. Three-pad front; two-pad rear. Discs: front 12¾in diameter,

The starter ring is attached to the centre of the clutch casing; no normal flywheel is used, the necessary flywheel effect being obtained by the mass of the clutch and ring.

rear 12¾in diameter. Total lining area: 75 sq in; 45 sq in front.

Steering.—Rack and pinion. Eight-toothed pinion. 1¾ turns from lock to lock.

Wheels and Tyres.—Dunlop light alloy, perforated disc, centre-lock wheels. 6.50-16in Dunlop racing tyres on 5.00-16in rims.

Electrical Equipment.—12-volt; 40-ampère-hour battery. Head lamps, 48- or 60-watt bulbs.

Fuel and Oil System.—37 Imp. gallons in two flexible tanks. Oil capacity 3½ gallons.

Main Dimensions.—Wheelbase 7ft 6in; track (front) 4ft 2in; (rear) 4ft. Overall length 12ft 10in. Width 5ft 5¼in. Height, at scuttle, 2ft 8in; at fin, 3ft 8in. Ground clearance 5¼in under sump. Frontal area 10.85 sq ft. Turning circle 32ft.

The JAGUAR "D" Type

S P E C I F I C A T I O N

ENGINE. Six cylinder 3½ litre Jaguar engine 83 mm. 106 mm., 3,442 c.c. Twin overhead camshafts driven by two stage chain. Cylinder head of high tensile aluminium alloy with hemi-spherical combustion chambers. Aluminium alloy pistons, steel connecting rods. Forced lubrication on dry sump principle. Cooling by pump.

TRANSMISSION. 4 speed synchromesh gearbox operated by central remote control lever. Triple dry plate clutch.

SUSPENSION. Independent front suspension incorporating transverse wishbones and torsion bars with telescopic shock absorbers. Rear suspension by trailing links and torsion bar with telescopic shock absorbers.

BRAKES. Dunlop disc type.

STEERING. Rack and pinion. Steering wheel adjustable for reach.

WHEELS AND TYRES. Dunlop light alloy perforated disc with centre lock hubs. Dunlop Racing tyres and tubes.

FUEL SUPPLY. By large S.U. electric pumps from rear mounted tanks.

ELECTRICAL EQUIPMENT. 12v. 40 amp-hour battery. Constant voltage controlled ventilated dynamo. Flush fitting headlamps and sidelamps, integral stop/tail lamps with built-in reflectors. Instrument panel light. Horn. Starter motor.

INSTRUMENTS. Revolution counter, oil pressure gauge, water thermometer gauge, ignition warning light.

FRAME AND BODY. Integral frame and body. Body of light alloy, constructed on monocoque principles. Two seater body complying with F.I.A. sports car regulations. Spare wheel carried horizontally in tail.

DIMENSIONS. Overall length 14' 8", overall width 5' 4½". Height at scuttle 2' 8", wheelbase 7' 6". Track (front) 4' 2", (rear) 4'.

J A G U A R   C A R S   L T D   .   C O V E N T R Y   .   E N G L A N D

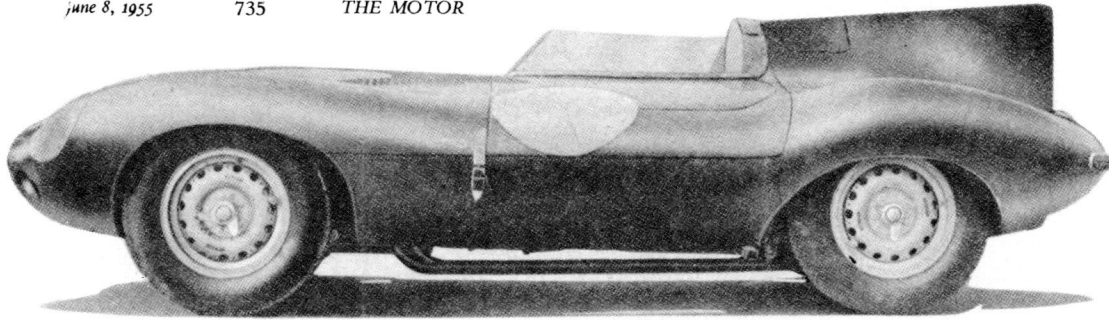

SLEEKER in appearance than last year's models, the 1955 Le Mans cars have lengthened nose sections and tail fins for better penetration and greater stability, and driver protection is increased by longer and deeper windshields.

JAGUARS for LE MANS

Latest D-type in Production Form Will be Raced with Detail Prototype Modifications

AS already stated in *The Motor* three weeks ago, the official team of Jaguar cars for Le Mans will be basically standard production D-types. These, however, differ in many important respects from the preproduction models which raced last year, when Rolt and Hamilton took second place at fractionally over 105 m.p.h., only 90 sec. behind the 4.9-litre Ferrari at the end of the 24 hours of racing which ended in appalling weather.

Changes incorporated for the production edition (which is beginning to come through the Coventry works in limited numbers) include the use of a separate frame built up of brazed steel tubes instead of the combined light-alloy frame-cum-body centre-section used originally, detail modifications to the tail and rear suspension, rearrangement of the cockpit to give more elbow room, the provision of a separate sub-frame at the front to carry the radiator and bonnet, and minor changes to the transmission.

These alterations have been effected with the triple purpose of facilitating production, making repair quicker and easier in the event of accidental damage, and incorporating improvements in the light of prototype experience.

In addition, the actual Le Mans entries have certain other prototype modifications which still further increase performance and suitability for the race. These include a new cylinder head and exhaust system (which puts up the power output from 250 b.h.p. at 6,000 r.p.m. to 285 b.h.p. at 5,750 r.p.m.), a supplementary fuel tank, and certain body changes to the nose, screen and tail fin to give improved penetration and stability as well as better driver protection on the faster sections of the circuit (where speeds exceeding 170 m.p.h. were recorded by the Moss-Walker Jaguar last year).

So much for the broad picture. In the description which

JAGUAR 1955 "D" TYPE

Engine dimensions		
Cylinders		6
Bore		83 mm.
Stroke		106 mm.
Cubic capacity		3,442 c.c.
Piston area		50.4 sq. in.
Valves		Overhead (twin o.h.c.)
Compression ratio		9 to 1

Engine performance		
	Production	Le Mans
Max. b.h.p.	250	285
at (r.p.m.)	6,000	5,750
Max. b.m.e.p.	174	190
at (r.p.m.)	4,000	5,500
B.H.P. per sq. in. piston area	4.96	5.65
Peak piston speed, ft. per min.	4,180	4,010

Engine details	
Carburetters	3 Weber (twin-choke) 45 mm.
Ignition	Coil
Plugs	Champion NA10
Fuel pump	2 S.U. electric
Fuel capacity	36 gallons
Oil filter	None
Oil capacity	3½ gallons
Cooling system	Pump
Water capacity	29 pints
Electrical system	12 volt
Battery capacity	38 amp./hr.

Transmission		
Clutch		Borg and Beck 7¼ in. triple plate
Gear ratios:	Production	Le Mans
Top	3.54	2.53
3rd	4.53	3.23
2nd	5.82	4.15
1st	7.59	5.42
Rev.	7.77	5.55
Prop. shaft	Open Hardy Spicer	
*Final drive	Salisbury hypoid (for alternative ratios, see footnote).	

Chassis details	
Brakes	Dunlop disc with Servo
Brake disc diameter	12¾ in.
Friction lining area	75 sq. in.
Suspension:	
Front	Independent, by wishbone and torsion bar
Rear	Trailing link, with torsion bar.
Shock absorbers	Girling telescopic
Wheel type	Dunlop light alloy disc
Tyre size	6.50—16
Steering gear	Rack and pinion
Steering wheel	16 in. light alloy

Dimensions		
Wheelbase		7 ft. 6½ in.
Track:		
Front		4 ft. 2 in.
Rear		4 ft. 2 in.
Overall length		12 ft. 10 in.
		(Le Mans 13 ft. 5½ in.)
Overall width		5 ft. 5½ in.
Overall height:		
At scuttle		31½ in.
Over fin		45 in.
Ground clearance		5½ in.
Turning circle		35 ft.
Dry weight		Approx. 1,940 lb.

Performance data		
Piston area, sq. in. per ton		58.2
Brake lining area, sq. in. per ton		86.6
Top gear m.p.h. per 1,000 r.p.m.	Production†	Le Mans
	24.2	33.9
Top gear m.p.h. at 2,500 ft/min. piston speed	87.2	122
Litres per ton-mile, dry	4,950	3,540

Notes—*On production models, alternative final drive ratios of 2.93, 3.31 and 3.92 are available.

†Based on 3.54 axle ratio.

ELBOW ROOM for the driver has been increased by structural changes; features visible here are the fly-off handbrake, central gearlever, tachometer and oil temperature gauges on the left and oil pressure and water temperature gauges on the right.

THREE twin-choke Weber carburetters supply mixture to the twin-o.h.c. engine which, in Le Mans form with special cylinder head and exhaust system, produces 285 b.h.p. Oil tank on the left and battery on the right, and coolant header tank between engine and radiator are features visible below.

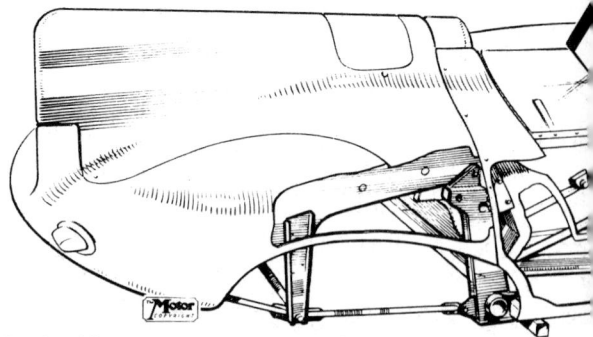

Jaguars for Le Mans - - - - Contd.

follows, the production D-type will be dealt with and details of special features of the Le Mans cars included where they apply.

The most fundamental difference between the production D-type and the cars which raced last year lies in the body-frame structure although, at a quick glance, the alterations might appear to be of a quite minor nature. The original D-type, it will be recalled, consisted basically of three structures, although two of them, the stressed-skin cockpit and the tubular framework carrying the engine and front suspension, were built up into a single indivisible unit, leaving only the tail unit readily detachable.

On the production D-type, the three units are quite separate entities. As before, the centre cockpit section of aluminium-magnesium alloy takes the form of an elliptical structure in which the bulkheads fore and aft act as stiffening diaphragms and there are, in addition, inverted L-shaped internal pressings running along the base on each side to form large-section longitudinal stiffeners, the whole forming an immensely strong stressed-skin foundation.

The triangulated tubular frame which mates with this structure is similar to the original design forward of the front bulkhead but the upper longitudinals slope downwards to meet the longitudinal base members at a point abreast of the rear bulkhead, thus both simplifying the structure and giving the driver much more elbow room. As before, an open A-shaped formation of tubes is superimposed on the forward part of the structure, with its apex just behind the radiator and the extremities of its legs mating up with the front bulkhead at the point of maximum width.

At the front, the framework is strutted and cross-braced

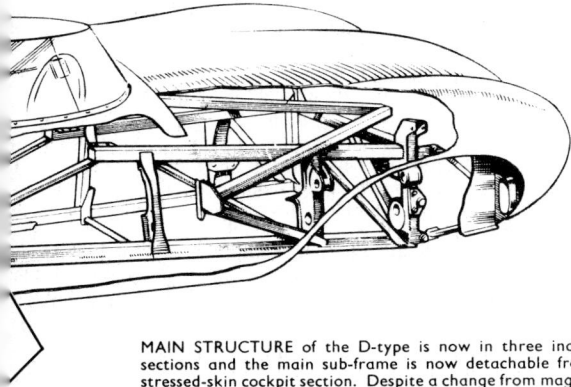

MAIN STRUCTURE of the D-type is now in three individual sections and the main sub-frame is now detachable from the stressed-skin cockpit section. Despite a change from magnesium alloy to high-tensile steel for the framework, its weight is slightly less.

SIMILAR in layout to previous D-types, the front suspension of the 1955 cars consists of unequal-length wishbones, with torsion bars attached to an extension of the lower wishbone, and therefore not concentric with the suspension pivot. The Dunlop disc brakes have three pairs of pads to each front wheel.

to form, in effect, a double cross member to carry the front suspension, whilst a detachable sub-frame (instead of an extension of the main framework) carries the water and oil radiators and acts as a pivot for the large one-piece bonnet and front wings. This sub-frame is of circular-section tubes whilst the main frame consists of rectangular or square-sections (flanged in the case of the base longerons to carry the floor), with circular section tubes for the lattice members.

Less Weight

A fundamental difference (which applies to the Le Mans cars as well as to the production types) is that this entire framework is fabricated from 50-ton high-tensile steel tubing with brazed joints instead of magnesium alloy with welded joints originally employed. Particularly interesting is the fact that the weight is stated to be very slightly less than before, due to a combination of the minor simplification which has been effected and the lighter-gauge tubing which the change from alloy to steel has made possible.

From a production and maintenance angle, the new design has great advantages. In the event of minor frontal damage, the radiator sub-frame can be removed by undoing four bolts, whilst the entire frame can be detached from the cockpit section with reasonable ease. Actually, it is secured by four bolts at the rear of the centre section, a series of bolts securing the floor to the base longerons and six bolts on each side where the top A-members mate with the forward bulkhead; when these have been removed, it is necessary only to cut away a small series of rivets where the battery and oil-tank compartments are attached to enable the frame to be withdrawn forwards.

As before, the aluminium-magnesium alloy tail is a separate unit, secured by four main bolts, plus a smaller series securing the top panelling. In construction, however, it differs considerably, having no internal framework but consisting of a stressed-skin structure in which internal diaphragm construction provides the necessary stiffeners. The new design is slightly lighter and provides more wheel clearance.

The production models have the same bonnet design as on the original D-types but for this year's Le Mans cars, the nose has been extended 7½ in. to give reduced drag and includes elaborate air ducting, as seen on the right.

The forward portions of the wing formations are cut away for the deeply-recessed headlamps and miniature side lamps but the lamp compartments are enclosed by shaped Perspex covers which conform to the wing contour. This year, lighting has been improved by omitting the separate road lamp but using 100-watt bulbs in the main lamps, necessitating a larger dynamo and battery.

Production D-types have the wrap-round windscreen and extended head fairing (but without tail fin) which

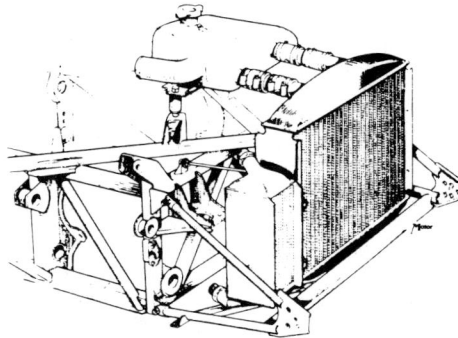

A SEPARATE tubular sub-frame now carries oil and water radiators, an arrangement which has obvious repair advantages over the main frame extension used previously.

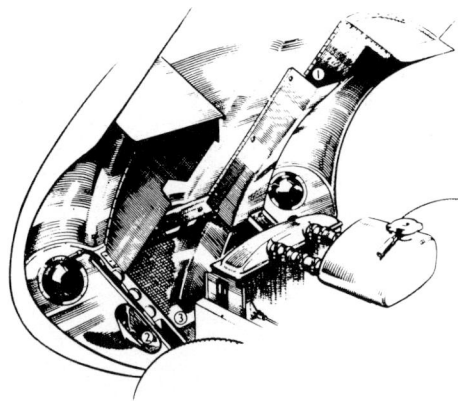

ELABORATE air ducting is a feature of the Le Mans cars this year, the hinged nose section having (1) a channel leading cool air to the carburetters, (2) ducts for brake cooling and (3) a mesh-covered intake for oil and water radiators.

Jaguars for Le Mans - - - - Contd.

represented such a great step forward in driver protection last year, but on this year's Le Mans cars the plan has been carried a step further. Instead of the semi-circular Perspex screen being tapered down to end short of the fairing, it now continues at almost full height to mate up with the headrest. This arrangement, in conjunction with a wider fairing, is designed to obviate the buffeting which drivers experienced down the Mulsanne straight. As before, the Le Mans cars will run with a tail fin.

Mechanically, production D-type models follow the original specification fairly closely, although a number of detail improvements are incorporated. The engine is the 250-b.h.p. edition of the XK engine and it is an interesting commentary on the extent to which the racing Jaguar models follow normal productions that the crankshaft, connecting rods and cylinder-block castings are taken from stock and, apart from minor additional machining, are identical with those used in the Mark VII saloon.

Main details of the production engine are given in the specification panel and need not be repeated here. For this year's Le Mans race, a prototype cylinder head is being used, in which special attention has been paid to improved filling at the top end of the power curve. As before two three-branch exhaust manifolds are used, but on these models the two exhaust pipes are not united but remain separate and are extended to a point under the tail with the idea of increasing the extractor effect.

Other changes for Le Mans include extended air intake pipes for the three twin-choke Weber carburetters and the omission of the large-diameter balance pipes between the intakes.

The nett result of these modifications is to increase the power output to 285 b.h.p. at 5,750 r.p.m.

Other D-type engine features of note include dry-sump lubrication (which saves 2¾ in. in overall height) with a separate tank and an oil radiator, whilst, also to save height, a separate water header tank is interposed between the cylinder head and the matrix. The fuel system, with twin electric pumps, is orthodox, but a notable feature is the use of a flexible aircraft-type fuel tank housed in the tail. Originally, a main and a supplementary tank were used, but the new tail construction has caused the latter to be omitted on the production D-type.

In unit with the engine are the clutch and gearbox, but a point of interest is that no normal flywheel is used, the mass of the three-plate clutch and starter ring being adequate at the high speeds involved. The close-ratio gearbox now has synchromesh on all four speeds, with

helical teeth for all except reverse. Another new feature is an oil pump giving a force-feed to every bearing.

Aft of the gearbox, a short open propeller shaft takes the drive to a conventional hypoid rear axle. Several final-drive ratios (see data panel) are available on the production examples. For Le Mans, however, the final drive ratio is stated to be 2.53 to 1, this giving a road speed of 33.9 m.p.h. per 1,000 engine r.p.m. with the standard 6.50-16-in. tyres, i.e. 195 m.p.h. on peak r.p.m.

The front suspension follows the already familiar D-type lines with wishbones of not quite equal length and longitudinal torsion bars, but the rear anchorage of the bars has been modified slightly although the front attachment remains, as before, to an inner extension of the lower wishbone instead of being concentric with the lower pivot point. This has the advantage that a bar can be changed without disturbing the main components and allowance is made in the suspension characteristics for the fact that the torsion bars bend slightly in operation as well as twisting. An anti-roll bar is fitted.

At the rear, the general arrangement of the torsion-bar suspension follows last-year's prototype design but has been modified in detail. The live axle is carried on a pair of parallel trailing links on each side which are formed of steel plates and, being in torsion during cornering, increase the roll stiffness. Transverse location is provided by an open A member, the apex of which is attached to the axle casing. A single transverse torsion bar, splined to the lower link bosses is used; it is housed in a large-diameter tube and has an enlarged centre section which is anchored in the centre of the tube so that the two halves act, in effect, as separate torsion bars.

The whole assembly is built up on a pair of fabricated suspension posts connected at the base by the tube housing, the torsion bar and by a smaller upper tube at the top; the posts are bolted to transverse box-section stiffeners formed in the rear bulkhead and the axle and suspension can thus be detached as a complete unit. As at the front, Girling telescopic dampers with built-in bump stops are employed.

Dunlop disc brakes with three pairs of pads at the front and two at the rear to give the necessary front/rear distribution are used and incorporate the usual automatic adjustment. Servo operation, with a fluid pump to increase the driver's effort, is employed, but the system has now been modified to increase the proportion of physical effort in relation to servo effort and thus give a more progressive action. For the hand brake, mechanical operation applies a separate pair of caliper pads on the rear discs.

The main dimensions are unchanged (except for the extended nose of the Le Mans cars).

FOR RACING, a metal cover encloses the passenger's seat alongside the driving compartment. The fuel filler is beneath a hinged flap behind the headrest, the spare wheel being housed in the extreme rear of the car.

Jaguar for Le Mans 1956

WITH three outright wins, two seconds and one third place, together with the honour of being, in 1953, the first make to win at an average speed above 100 m.p.h., Jaguars have dominated the post-war series of races in much the same way that Bentley did up to 1930. Their chance of drawing level with Bentley and Alfa Romeo, each of whom have won the race four times, is well within the realms of probability this year. Three works cars are entered, and the results of fuel consumption tests in practice will determine how many of them will have fuel injection or carburettors. The new regulations demand an average fuel consumption of about 12 m.p.g. to provide a safety margin, and the greater economy possible with fuel injection may weigh the balance in its favour. The cars are basic D-type production units, similar in specification to last year's winning car.

A neat solution has been reached for the full-width screen regulation this year. On the driver's side it is still fully wrapped round and merges into the head rest, with a joint in the portion occupied by the door. Instead of the previous metal tonneau cover over the passenger seat, a transparent plastic cover merges with the top of the screen to enclose the passenger's seat completely. In this way the eddies associated with an open screen have been avoided. In accordance with the regulations there is an electric screen wiper on the driver's side.

The same cylinder head as used last year—developed by Harry Weslake—is retained, with the inlet valves inclined at 35 deg and the exhaust at 40 deg from the cylinder centre line. Two plugs per cylinder were part of the original design, but development experience proved that dual ignition offered no advantages and only one plug is now used.

There are modifications only in detail to the front and rear suspension. The diameter of the front anti-roll bar has been increased by ⅛in to ¹¹⁄₁₆in diameter

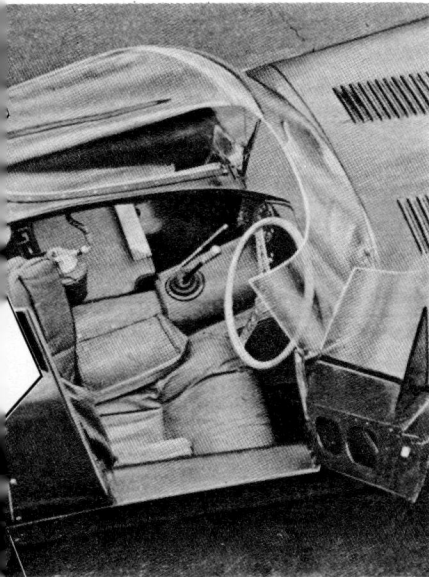

Jaguars' sleek bodies are fundamentally unchanged since last year. The clever low-drag compromise over the passenger's seat, to reduce the handicap of the regulation full-width screen, is clear in these two views

to increase the roll stiffness. At the rear the live axle, located by a pair of parallel trailing arms, is retained, but an anti-roll bar connects the upper links on each side to increase roll stiffness at the rear. Fuel tankage, by regulations, has been reduced from 36 to 28 gallons (126 litres) and this, in conjunction with other small modifications, has reduced the overall weight by approximately 50 lb.

Jaguars used fuel injection on one car at Sebring this year, and also at Rheims where they won the 12-hour sports car race, so that they have considerable race experience of this installation. In the Lucas system the fuel pressure pump is separated from the metering device, to eliminate vapour-lock troubles. There is an electrically driven fuel pump located at the rear of the car, which circulates the fuel continuously at 100 lb sq in, returning the surplus back to the tank. The pump incorporates a primary cloth filter as used on diesel engines; it feeds through a secondary filter, mounted on the bulkhead, to the metering distributor, which consists of a rotating sleeve, driven at camshaft speed from the front timing chain idler sprocket. The sleeve is hollow, and has one port for each cylinder. In the hollow portion of the sleeve a shuttle, or free piston, is forced back and forth by fuel under pressure, thus uncovering inlet and outlet ports. The travel of this piston is limited by a control stop, which is linked to a spring-loaded air piston the position of which is varied by manifold depression. There is an external adjustment for changes in barometric pressure and air temperature.

Fuel is delivered to the port by a spring-loaded, pintle-type nozzle which discharges at a pressure of 75 lb sq in, and sprays against the direction of the incoming air. The gate or slide-valve type of throttle is a single plate, with six holes corresponding in pitch and diameter with the ports. It is operated from a rack and pinion quadrant at the bulkhead end. This design ensures synchronization of opening, and gives an unobstructed path from the flared air intakes to the valve at the fully open position.

LE MANS

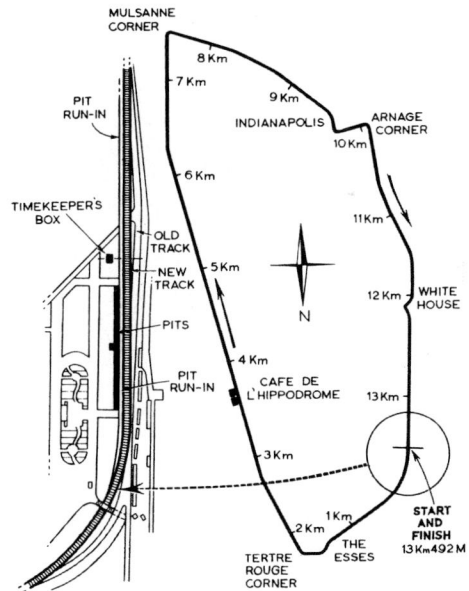

Diagram of the 8.4-mile circuit, with an enlarged plan of the pit and grandstand area to clarify this year's alterations. Signalling pits will be on the Mulsanne straight.

reprinted from

Auto Course

vol V no 5 1956

From race track to production line; clever organization allows the sports-racing D Type to be built by normal factory methods, rather than by the individualistic craftsmen of the development department

The D-Type Jaguar

BECAUSE of the innumerable successes of Jaguar in the leading sports car events of recent years, and the way in which popular opinion associates their name with Le Mans, many people have grown to accept the Coventry firm as a traditional part of the racing scene, and it requires conscious thought to remember that, in fact, they have only been racing for a very few years, and that the sum total of their racing experience is a fraction of that possessed by such of their rivals as Ferrari, Maserati and Mercedes-Benz. At the moment of writing, it is only five short years since the first sports/racing Jaguar was conceived on the design staffs' drawing boards, and until Le Mans in 1951 Jaguar competition experience had been limited to semi-official assistance of certain private owners, although, pre-war a team from the factory had won the coveted Manufacturers' Team Prize in the RAC Rally.

Attempts to clarify the relationship between the various D Types can, at first, be very confusing, as the differences between the 1954 and 1955 cars, and between both these models and the production D Type, are slight but important. Ignoring the power unit for a moment, the basic differences between the three cars are as follows. The 1954 D Type employed a monocoque elliptical central section, fabricated in magnesium alloy. Integral with this central section was a front section, constructed of square- and round-section aluminium tubing, which provided

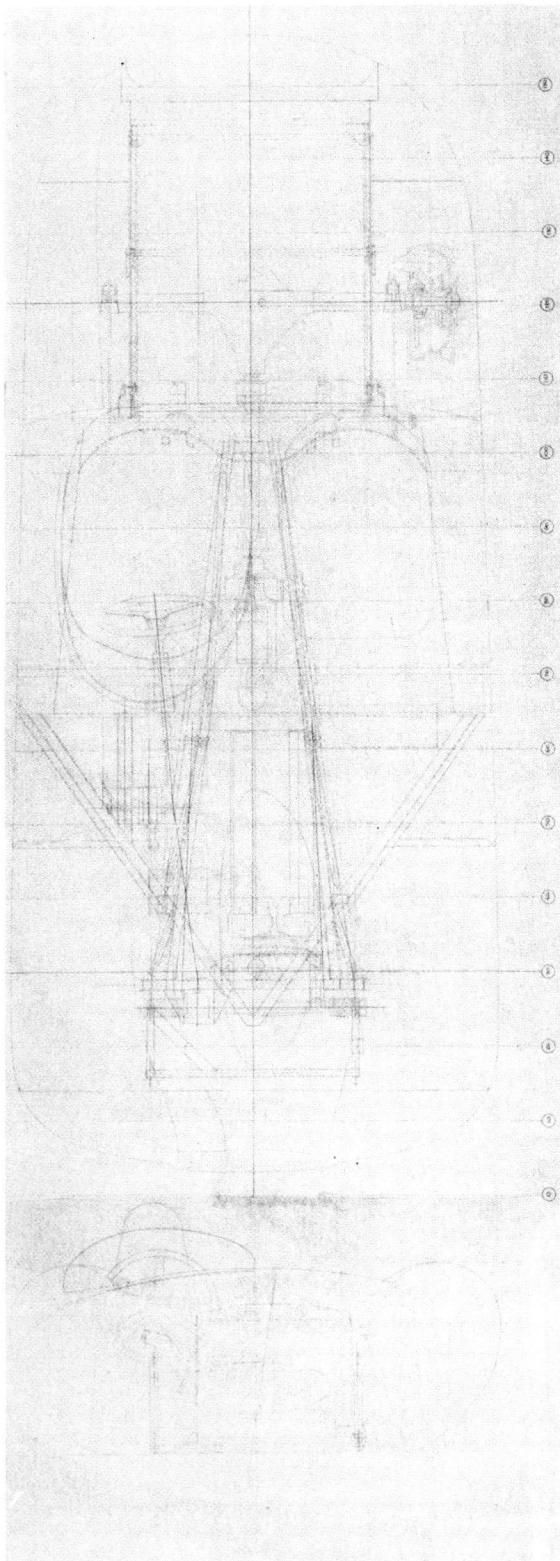

attachment points for both engine and front suspension. The 1955 cars retained the magnesium alloy central section, but the one-piece method of construction had been found in practice to be very costly and difficult to repair, as every joint was secured by Argon arc welding, so the front section – although retaining the same basic design – was changed to steel tubes. This was attached by bolts to the central section, as was the rear section, which carries the fuel tank and spare wheel. The present production D Type is, in effect, an amalgam of the works' cars of 1954 and 1955: the body and framework are of 1955 type, while the engine conforms in power output to the cars run officially in 1954.

The tubular steel frame is made from 45 tons per sq. in. tubing, the main structural members being of 18 s.w.g. thickness and those less heavily loaded are of 20 s.w.g. The new steel frame was found to be slightly lighter than its aluminium ancestor: the total weight, in fact, of the framework being 56 lb. The whole of the central body structure is riveted and welded from 18-gauge magnesium alloy.

It is an interesting reflexion of the longevity of the production

...the D-Type Jaguar...

XK140 engine that both the C and D types, in their various forms, have used that engine as a basis: the standard crankcase and cylinder block are used. Broadly speaking, development work has been confined to the obtaining of more power, and the factor of reliability has never been in question. Rather naturally, the manufacturers are reticent regarding detailed development as, until any particular detail is superseded, it would be pointless to publicize the reasons for success. The cylinder block and crankcase is a single iron casting, with the unusual bore : stroke ratio of $0.778 : 1$. Particularly adequate structural rigidity is secured by the internal webbing of the crankcase, and the arrangement of the housings for the seven main bearings. Within the bearings, which are indium lead bronze, runs the crankshaft of EN 16 steel. No flywheel is fitted, but a flywheel effect is obtained by the adequate torsional vibration damper fitted to the front of the crankshaft, and by the mass of the triple-plate clutch and the starter ring.

The most obvious external difference to the appearance of the engine, as compared with the normal XK series, is caused by the change from wet- to dry-sump system of lubrication. In addition to the reduction in engine height, which allowed the engine to be lowered in the car, without reducing the ground clearance, this has had the effect of lowering the centre of gravity of the heaviest mass of weight in the car. One of the main problems with dry-sump lubrication is to prevent aeration of the lubricant, and for this reason the Jaguar employs baffles inside the oil tank, from which a breather pipe connects with the crankcase. After being circulated through the engine bearings the oil falls to the base of the sump, but because oil offers much more resistance than air, it is necessary to return the oil to the tank very quickly, by means of a dual scavenge pump. Although the engine is basically the same as that used in even the Mk. VII saloon, considerably more power is obtained from it, but it is in other directions that one should look for the most important improvements that have been made to the sports/racing Jaguar since its first appearance. We have already discussed the changes in construction – the original 1955 C Type was built around a tubular frame, and the bodywork bore the slightest share of the load – but the way in which wind resistance

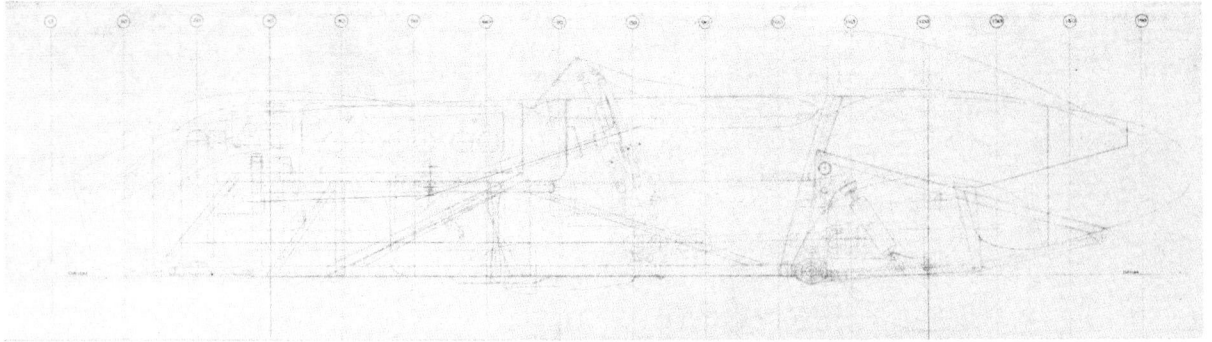

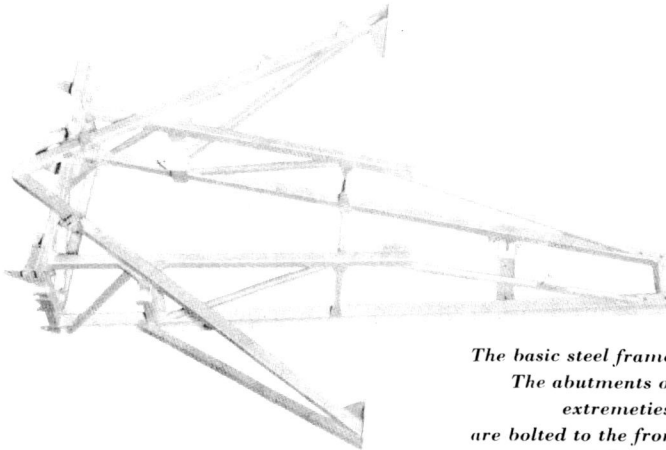

The basic steel framework.
The abutments on the lateral
extremeties of the frame
are bolted to the front bulkhead
of the central monocoque

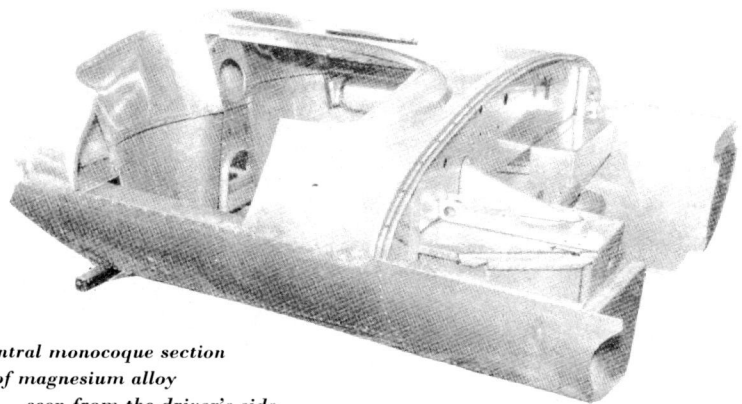

The central monocoque section
of magnesium alloy
seen from the driver's side

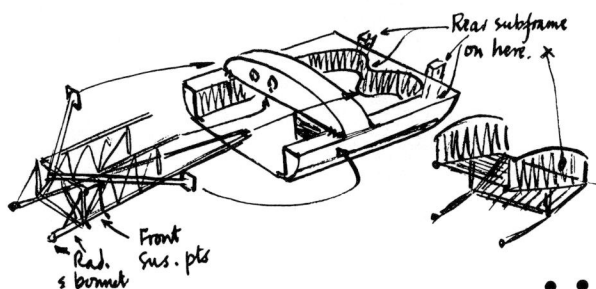

Rear subframe on here. ✗

Front sus. pts

Rad. & bonnet

...the D-Type Jaguar...

has been repeatedly reduced has been responsible to a considerable extent for the higher performance year by year. Accepting the drag coefficient of the 1953 C Type as being 100 per cent, subsequent models show the improvements effected. The 1953 prototype had a figure of 77 per cent, and this was reduced on the 1954 D Type to 72 per cent, while on the 1955 car – with relatively small visual changes – the figure was reduced to 64 per cent. As well as this reduction in the car's resistance to the atmosphere allowing a larger margin of the engine's developed power to be devoted to the main task of propelling the car at high speed, it permits the higher speed to be obtained without increase in the fuel consumption; this point is not unimportant at Le Mans, where a minimum distance is laid down between refuelling stops.

The three double-bodied Weber carburettors are set at a pronounced downward angle, so that when the engine is mounted in the car at its angle of 8 degrees from the vertical, the carburettors lie horizontally. The mounting of the engine at an angle solves two unrelated problems; the overall height of the bonnet is reduced and it is possible to mount the engine within the complexities of the forward sub-section of the framework. Without modification to the framework, and reduction in its rigidity, it would be impossible to mount the engine vertically. Since the XK series engine was first used, the total power extracted has jumped from 140, through 160, 210 and 250, to 285 b.h.p. Apart from any other aspect, it can easily be appreciated what a large margin of safety has been built into the engine, from which only 190 b.h.p. is extracted in the

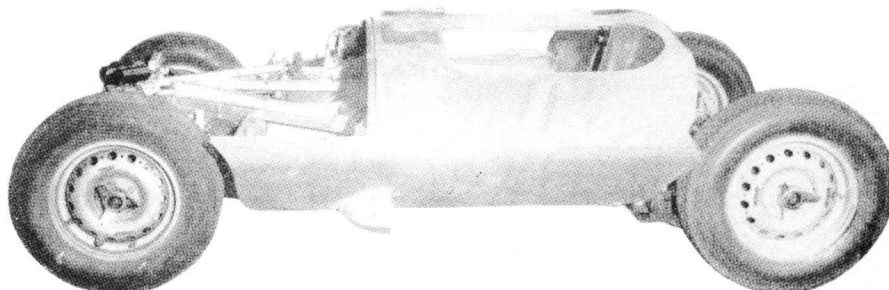

The 'complete chassis' of the D Type, less engine and plastic fuel tanks

Only the engine remains to be fitted

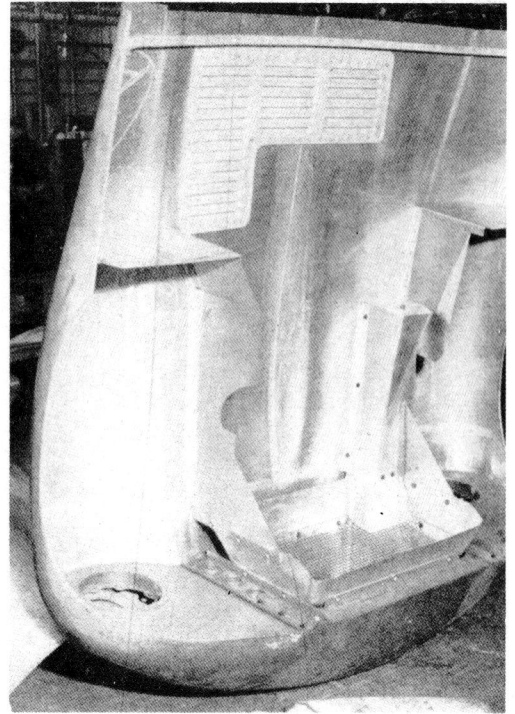

case of the saloon version. It is worth noting that the maximum power is obtained at 5,750 r.p.m., and that, with the top gear ratio used at Le Mans – 2·79 to 1 – and the tyre sizes employed, only 6,000 r.p.m. were required to attain a speed of 183 m.p.h. This is a considerably narrower margin of revolutions over the peak of the power curve to obtain maximum speed than is usual on medium-sized flow-production saloon cars.

The front suspension is by longitudinal torsion bars and upper and lower wishbones, and the inner fulcrum bearings are in line with the longitudinal centre-line of the chassis. The steering arms, which extend in front of the wheel centre line, connect with the rack-and-pinion steering unit which is carried above and in front of the main cross-member. The long steering column is provided with a universal joint. It is a feature of the Jaguar front suspension that the torsion bar can be changed without disturbance of the principal suspension parts, owing to the bar being offset from the centre line of the car by $2\frac{1}{2}$ degrees. A vernier arrangement of splines is provided, which enables the height of the car to be adjusted. The rear section sub-frame is only employed to carry the fuel tanks and the spare wheel, and the rear suspension units are attached to the rear bulkhead of the central monocoque, which is strengthened at the attachment points by two massive members of box section. The rear

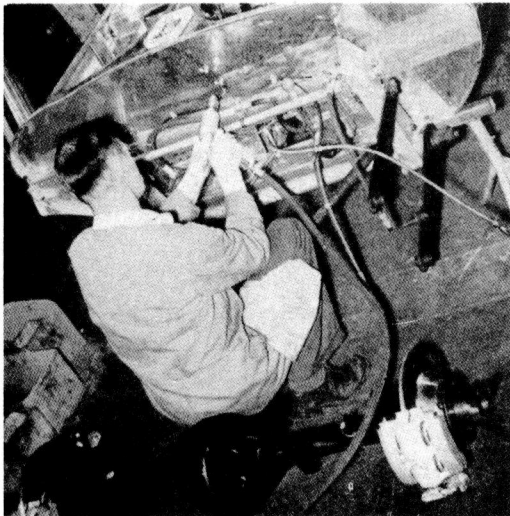

*This view shows the Salisbury rear axle
complete with Dunlop disc brakes.
One end of the A-bracket and the
method of attachment of the rear suspension
can also be seen*

*Prominent in this photograph are
the oil radiator; the header tank,
the oil tank, the reservoir of the
servo-assisted brakes, and the three
Weber DCO3 45 mm., twin-choke carburettors*

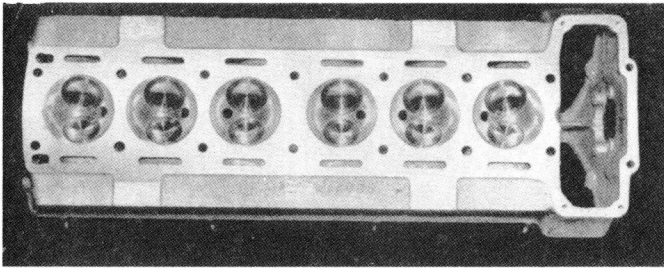

The aluminium alloy cylinder head

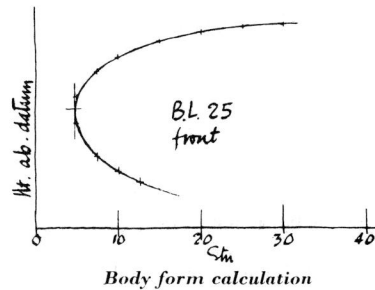

Body form calculation

A front view of the dry-sump 250 b.h.p. D type engine. Both the dynamo and the water pump are belt-driven

... the D-Type Jaguar ...

suspension is by two upper and two lower trailing links, and a single transverse torsion bar. The trailing links are of flat steel plate, of a section which will allow some flexibility as, under cornering, the links are in torsion, thus increasing the roll stiffness of the car. The four trailing links form a parallelogram. The single rear torsion bar has an enlarged centre section which is secured by a reaction plate, itself attached to the centre of the main body structure.

From the engine the power is transmitted through a triple-plate clutch to the synchromesh gearbox, in which close-ratio helical gears are used. A short Hardy Spicer propellor shaft carries the power to a Salisbury rear axle unit. With the exception of the ratio fitted and reduction in the length of the axle tubes, this unit is the same as those fitted to the everyday XK140. As the drag coefficient of the car has been so much reduced, so, too, has the retarding influence of the air resistance been cut down. Because of this, the load imposed on the braking system is a severe one. The Dunlop disc brakes have 12¾-inch discs, with three pairs of pads on the front brakes and two on the rear brakes; this gives the required distribution between front and rear. As a result of lessons learnt in the early stages of the D type, the volume of friction material was increased

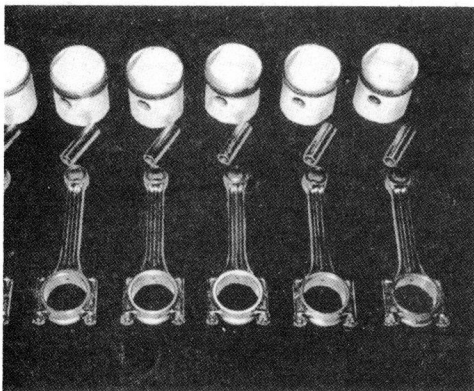

The pistons of the D Type give a compression ratio of 9 : 1. Indium lead-bronze Vandervell bearings are used in the connecting rods

Leica Studio Wörner

This photograph, Hawthorn at Arnage, shows the longer nose and the air entries which lowered the brake operating temperature by almost 200° F. on the 1955 factory D Type. This car differs from the production model in having an enveloping screen which blends with the finned head fairing. The tail was also lengthened.

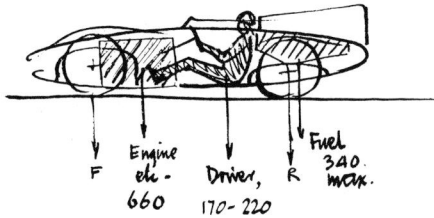

Distribution of the weight masses

F   Engine   Driver,   R   Fuel
     etc. -   170-220   340.
     660   max.

The very de luxe driving compartment
of the production car

in the interests of longevity. Because of the danger arising from the sharp temperature rise around the brake calipers, the hydraulic brake operating cylinders – a total of twenty are required – are attached to the calipers by bolts and distance pieces, which ensure an adequate flow of air. Because of the number of operating cylinders, only a small clearance can be allowed between the disc and the brake pad; otherwise, there would be appreciable lag on the pedal. With the brakes in the off position the clearance is only 0·010–0·015 in. This is maintained by a combination of retraction and automatic adjustment. Servo assistance is provided for the brakes by a Plessey pump driven from behind the gearbox, and a non-return valve is incorporated in the system, to prevent air from being drawn into the system when the propellor shaft's direction of rotation is changed by the use of reverse gear.

One particularly interesting feature of the D type's specification is that the fuel – 57 gallons – is carried in two flexible tanks, which are themselves mounted within two light-alloy boxes. Like similar fuel containers used during the war, these tanks are very resistant to damage, and appear to be a very worthwhile safety precaution. The cars raced during 1954 by the factory had head fairings, and a tail fin to assist in preserving

directional stability – especially during the frightening rush down the Mulsanne straight, with its cross-winds – but this feature was considerably improved on the 1955 cars. The fairing and fin were smoothed into the bodywork, and the enveloping windscreen became, in effect, a blister with the top cut off, and it, too, was smoothed into the body line. Apart from any increase in speed owing to the reduction of drag, these modifications had the effect of appreciably limiting the very tiring buffeting to which the drivers had been subjected.

There are many who doubt the statement that 'racing improves the breed', but the story of the competition Jaguar's development suggests that there is truth in it. Apart from having motored faster year by year, the latest D type is a better car than its predecessors. As well as having gone faster each year, the car has become more handsome, more economical and more comfortable for the driver. As the race regulations for many events likely to interest the Coventry firm are – at the moment of typing – still in a state of flux, it is too early to hazard a guess as to the future of the cars carrying the rampant Jaguar, but there can be little doubt that if their previous approach to the problems of racing is maintained a good share of success must follow.

R.N.

No one can deny that
this standard production car
was improved through racing

XK "SS"

*A Potent New
Super Sports Jaguar
for Touring or Racing*

DEVELOPED from the successful D-type racing sports car, a new 2-seater Jaguar has made its appearance in response to demand from America for a car combining racing performance with equipment and weather protection of touring-car standard. The new Jaguar, to be called the XK"SS" should meet this demand in a most potent and satisfying manner, for it follows the mechanical specification of the 3½-litre Le Mans cars in all essentials, yet has a full-width curved windscreen, folding hood, luggage grid and bumpers. The cockpit is properly trimmed, has well-upholstered seats and a full "touring" range of instruments. Features retained from the D-type include the large tail fuel tank, drilled lightweight steering wheel, and Dunlop disc brakes and light-alloy disc wheels with knock-off hubs. The car is initially for export only, and first deliveries will be made in February to the U.S.A., where the price is $6,900. The XK"SS" is an addition to the Jaguar range and will not supplant any existing models.

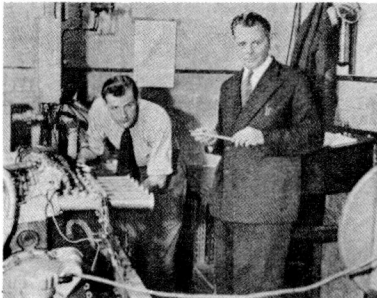

Re-assembled, the Ecurie Ecosse 3.78-litre engine with its Lucas fuel injection system undergoes test, supervised by W. E. Wilkinson, Jaguar's engine development engineer. Right : The cylinder head, valves and gasket as stripped. After removal of the carbon deposits the valves were lapped in and the head rebuilt for further arduous service

Tireless Athlete

JAGUAR ENGINE STILL FIGHTING FIT AFTER 6,000 RACING MILES

RACING certainly improves the breed, but it is not often one has evidence that racing also *proves* the breed. Few firms can claim that their competition models differ so little from those which can be bought in the showroom as do Jaguars. It was with great interest, therefore, that the engine of the Le Mans-winning Ecurie Ecosse Jaguar was dismantled for inspection at the works.

After completing bench tests, the 3.78-litre engine undertook the 24-hour Le Mans race and the Monza 500 miles event without any attention other than the normal checking of valve clearances, oil filters and the ignition settings. Including the period on the test bed, road-proving, practice and the races, this engine must have completed some 6,000 miles at racing speed, which would correspond to at least 30,000 miles of normal road use.

The only difference in these competition engines as compared with the production power unit is that the cylinder head is designed for improved breathing at high speeds, has bigger ports and valves, with larger tappets and stronger springs.

It was difficult to imagine that the engine had been subjected to such a severe test. There was no loss of tappet clearance on the exhaust valves. The inlets showed a maximum loss of 0.004in, with a minimum of 0.002in—doubtless due to dirt entering the induction side, for such engines are not fitted with air cleaners.

There was no measurable wear on the crankshaft which, in addition to Le Mans and Monza, had previously run at Le Mans and Rheims last year and Argentina this year. The maximum wear on one cylinder bore measured at the top was 0.002in, with an average of 0.0012in. After cleaning and the normal lapping in of valves, the engine was rebuilt; only gaskets were replaced.

The two camshafts with their springs and tappets (above right). The condition of the tappet faces was comparable with what would be expected after a normal endurance bench test

The amount of bore wear was negligible. There was no measurable wear on the crankshaft bearings. After cleaning, the pistons with their rings were replaced for further service

An intermediate and centre main bearing shell (below). There was no sign of spalling or overheating and the thin lead overlay was intact

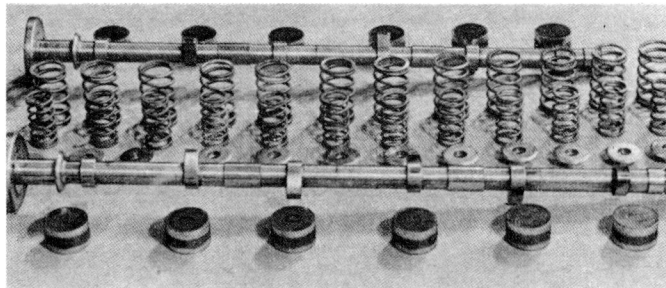

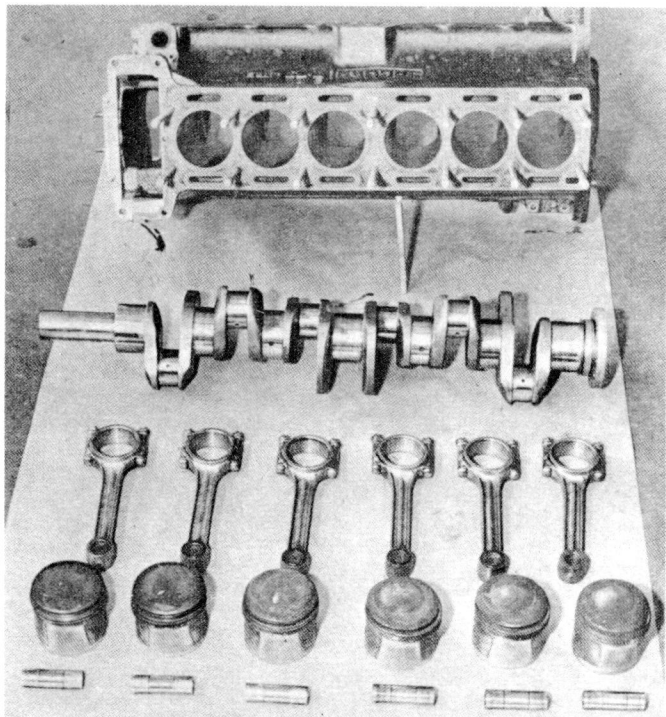

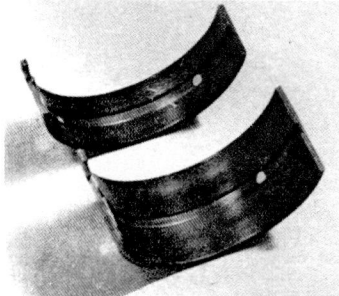

(Reproduced from Phil Weaver's Comp. Shop notebook, headed XKD 606)

Car involved in crash when being driven by Flockhart. Partially rebuilt in Service Dept – New frame, N/S/F susp. unit, bonnet etc.
Fitted Lucas P.I equipment + 3.75 litre engine in Comp. Dept. Axle ratio changed from 3.31/1 to 2.69/1.
Complete electrical check over
Oil system & filter cleaned out
Brakes vetted by Dunlop.
Gearbox stripped by Service Dept.
Windscreen removed – lower one fitted.

Starter: Fully modified 606.
Castor:- 2½°.   Camber:- 1¾°
Screen:- Full to 1957 Regs.
Tonneau Cover:- Plastic.

New material fitted.
   Clutch slave cylinder.
   Radiator.
   Oil cooler.
    " tank.
   R/A races & seals.
   Engine 3.75L.

Engine removed twice during test in order to cure oil leakage from c/shaft front oil seal. Finally cured by fitting new seal & using Jointing compound in housing.

Specification as prepared for Le Mans 1957.

Engine (3.75L).		E 5005-9.
Cyl. Head.		A 62 35×40.
P.I. metering Head.		D8 M7 C10.
P.I. H.P. Pump.		P15.
Gearbox.		GBD 306.
Rear Axle.		C 55/1 2.69/1 2F.
Calipers.	Front.	Single Pad S/N 390. MS
	Rear.	Wide 1¼" S/N 138.
Servo Pump.		20890.
Master Cyl.	F.P.	S/N 231.
Radiator.		238/3.
Oil Cooler.		24299.
Oil Tank.		Welded supports.
Sway Bars.	Front.	11/16" dia.
	Rear.	¾" dia.
Torsion Bars.	Front.	.766" dia.
	Rear.	.835" dia.
Dampers.		Std. Hand Settings
Track.		1/16" T.O.

1957 Le Mans.

Cont.
Drivers:-   Flockhart + Bueb.
Race No:-   3.
Result.   1st

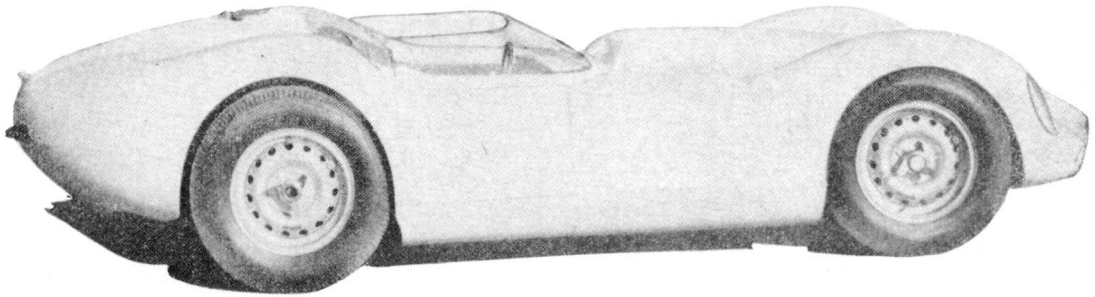

1958 COMPETITION CARS ▪▪ THE LISTER-

LAST week the first of two Lister-Jaguars was dispatched to Briggs Cunningham, who will enter the cars—one of 3.0 litres and one of 3.8 litres—in the Sebring 12-hour race on March 22. This is just the beginning of what looks like a busy season for Brian Lister (Light Engineering), Ltd., of Cambridge. Jaguar-engined cars, either complete or in component form, have been ordered by Ecurie Ecosse, the *Equipe Nationale Belge* and Peter Whitehead, and two more will be entered in British events by the works. Five cars to be fitted with 4.6-litre Chevrolet Corvette engines are already booked for the United States.

The major change and, of course, the most obvious one, in the 1958 cars is a completely new body (illustrated in *The Motor* last week) of attractive shape and extremely low frontal area. Faced with the combined problems of a tall engine and Appendix "C" regulations stipulating windscreen height, Lister has hit on the idea of a "power bulge" occupying most of the bonnet area, yet with a low scuttle behind it from which the windscreen height is measured. As a result, the top of the screen is still only 33 in. from the ground and Archie Scott-Brown is likely to appear once again apparently sitting on the road. A head fairing, into which is built a crash-bar to satisfy American requirements, projects slightly above the windscreen, which is curved backward and matched aerodynamically by a high tail. Further trials on the road and in races may result in some modifica-

tion, but at the moment the clean lines are broken only by quite small openings over the rear wheel arches which direct cool air to the inboard disc brakes. The bodies of the Cunningham cars, incidentally, are of Elektron.

Chassis changes are confined to larger brakes, a light-alloy final-drive unit and a fuel tank of increased capacity. To recapitulate, the Lister has a ladder-type frame of 3-in. steel tubes, tapering fore and aft from an unusually wide point

level with the driver's seat which enables him to sit right down inside the frame. At the front an extremely rigid box structure carries the front suspension, by Girling combined coil-spring and damper units, with equal-length wishbones which are made up of steel tubes reinforced by vertical flanges welded on at top and bottom. The steering swivels and hubs are of M.G. manufacture, and rack-and-pinion steering of Morris type, modified by Lister.

The high tail enables a new, 38-gallon fuel tank to be carried, with the five-gallon oil tank beneath it. The Girling-suspended de Dion rear axle is located by parallel trailing arms and a vertical sliding trunnion on the differential case. Disc brakes by Girling.

Engine : (3-litre Jaguar)	**Transmission—***Contd.*
Cylinders : 6	Alternative ratios: 2.93, 3.31, 3.54, 3.77, 4.09, 4.27, 4.55, 4.78
Bore and stroke: 83 mm. x 92 mm.	
Cubic capacity : 2,986 c.c.	**Chassis**
Piston area : 50.4 sq. in.	Brakes : Girling 12-in. disc.
Valves : Twin o.h. cam	Suspension :
Compression ratio : 10.5	Front : Wishbones and Girling coil spring suspension units.
Max. power : 254 b.h.p. at 6,000 r.p.m.	Rear : de Dion axle and Girling coil spring suspension units.
Carburetters : 3 Weber side draught	Tyre size : Front 6.00-16.
Oil capacity : 5 gallons	Rear 6.50-16.
Fuel capacity : 38 gallons	
Transmission :	**Dimensions**
Clutch : Borg and Beck 3-plate	Wheelbase : 7 ft. 6¾ in.
Gear ratios (3.54 final drive) all synchromesh	Track :
Top 3.54	Front : 4 ft. 4 in.
3rd 4.525	Rear : 4 ft. 5¼ in.
2nd 5.825	Overall length : 13 ft. 6 in.
1st 7.61	Overall width : 5 ft. 2¼ in.
Final drive : Salisbury, incorporating Power-Lok differential with ZF differential optional	Overall height : 3 ft. 3 in.
	Ground clearance : 4 in.
	Turning circle : 40 ft.
	Dry weight : 15¼ cwt.

LATEST VERSION OF ONE OF BRITAIN'S FASTEST SPORTS CARS

JAGUAR

The suspension as a whole follows what has now become the classic pattern, for a de Dion tube is used at the rear, sprung once more by Girling suspension units. Parallel radius arms locate it longitudinally, and a bronze sliding trunnion laterally. Girling are also responsible for the disc brakes, inboard rear and outboard front, which are now both of 12 in. diameter. Cars for America have Firestone tyres.

As usual, the Jaguar engine is tilted slightly in the chassis, mounted at two points forward on the frame side members and one rear point for the gearbox. The 3.4-litre, 3.8-litre or comparatively new 3.0-litre engine can be equally well accommodated. The last named is of course intended for international events run under Appendix "C," and serious competitors will presumably specify the 35-40 cylinder head with which the engine develops 254 b.h.p. at 6,300 r.p.m. on a compression ratio of 10.5 : 1. Cylinder dimensions are 83 mm. x 92 mm., making a capacity of 2,986 c.c. Apart from single ignition the engine is in other respects exactly like the normal D-type. The drive from the D-type, all-synchromesh gearbox passes through a short, open propeller shaft to the chassis-mounted Salisbury final drive unit, which now occupies an Elektron casing. Standard equipment includes a Powr-Lok differential, but a ZF limited-slip differential is available. There are eight possible final drive ratios, ranging from 2.93 : 1 to 4.78 : 1. On the normal ratio of 3.54 : 1, road speed per 1,000 r.p.m. in top gear is 24 m.p.h.

The new, high tail is largely filled by tankage, with a 38-gallon fuel tank which should considerably reduce the necessity for replenishment stops in long races, and a five-gallon oil tank to supply the dry-sump engine. At the opposite extreme of the car is a steeply sloping Marston radiator with an oil cooler by the same maker just in front of it. Dry weight of the car is quoted at 15½ cwt. The output of the largest engines available—the 3.8 Jaguar and the 4.6 Chevrolet—is of the order of 300 b.h.p.

Very small frontal area has been achieved, in spite of the tall engine, by sinking the scuttle (and hence the regulation windscreen) below the centre part of the bonnet. Front suspension is orthodox, with Girling suspension units and equal-length wishbones.

B31

Height of the tail fin is dictated by the greater height of the windscreen called for by the regulations

Jaguar New Competition Car

BRIGGS CUNNINGHAM'S PRIVATE ENTRY FOR LE MANS IS A LOGICAL DEVELOPMENT OF D-TYPE

BRITISH hopes for an outright win in the Le Mans 24-hour race, starting tomorrow, depend largely on the new competition Jaguar entered privately by American Briggs Cunningham. Jaguars have already five victories to their credit in the race, a record shared with Bentleys; of these outright wins two were achieved with cars privately entered by Ecurie Ecosse in 1956 and 1957.

This new car does not necessarily represent a try-out for future works entries. It is only natural for a company such as Jaguar, whose reputation has been enhanced by participation in racing, to continue development, even though they withdrew officially from competition at the end of the 1956 season. The position is that Briggs Cunningham has persuaded Sir William Lyons to place at his disposal one of the several models on which the company have continued development during the past five years. This new model is a logical development of the D-type, and probably represents the truest interpretation of the current regulations for open sports cars. In other words, Jaguar have designed a car to meet these regulations from its inception rather than adapt existing models to meet the new requirements. Thus the shape and proportions of the body are dictated by the latest windscreen regulation (9.84in. vertical height of transparent material), and it has a streamline form designed to produce the minimum drag within this frame-

work. Height of the scuttle, 2ft 10in., is very similar to that of the D-type, but the height to the top of the tail fin, 4ft 5½in., is considerably greater, as is the overall length of 14ft 2in. compared with 12ft 10in. This latter dimension is greater for two reasons—the wheelbase, at 8ft 0in., is 6in. longer, and more length of body form behind the driver's head fairing was required to obtain an efficient streamline shape because of the higher windscreen. Front and rear tracks are equal at 4ft 0in.; the D-type had 4ft 0in. front track, but a 4ft 2in. rear track.

Laminated safety glass is used for the windscreen, which is curved and metal-framed. With a screen of these proportions it is necessary for the driver to have vision through it, instead of over it, as was possible with the old regulations. It is, therefore, essential to have wipers which will clear the screen when it becomes obscured, and work efficiently at very high speeds. A considerable amount of development work has been necessary to solve these problems. Lucas have evolved a special heavy-duty motor which operates at 100 strokes per minute (the same as the high speed range in a normal two-speed motor), and Trico have assisted in the development of the special blades and washing equipment. There are two water jets inside a deflector shield, and tests have proved these to work satisfactorily with direct jets on to the screen at speeds as high as 160 m.p.h. A reservoir tank containing a mixture of

water and wood alcohol is located in the cockpit; adjacent to it is the wiper switch and operating plunger for the washing equipment.

From the engine bulkhead rearwards, a monocoque type of construction is used for the combined body-chassis unit. It is constructed entirely of aluminium alloy with riveted joints, and the outer panels are stressed members. Main load-carrying members are the scuttle structure, central backbone member and rear bulkhead-section. Within this rear bulkhead-section is housed the I.C.I. flexible rubber-and-fabric fuel tank, which has a capacity of 26.5 gallons. It is clipped to the constraining framework at several points to avoid complete collapse as the fuel is used. With fuel injection—Lucas port-type is used on this engine—it is important that air is kept out of the fuel system. To achieve this object, two anti-surge pots are fitted at each side of the tank, to avoid risk of fuel starvation during severe cornering either to the right or left. There is a fuel feed pipe from the bottom of each of these anti-surge pots to the inlet side of the continuously running fuel booster pump, which is electrically driven and operates at 100 p.s.i.; surplus fuel is returned to the tank. The effect of these anti-surge pots and baffling is so effective that in racing conditions the fuel can be used to within the last three pints of the tank capacity without starvation.

The fin section of the tail is hinged at

Left: The bulges aft of the doors are air scoops for brake cooling. Right: A feature is the air intake in the nose, flanked by faired head lamps.
Colour scheme is the American medium blue on white. The special windscreen washer shield is forward of the steering wheel

one side to provide access to the horizontally mounted spare wheel and to the compulsory luggage space above it, which must be able to contain a trunk measuring 25·6 × 15·75 × 7·875in.

As on the production series D-types, there is a front sub-frame on which the front suspension, steering and engine are mounted. This is bolted to the bulkhead of the monocoque structure, and is constructed largely of square-section steel tubes. For access to the engine bay, a one-piece light alloy nose cowl containing lamps and cooling ducts is hinged at its lower forward edge.

Most interesting technical innovation is the new independent rear suspension. The Salisbury hypoid bevel final drive unit is mounted directly to the chassis, with fixed length universal drive shafts to each wheel; these act also as the upper arms of the wishbone linkages. Main loads are absorbed in a massive wishbone arm of

fabricated box section steel, with widely based pivots attached to a separate small sub-frame. Because of the stiff section of this lower arm and the spread of the mounting points, there is no need for any other type of torque stay or radius arm. The outer end of each wishbone is pivoted to an aluminium housing, inside of which are two opposed taper roller bearings for the wheel hub. There are two suspension units, consisting of a Girling telescopic damper surrounded by a coil spring, for each wheel. They are mounted, one at either side of the drive shaft, to the common transverse pivot pin in the lower wishbone. From the forward mounting of each damper unit there is also a drop link connecting to a transverse anti-roll bar.

The Dunlop disc brakes are mounted inboard at the rear. This confers a big advantage in the reduction of unsprung

weight, but involved some severe problems during development of the car. It is more difficult to get rid of the generated heat during severe braking when they are mounted inboard, compared with the more usual position at the wheels. Two separate systems are provided for cooling the brakes. Projecting below the otherwise clean under-shield are two ducts to direct cooling air on to the forward and open sides of the discs. In addition, there is an entry duct above each wheel fairing, through which cooling air is directed with a reverse flow on to the rear-mounted calipers. In spite of this provision, it was found that a great deal of heat was being transferred inwards from the discs, through the drive shaft flanges to the lubricating oil of the final drive unit. The normal type of rubber or leather oil seals at the output flanges were found to be ineffective, and special

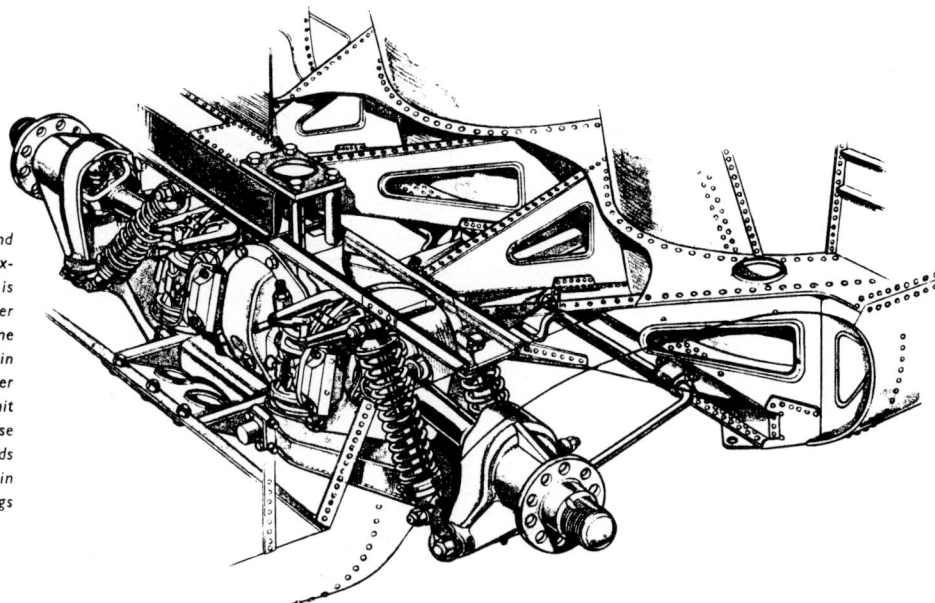

Independent rear suspension and inboard disc brakes. The box-section lower wishbone is mounted on opposed taper-roller bearings to a small sub-frame which is bolted to the main monocoque structure. Upper mounting for the final drive unit is a deep, box-section transverse member, from which the loads are transmitted to the main structure by diagonal bracings

JAGUAR
NEW COMPETITION
CAR . . .

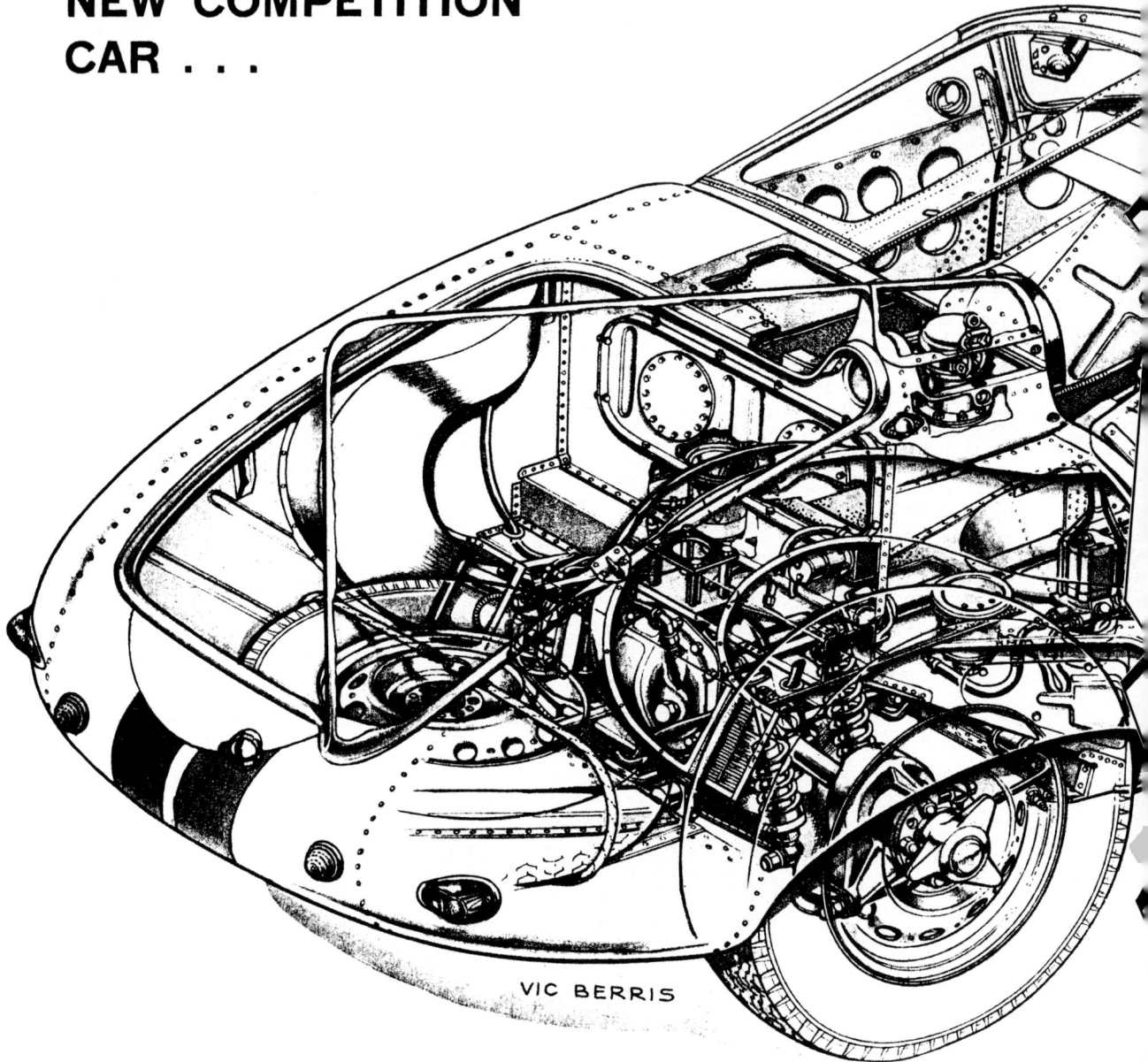

VIC BERRIS

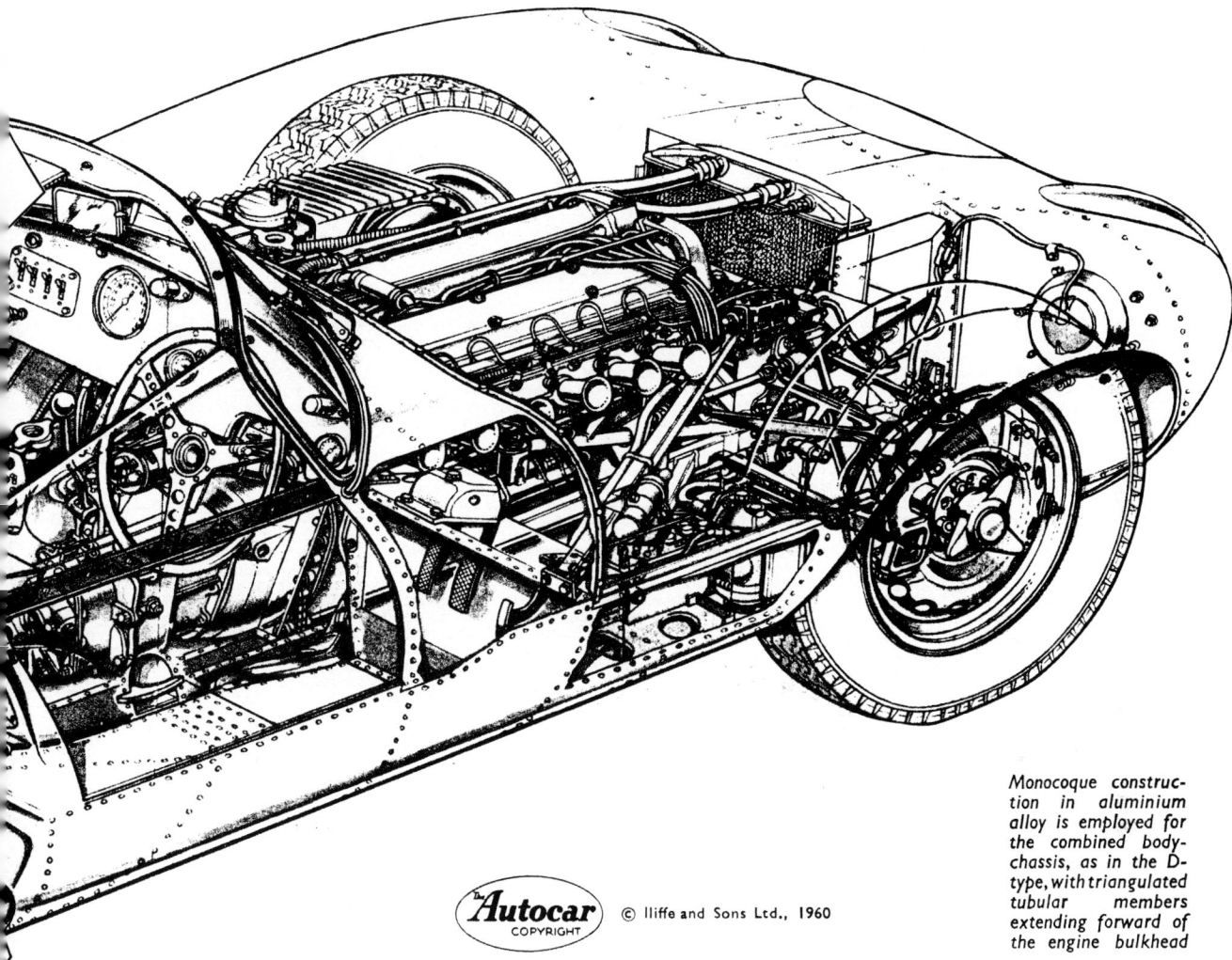

Monocoque construction in aluminium alloy is employed for the combined body-chassis, as in the D-type, with triangulated tubular members extending forward of the engine bulkhead

The Autocar COPYRIGHT © Iliffe and Sons Ltd., 1960

SPECIFICATION

ENGINE

No. of cylinders	6 in line
Bore and stroke	85 x 88mm (3·346 x 3·465in.)
Displacement	2,997 c.c. (183 cu. in.)
Valve position	Opposed in hemispherical combustion chamber; operated by 2 o.h.c.
Compression ratio	10·0 to 1
Max. b.h.p. (net)	295 at 6,800 r.p.m.
Carburation	Lucas port-type fuel injection
Fuel pump	Lucas
Tank capacity	26·5 Imp. gallons (120·5 litres)
Oil tank capacity	3·5 Imp. gallons (15·9 litres)
Oil filter	Full flow
Cooling system	Pressurized, pump without fan
Battery	12 volt, 48 amp. hr. Lucas lightweight

TRANSMISSION

Clutch	Borg and Beck 7·25in. dia triple plate
Gearbox	Four speeds, synchromesh on all ratios, central gear lever
Overall gear ratios	Top 3·31; 3rd 4·23; 2nd 5·44; 1st 7·10
Final drive	Hypoid bevel, ratio 3·31 to 1

CHASSIS

Brakes	12in. dia non-servo Dunlop discs (inboard at rear) with 2 segmental pads per disc
Suspension: front	Independent wishbones and torsion bar
rear	Independent wishbones with 2 combined telescopic dampers and coil springs per wheel
Dampers	Girling telescopic
Wheels	Dunlop light alloy with centre lock hubs
Tyre size	6·50 x 16 Dunlop Stabilia (low silhouette)
Steering	Rack and pinion
No. of turns lock to lock	2·5

DIMENSIONS
(Manufacturer's figures)

Wheelbase	8ft 0in. (243·8 cm)
Track	4ft 0in. (121·9 cm)
Overall length	14ft 2in. (431·8 cm)
Overall width	5ft 2·75in. (159·4 cm)
Overall height	4ft 5·25in. (135·2 cm) to fin, 3ft 8·75in. (113·7 cm) to screen
Ground clearance	6·5in. (16·5 cm)
Turning circle	38ft 4·5in. (11·7 m)
Kerb weight	17·2 cwt (1,925 lb) (872 Kg) (estimated)

GRAVITY ASSISTANCE
BETWEEN PUMP &
RADIATOR

S.U. PUMP

RADIATOR

DIFFERENTIAL

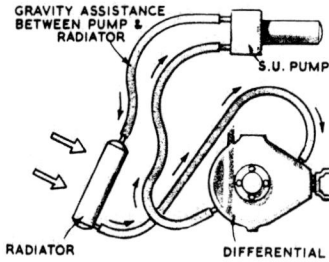

The driver can bring into circuit an oil cooler when the oil temperature of the chassis-mounted final drive unit reaches a predetermined figure. The oil is circulated by a S.U. fuel pump, as shown in the circuit diagram on the left

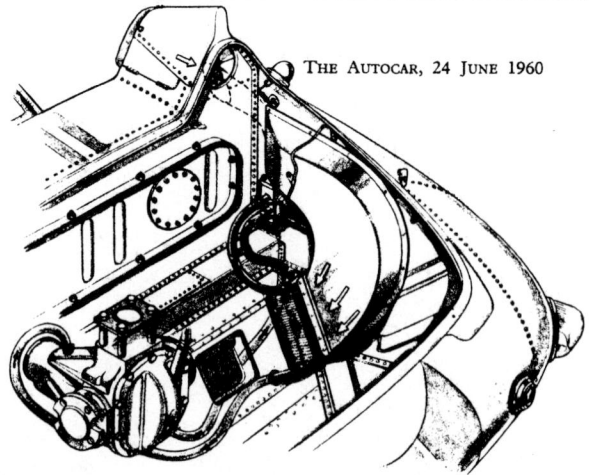

silicone types were developed. In addition, an oil cooler can be brought into circuit by the driver when the oil temperature approaches a critical stage, such as might occur after severe and sustained braking. A normal S.U. type of fuel pump circulates oil through a cooler which is situated in a by-pass from the reverse flow cooling ducts to the calipers. Front suspension and the forward-mounted rack-and-pinion steering is basically the same as on the earlier D-type, with detail improvement and changes in geometry to improve road-holding. The wishbones are steel forgings with ball pivots top and bottom, and incorporate an anti-roll bar. Among the improvements is a saving of 11lb on the unsprung weight of each assembly.

Since the car appeared at the official practice day on 9 April a tail fin has been added. This not only improved directional stability at high speed but enabled another 300 r.p.m. to be obtained in top gear by splitting the air flow across the tail and reducing turbulence. Above the passenger's seat there is a transparent plastic tonneau cover.

Among the new developments on the otherwise basically unchanged and well-known overhead camshaft engine is the use of an aluminium cylinder block and

crankcase with pressed-in dry-type cast-iron liners for the bores, as used on previous 3-litre versions of this engine, with bores of 85mm and strokes of 88mm.

In the version used on the 9 April practice day, titanium connecting rods were used. In its pure form titanium has an ultimate tensile strength of 30 tons per square inch but when alloyed with aluminium and magnesium, and depending on its heat treatment, this figure can be increased to 70 tons per square inch. Its main advantage is that its unit weight is only half that of steel. When used for connecting rods this reduces considerably the reciprocating weight and rotational mass of the crankshaft which, in turn, raises the point at which torsional oscillations become troublesome. The 3-litre Jaguar unit has a safe usable maximum speed of 7,000 r.p.m., maximum peak power of 295 b.h.p. being developed at 6,800 r.p.m.

The light-alloy cylinder head, with valves operated directly by two overhead camshafts and inverted tappets, is a development of the previous 30-40 competition units—indicating that the inlet valves are placed at 30deg and the exhausts at 40deg from the vertical axis. Carburation is by the Lucas port-type fuel injection sytem with gate-type throttle valves, as described in *The Autocar* of

9 November 1956. The one change from this earlier development is the use of a single-shuttle metering distributor.

The oil system is, of course, on the dry sump principle, with one pressure and two scavenge pumps which feed direct to the oil tank mounted just forward of the chassis bulkhead. On the pressure circuit, oil is drawn from the tank through gauze filters, passed through a cooler mounted forward of the main radiator and thence through a full flow filter to the crankcase gallery.

The gearbox, mounted in unit with the engine, has synchromesh on all forward ratios, as had earlier competition types. There is, however, no longer a Plessey pump to supply hydraulic servo assistance for the disc brakes; acceptable pedal loads have been obtained without the use of servo assistance. To comply with the Le Mans regulations, front and rear systems are operated from independent hydraulic circuits. This is achieved by the use of a tandem type of master cylinder in which the operating pistons abut mechanically in the event of an hydraulic failure in one of the independent circuits.

Over a timed section of the Sarthe circuit during the official practice day, this new Jaguar was faster than any of its rivals. If it performs reliably for 24 hours it could be the overall winner.

Left: Oil tank, showing the methods used for de-aerating. On the inlet side there is a fish-tail diffuser which leads the oil to a small weir, at which stage the air is separated out in the breather compartment. Further de-aeration is achieved as the oil passes over the drilled baffle plate above the static oil level. Right: Corner section of the windscreen, with the special highspeed wiper, the two water jets and a directional baffle plate, which also prevents the jets being blocked with flies or dirt

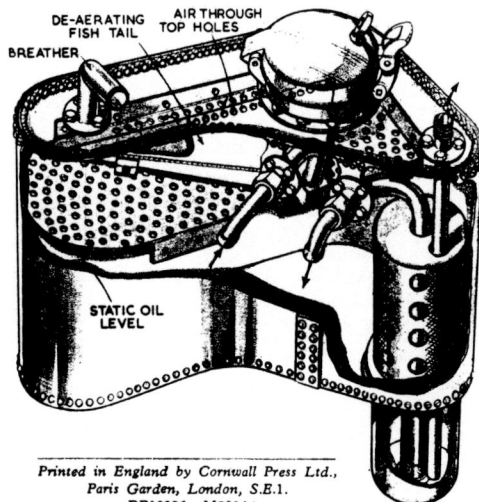

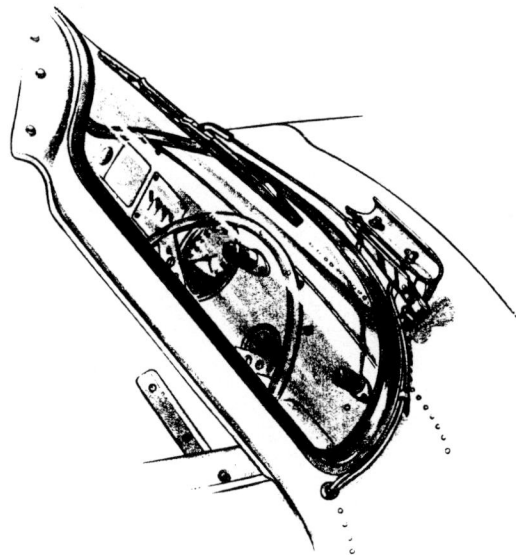

DE-AERATING
FISH TAIL

AIR THROUGH
TOP HOLES

BREATHER

STATIC OIL
LEVEL

Printed in England by Cornwall Press Ltd.,
Paris Garden, London, S.E.1.
RP10096—M8914

Left: Ecurie Ecosse D-type
Jaguar

LE MANS 1960 . . .

LE MANS 1960 . . .

CARS, ENTRANTS AND DRIVERS

(British entries in bold).

CAR	c.c.	ENTRANT	COUNTRY	DRIVERS
GRAND TOURING CATEGORY				
4,000 to 5,000 c.c.:				
1 Chevrolet-Corvette	4,640	B. S. Cunningham	U.S.A.	Cunningham, Duntov, Form
2 Chevrolet-Corvette	4,640	B. S. Cunningham	U.S.A.	Thompson, Windridge
3 Chevrolet-Corvette	4,640	B. S. Cunningham	U.S.A.	Grossman, Hugus, Fitch
4 Chevrolet-Corvette	4,640	Camoradi U.S.A.	U.S.A.	Lilley, Gamble
2,500 to 3,000 c.c.:				
14 Ferrari	2,953	Scuderia Serenissima	Italy	Abate, Balzarini
15 Ferrari	2,953	**A. G. Whitehead**	**G.B.**	**Whitehead, H. Taylor**
16 Ferrari	2,953	F. Tavano	France	Tavano, Loustel
17 Ferrari	2,953	N.A.R.T.	U.S.A.	P. & R. Rodriguez
18 Ferrari	2,953	N.A.R.T.	U.S.A.	Arents, Kimberley
19 Ferrari	2,953	N.A.R.T.	U.S.A.	Hugus, Pabst
20 Ferrari	2,953	N.A.R.T.	U.S.A.	Publicker
21 Ferrari	2,953	Equipe Nle Belge	Belgium	Beurlys, Blary, Swaters
22 Ferrari	2,953	Ecurie Francorchamps	Belgium	Dernier, Noblet
23 Austin-Healey	2,910	**J. C. Sears**	**G.B.**	**Sears, Riley**
1,300 to 1,600 c.c.:				
35 Porsche	1,588	Automobiles Porsche	Germany	Linge, Walter
1,150 to 1,300 c.c.:				
41 Lotus Elite	1,216	**D. Buxton**	**G.B.**	**Buxton, Allen**
42 Lotus Elite	1,216	**D. Buxton**	**G.B.**	**Wagstaff, Marsh**
43 Lotus Elite	1,216	**D. Buxton**	**G.B.**	**Baillie, Parks**
44 Lotus Elite	1,216	R. Masson	France	Masson, Laurent, Gallier
SPORTS CAR CATEGORY				
2,500 to 3,000 c.c.:				
5 Jaguar	2,997	**Ecurie Ecosse**	**G.B.**	**Flockhart, Halford**
6 Jaguar	2,996	Jaguar New York	U.S.A.	Hansgen, Gurney
7 Aston Martin	2,992	**Border Reivers**	**G.B.**	**Clark, Salvadori, Whitmore**
8 Aston Martin	2,992	**Major Baillie**	**G.B.**	**Baillie, Fairman**
9 Ferrari	2,953	Scuderia Ferrari	Italy	P. Hill, Ginther
10 Ferrari	2,953	Scuderia Ferrari	Italy	von Trips, Allison
11 Ferrari	2,953	Scuderia Ferrari	Italy	Frère, Gendebien
12 Ferrari	2,953	Scuderia Ferrari	Italy	Scarfiotti, Cabianca
24 Maserati	2,890	Camoradi U.S.A.	U.S.A.	Shelby, Gregory
25 Maserati	2,890	Camoradi U.S.A.	U.S.A.	—
26 Maserati	2,890	Camoradi U.S.A.	U.S.A.	Jeffords, Schappard, Casner
1,600 to 2,000 c.c.:				
28 Triumph	1,985	**Standard Triumph**	**G.B.**	**Sanderson, Rotschild, Boxall**
29 Triumph	1,985	**Standard Triumph**	**G.B.**	**Bolton, Becquart**
30 A.C.-Bristol	1,971	Equipe Lausannoise	France	Wicky, Gachang, Gretener
31 Lotus	1,964	**Lotus England**	**G.B.**	**Ireland,**
32 M.G.	1,762	**Ted Lund**	**G.B.**	**Lund, Escott, Bloor**
33 Porsche	1,606	Automobiles Porsche	Germany	Trintignant, Barth
34 Porsche	1,606	Automobiles Porsche	Germany	Bonnier, G. Hill
1,300 to 1,600 c.c.:				
36 Porsche	1,588	J. Kerguen	U.S.A.	Kerguen, Lacaze, Dewez
37 Osca	1,569	Automobiles Osca	Italy	—
38 Porsche	1,498	G. de Beaufort	Belgium	de Beaufort, Bootz
39 Porsche	1,498	Automobiles Porsche	Germany	Hermann
1,150 to 1,300 c.c.:				
40 Alfa-Romeo Conrero	1,290	Virgilio Conrero	France	de Leonibus
1,000 to 1,150 c.c.:				
45 Lola-Climax	1,098	**Lola Climax**	**G.B.**	**Vogele, Ashdown, Honeger**
850 to 1,000 c.c.:				
46 Austin-Healey	996	**Donald Healey**	**G.B.**	**Sprinzel, Colgate, Ross**
47 D.B. Panhard	954	Automobiles D.B.	France	Vinatier, Vidilles
48 D.B. Panhard	954	Automobiles D.B.	France	Jaeger, Bouharde
700 to 850 c.c.:				
49 Fiat Abarth	847	Abarth	Italy	Poltronieri
50 Fiat Abarth	847	Abarth	Italy	Cattini
51 D.B. Panhard	750	Automobiles D.B.	France	Cotton, van den Bruwaene
52 D.B. Panhard	750	Automobiles D.B.	France	Bartholoni, de Sait Auban
53 Osca	746	Automobiles Osca	Italy	Laroche, Simon
54 Osca	746	Hugus	U.S.A.	Bentley
55 Stanguellini	741	Stanguellini	Italy	de la Geneste, Revillon
56 D.B. Panhard	701	Automobiles D.B.	France	Laureau, Armagnac

* [This statement is incorrect. See D-type records. A.W]

Cunningham

BRIGGS CUNNINGHAM, a charming American, makes a welcome return to the Sarthe circuit after an absence of five years. In the years 1952, 1953 and 1954 he was so near to success with his cars; in 1952 co-driving with Spear he was placed fourth, in 1953 Walter and Fitch brought a Cunningham into third place, and Cunningham himself, driving a similar car with Spear, finished seventh, and the third team car tenth. Again, in 1954 Spear and Johnston finished third, and Briggs co-driving with Bent finished fifth. No one would be a more popular winner in 1960.

His main entry is undoubtedly the experimental new competition Jaguar (fully described on page 1000) which he has inveigled out of Sir William Lyons. This is to be driven by American sports car champion Walter Hansgen, who will have Dan Gurney as his co-driver. Gurney shared a Ferrari with Behra last year, and was leading the race until eliminated on the 129th lap. In addition to the Jaguar, Cunningham is entering three Chevrolet Corvettes, one of which Briggs will share with Arkus Duntov, who is the General Motors engineer responsible for the development of the Corvettes. The vee-8 engine has a capacity of 4,640 c.c., uses Rochester-type fuel injection, and a more powerful version of the engine than that used on 9 April practice day will be available for the race. The fourth Corvette is entered also by the Camoradi U.S.A. team. Although these cars have glass fibre bodies they are comparatively heavy, and the standard drum brakes may prove to be the weak link in 24 hours of racing.

Ecurie Ecosse

BECAUSE OF strong discouragement by Coopers against fitting the deep regulation screen to one of their cars, and the difficulty of providing centre-lock hubs in time for the race, the Cooper Monaco entered by Ecurie Ecosse will not be running. Ron Flockhart and Bruce Halford will share the driving of the other Ecurie Ecosse entry—a D-type Jaguar. This car will be competing in its fourth Le Mans race; it finished second in 1957 * and ran also in the Monza 500-mile race.

Jaguar are not assisting this year in preparation of the Ecurie Ecosse car, and "Wilkie" Wilkinson has built a new 3-litre engine, basically a modified 2.4 Jaguar unit, with cylinder bores opened out to 86mm and a new crankshaft giving a stroke also of 86mm. Three twin-choke Weber carburettors are used.

Luggage space is provided by a bulge beside the tail fin, and a transparent plastic cover fits between this and the top of the screen to reduce drag.

527

Appendix Five

Individual Histories

XKC/XKD 401 to 406
XKD 501 to 575 (including XKSS)
XKD 601 to 606

In the companion volume (to 1953) each individual C-type was listed, from XKC 001 to 054. Naturally, it is also important to put on record the early history of each D-type (or XKSS) where it is known. With the passing of time, however, I am even more reluctant than before to try to record recent history.

The authenticity factor

Except for the 1954 cars in their original guise, the basic structure of the D-type and XKSS consisted of a front frame bolted to, and easily detachable from, a monocoque centre section containing the front and rear bulkheads and, of course, the whole cockpit area. This tended to be called the body (and it did have a 'body' number), whereas the fairly small – though essential – engine-bearing frame was usually called the chassis (and it was stamped with the 'chassis' number). D-types and XKSSs, like most cars, derive their main identity from the chassis number; yet the centre section is the crucial monocoque portion which holds the whole thing together. In cases of dual identity, as does occur, it is usually because the frame and the monocoque have been separated. Anyone looking for a genuine car with a genuine history should satisfy himself – above all – that these two items are clearly related to one another. Naturally, like all competition cars, many D-types have had accidents in their time, or have been fitted with the incorrect engine, wheels, etc. If a component is beyond redemption, then, of course, it needs replacing; and that may include the frame, the monocoque or any other part. In my view, when cars are as valuable as these,

all major discarded parts should be retained by the owner and offered to the next owner for historical continuity.

The D-type is such an outstanding design, several companies and individuals have built brand new copies – either following the specification closely or re-creating the spirit of these great cars. The best-known ones are the creations of Guy Black and Bryan Wingfield in Britain and of Steve Sulis in Sydney, Australia, each of whom marks his new vehicles with identity numbers quite unrelated to the D-type's numbers, and thus establishing them as a different breed. The Australian copies, unlike the two British ones are, in effect, true reproductions of the original.

Some of the finest cars are those modern ones – and there are several – which have been built with as many genuine D-type spare parts as possible but cannot establish an identity for themselves. This would not matter, except where the owner wishes to race his faithful reproduction but finds that the sanctioning organisation will not accept an entry without an authenticating number. If it does not exist, what is the owner to do? Well, more than one racer has been known to invent a number and stamp it on his car. This kind of action should not be necessary, and it is time the authorities gave the 'clones' a chance. After all, as historic cars get older they become, more valuable. No wonder relatively few examples of the real thing are to be seen racing these days. Perhaps by the time this edition appears in 1987, something *will* have been done to permit enthusiasts to race their cars without having to identify them with a factory number – genuine or otherwise. There are other ways of deciding what is fair and what is not. I hope these words become outdated soon.

The numbering system – and numbers

The numbering system dates from the time prior to the D-type designation being established officially.

The XK120C had become the C-type. The letter 'C' stood for 'competition', and who would be likely to change it for future models?

On 18 March 1954, the deputy company secretary of Jaguar Cars Ltd, Percy Shortley, issued a memo to Alice Fenton – head of home sales as well as secretary to William Lyons – with the heading 'XKC Competition Cars'. It was copied to all the main vehicle and works engineers and read:

Will you please note that identity numbers for
XK120C Series 2 commences at XKC 201
Series 3 commences at XKC 301
Series 4 commences at XKC 401

The 'XK120C, Series 4' became the D-type, but the first three or four cars were made by the time that was decided. In due course, internal memos began referring to the new 'XK120D', and so the XKC prefix became XKD during the build period for the first six cars. XKC or XKD is, in my view, equally correct when applied at this stage. Certainly, each of the Comp. Shop's notebooks for these cars is headed 'XKC' from 401 to 406.

A more interesting memo was sent to a similar list of directors, managers and supervisors, and copied to Mr Lyons, by production manager John Silver on 30 August 1955:

Will you please note that it has been agreed that the 100 'D' type
complete cars originally ordered should be reduced to 67. The
balance of detail parts is to be transferred to Spares.

The figure of 67 works out correctly, too. There were 87 D-types altogether. If six '400' and six '600' series cars are added to the first eight 1955 cars (three 'pre-production' and five 'works') the total is 20 – thus leaving 67 cars made actually on the production 'system'. All 67 were complete structurally by the end of 1955, but many would not be sold until well into 1957.

Sixteen XKSS numbers were selected as a '700' series but they had been identified as D-types before conversion and that is the sequence in which I have placed them in this appendix. For cross-reference purposes, here are the numbers and their equivalents:

XKSS 701	=	XKD 555
XKSS 704	=	XKD 563
XKSS 707	=	XKD 564
XKSS 710	=	XKD 568
XKSS 713	=	XKD 569
XKSS 716	=	XKD 575
XKSS 719	=	XKD 572
XKSS 722	=	XKD 539
XKSS 725	=	XKD 562
XKSS 728	=	XKD 547
XKSS 754	=	XKD 542
XKSS 757	=	XKD 559

XKSS 760	=	XKD 557
XKSS 763	=	XKD 566
XKSS 766	=	XKD 567
XKSS 769	=	XKD 550

Some cars were modified to and from XKSS or similar specification after the above cars were converted in 1957. Technically, the D-type and the XKSS are one and the same thing and, if a restoration is to be done, I do not think it matters which style the owner chooses. The question of fitting a long nose and high tail fin is slightly different, in that no cars of that type were built for sale to the public.

Below the chassis number, in the following list, are the original colour, engine number, and (in some cases) registration number.

XKC 401
Unpainted,
then BRG
E2001-9
OVC 501

Still owned by Jaguar, this is the prototype, light-alloy frame D-type, registered OVC 501, but used for Spring 1954 Le Mans practice session with incorrect number (OKV 501). Used for later testing (including De Dion rear suspension) but never raced; soon loaned by works to Beaulieu Motor Museum. Some road mileage (notably to 1958 Geneva show). Slight damage in rail transit to Germany in 1964, for showing there by arrangement with David Kergon of Smiths Industries. Other shows included Geneva 1966 and Swallow/Jaguar 'half-century' exhibition, Coventry, 1972. Still a very original car, with modified and adapted XK120 wishbones, prototype oil cooler, special radiator (by Marston Excelsior of Wolverhampton) and other 'C' and 'XK' parts. Some refurbishing work carried out in 1980s out by John Pearson of Whittlebury. Car retains original 'XKC 401' punch mark on top of front shock-absorber mounting.

Above and overleaf:
Details of the prototype, XKD 401, photographed by the author at Whittlebury in the mid-1980s, including new and old radiators, roadgoing tyres, and original front end including unique wishbones.

Left:
XKC 401 being 'spring-cleaned' for Jaguar by John Pearson of Whittlebury. (This again shows the original wishbone clearly.)

Above:
XKC 401 cockpit.

Below and Inset:
XKC 401 as a road car: photographed by the author outside the Polly Tearoom in Marlborough, and in the New Forest (where the audience seems slightly more enthusiastic!) in 1971, during a delivery run to Beaulieu.

The author and XKC 401.

XKC 402
BRG
E2004-9
OKV 1

Works team car, second at Le Mans and Reims in 1954 (Hamilton/Rolt), then shown at Paris Salon before sale to Duncan Hamilton to be raced privately by him, replacing his C-type (XKC 038); victories at Goodwood, Silverstone and Snetterton, second at Montlhéry and third at Oporto. Also in 1955 Michael Head borrowed it to win at Helsinki. Converted in 1956 for John Goddard who used it in the occasional sprint and hill-climb in Europe and Australia, but above all as a road car. He damaged it quite badly in 1957. It was, at the time, registered 3 APB; subsequently EOV 165 in Australia (though 'OKV 1' was painted on the nose again).

Ian Cummins (see XKD 510) co-drove with Goddard on several old-style high-speed inter-city dashes through Australia, and aided in the auctioning of his friend's mainly automotive and maritime collection in 1984. ('Jumbo' Goddard had died in 1983.) Car returned to Britain in 1985 for successful bidder, Robin Davidson of Suffolk, who placed it in the National Motor Museum at Beaulieu in 1986, still in 'Goddard conversion' trims.

XKC 402 photographed by the author in its new guise and with its new registration number at the 1956 Brighton Speed trials in which it was driven by John Goddard. (Mike Salmon looks over Gillie Tyrer's C-type, background left.)

XKC 403
BRG
E2005-9
OKV 2

Works team car. 1954, retired Le Mans and Reims after leading (Moss/Walker); converted to 2·5 litres for 1954 TT, taking fifth place (Wharton/Whitehead). Rebuilt after TT with E2004-9 (3·4 litres) and used for winter driver tests at Silverstone. Sold to John Broadhead for Bob Berry to race; second at Goodwood, fifth at Oporto in 1955 before crashing in TT that year. Damage seemed slight, but Berry recalls that the frame was

Two pictures by Tom Groskritz, one showing the car in the 1970s when it was 'not for sale', and the other showing the Lynx rebuild in 1981 when, according to Groskritz 'XKD 548' was overstamped '403'. Car in the background is thought to be 'XKD 504' with '505' frame.

found to be out of true and was replaced by a new one of the early type – a difficult rebuild, this being one of the original welded-up constructions. The number on the new frame, if any, is uncertain.

Car painted lighter green for 1956, when Berry came third at Silverstone and first at Goodwood, virtually writing-off car later on in that Whitsun meeting. Engine believed retained and fitted into new 'OKV 2', created from XKD 548? – or 570? – or another? New structure painted dark green, usually called BRG.

On recovery, Berry raced at club level from late 1956; other drivers appointed by Broadhead included Flockhart, Fairman, Blond and even the racing cyclist Reg Harris. Engine change (E2004-9 to E2065-9) undertaken at works in 1958; car sold soon afterwards to Gerry Crozier, then on to Canada in early 1960s. Owned by George Gordon, James Mace and James Catto. Another driver racing the car for Catto was killed. After many years lying dormant 'OKV 2' was returned to Britain by Lynx Engineering who rebuilt it and sold it to James Wallis in the early 1980s, when the identity of the structure was still not established fully.

Original remains of the 1956 shunt were said to have been buried on Broadhead's premises, but Berry does not believe the story.

XKC 404
BRG
E2006-9
OKV 3

Works team car, 1954 Reims winner (Wharton/Whitehead); 1955 Brussels show; Silverstone lap record, 1955 (Hawthorn). Sold via John Coombs and several owners to M. G. F. Dickens. Resold to Africa, where first overseas owner, John Love, won 1960 Angola GP. R. W. Evans Pty (Pretoria) entered it for 1961 Kyalami 9-hr race in which Tony Maggs led initially but co-driver (and owner) Neville Austin crashed. Bought by Rondalia Touring Club of Pretoria, then by Paul Hawkins who brought it back to UK; he sold to John Melville-Smith. Martin Morris drove restored car but crashed in Snetterton race; so he purchased and rebuilt it, and made it very competitive. In 1976 the Morrises used the car for a tour of California, the main purpose of which was to win the main race at Laguna Seca's 'tribute to Jaguar' weekend. (Mission accomplished.) Morris was third in 1978 historic Le Mans event and voted Jaguar Driver of the Year. The car – much modified, though still in the spirit of the original – remained effective. Martin Morris won events in Monaco (1983), Germany (1985), and New Zealand (1987) – always touring in between times, accompanied by his wife.

Acknowledgement from Stirling Moss (Cooper) as John Love (XKC 404) makes room for him in the first post-war South African Grand Prix at East London, New Year 1960. They were to finish second and seventh respectively behind Paul Frère (Cooper). (*Courtesy: L. Symons*)

Above:
Neville Austin finishing sixth in the Border 100 *Formule Libre* race at East London, July 1961. Later that month he won the 150-mile street race at Lourenço Marques (Maputo) in Mozambique. (*Courtesy: L. Symons*)

Right:
Neville Austin could not afford to rebuild OKV 3 after this crash in the 1961 *Rand Daily Mail* Kyalami 9-hour race, and sold the car to the Rondalia Touring Club who cobbled it up and put it on show. (*Courtesy: L. Symons*)

Below:
Works photograph of OKV 3 after a works rebuild for Melville-Smith in the late 1960s. This was organised by Chris Butler and was the last major factory involvement in D-type repair work.

Martin Morris wins at Laguna Seca, California, 1976.

The Morrises drove to Monaco in 1983, won a motor race, drove to the Dordogne for a holiday, then drove home. Note passenger's windscreen. (*Courtesy: Martin Morris*)

XKC 405

This car was only partly completed, if built at all. The most likely reason for this was the decision taken, in autumn 1954, to alter the material and structure of the D-type for 1955 production – mainly to make repairs and replacement of frame-parts easier to deal with. The engine-bearing frame *could* have found its way into OKV 1 (XKD 402) which has had its number restamped at some stage; but I cannot find a works notebook for 405, so the evidence is circumstantial, in that 402 had several minor shunts before it went to Australia. Then again, the frame could have gone into XKD 403 after the 1955 TT – only to be destroyed with the rest of that car at Goodwood, Whitsun 1956. Either way, there was no XKD 405 as such.

*XKD 406
BRG
E2003-9
RRW 21
(later 3 CPF)

Works car, first raced in 1954 TT (Moss/Walker) with $2\frac{1}{2}$-litre engine, then fitted with $3\frac{1}{2}$ for motor show and driver-tests, then loaned to Briggs Cunningham in the USA. Lloyd, Spear, Walters and Cunningham himself first tested the car at Sebring on 26 January 1955. Then Phil Walters did 164 mph on Daytona Beach before sharing winning Sebring race drive with Mike Hawthorn in this car. Hamilton came 5th at Silverstone (May '55), then purchased car, lending it to George Abecassis and Michael Head for odd races. Sold (winter 1956/7) to J Forbes Clark of Wolverhampton, who used car for sprints and hill-climbs. Various subsequent owners include Peter Skidmore, Sir Nicholas Williamson (who took it up Shelsley Walsh in an impressive 37·3 seconds), John Beasley and Martin Hilton.

*N.B. The works notebook for this car is headed 'XKC 406', but 'XKD' was the established prefix by the time this car – the last of the original batch of six – was completed.

XKD 406, photographed by the author in May 1958, taking third place in its class at Prescott driven by J. Forbes Clark.

Duncan Hamilton renews his acquaintance with 406 at an AP special event. (Silverstone 1970)

Hill-climb ace Sir Nicholas Williamson leaves the
starting line at Shelsley Walsh with XKD 406 in 1972.
(*Courtesy: Paul Skilleter*)

XKD 501
EE blue
E2008-9
MWS 301

New 'production' D-type supplied to *Ecurie
Ecosse* for Silverstone meeting, May 1955;
checked-out in works Competition Shop
beforehand. Crashed in practice at Silverstone and Nürburgring (J. Stewart).
Rebuilt at works, then fastest finisher at
Wicklow and two Snetterton wins (Titterting-
ton). Titterington and Sanderson second in
Goodwood 9 hr race (Aug. '55). 'Wilkie' Wilkinson rolled car at Snetterton (March '56).
Car rebuilt in time for Flockhart and Sanderson to come fourth at Rheims and first at
Le Mans. Retired 1957 Mille Miglia (Flockhart). When car finally withdrawn from
racing, *EE* benefactor, Major Thomson, kept
it at his Peebles home. When the whole collection was subsequently auctioned at Glen-
eagles, Michael Nairn's bid ensured it stayed
in Scotland. A painstaking rebuild to 1956
Le Mans specification was carried out at
Raymond Fielding's Forres garage during
1971/2.

**An early victory for an *Ecurie Ecosse* D-type was
achieved by Desmond Titterington in the 'scratch' class
of the 1955 Leinster Trophy race on the Wicklow road
circuit. (He started from scratch and was fastest
finisher.) David Murray is seen here keeping a fatherly
eye on XKD 501 before the start. (*Courtesy: Barclay
Wilson*)**

537

Ron Flockhart during the last-ever Mille Miglia (1957) prior to retirement due to XKD 501 trying to shake itself apart.

Michael Nairn with (*left to right*) Jack Cox, Digby Larque, and Jim Suttle of Jaguar. He was cleaning-down XKD 501 (the 1956 Le Mans winner) after driving from Scotland for the 1978 works open day at Browns Lane.

XKD 502
EE blue
E2020-9
MWS 302

Of similar spec. to 501, and delivered at the same time; sixth in its first race at Silverstone in May 1955, driven by D. Titterington who came first in the Ulster Trophy (and second on handicap) at Dundrod a week later, before crashing, practising for the *Eifelrennen* (as Stewart did, too). Car rebuilt at works, then raced regularly including Sanderson victory at Aintree (Sept. '55), and further successes in spring and summer 1956. Sold by *EE* to Maurice Charles of Cardiff after '56 season; Charles obtained a new body from works, and made many modifications including fitting IRS in early sixties. Later owners included Jack Alderslade (who obtained an ex-Lambert wide-angle head in the mid-1960s, and had much test and development work done by Playfords), Michael McGrath, and the Hexagon company for whom Nick Faure raced it successfully in historic events in early seventies, when it had a long-nose bonnet. Later still, the car went through the hands of Vic Norman, Patrick Lindsay and Albert Obrist. There was a complete rebuild by Lynx before it went to Japan in the 1980s.

Above:
Maurice Charles and his ex-*Ecurie Ecosse* D-type, XKD 502, among the Lotuses at Silverstone for the 1957 750MC relay race.

Left:
Two views of the independent rear suspension fitted to XKD 502. (*Courtesy: Paul Skilleter*)

539

A sort-of-long-nose bonnet, as fitted to XKD 502. Michael McGrath (*left*) takes the sash from Martin Morris (XKC 404) in a Silverstone relay race, c. 1970.

XKD 503
Yellow
E2011-9

Works-prepared by arrangement with Joska Bourgeois (Belgian Motor Co.) for Le Mans 1955, finishing third driven by John Claes and Jacques Swaters. Returned to works afterwards for checking and testing, and finally delivered by Les Bottrill to docks for shipment to Belgium. This 'short-nose' car was then re-exported to the USA for Ernest Erickson of Chicago. He took third in main

event at inaugural 'Road America' meeting (Elkhart Lake, Wisconsin, Sept 1955). Later sold to Alfonso Gomez Mena, who had crashed his previous car (XKD 521) in 1956. Mena finished sixth in 1957 Havana GP, but retired at Sebring (engine), and vanished from the international scene. 'XKD 503' was seen on fake car in the 1980s.

XKD 503, brand-new, at Channel airport with Bob Berry in attendance. Also being delivered from the works to Le Mans (1955) is XKD 507, in the capable hands of Norman Dewis (*right*).

A quick sale: XKD 503, having finished third at Le Mans in 1955, is sent to the USA for the use of Ernie Erickson – one of the first D-type privateers in America.

XKD 504
BRG (then *EE* blue)
E3003-9

'Long-nose', 1955 works Le Mans spare car, then test vehicle for Lucas fuel-injection system. First raced by Fairman (Silverstone, May 1956), using carburetter engine E3002–9; retired with broken N/S driveshaft. Engine E4001-9 fitted Oct 1956. Sold to *Ecurie Ecosse* at end of 1956 season, as 'carburetter' car; best results second at Saint Étienne (John Lawrence) and sixth at Monza (Ninian Sanderson) in 1957. Later, Michael Salmon bought car to replace his C-type (XKC 011). His biggest win was 1961 Snetterton 3-hour race shortly before resale to Peter Sutcliffe of Huddersfield, who drove well until major damage to car in Snetterton crash in 1963. Car returned to works and may have received frame of XKD 505 at this or an earlier stage. Neil Corner bought car in 1966, and raced it successfully in early 'historic' sports car events (Griffiths Formula).

Total rebuild by Lynx for Paul Vestey in early eighties included removal of front sub-frame stamped 'XKD 505' (and sale of same to East Grinstead collector Bill Lake). Car believed otherwise generally intact.

XKD 504 in Mike Salmon's hands – Brands Hatch 1959.

Peter Sutcliffe's car, photographed from the author's office window (overlooking the Browns Lane service department doorway) in 1963 after its comprehensive Snetterton roll.

Right:

This front subframe stamped 'XKD 505' is, certainly, authentic. Guy Black (seen here) arranged for Lynx Engineering to build a new long-nose car around this item in the early 1980s.

XKD 505
BRG
E3002-9

1955 Le Mans winner (works 'long-nose' driven by Hawthorn and Bueb); then modified for Aintree, but not raced there. Completely overhauled for Dundrod TT race, and fitted with De Dion rear suspension (ex-XKC 401); car withdrawn before race as practice showed Metalastik coupling to be unreliable. Fuel injection engine E3003-9 fitted March 1956 for Easter Monday Goodwood; car withdrawn beforehand due to 'poor handling'. Hawthorn and Fairman tested car at Silverstone on 17 April 1956; Fairman crashed at Becketts causing damage to near-side front suspension assembly and bonnet. Tested at Silverstone on 14 September 1956 with fully independent rear suspension by Ivor Bueb and Mike Hawthorn. (IRS gave weight reduction of $44\frac{1}{2}$ lb by comparison with De Dion, and brought it down to normal 1955 works car dry weight of 18 cwt 3 qr 12 lbs) Test discontinued due to rear assembly coming loose, with three bolts lost altogether! Last recorded works (tyre) tests at MIRA included 932 miles covered at an average of 128 mph between 10 and 16 June 1958. Although Coundley correspondence (with factory) links 505 with 601, there is no record of 505 actually being sold as an entity – hence the probability of parts of 505 turning up in other cars, notably in 601 and 504. New long-nose style of car built by RS panels and Lynx using sub-frame numbered 505 (owned by Bill Lake) in early 1980s; resultant vehicle sold to David Lomas, UK.

XKD 506
BRG
E3003-9

1955 works 'long-nose', retired Le Mans with gearbox failure (Hamilton/Rolt); then fifth at Aintree (Hawthorn) and retired when second in TT (Hawthorn/Titterington) – stand-in car for 505 on both occasions (used engine E3007-9 each time). Fitted with E3005-9 in time for end-of-season Silverstone tests; but E3001-9 installed prior to shipment to Florida January 1956, repainted in Cunningham colours for Daytona and Sebring, where it retired with valve failure (as well as brake problems). Then it stayed on, on long-term loan to Cunningham team. Returned to works less engine and reduced to scrap/parts c. 1959.

XKD 507
White and blue
E3004-9

1955 works 'long-nose' car retired Le Mans with engine failure, driven as a Cunningham entry by Phil Walters and Bill Spear. Shipped to USA for Cunningham, whose driver Sherwood Johnston came second at Elkhart Lake then first at Watkins Glen and Hagerstown before the year was out. Car remained in Cunningham team for 1956 and 1957, and for part of 1958 when Cunningham team raced new Lister-Jaguars. It became a Briggs Cunningham museum exhibit in the 1960s and is still much as it was raced by Hansgen and others, with Alfred Momo's special fin fitted to the production tail which had to

be fitted after the Elkhart Lake accidents of 1956. It has 'production' cylinder head (35/35) and oil tank, but is otherwise very much to works Le Mans spec. with quick-change front brakes, etc.

XKD 507, newly painted outside the experimental department prior to being delivered to Le Mans by Norman Dewis in 1955.

Phil Hill leads Steve Griswold at Laguna Seca in 1976, when he was second to Martin Morris in the pre-1956 race driving Briggs Cunningham's car, XKD 507.

XKD 508
BRG
E3005-9

1955 works 'long-nose' retired Le Mans when Don Beauman (co-driver to Norman Dewis) stuck in sand at Mulsanne. Transferred to Cunningham for 1956 Sebring fitted with engine E3006-9 and painted in white and blue; Hamilton/Rolt retired with brake trouble which beset 506 and 507 too. Car stayed on in Cunningham team, acquiring some 'Momo mods'. Returned to works less engine c. 1959, and effectively junked.

XKD 509
BRG
E2015-9

Production 'short-nose' car sold via Charles Hornburg to Albert R Browne of Menlo Park, Calif., late 1955 and entered for Sebring 1956 (Brero/Weiss), running eighth before retiring. Louis Brero put in some stirring drives with this car, his most successful one being second to Carroll Shelby (Ferrari) at Elkhart Lake, 1956. December 1956 Brero

also scored a worthy third at Nassau in this car, which was painted in distinctive 'wasp' stripes.

Reported later owned by Brian Classick (UK), then Nigel Moores estate.

XKD 510
BRG
E2017-9
YPC 614

Sold new to Richard Wilkins but soon resold to Duncan Hamilton. Raced in Dakar GP March 1956 (Graham Whitehead, fifth); then loaned by Hamilton to protégé Tony Dennis who crashed fatally at Goodwood, Easter 1956, mis-selecting gear. Remains bought by Gerald Ashmore of West Bromwich, rebuilt and raced for several seasons prior to resale to Neville Taylor of Barnsley, who carried out some kind of partial 'XKSS' conversion. Jinx struck again after car bought by The Cycle & Carriage Co. Singapore. Driving in 1963 Johore GP, Yong Nam Kee

D-types at Sebring, 1956. Lou Brero, centre, runs for his car (XKD 509) at Le Mans-type start.

The forceful Lou Brero (XKD 509) wins at Stockton, San Francisco, March 1957. (Soon afterwards, he would be killed while driving a different car in Hawaii.)

was killed in enormous accident. Australian John Hallihan (already the owner of a C-type) heard about the wreck while returning home from UK in 1967, and arranged purchase (but did not get far with proposed rebuild). He sold to Ian Cummins whose meticulous and faithful re-creation of the car – using the original parts wherever he could – was completed in 1981 and led to a short production run of 'D-type' clones by his erstwhile partner Steve Sulis of Classic Autocraft, Sydney. (The whole project was aided greatly by Keith Berryman – see XKD 526.) Car auctioned at 1982 Sydney motor show and acquired at record price by Australian B.S. ('Bib') Stillwell, former owner-driver of XKD 520 (and purchaser of a Bryan Wingfield 'Dee-type' special). Stillwell – by now the Arizona-based President of Gates Learjet – returned to racing and was soon making his mark in North American historic car events.

Gerald Ashmore eventually spun to a halt near the finish line at Ragley Hall hill-climb in his efforts to keep the power on. This Harold Hastings picture (dating from April 1959) shows the beginning of the long, long moment for the rebuilt XKD 510.

Below:
Yong Nam Kee on the front row of the 1963 Johore GP, Singapore, in XKD 510.

Bottom photographs:
The Singapore accident: XKD 510, already partially cut down, was split in two by the impact of hitting a pole sideways at high speed, the front end landing on the water's edge. (The central bracing *was* important structurally.)

Using as many original parts as possible, Ian Cummins re-created XKD 510 in Sydney; this meticulous work would lead to a small production run of authentic reproductions.

The new XKD 510: Lofty England and the finished article, 1981.

XKD 511
BRG
E2019-9
TNG 959

Sold via Mann Egerton & Co. of Norwich, Sept. 1955, to Capt. Ian B. Baillie of the Life Guards whose main achievement was to take International Class 'C' speed records (up to 200 miles) at Monza despite rain and cross-winds, with 144·92 mph best lap, March 1957. Not so successful in racing. Sold to M. V. Mackie, then James Boothby. Owner from mid-sixties, former racing photographer Guy Griffiths whose daughter Penny (now Mrs Woodley) raced occasionally before car joined family collection. Painted white, car was being maintained in running condition in the UK by Roger and Penny Woodley in the 1980s.

In the 1956 Eastern Counties MC national 100-mile race (won by Les Leston in a Cooper-Climax) Ian Baillie was lying fifth when XKD 511 spun under braking for the Esses, dug in, and flipped over. He lay flat and was found to be suffering only from bruising when the car was lifted off him, just as Max Trimble went by in his C-type. (*Courtesy: Maxwell Trimble*)

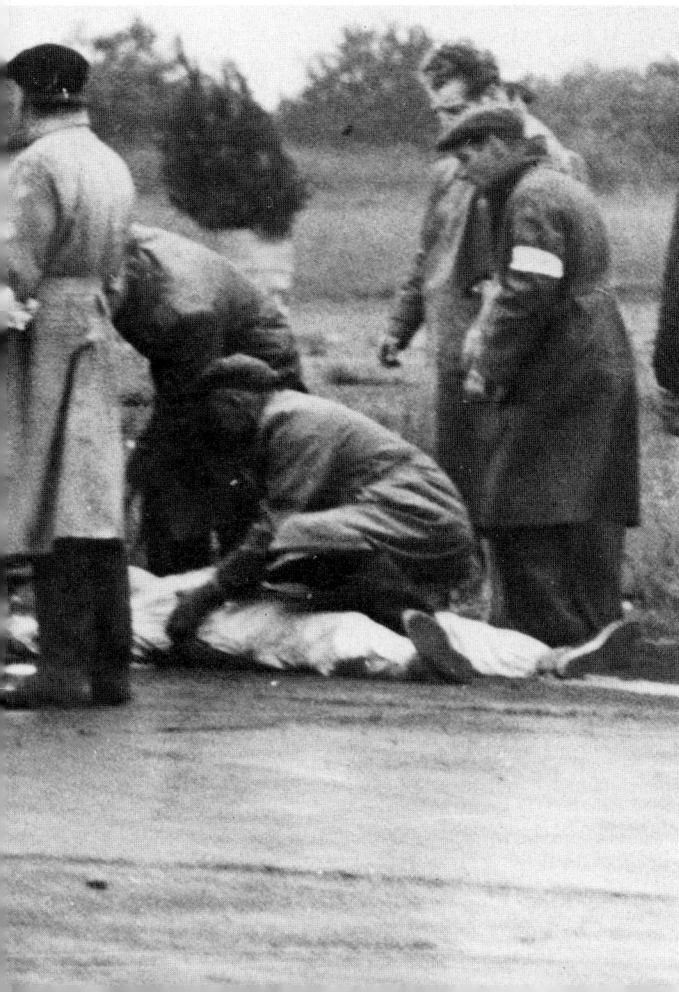

Above:

Penelope Griffiths in XKD 511 at Oulton Park for a Griffiths Formula event. (Her father, Guy, was an early promoter of affordable historic car racing.)

Below:

W. O. Bentley with Penny Griffiths and XKD 511 at Chipping Camden in the late 1960s.

The Griffiths collection of sports Jaguars: C-type, D-type, E2A, modified E-type coupé, lightweight E-type, with works 2+2 (Series Two). (*Courtesy: Guy Griffiths*)

XKD 512
BRG
E2014-9
J 26

Sold via St Helier Garages to Lord Louth, who took it from Jersey to South Africa where he raced it, selling it there in 1957 after taking a couple of seconds at a Jo'burg meeting. Local owners included Mr Watson (driver Malcolm Gardner), Jimmy de Villiers, and

Ian Brown. Later driven by Bruce Huntley and G. Pfaff without much success despite 3·8 conversion. Retired Kyalami 1961. Sold in UK (516 EYR) to Russ Taylor in 1962, Jack Epstein 1964, then to Nigel Moores in 1965.

XKD 512 (*left*) joined the Longbacon Engineering stable in the 1960s. The late Nigel Moores stands alongside; Paul Kelly is between XKSS 757 and XKD 515.

XKD 513
French blue
E2022-9

Sold via Ch. Delecroix, Paris, and dealer H. Peignaux, Lyon, to Jean-Marie Brussin who came third at Le Mans in 1957 with Jean Lucas co-driving. In 1958, now with 3-litre engine and sharing driving with Guelfi, Brussin was killed at the same circuit, after an accident involving Bruce Kessler's Maserati. At the Geneva show of 1963 the rebuilt wreck was reborn with an attractive GT body by Michelotti. This car, with *no* original body panels, spent many years in the USA. Later Lynx Engineering put the Michelotti body on an E-type chassis. The few remaining parts were used by Lynx for a 'total reconstruction' of XKD 513, which went to the USA in the early 1980s: Peter Giddings and Bob Baker were among the owners.

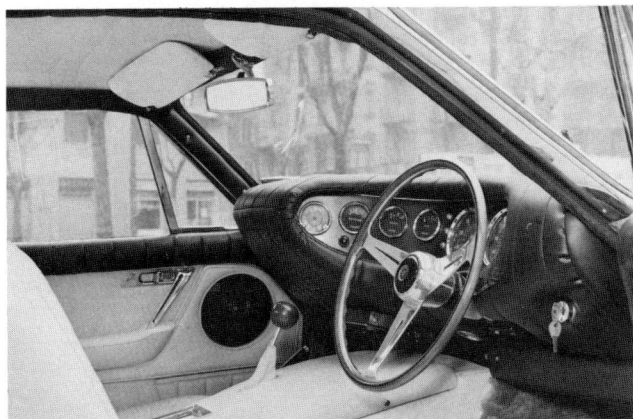

Parts of the remains of XKD 513 were used in the construction by Michelotti of this dramatic coupé for the 1963 Geneva show.

The Michelotti coupé during its American sojourn in 1971. The body would be given E-type mechanical components a decade later.

Norman Dewis testing XKD 513 at MIRA prior to Le Mans, 1958.

A new 'XKD 513' emerges at Lynx Engineering. How the bootlid from Boothby's D-type (see XKD 511) came to be 'found in a barn' and incorporated into the new body is one of many D-type mysteries.

XKD 514
Battleship grey
E2018-9
PWX 2

Sold via Messrs Glovers of Ripon to (Sir) Robert Ropner of Bedale, Yorkshire in August 1955 and used as road car. After one year, letter to Engineering Director Heynes said: '... the D continues to go like a bird. It has never failed to start or oiled-up a plug in 8000 miles....' Car converted to 3·8 litres in 1959 and retained by Ropner (and his son Bruce) for twenty years during which he took part in Catterick hill-climbs twice and lent it to his son (whose Cobra had broken down) for one relay race at Croft in 1965. The car was always maintained by the works or Wilkie Wilkinson of *Ecurie Ecosse* (and, later, BRM), and was used mainly for touring – mostly between Darlington and Aberdeenshire, and once to Italy. Bruce Ropner disposed of the car to Adrian Hamilton in Autumn 1975, in part-exchange for a Ford GT40 which was gutted by a petrol fire the first time he drove it. Hamilton had bought the car for Robert Danny, who never took delivery. Instead it was bought by Ole Sommer for his private collection, and painted BRG. The Sommer Collection of Naerum, Denmark, is open to members of the public.

XKD 515
Special blue
E2033-9
RRU 1

Sold via Henlys to Col Ronald J. Hoare, CBE, Director of F. English Ltd (Bournemouth main Ford dealers); used as road car then sold to John Coundley (early 1959); later bought back and resold to Nigel Moores.

XKD 514, seen when new at Bedale with the other Jaguars of shipping magnate Sir Robert Ropner. A most original car, it is still run regularly in Denmark by former Jaguar importer Ole Sommer.

XKD 515 driven at Crystal Palace in 1971 by 'Willie Eckerslyke', the name used by Littlewoods heir Nigel Moores when he went racing.

XKD 516
Cream
E2020-9

Sold via Max Hoffman, New York, to former XK 120 and C-type user Commander J. Rutherford of Palm Beach Florida. *Car* magazine, UK, tested it in 1977 by which time it was owned by musician Nick Mason, its long-term owner.

XKD 517
Pastel green
E2026-9
TKF 9

Sold via Henlys to Gillie Tyrer and raced quite successfully by Alex McMillan in late-1955 club racing. (McMillan was co-owner.) Purchased mid-1956 by Murkett Bros, Jaguar dealers of Huntingdon, painted white and driven by Henry Taylor (best results, a first at Snetterton and a third at Spa-Francorchamps, 1957). Owned in 1958 by Jock McBain and raced for Ian Scott Watson's 'Border Reivers' by Jim Clark in twenty events, finishing every time, including 12 'firsts'; eighth at Spa (Clark's first national *or* international meeting!). Sold to Alan Ensoll winter 1958/59; Ensoll cut car about, *á la* XKSS, then sold to Bob Duncan of Crumlin, who raced in N. Ireland in early sixties before selling to Jaguar collector Bryan Corser in 1964; restored to correct general shape and painted BRG. Purchased in 1979 by William Tuckett, Devon, and damaged in early eighties (historic racing), but repaired with Martin Morris's help.

Henry Taylor at Oulton Park for the Empire Trophy race in 1957, by which time XKD 517 (like many other Ds) had acquired a full-width windscreen.

Shrewsbury solicitor Bryan Corser and XKD 517 at Gaydon, c. 1970, with his lightweight E-type beyond.

XKD 518
Red
E2028-9
KDB 100

Sold via Henlys to Peter Blond (Manchester) whose best results were at Snetterton in 1956. Next owner Jonathan Sieff sold to M. R. G. Mostyn of Speedwell Garage, Twickenham; later owners included Jean Bloxham (Mrs M. Salmon), J. Coombs/R. Wilkins, and Clive Lacey. Exported to Germany in 1980s.

XKD 517 was crashed by Henry Taylor at Silverstone in 1956.

XKD 518 at Oulton Park. (*Courtesy: Paul Skilleter*)

M. R. G. ('Monty') Mostyn fitted an XKSS-type bonnet badge to XKD 518, seen here at the 1959 National West Essex CC speed trials on North Weald aerodrome. He was third (21·42 sec. for the half-mile) to Ron Brightman (20·37 sec; Lister-Chevrolet) and Patsy Burt (21·34 sec; Cooper-Climax F2).

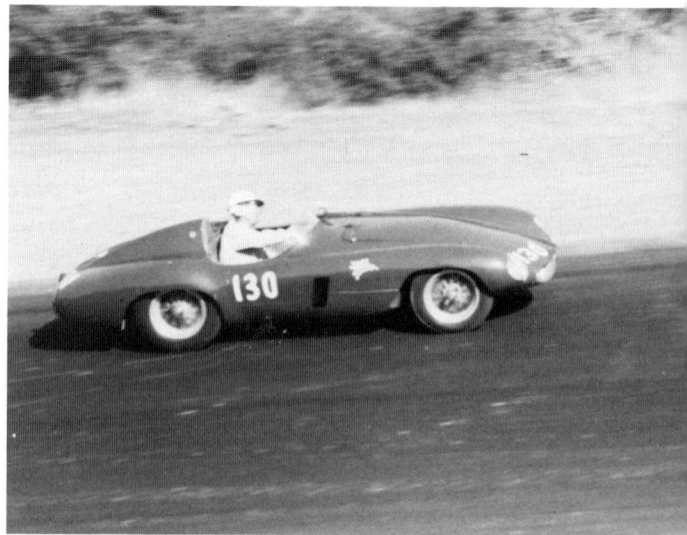

Bill Krause (XKD 519) chased by eventual winner Harrison Evans (Ferrari 750 Monza) at Paramount Ranch, August 1956. This circuit, in the Santa Monica mountains near Hollywood, was owned by the Paramount Motion Picture Studio. (*Courtesy: Jim Sitz*)

XKD 519
Pastel green
E2009-9

Sold via Charles Hornburg to A. R. Krause of Bellflower, Calif., an engineer who did a lot of modifying, and whose son Bill raced it quite successfully. Best result, after modification to 3·8 litres, was in 1958 'Sports Car GP' at Riverside, where Bill Krause was a strong third to Chuck Daigh (Scarab) and Dan Gurney (Ferrari). Later a Chevrolet engine was substituted to try and keep car competitive, a fairly popular but rarely successful USA ploy. Reported with Lynx in 1985.

XKD 520
BRG
E2021-9

Sold via Jack Bryson, Aussie importer, to 'Bib' Stillwell of Melbourne who finished second to Tony Gaze (HWM-Jaguar) first time out in Moomba TT at Albert Park despite second-gear failure, in March 1956. Later that spring, Stillwell won at Albert Park, and came third (and fastest sports car) at Bathurst, NSW. Soon afterwards he broke the sports car record at Rob Roy hill-climb and won the South Australia Trophy race at Port Wakefield, beating Stan Jones (Maserati 250F) on handicap and on scratch. Next owner was radio personality Jack Davey, who had it repainted red; but a 'friend' wrecked it in a road accident. Alan Standfield (Sydney body man) helped purchaser Frank Gardner

XKD 519 driven by Bill Krause and Porsche 550 Spyder of Ken Miles en route to third and fourth places respectively in the Pomona Fairground 1-hour race, California, June 1956. (*Courtesy: Jim Sitz*)

Bib Stillwell (XKD 520) ascends Mount Panorama on the Bathurst circuit, Easter Monday 1956, en route for third place behind two single-seater drivers – Lex Davison (Ferrari) and Reg Hunt (Maserati). The Jaguar was fastest of all on the notorious Conrod Straight, being timed at 148 mph despite a misfire. (*Courtesy: Les Hughes*)

rebuild car (painted white); Gardner raced car from April to October 1958. Gardner went abroad, selling car to Turramurra enthusiast David Finch who raced regularly for three years and had an imitation 'long-nose' made for it. Finch's biggest win was 1961 Queensland TT. Next owners were Ash Marshall, Peter Bradley, and Richard Parkinson. In 1967, Paul Hawkins arranged sale to racing driver and former Jaguar apprentice Richard Attwood in UK. Purchased by Lynx in 1970s and given major overhaul prior to sale to A. Spencer Nairn, Jersey.

XKD 521
Cream
E2037-9

Sold via Frank Seiglie of Distribuidora Jaguar SA, Havana, Cuba, to Alfonso Gomez Mena who finished eighth at Sebring 1956 (co-driver Santiago Gonzales). Later, car virtually written-off against house, but Mena tells works: 'Thanks to the well-engineered and strength of the car and God's will, I am at this moment alive and able to write to you'. After a £2000 Momo quote, Mena bought another car (XKD 503) second-hand rather than have his rebuilt.

XKD 522
Red
E2027-9

1955 Los Angeles show car, then entered for Palm Springs races that December by West Coast Jaguar agent Chuck Hornburg. Ignacio Lozano was chosen to drive as Sherwood Johnston not available; Lozano was unplaced on Saturday race, so Carroll Shelby was brought in to drive main Sunday event; retired due to uncompetitiveness, though Shelby 'impressed' by some aspects. Race preparation by Jay Chamberlain for Hornburg in whose premises it was badly damaged by fire. Sold and reported rebuilt with Chevrolet engine in Nevada, where car was wrecked in 1960s. Thomas Groskritz of California bought 'basket case' in Reno in 1971. (At the New York Jaguar 'great mark-down sale' that year, Groskritz also found and purchased many of the parts he needed.) In the 1980s, Groskritz (see also XKD 531) was using Lynx components as the basis for a resurrection of 522.

Frank Gardner with the rebuilt XKD 520 in 1958. (*Courtesy: Terry McGrath*)

David Finch with XKD 520 at Bathurst, shortly after acquisition from Frank Gardner. The Aston Martin DB3S is driven by Warren Blomfield. (*Courtesy: Spencer Martin*)

Jaguar's service manager for North America, Kenrick ('Buck') Hickman, at the wheel of XKD 522 – Charles ('Chuck') Hornburg's own car. Also present when it arrived at Burbank airport, California, were Jaguar west coast manager John Dugdale, Ken McDermot (*centre*) and Walter Taylor of Hornburg's service department.

553

XKD 522 at Los Angeles Auto Show, November 1955. (*Courtesy: Tom Groskritz*)

Unique picture of C-type and D-type with E2A on the occasion of the latter's one and only victory (by Walt Hansgen) at Bridgehampton in 1960. This line-up was for photographic purposes only, with Alfredo Momo in E2A, Jeff Scott in XKC 032, and Joe Grimaldi in XKD 523 – which already had a Buick V8 engine and was beginning to lose its identity.

Ignacio Lozano at Palm Springs, December 1955. This was the first race for the West Coast 'showroom' car, XKD 522, soon to be ruined by fire in Hornburg's workshop. (*Courtesy: Mrs Charles Hornburg*)

XKD 523
Black

Sold via Jaguar Cars New York to Roberts Harrison; resold within a year to Walter Huggler of Pennsylvania; also said to have been driven by George Constantine (see also 545) but I have not been able to verify. Joe Grimaldi (formerly of Fred Opert Racing team) fitted Buick V8 engine later, but next owner (Jeff Millstein) hunted up the Jaguar engine (finding it in a Lister which he is said to have bought and scrapped). Millstein's brother Bob, recalls that there were *two* rear body sections, one with fin, one without. Millstein sold car to Vintage Car Store, Nyack, NY, in 1970. On 13 September 1973, an *Autosport* advertisement caught the eye of UK enthusiast Bob Woods, who arranged to purchase what he believed to be a D-type. In fact there were some bits of *two* D-types – but nothing like all of *one*! For example, there was no centre-section which is so crucial to

completion of a genuine D-type rebuild. Woods lost interest at once and XKD 523 acquired a dual identity which it is unlikely to lose. One 'XKD 523' was built around the centre-section in the USA; the other was 're-created' by Lynx Engineering in the UK (see also XKD 529 and 560).

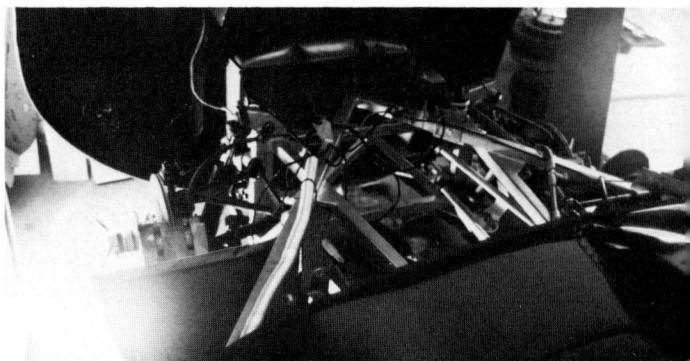

The 'American XKD 523' photographed in 1975, showing new frame.

554

The 'American XKD 523' photographed in the early 1980s by the then-owner, Ron Finger.

The 'British XKD 523' at Lynx Engineering in 1980 – a new car being built for Brian Angliss around parts of the original front frame, which had been cut about to take Grimaldi's Buick engine many years before.

XKD 524
Black
E2032-9

Sold via New York to Henry Carroll Inc., of Binghampton, NY. Car won a minor US sprint in 1956, driven by new owner Paul Pfohl. Then what?

'John' Gordon Benett in Briggs Cunningham's car, XKD 525, at Cumberland, Maryland, May 1956. Jack McAfee (Porsche 550) passed him and went on to finish second to Walter Hansgen in another D-type (XKD 529). (*Courtesy: C. Gordon Benett*)

XKD 525
BRG
E2033-9

Sold via NY to Briggs Cunningham, and soon repainted white and blue. This short-nosed production model was regarded as his 'personal' race car, but was almost certainly 'robbed' after his other three D-types all crashed on the same weekend. (Elkhart Lake, 1956.) Was .its tail-section built into XKD 507? Who knows?

XKD 526
BRG
E2042-9
NCN 040

Sold to Mr & Mrs Cyril Anderson of Andersons Agencies Pty, Brisbane, Jaguar distributors for Queensland, and raced for them originally by Bill Pitt. One memorable result was fourth in the 1956 Australian TT, beaten only by Moss and Behra in Maseratis and Wharton in a Ferrari, and finishing ahead of Stillwell in XKD 520. A week later, Pitt rolled it at the same circuit (Albert Park Melbourne) and was lucky to land in the road virtually unhurt. Pitt raced successfully until 1959 when the Andersons (and Pitt) became deeply involved with a 3·4 in touring car racing. NSW company Leaton Motors acquired the D-type, and it was raced for them by Frank Matich, Doug Chivas, and Barry Topen. During this period, a loose 'GT' class was established in Australia and Leaton fitted a neat hardtop to enable XKD 526 to take part; Frank Matich won 1961 national GT championship. Topen crashed car at Sandown in 1962. Keith Russell bought, rebuilt and raced it in 1965/66. Keith Berryman bought it in 1967 and raced it in early 1970s. Complete, lengthy rebuild by Cummins/Sulis followed, in parallel with that of XKD 510. Still owned by Berryman in 1980s.

Mrs Geordie Anderson tries out XKD 526 for herself. (*Courtesy: Terry McGrath*)

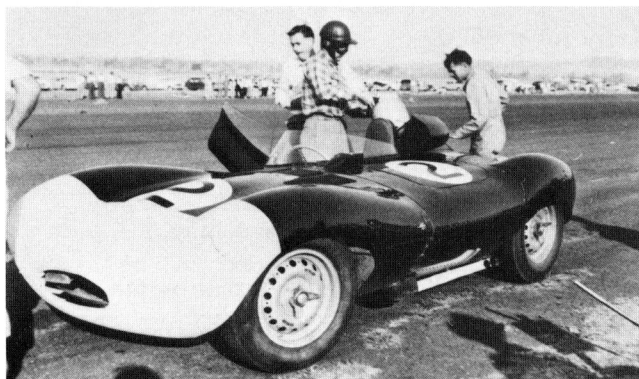
Bill Pitt fuels XKD 526 at Lowood where he won the Champions' Scratch Race and the Queensland TT (from Stillwell's XKD 520) in November 1956, shortly before his lucky escape in Melbourne. (*Courtesy: Terry McGrath*)

Frank Matich (*left*) and the men from Leaton Motors, Sydney, NSW, visit Lowood, Queensland, in 1959, to test and purchase XKD 526. (*Courtesy: Les Hughes*)

Two Bathurst angles on the fascinating conversion which enabled Frank Matich to win the Australian GT Championship with XKD 526 in 1961, its sixth year of racing. (*Courtesy: Spencer Martin*)

Superbly restored, XKD 526 was photographed by the author at Bathurst in 1985, when Keith Berryman took Tom Walkinshaw and Win Percy on a parade lap prior to the running of the James Hardie 1000.

A 1956 Momo advertisement.

XKD 527
BRG
E2025-9

Sold via Hornburg to Jerry Austin of Arcadia, Calif., who won the first big D-type victory on the west coast, the 1956 6-hr race at Torrey Pines; Sherwood Johnston was co-driver. Austin lent his car for press tests; he had no more big wins but good 'places' at Palm Springs and Santa Barbara in 1957. Owned in mid-sixties by M. A. Olson of Farmington, Utah. Peter van Rossem raced this car in UK in early 1970s. Later to Nigel Dawes collection, and still there in late 1980s.

XKD 527 being driven to victory in the Californian 6- hour race, January 1956, by Sherwood Johnston (seen here) and the car's owner Jerry Austin.
(*Courtesy: Jim Sitz*)

Peter van Rossem with XKD 527 at Silverstone in the 1970s.

XKD 528
Cream
E2039-9

Sold via Hornburg, owned by Continental Motors, Whittier, Calif., and raced by Pearce Woods. *Road & Track* borrowed it for 'road-test' (May '56 edition) after car illustrated on cover (XKD 527) had trouble at Palm Springs race and couldn't be used. Lent to Harold Erb who came third (to Ferraris of Carroll Shelby and Phil Hill) in Palm Springs National race, November 1956. Car bought for long-term ownership by Hollywood photographer Carlyle Blackwell Jr (who sold XKC 007 to buy it) in 1958, and acquired

3·8 engine with 35/40 cylinder head some ten years later. Blackwell's pictures of D-type, painted red, appeared in *R & T Salon* feature. Won 1959 6-hour race at Pomona, California, with expatriate Englishman (and top-class professional driver) Ken Miles and Blackwell driving. Car then yellow and black. Restored in late 1970s by Griswold for Ronald Laurie of San Francisco (also owner of Hageman Special).

Pearce Woods (XKD 528) at Pebble Beach, California, in April 1956. This was the last event to be run on public roads here. A new track, Laguna Seca, was built twenty miles inland in 1957. (*Courtesy: Jim Sitz*)

Photographs above:
Pearce Woods' win with XKD 528 (owned by Fran Lehum and Fred Woodward of Continental Motors, Whittier, California) at Honolulu in the spring of 1957. (*Courtesy: Mrs Charles Hornburg*)

Right:
Ken Miles tells Carlyle Blackwell the score as he hands over XKD 528 during their victory run in the 6-hour race at Pomona Fairgrounds, California, in 1959. (*Courtesy: Jim Sitz*)

Below:
Carlyle Blackwell and XKD 528 at Santa Barbara. (*Courtesy: Mrs Charles Hornburg*)

Top:

Totally reconstructed by Griswold, XKD 528 is seen with the Jaguar-powered Hageman Special; both were the property of Californian Ronald Laurie in the 1980s.

Above:

Two close-ups of XKD 528, as restored. (*Courtesy: Ron Laurie*)

XKD 529
BRG
E2039-9

Sold via Hoffman to Auto Engineering (Tage Hansen), Boston, and raced very successfully by Walt Hansgen who embarrassed the 'official' Cunningham team Jaguars before joining that team himself during 1956. Fame continued when Thomas Rutherford of Massachusetts achieved the highest speed ever officially recorded by an XK-engined Jaguar; at Bonneville, the carefully (but not extensively) modified car, with 3·8 engine, and 2·53 axle, was timed at 185·47 mph, in 1960. He wanted to modify further, to break 200 mph but was still talking about it four years later. Suffered tornado damage during ownership by George Boyd in seventies, before sale to Walter Hill of Florida who

completed restoration in 1980. Car later given 'Bonneville' visual spec. (*N.B. In the 1970s another USA-based car appeared, erroneously identified as 'XKD 529'. Later, the last figure was changed to a '3' for which there may have been some justification.*)

Young Tom Rutherford with the ex-Hansgen car, XKD 529, at the Utah salt flats in 1959, when he exceeded 185 mph. Note wheels and exhaust.

XKD 530
BRG
E2044-9

Sold via Suomen Maanviljelijain Kauppa Oy of Tampere to Finnish Davis Cup player and former C-type owner Curt Lincoln of Helsinki. Won over-2-litre race at Djurgard Park (May 1956) and raced thereafter with continued local success on ice, sand, and normal circuits. Major overhaul at Coventry winter 1959/60, when still owned by Lincoln. Timo Makinen raced this car before becoming one of first 'Flying Finns' of World-class rallying. Estonian engineer/writer Margus-Hans Kuuse suggests that this is the only D-type to have raced in the USSR – and it won! The event was the *Formule Libre* race of the CHAMK (Central Automobile Club of the USSR) in 1961; 'One of only four times in USSR history that our racers have competed directly against Westerners – twice in Leningrad, once in Tallinn, and once at Monza, Italy,' says Kuuse. At Tallinn, Curt Lincoln won the FJ and F3 races in that meeting but the D-type appears to have been on loan to another Finn named H. Hietarinta that day. Brought from Finland to join collection of Nigel Moores, 1966.

XKD 530 wears weird tailfin and full-width windscreen for Leningrad (CHAMK) race meeting in 1961. (*Courtesy: Margus-Hans Kuuse*)

XKD 531
BRG
E2034-9

First owner Jack Douglas of California changed colour to mustard yellow, and raced car from early 1956. Possibly his best result was to come second to John Barneson (Hageman Super Sports) in Great Salt Lake Trophy 100-mile race in June 1956. Ray Seher of Reno bought car (plus the remains of XKD 522 'for spares') in late 1950s. Next owner, Thomas Groskritz, bought and restored it, and still owned it in the 1980s. (See also XKD 522.)

Below and bottom photograph:
XKD 531 as rebuilt to *concours* standard by Tom Groskritz, and photographed by him at Riverside, California in the 1970s.

Timo Makinen on dirt track in Finland, with XKD 530 – the ex-Curt Lincoln car.

XKD 532
Red
E2030-9

Sold to Jack Parker (visiting Coventry from Australia) and road-tested for May 1957 issue of *Wheels* magazine by Pedr Davis. Car kept garaged at Bondi, Sydney, by 'Gelignite Jack' Murray — well-known rallyist, temporarily banned from racing because he had entered an 'unofficial' rally — who repainted it silver and raced occasionally between 1958 and 1961, when dealer and touring car racer Bob Jane of Victoria bought it. Apart from being driven out through the plate-glass window of his Parramatta Road, Sydney, showroom and left stranded on a central reservation by a would-be suicide one night in 1976, the car had a quiet life — in store, on display, or being maintained and restored by James Shepherd in Melbourne who drove it in the odd historic race. Sold in 1980 to George Parlby, Sydney.

XKD 533
French blue
E2040-9

Sold with 1956 regulation full-width screen via Delecroix (Paris) and Peignaux (Lyon) to Monnoyeur of Dijon. Best and possibly only major race result, seventh in Forez 6-hr race (Saint Étienne, May 1957). Monnoyeur was the man behind 'Los Amigos', the team that entered 513 for Le Mans in 1957/58. Both 'French' cars came back to Coventry in the spring of 1958 — 513 for Le Mans preparation, 533 for conversion to full 'XKSS' specification for its new owner, Pierre Chemin of Lyon, who kept it a long time. Later joined Philippe Renault's Jaguar collection. (Colour BRG, when converted to XKSS; but no change of chassis number.)

XKD 534
E2043-9

On show at Attwoods (Wolverhampton dealers) before sale in Independent Motor Sales, Wellington, New Zealand to Jack Shelly; Shelly's son Tony decided not to race in view of impending marriage, so car 'long-term loaned' to Robert Gibbons to prepare and drive. Best meeting was 1957 NZ GP, Ardmore, Auckland where Gibbons won (from Jack Brabham in fading Cooper Climax) in sports car race in which Ken Wharton (Ferrari) was killed, and came fifth in GP itself. Shellys sold car to Angus Hyslop in mid-1958, and two years later he reported (in a letter to 'Lofty' England) '... in last two seasons it has performed 100 per cent reliably and not caused any worry at all.' Later

owners were Simon Taylor (1961), Gary Bremer (1963) and Noel Foster of Auckland (1965); by then it had 3·8 engine, as did so many 'C' and 'D' Jaguars in later life. In 1986 *Australian Jaguar*, edited by Les Hughes, reported that Foster had averaged 1000 miles a year (mostly on the road) since buying it, and that he had just passed it on to his son in generally good condition.

XKD 535
Pastel blue
E2048-9
NVC 260

Sold via Madrid agent C. de Salamanca to Joaquin Palacios, formerly associated with Pegaso. All racing seems to have been done by Rodolfo Bay, who took eighth place in 1956 Oporto race, Portugal, and broke the record for the Galapagar hill-climb in Spain (previously held by a Pegaso) in 1957. Bay advertised it for sale (in 'perfect' condition) that autumn. This car found its rather scruffy way into the museum at Le Mans, though it never raced at that circuit.

XKD 536
Black
E2024-9

Sold via Hornburg to Loyal Katskee of Loyal's Foreign Cars, Omaha, who hit rocks while practising for first race (Nassau, December 1955); 'negligence on my part,' he said, 'the finest race car I've ever seen.' Damaged wheels at Sebring (1956). Returned to Britain by Herb Wetson in later life, having been fitted, typically, with a Chevrolet V8 engine. David Piper sold it to Tony Charnock. A 1976/77 Lynx restoration, this car was sold again in 1984, via Adrian Hamilton to Robert Cooper.

XKD 536 (rebuilt from engineless wreck) outside the original Lynx 'transplant surgery' at Northiam, Sussex, in July 1976 prior to delivery (with 35–40 3·8 engine) to John Lees. (*Courtesy: Rob Harcourt*)

XKD 534, owned by Noel Foster, in a New Zealand Jaguar meet line-up of the 1960s. (*Courtesy: Simon Taylor*)

XKD 537
Cream
E2047-9

Sold via J. M. Arfvidson of Imporsal (Importadora Salvadorena SA, San Salvador) to Mauricio Miranda mid 1956 and badly damaged in crash soon after. Sent back to works late in year, and still awaiting repair 'go-ahead' on 12 February 1957 when fire gutted much of Jaguar works including service department. Car totally destroyed, and replaced by XKD 549.

XKD 538
Ivory
E2030-9

Sold to Jack Ensley, President of Jaguar Midwest Distributors Inc. (Indianapolis), who with Bob Sweikert finished third at Sebring in 1956. Damaged car in British GP sports car race (Silverstone, July 1956); repaired at Coventry before shipment to USA in time for Ensley to finish second to George Constantine in Watkins Glen GP that September. Next two owners (Barney Devlin of Pennsylvania and Harry Heinl of Ohio) to mid-sixties; later owners included Preston Smith of Williamsport, Pennsylvania. Car up for sale by Vintage Car Store, Nyack, NY, in early 1980s.

Bob Sweikert saves the day for Jaguar at Sebring in 1956, sharing XKD 538 with owner Jack Ensley. (*Courtesy: Jim Sitz*)

XKD 539
Red
E2045-9
4 DPD

Completed as XKSS 722, and sold via Henlys to Coombs of Guildford in May 1957, road-tested in *Punch* by Basil Boothroyd with illustrations by Russell Brockbank. John Coombs first in class at Brighton Speed Trials (Sept 1957). Registered 'UDT 100' for Gibson Jarvie of UDT; then owned by Col Ronald Hoare, but little or no competition work until purchase by Bill Rigg in 1962. Rigg converted car back to D-type appearance in 1963, racing it in this form at Silverstone, Dunboyne and elsewhere. Rigg damaged the car at Silverstone in 1964 and was tragically killed in a Lotus Elite at Dunboyne two weekends later. Registration numbers 548 ARX and AWP 316B applied to this car. John Pearson, Northamptonshire, acquired the monocoque and many parts. Car later identified with Nigel Moores (Longbacon Engineering), still in D-type form.

XKD 540
BRG
E2029-9
WVM 3

Sold (after dealer-show use) via Coombs (1957) to Philip Scragg of Cheshire (hill-climb specialist) who had it converted at Coventry to full XKSS specification in winter of 1958/9 for new sports-car hill-climb championship. Sold at end of 1959 season to Jack Browning of Cheltenham, who also competed in hill-climbs; conversion to 3·8 at Works and registered BLH 7 when owned, briefly, by Betty Haig (1962). Sold via Jack Playford to Laurie O'Neill in Australia (late 1962) where it was featured in *Sports Car World* (July 1964) and registered NSW 567. In 1965 it went from Sydney to new owner, Colin Hyams of Melbourne. Bill Clemens used it for show purposes from 1968 to 1971 when Bryan Corser of Shrewsbury, UK, added it to his collection for many years. Sold to Peter Fowler, 1985.

Jack Browning hill-climbing at Prescott in 1960 with XKD 540, as converted to XKSS for first owner Phil Scragg.

Above:
Betty Haig with XKD 540 which she owned in the early sixties. (*Courtesy: Paul Skilleter*)

Left and below:
Jimmy Clark and Jackie Stewart (in Australia in 1967 for the Tasman race series) try out XKD 540 when owned by Colin Hyams. (*Courtesy: Eoin Young*)

XKD 540 in prize-winning form at Lilydale, Victoria, prior to sale by Bill Clemens to Bryan Corser in the early 1970s.

XKD 541
Pacific blue
E2049-9

Sold via Hornburg to Harold Fenner of New Mexico, then Charles Brown museum (Texas) before going east around 1970. Notable later owner was Roberts Harrison of Pennsylvania. Raced in historic events by Stephen Griswold.

Above:

Still in its original blue with grey leather upholstery, Roberts Harrison's D-type (XKD 541) was photographed in 1971 at his Pennsylvania estate, with his C-type (XKC 044) in the background. (*Courtesy: Tom Groskritz*)

Roberts Harrison with XKD 541 at Mount Equinox, Vermont, where Henry Wessells (*left*) drove it in 1984. (*Courtesy: Karen Miller*)

566

XKD 542
French blue
E2054-9

Completed as XKSS 754 and shipped to USA. Owned by Henry Black in Illinois, 1963. 1966 owner was John Scherer of Detroit; he restored it – crashed it in a hill-climb, then sold it to William Culbertson of Dayton, Ohio, in 1969. His painstaking restoration continued into the 1980s.

Stages in the outstanding Culbertson rebuild of XKSS 754 in the USA.

Old chassis and suspension units are married to new Lynx components for David Duffy, Autumn 1980. (Beyond are XKD 560, being built for Stephen Curtis, and a Lynx copy-car.)

XKSS 754 nears completion in the 1980s. (*Courtesy: William Culbertson*)

XKD 543 Black E2041-9	Still at factory after being used for dealer-shows at time of fire (Feb. 1957), and apparently too badly damaged to resurrect, though engine rebuilt, tested and possibly supplied to Tojeiro of Royston, Herts.
XKD 544 BRG E2039-9	Loaned by works to dealers (Brooklands of Bond Street, London) for display, then dismantled for spares. Some D-type items (*possibly* from this car) found their way into a plastic-bodied Austin-engined special in the Bromsgrove area (later in Wales). This special was sold to the father of XK enthusiast Peter Butt, then via John Pearson to David Cottingham. David Duffy bought it, and a new production-type car was created to their usual high standards by Lynx Engineering.

WKV 340 was, the author believes, a Coventry-registered special made by Harold Thompson (for whom he worked briefly in the Jaguar laboratory during his apprenticeship), c. 1957. Thompson was a specialist in glass fibre material when Jaguar was considering it seriously for use in E-type bonnets. A glass fibre D-type *was* made and driven, but the author can't be sure whether or not WKV 340's structure, seen here, originated from it. Either way, there is no doubt about the fact that XKD 544 never left the works as a complete car.

XKD 545 Pastel blue E2052-9	Sold via New York to unknown customer in eastern USA (author believes this may be the car George Constantine of Massachusetts campaigned successfully in 1956, including victory in that year's Watkins Glen GP). Bill Sadler and John Cannon of Canada were successive owners later on; Hugh Dixon also had this much-rebuilt car next and sold it to Vintage Car Store, Nyack, NY, in 1968/9. Peter Ashworth bought it and took it to the UK in 1969/70, when it was given the full-width screen complete with 1957-type Le Mans regulation soft-top. Ashworth registered it XKD 545J, and it appeared at several club meets. Later, it reverted to 'driver-only' windscreen. London dealers Coys sold it in 1980 to Peter Briggs. After release from bonded warehouse in Perth, WA, in 1982 it became a star exhibit of Briggs' York Motor Museum; later he had it sent to Sydney for the complete Classic Autocraft (Steve Sulis) treatment.

Below:
XKD 545, complete with hood, at Mallory Park for a club event in 1971, when it was owned by Peter Ashworth. Partly hiding it are Rixon Bucknall's XK 140 special and the ex-works SS Jaguar 100 competition car (Chassis No. 18008).

Chris Drake, seen here at Silverstone, kept XKD 546 active in the 1980s.

XKD 546
BRG
E2053-9

Sold to USA; various owners, then Robert Otten, Palo Alto, California, in 1972. Chris Drake (UK) owned it from 1976, racing it spiritedly from time to time. ('Major servicing' work carried out by Lynx after re-importation.)

XKD 547
BRG
E2051-9

Displayed at 1956 Barcelona Fair. Converted to XKSS 728 in 1957 and exported to USA. Later owners believed to include John Norcross, Chicago.

XKD 548
BRG
E2055-9

Displayed in Jaguar showrooms of Appleyard (Leeds) and Mansbridge (Lincoln) during 1956. Dismantled for spares in January 1957. Could this car have taken XKC 403's identity from 1956? (XKC 403 did become a 'production' type car then; but that leaves XKD 570 to be solved.)

XKD 549
BRG
E2059-9

Dealer shows, notably Rothwell & Milbourne of Malvern, during 1956; then earmarked for conversion to XKSS but exported to El Salvador instead, replacing the burned-out car XKD 537 and acquiring its identity for export purposes. No success for owner (Mauricio Miranda); car found its way to north-east USA and was traded around. Advertised for sale in *Competition Press* 1966, by Thomas Foreman, Flemington, New Jersey; car bright red and 'one of the best and least-run Ds remaining'. Herb Wetson of New York corresponded with Jaguar Cars Inc., about it as owner soon afterwards. 1977 owner believed to be Paul Petty, Connecticut.

XKD 550
BRG
E2062-9

Loaned to Appleyards (Leeds distributors) initially; then converted to XKSS 769 at works and sent to USA in 1957.

XKSS 769 – with rollbar, extra mirror, and several dents – at a late 1960s US club race meeting.

XKD 551
BRG
E2070-9
ULU 336

Dealer shows including Henlys of London and Jaguar-selling former TT rider Austin Munks of Boston, Lincs, before being sold to Coombs of Guildford (May 1957) as 'shop-soiled' car. Purchased that October by G. Sportoletti Baduel of London, and used by him as a road car, with regular servicing at Henlys. Converted to 'touring specification' similar to XKSS, including fitting of passenger door and removal of decking between seats; unique features were the windscreen (probably the rear screen of a saloon car) and the adaption of a second headrest/faring for the passenger. Regular Continental tours and two major works services (1959 and 1961). Offered for sale by the late Paul Hawkins in 1966 as 'built for Mille Miglia' (though the race was defunct). Later owners: Colin Crabbe, David Hoskison and Peter Agg of Trojan collection in Surrey. Sold via Coys of London in 1984, registered 77 EWW.

Two views of G. S. Baduel's road-going D-type, XKD 551.

Above centre:
1970 British GP parade at Brands Hatch was organised by Bryan Corser and led by Sir William Lyons. Pedro Rodriguez and François Cevert are seen here in XKD 551 and XKD 515 respectively. Higher windscreen of authentic XKSS can be seen on Robert Danny's car (XKSS 719) in the background.

XKD 552
Battleship grey
E2061-9

Dealer shows, including Hollingdrake of Colwyn Bay, North Wales: then returned to works and exported via Lowis & Hodgkiss of Nairobi (Jaguar Kenya distributor) for John Manussis who raced locally and then sold within a year to Nolis John Samaras of Dar-es-Salaam, Tanganyika. Re-exported (to Trinidad) from England during 1960 by Cliff Stuart; 1963 owner French-Canadian Roger Lucas of Montreal; car still in Canada in early seventies, later owners including George Phillips of Toronto. (Colour was changed to gold by Lucas.)

XKD 553
White
E2046-9

Dealer shows in UK in 1956; then prepared (with fin) and sent to USA for Jack Ensley (co-driver Pat O'Connor) who failed to finish at Sebring 1957. Late 1957 owner was John C. Rueter (regular ARCA competitor pre-war in Bugatti and 'Old Grey Mare' special; later an SCCA official, and author). New owner in winter 1958/9 was Edmund (Ed) Rahal of Savannah, Georgia, who had several wins, including at least two on Daytona 'road' circuit in September 1959 and January 1960. (CBS's coverage of the latter meeting was supposedly the first time motor-racing had been featured on television.) Car spent roughly ten more years in USA before returning to UK and various owners including Bob Roberts (Midland Motor Museum) and Paul Vestey. Purchased by Lynx and sold to Germany in 1980.

XKD 554
E2069-9

Sold via Armandora Mexicana SA to Julio Mariscal who had good victories locally at such locations as Puebla and Lago del Guad-

XKD 553 lays rubber as Ed Rahal sets off on his winning way in the televised Daytona sports car race, January 1960.

XKD 554 wins the Lago del Guadalupe 100 km sports car race in January 1957, driven by Julio Mariscal.

alupe. At the GP of Avandaro (near Mexico City, April 1957), Mariscal came second to Johnnie von Neumann (Testa Rossa Ferrari), and ahead of the 15-year-old Ricardo Rodriguez (Osca). Car also appeared in California occasionally, and was soon sold there to J. Fouch and H. Schlieske, Los Angeles; then Gene McManus (Ohio); then George Bullock (Georgia 1966); later back to the UK where it became the property of the late Hon. Patrick Lindsay (colour black), registered 2 HYY.

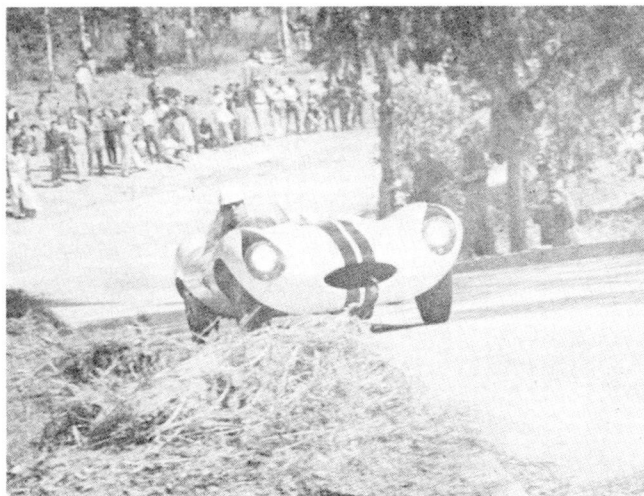

XKD 555
BRG
E2060-9

New York-based 'demonstrator' repainted Sherwood Green. First complete XKSS conversion done in experimental department (other conversions done in service dept); allocated new identity as XKSS 701. Conversion complete, 14 January 1957; announcement as new model, seven days later, sale price in USA, $6900. First raced by Jaguar USA Vice-Pres. C. Gordon Benett at Mansfield, Louisiana on 10 March 1957, having driven the car from New York. He won. First owner was Robert Stonedale of Houston, Texas. David Tallaksen also raced this car quite successfully and it was tested briefly by *Road & Track*, August 1957. Chevrolet-powered for a while (see photo), when owned by John Lee. Robert Sutherland sent it to Britain; Lynx bought it, turned it into a D-type, and sold it to Mr Takahashi, Japan, in 1983.

XKSS 701, as owned by John Lee in 1971, prior to sale to Herb Wetson, New York. (*Courtesy: Tom Groskritz*)

Chevrolet engine in XKSS 701, 1971. (*Courtesy: Tom Groskritz*)

XKSS 701, in the hands of Ali Lugo, USA, September 1975. The new front frame could have been the 'spare' which Herb Wetson bought with XKD 536. The rear wheels and axle were said to be from XKD 560. This vehicle was sold to Bob Sutherland, still incomplete.

XKD 556 Cream E2065-9	Report of 100-mile MIRA test from Les Bottrill to Lofty England dated 12/2/57. Car in service for attention that day; virtually destroyed in factory fire that evening. Stripped for possible salvage in March. Engine to be examined with a view to re-use (it would be fitted to XKC 403 in the spring of 1958).
XKD 557 Cream E2074-9	Converted to XKSS 760 and sold via Jaguar of Eastern Canada to Peter Hessler of Quebec City. A. H. Iler of Montreal was probably the second owner. (Circumstantial evidence is that this car was driven competitively in Canada as early as 1957, by a Peter Templar.) Later restored by Bill Strohm of Pasadena (using XKSS 707 as 'model'); then passed to musician James Dale based in Hollywood in the early 1970s, and then in Toronto.
XKD 558 Cream E2064-9	Sold to Oxford Motors (Plimley), Vancouver, early 1956, and retained by them, being seen on occasional sprint demonstrations at Abbotsford airport. Sold to James Rattenbury (a Vancouver engineer), first private owner, in October 1957; won its first race at Abbotsford that month. First again at same location, March 1958, then second to Pete Lovely (Testa Rossa Ferrari) at Shelton in April. Total of nine race meetings in 1958. Rattenbury, who had previously built three Crosley specials, made many modifications including lengthening wheelbase to 95 inches, added de Dion-type axle, Thornton differential, Roots-type blower, and Hillborn injection. Nine meetings and one win in 1959; same in 1960. Rattenbury (who was to turn to hydroplanes in midsixties after his 'first accident in 15 years of racing', in Genie) sold to Starr Calvert of Seattle in April 1961; victory in Barhdal Trophy, Pacific Raceway, won Calvert a trip to Indianapolis; shortly afterwards he hurt his back in damaging crash at West Delta

Park; not much done until Autumn 1964, when car rebuilt with 427 Ford V8, BW T10 transmission, wide Chevrolet wheels, etc. Difficult to handle but quite successful until Calvert was injured again when his brakes failed at Westwood, BC, September 1964; the *Vancouver Sun* claimed, 'Witnesses said trees were clipped off 20 ft from the ground' before the car demolished itself on landing, *and* suffered a carburetter fire! (Calvert had already advertised his old engine, which had probably been sold by this time.) Subsequent history led finally to correspondence (on the authenticity or otherwise of *two* 'rebuilds') in *Thoroughbred and Classic Cars* (April and June 1980). Original engine, gearbox and monocoque believed with Ian Newby in Canada; other remnants incorporated by Lynx Engineering in new long-nose car for Philippe Renault, France.

Some parts of XKD 558 went into this new long-nose car, built in the late 1970s by Lynx.

XKD 559 Cream E2071-9 (?)	Converted to XKSS 757 and sold via Gilman Motors (Hong Kong Jaguar importers) to K. Y. Cheang who registered it XX 120 and drove it for some 1400 miles on the road. Then in 1959, he sold it to AC-Bristol owner and senior Cathay Pacific airline pilot Ron Hardwick who entered it in Macau Grand Prix. Hardwick was third in practice and led the race, which was stopped immediately when a pedestrian bridge collapsed. Hardwick won the restarted race but sold car back to K. Y. Cheang. ('I have kicked myself ever since,' wrote Hardwick, more than twenty years later.) Car bought by Gilman's manager Martin Redfern who gave it its second Macau GP victory in 1960 when it looked more like a D-type than an XKSS (it had been rebuilt following some accident damage, including a new front sub-frame and other parts). The car was brought back to UK by Nigel Moores, Liverpool, in early 1966 when it was re-established as a dark green XKSS.

XKSS 757, partially re-converted to D-type body specifications at Macau in 1959. (*Courtesy: Ron Hardwick*)

Martin Redfern gives XKSS its second successive Macau Grand Prix victory (1960).

Martin Redfern, in the winning Jaguar, between Grant Wolfkill (Porsche) and Jan Bussell (Ferrari) – who would finish second and third respectively – at Macau in 1960.

XKSS with fin and wide screen, after Redfern's 1960 Macau win.

Paul Kelly on the road with XKSS in the mid-1960s.

XKD 560
Cream
E2050-9

Originally sent to USA in early 1956, this car seems to have disappeared as a unit. Some parts were found in the job-lot bought unseen by Bob Woods in 1973 and subsequently the subject of a *Sunday Times* feature by Chris Harvey. The misrepresentation appalled Woods and, having failed to get his money back, he sold his purchase to Stephen Curtis. With the help of Lynx Engineering's Guy Black, Curtis found he had parts of two cars – XKD 523 and XKD 560. The former parts he sold to Lynx; he also commissioned Lynx to re-create XKD 560 (which they did, acquiring Norman Buckley's *Miss Windermere* engine to fit into it).

Ron Flockhart dedicated this shot (of him in XKD 561 at Silverstone) to ex-works race mechanic Ron Gaudion and his *Ecurie Ecosse* colleagues. (*Courtesy: Ron Gaudion*)

Talbot historian Anthony Blight admires the Lynx re-creation (using some parts from XKD 560) owned by his son-in-law Stephen Curtis in the early 1980s.

Thumbs-up from Max Trimble (XKD 561) at the 1957 Easter Monday Goodwood meeting.

XKD 561
EE blue
E2036-9

Third 'short-nose' *Ecurie Ecosse* car, delivered Spring 1956 and used for that season only; driven to victory by Flockhart in its first race (Snetterton) and other successes. Bought by Maxwell Trimble in Winter 1956/57 and converted to 'App. C' screen, etc., at Jaguar works. (Trimble, from Walsall, had run an ex-*EE* C-type, XKC 046, the previous year.) Raced at Oulton Park and Goodwood in April, then crashed heavily at Spa (May 1957) suffering severe leg injuries; wrote to Lofty England within days, '. . . amazed how strong the car was, and feel that this coupled with my lightness of build saved my life'. Remains brought from Dover by David Shale (Healey 100S and Cooper-Jaguar driver) to his premises at Northampton. Back home in Walsall, Trimble considered fitting engine into Tojeiro – but 8 November 1957 *Autosport* read, 'offers, or will separate'. Purchaser was Berwyn Baxter of Kieft Cars, Birmingham, who sold the bits to Maurice Charles of Cardiff. Charles rebuilt the car; Clive Unsworth of Lancashire bought it and it was not seen in public afterwards very often. Its condition had deteriorated badly by the 1980s.

XKD 562
Cream
E2077-9

Like most other conversions, this car (finished in primer) was brought along the yard from storage sheds to service department at Browns Lane in January 1957. In due course it was fitted out as XKSS 725, painted, and shipped to USA – probably to California. In 1987 it was brought from Cuba by Colin Crabbe, and was due to join the Dönhoff collection after restoration (see also XKSS 766).

XKSS 725, photographed in Cuba in the 1980s.

Stirling Moss with Walter Hill's XKSS 704 (now painted red) in Florida in the early 1970s, to make a film about the history of the Sebring 12-hour race (won by a works D-type back in 1955).

Walter Hill's XKSS 704, photographed by the author at Road Atlanta, Georgia, in 1981.

XKD 563 Cream E2072-9	Converted to XKSS 704 and shipped to USA. Owned by David Causey and then, for many years, Ronald Scranton of Illinois. Later joined the Walter Hill, Florida, collection. (See also XKD 529 and 568.)
XKD 564 Cream E2066-9	Converted to XKSS 707 and shipped to America where Sidney Colberg of San Francisco bought it from Oxford Motors of Sacramento, and kept it for many years, having it restored by Ray Seher and E-type racer Merle Brennan at Reno in the early 1970s. California registration number was 'XKSS'. 'Major rebuild' by Lynx Engineering in UK. More recent owners included Chris Stewart and Campbell McClaren (the latter also acquiring one of the TWR Group A Jaguar XJ-S racing coupés as they began to become redundant during 1986).
XKD 565 Primer only E2075-9	Destroyed in February 1957 works fire, prior to conversion to XKSS.

XKSS 707 (*left*) in the 1970s when Chris Stewart owned it. Next to it is the original prototype Lynx copy of the D-type Jaguar. On the right is the ex-Hamilton C-type (XKC 004).

XKD 566
Carmen red
E2068-9

Converted to XKSS 763 and shipped to NY, where Momo Corporation sold it to E. Colasante of Long Island. Much more recent reports say first owner was Anthony Ruggerio of Newark, New Jersey. Bob Baker of Omaha purchased it as a 'one owner' car in March 1983. A most original car in good working order, it was reported sold to Richard Freshman, Los Angeles in 1985; then on to Herr Boettcher in Germany in 1986.

XKSS 763 photographed in about 1984 by its then owner, Bob Baker of Nebraska.

XKD 567
Mist grey
E2067-9

Converted to XKSS 766 and sold to J. B. del Cueto, New York. Car found in Cuba (likewise XKSS 725) and brought back to UK in 1987 by Colin Crabbe to be restored for Dönhoff Collection, Germany.

XKD 568
BRG
E2073-9

Converted to XKSS 710 and sold in USA to Don Horn, Memphis. Passed through several hands, including Bob Grossman's, before spending some time in possession of Harry Heinl, Toledo, Ohio, who owned 538 for most of same period. (1966 quote '.... the only production race cars suitable for street use ever built, with possible exception of pre-

XKSS 710, as converted back to D-type for Walter Hill, whose plan in 1987 was to take it to 1957 Sebring (longnose, 3·8, fuel injection) condition.

sent-day Ford GT40.') Heinl modified both cars for the road in various ways, including installation of twin 10-inch fans in front of radiator, 'completely eliminating all cooling problems'. Heinl sold to Delavan Lee. From circa 1970, car owned by Walter Hill (owner of several 'C' and 'D' Jaguars) in Florida who, by early 1987, was close to adapting it to the very last Works D-type state, visually, as run at Sebring in Cunningham colours just thirty years earlier, original fuel injection system and all!

Motoring super-star Steve McQueen with his own car, XKSS 713. (*Courtesy: Gordon Mackenzie*)

XKD 569
Cream
E2076-9

Converted to XKSS 713 and shipped to California for James Peterson when he was in charge of engineering the new Riverside circuit, mid-1957. (Peterson let *Road & Track* do acceleration tests with it on the mile-long straight there, to check against figures they'd obtained on 555; August 1957 edition.) Later repainted in a dark colour. Owned by film star and race-driver Steve McQueen, who was said to have logged 'at least 80,000 miles' in it on the road before passing it to the Harrah museum, Nevada in the 1960s. Car sold back to Steve McQueen in 1977, and auctioned in 1984 following his death. His former neighbour Richard Freshman was the successful bidder, and shipped car to Lynx for rebuild.

XKD 570
Bare metal
E2078-9

Car into Service Dept in bare metal state, 18 July 1956, with instruction to remove engine and gearbox and pass them to Bob Smart, the man in charge of Service Dept engine and gearbox administration. The timing of this work coincides with the period during which the badly damaged XKD 403 was being dealt with – mainly in the Competition Shop as opposed to Service Dept. Jack Broadhead (403's owner) was charged £1645 11s 1d – a fairly high sum then – and it is known that the result of 403's rebuild was much more like a production car. This supposition is, of course, based only on the circumstances. (See also XKD 548.)

XKD 571
Primer (?)
E2071-9

Destroyed in factory fire, 12 Feb 1957, prior to or during conversion to XKSS in service department.

XKD 572
White
E2082-9

Converted to XKSS 719 and sold via Jaguar Midwest (Jack Ensley) to James Grove of St Louis. Steven J. Earle (organiser of Laguna Seca historic races from mid-1970s) owned it for some years, in California. An *Autocar* article (24/8/72) suggests that Earle bought it back twice. Later, c.1970, it joined the Robert Danny collection in UK. Rebuilt by Lynx for Robert Baker (1982) who sold to Bill Tracy, of Virginia in 1983. Car on offer again in 1986.

XKD 573
Yellow
E2079-9

Sold via Joska Bourgeois to *Ecurie Francorchamps*. Works-prepared 'production short-nose', completed July 1956 for later-than-usual Le Mans, where Swaters/Rouselle came fourth. Best later result was second in Montlhéry Autumn Cup, 1956 (Pilette); then works-prepared once more for Le Mans 1957, including new engine using old number, result fourth (Frère/Rouselle). Also fourth at Spa (Rouselle), fifth at Saint Étienne (Bianchi) and sixth in Swedish GP (de Changy/Dubois). Sold winter 1957/58 to Baron Janssen de Limpens, who used it to commute between Brussels and his weekend home by the sea. He resold to Jacques de Clippel (Jaguar's Antwerp agent) in early 1962. De Clippel intended breaking N. Dewis's October 1953 Belgian National speed record but it rained on the day (May 1962), and the attempt wasn't made; he is thought to have sold the car after competing in only one hill-climb plus 'showroom' use. Gerard ('Jabby') Crombac was looking for a D-type on behalf of organisers of first Japanese GP, and was told of this one by Lucien Bianchi. Crombac's friend, Francis Francis Jr (a Paris-based

Right:
XKSS 719 when new, photographed by the then-owner, Steven Earle.

Below:
XKSS 719 in 1985, photographed by the then-owner, Bill Tracy.

Francis Francis with XKD 573 at Suzuka, 1963. (*Courtesy: Gérard Crombac*)

XKD 573, converted to 1955 Le Mans specification for John Coombs, who lent it to Jaguar. This 1970s shot in the old Browns Lane showroom includes Belgian former-racer Roger Laurent with (*from left*) Frank Rainbow, Gordon Gardner, Joe Sutton, Jock Thomson, Phil Weaver, Bob Penney, and Lofty England.

Briton) bought the car, Bianchi prepared it and Crombac arranged shipment to Japan for this inaugural event on the new Suzuka Circuit (1963) where Francis came eighth. Car shipped back to Bob Hicks' UK tuning shop whence Crombac arranged sale to John Coombs. Coombs' ace racing mechanic Roland Law completely rebuilt and converted from 1956/7 to 1955 (small screen) body specification. From the mid-1960s, the bright yellow car was on long-term loan to Browns Lane by Coombs.

XKD 574
Primer (?)
E2085-9

Destroyed in February 1957 in works fire while being prepared for conversion to XKSS.

XKD 575
BRG
E2080-9

Converted to XKSS 716 and sold via Jaguar of Eastern Canada to Stanley McRobert of Montreal, who won first time out at St Eugène. Later at same meeting it rained; McRobert raced with hood up and side-screens in place, but soon came in complaining about fumes. Generally successful for several seasons in Canadian races and hill-climbs. 1968 owner was Peter Kalikow of New York. 1980 owner John Harper raced it in UK after 'major work' by Lynx to turn it into a D-type again. Subsequently owned and raced by John Pearson of Whittlebury, prior to preparation and sale (via Brian Redman) in 1986 to IMSA racer, Don Marsh.

Gentleman John Pearson holds the door of XKSS 716 for Bob Tullius at Silverstone in 1983, watched by Jim Randle and John Egan.

Bob Tullius with XKSS 716, converted back to 1956 D-type specification. (*Courtesy: Gary Pearson*)

XKSS 716 meets XJR-5 during the latter's 1983 Silverstone evaluation tests, which helped Jaguar decide to return to Le Mans with Group 44 the following year. (*Courtesy: Gary Pearson*)

John Pearson, Brian Redman, and Don Marsh with
XKSS 716 at Pearson's Whittlebury works near
Silverstone, 1986.

XKD 601
BRG
E3005-9

First of the 1956 long-nose works cars with
lightened panels, first tested at Goodwood
in February 1956 with fuel injection fitted.
Hawthorn/Titterington had brake failure at
Sebring and halfshaft failure at Nürburgring.
Using E4002-9 carburetter engine, Hawthorn and Frère came second at Reims before
sale to Hamilton at end of 1956 season.
Works-prepared for Le Mans 1957 using 3·8-
litre carburetter engine E5006-9; Hamilton
and Gregory sixth. Car (registered 2 CPG)
used by Hamilton in other events, then sent
to works for preparation as 3-litre (EE 1201–
10) for Le Mans 1958, when Bueb co-drove
(Hamilton crashed when second). Car
returned to works, where major rebuild
almost certainly included parts from redun-
dant works car XKD 505. Later owners
include John Coundley, Anthony Bamford,
Peter Sargent, Jim Rogers, Bob Roberts and
Adrian Hamilton, who sold it to the USA in
1986.

Duncan Hamilton (XKD 601) photographed in a typical
driving pose by the author at Silverstone, 1958.

2 CPG at a London dealer show (H. R. Owen, South
Kensington) in 1977. On the right is Michael Barker –
manager of Bob Roberts' Midland Motor Museum. In
the centre is Phil Weaver; and on the left is Michael
Beasley – the man who has done such wonders for
Jaguar's manufacturing facilities in the 1980s.

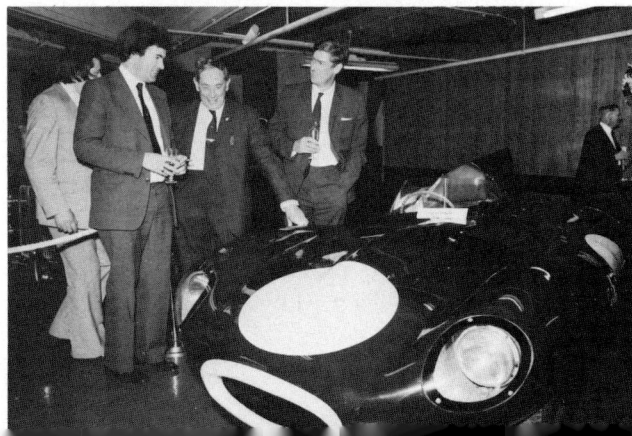

XKD 602
BRG
E4004-9

Works car first prepared for Le Mans 1956, with PI, for Wharton/Fairman. Fairman crashed avoiding XKD 603; see the following entry – and XKD 602 ceased to exist as a separate entity, as a result.

XKD 603
BRG
EXP 4

Works long-nose completed April 1956, with fuel injection; immediately converted to carburetters. Hawthorn retired Silverstone with steering seizure. E4002-9 carburetter engine fitted for Nürburgring where Frère crashed. E4003-9 carburetter engine fitted for Reims (Fairman and Titterington third). E4005-9 carburetter engine fitted for Le Manss (Frère crashed). Front chassis built into centre-section and tail units of XKD 602, to make one car – numbered XKD 603. Sold to *Ecurie Ecosse*, painted blue, and registered RSF 303 for 1957 when it was first at Saint Étienne (Flockhart) second at Le Mans, fourth in Argentina and Italy (500-mile race) and took part in at least four other races. Repaired in works after Gregory crashed at Nürburgring, 1958; fitted with 3-litre engine EE 1207-10 for Le Mans (retired); prepared at works again for 1959 Le Mans (again retired, broken con-rod). Finished sixth in its final race for *Ecurie Ecosse*, the 1959 TT at Goodwood (Flockhart and Bekaert). Sold to James Munro (USA) as 3·4-litre carburetter car. (Works did not sell any D-types with PI.) Later returned to UK for Anthony Bamford. Willy Green and Murray Smith successful in 1970s historic events.

The mighty *Ecurie Ecosse* team in the Monza 500-mile race, 1957. This was how they finished:
   No. 4, Fairman (3·4) XKD 603 – fourth
   No. 6, Sanderson (3·4) XKD 504 – sixth
   No. 2, Lawrence (3·8) XKD 606 – fifth.

XKD 604
BRG
E4003-9

Works long-nose car built March/April 1956 with fuel injection (later switched to carburetters) and experimental De Dion rear suspension. Titterington drove this car in its first race at Silverstone. Works notebook records: 'Crashed – complete write-off. Towed home on trailer and stripped down 7 & 8 May 1956.' Some bits doubtless cannibalised for other cars.

XKD 605 in the Biscaretti Museum, Turin, where it spent over twenty years before being returned to Browns Lane.

XKD 605
BRG
E4001-9

Built Feb/March 1956 as latest-spec works car with fuel injection. Attended Silverstone, but not raced ('reported unstable at rear'). Used for Reims tests and for 12-hour race there. Engine changed to E3005-9 in practice and retained for race, which it won driven by Hamilton and Bueb, the former being 'sacked' for not staying in second place as per team orders. (Modified 'A' link and drive-shafts fitted for this race, following two half-shaft failures in works cars already in 1956). E4007-9 fitted for Le Mans, in which broken PI pipe caused misfiring until discovered (Hawthorn and Bueb sixth). First works 3·8-litre engine fitted and car painted white/blue for Sebring 1957. (Hawthorn and Bueb third). Lent to Cunningham/Momo team – first to race, then for exhibition purposes, and eventual return to UK (1961). Later painted BRG again and sent to Biscaretti Museum, Turin, on long-term static loan. Returned to works in 1980s; still very original.

XKD 606
BRG
E4006-9

Sixth and last of the 1956 works long-nose cars with lightened body panels, completed 28 June and tested at Lindley on 2 July, using 3·4-litre carburetter engine. Titterington crashed in practice for Le Mans; damage superficial, but car not raced; returned to Coventry, rectified, repainted, tested and put in store. (Jaguar was giving up sports car racing.) E4004-9 carburetter 3·4-litre engine fitted for transfer to *Ecurie Ecosse*, November 1956. Now blue and registered RSF 301, returned to Coventry from Edinburgh after Flockhart's Argentine crash and partially rebuilt with new frame, bonnet, etc. in works service dept. Then passed to Competition Department for (loaned) 3·8-litre works PI engine and 2·69:1 axle ratio, and taken to Le Mans, finishing first. Then fifth at Monza a week later. Car also raced in Sweden and Belgium in August 1957. Raced with less success in 1958 and 1959. Fitted with regu-

XKD 606 with its high 1960 windscreen and 'luggage boot', at Silverstone in 1961 driven by Jack Wober, in company with David Hobbs' Lotus Elite.

lation 'luggage boot' and high screen for Le Mans 1960 (Flockhart and Halford retired.) Then raced in same trim at Watkins Glen (seventh) by Paul O'Shea in late-1960 USA tour. David Murray sold car to Jack Wober, Glasgow. Then, Richard Wrottesley crashed it heavily at Silverstone practice session, June 1962. A new frame was fabricated in Coundley workshops during this rebuild, and car sold later to E-type owner Pierre Bardinon, in France. Next owner was a member of the Chandon family. Victor Gauntlett (of Aston Martin Lagonda fame) acquired this car (*and a modern re-creation of it*) in the early 1980s. Lynx Engineering fitted fuel injection (sliding throttle type) *à la* 1957 Le Mans specification. Car sold to France again in mid-1980s. (*N.B. When the damaged front frame was removed in the 1960s, the UK logbook was also retained. These two items went to the Nigel Moores collection for which a duplicate 'XKD 606' was created subsequently.*)

A case for racing? This new monocoque and frame were being formed into an accurate copy of a D-type in the mid-1980s for John Pearson by Lynx Engineering. It made no pretence to lay claim to any existing numbers, yet seemed a much more genuine creation than certain numbered cars. Would such a car be eligible for historic car racing in the future?

John Pearson: To own a 'D' was always his dream. He had raced them, and restored them; but in the end, he had to go for a new structure, incorporating as many genuine components as he could.

Appendix Six

1955 Le Mans Summary

This appendix contains the post-race summary compiled by Malcolm Sayer, and based on the Jaguar team's timesheets. See Chapter 4 for a full account of the race.

CAR NO. 6 (HAWTHORN-BUEB)

SUMMARY.
152 laps by Hawthorn, average 4 m. 30 sec. = 111·5 m.p.h.
fastest 4 m. 6 sec. = 122·5 m.p.h.
155 laps by Bueb, average 4m. 41 sec. = 107·2 m.p.h.
fastest 4 m. 20 sec. = 115·7 m.p.h.

Total time in pits approx. 23 min. 6 secs.
Overall fuel consumption = 11·1 m.p.g. at average running speed of 108·6 m.p.h.
Tyres – two rears changed at approx. half distance. All four changed to cut treads three hours later.

DETAILS.

Time	Item	
4 pm	*1*	*36 laps by Hawthorn, average 4 m. 13 secs. = 119 m.p.h.*
		fastest 4 m. 06 secs. = 122·5 m.p.h.
6.30 pm	*2*	*Pit stop app. 1 m. 30 sec. Fuel 29 gals. = 10·4 m.p.g.*
		Oil 12 pts.
		Water 4 pts.
		45 laps by Bueb, average 4 m. 27 sec. = 112·7 m.p.h.
		fastest 4 m. 20 sec. = 115·7 m.p.h.
9.57 pm	*3*	*Pit stop app. 1 m. 30 sec. Fuel 33 gal. = 11·4 m.p.g.*
		40 laps by Hawthorn, average 4 m. 25 sec. = 113·5 m.p.h.
		fastest 4 m. 22 sec. = 115 m.p.h.
1 am	*4*	*Pit stop 1 m. 43 sec. Fuel 32 gal. = 10·5 m.p.g.*
		40 laps by Bueb, average 4 m. 38 sec. = 108·2 m.p.h.
		fastest 4 m. 23 sec. = 114·5 m.p.h.

4.10 am	5	Pit stop 2 m. 42 sec. Fuel 27 gal. = 12·4 m.p.g.
		2 rear tyres changed.
		37 laps by Hawthorn, average 4 m. 30 sec. = 111·5 m.p.h.
		fastest 4m. 21 sec. = 115·5 m.p.h.
		(Rain began at 5.50 am)
7.00 am	6	Pit stop 8 m. 07 sec. Fuel 30 gal. = 10·3 m.p.g.
		Oil in gearbox.
		4 tyres changed to cut treads.
		36 laps by Bueb, average 4 m. 39 sec. = 108 m.p.h.
		fastest 4 m. 29 sec. = 112 m.p.h.
10.0 am	7	Pit stop, 1 m. 25 sec. Fuel 26 gal. = 11·6 m.p.g.
		9 laps by Hawthorn, average 4 m. 59 sec. = 100·5 m.p.h.
		fastest 4 m. 40 sec. = 107·5 m.p.h.
10.40 am	8	Pit stop, 3 m. 0 sec. Clothes changes.
		27 laps by Hawthorn, average 4 m. 45 sec. = 104·5 m.p.h.
		fastest 4 m. 38 sec. = 108·5 m.p.h.
12.50 pm	9	Pit stop, 1 m. 27 sec. Fuel 26 gal. = 11·6 m.p.g.
		34 laps by Bueb, average 5 m. 00 sec. = 100·2 m.p.h.
		fastest 4 m. 46 sec. = 105·5 m.p.h.
3.40 pm	10	Pit stop, 1 m. 42 sec.
		3 laps by Hawthorn, average 6 m. 01 sec. = 83·5 m.p.h.

CAR NO. 7 (ROLT/HAMILTON)

SUMMARY

112 laps by Rolt, average 4 m. 26 sec. = 113·3 m.p.h.
fastest 4 m. 12 sec. = 119·5 m.p.h.
74 laps by Hamilton, average 4 m. 30 sec. = 111·5 m.p.h.
fastest 4 m. 18 sec. = 117·0 m.p.h.
Retired, gearbox U/S, after 186 laps, at 6.50 am.
Total time in pits approx. 32 m. 35 sec.
Overall fuel consumption 10·25 m.p.g. at average running speed of 110 m.p.h.
2 rear tyres changed after 12 hours.

DETAILS

Time	Item	
4 pm	1	36 laps by Rolt, average 4 m. 20 sec. = 115·6 m.p.h.
		fastest 4 m. 12 sec. = 119·5 m.p.h.
6.40 pm	2	Pit stop 2 m. 26 sec. Fuel 29 gal. = 10·4 m.p.g.
		Oil 12 pints.
		Water 4 pints.
		41 laps by Hamilton, average 4 m. 25 sec. = 113·5 m.p.h.
		fastest 4 m. 18 sec. = 117 m.p.h.
		(left course on 19th lap).
9.40 pm	3	Pit stop 1 m. 45 sec. Fuel 34 gal. = 10·1 m.p.g.
		25 laps by Rolt, average 4 m. 28 sec. = 112·3 m.p.h.
		fastest 4 m. 23 sec. = 114·5 m.p.h.
11.35 pm	4	Pit stop approx. 4 m. 50 sec. All plugs changed.
		19 laps by Rolt, average 4 m. 22 sec. = 115 m.p.h.
		fastest 4 m. 19 sec. = 116·3 m.p.h.
1 am	5	Pit stop 2 m. 07 sec. Fuel 36 gal. = 10·25 m.p.g.
		8 laps by Hamilton, average 4 m. 37 sec. = 108·6 m.p.h.
		fastest 4 m. 33 sec. = 110·3 m.p.h.
1.48 am	6	Pit stop 4 m. 01 sec. Throttle spring changed.
		Steering greased.
		3 laps by Hamilton, average 4 m. 36 sec. = 109 m.p.h.
2.0 am	7	Pit stop 10 m. 0 sec. Leak in oil tank caulked.
		22 laps by Hamilton, average 4 m. 35 sec. = 109·5 m.p.h.
		fastest 4 m. 30 sec. = 111·5 m.p.h.

4.0 am	8	Pit stop 5 m. 33 sec. 2 rear tyres changed.
		Fuel 26 gals. = 10·6 m.p.g.
		6 laps by Rolt, average 4 m. 33 sec. = 110·3 m.p.h.
		fastest 4 m. 28 sec. = 112·3 m.p.h.
4.40 am	9	Pit stop 1 m. 43 sec. Steering greased again.
		26 laps by Rolt, average 4 m. 33 sec. = 110·3 m.p.h.
		fastest 4 m. 22 sec. = 115 m.p.h.
6.50 am	10	Pit stop permanent. Fuel 27 gal. = 9·9 m.p.g.
		Hamilton failed to start, gearbox U/S. Plugs changed.

CAR NO. 8 (BEAUMAN-DEWIS)

SUMMARY

64 2/3 laps by Beauman, average 4 m. 27 sec. = 112·7 m.p.h.
fastest 4 m. 20 sec. = 115·7 m.p.h.
42 laps by Dewis, average 4 m. 27 sec. = 112·7 m.p.h.
fastest 4 m. 20 sec. = 115·7 m.p.h.
Driven into sandbank by Beauman at approx. midnight.
Total time in pits 4 m. 30 sec.
Overall fuel consumption 10·5 m.p.g. at average running speed of 112·5 m.p.h.

DETAILS.

Time	Item	
4 pm	1	36 laps by Beauman, average 4 m. 24 sec. = 114 m.p.h.
		fastest 4 m. 20 sec. = 115·7 m.p.h.
6.40 pm	2	Pit stop 1 m. 31 sec. Fuel, 29 gal. = 10·4 m.p.g.
		42 laps by Dewis, average 4 m. 27 sec. = 112·7 m.p.h.
		fastest 4 m. 20 sec. = 115·7 m.p.h.
9.50 pm	3	Pit stop 2 m. 59 sec. Fuel, 33 gal. = 10·7 m.p.g.
		28 2/3 laps by Beauman, average 4 m. 31 sec. = 111·2 m.p.h.
		fastest (= last lap) 4 m. 24 sec. = 114 m.p.h.
		Reported in sand at Arnage approx. midnight

CAR NO. 10 (SWATERS-CLAES)

SUMMARY

141 laps by Swaters, average 4 m. 39 sec. = 108 m.p.h.
fastest 4 m. 22 sec. = 115 m.p.h.
154 laps by Claes, average 4 m. 54 sec. = 102·5 m.p.h.
fastest 4 m. 29 sec. = 112 m.p.h.
Total time in pits = 19 m. 55 sec.
Overall fuel consumption = 11·2 m.p.g. at average running speed of 104 m.p.h.

DETAILS

Time	Item	
4 pm	1	34 laps by Swaters, average 4 m. 28 sec. = 112·3 m.p.h.
		fastest 4 m. 23 sec. = 114·5 m.p.h.
6.34 pm	2	Pit stop, 1 m. 58 sec. Fuel 28 gal. = 10·1 m.p.g.
		Oil 8 pints.
		Water 4 pints.
		36 laps by Claes, average 4 m. 34 sec. = 110 m.p.h.
		fastest 4 m. 29 sec. = 112 m.p.h.
9.20 pm	3	Pit stop, 1 m. 20 secs. Fuel 28 gal. = 110 m.p.g.
		Oil 8 pints.
		Water 2 pints
		36 laps by Swaters, average 4 m. 41 sec. = 107·3 m.p.h.
		fastest 4 m. 36 sec. = 109 m.p.h.

12.10 pm	*4*	*Pit stop 1 m. 45 sec. Fuel 26 gal. = 11·6 m.p.g.*
		19 laps by Claes, average 4 m. 46 sec. = 105·3 m.p.h.
		fastest 4 m. 41 sec. = 107·3 m.p.h.
1.45 pm	*5*	*Pit stop, 2 m. 46 sec. No. 1 plug changed*
		16 laps by Claes, average 4 m. 42 sec. = 106·8 m.p.h.
		fastest 4 m. 37 sec. = 109 m.p.h.
3.05 am	*6*	*Pit stop, 1 m. 55 sec. Fuel 26 gal. = 11·2 m.p.g.*
		36 laps by Swaters, average 4 m. 32 sec. = 110·6 m.p.h.
		fastest 4 m. 22 sec. = 115 m.p.h.
5.50 am	*7*	*Pit stop 1 m. 32 sec. Fuel 28 gal. = 10·8 m.p.g.*
		35 laps by Claes, average 4 m. 52 sec. = 103·3 m.p.h.
		fastest 4 m. 29 sec. = 112 m.p.h.
8.45 am	*8*	*Pit stop 5 m. 42 sec. Quart of oil in gearbox.*
		Fuel 26 gal. = 11·2 m.p.g.
		35 laps by Swaters, average 4 m. 56 sec. = 101·8 m.p.h.
		fastest 4 m. 34 sec. = 110 m.p.h.
11.40 pm	*9*	*Pit stop 1 m. 31 sec. Fuel 25 gal. = 11·7 m.p.g.*
		34 laps by Claes, average 5 m. 14 sec. = 96 m.p.h.
		fastest 5 m. 02 sec. = 99·7 m.p.h.
2.40 am	*10*	*Pit stop 1 m. 26 sec. Fuel 23 gal. = 12·4 m.p.g.*
		14 laps by Claes, average 5 m. 24 sec. = 93 m.p.h.
		fastest 5 m. 16 sec. = 95·4 m.p.h.

Appendix Seven

D-type MIRA Test Record

This appendix is based upon the test record 'diary' made by Les Bottrill of all sixty-seven production-line assembled D-types.

Diary Date (1955)	Car (XKD)	Comments
18 July	509	*Checking of rejects on first check.*
19 July	509	*1st test: 60 laps of MIRA. 30 items still need attention (200 miles).*
20 July	510	*Preliminary check: 50 chassis & 35 body items need attention.*
21 July	512	*Prelim. check: 54 chassis & 39 body items need attention.*
22 July	512	*1st test at MIRA: 6 chassis & 2 body items need attention (125 miles).*
25 July	509	*Rectification of test rejects.*
26 July	509	*Rectification; second MIRA test (165 miles); 10 items.*
27 July	(XKC052)	*(Working on Peter Blond's C-type, in service dept.)*
28 July	512	*Rectification of rejects.*
29 July	510	*First MIRA test (206 miles); 13 items.*
9 August	514	*1st check: 35 chassis & 17 body items.*
9 August	510	*Rectification.*
10 August	514	*1st MIRA test (200 miles); 12 items.*
11 August	510	*Rectification.*
12 August	509	*Ignition & carburation test at MIRA. 90 miles.*
13 August	514	*Rectification.*
15 August	514*	*2nd MIRA test (125 miles); checking gearbox and air box mods.*
16 August	509*	*4th MIRA test (100 miles), carb. & ignition check.*
17 August	514	*Rectification (also work on a car for Goodwood.) [XKD 514 despatched on 26 August]*
18 August	510	*Rectification.*
19 August	510	*More rectification; 2nd MIRA test (100 miles)*
22 August	509	*Rectify gearbox [Despatched 9 Nov]*
23 August	512	*Rectify gearbox*
24 August	512	*Rectify gearbox*
25 August	512*	*2nd MIRA test (165 miles) [despatched 20 Sept]*
27 August	513	*1st check*
28 August	513	*Rectify.*
29 August	513	*1st MIRA test (206 miles)*
30 August	518	*1st check & rectify*
31 August	518	*1st MIRA test (217 miles)*
1 Sept	522	*1st MIRA test (125 miles)*
2 Sept	522	*1st MIRA test cont'd. (100 miles)*
3 Sept	511	*1st check*
5 Sept	511	*1st MIRA test (200 miles)*
6 Sept	526	*1st MIRA test (211 miles)*

Date	No.	Description
7 Sept	513*	2nd MIRA test (70 miles) [despatched 26 Sept]
8 Sept	517	1st MIRA test (206 miles)
9 Sept	517*	Check (test?)(unclear)
10 Sept	513	Final check/rectify
	517	Final check/rectify [despatched 15 Sept]
11 Sept	511	Final check
12 Sept	515	1st MIRA test (235 miles)
13 Sept	515*	2nd(?) MIRA test (?) [despatched 21 Sept]
13 Sept	516	1st check
14 Sept	516	1st MIRA test (211 miles)
15 Sept	511*	('Final test – OK') [despatched 20 Sept]
16 Sept	518*	2nd MIRA test (80 miles)[despatched 29 Dec]
17/18 "	521	1st MIRA test (215 miles)
19 Sept	519	1st MIRA test (217 miles)
20 Sept	523	1st MIRA test (190 miles)
21 Sept	510*	3rd MIRA test (100 miles) [despatched 24 Sept]
21 Sept	516	2nd MIRA test (80 miles)
22 Sept	524	1st MIRA test (208 miles)
22 Sept	516	3rd MIRA test (70 miles)
23 Sept	525	1st MIRA test (200 miles)
23 Sept	(?)	(also 15 laps in P.I. car)
24 Sept	516	Rectify
24 Sept	519	Rectify
26 Sept	516*	4th MIRA test (70 miles) [despatched 12 Oct]
26 Sept	519	2nd MIRA test (75 miles)
27 Sept	522*	2nd MIRA test (80 miles) [despatched 11 Nov]
28 Sept	519	3rd MIRA test (50 miles)
28 Sept	526*	2nd MIRA test (110 miles) [despatched 13 Oct]
29 Sept	519*	4th MIRA test (100 miles) [despatched 9 Nov]
29 Sept	520	1st MIRA test (228 miles)
30 Sept	523*	2nd MIRA test (30 miles) [despatched 22 Nov]
1 Oct	527	1st MIRA test (210 miles)
2 Oct	528	1st check
3 Oct	528	1st MIRA test (200 miles)
3 Oct	521*	2nd MIRA test (80 miles) [despatched 21 Oct]
3 Oct	529	1st MIRA test (120 miles)
4 Oct	529	1st MIRA test cont'd (85 miles)
4 Oct	530	1st MIRA test (185 miles)
4 Oct	533	1st MIRA test (100 miles)
5 Oct	533	1st MIRA test (125 miles)
5 Oct	536	1st MIRA test (202 miles)
6 Oct	524	2nd MIRA test (115 miles)
6 Oct	525	2nd MIRA test (80 miles)
6 Oct	531	1st MIRA test (140 miles)
7 Oct	531	1st MIRA test cont'd (60 miles)
7 Oct	532	1st MIRA test (200 miles)
8 Oct	–	Rectification
9 Oct	534	1st MIRA test (100 miles)
10 Oct	534	1st MIRA test cont'd (100 miles)
10 Oct	530	2nd MIRA test (90 miles)
10 Oct	535	1st MIRA test (160 miles)
11 Oct	535	1st MIRA test cont'd (60 miles)
11 Oct	520	2nd MIRA test (95 miles)
11 Oct	529	2nd MIRA test (80 miles)
12 Oct	527*	2nd MIRA test (70 miles) [despatched 9 Nov]
12 Oct	528	2nd MIRA test (70 miles)
12 Oct	537	1st MIRA test (205 miles)
13 Oct	525	3rd MIRA test (100 miles)
13 Oct	529	3rd MIRA test (80 miles)
13 Oct	537	1st MIRA test cont'd (90 miles)
14 Oct	538	1st MIRA test (195 miles)
14 Oct	524	3rd MIRA test (60 miles)
14 Oct	520	3rd MIRA test (80 miles)
15 Oct	542	1st MIRA test (100 miles)
17 Oct	542	1st MIRA test cont'd (118 miles)
17 Oct	528	3rd MIRA test (85 miles)
17 Oct	539	1st MIRA test (95 miles)
18 Oct	540	1st MIRA test (208 miles)
18 Oct	537	Brake test (80 miles)
18 Oct	533	2nd MIRA test (95 miles)
19 Oct	546	1st MIRA test (200 miles)
20 Oct	531	2nd MIRA test (85 miles)
20 Oct	534	2nd MIRA test (80 miles)
20 Oct	537	Brake test (95 miles)
20 Oct	541	1st MIRA test (117 miles)
21 Oct	541	1st MIRA test cont'd (90 miles)
21 Oct	543	1st MIRA test (200 miles)
22 Oct	–	Rectification
23 Oct	537	Brake test (70 miles)
24 Oct	544	1st MIRA test (215 miles)
24 Oct	528*	4th MIRA test (40 miles) [despatched 9 Nov]
24 Oct	542	2nd MIRA test (80 miles)
24 Oct	530*	3rd MIRA test (50 miles) [despatched 13 Feb '56]
24 Oct	537	5th MIRA test (80 miles)
25 Oct	525	4th MIRA test (50 miles)
25 Oct	533	3rd MIRA test (65 miles)
25 Oct	542*	2nd MIRA test (50 miles) [Stock, 1956]
25 Oct	520*	4th MIRA test (40 miles) [despatched 14 Dec]
25 Oct	524	4th MIRA test (60 miles)
26 Oct	532	2nd MIRA test (87 miles)
26 Oct	529*	3rd MIRA test (60 miles) [despatched 1 Dec]
26 Oct	535	2nd MIRA test (80 miles)
26 Oct	538	2nd MIRA test (45 miles)
27 Oct	540	2nd MIRA test (70 miles)
27 Oct	538*	3rd MIRA test (140 miles) [see Appendix 5]
27 Oct	525	Brake test (100 miles)
28 Oct	548	1st MIRA test (200 miles)
28 Oct	548	Brake test (100 miles)
28 Oct	524*	5th MIRA test (30 miles) [despatched 20 Dec]
28 Oct	525	6th MIRA test (40 miles)
31 Oct	525	7th MIRA test (30 miles)
31 Oct	533	4th MIRA test (90 miles)

Date	No.	Test
31 Oct	(Berry)	Test – presumably XKC 403? (50 miles)
1 Nov	532	3rd MIRA test (90 miles)
1 Nov	534*	3rd MIRA test (60 miles) [despatched 6 Sept]
1 Nov	535	3rd MIRA test (80 miles)
1 Nov	541	2nd MIRA test (80 miles)
2 Nov	546*	2nd MIRA test (100 miles) [despatched 13 Dec]
2 Nov	537	6th MIRA test (60 miles)
2 Nov	525*	8th MIRA test (50 miles) [despatched 1 Dec]
3 Nov	543	2nd MIRA test (70 miles)
3 Nov	545	1st MIRA test (200 miles)
4 Nov	541*	3rd MIRA test (60 miles) [despatched 11 Nov]
4 Nov	547	1st MIRA test (200 miles)
7 Nov	537*	7th MIRA test (60 miles) [despatched 23 April '56]
8 Nov	543	3rd MIRA test (70 miles)
8 Nov	545	2nd MIRA test (75 miles)
9 Nov	531*	3rd MIRA test (70 miles) [despatched 1 Dec]
9 Nov	535*	4th MIRA test (85 miles) [depatched 5 April '56]
10 Nov	545*	3rd MIRA test (30 miles) [despatched 16 Dec]
10 Nov	543*	4th MIRA test (80 miles) [stock, 1956]
11 Nov	550	1st MIRA test (200 miles)
11 Nov	547*	2nd MIRA test (85 miles) [stock, 1956]
14 Nov	549	1st MIRA test (205 miles)
15 Nov	540*	3rd MIRA test (95 miles) [see Appendix 5]
15 Nov	533*	5th MIRA test (105 miles) [see Appendix 5]
15 Nov	551	1st MIRA test (200 miles)
16 Nov	554	1st MIRA test (200 miles)
16 Nov	560	1st MIRA test (200 miles)
17 Nov	550*	2nd MIRA test (80 miles) [stock, 1956]
17 Nov	539	2nd MIRA test (105 miles)
18 Nov	552	1st MIRA test (200 miles)
18 Nov	539	3rd MIRA test (75 miles)
19 Nov	553	1st MIRA test (200 miles)
20 Nov	549*	2nd MIRA test (95 miles) [stock, 1956]
20 Nov	551	2nd MIRA test (120 miles)
20 Nov	544	2nd MIRA test (95 miles)
21 Nov	532*	4th MIRA test (75 miles) [see Appendix 5]
22 Nov	560*	2nd MIRA test (75 miles) [despatched 7 Feb, '56]
22 Nov	558	1st MIRA test (200 miles)
23 Nov	539*	4th MIRA test (95 miles) [stock, 1956]
23 Nov	559	1st MIRA test (190 miles)
23 Nov	557	1st MIRA test (80 miles)
24 Nov	557	1st MIRA test cont'd (120 miles)
24 Nov	552*	2nd MIRA test (65 miles) [see Appendix 5]
25 Nov	555	1st MIRA test (200 miles)
25 Nov	544	3rd MIRA test (75 miles)
26 Nov	556*	1st MIRA test (200 miles) [stock, 1956]
28 Nov	558	2nd MIRA test (80 miles)
28 Nov	548*	2nd MIRA test (70 miles) [stock, 1956]
29 Nov	558*	3rd MIRA test (40 miles) [despatched 7 Feb '56]
29 Nov	554	2nd MIRA test (85 miles)
29 Nov	557*	2nd MIRA test (90 miles) [stock, 1956]
30 Nov	561	1st MIRA test (?)
1 Dec	561	1st MIRA test cont'd (200 miles)
1 Dec	551*	3rd MIRA test (130 miles) [stock, 1956]
1 Dec	562	1st MIRA test (130 miles)
2 Dec	562	1st MIRA test cont'd (70 miles)
2 Dec	559*	2nd MIRA test (70 miles) [stock, 1956]
2 Dec	555	2nd MIRA test (50 miles)
3 Dec	563	1st MIRA test (200 miles)
3 Dec	561*	2nd MIRA test (80 miles) [despatched 28 Feb '56]
4 Dec	567	1st MIRA test (200 miles)
4 Dec	554*	3rd MIRA test (100 miles) [despatched 20 Jan '56]
5 Dec	570	1st MIRA test (185 miles)
6 Dec	569	1st MIRA test (195 miles)
7 Dec	553	2nd MIRA test (75 miles)
7 Dec	555*	3rd MIRA test (50 miles) [stock, 1956]
7 Dec	562*	2nd MIRA test (65 miles) [stock, 1956]
8 Dec	565	1st MIRA test (200 miles)
8 Dec	564*	1st MIRA test (200 miles) [stock, 1956]
9 Dec	563	2nd MIRA test (50 miles)
9 Dec	570*	2nd MIRA test (70 miles) [stock, 1956]
9 Dec	553*	3rd MIRA test (?) [stock, 1956]
10 Dec	568	1st MIRA test (200 miles)
10 Dec	567	2nd MIRA test (75 miles)
12 Dec	569*	2nd MIRA test (30 miles) [stock, 1956]
12 Dec	565*	2nd MIRA test (70 miles) [stock, 1956]
13 Dec	566*	1st MIRA test (185 miles) [stock, 1956]
13 Dec	567	Final check
14 Dec	564*	Final check [stock, 1956]
14 Dec	568*	Final check [stock, 1956]
15 Dec	571	1st MIRA test (200 miles)
15 Dec	572	1st MIRA test (200 miles)
16 Dec	566*	2nd test (road) MIRA (30 miles) [stock, 1956]
17 Dec	573	1st MIRA test (180 miles)
17 Dec	574	1st MIRA test (180 miles)
20 Dec	571*	Final check [stock, 1956]
20 Dec	572*	Final check [stock, 1956]
21 Dec	575	1st MIRA test (200 miles)

23 Dec	574*	2nd MIRA test (80 miles) [stock, 1956]
23 Dec	573*	2nd MIRA test (80 miles)
28 Dec	573	Final check [see Appendix 5]
28 Dec	574	Final check
28 Dec	575*	2nd test (? miles) [stock, 1956]

| 28 Dec | 575 | Final check |

*The asterisk suggests the date on which each production-line D-type had its final test run before being passed for final painting and despatch (or storage).

Appendix Eight

1964 Le Mans Report

errick White's account of the 1964 Le Mans, which follows, is significant because it covers the very last works-preparation of a Jaguar for Le Mans *and* the last running of a Jaguar there for twenty years. The light-weight E-type's main faults – alloy-block cracks and gearbox seal failures – came to light once again. Handling and performance, already improved on the works/Coombs car and yet found wanting by Graham Hill and Jackie Stewart, showed that much more development was needed. Instead the LWE project was soon dropped and, in effect, replaced by the XJ13.

LE MANS 1964

Two 1963 Competition 'E' Types obtained entries for the 1964 Le Mans race – Lindner and Lumsden. Lindner's car was prepared by Jaguar Competition Department while Lumsden's car was prepared by Playford Motors. The bodies of both cars were altered to reduce drag – Lindner's 'E' having an aluminium hardtop and new windscreen of the same type as fitted to the 1962 low drag couple now owned by Protheroe, whilst Lumsden's 'E' had a different shaped hardtop and windscreen, (based on sketches supplied by Mr. Sayer for their 1962 car) and a modified bonnet nose.

Additional modifications to the cars since 1963 were the lowering of Lumsden's car by 1½"; the fitting of cast magnesium wheels with rim widths of 7" at the front and 7½" at the rear

instead of 6"; 725L × 15 R6 tyres at the rear instead of 650L or 700L; larger anti-roll bars – 1" diam. front and 13/16" diam. rear instead of 15/16" and 11/16" respectively; and front and rear dampers with stiffer leak settings. Also both cars were fitted with five speed ZF gearboxes and Lindner's engine was fitted with 15/32" camshafts and a slide throttle system.

Lindner's car was sent to Le Mans April test weekend with a flexibly mounted steering rack housing, whilst Lumsden's car had a solidly mounted rack. This involved replacing the rubber mounting with an aluminium packing piece and altering the height of the rack by approximately ¼" to the ideal position for correct steering geometry.

TEST WEEKEND – 18/19TH APRIL 1964

C.W. and P = 3·31 : 1 in both cars.

Saturday. 9.0 a.m. to 4.45 p.m. – Dry for first 20–30 minutes, then rain or drizzle all day. No wind – 15°C ambient.

Neither Lindner nor Nocker had driven at Le Mans before. Lindner did spells of 1, 7, 2, 9 and 5 laps, totalling 24 – best time 4/29·1 on 22nd lap. Nocker did two spells of 6 laps each – best time 4/29·1 on 11th lap. All these laps were done during rain.

Max. 5th gear = 5·100 r.p.m. = 162 m.p.h. calc.
  (Official max. speed = 260 k.p.h. = 161 m.p.h.)
Water Temp = 70°c
Oil Press. = 70 p.s.i.
Oil Temp = 85°c
Axle Temp = 100°c. pump on, 120°c pump off.
Fuel cons. = 3·91 litre/lap. = 35 laps maximum.
Oil for 27 laps – 1·85 litre = 3¼ pints
Tyre Life – laps (D12)   NSF   OSF   58   173
                       NSR   OSR   25   25

Both drivers mentioned that the brake pedal effort was high, and Nocker complained of understeer – probably due to – 1° front wheel camber instead of – 2° as requested. Also accelerator pedal travel was too long and the drivers could not 'heel and toe' when changing gear.

Tyre pressures used were Ft. 45 p.s.i, Rear 50 p.s.i. initially and finally the rears were dropped to 45 p.s.i. to reduce the understeer.

Drivers changed gear at 6500 r.p.m.

Sunday – 9 a.m. to 12.45 p.m. 2.45 p.m. to 4.45 p.m. Rain until 2 p.m., then sun and approx. 10 m.p.h. wind drying track; 45° headwind on Mulsanne straight. 15°c ambient.

Lindner's 'E' C.W & P changed from 3·31 to 3·54 : 1 Ture pressures 45 p.s.i cold – D 12 tyres. Nocker did spells of 9, 5 and 4 laps, = 18 and Lindner did 13, 11, 1 and 1 = 26. Total laps for two days, = 80. As it dried out during the afternoon, lap times improved. Nocker registering 4/07·1 (4/07·3 official) on his 17th lap, Lindner 4/10·4 and the Lumsden/Sargent 'E' also did 4·07·3.

Max 5th gear = 5,550 r.p.m. = 165 m.p.h. calc.
Water temp. = 70°c with 3" blanking.
Oil press. = 50–60 p.s.i. 105–110°c.
Axle Temp = 125°c pump on, 140°c pump off.
Fuel cons. = 4·3 litre/lap = 32 laps max.
Oil for 27 laps – 1·74 litre = 3·05 pints.

Brake pad wear/lap = Front = ·0027", Rear = ·0025"

Therefore Max. pad life – Front (·850" new) = 222 laps
                                 Rear (·750" new) = 200 laps

During the last few minutes of practice all the tyres on the car were replaced by 650 L × 15 R6 D9 at 57 p.s.i cold and the car was driven for two laps to check the engine revs and max. speed. The engine revs rose from 5,550 to 6,000 r.p.m. in 5th gear giving a calculated road speed of 169 m.p.h, i.e. a rise of 4 m.p.h. when compared with the 725 L tyres and 3·54 : 1 CW and P and an increase of 7/8 m.p.h. when compared with the 725L tyres and 3·31 CW and P.

G.T. Section	Driver	Best Lap Time	Speed m.p.h.
Cobra Coupe	Schlesser	4/02·3	180
Lindner 'E'	Nocker	4/07·3	161 (3·31 : 1)
Lumsden 'E'	Sargent	4/07·3	168 (suspect)
Ferrari GTO	Dumay	4/12·7	–
Porsche 2L	Buchet	4/20·4	165
G.T. Prototypes			
Ferrari 3·3L	Scarfiotti	3/43·8	189
Ferrari 4·0L	Surtees	3/45·9	194
Ferrari 3·3L	Parkes	3/47·1	189
Maserati 5·0L	Simon	3/56·1	–
Porsche 8 cyl.	Lige	4/13·7	163
Ford 4·2L	Schlesser	4/21·8	–

WORK DONE – JAGUAR COMPETITION DEPT.

The car was returned to Jaguars and work was done to reduce the wind resistance, increase the engine power and improve the brakes.

Aerodynamics. The engine oil cooler was moved from underneath the radiator to in front of the radiator with its own intake and outlet air ducts; the underside of the bonnet nose was deepened and a panel fitted under the radiator: the front sidelight/flasher light unit was removed and separate lights recessed into the bonnet nose behind flat perspex; the bonnet straps were removed; the headlamp perspex covers were fitted with dum-dum to prevent air leakage and the overhang of the rear wheel arches was reduced. A flush fitting aluminium windscreen frame was tried to replace the rubber moulding which protruded 3/8" to ½", but shortage of time did not allow a good enough fit to be achieved and the scheme was abandoned when the windscreen cracked on assembly. In this respect Lumsden's car was much better – the windscreen was fitted into a flush-fitting metal frame with 7 or 8 lugs. A new windscreen/frame unit could be fitted in about a minute by unscrewing and replacing the 7 or 8 countersunk screws in the lugs.

Engine. A new exhaust system was made up to Mr Buck's requirements: 6 primary pipes 1·5/8" bore × 40", into two tail pipes 1·7/8" bore × 34" – slip joints at the primary pipe/tail pipe junction and imitation "silencers" welded on the outside of the tailpipes. The power figures were now as follows:

	Test Days April 18/19	Practice & Race, 20th June.
5000 r.p.m.	286 b.h.p. corr.	288 b.h.p. (calc.)
5500 r.p.m.	308	318
5750 r.p.m.	319	339
6000 r.p.m.	322	345
6500 r.p.m.	–	–

Brakes. To reduce the brake pedal effort the wheel cylinder sizes were increased from 2·1/8" to 2½" at the front from 1·5/8" 1·7/8" at the rear (approx. 38% increase at the front and 33% at the rear). A similar modification on Coombs 63/64 'E' gave the following results on test at M.I.R.A. at 60 m.p.h with D.S.11 pads:-

591

Deceleration – Pedal Effort – Line Pressure.
·5G   –   65 lb – 360 p.s.i
·875G – 110 lb – 600 p.s.i
1·00 G – 140 lb – 800 p.s.i

On Lumsden's 'E' the pedal effort was reduced by increasing
the pedal ratio numerically.

Steering. The steering geometry was checked from full bump to
full rebound and was found to be badly in error. This was corrected
by lifting the rack approx. 5/16". and the rack housing was then
attached solidly to the frame.

Suspension. The front wheel camber was altered from $-1°$ to $-2°$
to reduce understeer.

General. The cockpit was trimmed with carpets, padded facia,
door panels, headlining etc. and the boot was provided with
a mat and side panels.

Bumpers were made but not used as their absence was not noticed
during scrutineering.

Separate ignition switch and starter button fitted.

Oil pressure warning light fitted but not used as it cut out
at approx. 70 p.s.i instead of 30–35 p.s.i as requested.

*New ZF gearbox fitted to replace box damaged by Nurburgring
1000 km race.*

*Cockpit ventilation increased by additional air scoop above driver's
head.*

Bug deflector fitted.

Smiths chronometric rev. counter fitted.

*Engine originally spare intended for Le Mans – Lindner's engine
number RA-1347-9S stamped on.*

*During tests at M.I.R.A. the rev. counter showed 4800 r.p.m.
instead of the expected 5800 r.p.m. Checks were then carried out
which confirmed that the CW and P was 3·54 : 1, that 4th
gear was 1·0 : 1, that 5th gear was 0·834 : 1 and that the rev.
counter was 1% fast at 5000 r.p.m. The car was easy to push on
a flat concrete surface.*

LE MANS PRACTICE AND RACE – 17/21 JUNE 64.

The car passed through scrutineering with no trouble at all.
Weight (138 litres in fuel tank) = 1170 kg = 2570 lbs.
   (Weight with no full) = 2360 lb)
Lumsden's 'E' – fuel tank = 1141 kg = 2520 lb.
Ford G.T. Prototype (ex Lola) = 1065 kg = 2350 lb.

Practice, Wednesday – 7 p.m. to 11 p.m.
   Dry, 5–10 m.p.h. tailwind, 25°c ambient.
   Tyres – Ft. 700L × 15 R6 D9 55 p.s.i cold.
         Rr. 725 L × 15 R6 D9 50 p.s.i cold.

Lindner did 8 + 4 + 6 = 18 laps – best time 4/06·3 on 6th
lap (daylight).
Nocker did 7 + 8 = 15 laps – best time 4/10·6 on 10th lap
(daylight).

Both drivers reported that the engine felt stiff – drivers
changed gear at 5900 r.p.m.

Throttle stuck open and Lindner slid into sandbank on 33rd lap.

Time was lost investigating a misfire – proved to be due to
H.T. lead coming loose from distributor cap.

Max. 5th gear – 56/5700 r.p.m. = 167/170 m.p.h. calc.
Water temp = 70°c – no radiator blanking.
Oil press = 60/65 p.s.i
Oil temp = 80/85°c
Axle temp = 95/100°c – pump on.
Cockpit temp = 32°c on instrument panel.
Fuel cons. = 4·28 litre/lap = 32 laps max.

Oil for 27 laps – $1\frac{1}{2}$ litres = 2·6 pints.
Brake pad wear/lap – front =   rear = ·002"

Therefore, max. pad life – Front-(·850" new) =
                           Rear-(·750" new) = 250 laps.

Tyre life – D9 – Front – 520 laps

Practice Thursday 18th June 6 p.m. to 11 p.m.
   Dry, wind variable in direction, approx. 10–20 m.p.h
   23°c ambient.
   Tyres as for Wendesdays practice.
   CW & P now 3·77 : 1 instead of 3·54 : 1

Lindner did 7 laps – best time 4/08·3 on 5th lap.
Nocker did 10 + 3 + 4 = 17 laps – best time 4/05·9 on
8th lap (daylight).
The last 3/4 hours was used to bed in brake pads, tyres etc.
This should have been done earlier as the final run on the
race tyres and pads was missed when the rear pads proved
difficult to change.

Nocker reported that the car felt "twitchy" over crests of
hills with an almost empty tank.

Maximum tyre tread wear at front and rear at 1/3rd of tread
width, nearer centre of car. Suggest trying wheel cambers
of $-1°$ instead of $-2°$ in future long distance races.

Max 5th gear = 6050 r.p.m. = 169 m.p.hcalc.
(6400 + r.p.m. when slipstreaming Cobra).
Water temp = 60/65°c
Oil press = 60 + p.s.i
Oil temp = 75°c after 10 laps
Axle temp = 128°c after 10 laps, 120° after 17 laps.
Cockpit temp = 30°c (pump on)
Disc temp (braking hard before pits.)
   N.S.F. = 800°F   N.S.R. = 700 –°F
Fuel cons. = 4·55 litre/lap – 30 laps max.
Tyre life (from J. Leonard – Dunlop)
   Front – no change
   Rear – change after $11\frac{3}{4}$ hours +
Water added for first time – cylinder head nuts tightened
   considerably and Barseal added and Loy over split
   in inlet manifold flange.

Before the race the car was checked over, oil and filter
changed, etc. a spade, torch, hydraulic jack and tool bag
fitted and a blue identification light fitted on the roof

of the car. Also the instruments were marked with "Scotlite" as follows:

R.P.M.   –   6000
Water   –   95 to 100°c
Oil   –   25–30 p.s.i
Oil   –   125–128°c
Axle   –   130–133°c
Speedo   –   6000 r.p.m. in 1st, 2nd, 3rd, 4th, 5th.

The car started the race with the following tyres.

Front – 700L × 15 R6D9 – 55 p.s.i. cold
Rear – 725L × 15 R6 D9 (C4821) – 50 p.s.i.

No radiator blanking
Fuel pump and axle pump switches ON
N.3 plugs were fitted.

Competitors Practice Times. – Official.

G.T.Section –	Best Lap Time.
Cobra –	3/56·1
Cobra –	3/58·2
Aston Martin –	3/58·6
Cobra –	4/01·3
Ferrari G.T.O. –	4/03·4
Ferrari G.T.O. –	4/04·5
Ferrari G.T.O. –	4/04·9
Jaguar 'E' –	4/05·9 (Nocker)
Ferrari G.T.O. –	4/14·1
Porsche 4 cyl. –	4/15·6
Jaguar 'E' –	4/16 (Sargent)
Porsche 4 cyl. –	4/16

Prototype Section – Best Lap Time.

Ferrari 3·3L –	3/42·0 (Surtees)
Ford 4·2L –	3/45·3
Ferrari 4·0L –	3/45·3
Ford 4·2L –	3/45·9
Ferrari 3·0L –	3/45·9
Ferrari 3·3L –	3/49
Porsche 8 cyl. –	4/02·1

RACE – SATURDAY 4. P.M. – Ambient 29°c.

Dry throughout.
Agreed to lap at 4/10 to 4/15
4 p.m. – 5.45 p.m. 27 laps. Lindner lay 12th overall after first lap, and 15th overall (5th G.T. car) after 3 laps.
Minus 50 sec. on leading G.T. car (Cobra No.3) after 4 laps.
Plus 2 sec. on Lumsden after 5 laps.
Minus 90 secs. on leading prototype (Ford) after 6 laps.
Lapped by leading prototype (Ford) after 11 laps.
8th in G.T. class after 13 laps.
Daytona Cobra (Gurney) lapping 4/01
Aston Martin (Salmon) lapping 4/05
Ford (Ginther) lapping 3/57·2, 3/54
Ford (P. Hill) lapping 3/54

5.54 p.m. Pit stop – 1 min. 35 sec.

Max. 5th = 6300 = 176 m.p.h. (calc)

Note Revs up by 250 r.p.m. (7 m.p.h.), compared to Thursdays practice (due to engine, gearbox and axle now being run in ?)
Water temp. = 'low' – possibly 60°c ?
Oil pressure = 60 + p.s.i
Oil temp = 60°c
Axle temp. = 110°c – pump on
Fuel cons. = 4·45 litre/lap = 30 laps max.
Tyre life – (J. Leonard – Dunlop)
   Front – no change
   Rear – Change after 14 hours.
No oil added after checking.
No water added after checking.
'Brake pedal soft initially, later O.K.' – P.L.
'Cockpit temp. O.K.' – P.L.
'Passed Lumsden easily on straight at 6300' – P.L.
(Note. Lumsden officially timed at 174 m.p.h.)

5.56 to 7.58 p.m. 28 laps – Sunny, hot, dry.
Nocker proceeded to lap around 4/15 until his 26th lap when he slowed as the water temp. gauge had reached 100°c.
Steam or smoke had been seen under the car on lap 23.

5th in G.T. class on lap 38.
Leading G.T. car (Cobra) lapping 4/02, 4/04.
Lumsden 3rd in G.T. class.
G.T. class positions on 38th lap –

   Cobra (Gurney/Bondurant)
   Cobra (Neerpach/Amon)
   Jaguar 'E' (Lumsden/Sargent)
   Ferrari G.T.O. (Beurlys/Bianchi)
   Jaguar 'E' (Lindner/Nocker)
   Cobra (Sears/Bolton)
   Ferrari G.T.O. (Hugus/Rosinski)
   Aston Martin (Salmon/Sutcliffe)

7.58 p.m. Pit Stop – 7 min. 40 sec.
NO WATER IN ENGINE – water added
'Water temp. rose steadily while driving' – P.N.
Oil press = 60 p.s.i
Oil temp. = 60/80°c
Axle temp. = 110°c
Fuel cons. = 4·4 litres/lap = 31 laps max.

8.06–10.30 p.m. approx. 25 laps.
Lindner drove at a much reduced pace (4/25 to 7/00) in 4th and 5th gears (trying to last the compulsory 25 laps before water could be added). The engine still responded perfectly and all gauge readings were all right apart from the water temperature which rose steadily to 100/110°c and then dropped when the radiator header tank was empty.

10.30–1.30 a.m. Pit stop 3 hours 8 mins.

Cylinder head and gasket changed by F. Rainbow and R. Penney under difficult conditions – plugs changed.
Barseal added to water.
Gearbox oil checked – O.K.

3 litres engine oil added.
During this pit stop a Ferrari rear axle disintegrated as the car passed the pits at approx. 160 m.p.h – the pinion, bearings and surrounding alum. casting hit the N.S.R. of the 'E' type and caused considerable damage including destroying the brake and parking lights. Fortunately, the auxiliary tail lights which had previously been fitted allowed the car to continue in the race.

By 11 p.m. the Lumsden 'E' type had been retired due to loss of gearbox oil (nose oil seal failure?) after completing 80 laps.

By 1.0 a.m. the Lindner 'E' was 20 laps behind the leading G.T. Cobra, and 24 laps behind the leading prototype Ferrari.

1.30 a.m.–3.22 a.m. – 25 laps.
Nocker lapped at 4/15 to 4/25 until the water temp. gauge again registered 110°c after 19 laps.

3.22 a.m. Pit stop 5/13 sec.
2 gall. water added and Barseal.
106 litres fuel added
1 litre oil added

3.27 a.m.–5.25 a.m. – 25 laps – Total 130 laps.
Lindner – lapped at 4/10 until 4 a.m. to avoid disqualification – then at 5/00 to 6/00 minutes.

5.25 a.m. – Pit Stop
2 gall. water added and 'Never Leak'
114 litres fuel added
3 litres oil added.

5.31 a.m. to 7.30 a.m. approx.
Nocker lapped at 4/20 approx. until water temperature rose to 110°c.

Car retired at 7.30 a.m.

After 24 hours the positions (subject to protests etc.) were as follows:

Position Overall	Position G.T. Section	Make.	Laps.
1		Ferrari	348
2		Ferrari	343
3		Ferrari	336
4	1	Cobra	333
5	2	Ferrari	332
6	3	Ferrari	327
7	4	Porsche	322
8	5	Porsche	318
9	6	Ferrari	314
10	7	Porsche	314
11	8	Porsche	308
12	9	Porsche	307
13	10	Alfa Romeo	306
14		Iso Rivolta	306

25 cars finished – 30 cars retired.

CONCLUSIONS

The 'E' types were 10 seconds slower than the 4.7 litre Cobra Coupes in practice, 7 seconds slower than the Aston Martin, and 2 seconds slower than the G.T.O. Ferraris. By official timing they were 7 m.p.h. slower than the Cobras and 2 m.p.h. slower than the G.T.O. Ferraris in the middle of the Mulsanne straight.

In order to win the G.T. section it would have been necessary to lap at 4/14, assuming 12 pit stops of 1/30 and 1 pit stop of 4/00, and no other time lost. This would have beaten the leading G.T. Cobra, which was delayed twice with oil cooler problems. It is not known for how long this car was delayed, but its normal lap time during the first 6 hours of the race appeared to be faster than 4/05.

To be competitive with the Coupe Cobras at Le Mans the maximum speed of the 'E' types will have to be raised at least 10–12 m.p.h. and acceleration improved considerably by a) increased mid range power and b) decreased weight of car. It is thought that the handling of the car can be improved by reduction of steered angles of the rear wheels due to the rubber mounting of the rear suspension, and acceleration and braking should both be improved (at the slight expense of cornering speed) by reducing the camber of front and rear wheels from −2° to −1°. (for long races only).

An enormous amount of labour was wasted between practice periods on the task of changing the axle ratio – fitting a 3·77 : 1 axle unit into a spare rear suspension unit assembly and fitting this into the car took 15–20 man hours – compared to 15 minutes for one man to alter the transmission ratio on a Formula 1 B.R.M. It is impossible to alter gear ratios on the 'E' type.

A lot of time was spent between practice periods fitting the following items – all of these items should in future be fitted at Jaguars:

> Identification lights.
> Fire extinguisher.
> Shovel.
> Tool kit.
> Drink bottle or Thermos Flask with tube.

Mr Lindner has assembled a good team of people – drivers, mechanic, timekeepers and signallers, etc., and they went about their work in an efficient manner.

D.A.WHITE.

Oddballs: **This photograph, supplied by Cecil Winby (formerly of Brico) is dated August 1964, and shows a piston top pounded into three spheres. The engine is from the Lindner E-type, presumably used at Le Mans.**

Author's note: After Le Mans Lindner took his car to Goodwood where he invited Peter Sutcliffe to try to help cure a problem during TT practice. Sutcliffe crashed and the car was rebuilt at the works in time to take part in the Montlhéry 1000 km race which, tragically claimed Lindner's life.

The next appendix list all the works-built lightweight E-types including the Lindner car.

Special-build
E-type-Individual Histories

This appendix includes a brief history of all the ex-works special-build E-types to leave Browns Lane.

Body:	EC1001
Chassis:	EC1001
Engine:	E5033-9
Gearbox:	C7513
Delivered:	June 1963

Built in 1961/2, one of an otherwise still-born batch of E-types with light-gauge steel centre-section, projected for GT racing. Owned from June 1963 and raced successfully by Elmer Richard Protheroe, with John Coundley co-driving in longer events. Later owned by Robert Gordon. Driven into Oulton Park lake by David Wansborough in practice for 1965 TT, but still raced. Successful hill-climb car in late sixties, driven by Shropshire farmer-turned-trucker Michael Wright. Ultimately shipped to Florida to join the magnificent Walter Hill collection of competition Jaguars.

Body:	R5859
Chassis:	S850006
Engine:	RA1343-9S
Gearbox:	EB126CR
Delivered:	March 1963

Rebuild of early production car bought by Coombs of Guildford, first raced at Oulton Park April 1961 and effectively written-off at Goodwood Easter 1962 (Roy Salvadori both times). Triple Weber carburetters and 35/40 head in 1962; then full 'lightweight' spec. for '63 season, when Graham Hill took major UK sprint-race wins. Other occasional drivers of this development car included Sears, Stewart, Gurney and MacDowel (by then a Coombs employee). Sold by Coombs to Red Rose Motors, this car won more than a dozen races in 1965 driven by Brian Redman. Later owned for many years by ship's engineer Gordon Brown.

Body:	R5860
Chassis:	S850659
Engine:	RA1345-9S
Gearbox:	EB9376CR
Delivered:	March 1963

First Cunningham team car, ready for Sebring where it came eighth. Returned to works for many modifications including new four-speed synchromesh gearbox (4FS/3), 2·79:1 axle ratio, $30\frac{3}{4}$ gallon fuel tank in boot-well with spare wheel above; mods to brakes and dampers; new front and rear anti-roll bars fitted. Registered 5115 WK. Finished ninth at Le Mans (July '63). Brake pedal mod, applicable to whole series in June '63. New ZF five-speed gearbox (No.73) fitted. Stiffer engine and gearbox mountings. Owned in the 1980s by Nigel Dawes; fitted with engine numbered as from 5116 WK.

Body: R5861
Chassis: S850660
Engine: RA1344-9S
Gearbox: EB9375CR
Delivered: March 1963

Raced to seventh at Sebring 1963 for San Francisco-based entrant Kjell Qvale by Ed Leslie and Frank Morrill. Car preparation by Joe Huffaker. Brake pedal mod advised June 1963.

Body: R5862
Chassis: S850661
Engine: RA1346-9S
Gearbox: EB9813CR
Delivered: April 1963

Run by Salvadori through 1963 for his sponsor C. T. Atkins. No wins but Silverstone GT lap record and a good third in TT race. Mods included ZF five-speed gearbox No.72 in July '63. many successes by Roger Mac in 1964. Fewer results from next owner Peter Mould. Sprinted and hill-climbed by Penny Griffiths (Woodley) in late 1960s and still in the family collection.

Body: R5863
Chassis: S850662
Engine: RA1347-9S
Gearbox: EB9642CR
Delivered: May 1963

Peter Lindner and Peter Nöcker of Germany very fast with this car, many end-of-season modifications, including low drag roof similar to EC1001. Works-prepared for Le Mans 1964 (See previous appendix). Crashed in pouring rain, Montlhéry late 1964. Car written-off and locked up by French authorities. Remains freed in late 1970s; new car subsequently constructed by Lynx Engineering, using pictures of original for reference. Roof remade after dissatisfaction with first attempt. Re-created car returned to Germany and run in historic events mid 1980s.

Body: R5864
Chassis: S850663
Engine: RA1348-9S
Gearbox: 455-1 (all synchro)
Delivered: May 1963

Crashed by owner Peter Lumsden in first race, Nürburgring 1000 km, May 1963. Returned to works for new body and frame. Raced by Lumsden and Sargent 1963, and again in modified form (Costin low drag body) in 1964. Later owners to race car in UK club events include John Scott-Davies and John Carden. Later to USA and concours condition. (Driven for Howard Cohen by Stephen Griswold at 1980 Laguna Seca historic races. Later transferred to other ownership.)

Body: R5865
Chassis: S850664
Engine: RA1349-9S
Gearbox: 4-speed all-synchro
Delivered: June 1963

Cunningham team car 5114 WK for Le Mans 1963 driven by Hansgen/Pabst to early retirement (gearbox trouble). Front portion of bonnet fitted to 5115WK for latter part of race, with numbers removed (leading to subsequent identity mix-up). New ZF five-speed No.68 fitted afterwards and other mods before shipment to USA. Various owners on both sides of the Atlantic. Restored by John Freshman (USA) with iron block, but alloy block retained for authenticity. In 1987, Campbell McLaren acquired car (for the second time!) and had XK Engineering of Nuneaton prepare it for historic events.

Body: R5866
Chassis: S85665
Engine: RA1350-9S
Gearbox: 4-speed all-synchro
Delivered: June 1963

Cunningham team car registered 5116 WK for Salvadori/Richards. Written off at Le Mans, 1963 and returned to works; engine salvaged (reported fitted to Dawes car in 1980s.)

Body: R5867
Chassis: S850666
Engine: RA1351-9S
Gearbox: EB162CR
Delivered: July 1963

Peter Sutcliffe raced regularly between 1963 and 1965; it was shunted several times. Successful in UK, Belgium, France and South Africa. Richard Bond, Bob Vincent and Bob Jennings were later owners, the latter lending it to Michael MacDowel for hill-climbs in 1968. Car was later owned by Bryan Corser for many years; then to Walter Hill collection, Florida.

Body: R5868
Chassis: S850667
Engine: RA1353-9S
Gearbox: EB9813CR (ex Atkins?)
Delivered: October 1963

Brysons (Australian importers) ordered this car for dealer Bob Jane, already an outstanding Jaguar driver down under. Jane won Australian GT championship at Calder, December 1963, and had good results in early 1964. Brought car to UK (raced Brands Hatch July '64) then returned car to works for mods (including ZF box). Raced by Jane in Australia in 1965 and by him and Spencer Martin in 1966. Car retained by original owner in show condition until auctioned 1980 and transferred from Victoria to York Motor Museum, Western Australia.

Body: R5869
Chassis: S850668
Engine: RA1354-9S
Gearbox: ZF73
Delivered: December 1963

Bought by Richard Wilkins, but not raced by him. Various later owners including Philip Scragg and Tony Harrison. Car registered 2GXO.

Body: R5870
Chassis: S850669
Engine: RA1355-9S
Gearbox: ZF69
Delivered: January 1964

Philip Scragg's first 'lightweight', soon sold partly due to annoyance of GT class opposition, and consequent re-classification in BARC events. Car registered PS1175. Later owners included the composer Anthony Hopkins, presenter of BBC's 'Talking about Music', and author of numerous book including *Beating Time* in which he admits to having owned 14 Jaguars. This one suffered the usual trouble – cracks towards the rear of the alloy block. Bob Vincent brought this car to Brands Hatch for the 1970 British Grand Prix parade of Jaguars.

Body: 7501 (steel)
Chassis: S850817
Engine: RA1357-9S
Gearbox: ZF445
Delivered: July 1964

Road car for Sir Robert Ropner, with cast-iron block wet-sump engine, 35/40 head and triple Weber carburetters rather than fuel injection. Later owned by John Foster.

Body: 7685 (steel)
Chassis: S890193
Engine: RA1356-9S
Gearbox: ZF447
Delivered: July 1964

Production steel coupé (i.e. hatchback) with wet sump 35/40 fuel injection alloy-block engine, and most usual lightweight E-type components. Built for Pierre Bardinon, France. Later owned by Philippe Renault.

Appendix Ten

Racing XK Engine Test Results

This appendix contains a selection of Browns Lane XK racing engine test results from 1954 to 1964. Also included is a facsimile of a test comparison made between a Ferrari GTO engine and an (unidentified) 3-litre example of Jaguar's alloy-block XK competition engine.

	April 1954	April 1954	May 1954	September 1954	April 1955
Engine No	E1005-8	E1054-9	E2004-9	E2005-9	E2006-9
Prepared for	XKC011	XKC054	XKC402	XKC403	XKC404
(chassis/event)	Reims	Reims	Le Mans	TT race	Silverstone May meeting
cc	3441	3441	3441	2482	3441
Bore (mm)	83	83	83	83	83
Stroke (mm)	106	106	106	76·5	106
Camshaft lift (in)	3/8	3/8	3/8	3/8	7/16
Inlet valve dia (in)	1 3/4	1 7/8	1 7/8	1 7/8	1 29/32
Exhaust valve dia (in)	1 5/8	1 5/8	1 5/8	1 5/8	1 11/16
Fuel supply	2 × SU H8	3 × DCO3 (Weber)	3 × DCO3	3 × DCO3	3 × DCO3
Gross bhp	214·5	246	255·5	190	272·5
at rpm	5750	6000	6000	6000	5500
Notes	*Fitted to XK120C with alloy disc wheels (wet sump)*	*Fitted to experimental car also known as 'XP11' and 'XKC201' (wet sump)*	*First race for the D-type Jaguar. This car came second*	*Sleeved 3½-litre block with 76½ mm stroke crankshaft*	*Compression ratio recorded as 9·4 to 1*

598

	July 1955	September 1955	December 1955	February 1956	February 1956
Engine No	E3007-9*	E3002-9	EXP 8	E3005-8	E2084-9
Prepared for	XKD 506	XKD 506	XKD 506	XKD 601	(Production unit)
(Chassis/event)	Le Mans spare	TT race	'Experimental high-speed' unit	Sebring 12-hour	
cc	3441	3441	2482	3441	3441
Bore (mm)	83	83	83	83	83
Stroke (mm)	106	106	76·5	106	106
Camshift lift (in)	7/16	7/16	7/16	7/16	3/8
Inlet valve dia (in)	2	2	1 29/32	2	1 7/8
Exhaust valve dia (in)	1 11/16	1 11/16	1 11/16	1 11/16	1 5/8
Fuel supply	3 × DCO3	3 × DCO3	3 × DCO3	Lucas PI	3 × DCO3
Gross bhp	270·8	270·5	220·2	254	252·5
at rpm	6000	5750	7000	5250	6000

Notes	Spare engine fitted to XKD 506 after Le Mans	Hawthorn and Titterington car	Special exhaust (Engine sent to Harry Weslake for test in 1956)	First use of PI in a race	Sample from Production Dept to Engineering Dept 'for test and approval'

	May 1956	May 1956	May 1956	May 1956	July 1956
Engine No	E4001-9	E4002-9	E4002-9	E4002-9	E4007-9
Prepared for	–	(See below)	(See below)	(See below)	XKD 605
(Chassis/event)	Silverstone race	(See below)	(See below)	(See below)	Le Mans race
cc	3441	3441	3441	3441	3441
Bore (mm)	83	83	83	83	83
Stroke (mm)	106	106	106	106	106
Camshaft lift (in)	7/16	7/16	7/16	7/16	7/16
Inlet valve dia (in)	2	2	2	2	2
Exhaust valve dia (in)	1 11/16	1 11/16	1 11/16	1 11/16	1 11/16
Fuel supply	Lucas PI	3 × DCO3	3 × SU	Lucas PI	Lucas PI
Gross bhp	269·8	273	271	268·5	263·5
at rpm	6000	6000	5750	5750	6000

Notes	Also showed 269·0 bhp at 5500 rpm and 270 lb ft torque at 4500 rpm	This test dated 30/5/56, was done to compare 45 mm Weber carburetter, SU horizontal carburetter (1 3/8 in dia throttle) and 45 mm Lucas petrol injection (with modified induction manifold and revised injection position). It was probably also the last engine test conducted by Jack Emerson			Reports on six 1956 Le Mans engines were made by W. Wilkinson ('Bill')

	July 1956	November 1956	January 1957	January 1957
Engine No	E4006-9	E4004-9	E2083-9	E2083-10·7
Prepared for	XKD 606	ex-XKD 602	(Production D engine, before conversion)	(Conversion by A. Momo, returned for test)
(Chassis/event)	Le Mans (practice only)	End-of-season prior to sale		
cc	3441	3441	3441	3807
Bore (mm)	83	83	83	87·3
Stroke (mm)	106	106	106	106
Camshaft lift (in)	7/16	7/16	3/8	(XM2)
Inlet valve dia (in)	2	2	1 7/8	1 7/8
Exhaust valve dia (in)	1 11/16	1 11/16	1 5/8	1 5/8
Fuel supply	3 × DCO3	3 × DCO3	3 × DCO3	3 × DCO3
Gross bhp	277·5	279	250	284
at rpm	6000	5750	6000	6000

Notes	Reports on six 1956 Le Mans engines were made by W. Wilkinson ('Bill')	Engine for Ecurie Ecosse 'outstanding bench performance'. (279 bhp also at 6000 rpm – best 3·4 figure ever)	Two of several tests done at Jaguar works, to assess the value of engine capacity increase carried-out by Alfred Momo on behalf of Briggs Cunningham, (full details printed separately)	

	March 1957	May 1957	July 1957	July 1957	July 1957
Engine No	E5001-10	E5005-9	E5008-10	E5007-9	E5006-10
Prepared for	XKD 605	XKD 606	–	(First 3·8 for Lister)	For D. Hamilton
(Chassis/event)	Sebring race	Le Mans race	North American racing		
cc	3781	3781	3781	3781	3781
Bore (mm)	87	87	87	87	87
Stroke (mm)	106	106	106	106	106
Camshaft lift (in)	7/16	7/16	7/16	7/16	7/16
Inlet valve dia (in)	2	2	2	2	2
Exhaust valve dia (in)	1 11/16	1 11/16	1 11/16	1 11/16	1 11/16
Fuel supply	Lucas PI	Lucas PI	3 × DCO3	3 × DCO3	3 × DCO3
Gross bhp	306·5	297·5	297	290	294
at rpm	5500	55/5750	5500	5500	5750
Notes	*E5003 and E2083 also prepared for Sebring. (3·8 litres, Weber carbs)*	*Works engine prepared and fitted to Ecurie Ecosse car in Coventry*	*Another 3·8 engine for Cunningham team (E5009-10) gave 295 bhp at 5500 rpm*	*Result of unexpected early season success of Archie Scott-Brown (Lister-Jaguar)*	*Max power sustained at 6000 rpm*

	August 1957	November 1957	December 1957	December 1958
Engine No	W5029-9		E4007	EXP 16
Prepared for (Chassis/event)	Marine application (N. Buckley)	Modified D-type unit (Ecurie Ecosse)	Works-modified D-type unit	'For Fitment in the green "E" type car'
cc	3441	2954	2987	2997
Bore (mm)	83	83	83	85
Stroke (mm)	106	91	92	88
Camshaft lift (in)	7/16	3/8	7/16	7/16
Inlet valve dia (in)	2	1 7/8	2	2 3/32
Exhaust valve dia (in)	1 11/16	1 5/8	1 11/16	1 11/16
Fuel supply	3 × DCO3	3 × DCO3	3 × DCO3	3 × DCO3
Gross bhp	267	234	254	272
at rpm	5750	6100	6300	6750
Notes	*Modified XK120 engine with new 35/40 head giving improvement of about 35 bhp*	*Ecurie Ecosse's own modified D-type unit, as tested by Jaguar. 9·17 to 1 CR*	*One of two 10·25 to 1 CR works prepared units for Ecurie Ecosse*	*Cast iron block 10·25 to 1 CR*

	March 1959	June 1960	August 1960	May 1961
Engine No	EE1302-10	E1307-10	E5028-10	R1027-9·5
Prepared for	Lister			Sopwith entry
(Chassis/event)	Sebring	Le Mans race	USA racing	Spa GT race
cc	2997	2997	3781	3781
Bore (mm)	85	85	87	87
Stroke (mm)	88	88	106	106
Camshaft lift (in)	7/16	7/16	7/16	(XM3)
Inlet valve dia (in)	2 3/32	2 3/32	2 3/32	1 3/4
Exhaust valve dia (in)	1 11/16	1 11/16	1 11/16	1 5/8
Fuel supply	3 × DCO3	Lucas PI	3 × DCO3	3 × SU HD8
Gross bhp	258	294	294	276
at rpm	6000	6750	5500	5750
Notes	*Two similar engines for Cunningham's Listers in same batch*	*Alloy block unit for 'E2A' (Cunningham entry)*	*Cast iron block '3·8' for 'E2A' on loan to Cunningham*	*Basically production 3·8 E-type 9·5 to 1 CR Iskendenan XM3 camshaft*

	April 1962	May 1962	June 1962	April 1964
Engine No	R1028-9·8	E5033-9	R5909-9	RA1347-9·5
Prepared for	Coombs entry	'for Light Weight		Lindner
(Chassis/event)	for Goodwood	"E"-type car'	Le Mans race	Lightweight
cc	3781	3781	3781	3781
Bore (mm)	87	87	87	87
Stroke (mm)	106	106	106	106
Camshaft lift (in)	7/16	15/32	7/16	15/32
Inlet valve dia (in)	2 3/32	2 3/32	2 3/32	2 3/32
Exhaust valve dia (in)	1 11/16	1 11/16	1 11/16	1 11/16
Fuel supply	3 × DCO3	Lucas PI	3 × DCO3	Lucas PI
Gross bhp	296	324	296	344
at rpm	5750	6000	5500	6500
Notes	*Cast iron block 3·8*	*For Coombs car*	*For Cunningham fhc*	*Special exhaust or test bed*

From: Mr.Wilkinson   EXPERIMENTAL DEPARTMENT

To: Mr.Heynes   21st May 1957

Copy to: Mr.Baily   EXP/1551/WW

SUBJECT   LE MANS RACE ENTRY

Herewith details and Full Load performance curve of the XK 'D' 3.75 litre Petrol Injection engine prepared for "Ecurie Ecosse" for the above race entry.

ENGINE DETAIL

Engine No. & Type	E 5005-9 3.75 Litre. Bore 87mm Stroke 106mm.
Specification	A 125
Cylinder Head	A 62 35°/40° XK 2351
Compression Ratio	9.13:1
Inlet Valve	Nimonic 2" Head Dia. XK 2133
Exhaust Valve	Nimonic 1 11/16" Head Dia. XK 1981
Camshaft	7/16" lift Steel Wide Timing XK 1815-6
Valve Timing	Inlet opens 35° B.T.D.C. closes 62° A.T.D.C., Exhaust opens 63° B.T.D.C. closes 35° A.T.D.C.
Valve Springs	Terry Chrome Vanadium Red Stripe XK 2097-8 7/16" lift.
Tappet Clearance	Inlet .010" Exhaust .015"
Camshaft	XK 1958 Nitrided
Piston	Brico "Full Skirt" EXP 6086 9:1
Fuel Injection	Lucas 45mm. Petrol Injection System Timing 10°
Air Entry	Trumpets 6½" long
Distributor	Lucas LT 16373 Series J 20
Static Setting	10 Crank Degrees
Sparking Plug	Champion N.A.10
Coil	H.V.12
Exhaust System	1956 Le Mans Competition System 114" long
Fuel	Shell Premium
Engine Oil	Double Shell SAE 30

Test Detail

Test No.1   Date: 3.5.57   Baro 29.80" Hg

R.P.M.	N.T.P. B.H.P.	B.M.E.P.	TORQUE	PTS BHP/HR
1250	45.1	124.2	190.0	.787
1750	87.5	172.0	262.5	.568
2000	100.2	172.3	262.6	.568
2500	123.5	170.0	259.5	.581
3000	159.0	182.2	278.5	.538
3500	189.8	186.8	285.0	.534
4000	219.5	188.8	188.0	.534
4500	254.5	194.5	297.0	.511
5000	275.5	189.6	290.0	.533
5500	297.5	186.0	284.0	.537
5750	297.5	177.8	279.0	.541
6000	292.0	167.2	255.5	.572

Max.B.H.P. = 297.5 at 5,750 R.P.M.
Max.B.M.E.P. lb.sq.in. = 194.5 at 4,500 R.P.M.
Max.Torque lb.ft. = 297.0 at 4,500 R.P.M.

Speed at $\frac{\text{Max. B.H.P.}}{\text{Max. Torque}}$ = $\frac{1.28}{1}$

B.M.E.P. at Max.Power = 177.8 = 91.5% of Max. B.H.E.P.

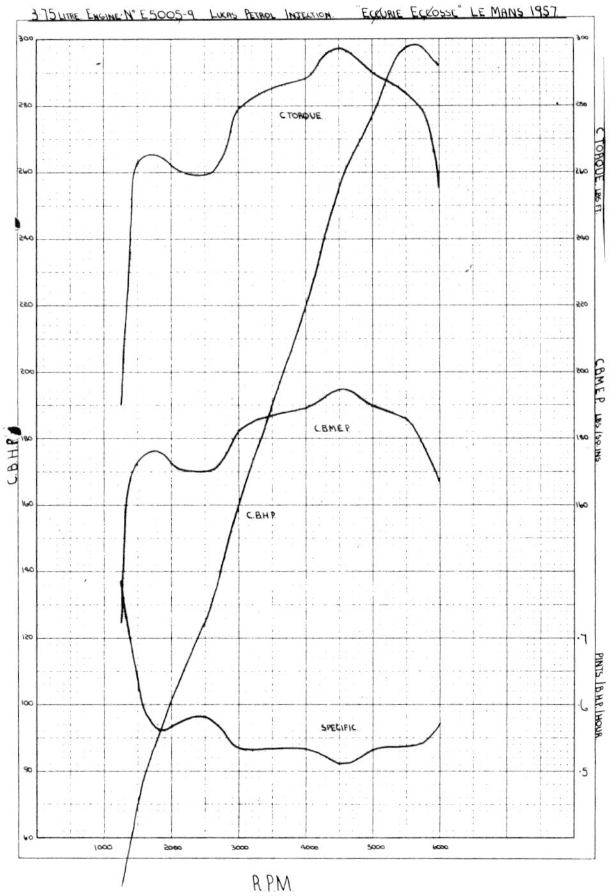

From: Mr.G.Buck   EXPERIMENTAL DEPARTMENT

To: Mr.Heynes   1st October 1962

Copy to: Mr.Baily   EXP/1±16/GB

FERRARI 250 G.T.O. ENGINE

The results of the bench tests on the 3 litre V 12 Ferrari engine are appended hereto. The figures for the Jaguar 3 litre alloy engine are included for comparison.

The peak B.H.P. is limited by valve bounce which commences at approximately 7800 r.p.m. This condition has been demonstrated by Mr.Dewis as being easily obtainable in the car and indeed was the limiting factor to performance on the roads. It was noticed during valve timing check that the valves are controlled in this particular engine by relatively low rate coil springs.

This engine has a much greater piston area than our own 3 litre and this explains the lower B.M.E.P.s at similar B.H.P. readings. One would expect therefore a high degree of reliability from this engine with its present specification, and that it would be capable of being further developed.

Because of the very limited time for which the engine was at our disposal no comparison of port dimension valve sizes and compression ratio etc could be made. All the data obtained in given on the attached results sheet.

Engine	JAGUAR	FERRARI
Specification	3.0 L.Alloy	250 G.T.O. V.12
Capacity	2996.7 cc	2953.2 cc
Bore	85mm	73mm
Stroke	88mm	58mm
Piston area	52.7 sq.ins.	77.8 sq.ins.
C.R.	10:1	
Cyl.Head	35/40 Squish type 2 3/32" inlet	
Camshaft	7/16" lift	.3854" lift
	I.O.35° B.T.D.C.	I.O.43° B.T.D.C.
	I.C.55° A.B.D.C.	I.C.75° A.B.D.C.
	Ex.O. 55° B.B.D.C.	Ex.O. 70° B.B.D.C.
	Ex.C. 35° A.T.D.C.	Ex.C. 43° A.T.D.C.
Tappet Clearance	In. .010" Ex. .015"	In. .006" Ex. .009"
Induction	45mm 14° Slope	Down Draught
Carburation	Lucas P.I.	Weber 38 D.C.N. (Six Double Choke)
Settings	15° B.T.D.C.	Ch. 33mm Main 120 Air 140 Pump 50 S.R. 60
Air intake	3" Trumpets	2 1/4" Trumpets
Distributor	Lucas LT ±6373	Marelli set 190° B.T.D.C.
Coil	Lucas HV 12	Marelli 12 V
Sparking plugs	Champion N 58R	Marchal HFS 34 (.025" gap)
Fuel	Super Shell 100	Super Shell 100
Oil	Shell SAE 30	Esso 30
Exhaust system	84" F type	Car system 131"

	JAGUAR		FERRARI	
R.P.M.	C. B.H.P.	C. B.M.E.P.	C. B.H.P.	C. B.M.E.P.
4000	161.0	174.0	128.0	133.0
4500	188.0	181.0		
5000	220.5	191.0	170.6	142.0
5500	245.5	193.0		
6000	261.5	189.0	220.0	152.7
6500	292.5	194.5	241.5	154.3
6750	293.5	188.1		
7000	291.7	180.5	270.8	162.0
7500			286.3	158.0
7750			288.0	154.5

R.P.M.	PTS/BHP/HR	C.TORQUE	PTS/BHP/HR	C.TORQUE
4000	.535	211.0	.640	168.1
4500	.513	219.5		
5000	.493	231.5	.655	179.1
5500	.494	234.0		
6000	.498	229.2	.672	192.7
6500	.485	236.0	.694	195.0
6750	.497	228.0		
7000	.526	219.0	.651	203.5
7500			.650	200.7
7750			.660	195.0

G.BUCK

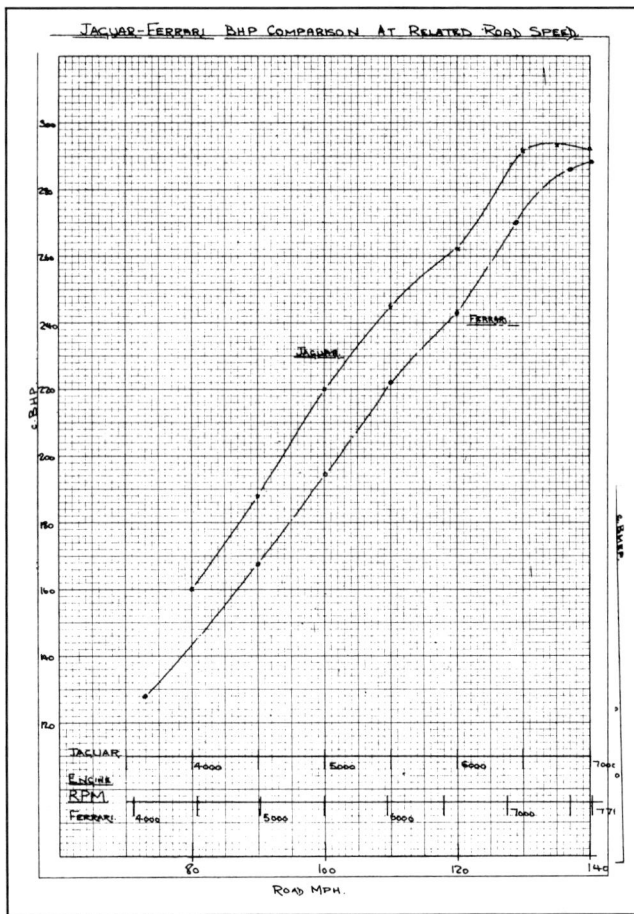

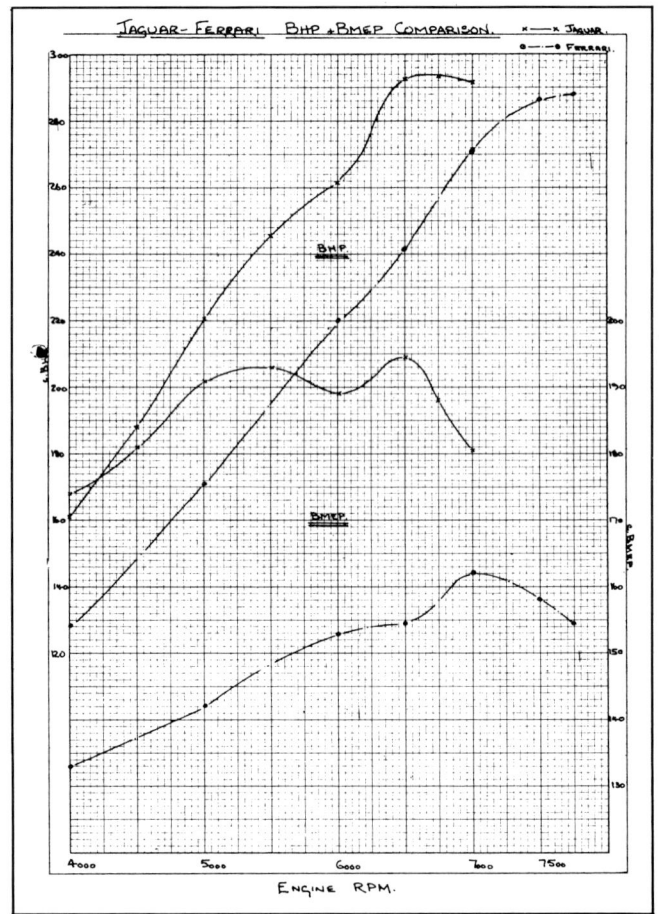

A fascinating pair of profiles: EC 1001 and Coombs's GTO behind the Browns Lane experimental department, 1962. (John Coombs was not amused when he heard that some nuts and bolts had been swept up by mistake; but when he thought about it, he realised that he could hardly expect Jaguar NOT to take the latest Ferrari apart once they'd got their hands on it.)

604

Appendix Eleven

XJ13 Test Reports

This appendix contains two reports from Mike Kimberley to Bill Heynes concerning testing of the XJ13 carried out at MIRA in 1967, and associated work. See Chapter 12 for context.

XJ13 DEVELOPMENT – INTERIM REPORT   *7th March 1967.*

FROM:— M. J. KIMBERLEY.
TO:— MR. W. M. HEYNES.
COPIES TO: MESSRS. W. T. F. HASSAN, R. J. KNIGHT, C. W. L. BAILY, H. MUNDY,
DR. J. N. TAIT, T. C. JONES, M. G. SAYER, W. WILKINSON, N. DEWIS,
E. BROOKES.
INFORMATION COPY: SIR WILLIAM LYONS.

Tests carried out at MIRA on 5.3.67, Driver N. Dewis.

1ST TEST

   Conditions: *Wet track, temperature 45°F*
                 Wind approx. 4 m.p.h. SW.
Silencer fitted on first test.
9 laps of No. 1 Circuit (26 miles).
Fastest lap 1 min. 43 secs. (101 m.p.h.)

Driver's Comments.
General feel – smooth – no vibrations, straight line running good.
Rear Suspension – very good.
Front Suspension. One front wheel out of balance (wheel kick),
vertical 'bounce' when car hits bumpy road surfaces, deflects steering.
Very strong castor feel.

General.
Driver unable to detect change in engine r.p.m. from 4th to top
(1100 r.p.m. at 140 m.p.h.) – possible clutch slip.

No water temperature reading, radiator and pipe over engine stone cold.
Bad water leaks – cockpit awash.
Oil pressure 100 lb/in.
Transmission Oil temperature   80°c.

2ND TEST

Weather conditions as Test 1, but track drying out.
Car condition as Test 1 except for the following. . . . . . . – front tyre
pressures lowered to 40 p.s.i., spare wheel removed and radiator partially
blanked off, leaving 100 square inches (22%).
6 laps of No. 1. Circuit (17·4 miles).
Fastest lap 1 min. 25 secs. (123 m.p.h.)

Driver's Comments
Oil blowing out of de-aerator tank breather.
Front wheel bounce slightly improved.
Still no noticeable change in revs. from 4th to top.

General.
Water temperature 85°c.
Oil pressure 85 lb/sq. in.
Exhaust Shield temperature 272°c.
Transmission oil temperature 100°c.

3RD TEST

Weather conditions as Test 2.
Car condition as Test 2 except for the following:—
Water radiator blanking reduced, giving 60% effective area (280 sq. in.).
Weight added to front (78 lbs).
7 Laps of No. 1 Circuit (20·3 miles)
Fastest lap 1 min. 16 secs. (137 m.p.h.)

Driver's Comments
Oil still blowing on to exhaust shields from de-aerator breather.
Clutch slipping badly.
Handling better, still small amount of vertical 'bounce' at front.
Very smooth feel to car on straight, i.e. no vibration periods, or
wheel kick, apart from wheel out of balance.
Rear end feels extremely good.
Possible use of higher cw & p ratio (revs 7,000 plus)

General
Water temperature   55°c.
Transmission oil temperature 150°c.

4TH TEST

Weather conditions ... Temperature 50°F.
                    Wind approx 4 m.p.h. W.SW.
                    Track dry with damp patches,

Car Condition.
As test 3 except for the following:

Castor angle reduced by $\frac{1}{2}$°.
Clutch free play increased.
Pipe taken out of top of de-aerator tank to separate catch tank.
Engine oil level checked.

$1\frac{3}{4}$ laps of No. 1 circuit (5·0 miles).

Driver's Comments.
Rapid fluctuations of oil pressure – needle fluctuated to zero
twice before engine was cut off.
Adequate supply of oil still in oil tank.
Fabricated steel lower oil sump pan fractured along welded seam.
Clutch slipping badly.
Instruments (Rev. Counter, Oil Pressure and Water Temperature) not
easily readable with present positioning.

---

*Testing discontinued due to clutch slip and possible engine big end
bearing failure.*

---

*N.B.   Engine oil continued to leak from the fractured lower
        sump pan for $2\frac{1}{2}$ hours, due to head of oil in tank, before
        final amount remaining was measured. Amount remaining
        approximately $1\frac{1}{4}$ gallons (capacity 6 gallons).*

        Catch tank held approximately $\frac{1}{4}$ pint oil.

                                        (M. J. Kimberley).

FROM:—   M. J. KIMBERLEY.
TO:—   MR. W. M. HEYNES.
COPIES TO:—   MESSRS. W. T. F. HASSAN, R. J. KNIGHT, C. W. L. BAILY,
            H. MUNDY, J. N. H. TAIT, T. C. JONES, M. G. SAYER,
            W. WILKINSON, N. DEWIS, G. BUCK, E. BROOKES.
INFORMATION COPIES TO: SIR WILLIAM LYONS, MR. F. R. W. ENGLAND.

XJ 13 DEVELOPMENT.
SUMMARY OF INTERIM REPORT NO. 8

*Stringent tests carried out at M.I.R.A. on 9.7.67, mostly on No. 2
(inner) circuit, to subject car and components to severest
conditions that could be met.*

Mileage covered..........   204 miles.   Driver: D. Hobbs.

Fastest Laps: No. 1 (Outer)   62·8 secs, giving 161·6 m.p.h.
            No. 2 (Inner)   80.4 secs, giving 106.1 m.p.h.

            *112ft radius on steering rad.   33·8 secs giving 1·079 G
                                lateral acceleration.*

*Handling was much improved but mods to the ZF transmission unit now
in hand should improve straight line running.*

*Ride was now acceptable except for wheel hop under max. deceleration,
to be eliminated by changing spring rates.*

Brakes improved, but more efficient cooling ducts being made.

Clutch adaptor ring broke so stronger one being fitted.

Wheels, drive pegs loosened – Dunlops are making suitable mods.

Tyres, white spot tyres gave only fair adhesion – new type to be tried.

*Misc. Driver's door catch to be improved.
        Plug lead connectors still need improvement.*

                                        M. J. Kimberley

                                        19th July, 1967.

Testing carried out at M.I.R.A. on 9.7.67.
Driver: D. Hobbs.

1st Test

Weather conditions   Wind N.W. 5 m.p.h.
Temperature   57°F
Pressure   29·8
Humidity   ·47

Car Condition   See attached specification sheet.

Test Reason   Warming up.

10 laps No. 1 Circuit.

Driver's Comments.   Front wheel patter considerably reduced and now acceptable. Oversteer going into banking. Induced weave damped out quicker. Straight line running slightly better but must be further improved.
Bump steer at 100 m.p.h. plus.

General.
Engine oil pressure   90 p.s.i.
Engine oil temperature   60°c
Water temperature   70°c
Transmission oil temperature   110°c

Oil leak from cam covers.
7000 r.p.m. in 4th coming off banking (148 m.p.h.)

2nd Test

Car Condition
$1\frac{1}{2}$ galls. engine oil added.
Tyre pressures set to 42F/45R hot.

Test Reason.   To check handling on steering pad and test new halfshaft drive flange location.

6 Clockwise laps approx. 112ft radius.
Best time for three laps 33·8 secs, giving 1·079G lateral acceleration.

Driver's Comments.
Too much O/steer.

3rd Test

Car Condition
Rear A.R.B. removed.

Test Reason: As Test 2
3 laps 112ft rad. clockwise – 34·2 secs (1·054G)
3 laps 112ft rad. anti-clockwise – 35·2 secs.

Driver's Comments.
Neutral steer with slight O/steer tendency.
Driver's door again flying open.

4th Test

Test Reason: To ascertain ride and handling characteristics. To make car and components undergo severest conditions that could be met.

7 laps No. 2 Circuit.

Driver's Comments.
Handling quite good – neutral steer with slight 'power on' oversteer. Feels as though car adhesion diminishing during max, cornering, but this is known characteristic of 'M' section white spot Dunlop tyres.

Brakes much better but still not as good as other comparable cars. Judder feel under hard deceleration.

Dampers   A little soft – adjust to harder settings.

Engine   Oil leaking from jackshaft seal.

General   Engine oil pressure   70 p.s.i.
Engine oil temperature   65°c
Transmission oil temperature   117°c

5th Test

Car Condition
Dampers up one setting, front and rear.

Test Reason   As previous test and to check tyre and disc temps.
4 laps No. 2 Circuit (Fastest lap 1m. 22 secs)

Driver's Comments.
When braking and negotiating bumpy surface – judder from rear then whole car judders. Brakes could not be locked.

General
Engine oil pressure   70 p.s.i.
Engine oil temperature   70°c
Water temperature   80°c
Transmission oil temperature   124°c

Tyre Temps:—	Front	Rear
Outside edge	27°c	49°c
Crown	49°c	79°c
Inside edge	45°c	65°c

Disc Temps.   Front 255°c
Rear 255°c

6th Test

Car Condition
Balance bar ratio modified to give 66% Front (1·54 : 1)
1 lap No. 2 Circuit.

Driver's comments.
Peculiar weave – O/S rear wheel loose.

General
Tyre pressure hot: Front   46 p.s.i.
Rear   48 p.s.i.

All rear wheel drive pegs loose.
Rear O/S pads picked up slightly and all pads flaked.

7th Test

Weather: Wind N.W.N.   5 m.p.h.
Temperature   63°F
Pressure   29·85
Humidity   ·415

Car Condition
Front tyre pressures lowered to 43 p.s.i. hot
Discs cleaned.
Car checked and wheel pegs locked and re-peened over.
O/S steering ball joint gaiter split.
One strip removed from base of water radiator giving 215in² area unblanked.   Check carried out to ascertain halfshaft drive flange location wear condition and check for clearance increases at rear:

Rear wheel alignment – ML – 30' in
400 lb.ft torque applied to wheels alternately clock and anti-clockwise.

607

Condition	O/S	N/S
Clockwise	40' in	40' in
Anti-clockwise	40' in	40' in

Thus no change in rear wheel steer effect.

Test Reason   Check B.B. ratio, disc temps. and change in judder condition.

4 laps No. 2 Circuit (fastest lap 1 min. 22 secs)

Driver's Comments.
Still cannot get front wheels to lock. Still bad judder – slightly worse than previous test.

General

Tyre temps.	Front	Rear
Crown	50°c	50°c

Disc Temps.   N/S Front – 597°c
N/S Rear – 399°c

Speeds: 6000 r.p.m. in top – 148 m.p.h.
7200 r.p.m. in 4th – 151 m.p.h.

8th Test

Car Condition
B.B.R. changed to 1·26 : 1 to give 61% front.
Decelerometer fitted to car.

Test Reason   To check effect of braking ratio change on braking and judder and to check decel.

4 laps No. 2 Circuit (Fastest lap 1m. 20·4 secs) giving 106·1 m.p.h.

Driver's Comments.
No change in braking feel or judder but long pedal which requires pumping before braking – possible shake back. Difficult to engage 3rd gear.

General
Water temperature   80°c

Max. braking condition:—   125 m.p.h. – 0·9G obtained
148 m.p.h. – 0·8G obtained

Disc Temps.   Front   597°c O/S   473°c N/S
Rear   417°c O/S   454°c N/S

Slight oil leak from halfshaft drive flange seal.

9th Test

Weather condition   Wind W..N.W.
Temperature   67°F
Pressure   29·85
Humidity   ·39

Car Condition
Air Pipes to rear discs.
Air scoops fitted to front.
Pip pin missing from N/S rear brake keep rate.
Dampers up two settings on front (15)

Test Reason.
Check disc temperature and effect of stiffer damper settings on judder, ride and bump steer.

2 laps No. 2 Circuit.

Driver's Comments.
Engine missing   plug lead off.
Damper settings much better.

10th Test

Car Condition.
Dampers up two settings on front (17).

Test Reason: As 9th test.
4 laps No. 2 Circuit (fastest lap 1 m. 20·8 secs)

Driver's Comments.
Judder appears to start from rear.
Rear wheel bump steer a little better.
Ride feel better.

General
Engine oil temperature   –   80°c
Water temperature   –   85°c
Transmission oil temperature –   114°c

Tyre Temps.	Front	Rear
Crown	49°c O/S	67°c O/S
	45°c N/S	63°c N/S

Disc Temps.
Front
Rear   601°c O/S and N/S
477°c O/S (7 secs) & 513°c N/S

11th Test

Car Condition
As previous test except dampers up four settings front and rear 21F

Test Reason   Driver felt that increased stiffness would improve judder and ride feel.

4 laps No. 2 circuit (fastest lap 1 m 21 secs)

Driver's Comments.
Upon max. obtainable braking fronts locked and then front and rear bounce coupling occurred. This condition occurs under max. deceleration obtained with engine braking and seems to be excited by bumpy surface. Brake pedal very long, especially after stops – vapourisation of fluid.

General
Engine Oil pressure   –   65 p.s.i.
Engine Oil Temperature   –   85°c
Transmission oil temperature –   120°c

12th Test

Car Condition
Dampers reset to 10 front and 10 and 15 rear.
$\frac{1}{2}$ gallon engine oil added.
Brake pedal down to floor after stopping – fluid vapourisation.

Test Reason.   To compare minm. setting with max. and effect on wheel hop.

1 lap No. 2 Circuit

Dampers up to max. settings – 19 front 20 O/S rear and 24 N/S rear.
1 lap No. 2 Circuit

Driver's Comments.
Slightly better with stiffer settings but still bad wheel hop, apparent bounce coupling occurring.

13th Test

Car Condition   As Test 12 but 200 lbs added to rear of car to reduce rear frequency to 105 cycles/min and increase frequency ratio front/rear to 1·23 : 1

Test Reason: To check for elimination of front and rear bounce coupling.

2 laps No. 2 Circuit.

Driver's Comments.
Wheel hop completely cured.
Braking now far better – fronts locked car stopped in straight line without any trace of wheel hop.

14th Test

(a) *Car condition*   As Test 13 except blanking strip removed from radiator giving 315 in² unblanked area.

   Test Reason   To determine effect of front tyre section on straight line running at speed.

   2 laps No. 1 circuit using 600M × 15 D15
   1 lap No. 1 circuit using 650L × 15

   Driver's Comments.
   No apparent change in straight line running. Stopped for plug lead to be refitted.

   General

Engine Oil Pressure	–	85 p.s.i.
Engine Oil Temperature	–	80°c
Water Temperature	–	70°c
Transmission oil Temperature	–	120°c

14th Test

(b) *Car Condition as (a) but with 27½ galls. fuel added. (in error).*

   7 laps No. 1 circuit (fastest lap 62·8 secs giving lap speed 161·6 m.p.h.)

   Driver's Comments.
   Oscillatory yaw damping slightly better but straight line running still requires improvement.

   General

Engine Oil Pressure	–	65–75 p.s.i.
Engine Oil Temperature	–	80°c
Water Temperature	–	70°c

Tyre pressure hot	Front	44 p.s.i.
	Rear	52 p.s.i.

   Speeds:—   Into banking 6800 r.p.m. in 4th (142 m.p.h.)
   7100 r.p.m. approx. out of banking (149 m.p.h.)
   Changing from 4th to top at 7400 r.p.m. (156 m.p.h.)
   Max. revs down straight approx. 7000 in top (176 m.p.h.)

15th Test

   Car Condition as previous test with 200 lb. in rear.

   Test Reason   To check effect of 6·5L section tyres on wheel hop.
   2 laps No. 2 circuit.

   Driver's Comments.
   Wheel hop not experienced under any condition of deceleration.

16th Test

   Car Condition   As 15th Test but 200 lbs. removed from rear of car.

   Test Reason   As 15
   1 Lap No. 2 Circuit.

   Driver's Comments.
   Bad wheel hop under high decel. conditions.

17th Test.

(a) *Car Condition   As Test 16 except rear tyres changed and 700M × 15 non D15 fitted with 40 p.s.i. cold, 600M × 15 D15 front tyres refitted 38 p.s.i. cold.*

   1 lap No. 2 Circuit.

   Driver's Comments.
   As Test 16.

17th Test

(b) *Car Condition   Tyre pressures reset hot to 43 front and 48 rear.*

   Driver's Comments.
   As Test 16.

18th Test

   Car Condition   As 17(b) except 200 lbs. weight added to front of car.
   1 lap No. 1 Circuit.

   Driver's Comments.
   Wheel hop still experienced.
   Testing discontinued at 5.10 p.m. after intermittent metallic rattle heard from engine locality. Investigation showed clutch adaptor ring (LM4) to have fractured. (Borg and Beck Specn.)

Mileage covered on 9.7.67	–	204 miles.
Total mileage of car	–	1157 miles.

CAR CONDITION FOR TEST 1 ON 9.7.67

As Interim Report No. 7 except for the following:

Front Suspension
   New front suspension bearings fitted.

   Geometry: Camber 1° – VE,   Castor 5° + VE
   Alignment   15' in ML, B & R.B.

Rear Suspension
   5/8" dia. A.R.B. fitted giving 165 lb/in at wheel with 7.756" radius arm.

   Geometry: Camber 1° – VE.
   Alignment 30' in ML, B & R.B.

Brakes.
   Balance bar ratio 1.26 : 1 (61% F)

Clutch
   New Hoffman release bearing fitted.

Transmission Unit.
   New drive shaft location using 0.1" thick thrust washer on inner location.
   'O' ring fitted to speedo drive to eliminate oil leak

Engine
   New cam cover gaskets fitted.

Misc.   New speedo fitted calibrated to 4 : 1 CW & P
   O/S door refitted
   Front side valance location effected with Zues fasteners.

Damper Settings   11 Front – 11 and 16 rear.

Brakes

Brake investigation showed that temperatures far higher than those recorded must have been attained. (Comark meters checked at 600°c and found to be reading low – rubbing thermo-couples and recorder to be used during next test) Results of investigation revealed:

Front   *Discs slightly crazed.*
        Seal nip reduced by ·015″ to ·015″
        Pads tapered and reduced in width to 9/16″.
        O/S brake condition worse than N/S

Rear   *Discs good*
        Seal nip reduced by ·028″ to only ·002″.
        High temperatures necessary to cause deformation of seal would also cause bad vapourisation of fluid.

The above conditions show that the air scoops used in the front and the air pipe at rear were not adequate to cool the brakes and correct ducting should, therefore, be fitted.

Straight Line Running.

Although the factors contributing to poor straight line running have been traced, their elimination necessitates a modification to the ZF5D S25 transmission unit. ZF have been notified of our requirements in this respect and new parts are awaited.

Wheel Hop

Testing carried out to date indicates that an increase in frequency ratio to 1·23 : 1 is necessary to obviate the apparent front and rear bounce coupling. Reduction in front bounce frequency of 10c/min completely cured the wheel 'patter' problem but reduced the F/R ratio to 1·1 : 1. 200 lbs added to rear of car reduced rear bounce frequency to 105c/min, (thus increasing ratio F/R to 1·23 : 1) and completely cured wheel 'hop' problem under all conditions of high deceleration.
A new range of springs giving various front/rear ratio combinations will be available by 31st July.

Clutch

New adaptor ring in LM8WP (forging) to be used in place of LM4. Borg & Beck now state that this problem was experienced some time ago and that LM8WP has since been used without failure. Test carried out for Jaguar on 12.7.67 showed that new material fractured at 11,500 r.p.m. (max. allowable V12 engine revs 7,750).

Wheels.

Locating pegs repinned (using 3 pins instead of only 1) and heavily peened over by Dunlop.

Tyres.

New tyres in 184 Mix being fitted.

Hubs

New oil seals and bearings fitted to front and rear hubs. Rear O/S hub, inner oil seal (C15231) failure.

13th July, 1967.

FROM:— M. J. KIMBERLEY
TO:— MR. E. BROOKES.
COPIES TO: MR. W. M. HEYNES, MR. M. G. SAYER, MR. W. WILKINSON, MR. G. BUCK, MR. N. DEWIS.

XJ13 DEVELOPMENT.
WORK LIST

1. *Weigh car side to side, front and rear.*
2. *Remove transmission and replace clutch, modified flywheel, starter motor and bell housing – aluminium clutch spacing ring in LM 8 WP to be manufactured and fitted together with three new locating dowels.*
3. *Strip all brakes – check for seal nip, pad. condition and disc run-out.*
4. *Strip front and rear hubs – replace bearings and oil seals (fit new inner oil seals in rear hubs if available).*
5. *Remove all tyres and send rear wheels to Dunlop Rim and Wheel for replacement and relocation of drive pegs.*
6. *New tyres to be fitted all round in 184 mix if available.*
7. *Fit split rings in Halfshaft drive flange circlip groove and test to determine reduction in end float. Check effect of wider circlip and twin circlips.*
8. *Fit new road springs to design specification.*
9. *Manufacture new rear A.R.B.'s.*
10. *Replace sparking plug connectors.*
11. *Fit 4.0 : 1 C.W. & P Trans. unit.*
12. *Replace steering and front suspension ball joint gaiters and fit heat shields if possible.*
13. *Check spring rates.*
14. *Recard all dampers.*
15. *Eliminate jackshaft oil seal leak.*
16. *Refit O/S door – new catches.*
17. *Repair Rr. body.*
18. *Check front suspension for end float.*
19. *Fit front and rear brake ducts.*
20. *Fit rubbing thermo couples on front and rear discs and install recorder.*
21. *Fit Cov. Rad. transmission oil cooler.*

M. J. Kimberley

Le Mans: A Last Word

When Volume 1 was published in 1982 Jaguar was preoccupied with its survival programme. The XJR-5 was on the drawing board in the USA, but TWR did not yet have the company's official support.

During the preparation of this book – Volume 2, in effect – the emergence of Jaguar from near-extinction proceeded in meteoric fashion, as did its return to the world of motor racing. Up to then the BL-Broadspeed affair was still fairly fresh in the mind; and in any case it was difficult to imagine any XJ variant being adaptable for touring car racing. Jaguar had looked at the XJ-S, but not as a Group A car. It had taken Walkinshaw logic to persuade the company that the possibility was there.

By the end of 1982, when Volume 1 reached the shops, the Group A Jaguar had scored four ETC victories and was about to be 'adopted' by the Coventry company. Group 44 had raced the XJR-5 in the USA and would soon give the mid-engined car its first IMSA win. On the face of it, two teams were running totally separate race programmes for Jaguar; but there *was* a common goal. All three parties wanted to see Jaguar relive its former glory at the very highest level of public awareness: that meant only one thing – Le Mans. A Le Mans victory still meant more to the marque than a victory anywhere else.

Jaguar, as recorded in both volumes, made its name in the 1950s by designing and building the C-type and the D-type for Le Mans. The five victories those cars achieved have influenced the character of the marque more than any other single factor apart from the brilliant perception of the late Sir William Lyons.

Although the North American IMSA GTP series became its battleground, the Jaguar V12-powered XJR-5/7 was undoubtedly built more with Le Mans in mind than anything else. It was brought to Britain for assessment in 1983 and was run at Le Mans in 1984 and 1985. On the first occasion both cars failed to finish, but ran very competitively before that. Mechanical and fuel consumption problems dogged them in 1985; but a very dogged Bob Tullius did bring one of them to the finish – the first time in 22 years that a Jaguar had been classified as a finisher. On both occasions, the team's home programme suffered; and this was one reason why the distinctive projectiles did not return in 1986. There were other reasons, too.

By 1985, Tom Walkinshaw had begun to set his sights on Le Mans, although he was not ready to take up the tentative entries that had been reserved for him that year. Soon afterwards, his British-designed Group C machine, the XJR-6, was being raced with great promise. It scored its first victory at Silverstone in May 1986, and promptly went to Le Mans for testing. A three-car team was entered, and each performed with credit before succumbing to failures that were incidental rather than basic to the car's design or construction. The last one to go, on Sunday morning, had been running strongly with every chance of finishing second until a blowout wrecked the rear end beyond reasonable hope of repair within the scope of the regulations. (In 1987 on XJR-8 would complete the 24 hours, coming fifth overall.)

Second place is not the same as winning, as most people

Above:
The 6.9-litre 700bhp-plus TWR Jaguar V12 Group C engine, as prepared by Allan Scott's engineers for the 1987 season when – more than at any time in thirty years – an outright victory at Le Mans was on the cards for Jaguar.

Opposite page top:
On the startline again: a Jaguar at Le Mans! The Watson/Adamowicz/Ballot-Lena XJR-5, 1984.

Right:
The Tullius/Redman/Bundy XJR-5 passes the fairground in 1984, the year of Jaguar's return to Le Mans.

agree and as Jaguar discovered at Le Mans in 1954. As recorded in this book, that was the D-type's début and it was a very exciting race; but Ferrari had been first and Jaguar second. That is why there was no question of second place being sufficient for Jaguar or for TWR, now that the latter had taken over the mantle of this particular responsibility from Group 44. It would have been wonderful to record a modern-day Le Mans victory here, but

Julia and John Egan with a thoughtful Graham Whitehead (*right*) and Jaguar's head of communications and public affairs, David Boole. Egan was to be knighted within two years, in recognition of the success he had achieved in restoring Jaguars profitability and reputation – a major element of the latter being attributable to competition results. This picture, one of many in this book taken by Jaguar's own photographers, dates from Le Mans 1984.

it cannot be done. This book has been hanging-fire long enough, already.

What *can* be recorded is the sudden emergence of Jaguar as the dominant sports-prototype marque of 1987. The XJR-6 had been lapping in about 1 min. 12·6 sec. at Sil-

Jaguar's popularity at Le Mans was reflected in the programme cover picture for 1985, based upon a painting by Michael Turner.

24 HEURES DU MANS
15-16 JUIN 1985
Girling
Lucas
JAGUAR
44

CHAMPIONNAT DU MONDE D'ENDURANCE
AUTOMOBILE CLUB DE L'OUEST

No longer is there a fast approach to the pits at Le Mans. This is what drivers see as they take the series of swerves before accelerating past the grandstands. (1985 picture features XJR-5).

The XJR-5s running in close company in the early stages of Le Mans 1985, when the drivers were Tullius/Robinson/ Ballot-Léna and Haywood/Redman/Adams.

Photographed by the author during its long final pitstop – the XJR-5 which Tullius brought home thirteenth at Le Mans in 1985.

verstone in race trim in winter testing – a time equivalent to Stuck's best qualifying time for the 1986 1000 km race and measurably slower only than the super-boosted Lancia LC2 of Andrea de Cesaris which did 1 min. 10·82 sec. in practice and then 1 min. 13·95 sec. to create a new Group C Silverstone race-lap record. Low 'one-elevens', Silman felt, were not far away.

The sudden changes first announced by FISA in Autumn 1986 were gradually modified during the following winter, and the fear that a Jaguar-powered Group C car might not be competitive were diminishing. (The very bulk of the Jaguar engine would penalise a flat-bottomed sports-car relatively heavily in terms of aero-dynamics.) In its existing concept, as a ground-effect car,

the 1987 version had been wind-tunnel tested and found to have more downforce *and* considerably improved drag. The aerodynamics devised by Tony Southgate had been more advanced than the chassis technology initially; but now each worked better for the other, and the XJR-6's temperament on the track was better-balanced than it had ever been – and it had been praised highly on a number of occasions in 1986.

For 1987, more than ever, the Silk Cut Jaguar team was run by Silman for TWR in an independent fashion. Walkinshaw's contract with the works was to provide a complete racing service, and that included fabrication of components and their purchase where necessary. Apart from matters related to the image of the marque – naturally a Coventry responsibility – the main co-operation from the works continued to be in the field of advanced component development and testing. One of the main items in this category had been the constant-velocity joints

1986 Le Mans action, photographed for Jaguar by Malcom Bryan. None of the three Silk Cut Jaguar Team XJR-6s finished the race, but their preparers (TWR) gained valuable experience.

which, on several occasions, had failed at crucial moments; Jaguar's own facilities, as well as its authority in dealing with its own suppliers, eased the TWR burden from time to time. On the other hand, Allan Scott preferred to carry out all his own development work at Kidlington with little or no Browns Lane involvement – a logical preference, since the Group C engine could include much more freedom of expression than the Group A one; and the 48-valve power unit – once tried in an ex-Tullius car – appeared to have been eliminated from the development programme, certainly from a competition point of view.

Since this book was first published in June 1987, the Silk Cut Jaguar Team has swept to prominence, and TWR has also taken on the Jaguar IMSA programme, sponsored by Castrol. The achievements of 1987 are covered in detail in a separate book, *Jaguar – World Champions* from this publisher, although it *has* been possible to include the basic facts in this revised edition, published in March 1988. (*See Pages 340–344, 426–427 and the Endpaper.*)

Despite the brilliant success of the XJR-8 in winning the 1987 world team and drivers' titles, and the promise shown by its successor the XJR-9, Jaguar remained frustrated at Le Mans. As in the previous year, however, the early weeks of 1988 brought fresh inspiration and hope. Success breeds success and, with thirty race victories for Jaguar behind it – twenty in Group A and ten in Group C – Tom Walkinshaw Racing had every reason to look confident. But, as Walkinshaw put it at the Jaguar Racing press conference on 14 January 1988, it doesn't take an Einstein to know that there is nothing quite like the 'Le Mans Experience', and that force of numbers has been the key to so many victories at the Sarthe circuit. He and his team looked forward to 1988's great marathon with eager anticipation nonetheless.

And there was a new affinity between the factory and the team. By 1988, Jim Randle's vast new Jaguar engineering centre at Whitley, Coventry, was operational – and, through linkman Peter Dodd – it was able to offer TWR a number of rig-test and other proving facilities. Such assistance could reduce laborious endurance testing on the

race track to a minimum, and enable the team to get on with other work more directly related to the racing itself.

Racing was back in Jaguar's blood again, certainly until that sixth victory at Le Mans had been achieved. Sir John Egan, the man who put Jaguar back together again in the 1980s, had no doubt at all that Jaguar customers expected their car to have a racing pedigree. Le Mans was not the only place to acquire a pedigree, but it remained the most important one. Would 1988 be Jaguar's year? An answer to that question was due soon after this edition went on sale.

The man who followed Bob Tullius as Jaguar's banner-carrier at Le Mans in the late 1980s: Tom Walkinshaw, seen here in 1984 with the XJ-S which brought him the 1984 European Touring Car Championship. He continued to drive touring cars, but employed others to race Group C machines. His company, Tom Walkinshaw Racing, was spreading its wings wider in 1988, still racing for Jaguar with Le Mans as the most-wanted goal. (*Courtesy: Neville Marriner,* Daily Mail)

Below:
The XJR-8LM of Boesel, Cheever, and Lammers – sole surviving Jaguar of 1987 Le Mans – sets off for fifth place and towards a gruelling journey's end.

Index

621